KU-471-372

Sweet & Maxwell's

Intellectual Property Statutes
2004/05

1st Edition

Helen Norman, LLM,
Barrister (Non-Practising),
Senior Lecturer in Law, University of Bristol

LONDON
SWEET & MAXWELL
2004

First Edition. 2004
Published in 2004 by Sweet & Maxwell Ltd
of 100 Avenue Road, London NW3 3PF
Typeset by Sweet & Maxwell Ltd, 100 Avenue Road, London NW3 3PF
Printed in Great Britain by Ashford Colour Printers Hants

No natural forests were destroyed to make this product; only farmed timber
was used and replanted

ISBN 0 421 892 005

All rights reserved. Crown copyright material is reproduced with the
permission of the Controller of HMSO and the Queen's Printer for
Scotland.

No part of this publication may be reproduced or transmitted in any form or
by any means, or stored in any retrieval system of any nature without prior
written permission, except for permitted fair dealing under the Copyright,
Designs and Patents Act 1988, or in accordance with the terms of a
licence issued by the Copyright Licensing Agency in respect of
photocopying and/or reprographic reproduction. Application for permission
for other use of copyright material including permission to reproduce
extracts in other published works shall be made to the publishers. Full
acknowledgment of author, publisher and source must be given.

Grateful acknowledgement is made to the UPOV for permission to
reproduce the International Convention for the Protection of New Varieties
of Plants; the WIPO for permission to reproduce the Convention for the
Protection of Producers of Phonograms Against Unauthorized Duplication
of Their Phonograms, the WIPO Copyright Treaty, the Agreed Statements
Concerning the WIPO Copyright Treaty, the Agreed Statements
Concerning the WIPO Performances and Phonograms Treaty; the
UNESCO for the permission to reproduce the Universal Copyright
Convention; the Council of Eurpoe for permission to reproduce the
European Patent Convention and the World Trade Organisation for
permission to reproduce the Agreement on Trade-Related Aspects of
Intellectual Property Rights.

Learning Resources
Centre

©
Sweet & Maxwell Limited
2004

12828548

PREFACE

Sweet & Maxwell's Intellectual Property Law Statutes is intended as a reference work for undergraduate and postgraduate students of intellectual property law. Its aim is to provide a collection of the core domestic, European and international materials in the principal areas of patents, designs, trade marks, copyright and plant variety protection.

Intellectual Property law in the last 15 years has seen an unprecedented volume of new measures, mainly as a result of the European Union's drive to attain the internal market, but also as a result of the international response to digital technology and advances in biotechnological science. With the exception of the Trade Marks Act 1994, the response of the United Kingdom Government has not been to pass new legislation, but to amend existing Acts by means of statutory instrument. This has produced primary legislation of needless complexity and detail, as evidenced by the heavily revised text of the Registered Designs Act 1949 and the Copyright, Designs and Patents Act 1988. Similar revisions to the Patents Act 1977 are anticipated, hence the principal provisions of the Patents Bill 2004 and the Regulatory Reform (Patents) Order 2004 are included in advance of their likely implementation date of December 2004. Further changes to primary legislation may be expected in the next two years as a result of the Directive of the European Parliament and of the Council on the enforcement of intellectual property rights and the (possible) agreement on the Community Patent.

The materials are presented in the following sequence. First, United Kingdom primary legislation dealing with (in chronological order) registered designs, patents, copyright, trade marks and plant varieties. Textual amendments up to May 2004 have been included so as to produce a consolidated version of each principal Act. For convenience, the reforms to patent law are included immediately after the Patents Act, and the Trade Marks (Amendment) Rules (setting out the classification of goods and services) follow immediately after the principal Act. Next, United Kingdom secondary legislation (in so far as not consolidated with primary legislation) is set out, again in chronological order. There follows EU legislation. This is in two parts, reflecting the Commission's twin track approach of creating pan-European rights by means of Regulations (in respect of plant varieties, trade marks and designs) and harmonising national law by means of Directives. Last, International Conventions are set out, from the Paris Convention of 1883 through to the WIPO Copyright and the Phonograms and Performers Treaties of 1996, and encompassing the European Patent Convention 1973 (which it should be remembered is not an EU measure) and the Agreement on Trade-Related Aspects of Intellectual Property Rights 1994.

Helen Norman
Bristol, July 2004

CONTENTS

CHRONOLOGICAL CONTENTS

STATUTES

STATUTORY INSTRUMENTS

EU MATERIALS

INTERNATIONAL MATERIALS

ALPHABETICAL CONTENTS

STATUTES

STATUTORY INSTRUMENTS

EU MATERIALS

INTERNATIONAL MATERIALS

Registered Designs Act 1949

(12, 13 & 14 GEO. 6, C. 88)

Registrable designs and proceedings for registration

[Registration of designs

1.—(1) A design may, subject to the following provisions of this Act, be **1-001** registered under this Act on the making of an application for registration.

(2) In this Act "design" means the appearance of the whole or a part of a product resulting from the features of, in particular, the lines, contours, colours, shape, texture or materials of the product or its ornamentation.

(3) In this Act—

"complex product" means a product which is composed of at least two replaceable component parts permitting disassembly and reassembly of the product; and

"product" means any industrial or handicraft item other than a computer program; and, in particular, includes packaging, get-up, graphic symbols, typographic type-faces and parts intended to be assembled into a complex product.][1]

[Substantive grounds for refusal of registration

1A.—(1) The following shall be refused registration under this Act— **1-002**

(a) anything which does not fulfil the requirements of section 1(2) of this Act;

(b) designs which do not fulfil the requirements of sections 1B to 1D of this Act;

(c) designs to which a ground of refusal mentioned in Schedule A1 to this Act applies.

(2) A design ("the later design") shall be refused registration under this Act if it is not new or does not have individual character when compared with a design which—

(a) has been made available to the public on or after the relevant date; but

(b) is protected as from a date prior to the relevant date by virtue of registration under this Act [or the Community Design Regulation][2] or an application for such registration.

(3) In subsection (2) above "the relevant date" means the date on which the application for the registration of the later design was made or is treated by virtue of section 3B(2), (3) or (5) or 14(2) of this Act as having been made.][3]

[Requirement of novelty and individual character

1B.—(1) A design shall be protected by a right in a registered design to the **1-003** extent that the design is new and has individual character.

(2) For the purposes of subsection (1) above, a design is new if no identical design or no design whose features differ only in immaterial details has been made available to the public before the relevant date.

---

[1] Substituted by SI 2001/3949 reg 2

[2] Words inserted by SI 2003/550 reg 2 (2)

[3] Inserted by SI 2001/3949 reg 2

(3) For the purposes of subsection (1) above, a design has individual character if the overall impression it produces on the informed user differs from the overall impression produced on such a user by any design which has been made available to the public before the relevant date.

(4) In determining the extent to which a design has individual character, the degree of freedom of the author in creating the design shall be taken into consideration.

(5) For the purposes of this section, a design has been made available to the public before the relevant date if—

(a) it has been published (whether following registration or otherwise), exhibited, used in trade or otherwise disclosed before that date; and

(b) the disclosure does not fall within subsection (6) below.

(6) A disclosure falls within this subsection if—

(a) it could not reasonably have become known before the relevant date in the normal course of business to persons carrying on business in the European Economic Area and specialising in the sector concerned;

(b) it was made to a person other than the designer, or any successor in title of his, under conditions of confidentiality (whether express or implied);

(c) it was made by the designer, or any successor in title of his, during the period of 12 months immediately preceding the relevant date;

(d) it was made by a person other than the designer, or any successor in title of his, during the period of 12 months immediately preceding the relevant date in consequence of information provided or other action taken by the designer or any successor in title of his; or

(e) it was made during the period of 12 months immediately preceding the relevant date as a consequence of an abuse in relation to the designer or any successor in title of his.

(7) In subsections (2), (3), (5) and (6) above "the relevant date" means the date on which the application for the registration of the design was made or is treated by virtue of section 3B(2), (3) or (5) or 14(2) of this Act as having been made.

(8) For the purposes of this section, a design applied to or incorporated in a product which constitutes a component part of a complex product shall only be considered to be new and to have individual character—

(a) if the component part, once it has been incorporated into the complex product, remains visible during normal use of the complex product; and

(b) to the extent that those visible features of the component part are in themselves new and have individual character.

(9) In subsection (8) above "normal use" means use by the end user; but does not include any maintenance, servicing or repair work in relation to the product.][1]

[Designs dictated by their technical function

1-004   **1C.**—(1) A right in a registered design shall not subsist in features of appearance of a product which are solely dictated by the product's technical function.

(2) A right in a registered design shall not subsist in features of appearance of a product which must necessarily be reproduced in their exact form and dimensions so as to permit the product in which the design is incorporated or to

---

[1] Inserted by SI 2001/3949 reg 2

which it is applied to be mechanically connected to, or placed in, around or against, another product so that either product may perform its function.

(3) Subsection (2) above does not prevent a right in a registered design subsisting in a design serving the purpose of allowing multiple assembly or connection of mutually interchangeable products within a modular system.]¹

[Designs contrary to public policy or morality

1D. A right in a registered design shall not subsist in a design which is **1-005** contrary to public policy or to accepted principles of morality.]²

Proprietorship of designs

2.—[(1) The author of a design shall be treated for the purposes of this Act **1-006** as the original proprietor of the design, subject to the following provisions.

(1A) Where a design is created in pursuance of a commission for money or money's worth, the person commissioning the design shall be treated as the original proprietor of the design.

(1B) Where, in a case not falling within subsection (1A), a design is created by an employee in the course of his employment, his employer shall be treated as the original proprietor of the design.]³

(2) Where a design [...]⁴ becomes vested, whether by assignment, transmission or operation of law, in any person other than the original proprietor, either alone or jointly with the original proprietor, that other person, or as the case may be the original proprietor and that other person, shall be treated for the purposes of this Act as the proprietor of the design [...]⁵.

[(3) In this Act the 'author' of a design means the person who creates it.

(4) In the case of a design generated by computer in circumstances such that there is no human author, the person by whom the arrangements necessary for the creation of the design are made shall be taken to be the author.]⁶

[Applications for registration

3.—(1) An application for the registration of a design shall be made in the **1-007** prescribed form and shall be filed at the Patent Office in the prescribed manner.

(2) An application for the registration of a design shall be made by the person claiming to be the proprietor of the design.

(3) An application for the registration of a design in which national unregistered design right subsists shall be made by the person claiming to be the design right owner.

(4) For the purpose of deciding whether, and to what extent, a design is new or has individual character, the registrar may make such searches (if any) as he thinks fit.

(5) An application for the registration of a design which, owing to any default or neglect on the part of the applicant, has not been completed so as to enable registration to be effected within such time as may be prescribed shall be deemed to be abandoned.]⁷

---

¹ Inserted by SI 2001/3949 reg 2
² Inserted by SI 2001/3949 reg 2
³ Substituted by Copyright, Designs and Patents Act 1988 c.48 s 267 (2)
⁴ Words repealed by SI 2001/3949 Sch 2 para 1
⁵ Words repealed by SI 2001/3949 Sch 2 para 1
⁶ Inserted by Copyright, Designs and Patents Act 1988 c.48 s 267 (3) (4)
⁷ Substituted by SI 2001/3949 reg 4

[Determination of applications for registration

1-008   **3A.**—(1) Subject as follows, the registrar shall not refuse an application for the registration of a design.

(2) If it appears to the registrar that an application for the registration of a design has not been made in accordance with any rules made under this Act, he may refuse the application.

(3) If it appears to the registrar that an application for the registration of a design has not been made in accordance with sections 3(2) and (3) and 14(1) of this Act, he shall refuse the application.

(4) If it appears to the registrar that any ground for refusal of registration mentioned in section 1A of this Act applies in relation to an application for the registration of a design, he shall refuse the application.]¹

[Modification of applications for registration

1-009   **3B.**—(1) The registrar may, at any time before an application for the registration of a design is determined, permit the applicant to make such modifications of the application as the registrar thinks fit.

(2) Where an application for the registration of a design has been modified before it has been determined in such a way that the design has been altered significantly, the registrar may, for the purposes of deciding whether and to what extent the design is new or has individual character, direct that the application shall be treated as having been made on the date on which it was so modified.

(3) Where—

    (a) an application for the registration of a design has disclosed more than one design and has been modified before it has been determined to exclude one or more designs from the application; and

    (b) a subsequent application for the registration of a design so excluded has, within such period (if any) as has been prescribed for such applications, been made by the person who made the earlier application or his successor in title,

the registrar may, for the purpose of deciding whether and to what extent the design is new or has individual character, direct that the subsequent application shall be treated as having been made on the date on which the earlier application was, or is treated as having been, made.

(4) Where an application for the registration of a design has been refused on any ground mentioned in section 1A(1)(b) or (c) of this Act, the application may be modified by the applicant if it appears to the registrar that—

    (a) the identity of the design is retained; and

    (b) the modifications have been made in accordance with any rules made under this Act.

(5) An application modified under subsection (4) above shall be treated as the original application and, in particular, as made on the date on which the original application was made or is treated as having been made.

(6) Any modification under this section may, in particular, be effected by making a partial disclaimer in relation to the application.]²

---

¹ Inserted by SI 2001/3949 reg 4
² Inserted by SI 2001/3949 reg 4

[Date of registration of designs

3C.—(1) Subject as follows, a design, when registered, shall be registered as **1-010** of the date on which the application was made or is treated as having been made.

(2) Subsection (1) above shall not apply to an application which is treated as having been made on a particular date by section 14(2) of this Act or by virtue of the operation of section 3B(3) or (5) of this Act by reference to section 14(2) of this Act.

(3) A design, when registered, shall be registered as of—

    (a) in the case of an application which is treated as having been made on a particular date by section 14(2) of this Act, the date on which the application was made;

    (b) in the case of an application which is treated as having been made on a particular date by virtue of the operation of section 3B(3) of this Act by reference to section 14(2) of this Act, the date on which the earlier application was made;

    (c) in the case of an application which is treated as having been made on a particular date by virtue of the operation of section 3B(5) of this Act by reference to section 14(2) of this Act, the date on which the original application was made.][1]

[Appeals in relation to applications for registration

3D. An appeal lies from any decision of the registrar under section 3A or 3B **1-011** of this Act.][2]

Provisions for secrecy of certain designs

5.—(1) Where, either before or after the commencement of this Act, an appli- **1-012** cation for the registration of a design has been made, and it appears to the registrar that the design is one of a class notified to him by [the Secretary of State][3] as relevant for defence purposes, he may give directions for prohibiting or restricting the publication of information with respect to the design, or the communication of such information to any person or class of persons specified in the directions.

Effect of registration, etc

[Right given by registration

7.—(1) The registration of a design under this Act gives the registered **1-013** proprietor the exclusive right to use the design and any design which does not produce on the informed user a different overall impression.

(2) For the purposes of subsection (1) above and section 7A of this Act any reference to the use of a design includes a reference to—

    (a) the making, offering, putting on the market, importing, exporting or using of a product in which the design is incorporated or to which it is applied; or

    (b) stocking such a product for those purposes.

---

[1] Inserted by SI 2001/3949 reg 4
[2] Inserted by SI 2001/3949 reg 4
[3] Words substituted by Copyright, Designs and Patents Act 1988 c.48 s 272, Sch 3 para 3 (2)

(3) In determining for the purposes of subsection (1) above whether a design produces a different overall impression on the informed user, the degree of freedom of the author in creating his design shall be taken into consideration.

(4) The right conferred by subsection (1) above is subject to any limitation attaching to the registration in question (including, in particular, any partial disclaimer or any declaration by the registrar or a court of partial invalidity).][1]

[Infringements of rights in registered designs

1-014　**7A.**—(1) Subject as follows, the right in a registered design is infringed by a person who, without the consent of the registered proprietor, does anything which by virtue of section 7 of this Act is the exclusive right of the registered proprietor.

(2) The right in a registered design is not infringed by—

　(a) an act which is done privately and for purposes which are not commercial;

　(b) an act which is done for experimental purposes;

　(c) an act of reproduction for teaching purposes or for the purposes of making citations provided that the conditions mentioned in subsection (3) below are satisfied;

　(d) the use of equipment on ships or aircraft which are registered in another country but which are temporarily in the United Kingdom;

　(e) the importation into the United Kingdom of spare parts or accessories for the purposes of repairing such ships or aircraft; or

　(f) the carrying out of repairs on such ships or aircraft.

(3) The conditions mentioned in this subsection are—

　(a) the act of reproduction is compatible with fair trade practice and does not unduly prejudice the normal exploitation of the design; and

　(b) mention is made of the source.

(4) The right in a registered design is not infringed by an act which relates to a product in which any design protected by the registration is incorporated or to which it is applied if the product has been put on the market in the European Economic Area by the registered proprietor or with his consent.

(5) The right in a registered design of a component part which may be used for the purpose of the repair of a complex product so as to restore its original appearance is not infringed by the use for that purpose of any design protected by the registration.

(6) No proceedings shall be taken in respect of an infringement of the right in a registered design committed before the date on which the certificate of registration of the design under this Act is granted.][2]

Duration of right in registered design

1-015　**8.**—(1) The right in a registered design subsists in the first instance for a period of five years from the date of the registration of the design.

(2) The period for which the right subsists may be extended for a second, third, fourth and fifth period of five years, by applying to the registrar for an extension and paying the prescribed renewal fee.

(3) If the first, second, third or fourth period expires without such application and payment being made, the right shall cease to have effect; and the registrar shall, in accordance with rules made by the Secretary of State, notify the proprietor of that fact.

---

[1] Substituted by SI 2001/3949 reg 5
[2] Inserted by SI 2001/3949 reg 5

(4) If during the period of six months immediately following the end of that period an application for extension is made and the prescribed renewal fee and any prescribed additional fee is paid, the right shall be treated as if it had never expired, with the result that—

(a) anything done under or in relation to the right during that further period shall be treated as valid,

(b) an act which would have constituted an infringement of the right if it has not expired shall be treated as an infringement, and

(c) an act which would have constituted use of the design for the services of the Crown if the right had not expired shall be treated as such use.

Exemption of innocent infringer from liability for damages

9.—(1) In proceedings for the infringement of [the right in a registered **1-016** design]¹ damages shall not be awarded against a defendant who proves that at the date of the infringement he was not aware, and had nor reasonable ground for supposing, that the design was registered; and a person shall not be deemed to have been aware or to have had reasonable grounds for supposing as aforesaid by reason only of the marking of [a product]² with the word "registered" or any abbreviation thereof, or any word or words expressing or implying that the design applied to [, or incorporated in, the product]³ has been registered, unless the number of the design accompanied the word or words or the abbreviation in question.

(2) Nothing in this section shall affect the power of the court to grant an injunction in any proceedings for infringement of [the right in a registered design]⁴.

[Cancellation of registration

11. The registrar may, upon a request made in the prescribed manner by the **1-017** registered proprietor, cancel the registration of a design.]⁵

[Grounds for invalidity of registration

11ZA.—(1) The registration of a design may be declared invalid on any of **1-018** the grounds mentioned in section 1A of this Act.

(2) The registration of a design may be declared invalid on the ground of the registered proprietor not being the proprietor of the design and the proprietor of the design objecting.

(3) The registration of a design involving the use of an earlier distinctive sign may be declared invalid on the ground of an objection by the holder of rights to the sign which include the right to prohibit in the United Kingdom such use of the sign.

(4) The registration of a design constituting an unauthorised use of a work protected by the law of copyright in the United Kingdom may be declared invalid on the ground of an objection by the owner of the copyright.

(5) In this section and sections 11ZB, 11ZC and 11ZE of this Act (other than section 11ZE(1)) references to the registration of a design include references to the

---

¹ Words substituted by Copyright, Designs and Patents Act 1988 c.48 s 272 Sch 3 para 5
² Words substituted by SI 2001/3949 Sch 1 para 3 (a)
³ Words substituted by SI 2001/3949 Sch 1 para 3 (b)
⁴ Words substituted by Copyright, Designs and Patents Act 1988 c.48 s 272 Sch 3 para 5
⁵ Substituted by SI 2001/3949 reg 7

former registration of a design; and these sections shall apply, with necessary modifications, in relation to such former registrations.]¹

[Applications for declaration of invalidity

1-019   **11ZB.**—(1) Any person interested may make an application to the registrar for a declaration of invalidity on the ground mentioned in section 1A(1)(a) or (b) of this Act.

(2) Any person concerned by the use in question may make an application to the registrar for a declaration of invalidity on the ground mentioned in section 1A(1)(c) of this Act.

(3) The relevant person may make an application to the registrar for a declaration of invalidity on the ground mentioned in section 1A(2) of this Act.

(4) In subsection (3) above "the relevant person" means, in relation to an earlier design protected by virtue of registration under this Act [or the Community Design Regulation]² or an application for such registration, the registered proprietor of the design [,the holder of the registered Community design]³ or (as the case may be) the applicant.

(5) The person able to make an objection under subsection (2), (3) or (4) of section 11ZA of this Act may make an application to the registrar for a declaration of invalidity on the ground mentioned in that subsection.

(6) An application may be made under this section in relation to a design at any time after the design has been registered.]⁴

[Determination of applications for declaration of invalidity

1-020   **11ZC.**—(1) This section applies where an application has been made to the registrar for a declaration of invalidity in relation to a registration.

(2) If it appears to the registrar that the application has not been made in accordance with any rules made under this Act, he may refuse the application.

(3) If it appears to the registrar that the application has not been made in accordance with section 11ZB of this Act, he shall refuse the application.

(4) Subject to subsections (2) and (3) above, the registrar shall make a declaration of invalidity if it appears to him that the ground of invalidity specified in the application has been established in relation to the registration.

(5) Otherwise the registrar shall refuse the application.

(6) A declaration of invalidity may be a declaration of partial invalidity.]⁵

[Modification of registration

1-021   **11ZD.**—(1) Subsections (2) and (3) below apply where the registrar intends to declare the registration of a design invalid on any ground mentioned in section 1A(1)(b) or (c) or 11ZA(3) or (4) of this Act.

(2) The registrar shall inform the registered proprietor of that fact.

(3) The registered proprietor may make an application to the registrar for the registrar to make such modifications to the registration of the design as the registered proprietor specifies in his application.

(4) Such modifications may, in particular, include the inclusion on the register of a partial disclaimer by the registered proprietor.

---

¹ Inserted by SI 2001/3949 reg 7
² Words inserted by SI 2003/550 reg 2 (3) (a)
³ Words inserted by SI 2003/550 reg 2 (3) (b)
⁴ Inserted by SI 2001/3949 reg 7
⁵ Inserted by SI 2001/3949 reg 7

(5) If it appears to the registrar that the application has not been made in accordance with any rules made under this Act, the registrar may refuse the application.

(6) If it appears to the registrar that the identity of the design is not retained or the modified registration would be invalid by virtue of section 11ZA of this Act, the registrar shall refuse the application.

(7) Otherwise the registrar shall make the specified modifications.

(8) A modification of a registration made under this section shall have effect, and be treated always to have had effect, from the grant of registration.][1]

[Effect of cancellation or invalidation of registration

11ZE.—(1) A cancellation of registration under section 11 of this Act takes **1-022** effect from the date of the registrar's decision or from such other date as the registrar may direct.

(2) Where the registrar declares the registration of a design invalid to any extent, the registration shall to that extent be treated as having been invalid from the date of registration or from such other date as the registrar may direct.][2]

[Appeals in relation to cancellation or invalidation

11ZF. An appeal lies from any decision of the registrar under section 11 to **1-023** 11ZE of this Act.][3]

[Powers exercisable for protection of the public interest

11A.—(1) Where a report of the [Competition Commission][4] has been laid **1-024** before Parliament containing conclusions to the effect—

   (c) on a competition reference, that a person was engaged in an anti-competitive practice which operated or may be expected to operate against the public interest, or

   (d) on a reference under section 11 of the Competition Act 1980 (reference of public bodies and certain other persons), that a person is pursuing a course of conduct which operates against the public interest,

the appropriate Minister or Ministers may apply to the registrar to take action under this section.

(2) Before making an application the appropriate Minister or Ministers shall publish, in such a manner as he or they think appropriate, a notice describing the nature of the proposed application and shall consider any representations which may be made within 30 days of such publication by persons whose interests appear to him or them to be affected.

(3) If on an application under this section it appears to the registrar that the matters specified in the Commission's report as being those which in the Commission's opinion operate or operated or may be expected to operate against the public interest include—

   (a) conditions in licences granted in respect of a registered design by its proprietor restricting the use of the design by the licensee or the right of the proprietor to grant other licences, [...][5]

   (b) [...][6]

---

[1] Inserted by SI 2001/3949 reg 7
[2] Inserted by SI 2001/3949 reg 7
[3] Inserted by SI 2001/3949 reg 7
[4] Words substituted by SI 1999/506 Pt II art 9
[5] Words repealed by SI 2001/3949 Sch 2 para 1
[6] Repealed by SI 2001/3949 Sch 2 para 1

he may by order cancel or modify any such condition.

(6) An appeal lies from any order of the registrar under this section.

(7) In this section "the appropriate Minister or Ministers" means the Minister or Ministers to whom the report of the [Competition Commission][1] was made.][2]

Use for services of the Crown

1-025 **12.** The provisions of the First Schedule to this Act shall have effect with respect to the use of registered designs for the services of the Crown and the rights of third parties in respect of such use.

International Arrangements

Orders in Council as to convention countries

1-026 **13.**—(1) His Majesty may, with a view to the fulfilment of a treaty, convention, arrangement or engagement, by Order in Council declare that any country specified in the Order is a convention country for the purposes of this Act:

Provided that a declaration may be made as aforesaid for the purposes either of all or of some only of the provisions of this Act, and a country in the case of which a declaration made for the purposes of some only of the provisions of this Act is in force shall be deemed to be a convention country for the purposes of those provisions only.

(2) His Majesty may by Order in Council direct that any of the Channel Islands, any colony, [...][3] shall be deemed to be a convention country for the purposes of all or any of the provisions of this Act; and an Order made under this subsection may direct that any such provisions shall have effect, in relation to the territory in question, subject to such conditions or limitations, if any, as may be specified in the Order.

(3) For the purposes of subsection (1) of this section, every colony, protectorate, territory subject to the authority or under the suzerainty of another country, and territory administered by another country [...][4] under the trusteeship system of the United Nations, shall be deemed to be a country in the case of which a declaration may be made under that subsection.

Registration of design where application for protection in convention country has been made

1-027 **14.**—(1) An application for registration of a design in respect of which protection has been applied for in a convention country may be made in accordance with the provisions of this Act by the person by whom the application for protection was made or his personal representative or assignee:

Provided that no application shall be made by virtue of this section after the expiration of six months from the date of the application for protection in a convention country or, where more than one such application for protection has been made, from the date of the first application.

[(2) Where an application for registration of a design is made by virtue of this section, the application shall be treated, for the purpose of determining

---

[1] Words substituted by SI 1999/506 Pt II art 9
[2] Inserted by Copyright, Designs and Patents Act 1988 c.48 ss 266 (5) 270
[3] Words repealed by Statute Law (Repeals) Act 1986 c.12 s 1 (1) Sch 1 Pt VI
[4] Words repealed by Statute Law (Repeals) Act 1986 c.12 s 1 (1) Sch 1 Pt VI

whether [(and to what extent)]¹ that or any other design is new [or has individual character]², as made on the date of the application for protection in the convention country or, if more than one such application was made, on the date of the first such application.

(3) Subsection (2) shall not be construed as excluding the power to give directions under [section 3B(2) or (3)]³ of this Act in relation to an application made by virtue of this section.]⁴

(4) Where a person has applied for protection for a design by an application which—

    (a) in accordance with the terms of a treaty subsisting between two or more convention countries, is equivalent to an application duly made in any one of those convention countries; or

    (b) in accordance with the law of any convention country, is equivalent to an application duly made in that convention country.

he shall be deemed for the purposes of this section to have applied in that convention country.

Register of designs, etc

[Register of designs etc

17.—(1) The registrar shall maintain the register of designs, in which shall be **1-028** entered—

    (a) the names and addresses of proprietors of registered designs;

    (b) notices of assignments and of transmissions of registered designs; and

    (c) such other matters as may be prescribed or as the registrar may think fit.

(2) No notice of any trust, whether express, implied or constructive, shall be entered in the registrar of designs, and the registrar shall not be affected by any such notice.

(3) The register need not be kept in documentary form.

(4) Subject to the provisions of this Act and to rules made by the Secretary of State under it, the public shall have a right to inspect the register at the Patent Office at all convenient times.]⁵

Certificate of registration

18.—(1) The registrar shall grant a certificate of registration in the **1-029** prescribed form to the registered proprietor of a design when the design is registered.

Registration of assignments, etc

19.—(1) Where any person becomes entitled by assignment, transmission or **1-030** operation of law to a registered design or to a share in a registered design, or becomes entitled as mortgagee, licensee or otherwise to any other interest in a registered design, he shall apply to the registrar in the prescribed manner for the registration of his title as proprietor or co-proprietor or, as the case may be, of notice of his interest, in the register of designs.

---

¹ Words inserted by SI 2001/3949 Sch 1 para 4 (2) (a)
² Words inserted by SI 2001/3949 Sch 1 para 4 (2) (b)
³ Words substituted by SI 2001/3949 Sch 1 para 4 (3)
⁴ Substituted by Copyright, Designs and Patents Act 1988 c.48 s 272 Sch 3 para 7
⁵ Substituted by Patents, Designs and Marks Act 1986 c.39 s 1 Sch 1 para 3

(2) Without prejudice to the provisions of the foregoing subsection, an application for the registration of the title of any person becoming entitled by assignment to a registered design or a share in a registered design, or becoming entitled by virtue of a mortgage, licence or other instrument to any other interest in a registered design, may be made in the prescribed manner by the assignor, mortgagor, licensor or other party to that instrument, as the case may be.

(3) Where application is made under this section for the registration of the title of any person, the registrar shall, upon proof of title to his satisfaction—

    (a) where that person is entitled to a registered design or a share in a registered design, register him in the register of designs as proprietor or co-proprietor of the design, and enter in that register particulars of the instrument or event by which he derives title; or

    (b) where that person is entitled to any other interest in the registered design, enter in that register notice of his interest, with particulars of the instrument (if any) creating it.

[(3A) Where [national unregistered design right][1] subsists in a registered design, the registrar shall not register an interest under subsection (3) unless he is satisfied that the person entitled to that interest is also entitled to a corresponding interest in the [national unregistered design right][2].

(3B) Where [national unregistered design right][3] subsists in a registered design and the proprietor of the registered design is also the design right owner, an assignment of the [national unregistered design right][4] shall be taken to be also an assignment of the right in the registered design, unless a contrary intention appears.][5]

(4) Subject to any rights vested in any other person of which notice is entered in the register of designs, the person or persons registered as proprietor of a registered design shall have power to assign, grant licences under, or otherwise deal with the design, and to give effectual receipts for any consideration for any such assignment, licence or dealing:

Provided that any equities in respect of the design may be enforced in like manner as in respect of any other personal property.

(5) Except for the purposes of an application to rectify the register under the following provisions of this Act, a document in respect of which no entry has been made in the register of designs under subsection (3) of this section shall not be admitted in any court as evidence of the title of any person to a registered design or share of or interest in a registered design unless the court otherwise directs.

Rectification of register

1-031   **20.**—(1) The court may, on the application of [the relevant person][6], order the register of designs to be rectified by the making of any entry therein or the variation or deletion of any entry therein.

    [(1A) In subsection (1) above

        "the relevant person" means—

---

[1] Words substituted by SI 2001/3949 Sch 1 para 6 (2)
[2] Words substituted by SI 2001/3949 Sch 1 para 6 (2)
[3] Words substituted by SI 2001/3949 Sch 1 para 6 (3)
[4] Words substituted by SI 2001/3949 Sch 1 para 6 (3)
[5] Inserted by Copyright, Designs and Patents Act 1988 c.48 s 272 Sch 3 para 10
[6] Words substituted by SI 2001/3949 reg 8 (2)

(a) in the case of an application invoking any ground referred to in section 1A(1)(c) of this Act, any person concerned by the use in question;

(b) in the case of an application invoking the ground mentioned in section 1A(2) of this Act, the appropriate person;

(c) in the case of an application invoking any ground mentioned in section 11ZA(2), (3) or (4) of this Act, the person able to make the objection;

(d) in any other case, any person aggrieved.

(1B) In subsection (1A) above "the appropriate person" means, in relation to an earlier design protected by virtue of registration under this Act [or the Community Design Regulation]¹ or an application for such registration, the registered proprietor of the design [, the holder of the registered Community design]² or (as the case may be) the applicant.]³

(2) In proceedings under this section the court may determine any question which it may be necessary or expedient to decide in connection with the rectification of the register.

(3) Notice of any application to the court under this section shall be given in the prescribed manner to the registrar, who shall be entitled to appear and be heard on the application, and shall appear if so directed by the court.

(4) Any order made by the court under this section shall direct that notice of the order shall be served on the registrar in the prescribed manner; and the registrar shall, on receipt of the notice, rectify the register accordingly.

[(5) A rectification of the register under this section has effect as follows—

(a) an entry made has effect from the date on which it should have been made,

(b) an entry varied has effect as if it had originally been made in its varied form, and

(c) an entry deleted shall be deemed never to have had effect,

unless, in any case, the court directs otherwise.]⁴

[(6) Orders which may be made by the court under this section include, in particular, declarations of partial invalidity.]⁵

Power to correct clerical errors

21.—(1) The registrar may, in accordance with the provisions of this section, **1-032** correct any error in an application for the registration or in the representation of a design, or any error in the register of designs.

(2) A correction may be made in pursuance of this section either upon a request in writing made by any person interested and accompanied by the prescribed fee, or without such a request.

(3) Where the registrar proposes to make any such correction as aforesaid otherwise than in pursuance of a request made under this section, he shall give notice of the proposal to the registered proprietor or the applicant for registration of the design, as the case may be, and to any other person who appears to him to be concerned, and shall give them an opportunity to be heard before making the correction.

¹ Words inserted by SI 2003/550 reg 2 (4) (b)
² Words inserted by SI 2003/550 reg 2 (4) (a)
³ Inserted by SI 2001/3949 reg 8 (3)
⁴ Inserted by Copyright, Designs and Patents Act 1988 c.48 s 272 Sch 3 para 11
⁵ Inserted by SI 2001/3949 reg 8 (4)

Inspection of registered designs

1-033   **22.**—[(1) Where a design has been registered under this Act, there shall be open to inspection at the Patent Office on and after the day on which the certificate of registration is issued—
>   (a) the representation or specimen of the design [...][1]
>   (b) [...][2]

This subsection has effect subject to the following provisions of this section and to any rules made under section 5(2) of this Act.][3]

Legal proceedings and Appeals

Certificate of contested validity of registration

1-034   **25.**—(1) If in any proceedings before the court the validity of the registration of a design is contested, and it is found by the court that the design is [, to any extent,][4] validly registered, the court may certify that the validity of the registration of the design was contested in those proceedings.

(2) Where any such certificate has been granted, then if in any subsequent proceedings before the court for infringement of [the right in the registered design][5] or for [invalidation][6] of the registration of the design, a final order or judgment is made or given in favour of the registered proprietor, he shall, unless the court otherwise directs, be entitled to his costs as between solicitor and client:

Provided that this subsection shall not apply to the costs of any appeal in any such proceedings as aforesaid.

Remedy for groundless threats of infringement proceedings

1-035   **26.**—(1) Where any person (whether entitled to or interested in a registered design or an application for registration of a design or not) by circulars, advertisements or otherwise threatens any other person with proceedings for infringement of [the right in a registered design][7], any person aggrieved thereby may bring an action against him for any such relief as is mentioned in the next following subsection.

(2) Unless in any action brought by virtue of this section the defendant proves that the acts in respect of which proceedings were threatened constitute or, if done, would constitute, an infringement of [the right in a registered design][8] the registration of which is not shown by the plaintiff to be invalid, the plaintiff shall be entitled to the following relief, that is to say:—
>   (a) a declaration to the effect that the threats are unjustifiable;
>   (b) an injunction against the continuance of the threats; and
>   (c) such damages, if any, as he has sustained thereby.

[(2A) Proceedings may not be brought under this section in respect of a threat to bring proceedings for an infringement alleged to consist of the making or importing of anything.][9]

---

[1] Word repealed by SI 2001/3949 Sch 2 para 1
[2] Repealed by SI 2001/3949 Sch 2 para 1
[3] Substituted by Copyright, Designs and Patents Act 1988 c.48 s 272 Sch 3 para 12 (2)
[4] Words inserted by SI 2001/3949 Sch 1 para 8 (2)
[5] Words substituted by Copyright, Designs and Patents Act 1988 c.48 s 272 Sch 3 para 14
[6] Word substituted by SI 2001/3949 Sch 1 para 8 (3)
[7] Words substituted by Copyright, Designs and Patents Act 1988 c.48 s 272 Sch 3 para 15 (2)
[8] Words substituted by Copyright, Designs and Patents Act 1988 c.48 s 272 Sch 3 para 15 (2)
[9] Inserted by Copyright, Designs and Patents Act 1988 c.48 s 272 Sch 3 para 15 (3)

(3) For the avoidance of doubt it is hereby declared that a mere notification that a design is registered does not constitute a threat of proceedings within the meaning of this section.

The Appeal Tribunal

28.—(1) Any appeal from the registrar under this Act shall lie to the Appeal Tribunal.   **1-036**

[(2) The Appeal Tribunal shall consist of—
  (a) one or more judges of the High Court nominated by the Lord Chancellor, and
  (b) one judge of the Court of Session nominated by the Lord President of that Court.][1]

(7) Upon any appeal under this Act the Appeal Tribunal may exercise any power which could have been exercised by the registrar in the proceeding from which the appeal is brought.

Offences

Fine for falsely representing a design as registered

35.—(1) If any person falsely represents that a design applied to [, or incorpo-   **1-037** rated in, any product][2] sold by him is registered [...][3], he shall be liable on summary conviction to [a fine not exceeding level 3 on the standard scale][4]; and for the purposes of this provision a person who sells [a product][5] having stamped, engraved or impressed thereon or otherwise applied thereto the word "registered", or any other word expressing or implying that the design applied to [, or incorporated in, the product][6] is registered, shall be deemed to represent that the design applied to [, or incorporated in, the product][7] is registered [...][8].

(2) If any person, after [the right in a registered design][9] has expired, marks [any product][10] to which the design has been applied [or in which it has been incorporated][11] with the word "registered", or any word or words implying that there is a [subsisting right in the design under this Act][12], or causes any [such product][13] to be so marked, he shall be liable on summary conviction to [a fine not exceeding level 1 on the standard scale][14]

[Offence by body corporate: liability of officers

35A.—(1) Where an offence under this Act committed by a body corporate   **1-038** is proved to have been committed with the consent or connivance of a director, manager, secretary or other similar officer of the body, or a person purporting to

---

[1] Substituted by Copyright, Designs and Patents Act 1988 c.48 s 272 Sch 3 para 17 (2)
[2] Words substituted by SI 2001/3949 Sch 1 para 10 (2) (a)
[3] Words repealed by SI 2001/3949 Sch 2 para 1
[4] Words substituted by Copyright, Designs and Patents Act 1988 c.48 s 272 Sch 3 para 24 (2) (4)
[5] Words substituted by SI 2001/3949 Sch 1 para 10 (2) (c)
[6] Words substituted by SI 2001/3949 Sch 1 para 10 (2) (d)
[7] Words substituted by SI 2001/3949 Sch 1 para 10 (2) (d)
[8] Words repealed by SI 2001/3949 Sch 2 para 1
[9] Words substituted by Copyright, Designs and Patents Act 1988 c.48 s 272 Sch 3 para 24 (3) (a)
[10] Words substituted by SI 2001/3949 Sch 1 para 10 (3) (a)
[11] Words inserted by SI 2001/3949 Sch 1 para 10 (3) (b)
[12] Words substituted by Copyright, Designs and Patents Act 1988 c.48 s 272 Sch 3 para 24 (3) (b)
[13] Words substituted by SI 2001/3949 Sch 1 para 10 (3) (c)
[14] Words substituted by Copyright, Designs and Patents Act 1988 c.48 s 272 Sch 3 para 24 (3) (c)

act in any such capacity, he as well as the body corporate is guilty of the offence and liable to be proceeded against and punished accordingly.

(2) In relation to a body corporate whose affairs are managed by its members "director" means a member of the body corporate.][1]

Supplemental

Interpretation

1-039   **44.**—(1) In this Act, except where the context otherwise requires, the following expressions have the meanings hereby respectively assigned by them, that is to say—

["Appeal Tribunal" means the Appeal Tribunal constituted and acting in accordance with section 28 of this Act as amended by the Administration of Justice Act 1969;][2]

"assignee" includes the personal representative of a deceased assignee, and references to the assignee of any person include references to the assignee of the personal representative or assignee of that person;

["author" in relation to a design, has the meaning given by section 2(3) and (4);][3]

[["Community Design Regulation" means Council Regulation (EC) 6/2002 of 12th December 2001 on Community Designs;][4]

"complex product" has the meaning assigned to it by section 1(3) of this Act;][5]

["the court" shall be construed in accordance with section 27 of this Act;][6]

"design" has the meaning assigned to it by [[section 1(2)][7] of this Act][8];

["employee", "employment" and "employer" refer to employment under a contract of service or of apprenticeship,][9]

["national unregistered design right" means design right within the meaning of Part III of the Copyright, Designs and Patents Act 1988;][10]

"prescribed" means prescribed by rules made by [the Secretary of State][11] under this Act;

["product" has the meaning assigned to it by section 1(3) of this Act;][12]

"proprietor" has the meaning assigned to it by section two of this Act;

["registered Community design" means a design that complies with the conditions contained in, and is registered in the manner provided for in, the Community Design Regulation;][13]

"registered proprietor" means the person or persons for the time being entered in the register of designs as proprietor of the design;

---

[1] Inserted by Copyright, Designs and Patents Act 1988 c.48 s 272 Sch 3 para 25 (1) (2)
[2] Substituted by Administration of Justice Act 1969 c.58 Sch 1
[3] Inserted by Copyright, Designs and Patents Act 1988 c.48 s 272 Sch 3 para 31 (3)
[4] Inserted by SI 2003/550 reg 2 (5)
[5] Inserted by SI 2001/3949 Sch 1 para 14 (3)
[6] Substituted by Copyright, Designs and Patents Act 1988 c.48 s 272 Sch 3 para 31 (6)
[7] Words substituted by SI 2001/3949 Sch 1 para 14 (2)
[8] Words substituted by Copyright, Designs and Patents Act 1988 c.48 s 272 Sch 3 para 31 (7)
[9] Inserted by Copyright, Designs and Patents Act 1988 c.48 s 272 Sch 3 para 31 (8)
[10] Inserted by SI 2001/3949 Sch 1 para 14 (3)
[11] Words substituted by Copyright, Designs and Patents Act 1988 c.48 s 272 Sch 3 para 31 (10)
[12] Inserted by SI 2001/3949 Sch 1 para 14 (3)
[13] Inserted by SI 2003/550 reg 2 (5)

"registrar" means the Comptroller-General of Patents Designs and Trade Marks;

(4) For the purposes of [subsection (1) of section 14]¹ of this Act, the expression "personal representative", in relation to a deceased person, includes the legal representative of the deceased appointed in any country outside the United Kingdom.

Application to Scotland

45. In the application of this Act to Scotland—   **1-040**

(3) The expression "injunction" means "interdict"; the expression "arbitrator" means "arbiter" the expression "plaintiff" means "pursuer"; the expression "defendant" means "defender".

[(4) References to the Crown shall be construed as including references to the Crown in right of the Scottish Administration.]²

Application to Northern Ireland

46. In the application of this Act to Northern Ireland—   **1-041**

[(3) References to enactments include enactments comprised in Northern Ireland legislation:]³

[(3A) References to the Crown include the Crown in right of Her Majesty's Government in Northern Ireland:]⁴

(4) References to a Government department shall be construed as including references to [a Northern Ireland department]⁵ [and in relation to a Northern Ireland department references to the Treasury shall be construed as references to the Department of Finance and Personnel]⁶:

[Application to Isle of Man

47. This Act extends to the Isle of Man, subject to any modifications **1-042** contained in an Order made by Her Majesty in Council, and accordingly, subject to any such Order, references in this Act to the United Kingdom shall be construed as including the Isle of Man.]⁷

[Territorial waters and the Continental shelf

47A.—(1) For the purposes of this Act the territorial waters of the United **1-043** Kingdom shall be treated as part of the United Kingdom.

(2) This Act applies to things done in the United Kingdom sector of the continental shelf on a structure or vessel which is present there for purposes directly connected with the exploration of the sea bed or subsoil or the exploitation of their natural resources as it applies to things done in the United Kingdom.

(3) The United Kingdom sector of the continental shelf means the areas designated by order under section 1(7) of the Continental Shelf Act 1964.]⁸

---

¹ Words substituted by SI 2001/3949 Sch 1 para 14 (4)
² Inserted by SI 1999/1820 Sch 2 Pt I para 25
³ Substituted by Copyright, Designs and Patents Act 1988 c.48 s 272 Sch 3 para 33 (3)
⁴ Inserted by Copyright, Designs and Patents Act 1988 c.48 s 272 Sch 3 para 33 (4)
⁵ Words substituted by Copyright, Designs and Patents Act 1988 c.48 ss 272 305 (3) Sch 3 para 33 (5)
⁶ Words inserted by Copyright, Designs and Patents Act 1988 c.48 s 272 Sch 3 para 33 (5)
⁷ Substituted by Copyright, Designs and Patents Act 1988 c.48 s 272 Sch 3 para 34
⁸ Inserted by Copyright, Designs and Patents Act 1988 c.48 s 272 Sch 3 para 35

SCHEDULES

[Schedule A1

GROUNDS FOR REFUSAL OF REGISTRATION IN RELATION TO EMBLEMS ETC

Grounds for refusal in relation to certain emblems etc

1-044   1.—(1) A design shall be refused registration under this Act if it involves the use of—

(a) the Royal arms, or any of the principal armorial bearings of the Royal arms, or any insignia or device so nearly resembling the Royal arms or any such armorial bearing as to be likely to be mistaken for them or it;

(b) a representation of the Royal crown or any of the Royal flags;

(c) a representation of Her Majesty or any member of the Royal family, or any colourable imitation thereof; or

(d) words, letters or devices likely to lead persons to think that the applicant either has or recently has had Royal patronage or authorisation;

unless it appears to the registrar that consent for such use has been given by or on behalf of Her Majesty or (as the case may be) the relevant member of the Royal family.

(2) A design shall be refused registration under this Act if it involves the use of—

(a) the national flag of the United Kingdom (commonly known as the Union Jack); or

(b) the flag of England, Wales, Scotland, Northern Ireland or the Isle of Man,

and it appears to the registrar that the use would be misleading or grossly offensive.

(3) A design shall be refused registration under this Act if it involves the use of—

(a) arms to which a person is entitled by virtue of a grant of arms by the Crown; or

(b) insignia so nearly resembling such arms as to be likely to be mistaken for them;

unless it appears to the registrar that consent for such use has been given by or on behalf of the person concerned and the use is not in any way contrary to the law of arms.

(4) A design shall be refused registration under this Act if it involves the use of a controlled representation within the meaning of the Olympic Symbol etc. (Protection) Act 1995 unless it appears to the registrar that—

(a) the application is made by the person for the time being appointed under section 1(2) of the Olympic Symbol etc. (Protection) Act 1995 (power of Secretary of State to appoint a person as the proprietor of the Olympics association right); or

(b) consent for such use has been given by or on behalf of the person mentioned in paragraph (a) above.][1]

Grounds for refusal in relation to emblems etc. of Paris Convention countries

1-045   2.—(1) A design shall be refused registration under this Act if it involves the use of the flag of a Paris Convention country unless—

(a) the authorisation of the competent authorities of that country has been given for the registration; or

(b) it appears to the registrar that the use of the flag in the manner proposed is permitted without such authorisation.

(2) A design shall be refused registration under this Act if it involves the use of the armorial bearings or any other state emblem of a Paris Convention country which is protected under the Paris Convention unless the authorisation of the competent authorities of that country has been given for the registration.

(3) A design shall be refused registration under this Act if—

(a) the design involves the use of an official sign or hallmark adopted by a Paris Convention country and indicating control and warranty;

(b) the sign or hallmark is protected under the Paris Convention; and

(c) the design could be applied to or incorporated in goods of the same, or a similar, kind as those in relation to which the sign or hallmark indicates control and warranty;

unless the authorisation of the competent authorities of that country has been given for the registration.

(4) The provisions of this paragraph as to national flags and other state emblems, and official signs or hallmarks, apply equally to anything which from a heraldic point of view imitates any such flag or other emblem, or sign or hallmark.

---

[1] Inserted by SI 2001/3949 reg 3

(5) Nothing in this paragraph prevents the registration of a design on the application of a national of a country who is authorised to make use of a state emblem, or official sign or hallmark, of that country, notwithstanding that it is similar to that of another country.

Grounds for refusal in relation to emblems etc. of certain international organisations

3.—(1) This paragraph applies to—
    (a) the armorial bearings, flags or other emblems; and
    (b) the abbreviations and names,
of international intergovernmental organisations of which one or more Paris Convention countries are members.

1-046

(2) A design shall be refused registration under this Act if it involves the use of any such emblem, abbreviation or name which is protected under the Paris Convention unless—
    (a) the authorisation of the international organisation concerned has been given for the registration; or
    (b) it appears to the registrar that the use of the emblem, abbreviation or name in the manner proposed—
        (i) is not such as to suggest to the public that a connection exists between the organisation and the design; or
        (ii) is not likely to mislead the public as to the existence of a connection between the user and the organisation.

(3) The provisions of this paragraph as to emblems of an international organisation apply equally to anything which from a heraldic point of view imitates any such emblem.

(4) Nothing in this paragraph affects the rights of a person whose *bona fide* use of the design in question began before 4th January 1962 (when the relevant provisions of the Paris Convention entered into force in relation to the United Kingdom).

Paragraphs 2 and 3: supplementary

4.—(1) For the purposes of paragraph 2 above state emblems of a Paris Convention country (other than the national flag), and official signs or hallmarks, shall be regarded as protected under the Paris Convention only if, or to the extent that—
    (a) the country in question has notified the United Kingdom in accordance with Article 6*ter*(3) of the Convention that it desires to protect that emblem, sign or hallmark;
    (b) the notification remains in force; and
    (c) the United Kingdom has not objected to it in accordance with Article 6*ter*(4) or any such objection has been withdrawn.

1-047

(2) For the purposes of paragraph 3 above the emblems, abbreviations and names of an international organisation shall be regarded as protected under the Paris Convention only if, or to the extent that—
    (a) the organisation in question has notified the United Kingdom in accordance with Article 6*ter*(3) of the Convention that it desires to protect that emblem, abbreviation or name;
    (b) the notification remains in force; and
    (c) the United Kingdom has not objected to it in accordance with Article 6*ter*(4) or any such objection has been withdrawn.

(3) Notification under Article 6*ter*(3) of the Paris Convention shall have effect only in relation to applications for the registration of designs made more than two months after the receipt of the notification.

Interpretation

5. In this Schedule—
    "a Paris Convention country" means a country, other than the United Kingdom, which is a party to the Paris Convention; and
    "the Paris Convention" means the Paris Convention for the Protection of Industrial Property of 20th March 1883.]¹

1-048

---

¹ Inserted by SI 2001/3949 reg 3

Patents Act 1977

CHAPTER 37

PART I

NEW DOMESTIC LAW

Patentability

Patentable inventions

2-001 **1.**—(1) A patent may be granted only for an invention in respect of which the following conditions are satisfied, that is to say—
   (a) the invention is new;
   (b) it involves an inventive step;
   (c) it is capable of industrial application;
   (d) the grant of a patent for it is not excluded by subsections (2) and (3) below;
and references in this Act to a patentable invention shall be construed accordingly.

(2) It is hereby declared that the following (among other things) are not inventions for the purposes of this Act, that is to say, anything which consists of—
   (a) a discovery, scientific theory or mathematical method;
   (b) a literary, dramatic, musical or artistic work or any other aesthetic creation whatsoever;
   (c) a scheme, rule or method for performing a mental act, playing a game or doing business, or a program for a computer;
   (d) the presentation of information;
but the foregoing provision shall prevent anything from being treated as an invention for the purposes of this Act only to the extent that a patent or application for a patent relates to that thing as such.

[(3) A patent shall not be granted for an invention the commercial exploitation of which would be contrary to public policy or morality.

(4) For the purposes of subsection (3) above exploitation shall not be regarded as contrary to public policy or morality only because it is prohibited by any law in force in the United Kingdom or any part of it.][1]

(5) The Secretary of State may by order vary the provisions of subsection (2) above for the purpose of maintaining them in conformity with developments in science and technology; and no such order shall be made unless a draft of the order has been laid before, and approved by resolution of, each House of Parliament.

Novelty

2-002 **2.**—(1) An invention shall be taken to be new if it does not form part of the state of the art.

(2) The state of the art in the case of an invention shall be taken to comprise all matter (whether a product, a process, information about either, or anything

---

[1] Substituted by SI 2000/2037 reg 3

else) which has at any time before the priority date of that invention been made available to the public (whether in the United Kingdom or elsewhere) by written or oral description, by use or in any other way.

(3) The state of the art in the case of an invention to which an application for a patent or a patent relates shall be taken also to comprise matter contained in an application for another patent which was published on or after the priority date of that invention, if the following conditions are satisfied, that is to say—

(a) that matter was contained in the application for that other patent both as filed and as published; and

(b) the priority date of that matter is earlier than that of the invention.

(4) For the purposes of this section the disclosure of matter constituting an invention shall be disregarded in the case of a patent or an application for a patent if occurring later than the beginning of the period of six months immediately preceding the date of filing the application for the patent and either—

(a) the disclosure was due to, or made in consequence of, the matter having been obtained unlawfully or in breach of confidence by any person—

(i) from the inventor or from any other person to whom the matter was made available in confidence by the inventor or who obtained it from the inventor because he or the inventor believed that he was entitled to obtain it; or

(ii) from any other person to whom the matter was made available in confidence by any person mentioned in sub-paragraph (i) above or in this sub-paragraph or who obtained it from any person so mentioned because he or the person from whom he obtained it believed that he was entitled to obtain it;

(b) the disclosure was made in breach of confidence by any person who obtained the matter in confidence from the inventor or from any other person to whom it was made available, or who obtained it, from the inventor; or

(c) the disclosure was due to, or made in consequence of the inventor displaying the invention at an international exhibition and the applicant states, on filing the application, that the invention has been so displayed and also, within the prescribed period, files written evidence in support of the statement complying with any prescribed conditions.

(5) In this section references to the inventor include references to any proprietor of the invention for the time being.

(6) In the case of an invention consisting of a substance or composition for use in a method of treatment of the human or animal body by surgery or therapy or of diagnosis practised on the human or animal body, the fact that the substance or composition forms part of the state of the art shall not prevent the invention from being taken to be new if the use of the substance or composition in any such method does not form part of the state of the art.

Inventive step

3. An invention shall be taken to involve an inventive step if it is not obvious **2-003** to a person skilled in the art, having regard to any matter which forms part of the state of the art by virtue only of section 2(2) above (and disregarding section 2(3) above).

Industrial application

2-004   **4.**—(1) Subject to subsection (2) below, an invention shall be taken to be capable of industrial application if it can be made or used in any kind of industry, including agriculture.

(2) An invention of a method of treatment of the human or animal body by surgery or therapy or of diagnosis practised on the human or animal body shall not be taken to be capable of industrial application.

(3) Subsection (2) above shall not prevent a product consisting of a substance or composition being treated as capable of industrial application merely because it is invented for use in any such method.

Priority date

2-005   **5.**—(1) For the purposes of this Act the priority date of an invention to which an application for a patent relates and also of any matter (whether or not the same as the invention) contained in any such application is, except as provided by the following provisions of this Act, the date of filing the application.

(2) If in or in connection with an application for a patent (the application in suit) a declaration is made, whether by the applicant or any predecessor in title of his, complying with the relevant requirements of rules and specifying one or more earlier relevant applications for the purposes of this section made by the applicant or a predecessor in title of his and each having a date of filing during the period of twelve months immediately preceding the date of filing the application in suit, then—

(a) if an invention to which the application in suit relates is supported by matter disclosed in the earlier relevant application or applications, the priority date of that invention shall instead of being the date of filing the application in suit be the date of filing the relevant application in which that matter was disclosed, or, if it was disclosed in more than one relevant application, the earliest of them;

(b) the priority date of any matter contained in the application in suit which was also disclosed in the earlier relevant application or applications shall be the date of filing the relevant application in which that matter was disclosed or, if it was disclosed in more than one relevant application, the earliest of them.

(3) Where an invention or other matter contained in the application in suit was also disclosed in two earlier relevant applications filed by the same applicant as in the case of the application in suit or a predecessor in title of his and the second of those relevant applications was specified in or in connection with the application in suit, the second of those relevant applications shall, so far as concerns that invention or matter, be disregarded unless—

(a) it was filed in or in respect of the same country as the first; and

(b) not later than the date of filing the second, the first (whether or not so specified) was unconditionally withdrawn, or was abandoned or refused, without—

(i) having been made available to the public (whether in the United Kingdom or elsewhere);

(ii) leaving any rights outstanding; and

(iii) having served to establish a priority date in relation to another application, wherever made.

(4) The foregoing provisions of this section shall apply for determining the priority date of an invention for which a patent has been granted as they apply for

determining the priority date of an invention to which an application for that patent relates.

(5) In this section "relevant application" means any of the following applications which has a date of filing, namely—

(a) an application for a patent under this Act;

(b) an application in or for a convention country (specified under section 90 below) for protection in respect of an invention or an application which, in accordance with the law of a convention country or a treaty or international convention to which a convention country is a party, is equivalent to such an application.

[(6) References in subsection (5) above to a convention country include references to a country, other than the United Kingdom, which is a member of the World Trade Organisation.][1]

Disclosure of matter, etc., between earlier and later applications

6.—(1) It is hereby declared for the avoidance of doubt that where an applica- **2-006** tion (the application in suit) is made for a patent and a declaration is made in accordance with section 5(2) above in or in connection with that application specifying an earlier relevant application, the application in suit and any patent granted in pursuance of it shall not be invalidated by reason only of relevant intervening acts.

(2) In this section—

"relevant application" has the same meaning as in section 5 above; and

"relevant intervening acts" means acts done in relation to matter disclosed in an earlier relevant application between the dates of the earlier relevant application and the application in suit, as for example, filing another application for the invention for which the earlier relevant application was made, making information available to the public about that invention or that matter or working that invention, but disregarding any application, or the disclosure to the public of matter contained in any application, which is itself to be disregarded for the purposes of section 5(3) above.

Right to apply for and obtain a patent and be mentioned as inventor

Right to apply for and obtain a patent

7.—(1) Any person may make an application for a patent either alone or **2-007** jointly with another.

(2) A patent for an invention may be granted—

(a) primarily to the inventor or joint inventors;

(b) in preference to the foregoing, to any person or persons who, by virtue of any enactment or rule of law, or any foreign law or treaty or international convention, or by virtue of an enforceable term of any agreement entered into with the inventor before the making of the invention, was or were at the time of the making of the invention entitled to the whole of the property in it (other than equitable interests) in the United Kingdom;

(c) in any event, to the successor or successors in title of any person or persons mentioned in paragraph (a) or (b) above or any person so

---

[1] Inserted by SI 1999/1899 Pt II reg 7 (1)

mentioned and the successor or successors in title of another person so mentioned;

and to no other person.

(3) In this Act "inventor" in relation to an invention means the actual deviser of the invention and "joint inventor" shall be construed accordingly.

(4) Except so far as the contrary is established, a person who makes an application for a patent shall be taken to be the person who is entitled under subsection (2) above to be granted a patent and two or more persons who make such an application jointly shall be taken to be the persons so entitled.

Determination before grant of questions about entitlement to patents, etc

2-008   **8.**—(1) At any time before a patent has been granted for an invention (whether or not an application has been made for it)—

(a) any person may refer to the comptroller the question whether he is entitled to be granted (alone or with any other persons) a patent for that invention or has or would have any right in or under any patent so granted or any application for such a patent; or

(b) any of two or more co-proprietors of an application for a patent for that invention may so refer the question whether any right in or under the application should be transferred or granted to any other person;

and the comptroller shall determine the question and may make such order as he thinks fit to give effect to the determination.

Determination after grant of questions referred before grant

2-009   **9.** If a question with respect to a patent or application is referred by any person to the comptroller under section 8 above, whether before or after the making of an application for the patent, and is not determined before the time when the application is first in order for a grant of a patent in pursuance of the application, that fact shall not prevent the grant of a patent, but on its grant that person shall be treated as having referred to the comptroller under section 37 below any question mentioned in that section which the comptroller thinks appropriate.

Handling of application by joint applicants

2-010   **10.** If any dispute arises between joint applicants for a patent whether or in what manner the application should be proceeded with, the comptroller may, on a request made by any of the parties, give such directions as he thinks fit for enabling the application to proceed in the name of one or more of the parties alone or for regulating the manner in which it shall be proceeded with, or for both those purposes, according as the case may require.

Determination of questions about entitlement to foreign and convention patents, etc

2-011   **12.**—(1) At any time before a patent is granted for an invention in pursuance of an application made under the law of any country other than the United Kingdom or under any treaty or international convention (whether or not that application has been made)—

(a) any person may refer to the comptroller the question whether he is entitled to be granted (alone or with any other persons) any such patent for that invention or has or would have any right in or under any such patent or an application for such a patent; or

(b) any of two or more co-proprietors of an application for such a patent for that invention may so refer the question whether any right in or under the application should be transferred or granted to any other person;

and the comptroller shall determine the question so far as he is able to and may make such order as he thinks fit to give effect to the determination.

Mention of inventor

13.—(1) The inventor or joint inventors of an invention shall have a right to **2-012** be mentioned as such in any patent granted for the invention and shall also have a right to be so mentioned if possible in any published application for a patent for the invention and, if not so mentioned, a right to be so mentioned in accordance with rules in a prescribed document.

(2) Unless he has already given the Patent Office the information hereinafter mentioned, an applicant for a patent shall within the prescribed period file with the Patent Office a statement—

(a) identifying the person or persons whom he believes to be the inventor or inventors; and

(b) where the applicant is not the sole inventor or the applicants are not the joint inventors, indicating the derivation of his or their right to be granted the patent;

and, if he fails to do so, the application shall be taken to be withdrawn.

(3) Where a person has been mentioned as sole or joint inventor in pursuance of this section, any other person who alleges that the former ought not to have been so mentioned may at any time apply to the comptroller for a certificate to that effect, and the comptroller may issue such a certificate; and if he does so, he shall accordingly rectify any undistributed copies of the patent and of any documents prescribed for the purposes of subsection (1) above.

Applications

Making of application

14.—(1) Every application for a patent— **2-013**

(a) shall be made in the prescribed form and shall be filed at the Patent Office in the prescribed manner; and

(b) shall be accompanied by the fee prescribed for the purposes of this subsection (hereafter in this Act referred to as the filing fee).

(2) Every application for a patent shall contain—

(a) a request for the grant of a patent;

(b) a specification containing a description of the invention, a claim or claims and any drawing referred to in the description or any claim; and

(c) an abstract;

but the foregoing provision shall not prevent an application being initiated by documents complying with section 15(1) below.

(3) The specification of an application shall disclose the invention in a manner which is clear enough and complete enough for the invention to be performed by a person skilled in the art.

(5) The claim or claims shall—

(a) define the matter for which the applicant seeks protection;

(b) be clear and concise;

    (c) be supported by the description; and

    (d) relate to one invention or to a group of inventions which are so linked as to form a single inventive concept.

(6) Without prejudice to the generality of subsection (5)(d) above, rules may provide for treating two or more inventions as being so linked as to form a single inventive concept for the purposes of this Act.

(7) The purpose of the abstract is to give technical information and on publication it shall not form part of the state of the art by virtue of section 2(3) above, and the comptroller may determine whether the abstract adequately fulfils its purpose and, if it does not, may reframe it so that it does.

(9) An application for a patent may be withdrawn at any time before the patent is granted and any withdrawal of such an application may not be revoked.

Date of filing application

2-014   **15.**—(1) The date of filing an application for a patent shall, subject to the following provisions of this Act, be taken to be the earliest date on which the following conditions are satisfied in relation to the application, that is to say—

    (a) the documents filed at the Patent Office contain an indication that a patent is sought in pursuance of the application;

    (b) those documents identify the applicant or applicants for the patent;

    (c) those documents contain a description of the invention for which a patent is sought (whether or not the description complies with the other provisions of this Act and with any relevant rules); and

    (d) the applicant pays the filing fee.

(2) If any drawing referred to in any such application is filed later than the date which by virtue of subsection (1) above is to be treated as the date of filing the application, but before the beginning of the preliminary examination of the application under section 17 below, the comptroller shall give the applicant an opportunity of requesting within the prescribed period that the date on which the drawing is filed shall be treated for the purposes of this Act as the date of filing the application, and—

    (a) if the applicant makes any such request, the date of filing the drawing shall be so treated; but

    (b) otherwise any reference to the drawing in the application shall be treated as omitted.

(3) If on the preliminary examination of an application under section 17 below it is found that any drawing referred to in the application has not been filed, then—

    (a) if the drawing is subsequently filed within the prescribed period, the date on which it is filed shall be treated for the purposes of this Act as the date of filing the application; but

    (b) otherwise any reference to the drawing in the application shall be treated as omitted.

[(3A) Nothing in subsection (2) or (3) above shall be construed as affecting the power of the comptroller under section 17(1) below to correct errors or mistakes with respect to the filing of drawings.][1]

(4) Where, after an application for a patent has been filed and before the patent is granted, a new application is filed by the original applicant or his successor in title in accordance with rules in respect of any part of the matter contained in the earlier application and the conditions mentioned in subsection

---

[1] Inserted by Copyright, Designs and Patents Act 1988 c.48 s 295 Sch 5 para 2

(1) above are satisfied in relation to the new application (without the new application contravening section 76 below) the new application shall be treated as having, as its date of filing, the date of filing the earlier application.

(5) An application which has a date of filing by virtue of the foregoing provisions of this section shall be taken to be withdrawn at the end of the relevant prescribed period, unless before that end the applicant—

    (a) files at the Patent Office one or more claims for the purposes of the application and also the abstract; and

    (b) makes a request for a preliminary examination and search under the following provisions of this Act and pays the search fee.

Publication of application

16.—(1) Subject to section 22 below, where an application has a date of **2-015** filing, then, as soon as possible after the end of the prescribed period, the comptroller shall, unless the application is withdrawn or refused before preparations for its publication have been completed by the Patent Office, publish it as filed (including not only the original claims but also any amendments of those claims and new claims subsisting immediately before the completion of those preparations) and he may, if so requested by the applicant, publish it as aforesaid during that period, and in either event shall advertise the fact and date of its publication in the journal.

(2) The comptroller may omit from the specification of a published application for a patent any matter—

    (a) which in his opinion disparages any person in a way likely to damage him, or

    (b) the publication or exploitation of which would in his opinion be generally expected to encourage offensive, immoral or anti-social behaviour.

Examination and search

Preliminary examination and search

17.—(1) Where an application for a patent has a date of filing and is not **2-016** withdrawn, and before the end of the prescribed period—

    (a) a request is made by the applicant to the Patent Office in the prescribed form for a preliminary examination and a search; and

    (b) the prescribed fee is paid for the examination and search (the search fee);

the comptroller shall refer the application to an examiner for a preliminary examination and search, except that he shall not refer the application for a search until it includes one or more claims.

(2) On a preliminary examination of an application the examiner shall determine whether the application complies with those requirements of this Act and the rules which are designated by the rules as formal requirements for the purposes of this Act and shall report his determination to the comptroller.

(3) If it is reported to the comptroller under subsection (2) above that not all the formal requirements are complied with, he shall give the applicant an opportunity to make observations on the report and to amend the application within a specified period (subject to section 15(5) above) so as to comply with those requirements (subject, however, to section 76 below), and if the applicant fails to do so the comptroller may refuse the application.

(4) Subject to subsections (5) and (6) below, on a search requested under this section, the examiner shall make such investigation as in his opinion is reasonably practicable and necessary for him to identify the documents which he thinks will be needed to decide, on a substantive examination under section 18 below, whether the invention for which a patent is sought is new and involves an inventive step.

(5) On any such search the examiner shall determine whether or not the search would serve any useful purpose on the application as for the time being constituted and—

> (a) if he determines that it would serve such a purpose in relation to the whole or part of the application, he shall proceed to conduct the search so far as it would serve such a purpose and shall report on the results of the search to the comptroller; and
>
> (b) if he determines that the search would not serve such a purpose in relation to the whole or part of the application, he shall report accordingly to the comptroller;

and in either event the applicant shall be informed of the examiner's report.

(6) If it appears to the examiner, either before or on conducting a search under this section, that an application relates to two or more inventions, but that they are not so linked as to form a single inventive concept, he shall initially only conduct a search in relation to the first invention specified in the claims of the application, but may proceed to conduct a search in relation to another invention so specified if the applicant pays the search fee in respect of the application so far as it relates to that other invention.

(7) After a search has been requested under this section for an application the comptroller may at any time refer the application to an examiner for a supplementary search, and [subsections (4) and (5) above][1] above shall apply in relation to a supplementary search as [they apply][2] in relation to any other search under this section.

[(8) A reference for a supplementary search in consequence of—

> (a) an amendment of the application made by the applicant under section 18(3) or 19(1) below, or
>
> (b) a correction of the application, or of a document filed in connection with the application, under section 117 below,

shall be made only on payment of the prescribed fee, unless the comptroller directs otherwise.][3]

Substantive examination and grant or refusal of patent

2-017   **18.**—(1) Where the conditions imposed by section 17(1) above for the comptroller to refer an application to an examiner for a preliminary examination and search are satisfied and at the time of the request under that subsection or within the prescribed period—

> (a) a request is made by the applicant to the Patent Office in the prescribed form for a substantive examination; and
>
> (b) the prescribed fee is paid for the examination;

the comptroller shall refer the application to an examiner for a substantive examination; and if no such request is made or the prescribed fee is not paid within that period, the application shall be treated as having been withdrawn at the end of that period.

---

[1] Words substituted by Copyright, Designs and Patents Act 1988 c.48 s 295 Sch 5 para 3 (2)
[2] Words substituted by Copyright, Designs and Patents Act 1988 c.48 s 295 Sch 5 para 3 (2)
[3] Inserted by Copyright, Designs and Patents Act 1988 c. 48 s 295 Sch 5 para 3 (3)

[(1A) If the examiner forms the view that a supplementary search under section 17 above is required for which a fee is payable, he shall inform the comptroller, who may decide that the substantive examination should not proceed until the fee is paid; and if he so decides, then unless within such period as he may allow—

(a) the fee is paid, or

(b) the application is amended so as to render the supplementary search unnecessary,

he may refuse the application.][1]

(2) On a substantive examination of an application the examiner shall investigate, to such extent as he considers necessary in view of any examination and search carried out under section 17 above, whether the application complies with the requirements of this Act and the rules and shall determine that question and report his determination to the comptroller.

(3) If the examiner reports that any of those requirements are not complied with, the comptroller shall give the applicant an opportunity within a specified period to make observations on the report and to amend the application so as to comply with those requirements (subject, however, to section 76 below), and if the applicant fails to satisfy the comptroller that those requirements are complied with, or to amend the application so as to comply with them, the comptroller may refuse the application.

(4) If the examiner reports that the application, whether as originally filed or as amended in pursuance of section 17 above, this section or section 19 below, complies with those requirements at any time before the end of the prescribed period, the comptroller shall notify the applicant of that fact and, subject to subsection (5) and sections 19 and 22 below and on payment within the prescribed period of any fee prescribed for the grant, grant him a patent.

(5) Where two or more applications for a patent for the same invention having the same priority date are filed by the same applicant or his successor in title, the comptroller may on that ground refuse to grant a patent in pursuance of more than one of the applications.

General power to amend application before grant

19.—(1) At any time before a patent is granted in pursuance of an application 2-018 the applicant may, in accordance with the prescribed conditions and subject to section 76 below, amend the application of his own volition.

(2) The comptroller may, without an application being made to him for the purpose, amend the specification and abstract contained in an application for a patent so as to acknowledge a registered trade mark.

Failure of application

20.—(1) If it is not determined that an application for a patent complies 2-019 before the end of the prescribed period with all the requirements of this Act and the rules, the application shall be treated as having been refused by the comptroller at the end of that period, and section 97 below shall apply accordingly.

Observations by third party on patentability

21.—(1) Where an application for a patent has been published but a patent 2-020 has not been granted to the applicant, any other person may make observations in writing to the comptroller on the question whether the invention is a patentable

---

[1] Inserted by Copyright, Designs and Patents Act 1988 c.48 s 295 Sch 5 para 4

invention, stating reasons for the observations, and the comptroller shall consider the observations in accordance with rules.

(2) It is hereby declared that a person does not become a party to any proceedings under this Act before the comptroller by reason only that he makes observations under this section.

Security and safety

Information prejudicial to defence of realm or safety of public

2-021 **22.**—(1) Where an application for a patent is filed in the Patent Office (whether under this Act or any treaty or international convention to which the United Kingdom is a party and whether before or after the appointed day) and it appears to the comptroller that the application contains information of a description notified to him by the Secretary of State as being information the publication of which might be prejudicial to the defence of the realm, the comptroller may give directions prohibiting or restricting the publication of that information or its communication to any specified person or description of persons.

(2) If it appears to the comptroller that any application so filed contains information the publication of which might be prejudicial to the safety of the public, he may give directions prohibiting or restricting the publication of that information or its communication to any specified person or description of persons until the end of a period not exceeding three months from the end of the period prescribed for the purposes of section 16 above.

Restrictions on applications abroad by United Kingdom residents

2-022 **23.**—(1) Subject to the following provisions of this section, no person resident in the United Kingdom shall, without written authority granted by the comptroller, file or cause to be filed outside the United Kingdom an application for a patent for an invention unless—

  (a) an application for a patent for the same invention has been filed in the Patent Office (whether before, on or after the appointed day) not less than six weeks before the application outside the United Kingdom; and

  (b) either no directions have been given under section 22 above in relation to the application in the United Kingdom or all such directions have been revoked.

(2) Subsection (1) above does not apply to an application for a patent for an invention for which an application for a patent has first been filed (whether before or after the appointed day) in a country outside the United Kingdom by a person resident outside the United Kingdom.

Provisions as to patents after grant

Publication and certificate of grant

2-023 **24.**—(1) As soon as practicable after a patent has been granted under this Act the comptroller shall publish in the journal a notice that it has been granted.

(2) The comptroller shall, as soon as practicable after he publishes a notice under subsection (1) above, send the proprietor of the patent a certificate in the prescribed form that the patent has been granted to the proprietor.

(3) The comptroller shall, at the same time as he publishes a notice under subsection (1) above in relation to a patent publish the specification of the patent, the names of the proprietor and (if different) the inventor and any other matters constituting or relating to the patent which in the comptroller's opinion it is desirable to publish.

Term of patent

25.—(1) A patent granted under this Act shall be treated for the purposes of **2-024** the following provisions of this Act as having been granted, and shall take effect, on the date on which notice of its grant is published in the journal and, subject to subsection (3) below, shall continue in force until the end of the period of 20 years beginning with the date of filing the application for the patent or with such other date as may be prescribed.

Patent not to be impugned for lack of unity

26. No person may in any proceeding object to a patent or to an amendment **2-025** of a specification of a patent on the ground that the claims contained in the specification of the patent, as they stand or, as the case may be, as proposed to be amended, relate—
    (a) to more than one invention, or
    (b) to a group of inventions which are not so linked as to form a single inventive concept.

General power to amend specification after grant

27.—(1) Subject to the following provisions of this section and to section 76 **2-026** below, the comptroller may, on an application made by the proprietor of a patent, allow the specification of the patent to be amended subject to such conditions, if any, as he thinks fit.

Restoration of lapsed patents

28.—[(1) Where a patent has ceased to have effect by reason of a failure to **2-027** pay any renewal fee, an application for the restoration of the patent may be made to the comptroller within the prescribed period.

(1A) Rules prescribing that period may contain such transitional provisions and savings as appear to the Secretary of State to be necessary or expedient.][1]

(2) An application under this section may be made by the person who was the proprietor of the patent or by any other person who would have been entitled to the patent if it had not ceased to have effect; and where the patent was held by two or more persons jointly, the application may, with the leave of the comptroller, be made by one or more of them without joining the others.

[(2A) Notice of the application shall be published by the comptroller in the prescribed manner.][2]

(3) If the comptroller is satisfied that—
    (a) the proprietor of the patent took reasonable care to see that any renewal fee was paid within the prescribed period or that that fee and

---

[1] Substituted by Copyright, Designs and Patents Act 1988 c.48 s 295 Sch 5 para 6 (2)
[2] Inserted by Copyright, Designs and Patents Act 1988 c.48 s 295 Sch 5 para 6 (3)

any prescribed additional fee were paid within the six months immediately following the end of that period, [...][1]

(b) [...][2]

the comptroller shall by order restore the patent on payment of any unpaid renewal fee and any prescribed additional fee.

[Effect of order for restoration of patent

2-028　　**28A.**—(1) The effect of an order for the restoration of a patent is as follows.

(2) Anything done under or in relation to the patent during the period between expiry and restoration shall be treated as valid.

(3) Anything done during that period which would have constituted an infringement if the patent had not expired shall be treated as an infringement—

    (a) if done at a time when it was possible for the patent to be renewed under section 25(4), or

    (b) if it was a continuation or repetition of an earlier infringing act.

(4) If after it was no longer possible for the patent to be so renewed, and before publication of notice of the application for restoration, a person—

    (a) began in good faith to do an act which would have constituted an infringement of the patent if it had not expired, or

    (b) made in good faith effective and serious preparations to do such an act,

he has the right to continue to do the act or, as the case may be, to do the act, notwithstanding the restoration of the patent; but this right does not extend to granting a licence to another person to do the act.

(5) If the act was done, or the preparations were made, in the course of a business, the person entitled to the right conferred by subsection (4) may—

    (a) authorise the doing of that act by any partners of his for the time being in that business, and

    (b) assign that right, or transmit it on death (or in the case of a body corporate on its dissolution), to any person who acquires that part of the business in the course of which the act was done or the preparations were made.

(6) Where a product is disposed of to another in exercise of the rights conferred by subsection (4) or (5), that other and any person claiming through him may deal with the product in the same way as if it had been disposed of by the registered proprietor of the patent.

(7) The above provisions apply in relation to the use of a patent for the services of the Crown as they apply in relation to infringement of the patent.][3]

Surrender of patents

2-029　　**29.**—(1) The proprietor of a patent may at any time by notice given to the comptroller offer to surrender his patent.

---

[1] Word repealed by Copyright, Designs and Patents Act 1988 c.48 ss 295, 303 (2) Sch 5 para 6 (4) Sch 8

[2] Repealed by Copyright, Designs and Patents Act 1988 c.48 ss 295, 303 (2) Sch 5 para 6 (4) Sch 8

[3] Inserted by Copyright, Designs and Patents Act 1988 c.48 s 295 Sch 5 para 7

Property in patents and applications, and registration

Nature of, and transactions in, patents and applications for patents

30.—(1) Any patent or application for a patent is personal property (without **2-030** being a thing in action), and any patent or any such application and rights in or under it may be transferred, created or granted in accordance with subsections (2) to (7) below.

(2) Subject to section 36(3) below, any patent or any such application, or any right in it, may be assigned or mortgaged.

(3) Any patent or any such application or right shall vest by operation of law in the same way as any other personal property and may be vested by an assent of personal representatives.

(4) Subject to section 36(3) below, a licence may be granted under any patent or any such application for working the invention which is the subject of the patent or the application; and—

  (a) to the extent that the licence so provides, a sub-licence may be granted under any such licence and any such licence or sub-licence may be assigned or mortgaged; and

  (b) any such licence or sub-licence shall vest by operation of law in the same way as any other personal property and may be vested by an assent of personal representatives.

(5) Subsections (2) to (4) above shall have effect subject to the following provisions of this Act.

(6) Any of the following transactions, that is to say—

  (a) any assignment or mortgage of a patent or any such application, or any right in a patent or any such application;

  (b) any assent relating to any patent or any such application or right;

shall be void unless it is in writing and is signed by or on behalf of the parties to the transaction (or, in the case of an assent or other transaction by a personal representative, by or on behalf of the personal representative) or in the case of a body corporate is so signed or is under the seal of that body.

(7) An assignment of a patent or any such application or a share in it, and an exclusive licence granted under any patent or any such application, may confer on the assignee or licensee the right of the assignor or licensor to bring proceedings by virtue of section 61 or 69 below for a previous infringement or to bring proceedings under section 58 below for a previous act.

Nature of, and transactions in, patents and applications for patents in Scotland

31.—(1) Section 30 above shall not extend to Scotland, but instead the **2-031** following provisions of this section shall apply there.

(2) Any patent or application for a patent, and any right in or under any patent or any such application, is incorporeal moveable property, and the provisions of the following sub-sections and of section 36(3) below shall apply to any grant of licences, assignations and securities in relation to such property.

(3) Any patent or any such application, or any right in it, may be assigned and security may be granted over a patent or any such application or right.

(4) A licence may be granted, under any patent or any application for a patent, for working the invention which is the subject of the patent or the application.

(5) To the extent that any licence granted under subsection (4) above so provides, a sub-licence may be granted under any such licence and any such licence or sub-licence may be assigned and security may be granted over it.

(6) Any assignation or grant of security under this section may be carried out only by writing [subscribed in accordance with the Requirements of Writing (Scotland) Act 1995][1].

(7) An assignation of a patent or application for a patent or a share in it, and an exclusive licence granted under any patent or any such application, may confer on the assignee or licensee the right of the assignor or licensor to bring proceedings by virtue of section 61 or 69 below for a previous infringement or to bring proceedings under section 58 below for a previous act.

[Register of patents etc

2-032   **32.**—(1) The comptroller shall maintain the register of patents, which shall comply with rules made by virtue of this section and shall be kept in accordance with such rules.

(2) Without prejudice to any other provision of this Act or rules, rules may make provision with respect to the following matters, including provision imposing requirements as to any of those matters—

(a) the registration of patents and of published applications for patents;

(b) the registration of transactions, instruments or events affecting rights in or under patents and applications;

(c) the furnishing to the comptroller of any prescribed documents or description of documents in connection with any matter which is required to be registered;

(d) the correction of errors in the register and in any documents filed at the Patent Office in connection with registration; and

(e) the publication and advertisement of anything done under this Act or rules in relation to the register.

(3) Notwithstanding anything in subsection (2)(b) above, no notice of any trust, whether express, implied or constructive, shall be entered in the register and the comptroller shall not be affected by any such notice.

(4) The register need not be kept in documentary form.

(5) Subject to rules, the public shall have a right to inspect the register at the Patent Office at all convenient times.

(6) Any person who applies for a certified copy of an entry in the register or a certified extract from the register shall be entitled to obtain such a copy or extract on payment of a fee prescribed in relation to certified copies and extracts; and rules may provide that any person who applies for an uncertified copy or extract shall be entitled to such a copy or extract on payment of a fee prescribed in relation to uncertified copies and extracts.

(7) Applications under subsection (6) above or rules made by virtue of that subsection shall be made in such manner as may be prescribed.

(8) In relation to any portion of the register kept otherwise than in documentary form—

(a) the right of inspection conferred by subsection (5) above is a right to inspect the material on the register; and

(b) the right to a copy or extract conferred by subsection (6) above or rules is a right to a copy or extract in a form in which it can be taken away and in which it is visible and legible.

---

[1] Words substituted by Requirements of Writing (Scotland) Act 1995 c.7 Sch 4 (2) para 49

(9) Subject to subsection (12) below, the register shall be prima facie evidence of anything required or authorised by this Act or rules to be registered and in Scotland shall be sufficient evidence of any such thing.

(10) A certificate purporting to be signed by the comptroller and certifying that any entry which he is authorised by this Act or rules to make has or has not been made, or that any other thing which he is so authorised to do has or has not been done, shall be prima facie evidence, and in Scotland shall be sufficient evidence, of the matters so certified.

(11) Each of the following, that is to say—

(a) a copy of an entry in the register or an extract from the register which is supplied under subsection (6) above;

(b) a copy of any document kept in the Patent Office or an extract from any such document, any specification of a patent or any application for a patent which has been published,

which purports to be a certified copy or a certified extract shall, subject to subsection (12) below, be admitted in evidence without further proof and without production of any original; and in Scotland such evidence shall be sufficient evidence.

(13) In this section "certified copy" and "certified extract" means a copy and extract certified by the comptroller and sealed with the seal of the Patent Office.

(14) In this Act, except so far as the context otherwise requires—

"register", as a noun, means the register of patents;

"register", as a verb, means , in relation to any thing, to register or register particulars, or enter notice, of that thing in the register and, in relation to a person, means to enter his name in the register;

and cognate expressions shall be construed accordingly.][1]

Effect of registration, etc., on rights in patents

33.—(1) Any person who claims to have acquired the property in a patent or **2-033** application for a patent by virtue of any transaction, instrument or event to which this section applies shall be entitled as against any other person who claims to have acquired that property by virtue of an earlier transaction, instrument or event to which this section applies if, at the time of the later transaction, instrument or event—

(a) the earlier transaction, instrument or event was not registered, or

(b) in the case of any application which has not been published, notice of the earlier transaction, instrument or event had not been given to the comptroller, and

(c) in any case, the person claiming under the later transaction, instrument or event, did not know of the earlier transaction, instrument or event.

(2) Subsection (1) above shall apply equally to the case where any person claims to have acquired any right in or under a patent or application for a patent, by virtue of a transaction, instrument or event to which this section applies, and that right is incompatible with any such right acquired by virtue of an earlier transaction, instrument or event to which this section applies.

(3) This section applies to the following transactions, instruments and events:—

(a) the assignment or assignation of a patent or application for a patent, or a right in it;

---

[1] Substituted by Patents, Designs and Marks Act 1986 c.39 s 1 Sch 1 para 4

(b) the mortgage of a patent or application or the granting of security over it;

(c) the grant, assignment or assignation of a licence or sub-licence, or mortgage of a licence or sub-licence, under a patent or application;

(d) the death of the proprietor or one of the proprietors of any such patent or application or any person having a right in or under a patent or application and the vesting by an assent of personal representatives of a patent, application or any such right; and

(e) any order or directions of a court or other competent authority—
  (i) transferring a patent or application or any right in or under it to any person; or
  (ii) that an application should proceed in the name of any person;

and in either case the event by virtue of which the court or authority had power to make any such order or give any such directions.

(4) Where an application for the registration of a transaction, instrument or event has been made, but the transaction, instrument or event has not been registered, then, for the purposes of subsection (1)(a) above, registration of the application shall be treated as registration of the transaction, instrument or event.

Rectification of register

2-034   **34.**—(1) The court may, on the application of any person aggrieved, order the register to be rectified by the making, or the variation or deletion, of any entry in it.

Co-ownership of patents and applications for patents

2-035   **36.**—(1) Where a patent is granted to two or more persons, each of them shall, subject to any agreement to the contrary, be entitled to an equal undivided share in the patent.

(2) Where two or more persons are proprietors of a patent, then, subject to the provisions of this section and subject to any agreement to the contrary—

(a) each of them shall be entitled, by himself or his agents, to do in respect of the invention concerned, for his own benefit and without the consent of or the need to account to the other or others, any act which would apart from this subsection and section 55 below, amount to an infringement of the patent concerned; and

(b) any such act shall not amount to an infringement of the patent concerned.

(3) Subject to the provisions of sections 8 and 12 above and section 37 below and to any agreement for the time being in force, where two or more persons are proprietors of a patent one of them shall not without the consent of the other or others grant a licence under the patent or assign or mortgage a share in the patent or in Scotland cause or permit security to be granted over it.

(4) Subject to the provisions of those sections, where two or more persons are proprietors of a patent, anyone else may supply one of those persons with the means, relating to an essential element of the invention, for putting the invention into effect, and the supply of those means by virtue of this subsection shall not amount to an infringement of the patent.

(5) Where a patented product is disposed of by any of two or more proprietors to any person, that person and any other person claiming through him shall be entitled to deal with the product in the same way as if it had been disposed of by a sole registered proprietor.

(6) Nothing in subsection (1) or (2) above shall affect the mutual rights or obligations of trustees or of the personal representatives of a deceased person, or their rights or obligations as such.

(7) The foregoing provisions of this section shall have effect in relation to an application for a patent which is filed as they have effect in relation to a patent and—

   (a) references to a patent and a patent being granted shall accordingly include references respectively to any such application and to the application being filed; and

   (b) the reference in subsection (5) above to a patented product shall be construed accordingly,

Determination of right to patent after grant

37.—[(1) After a patent has been granted for an invention any person having **2-036** or claiming a proprietary interest in or under the patent may refer to the comptroller the question—

   (a) who is or are the true proprietor or proprietors of the patent,

   (b) whether the patent should have been granted to the person or persons to whom it was granted, or

   (c) whether any right in or under the patent should be transferred or granted to any other person or persons;

and the comptroller shall determine the question and make such order as he thinks fit to give effect to the determination.][1]

(2) Without prejudice to the generality of subsection (1) above, an order under that subsection may contain provision—

   (a) directing that the person by whom the reference is made under that subsection shall be included (whether or not to the exclusion of any other person) among the persons registered as proprietors of the patent;

   (b) directing the registration of a transaction, instrument or event by virtue of which that person has acquired any right in or under the patent;

   (c) granting any licence or other right in or under the patent;

   (d) directing the proprietor of the patent or any person having any right in or under the patent to do anything specified in the order as necessary to carry out the other provisions of the order.

(3) If any person to whom directions have been given under subsection (2)(d) above fails to do anything necessary for carrying out any such directions within 14 days after the date of the order containing the directions, the comptroller may, on application made to him by any person in whose favour or on whose reference the order containing the directions was made, authorise him to do that thing on behalf of the person to whom the directions were given.

(4) Where the comptroller finds on a reference under [this section][2] above that the patent was granted to a person not entitled to be granted that patent (whether alone or with other persons) and on an application made under section 72 below makes an order on that ground for the conditional or unconditional revocation of the patent, the comptroller may order that the person by whom the application was made or his successor in title may, subject to section 76 below, make a new application for a patent—

---

[1] Substituted by Copyright, Designs and Patents Act 1988 c.48 s 295 Sch 5 para 9 (2)

[2] Words substituted by Copyright, Designs and Patents Act 1988 c.48 s 295 Sch 5 para 9 (3) (a)

(a) in the case of unconditional revocation, for the whole of the matter comprised in the specification of that patent; and

(b) in the case of conditional revocation, for the matter which in the opinion of the comptroller should be excluded from that specification by amendment under section 75 below;

(5) On any such reference no order shall be made under this section transferring the patent to which the reference relates on the ground that the patent was granted to a person not so entitled, and no order shall be made under subsection (4) above on that ground, if the reference was made after the end of the period of two years beginning with the date of the grant, unless it is shown that any person registered as a proprietor of the patent knew at the time of the grant or, as the case may be, of the transfer of the patent to him that he was not entitled to the patent.

(6) An order under this section shall not be so made as to affect the mutual rights or obligations of trustees or of the personal representatives of a deceased person, or their rights or obligations as such.

Employees' inventions

Right to employees' inventions

2-037   **39.**—(1) Notwithstanding anything in any rule of law, an invention made by an employee shall, as between him and his employer, be taken to belong to his employer for the purposes of this Act and all other purposes if—

(a) it was made in the course of the normal duties of the employee or in the course of duties falling outside his normal duties, but specifically assigned to him, and the circumstances in either case were such that an invention might reasonably be expected to result from the carrying out of his duties; or

(b) the invention was made in the course of the duties of the employee and, at the time of making the invention, because of the nature of his duties and the particular responsibilities arising from the nature of his duties he had a special obligation to further the interests of the employer's undertaking.

(2) Any other invention made by an employee shall, as between him and his employer, be taken for those purposes to belong to the employee.

[(3) Where by virtue of this section an invention belongs, as between him and his employer, to an employee, nothing done—

(a) by or on behalf of the employee or any person claiming under him for the purposes of pursuing an application for a patent, or

(b) by any person for the purpose of performing or working the invention, shall be taken to infringe any copyright or design right to which, as between him and his employer, his employer is entitled in any model or document relating to the invention.][1]

Compensation of employees for certain inventions

2-038   **40.**—(1) Where it appears to the court or the comptroller on an application made by an employee within the prescribed period that the employee has made an invention belonging to the employer for which a patent has been granted, that the patent is (having regard among other things to the size and nature of the employer's undertaking) of outstanding benefit to the employer and that by

---
[1] Inserted by Copyright, Designs and Patents Act 1988 c.48 s 295 Sch 5 para 11 (1)

reason of those facts it is just that the employee should be awarded compensation to be paid by the employer, the court or the comptroller may award him such compensation of an amount determined under section 41 below.

(2) Where it appears to the court or the comptroller on an application made by an employee within the prescribed period that—

(a) a patent has been granted for an invention made by and belonging to the employee;

(b) his rights in the invention, or in any patent or application for a patent for the invention, have since the appointed day been assigned to the employer or an exclusive licence under the patent or application has since the appointed day been granted to the employer;

(c) the benefit derived by the employee from the contract of assignment, assignation or grant or any ancillary contract ("the relevant contract") is inadequate in relation to the benefit derived by the employer from the patent; and

(d) by reason of those facts it is just that the employee should be awarded compensation to be paid by the employer in addition to the benefit derived from the relevant contract;

the court or the comptroller may award him such compensation of an amount determined under section 41 below.

(3) Subsections (1) and (2) above shall not apply to the invention of an employee where a relevant collective agreement provides for the payment of compensation in respect of inventions of the same description as that invention to employees of the same description as that employee.

(4) Subsection (2) above shall have effect notwithstanding anything in the relevant contract or any agreement applicable to the invention (other than any such collective agreement).

(5) If it appears to the comptroller on an application under this section that the application involves matters which would more properly be determined by the court, he may decline to deal with it.

(6) In this section—

"the prescribed period", in relation to proceedings before the court, means the period prescribed by rules of court, and

"relevant collective agreement" means a collective agreement within the meaning of [the Trade Union and Labour Relations (Consolidation) Act 1992][1], made by or on behalf of a trade union to which the employee belongs, and by the employer or an employers' association to which the employer belongs which is in force at the time of the making of the invention.

(7) References in this section to an invention belonging to an employer or employee are references to it so belonging as between the employer and the employee.

Amount of compensation

41.—(1) An award of compensation to an employee under section 40(1) or **2-039** (2) above in relation to a patent for an invention shall be such as will secure for the employee a fair share (having regard to all the circumstances) of the benefit which the employer has derived, or may reasonably be expected to derive, from the patent or from the assignment, assignation or grant to a person connected

---

[1] Words substituted by Trade Union and Labour Relations (Consolidation) Act 1992 c.52 Sch 2 para 9

with the employer of the property or any right in the invention or the property in, or any right in or under, an application for that patent.

(2) For the purposes of subsection (1) above the amount of any benefit derived or expected to be derived by an employer from the assignment, assignation or grant of—

(a) the property in, or any right in or under, a patent for the invention or an application for such a patent; or

(b) the property or any right in the invention;

to a person connected with him shall be taken to be the amount which could reasonably be expected to be so derived by the employer if that person had not been connected with him.

(3) Where the Crown or a Research Council in its capacity as employer assigns or grants the property in, or any right in or under, an invention, patent or application for a patent to a body having among its functions that of developing or exploiting inventions resulting from public research and does so for no consideration or only a nominal consideration, any benefit derived from the invention, patent or application by that body shall be treated for the purposes of the foregoing provisions of this section as so derived by the Crown or, as the case may be, Research Council.

In this subsection "Research Council" means a body which is a Research Council for the purposes of the Science and Technology Act 1965.

(4) In determining the fair share of the benefit to be secured for an employee in respect of a patent for an invention which has always belonged to an employer, the court or the comptroller shall, among other things, take the following matters into account, that is to say—

(a) the nature of the employee's duties, his remuneration and the other advantages he derives or has derived from his employment or has derived in relation to the invention under this Act;

(b) the effort and skill which the employee has devoted to making the invention;

(c) the effort and skill which any other person has devoted to making the invention jointly with the employee concerned, and the advice and other assistance contributed by any other employee who is not a joint inventor of the invention; and

(d) the contribution made by the employer to the making, developing and working of the invention by the provision of advice, facilities and other assistance, by the provision of opportunities and by his managerial and commercial skill and activities.

(5) In determining the fair share of the benefit to be secured for an employee in respect of a patent for an invention which originally belonged to him, the court or the comptroller shall, among other things, take the following matters into account, that is to say—

(a) any conditions in a licence or licences granted under this Act or otherwise in respect of the invention or the patent;

(b) the extent to which the invention was made jointly by the employee with any other person; and

(c) the contribution made by the employer to the making, developing and working of the invention as mentioned in subsection (4)(d) above.

(6) Any order for the payment of compensation under section 40 above may be an order for the payment of a lump sum or for periodical payment, or both.

(7) Without prejudice to [section 12 or section 14 of the Interpretation Act 1978][1], the refusal of the court or the comptroller to make any such order on an application made by an employee under section 40 above shall not prevent a further application being made under that section by him or any successor in title of his.

(8) Where the court or the comptroller has made any such order, the court or he may on the application of either the employer or the employee vary or discharge it or suspend any provision of the order and revive any provision so suspended, and section 40(5) above shall apply to the application as it applies to an application under that section.

(9) In England and Wales any sums awarded by the comptroller under section 40 above shall, if a county court so orders, be recoverable by execution issued from the county court or otherwise as if they were payable under an order of that court.

(10) In Scotland an order made under section 40 above by the comptroller for the payment of any sums may be enforced in like manner as a recorded decree arbitral.

(11) In Northern Ireland an order made under section 40 above by the comptroller for the payment of any sums may be enforced as if it were a money judgment.

Enforceability of contracts relating to employees' inventions

42.—(1) This section applies to any contract (whenever made) relating to **2-040** inventions made by an employee, being a contract entered into by him—

    (a) with the employer (alone or with another); or

    (b) with some other person at the request of the employer or in pursuance of the employee's contract of employment.

(2) Any term in a contract to which this section applies which diminishes the employee's rights in inventions of any description made by him after the appointed day and the date of the contract, or in or under patents for those inventions or applications for such patents, shall be unenforceable against him to the extent that it diminishes his rights in an invention of that description so made, or in or under a patent for such an invention or an application for any such patent.

(3) Subsection (2) above shall not be construed as derogating from any duty of confidentiality owed to his employer by an employee by virtue of any rule of law or otherwise.

(4) This section applies to any arrangement made with a Crown employee by or on behalf of the Crown as his employer as it applies to any contract made between an employee and an employer other than the Crown, and for the purposes of this section "Crown employee" means a person employed under or for the purposes of a government department or any officer or body exercising on behalf of the Crown functions conferred by any enactment [or a person serving in the naval, military or air forces of the Crown.][2]

Supplementary

43.—(1) Sections 39 to 42 above shall not apply to an invention made before **2-041** the appointed day.

---

[1] Words substituted by Interpretation Act 1978 c. 30 s 25 (2)
[2] Words inserted by Armed Forces Act 1981 c.55 s 22 (1) (2)

(2) Sections 39 to 42 above shall not apply to an invention made by an employee unless at the time he made the invention one of the following conditions was satisfied in his case, that is to say—

    (a) he was mainly employed in the United Kingdom; or

    (b) he was not mainly employed anywhere or his place of employment could not be determined, but his employer had a place of business in the United Kingdom to which the employee was attached, whether or not he was also attached elsewhere.

(3) In sections 39 to 42 above and this section, except so far as the context otherwise requires, references to the making of an invention by an employee are references to his making it alone or jointly with any other person, but do not include references to his merely contributing advice or other assistance in the making of an invention by another employee.

(4) Any references [in sections 39 to 42][1] above to a patent and to a patent being granted are respectively references to a patent or other protection and to its being granted whether under the law of the United Kingdom or the law in force in any other country or under any treaty or international convention.

(5) For the purposes of sections 40 and 41 above the benefit derived or expected to be derived by an employer from a patent shall, where he dies before any award is made under section 40 above in respect of the patent, include any benefit derived or expected to be derived from the patent by his personal representatives or by any person in whom it was vested by their assent.

(6) Where an employee dies before an award is made under section 40 above in respect of a patented invention made by him, his personal representatives or their successors in title may exercise his right to make or proceed with an application for compensation under subsection (1) or (2) of that section.

(7) In sections 40 and 41 above and this section "benefit" means benefit in money or money's worth.

(8) Section 533 of the Income and Corporation Taxes Act 1970 (definition of connected persons) shall apply for determining for the purposes of section 41(2) above whether one person is connected with another as it applies for determining that question for the purposes of the Tax Acts.

Contracts as to patented products, etc

Licences of right and compulsory licences

Patentee's application for entry in register that licences are available as of right

2-042   **46.**—(1) At any time after the grant of a patent its proprietor may apply to the comptroller for an entry to be made in the register to the effect that licences under the patent are to be available as of right.

(2) Where such an application is made, the comptroller shall give notice of the application to any person registered as having a right in or under the patent and, if satisfied that the proprietor of the patent is not precluded by contract from granting licences under the patent, shall make that entry.

(3) Where such an entry is made in respect of a patent—

    (a) any person shall, at any time after the entry is made, be entitled as of right to a licence under the patent on such terms as may be settled by agreement or, in default of agreement, by the comptroller on the appli-

---

[1] Words substituted by Copyright, Designs and Patents Act 1988 c.48 s 295 Sch 5 para 11 (2)

cation of the proprietor of the patent or the person requiring the licence;

(b) the comptroller may, on the application of the holder of any licence granted under the patent before the entry was made, order the licence to be exchanged for a licence of right on terms so settled;

(c) if in proceedings for infringement of the patent (otherwise than by the importation of any article [from a country which is not a member State of the European Economic Community][1]) the defendant or defender undertakes to take a licence on such terms, no injunction or interdict shall be granted against him and the amount (if any) recoverable against him by way of damages shall not exceed double the amount which would have been payable by him as licensee if such a licence on those terms had been granted before the earliest infringement;

(d) the renewal fee payable in respect of the patent after the date of the entry shall be half the fee which would be payable if the entry had not been made.

[(3A) An undertaking under subsection (3)(c) above may be given at any time before final order in the proceedings, without any admission of liability.][2]

(4) The licensee under a licence of right may (unless, in the case of a licence the terms of which are settled by agreement, the licence otherwise expressly provides) request the proprietor of the patent to take proceedings to prevent any infringement of the patent; and if the proprietor refuses or neglects to do so within two months after being so requested, the licensee may institute proceedings for the infringement in his own name as if he were proprietor, making the proprietor a defendant or defender.

(5) A proprietor so added as defendant or defender shall not be liable for any costs or expenses unless he enters an appearance and takes part in the proceedings.

Cancellation of entry made under s. 46

47.—(1) At any time after an entry has been made under section 46 above in respect of a patent, the proprietor of the patent may apply to the comptroller for cancellation of the entry. **2-043**

[Compulsory licences: general

48.—(1) At any time after the expiration of three years, or of such other period as may be prescribed, from the date of the grant of a patent, any person may apply to the comptroller on one or more of the relevant grounds— **2-044**

(a) for a licence under the patent;

(b) for and entry to be made in the register to the effect that licences under the patent are to be available as of right; or

(c) where the applicant is a government department, for the grant to any person specified in the application of a licence under the patent.

(2) Subject to sections 48A and 48B below, if he is satisfied that any of the relevant grounds are established, the comptroller may—

(a) where the application is under subsection (1)(a) above, order the grant of a licence to the applicant on such terms as the comptroller thinks fit;

(b) where the application is under subsection (1)(b) above, make such an entry as is there mentioned;

---

[1] Words inserted by Copyright, Designs and Patents Act 1988 c.48 s 295 Sch 5 para 12 (2)

[2] Inserted by Copyright, Designs and Patents Act 1988 c.48 s 295 Sch 5 para 12 (3)

(c) where the application is under subsection (1)(c) above, order the grant of a licence to the person specified in the application on such terms as the comptroller thinks fit.

(3) An application may be made under this section in respect of a patent even though the applicant is already the holder of a licence under the patent; and no person shall be estopped or barred from alleging any of the matters specified in the relevant grounds by reason of any admission made by him, whether in such a licence or otherwise, or by reason of his having accepted a licence.

(4) In this section 'the relevant grounds' means—

(a) in the case of an application made in respect of a patent whose proprietor is a WTO proprietor, the grounds set our in section 48B(1) below;

(b) in any other case, the grounds set out in section 48B(1) below.

(5) A proprietor is a WTO proprietor for the purposes of this section and sections 48A, 48B, 50 and 52 below if—

(a) he is a national of, or is domiciled in, a country which is a member of the World Trade Organisation; or

(b) he has a real and effective industrial or commercial establishment in such a country.

(6) A rule prescribing any such other period under subsection (1) above shall not be made unless a draft of the rule has been laid before, and approved by resolution of, each House of Parliament.]¹

[Compulsory licences: WTO proprietors

2-045   **48A.**—(1) In the case of an application made under section 48 above in respect of a patent whose proprietor is a WTO proprietor, the relevant grounds are—

(a) where the patented invention is a product, that a demand in the United Kingdom for that product is not being met on reasonable terms;

(b) that by reason of the refusal of the proprietor of the patent concerned to grant a licence or licences on reasonable terms—

(i) the exploitation in the United Kingdom of any other patented invention which involves an important technical advance of considerable economic significance in relation to the invention for which the patent concerned was granted is prevented of hindered, or

(ii) the establishment or development of commercial or industrial activities in the United Kingdom is unfairly prejudiced;

(c) that by reason of conditions imposed by the proprietor of the patent concerned on the grant of licences under the patent, or on the disposal or use of the patented product or on the use of the patented process, the manufacture, use or disposal of materials not protected by the paten, or the establishment or development of commercial or industrial activities in the United Kingdom, is unfairly prejudiced.

(2) No order or entry shall be made under section 48 above in respect of a patent whose proprietor is a WTO proprietor unless—

(a) the applicant has made efforts to obtain a licence from the proprietor on reasonable commercial terms and conditions; and

(b) his efforts have not been successful within a reasonable period.

(3) No order or entry shall be so made if the patented invention is in the field of semi-conductor technology.

---

¹ Substituted by SI 1999/1899 Pt II reg 3

(4) No order or entry shall be made under section 48 above in respect of a patent on the ground mentioned in subsection (1)(b)(i) above unless the comptroller is satisfied that the proprietor of the patent for the other invention is able and willing to grant the proprietor of the patent concerned and his licensees a licence under the patent for the other invention on reasonable terms.

(5) A licence granted in pursuance of an order or entry so made shall not be assigned except to a person to whom the patent for the other invention is also assigned.

(6) A licence granted in pursuance of an order or entry made under section 48 above in respect of a patent whose proprietor is a WTO proprietor –

(a) shall not be exclusive;

(b) shall not be assigned except to a person to whom there is also assigned the part of the enterprise that enjoys the use of the patented invention, or the part of the goodwill that belongs to that part;

(c) shall be predominantly for the supply of the market in the United Kingdom;

(d) shall include conditions entitling the proprietor of the patent concerned to remuneration adequate in the circumstances of the case, taking into account the economic value of the licence; and

(e) shall be limited in scope and in duration to the purpose for which the licence was granted.][1]

[Compulsory licences: other cases

48B—(1) In the case of an application made under section 48 above in **2-046** respect of a patent whose proprietor is not a WTO proprietor, the relevant grounds are –

(a) where the patented invention is capable of being commercially worked in the United Kingdom, that it is not being so worked or is not being so worked to the fullest extent that is reasonably practicable;

(b) where the patented invention is a product, that a demand for the product in the United Kingdom –

　(i) in not being met on reasonable terms, or

　(ii) is being met to a substantial extent by importation from a country which is not a member State;

(c) where the patented invention is capable of being commercially worked in the United Kingdom, that it is being prevented or hindered from being so worked –

　(i) where the invention is a product, by the importation of the product from a country which is not a member State;

　(ii) where the invention is a process, by the importation from such a country of a product obtained directly by means of the process or to which the process has been applied;

(d) that by reason of the refusal of the proprietor of the patent to grant a licence of licences on reasonable terms –

　(i) a market for the export of any patented product made in the United Kingdom is not being supplied, or

　(ii) the working or efficient working in the United Kingdom of any other patented invention which makes a substantial contribution to the art is prevented or hindered, or

　(iii) the establishment or development of commercial or industrial activities in the United Kingdom is unfairly prejudiced;

---

[1] Inserted by SI 1999/1899 Pt II reg 4

(e)   that by reason of conditions imposed by the proprietor of the patent on the grant of licences under the patent, or on the disposal or use of the patented product or on the use of the patented process, the manufacture, use or disposal of materials not protected by the patent, or the establishment or development of commercial or industrial activities in the United Kingdom, is unfairly prejudiced.

(2)   Where–

(a)   an application is made on the ground that the patented invention is not being commercially worked in the United Kingdom or is not being so worked to the fullest extent that is reasonable practicable; and

(b)   it appears to the comptroller that the time which has elapsed since the publication in the journal of a notice of the grant of the patent has for any reason been insufficient to enable the invention to be so worked,

he may by order adjourn the application for such period as will in his opinion give sufficient time for the invention to be so worked.

(3)   No order or entry shall be made under section 48 above in respect of a patent on the ground mentioned in subsection (1)(a) above if–

(a)   the patented invention is being commercially worked in a country which is a member State; and

(b)   demand in the United Kingdom is being met by importation from that country.

(4)   No entry shall be made in the register under section 48 above on the ground mentioned in subsection (1)(d)(i) above, and any licence granted under section 48 above on that ground shall contain such provisions as appear to the comptroller to be expedient for restricting the countries in which any product concerned may be disposed of or used by the licensee.

(5)   No order or entry shall be made under section 48 above in respect of a patent on the ground mentioned in subsection (1)(d)(ii) above unless the comptroller is satisfied that the proprietor of the patent for the other invention is able and willing to grant to the proprietor of the patent concerned and his licensees a licence under the patent for the other invention on reasonable terms.][1]

Provisions about licences under s. 48

2-047   **49.**—(1) Where the comptroller is satisfied, on an application made under section 48 above in respect of a patent, that the manufacture, use or disposal of materials not protected by the patent is unfairly prejudiced by reason of conditions imposed by the proprietor of the patent on the grant of licences under the patent, or on the disposal or use of the patented product or the use of the patented process, he may (subject to the provisions of that section) order the grant of licences under the patent to such customers of the applicant as he thinks fit as well as to the applicant.

(2)   Where an application under section 48 above is made in respect of a patent by a person who holds a licence under the patent, the comptroller—

(a)   may, if he orders the grant of a licence to the applicant, order the existing licence to be cancelled, or

(b)   may, instead of ordering the grant of a licence to the applicant, order the existing licence to be amended.

(4)   Section 46(4) and (5) above shall apply to a licence granted in pursuance of an order under section 48 above and to a licence granted by virtue of an entry under that section as it applies to a licence granted by virtue of an entry under section 46 above.

---

[1] Inserted by SI 1999/1899 Pt II reg 5

Exercise of powers on applications under s. 48

50.—(1) The powers of the comptroller on an application under section 48 2-048
above in respect of a patent [whose proprietor is not a WTO proprietor][1]shall be
exercised with a view to securing the following general purposes:—

    (a) that inventions which can be worked on a commercial scale in the
United Kingdom and which should in the public interest be so worked
shall be worked there without undue delay and to the fullest extent that is
reasonably practicable;

    (b) that the inventor or other person beneficially entitled to a patent shall
receive reasonable remuneration having regard to the nature of the
invention;

    (c) that the interests of any person for the time being working or
developing an invention in the United Kingdom under the protection of
a patent shall not be unfairly prejudiced.

(2) Subject to subsection (1) above, the comptroller shall, in determining
whether to make an order or entry in pursuance of [any application under section
48 above][2], take account of the following matters, that is to say—

    (a) the nature of the invention, the time which has elapsed since the publi-
cation in the journal of a notice of the grant of the patent and the
measures already taken by the proprietor of the patent or any licensee to
make full use of the invention;

    (b) the ability of any person to whom a licence would be granted under
the order concerned to work the invention to the public advantage;
and

    (c) the risks to be undertaken by that person in providing capital and
working the invention if the application for an order is granted,

but shall not be required to take account of matters subsequent to the making of
the application.

[Powers exercisable following merger and market investigations

50A—(1) Subsection (2) below applies where— 2-049

    (a) section 41(2), 55(2), 66(6), 75(2), 83(2), 138(2), 147(2) or 160(2) of, or
paragraph 5(2) or 10(2) of Schedule 7 to, the Enterprise Act 2002
(powers to take remedial action following merger or market investigations) applies;

    (b) the Competition Commission or (as the case may be) the Secretary of
State considers that it would be appropriate to make an application
under this section for the purpose of remedying, mitigating or
preventing a matter which cannot be dealt with under the enactment
concerned; and

    (c) the matter concerned involves—

        (i) conditions in licences granted under a patent by its proprietor
restricting the use of the invention by the licensee or the right of the
proprietor to grant other licences; or

        (ii) a refusal by the proprietor of a patent to grant licences on
reasonable terms.

(2) The Competition Commission or (as the case may be) the Secretary of
State may apply to the comptroller to take action under this section.

[1] Words inserted by SI 1999/1899 Pt II reg 7 (2)
[2] Words substituted by SI 1999/1899 Pt II reg 7 (3)

(3) Before making an application the Competition Commission or (as the case may be) the Secretary of State shall publish, in such manner as it or he thinks appropriate, a notice describing the nature of the proposed application and shall consider any representations which may be made within 30 days of such publication by persons whose interests appear to it or him to be affected.

(4) The comptroller may, if it appears to him on an application under this section that the application is made in accordance with this section, by order cancel or modify any condition concerned of the kind mentioned in subsection (1)(c)(i) above or may, instead or in addition, make an entry in the register to the effect that licences under the patent are to be available as of right.

(5) References in this section to the Competition Commission shall, in cases where section 75(2) of the Enterprise Act 2002 applies, be read as references to the Office of Fair Trading.

(6) References in section 35, 36, 47, 63, 134 or 141 of the Enterprise Act 2002 (questions to be decided by the Competition Commission in its reports) to taking action under section 41(2), 55, 66, 138 or 147 shall include references to taking action under subsection (2) above.

(7) Action taken by virtue of subsection (4) above in consequence of an application under subsection (2) above where an enactment mentioned in subsection (1)(a) above applies shall be treated, for the purposes of sections 91(3), 92(1)(a), 162(1) and 166(3) of the Enterprise Act 2002 (duties to register and keep under review enforcement orders etc.), as if it were the making of an enforcement order (within the meaning of the Part concerned) under the relevant power in Part 3 or (as the case may be) 4 of that Act.]¹

[Powers exercisable in consequence of report of Monopolies and Mergers Commission

2-050   **51.**—(1) Where a report of the [Competition Commission]² has been laid before Parliament containing conclusions to the effect—

(b) [...]³

(c) on a competition reference, that a person was engaged in an anti-competitive practice which operated or may be expected to operate against the public interest, or

(d) on a reference under section 11 of the Competition Act 1980 (reference of public bodies and certain other persons), that a person is pursuing a course of conduct which operates against the public interest,

the appropriate Minister or Ministers may apply to the comptroller to take action under this section.

(2) Before making an application the appropriate Minister or Ministers shall publish, in such manner as he or they think appropriate, a notice describing the nature of the proposed application and shall consider any representations which may be made within 30 days of such publication by persons whose interests appear to him or them to be affected.

[(2A) Where—

(a) on a reference under section 5 of the Competition Act 1980, a report of the Commission, as laid before Parliament, contains conclusions to the effect that—

(i) any person was engaged in an anti-competitive practice in relation to a description of goods which consist of or include

---

¹ Inserted by Enterprise Act 2002 c.40 Sch 25 para 8 (2)
² Words substituted by SI 1999/506 Pt II art 17
³ Repealed by Enterprise Act 2002 c.40 Sch 26 para 1

patented products or in relation to a description of services in which a patented product or process is used, and

    (ii) that practice operated or might be expected to operate against the public interest; or

(b) on a reference under section 11 of that Act, such a report contains conclusions to the effect that—

    (i) any person is pursuing a course of conduct in relation to such a description of goods or services, and

    (ii) that course of conduct operates against the public interest,

the appropriate Minister or Ministers may, subject to subsection (3) below, apply to the comptroller for relief under subsection (5A) below in respect of the patent.][1]

(3) If on an application under this section it appears to the comptroller that the matters specified in the Commission's report as being those which in the Commission's opinion operate, or operated or may be expected to operate, against the public interest include—

(a) conditions in licences granted under a patent by its proprietor restricting the use of the invention by the licensee or the right of the proprietor to grant other licences, or

(b) a refusal by the proprietor of a patent to grant licences on reasonable terms

he may by order cancel or modify any such condition or may, instead or in addition, make an entry in the register to the effect that licences under the patent are to be available as of right.

(4) In this section "the appropriate Minister or Ministers" means the Minister or Ministers to whom the report of the Commission was made.][2]

[Opposition, appeal and arbitration

52.—(1) The proprietor of the patent concerned or any other person wishing   **2-051** to oppose an application under sections 48 to 51 above may, in accordance with rules, give to the comptroller notice of opposition; and the comptroller shall consider any opposition in deciding whether to grant the application.][3]

Compulsory licences; supplementary provisions

53.—(4) An entry made in the register under sections 48 to 51 above shall for   **2-052** all purposes have the same effect as an entry made under section 46 above.

(5) No order or entry shall be made in pursuance of an application under sections 48 to 51 above which would be at variance with any treaty or international convention to which the United Kingdom is a party.

Use of patented inventions for services of the Crown

Use of patented inventions for services of the Crown

55.—(1) Notwithstanding anything in this Act, any government department   **2-053** and any person authorised in writing by a government department may, for the services of the Crown and in accordance with this section, do any of the following acts in the United Kingdom in relation to a patented invention without the consent of the proprietor of the patent, that is to say—

---

[1] Inserted by Competition Act 1980 c.21 s 14 (1)
[2] Substituted by Copyright, Designs and Patents Act 1988 c.48 s 295 Sch 5 para 14
[3] Substituted by SI 1999/1899 Pt II reg 6

    (a) where the invention is a product, may—
        (i) make, use, import or keep the product, or sell or offer to sell it where to do so would be incidental or ancillary to making, using, importing or keeping it; or
        (ii) in any event, sell or offer to sell it for foreign defence purposes or for the production or supply of specified drugs and medicines, or dispose or offer to dispose of it (otherwise than by selling it) for any purpose whatever;
    (b) where the invention is a process, may use it or do in relation to any product obtained directly by means of the process anything mentioned in paragraph (a) above;
    (c) without prejudice to the foregoing, where the invention or any product obtained directly by means of the invention is a specified drug or medicine, may sell or offer to sell the drug or medicine;
    (d) may supply or offer to supply to any person any of the means, relating to an essential element of the invention, for putting the invention into effect;
    (e) may dispose or offer to dispose of anything which was made, used, imported or kept in the exercise of the powers conferred by this section and which is no longer required for the purpose for which it was made, used, imported or kept (as the case may be),

and anything done by virtue of this subsection shall not amount to an infringement of the patent concerned.

Interpretation, etc., of provisions about Crown use

2-054   **56.**—(1) Any reference in section 55 above to a patented invention, in relation to any time, is a reference to an invention for which a patent has before that time been, or is subsequently, granted.

    (2) In this Act, except so far as the context otherwise requires, "the services of the Crown" includes—
    (a) the supply of anything for foreign defence purposes;
    (b) the production or supply of specified drugs and medicines; and
    (c) such purposes relating to the production or use of atomic energy or research into matters connected therewith as the Secretary of State thinks necessary or expedient;

and "use for the services of the Crown" shall be construed accordingly

Rights of third parties in respect of Crown use

2-055   **57.**—(1) In relation to—
    (a) any use made for the services of the Crown of an invention by a government department, or a person authorised by a government department, by virtue of section 55 above, or
    (b) anything done for the services of the Crown to the order of a government department by the proprietor of a patent in respect of a patented invention or by the proprietor of an application in respect of an invention for which an application for a patent has been filed and is still pending,

the provisions of any licence, assignment, assignation or agreement to which this subsection applies shall be of no effect so far as those provisions restrict or regulate the working of the invention, or the use of any model, document or information relating to it, or provide for the making of payments in respect of, or calculated by reference to, such working or use; and the reproduction or publication of any model or document in connection with the said working or use shall not be deemed to be an infringement of any copyright [or design right][1] subsisting in the model or document [or of any topography right][2].

(2) Subsection (1) above applies to a licence, assignment, assignation or agreement which is made, whether before or after the appointed day, between (on the one hand) any person who is a proprietor of or an applicant for the patent, or anyone who derives title from any such person or from whom such person derives title, and (on the other hand) any person whatever other than a government department.

[Compensation for loss of profit

57A.—(1) Where use is made of an invention for the services of the Crown, **2-056** the government department concerned shall pay—

  (a) to the proprietor of the patent, or
  (b) if there is an exclusive licence in force in respect of the patent, to the exclusive licensee,

compensation for any loss resulting from his not being awarded a contract to supply the patented product or, as the case may be, to perform the patented process or supply a thing made by means of the patented process.

(2) Compensation is payable only to the extent that such a contract could have been fulfilled from his existing manufacturing or other capacity; but is payable notwithstanding the existence of circumstances rendering him ineligible for the award of such a contract.

(3) In determining the loss, regard shall be had to the profit which would have been made on such a contract and to the extent to which any manufacturing or other capacity was under-used.

(4) No compensation is payable in respect of any failure to secure contracts to supply the patented product or, as the case may be, to perform the patented process or supply a thing made by means of the patented process, otherwise than for the services of the Crown.

(5) The amount payable shall, if not agreed between the proprietor or licensee and the government department concerned with the approval of the Treasury, be determined by the court on a reference under section 58, and is in addition to any amount payable under section 55 or 57.

(6) In this section 'the government department concerned', in relation to any use of an invention for the services of the Crown, means the government department by whom or on whose authority the use was made.

(7) In the application of this section to Northern Ireland, the reference in subsection (5) above to the Treasury shall, where the government department concerned is a department of the Government of Northern Ireland, be construed as a reference to the Department of Finance and Personnel.][3]

References of disputes as to Crown use

58.—[(1) Any dispute as to—   **2-057**

  (a) the exercise by a government department, or a person authorised by a government department, of the powers conferred by section 55 above,
  (b) terms for the use of an invention for the services of the Crown under that section,

---

[1] Words inserted by Copyright, Designs and Patents Act 1988 c.48 s 303 (1) Sch 7 para 20
[2] Words inserted by SI 1987/1497 reg 9 (2) para 2
[3] Inserted by Copyright, Designs and Patents Act 1988 c.48 s 295 Sch 5 para 16 (1) (4)

Malayan Credit Ltd v Jack Chia—MPH Ltd [1986] - Business partner
Tenant in common

(c) the right of any person to receive any part of a payment made in pursuance of subsection (4) of that section, or

(d) the right of any person to receive a payment under section 57A,

may be referred to the court by either party to the dispute after a patent has been granted for the invention.][1]

(2) If in such proceedings any question arises whether an invention has been recorded or tried as mentioned in section 55 above, and the disclosure of any document recording the invention, or of any evidence of the trial thereof, would in the opinion of the department be prejudicial to the public interest, the disclosure may be made confidentially to counsel for the other party or to an independent expert mutually agreed upon.

Infringement

Meaning of infringement

2-058   **60.**—(1) Subject to the provisions of this section, a person infringes a patent for an invention if, but only if, while the patent is in force, he does any of the following things in the United Kingdom in relation to the invention without the consent of the proprietor of the patent, that is to say—

(a) where the invention is a product, he makes, disposes of, offers to dispose of, uses or imports the product or keeps it whether for disposal or otherwise;

(b) where the invention is a process, he uses the process or he offers it for use in the United Kingdom when he knows, or it is obvious to a reasonable person in the circumstances, that its use there without the consent of the proprietor would be an infringement of the patent;

(c) where the invention is a process, he disposes of, offers to dispose of, uses or imports any product obtained directly by means of that process or keeps any such product whether for disposal or otherwise.

(2) Subject to the following provisions of this section, a person (other than the proprietor of the patent) also infringes a patent for an invention if, while the patent is in force and without the consent of the proprietor, he supplies or offers to supply in the United Kingdom a person other than a licensee or other person entitled to work the invention with any of the means, relating to an essential element of the invention, for putting the invention into effect when he knows, or it is obvious to a reasonable person in the circumstances, that those means are suitable for putting, and are intended to put, the invention into effect in the United Kingdom.

(3) Subsection (2) above shall not apply to the supply or offer of a staple commercial product unless the supply or the offer is made for the purpose of inducing the person supplied or, as the case may be, the person to whom the offer is made to do an act which constitutes an infringement of the patent by virtue of subsection (1) above.

(5) An act which, apart from this subsection, would constitute an infringement of a patent for an invention shall not do so if—

(a) it is done privately and for purposes which are not commercial;

(b) it is done for experimental purposes relating to the subject-matter of the invention;

(c) it consists of the extemporaneous preparation in a pharmacy of a medicine for an individual in accordance with a prescription given by a

[1] Substituted by Copyright, Designs and Patents Act 1988 c.48 s 295 Sch 5 para 16 (2) (4)

registered medical or dental practitioner or consists of dealing with a medicine so prepared;

(d) it consists of the use, exclusively for the needs of a relevant ship, of a product or process in the body of such a ship or in its machinery, tackle, apparatus or other accessories, in a case where the ship has temporarily or accidentally entered the internal or territorial waters of the United Kingdom;

(e) it consists of the use of a product or process in the body or operation of a relevant aircraft, hovercraft or vehicle which has temporarily or accidentally entered or is crossing the United Kingdom (including the air space above it and its territorial waters) or the use of accessories for such a relevant aircraft, hovercraft or vehicle;

(f) it consists of the use of an exempted aircraft which has lawfully entered or is lawfully crossing the United Kingdom as aforesaid or of the importation into the United Kingdom, or the use or storage there, of any part or accessory for such an aircraft.

[(g) it consists of the use by a farmer of the product of his harvest for propagation or multiplication by him on his own holding, where there has been a sale of plant propagating material to the farmer by the proprietor of the patent or with his consent for agricultural use;

(h) it consists of the use of an animal or animal reproductive material by a farmer for an agricultural purpose following a sale to the farmer, by the proprietor of the patent or with his consent, of breeding stock or other animal reproductive material which constitutes or contains the patented invention.][1]

(6) For the purposes of subsection (2) above a person who does an act in relation to an invention which is prevented only by virtue of paragraph (a), (b) or (c) of subsection (5) above from constituting an infringement of a patent for the invention shall not be treated as a person entitled to work the invention, but—

(a) the reference in that subsection to a person entitled to work an invention includes a reference to a person so entitled by virtue of section 55 above, and

(b) a person who by virtue of [section 28A(4) or (5)][2] above or section 64 below is entitled to do an act in relation to the invention without it constituting such an infringement shall, so far as concerns that act, be treated as a person entitled to work the invention.

[(6A) Schedule A1 contains–

(a) provisions restricting the circumstances in which subsection (5)(g) applies; and

(b) provisions which apply where an act would constitute an infringement of a patent but for subsection (5)(g).

(6B) For the purposes of subsection (5)(h), use for an agricultural purpose–

(a) includes making an animal or animal reproductive material available for the purposes of pursuing the farmer's agricultural activity; but

(b) does not include sale within the framework, or for the purposes, of a commercial reproduction activity.

(6C) In paragraphs (g) and (h) of subsection (5) "sale" includes any other form of commercialisation.][3]

(7) In this section—

---

[1] Inserted by SI 2000/2037 reg 4 (a)

[2] Words substituted by Copyright, Designs and Patents Act 1988 c.48 s 295 Sch 5 para 8 (a)

[3] Inserted by SI 2000/2037 reg 4 (b)

"relevant ship" and "relevant aircraft, hovercraft or vehicle" mean respectively a ship and an aircraft, hovercraft or vehicle registered in, or belonging to, any country, other than the United Kingdom, which is a party to the Convention for the Protection of Industrial Property signed at Paris on 20th March 1883 [or which is a member of the World Trade Organisation][1]; and

"exempted aircraft" means an aircraft to which [section 89 of the Civil Aviation Act 1982][2] (aircraft exempted from seizure in respect of patent claims) applies.

Proceedings for infringement of patent

2-059   **61.**—(1) Subject to the following provisions of this Part of this Act, civil proceedings may be brought in the court by the proprietor of a patent in respect of any act alleged to infringe the patent and (without prejudice to any other jurisdiction of the court) in those proceedings a claim may be made—

(a) for an injunction or interdict restraining the defendant or defender from any apprehended act of infringement;

(b) for an order for him to deliver up or destroy any patented product in relation to which the patent is infringed or any article in which that product is inextricably comprised;

(c) for damages in respect of the infringement;

(d) for an account of the profits derived by him from the infringement;

(e) for a declaration or declarator that the patent is valid and has been infringed by him.

(2) The court shall not, in respect of the same infringement, both award the proprietor of a patent damages and order that he shall be given an account of the profits.

(3) The proprietor of a patent and any other person may by agreement with each other refer to the comptroller the question whether that other person has infringed the patent and on the reference the proprietor of the patent may make any claim mentioned in subsection (1)(c) or (e) above.

(4) Except so far as the context requires, in the following provisions of this Act—

(a) any reference to proceedings for infringement and the bringing of such proceedings includes a reference to a reference under subsection (3) above and the making of such a reference;

(b) any reference to a plaintiff or pursuer includes a reference to the proprietor of the patent; and

(c) any reference to a defendant or defender includes a reference to any other party to the reference.

(5) If it appears to the comptroller on a reference under subsection (3) above that the question referred to him would more properly be determined by the court, he may decline to deal with it and the court shall have jurisdiction to determine the question as if the reference were proceedings brought in the court.

(6) Subject to the following provisions of this Part of this Act, in determining whether or not to grant any kind of relief claimed under this section and the extent of the relief granted the court or the comptroller shall apply the principles applied by the court in relation to that kind of relief immediately before the appointed day.

---

[1] Words inserted by SI 1999/1899 Pt II reg 7 (5)
[2] Words substituted by Civil Aviation Act 1982 c.16 s 109 Sch 15 para 19

Restrictions on recovery of damages for infringement

62.—(1) In proceedings for infringement of a patent damages shall not be **2-060** awarded, and no order shall be made for an account of profits, against a defendant or defender who proves that at the date of the infringement he was not aware, and had no reasonable grounds for supposing, that the patent existed; and a person shall not be taken to have been so aware or to have had reasonable grounds for so supposing by reason only of the application to a product of the word "patent" or "patented", or any word or words expressing or implying that a patent has been obtained for the product, unless the number of the patent accompanied the word or words in question.

(2) In proceedings for infringement of a patent the court or the comptroller may, if it or he thinks fit, refuse to award any damages or make any such order in respect of an infringement committed during any further period specified under section 25(4) above, but before the payment of the renewal fee and any additional fee prescribed for the purposes of that subsection.

(3) Where an amendment of the specification of a patent has been allowed under any of the provisions of this Act, no damages shall be awarded in proceedings for an infringement of the patent committed before the decision to allow the amendment unless the court or the comptroller is satisfied that the specification of the patent as published was framed in good faith and with reasonable skill and knowledge.

Relief for infringement of partially valid patent

63.—(1) If the validity of a patent is put in issue in proceedings for infringe- **2-061** ment of the patent and it is found that the patent is only partially valid, the court or the comptroller may, subject to subsection (2) below, grant relief in respect of that part of the patent which is found to be valid and infringed.

(2) Where in any such proceedings it is found that a patent is only partially valid, the court or the comptroller shall not grant relief by way of damages, costs or expenses, except where the plaintiff or pursuer proves that the specification for the patent was framed in good faith and with reasonable skill and knowledge, and in that event the court or the comptroller may grant relief in respect of that part of the patent which is valid and infringed, subject to the discretion of the court or the comptroller as to costs or expenses and as to the date from which damages should be reckoned.

(3) As a condition of relief under this section the court or the comptroller may direct that the specification of the patent shall be amended to its or his satisfaction upon an application made for that purpose under section 75 below, and an application may be so made accordingly, whether or not all other issues in the proceedings have been determined. *severance under statute (written notice under LPA 1925 S36(2))*

[Right to continue use begun before priority date

② unilateral
64.—(1) Where a patent is granted for an invention, a person who in the **2-062** United Kingdom before the priority date of the invention—

  (a) does in good faith an act which would constitute an infringement of the patent if it were in force, or
  (b) makes in good faith effective and serious preparations to do such an act,

has the right to continue to do the act or, as the case may be, to do the act, notwithstanding the grant of the patent; but this right does not extend to granting a licence to another person to do the act.

S → Kinch v. Bullard [1999] - serve by post, not read but sufficient.
last known abode

(2) If the act was done, or the preparations were made, in the course of a business, the person entitled to the right conferred by subsection (1) may—

    (a) authorise the doing of that act by any partners of his for the time being in that business, and

    (b) assign that right, or transmit it on death (or in the case of a body corporate on its dissolution), to any person who acquires that part of the business in the course of which the act was done or the preparations were made.

(3) Where a product is disposed of to another in exercise of the rights conferred by subsection (1) or (2), that other and any person claiming through him may deal with the product in the same way as if it had been disposed of by the registered proprietor of the patent.][1]

Certificate of contested validity of patent

2-063   **65.**—(1) If in any proceedings before the court or the comptroller the validity of a patent to any extent is contested and that patent is found by the court or the comptroller to be wholly or partially valid, the court or the comptroller may certify the finding and the fact that the validity of the patent was so contested.

(2) Where a certificate is granted under this section, then, if in any subsequent proceedings before the court or the comptroller for infringement of the patent concerned or for revocation of the patent a final order or judgment or interlocutor is made or given in favour of the party relying on the validity of the patent as found in the earlier proceedings, that party shall, unless the court or the comptroller otherwise directs, be entitled to his costs or expenses as between solicitor and own client (other than the costs or expenses of any appeal in the subsequent proceedings).

Proceedings for infringement by a co-owner

2-064   **66.**—(1) In the application of section 60 above to a patent of which there are two or more joint proprietors the reference to the proprietor shall be construed—

    (a) in relation to any act, as a reference to that proprietor or those proprietors who, by virtue of section 36 above or any agreement referred to in that section, is or are entitled to do that act without its amounting to an infringement; and

    (b) in relation to any consent, as a reference to that proprietor or those proprietors who, by virtue of section 36 above or any such agreement, is or are the proper person or persons to give the requisite consent.

(2) One of two or more joint proprietors of a patent may without the concurrence of the others bring proceedings in respect of an act alleged to infringe the patent, but shall not do so unless the others are made parties to the proceedings; but any of the others made a defendant or defender shall not be liable for any costs or expenses unless he enters an appearance and takes part in the proceedings.

Proceedings for infringement by exclusive licensee

2-065   **67.**—(1) Subject to the provisions of this section, the holder of an exclusive licence under a patent shall have the same right as the proprietor of the patent to bring proceedings in respect of any infringement of the patent committed after

---

[1] Substituted by Copyright, Designs and Patents Act 1988 c.48 s 295 Sch 5 para 17

the date of the licence; and references to the proprietor of the patent in the provisions of this Act relating to infringement shall be construed accordingly.

(2) In awarding damages or granting any other relief in any such proceedings the court or the comptroller shall take into consideration any loss suffered or likely to be suffered by the exclusive licensee as such as a result of the infringement, or, as the case may be, the profits derived from the infringement, so far as it constitutes an infringement of the rights of the exclusive licensee as such.

(3) In any proceedings taken by an exclusive licensee by virtue of this section the proprietor of the patent shall be made a party to the proceedings, but if made a defendant or defender shall not be liable for any costs or expenses unless he enters an appearance and takes part in the proceedings.

Effect of non-registration on infringement proceedings

68. Where by virtue of a transaction, instrument or event to which section 33 **2-066** above applies a person becomes the proprietor or one of the proprietors or an exclusive licensee of a patent and the patent is subsequently infringed, the court or the comptroller shall not award him damages or order that he be given an account of the profits in respect of such a subsequent infringement occurring before the transaction, instrument or event is registered unless—

  (a) the transaction, instrument or event is registered within the period of six months beginning with its date; or

  (b) the court or the comptroller is satisfied that it was not practicable to register the transaction, instrument or event before the end of that period and that it was registered as soon as practicable thereafter.

Infringement of rights conferred by publication of application

69.—(1) Where an application for a patent for an invention is published, **2-067** then, subject to subsections (2) and (3) below, the applicant shall have, as from the publication and until the grant of the patent, the same right as he would have had, if the patent had been granted on the date of the publication of the application, to bring proceedings in the court or before the comptroller for damages in respect of any act which would have infringed the patent; and (subject to subsections (2) and (3) below) references in sections 60 to 62 and 66 to 68 above to a patent and the proprietor of a patent shall be respectively construed as including references to any such application and the applicant, and references to a patent being in force, being granted, being valid or existing shall be construed accordingly.

(2) The applicant shall be entitled to bring proceedings by virtue of this section in respect of any act only—

  (a) after the patent has been granted; and

  (b) if the act would, if the patent had been granted on the date of the publication of the application, have infringed not only the patent, but also the claims (as interpreted by the description and any drawings referred to in the description or claims) in the form in which they were contained in the application immediately before the preparations for its publication were completed by the Patent Office.

(3) Section 62(2) and (3) above shall not apply to an infringement of the rights conferred by this section, but in considering the amount of any damages for such an infringement, the court or the comptroller shall consider whether or not it would have been reasonable to expect, from a consideration of the application as published under section 16 above, that a patent would be granted conferring on the proprietor of the patent protection from an act of the same

description as that found to infringe those rights, and if the court or the comptroller finds that it would not have been reasonable, it or he shall reduce the damages to such an amount as it or he thinks just.

Remedy for groundless threats of infringement proceedings

2-068   **70.**—(1) Where a person (whether or not the proprietor of, or entitled to any right in, a patent) by circulars, advertisements or otherwise threatens another person with proceedings for any infringement of a patent, a person aggrieved by the threats (whether or not he is the person to whom the threats are made) may, subject to subsection (4) below, bring proceedings in the court against the person making the threats, claiming any relief mentioned in subsection (3) below.

(2) In any such proceedings the plaintiff or pursuer shall, if he proves that the threats were so made and satisfies the court that he is a person aggrieved by them, be entitled to the relief claimed unless—

(a) the defendant or defender proves that the acts in respect of which proceedings were threatened constitute or, if done, would constitute an infringement of a patent; and

(b) the patent alleged to be infringed is not shown by the plaintiff or pursuer to be invalid in a relevant respect.

(3) The said relief is—

(a) a declaration or declarator to the effect that the threats are unjustifiable;

(b) an injunction or interdict against the continuance of the threats; and

(c) damages in respect of any loss which the plaintiff or pursuer has sustained by the threats.

(4) Proceedings may not be brought under this section for a threat to bring proceedings for an infringement alleged to consist of making or importing a product for disposal or of using a process.

(5) It is hereby declared that a mere notification of the existence of a patent does not constitute a threat of proceedings within the meaning of this section.

Declaration or declarator as to non-infringement

2-069   **71.**—(1) Without prejudice to the court's jurisdiction to make a declaration or declarator apart from this section, a declaration or declarator that an act does not, or a proposed act would not, constitute an infringement of a patent may be made by the court or the comptroller in proceedings between the person doing or proposing to do the act and the proprietor of the patent, notwithstanding that no assertion to the contrary has been made by the proprietor, if it is shown—

(a) that that person has applied in writing to the proprietor for a written acknowledgment to the effect of the declaration or declarator claimed, and has furnished him with full particulars in writing of the act in question; and

(b) that the proprietor has refused or failed to give any such acknowledgment.

(2) Subject to section 72(5) below, a declaration made by the comptroller under this section shall have the same effect as a declaration or declarator by the court.

Revocation of patents

Power to revoke patents on application

72.—(1) Subject to the following provisions of this Act, the court or the comp- **2-070** troller may on the application of any person by order revoke a patent for an invention on (but only on) any of the following grounds, that is to say—

    (a) the invention is not a patentable invention;

    [(b) that the patent was granted to a person who was not entitled to be granted that patent;]¹

    (c) the specification of the patent does not disclose the invention clearly enough and completely enough for it to be performed by a person skilled in the art;

    (d) the matter disclosed in the specification of the patent extends beyond that disclosed in the application for the patent, as filed, or, if the patent was granted on a new application filed under section 8(3), 12 or 37(4) above or as mentioned in section 15(4) above, in the earlier application, as filed;

    (e) the protection conferred by the patent has been extended by an amendment which should not have been allowed.

(2) An application for the revocation of a patent on the ground mentioned in subsection (1)(b) above—

    (a) may only be made by a person found by the court in an action for a declaration or declarator, or found by the court or the comptroller on a reference under section 37 above, to be entitled to be granted that patent or to be granted a patent for part of the matter comprised in the specification of the patent sought to be revoked; and

    (b) may not be made if that action was commenced or that reference was made after the end of the period of two years beginning with the date of the grant of the patent sought to be revoked, unless it is shown that any person registered as a proprietor of the patent knew at the time of the grant or of the transfer of the patent to him that he was not entitled to the patent.

(4) An order under this section may be an order for the unconditional revocation of the patent or, where the court or the comptroller determines that one of the grounds mentioned in subsection (1) above has been established, but only so as to invalidate the patent to a limited extent, an order that the patent should be revoked unless within a specified time the specification is amended under section 75 below to the satisfaction of the court or the comptroller, as the case may be.

(5) A decision of the comptroller or on appeal from the comptroller shall not estop any party to civil proceedings in which infringement of a patent is in issue from alleging invalidity of the patent on any of the grounds referred to in subsection (1) above, whether or not any of the issues involved were decided in the said decision.

(6) Where the comptroller refuses to grant an application made to him by any person under this section, no application (otherwise than by way of appeal or by way of putting validity in issue in proceedings for infringement) may be made to the court by that person under this section in relation to the patent concerned, without the leave of the court.

---

¹ Substituted by Copyright, Designs and Patents Act 1988 c.48 s 295 Sch 5 para 18

(4) Gore & Shell v. Carpenter (1990) — proposal is not sufficient severance

(7) Where the comptroller has not disposed of an application made to him under this section, the applicant may not apply to the court under this section in respect of the patent concerned unless either—

(a) the proprietor of the patent agrees that the applicant may so apply, or

(b) the comptroller certifies in writing that it appears to him that the question whether the patent should be revoked is one which would more properly be determined by the court.

Comptroller's power to revoke patents on his own initiative

2-071 **73.**—(1) If it appears to the comptroller that an invention for which a patent has been granted formed part of the state of the art by virtue only of section 2(3) above, he may on his own initiative by order revoke the patent, but shall not do so without giving the proprietor of the patent an opportunity of making any observations and of amending the specification of the patent so as to exclude any matter which formed part of the state of the art as aforesaid without contravening section 76 below.

[(2) If it appears to the comptroller that a patent under this Act and a European patent (UK) have been granted for the same invention having the same priority date, and that the applications for the patents were filed by the same applicant or his successor in title, he shall give the proprietor of the patent under this Act an opportunity of making observations and of amending the specification of the patent, and if the proprietor fails to satisfy the comptroller that there are not two patents in respect of the same invention, or to amend the specification so as to prevent there being two patents in respect of the same invention, the comptroller shall revoke the patent.][1]

[(3) The comptroller shall not take action under subsection (2) above before—

(a) the end of the period for filing an opposition to the European patent (UK) under the European Patent Convention, or

(b) if later, the date on which opposition proceedings are finally disposed of;

and he shall not then take any action if the decision is not to maintain the European patent or if it is amended so that there are not two patents in respect of the same invention.][2]

[(4) The comptroller shall not take action under subsection (2) above if the European patent (UK) has been surrendered under section 29(1) above before the date on which by virtue of section 25(1) above the patent under this Act is to be treated as having been granted or, if proceedings for the surrender of the European patent (UK) have been begun before that date, until those proceedings are finally disposed of; and he shall not then take any action if the decision is to accept the surrender of the European patent.][3]

Putting validity in issue

Proceedings in which validity of patent may be put in issue

2-072 **74.**—(1) Subject to the following provisions of this section, the validity of a patent may be put in issue—

[1] Substituted by Copyright, Designs and Patents Act 1988 c.48 s 295 Sch 5 para 19
[2] Substituted by Copyright, Designs and Patents Act 1988 c.48 s 295 Sch 5 para 19
[3] Inserted by Copyright, Designs and Patents Act 1988 c.48 s 295 Sch 5 para 19

(a) by way of defence, in proceedings for infringement of the patent under section 61 above or proceedings under section 69 above for infringement of rights conferred by the publication of an application;

(b) in proceedings under section 70 above;

(c) in proceedings in which a declaration in relation to the patent is sought under section 71 above;

(d) in proceedings before the court or the comptroller under section 72 above for the revocation of the patent;

(e) in proceedings under section 58 above.

(2) The validity of a patent may not be put in issue in any other proceedings and, in particular, no proceedings may be instituted (whether under this Act or otherwise) seeking only a declaration as to the validity or invalidity of a patent.

(3) The only grounds on which the validity of a patent may be put in issue (whether in proceedings for revocation under section 72 above or otherwise) are the grounds on which the patent may be revoked under that section.

(4) No determination shall be made in any proceedings mentioned in subsection (1) above on the validity of a patent which any person puts in issue on the ground mentioned in section 72(1)(b) above unless—

(a) it has been determined in entitlement proceedings commenced by that person or in the proceedings in which the validity of the patent is in issue that the patent should have been granted to him and not some other person; and

(b) except where it has been so determined in entitlement proceedings, the proceedings in which the validity of the patent is in issue are commenced before the end of the period of two years beginning with the date of the grant of the patent or it is shown that any person registered as a proprietor of the patent knew at the time of the grant or of the transfer of the patent to him that he was not entitled to the patent.

(5) Where the validity of a patent is put in issue by way of defence or counter-claim the court or the comptroller shall, if it or he thinks it just to do so, give the defendant an opportunity to comply with the condition in subsection (4)(a) above.

(6) In subsection (4) above "entitlement proceedings", in relation to a patent, means a reference under [section 37(1) above][1] on the ground that the patent was granted to a person not entitled to it or proceedings for a declaration or declarator that it was so granted.

(7) Where proceedings with respect to a patent are pending in the court under any provision of this Act mentioned in subsection (1) above, no proceedings may be instituted without the leave of the court before the comptroller with respect to that patent under section 61(3), 69, 71 or 72 above.

(8) It is hereby declared that for the purposes of this Act the validity of a patent is not put in issue merely because the comptroller is considering its validity in order to decide whether to revoke it under section 73 above.

General provisions as to amendment of patents and applications

Amendment of patent in infringement or revocation proceedings

75.—(1) In any proceedings before the court or the comptroller in which the **2-073** validity of a patent is put in issue the court or, as the case may be, the comptroller

---

[1] Words substituted by Copyright, Designs and Patents Act 1988 c.48 s 295 Sch 5 para 10

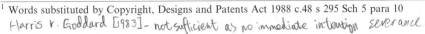 Harris v. Goddard [1983] - not sufficient as no immediate intention severance

may, subject to section 76 below, allow the proprietor of the patent to amend the specification of the patent in such manner, and subject to such terms as to advertising the proposed amendment and as to costs, expenses or otherwise, as the court or comptroller thinks fit.

(2) A person may give notice to the court or the comptroller of his opposition to an amendment proposed by the proprietor of the patent under this section, and if he does so the court or the comptroller shall notify the proprietor and consider the opposition in deciding whether the amendment or any amendment should be allowed.

(3) An amendment of a specification of a patent under this section shall have effect and be deemed always to have had effect from the grant of the patent.

(4) Where an application for an order under this section is made to the court, the applicant shall notify the comptroller, who shall be entitled to appear and be heard and shall appear if so directed by the court.

[Amendments of applications and patents not to include added matter

2-074   **76.**—(1) An application for a patent which—

    (a) is made in respect of matter disclosed in an earlier application, or in the specification of a patent which has been granted, and

    (b) discloses additional matter, that is, matter extending beyond that disclosed in the earlier application, as filed, or the application for the patent, as filed,

may be filed under section 8(3), 12 or 37(4) above, or as mentioned in section 15(4) above, but shall not be allowed to proceed unless it is amended so as to exclude the additional matter.

(2) No amendment of an application for a patent shall be allowed under section 17(3), 18(3) or 19(1) if it results in the application disclosing matter extending beyond that disclosed in the application as filed.

(3) No amendment of the specification of a patent shall be allowed under section 27(1), 73 or 75 if it—

    (a) results in the specification disclosing additional matter, or

    (b) extends the protection conferred by the patent.][1]

[Biotechnological inventions

2-075   **76A.**—(1) Any provision of, or made under, this Act is to have effect in relation to a patent or an application for a patent which concerns a biotechnological invention, subject to the provisions of Schedule A2.

(2) Nothing in this section or Schedule A2 is to be read as affecting the application of any provision in relation to any other kind of patent or application for a patent.][2]

---

[1] Substituted by Copyright, Designs and Patents Act 1988 c.48 s 295 Sch 5 para 20
[2] Inserted by SI 2000/2037 reg 5

PART II

PROVISIONS ABOUT INTERNATIONAL CONVENTIONS

European patents and patent applications

Effect of European patent (UK)

77.—(1) Subject to the provisions of this Act, a European patent (UK) shall, **2-076** as from the publication of the mention of its grant in the European Patent Bulletin, be treated for the purposes of Parts I and III of this Act as if it were a patent under this Act granted in pursuance of an application made under this Act and as if notice of the grant of the patent had, on the date of that publication, been published under section 24 above in the journal; and—

(a) the proprietor of a European patent (UK) shall accordingly as respects the United Kingdom have the same rights and remedies, subject to the same conditions, as the proprietor of a patent under this Act;

(b) references in Parts I and III of this Act to a patent shall be construed accordingly; and

(c) any statement made and any certificate filed for the purposes of the provision of the convention corresponding to section 2(4)(c) above shall be respectively treated as a statement made and written evidence filed for the purposes of the said paragraph (c).

(2) Subsection (1) above shall not affect the operation in relation to a European patent (UK) of any provisions of the European Patent Convention relating to the amendment or revocation of such a patent in proceedings before the European Patent Office.

[(3) Where in the case of a European patent (UK)—

(a) proceedings for infringement, or proceedings under section 58 above, have been commenced before the court or the comptroller and have not been finally disposed of, and

(b) it is established in proceedings before the European Patent Office that the patent is only partially valid,

the provisions of section 63 or, as the case may be, of subsections (7) to (9) of section 58 apply as they apply to proceedings in which the validity of a patent is put in issue and in which it is found that the patent is only partially valid.]¹

[(4) Where a European patent (UK) is amended in accordance with the European Patent Convention, the amendment shall have effect for the purposes of Parts I and III of this Act as if the specification of the patent had been amended under this Act; but subject to subsection (6)(b) below.]²

[(4A) Where a European patent (UK) is revoked in accordance with the European Patent Convention, the patent shall be treated for the purposes of Parts I and III of this Act as having been revoked under this Act.]³

(5) Where—

(a) under the European Patent Convention a European patent (UK) is revoked for failure to observe a time limit and is subsequently restored; and

(b) between the revocation and publication of the fact that it has been restored a person begins in good faith to do an act which would, apart

---

¹ Substituted by Copyright, Designs and Patents Act 1988 c.48 s 295 Sch 5 para 21 (2)
² Substituted by Copyright, Designs and Patents Act 1988 c.48 s 295 Sch 5 para 21 (3)
³ Inserted by Copyright, Designs and Patents Act 1988 c.48 s 295 Sch 5 para 21 (3)

from section 55 above, constitute an infringement of the patent or makes in good faith effective and serious preparations to do such an act;

he shall have the rights conferred by [section 28A(4) and (5) above, and subsections (6) and (7) of that section shall apply accordingly.][1]

(6) While this subsection is in force—

(a) subsection (1) above shall not apply to a European patent (UK) the specification of which was published in French or German, unless a translation of the specification into English is filed at the Patent Office and the prescribed fee is paid before the end of the prescribed period;

(b) subsection (4) above shall not apply to an amendment made in French or German unless [a translation into English of the specification as amended][2] is filed at the Patent Office and the prescribed fee is paid before the end of the prescribed period.

(7) Where [such a translation is not filed][3], the patent shall be treated as always having been void.

(8) The comptroller shall publish any translation filed at the Patent Office under subsection (6) above.

Effect of filing an application for a European patent (UK)

2-077   **78.**—(1) Subject to the provisions of this Act, an application for a European patent (UK) having a date of filing under the European Patent Convention shall be treated for the purposes of the provisions of this Act to which this section applies as an application for a patent under this Act having that date as its date of filing and having the other incidents listed in subsection (3) below, but subject to the modifications mentioned in the following provisions of this section.

(2) This section applies to the following provisions of this Act:—

section 2(3) and so much of section 14(7) as relates to section 2(3);

section 5;

section 6;

so much of section 13(3) as relates to an application for and issue of a certificate under that subsection;

sections 30 to 33;

section 36;

sections 55 to 69;

section 74, so far as relevant to any of the provisions mentioned above;

section 111; and

section 125.

(3) The incidents referred to in subsection (1) above in relation to an application for a European patent (UK) are as follows:—

(a) any declaration of priority made in connection with the application under the European Patent Convention shall be treated for the purposes of this Act as a declaration made under section 5(2) above;

(b) where a period of time relevant to priority is extended under that convention, the period of twelve months specified in section 5(2) above shall be so treated as altered correspondingly;

(c) where the date of filing an application is re-dated under that convention to a later date, that date shall be so treated as the date of filing the application;

---

[1] Words substituted by Copyright, Designs and Patents Act 1988 c.48 s 295 Sch 5 para 8 (b)
[2] Words substituted by Copyright, Designs and Patents Act 1988 c.48 s 295 Sch 5 para 21 (4)
[3] Words substituted by Copyright, Designs and Patents Act 1988 c.48 s 295 Sch 5 para 21 (5)

(d) the application, if published in accordance with that convention, shall, subject to subsection (7) and section 79 below, be so treated as published under section 16 above;

(e) any designation of the inventor under that convention or any statement under it indicating the origin of the right to a European patent shall be treated for the purposes of section 13(3) above as a statement filed under section 13(2) above;

(f) registration of the application in the register of European patents shall be treated as registration under this Act.

(4) Rules under section 32 above may not impose any requirements as to the registration of applications for European patents (UK) but may provide for the registration of copies of entries relating to such applications in the European register of patents.

[(5) Subsections (1) to (3) above shall cease to apply to an application for a European patent (UK), except as mentioned in subsection (5A) below, if—

(a) the application is refused or withdrawn or deemed to be withdrawn, or

(b) the designation of the United Kingdom in the application is withdrawn or deemed to be withdrawn,

but shall apply again if the rights of the applicant are re-established under the European Patent Convention, as from their re-establishment.][1]

[(5A) The occurrence of any of the events mentioned in subsection (5)(a) or (b) shall not affect the continued operation of section 2(3) above in relation to matter contained in an application for a European patent (UK) which by virtue of that provision has become part of the state of the art as regards other inventions.][2]

(6) Where between those subsections ceasing to apply to any such application and the re-establishment of the rights of the applicant a person begins in good faith to do an act which would, apart from section 55 above, constitute an infringement of the application if those subsections then applied, or makes in good faith effective and serious preparations to do such an act, he shall have the rights conferred by [section 28A(4) and (5) above, and subsections (6) and (7) of that section shall apply accordingly.][3]

(7) While this subsection is in force, an application for a European patent (UK) published by the European Patent Office under the European Patent Convention in French or German shall be treated for the purposes of sections 55 and 69 above as published under section 16 above when a translation into English of the claims of the specification of the application has been filed at and published by the Patent Office and the prescribed fee has been paid, but an applicant—

(a) may recover a payment by virtue of section 55(5) above in respect of the use of the invention in question before publication of that translation; or

(b) may bring proceedings by virtue of section 69 above in respect of an act mentioned in that section which is done before publication of that translation;

if before that use or the doing of that act he has sent by post or delivered to the government department who made use or authorised the use of the invention, or, as the case may be, to the person alleged to have done the act, a translation into English of those claims.

---

[1] Substituted by Copyright, Designs and Patents Act 1988 c.48 s 295 Sch 5 para 22
[2] Inserted by Copyright, Designs and Patents Act 1988 c.48 s 295 Sch 5 para 22
[3] Words substituted by Copyright, Designs and Patents Act 1988 c.48 s 295 Sch 5 para 8 (b)

(8) Subsection (7) above shall come into force on a day appointed for the purpose by rules and shall cease to have effect on a day so appointed, without prejudice, however, to the power to bring it into force again.

Operation of s. 78 in relation to certain European patent applications

2-078   **79.**—(1) Subject to the following provisions of this section, section 78 above, in its operation in relation to an international application for a patent (UK) which is treated by virtue of the European Patent Convention as an application for a European patent (UK), shall have effect as if any reference in that section to anything done in relation to the application under the European Patent Convention included a reference to the corresponding thing done under the Patent Co-operation Treaty.

(2) Any such international application which is published under that treaty shall be treated for the purposes of section 2(3) above as published only when a copy of the application has been supplied to the European Patent Office in English, French or German and the relevant fee has been paid under that convention.

(3) Any such international application which is published under that treaty in a language other than English, French or German shall, subject to section 78(7) above, be treated for the purposes of sections 55 and 69 above as published only when it is re-published in English, French or German by the European Patent Office under that convention.

Convention countries

Orders in Council as to convention countries

2-079   **90.**—(1) Her Majesty may with a view to the fulfilment of a treaty or international convention, arrangement or engagement, by Order in Council declare that any country specified in the Order is a convention country for the purposes of section 5 above.

(2) Her Majesty may by Order in Council direct that any of the Channel Islands, any colony [...]¹ shall be taken to be a convention country for those purposes.

(3) For the purposes of subsection (1) above every colony, protectorate, and territory subject to the authority or under the suzerainty of another country, and every territory administered by another country under the trusteeship system of the United Nations shall be taken to be a country in the case of which a declaration may be made under that subsection.

Miscellaneous

Evidence of conventions and instruments under conventions

2-080   **91.**—(1) Judicial notice shall be taken of the following, that is to say—
    (a) the European Patent Convention, the Community Patent Convention and the Patent Co-operation Treaty (each of which is hereafter in this section referred to as the relevant convention);
    (b) any bulletin, journal or gazette published under the relevant convention and the register of European or Community patents kept under it; and

¹ Words repealed by Statute Law (Repeals) Act 1986 c.12 s 1 (1) Sch 1 Pt VI

(c) any decision of, or expression of opinion by, the relevant convention court on any question arising under or in connection with the relevant convention.

PART III

MISCELLANEOUS AND GENERAL

Legal Proceedings

Appeals from the comptroller

97.—(1) Except as provided by subsection (4) below, an appeal shall lie to the **2-081** Patents Court from any decision of the comptroller under this Act or rules except any of the following decisions, that is to say—

(a) a decision falling within section 14(7) above;

(b) a decision under section 16(2) above to omit matter from a specification;

(c) a decision to give directions under subsection (1) or (2) of section 22 above;

(d) a decision under rules which is excepted by rules from the right of appeal conferred by this section.

Burden of proof in certain cases

100.—(1) If the invention for which a patent is granted is a process for **2-082** obtaining a new product, the same product produced by a person other than the proprietor of the patent or a licensee of his shall, unless the contrary is proved, be taken in any proceedings to have been obtained by that process.

(2) In considering whether a party has discharged the burden imposed upon him by this section, the court shall not require him to disclose any manufacturing or commercial secrets if it appears to the court that it would be unreasonable to do so.

Offences

Falsification of register etc

109. If a person makes or causes to be made a false entry in any register kept **2-083** under this Act, or a writing falsely purporting to be a copy or reproduction of an entry in any such register, or produces or tenders or causes to be produced or tendered in evidence any such writing, knowing the entry or writing to be false, he shall be liable—

(a) on summary conviction, to a fine not exceeding [the prescribed sum][1],

(b) on conviction on indictment, to imprisonment for a term not exceeding two years or a fine, or both.

Unauthorised claim of patent rights

110.—(1) If a person falsely represents that anything disposed of by him for **2-084** value is a patented product he shall, subject to the following provisions of this

---
[1] Words substituted by virtue of Magistrates Court Act 1980 s 32 (2)

section, be liable on summary conviction to a fine not exceeding [level 3 on the standard scale][1].

(2) For the purposes of subsection (1) above a person who for value disposes of an article having stamped, engraved or impressed on it or otherwise applied to it the word "patent" or "patented" or anything expressing or implying that the article is a patented product, shall be taken to represent that the article is a patented product.

(3) Subsection (1) above does not apply where the representation is made in respect of a product after the patent for that product or, as the case may be, the process in question has expired or been revoked and before the end of a period which is reasonably sufficient to enable the accused to take steps to ensure that the representation is not made (or does not continue to be made).

(4) In proceedings for an offence under this section it shall be a defence for the accused to prove that he used due diligence to prevent the commission of the offence.

Unauthorised claim that patent has been applied for

2-085   111.—(1) If a person represents that a patent has been applied for in respect of any article disposed of for value by him and—

(a) no such application has been made, or

(b) any such application has been refused or withdrawn,

he shall, subject to the following provisions of this section, be liable on summary conviction to a fine not exceeding [level 3 on the standard scale][2].

(2) Subsection (1)(b) above does not apply where the representation is made (or continues to be made) before the expiry of a period which commences with the refusal or withdrawal and which is reasonably sufficient to enable the accused to take steps to ensure that the representation is not made (or does not continue to be made).

(3) For the purposes of subsection (1) above a person who for value disposes of an article having stamped, engraved or impressed on it or otherwise applied to it the words "patent applied for" or "patent pending", or anything expressing or implying that a patent has been applied for in respect of the article, shall be taken to represent that a patent has been applied for in respect of it.

(4) In any proceedings for an offence under this section it shall be a defence for the accused to prove that he used due diligence to prevent the commission of such an offence.

Administrative provisions

Correction of errors in patents and applications

2-086   117.—(1) The comptroller may, subject to any provision of rules, correct any error of translation or transcription, clerical error or mistake in any specification of a patent or application for a patent or any document filed in connection with a patent or such an application.

(2) Where the comptroller is requested to correct such an error or mistake, any person may in accordance with rules give the comptroller notice of opposition to the request and the comptroller shall determine the matter.

---

[1] Words substituted (England, Wales) by Criminal Justice Act 1982 c.48 s 46 and (Scotland) by Criminal Procedure (Scotland) Act 1975 c.21 s 289G

[2] Words substituted (England, Wales) by Criminal Justice Act 1982 c.48 s 46 and (Scotland) by Criminal Procedure (Scotland) Act 1975 c.21 s 289G

Information about patent applications and patents, and inspection of documents

118.—(1) After publication of an application for a patent in accordance with **2-087** section 16 above the comptroller shall on a request being made to him in the prescribed manner and on payment of the prescribed fee (if any) give the person making the request such information, and permit him to inspect such documents, relating to the application or to any patent granted in pursuance of the application as may be specified in the request, subject, however, to any prescribed restrictions.

[Supplemental][1]

[Extent of invention

125.—(1) For the purposes of this Act an invention for a patent for which an **2-088** application has been made or for which a patent has been granted shall, unless the context otherwise requires, be taken to be that specified in a claim of the specification of the application or patent, as the case may be, as interpreted by the description and any drawings contained in that specification, and the extent of the protection conferred by a patent or application for a patent shall be determined accordingly.

(2) It is hereby declared for the avoidance of doubt that where more than one invention is specified in any such claim, each invention may have a different priority date under section 5 above.

(3) The Protocol on the Interpretation of Article 69 of the European Patent Convention (which Article contains a provision corresponding to subsection (1) above) shall, as for the time being in force, apply for the purposes of subsection (1) above as it applies for the purposes of that Article.][2]

Application of Act to Crown

129. This Act does not affect Her Majesty in her private capacity but, subject **2-089** to that, it binds the Crown.

Interpretation

130.—(1) In this Act, except so far as the context otherwise requires— **2-090**
"application for a European patent (UK)" and "international application for a patent (UK)" each mean an application of the relevant description which, on its date of filing, designates the United Kingdom;
"appointed day", in any provision of this Act, means the day appointed under section 132 below for the coming into operation of that provision;
["biological material" means any material containing genetic information and capable of reproducing itself or being reproduced in a biological system;
"biotechnological invention" means an invention which concerns a product consisting of or containing biological material or a process by means of which biological material is produced, processed or used;][3]

---

[1] Inserted by SI 2003/512 art 2
[2] Inserted by Copyright, Designs and Patents Act 1988 c.48 s 295 Sch 5 para 30
[3] Inserted by SI 2000/2037 reg 7

"Community Patent Convention" means the Convention for the European Patent for the Common Market and "Community patent" means a patent granted under that convention;

"comptroller" means the Comptroller-General of Patents, Designs and Trade Marks;

"Convention on International Exhibitions" means the Convention relating to International Exhibitions signed in Paris on 22nd November 1928, as amended or supplemented by any protocol to that convention which is for the time being in force;

"court" means

[(a) as respects England and Wales, the High Court or any patents county court having jurisdiction by virtue of an order under section 287 of the Copyright, Designs and Patents Act 1988;][1]

(b) as respects Scotland, the Court of Session;

(c) as respects Northern Ireland, the High Court in Northern Ireland;

"date of filing" means —

(a) in relation to an application for a patent made under this Act, the date which is the date of filing that application by virtue of section 15 above; and

(b) in relation to any other application, the date which, under the law of the country where the application was made or in accordance with the terms of a treaty or convention to which that country is a party, is to be treated as the date of filing that application or is equivalent to the date of filing an application in that country (whatever the outcome of the application);

"designate" in relation to an application or a patent, means designate the country or countries (in pursuance of the European Patent Convention or the Patent Co-operation Treaty) in which protection is sought for the invention which is the subject of the application or patent;

["electronic communication" has the same meaning as in the Electronic Communications Act 2000;][2]

"employee" means a person who works or (where the employment has ceased) worked under a contract of employment or in employment under or for the purposes of a government department [or a person who serves (or served) in the naval, military or air forces of the Crown][3];

"employer", in relation to an employee, means the person by whom the employee is or was employed;

"European Patent Convention" means the Convention on the Grant of European Patents, "European patent" means a patent granted under that convention, "European patent (UK)" means a European patent designating the United Kingdom, "European Patent Bulletin" means the bulletin of that name published under that convention, and "European Patent Office" means the office of that name established by that convention;

"exclusive licence" means a licence from the proprietor of or applicant for a patent conferring on the licensee, or on him and persons authorised by him, to the exclusion of all other persons (including the proprietor or applicant), any right in respect of the invention to which the patent or appli-

---

[1] Substituted by Copyright, Designs and Patents Act 1988 c.48 s 303 (1) Sch 7 para 23

[2] Inserted by SI 2003/512 art 3

[3] Words inserted by Armed Forces Act 1981 c.55 s 22 (1) (3)

cation relates, and "exclusive licensee" and "non-exclusive licence" shall be construed accordingly;

"filing fee" means the fee prescribed for the purposes of section 14 above;

"formal requirements" means those requirements designated as such by rules made for the purposes of section 17 above;

"international application for a patent" means an application made under the Patent Co-operation Treaty;

"International Bureau" means the secretariat of the World Intellectual Property Organization established by a convention signed at Stockholm on 14th July 1967;

"international exhibition" means an official or officially recognised international exhibition falling within the terms of the Convention on International Exhibitions or falling within the terms of any subsequent treaty or convention replacing that convention;

"inventor" has the meaning assigned to it by section 7 above;

"journal" has the meaning assigned to it by section 123(6) above;

"mortgage", when used as a noun, includes a charge for securing money or money's worth and, when used as a verb, shall be construed accordingly;

"1949 Act" means the Patents Act 1949;

"patent" means a patent under this Act;

"Patent Co-operation Treaty" means the treaty of that name signed at Washington on 19th June 1970;

"patented invention" means an invention for which a patent is granted and "patented process" shall be construed accordingly;

"patented product" means a product which is a patented invention or, in relation to a patented process, a product obtained directly by means of the process or to which the process has been applied;

"prescribed" and "rules" have the meanings assigned to them by section 123 above;

"priority date" means the date determined as such under section 5 above;

"published" means made available to the public (whether in the United Kingdom or elsewhere) and a document shall be taken to be published under any provision of this Act if it can be inspected as of right at any place in the United Kingdom by members of the public, whether on payment of a fee or not; and "republished" shall be construed accordingly;

"register" and cognate expressions have the meanings assigned to them by section 32 above;

"relevant convention court", in relation to any proceedings under the European Patent Convention, the Community Patent Convention or the Patent Co-operation Treaty, means that court or other body which under that convention or treaty has jurisdiction over those proceedings, including (where it has such jurisdiction) any department of the European Patent Office;

"right", in relation to any patent or application, includes an interest in the patent or application and, without prejudice to the foregoing, any reference to a right in a patent includes a reference to a share in the patent;

"search fee" means the fee prescribed for the purposes of [section 17(1) above][1];

"services of the Crown" and "use for the services of the Crown" have the meanings assigned to them by section 56(2) above, including, as respects

[1] Words substituted by Copyright, Designs and Patents Act 1988 c.48 s 295 Sch 5 para 5

any period of emergency within the meaning of section 59 above, the meanings assigned to them by the said section 59.

(2) Rules may provide for stating in the journal that an exhibition falls within the definition of international exhibition in subsection (1) above and any such statement shall be conclusive evidence that the exhibition falls within that definition.

(3) For the purposes of this Act matter shall be taken to have been disclosed in any relevant application within the meaning of section 5 above or in the specification of a patent if it was either claimed or disclosed (otherwise than by way of disclaimer or acknowledgment of prior art) in that application or specification.

(4) References in this Act to an application for a patent, as filed, are references to such an application in the state it was on the date of filing.

(5) References in this Act to an application for a patent being published are references to its being published under section 16 above.

(6) References in this Act to any of the following conventions, that is to say—

(a) The European Patent Convention;
(b) The Community Patent Convention;
(c) The Patent Co-operation Treaty;

are references to that convention or any other international convention or agreement replacing it, as amended or supplemented by any convention or international agreement (including in either case any protocol or annex), or in accordance with the terms of any such convention or agreement, and include references to any instrument made under any such convention or agreement.

(7) Whereas by a resolution made on the signature of the Community Patent Convention the governments of the member states of the European Economic Community resolved to adjust their laws relating to patents so as (among other things) to bring those laws into conformity with the corresponding provisions of the European Patent Convention, the Community Patent Convention and the Patent Co-operation Treaty, it is hereby declared that the following provisions of this Act, that is to say, sections 1(1) to (4), 2 to 6, 14(3), (5) and (6), 37(5), 54, 60, 69, 72(1) and (2), 74(4), 82, 83, [...][1], 100 and 125, are so framed as to have, as nearly as practicable, the same effects in the United Kingdom as the corresponding provisions of the European Patent Convention, the Community Patent Convention and the Patent Co-operation Treaty have in the territories to which those Conventions apply.

(8) [Part I of the Arbitration Act 1996][2] shall not apply to any proceedings before the comptroller under this Act.

(9) Except so far as the context otherwise requires, any reference in this Act to any enactment shall be construed as a reference to that enactment as amended or extended by or under any other enactment, including this Act.

Northern Ireland

2-091　　131. In the application of this Act to Northern Ireland—

(a) "enactment" includes an enactment of the Parliament of Northern Ireland and a Measure of the Northern Ireland Assembly;
(b) any reference to a government department includes a reference to a Department of the Government of Northern Ireland;

---

[1] Words repealed by Copyright, Designs and Patents Act 1988 c.48 s 303 (2) Sch 8
[2] Words substituted by Arbitration Act 1996 c.23 Sch 3 para 33

(c) any reference to the Crown includes a reference to the Crown in right of Her Majesty's Government in Northern Ireland;

(d) any reference to the [Companies Act 1985][1] includes a reference to the corresponding enactments in force in Northern Ireland; and

Short title, extent, commencement, consequential amendments and repeals

132.—(1) This Act may be cited as the Patents Act 1977.   2-092

(2) This Act shall extend to the Isle of Man, subject to any modifications contained in an Order made by Her Majesty in Council, and accordingly, subject to any such order, references in this Act to the United Kingdom shall be construed as including references to the Isle of Man.

(3) For the purposes of this Act the territorial waters of the United Kingdom shall be treated as part of the United Kingdom.

(4) This Act applies to acts done in an area designated by order under section 1(7) of the Continental Shelf Act 1964, [or specified by Order under [section 10(8) of the Petroleum Act 1998][2] in connection with any activity falling within [section 11(2)][3] of that Act][4], as it applies to acts done in the United Kingdom.

(5) This Act (except sections 77(6), (7) and (9), 78(7) and (8), this subsection and the repeal of section 41 of the 1949 Act) shall come into operation on such day as may be appointed by the Secretary of State by order, and different days may be appointed under this subsection for different purposes.

SCHEDULES

Section 76A   Schedule A2

Biotechnological Inventions

[1. An invention shall not be considered unpatentable solely on the ground that it concerns—   2-093
  (a) a product consisting of or containing biological material; or
  (b) a process by which biological material is produced, processed or used.][5]

[2. Biological material which is isolated from its natural environment or produced by means of a 2-094
technical process may be the subject of an invention even if it previously occurred in nature.][6]

[3. The following are not patentable inventions—   2-095
  (a) the human body, at the various stages of its formation and development, and the simple discovery of one of its elements, including the sequence or partial sequence of a gene;
  (b) processes for cloning human beings;
  (c) processes for modifying the germ line genetic identity of human beings;
  (d) uses of human embryos for industrial or commercial purposes;
  (e) processes for modifying the genetic identity of animals which are likely to cause them suffering without any substantial medical benefit to man or animal, and also animals resulting from such processes;

---

[1] Words substituted by Companies Consolidation (Consequential Provisions) Act 1985 c.9 s 30 Sch 2
[2] Words substituted by Petroleum Act 1998 c.17 Sch 4 para 14 (a)
[3] Words substituted by Petroleum Act 1998 c.17 Sch 4 para 14 (b)
[4] Words substituted by Oil and Gas (Enterprise) Act 1982 c.23 Sch 3 para 39
[5] Inserted by SI 2000/2037 Sch 2 para 1
[6] Inserted by SI 2000/2037 Sch 2 para 1

(f) any variety of animal or plant or any essentially biological process for the production of animals or plants, not being a micro-biological or other technical process or the product of such a process.][1]

2-096   [**4.** Inventions which concern plants or animals may be patentable if the technical feasibility of the invention is not confined to a particular plant or animal variety.][2]

2-097   [**5.** An element isolated from the human body or otherwise produced by means of a technical process, including the sequence or partial sequence of a gene, may constitute a patentable invention, even if the structure of that element is identical to that of a natural element.][3]

2-098   [**6.** The industrial application of a sequence or partial sequence of a gene must be disclosed in the patent application as filed.][4]

2-099   [**7.** The protection conferred by a patent on a biological material possessing specific characteristics as a result of the invention shall extend to any biological material derived from that biological material through propagation or multiplication in an identical or divergent form and possessing those same characteristics.][5]

2-100   [**8.** The protection conferred by a patent on a process that enables a biological material to be produced possessing specific characteristics as a result of the invention shall extend to biological material directly obtained through that process and to any other biological material derived from the directly obtained biological material through propagation or multiplication in an identical or divergent form and possessing those same characteristics.][6]

2-101   [**9.** The protection conferred by a patent on a product containing or consisting of genetic information shall extend to all material, save as provided for in paragraph 3(a) above, in which the product is incorporated and in which the genetic information is contained and performs its function.][7]

2-102   [**10.** The protection referred to in paragraphs 7, 8 and 9 above shall not extend to biological material obtained from the propagation or multiplication of biological material placed on the market by the proprietor of the patent or with his consent, where the multiplication or propagation necessarily results from the application for which the biological material was marketed, provided that the material obtained is not subsequently used for other propagation or multiplication.][8]

2-103   [**11.** In this Schedule:
"essentially biological process" means a process for the production of animals and plants which consists entirely of natural phenomena such as crossing and selection;
"microbiological process" means any process involving or performed upon or resulting in microbiological material;
"plant variety" means a plant grouping within a single botanical taxon of the lowest known rank, which grouping can be:
(a) defined by the expression of the characteristics that results from a given genotype or combination of genotypes; and
(b) distinguished from any other plant grouping by the expression of at least one of the said characteristics; and
(c) considered as a unit with regard to its suitability for being propagated unchanged.][9]

---

[1] Inserted by SI 2000/2037 Sch 2 para 1
[2] Inserted by SI 2000/2037 Sch 2 para 1
[3] Inserted by SI 2000/2037 Sch 2 para 1
[4] Inserted by SI 2000/2037 Sch 2 para 1
[5] Inserted by SI 2000/2037 Sch 2 para 1
[6] Inserted by SI 2000/2037 Sch 2 para 1
[7] Inserted by SI 2000/2037 Sch 2 para 1
[8] Inserted by SI 2000/2037 Sch 2 para 1
[9] Inserted by SI 2000/2037 Sch 2 para 1

Patents Bill 2004

[As Amended in Standing Committee D]

To Amend the law relating to patents.

BE IT ENACTED by the Queen's most Excellent Majesty, by and with the advice and consent of the Lords Spiritual and Temporal, and Commons, in this present Parliament assembled, and by the authority of the same, as follows:–

Amendments of the 1977 Act relating to international obligations

Methods of treatment or diagnosis

1. After section 4 of the Patents Act 1977 (c. 37) ("the 1977 Act") there is inserted— **3-001**
  "4A Methods of treatment or diagnosis
  (1) A patent shall not be granted for the invention of–
    (a) a method of treatment of the human or animal body by surgery or therapy, or
    (b) a method of diagnosis practised on the human or animal body.
  (2) Subsection (1) above does not apply to an invention consisting of a substance or composition for use in any such method.
  (3) In the case of an invention consisting of a substance or composition for use in any such method, the fact that the substance or composition forms part of the state of the art shall not prevent the invention from being taken to be new if the use of the substance or composition in any such method does not form part of the state of the art.
  (4) In the case of an invention consisting of a substance or composition for a specific use in any such method, the fact that the substance or composition forms part of the state of the art shall not prevent the invention from being taken to be new if that specific use does not form part of the state of the art."

Amendment of patents after grant

2.—(1) In section 27 of the 1977 Act (general power to amend after grant), after subsection (5) there is inserted— **3-002**
    "(6) In considering whether or not to allow an application under this section, the comptroller shall have regard to any relevant principles applicable under the European Patent Convention."
  (3) In section 62 of that Act (restrictions on recovery of damages for infringement), in subsection (3), after "satisfied that" there is inserted "(a)" and at the end there is inserted "and
    (b) the proceedings are brought in good faith."
  (4) In section 63 of that Act (relief for infringement of partially valid patent), in subsection (2), after "proves that" there is inserted "(a)" and after "knowledge, and" there is inserted—
    "(b) the proceedings are brought in good faith,
and".
  (5) In section 75 of that Act (amendment in infringement or revocation proceedings), after subsection (4) there is inserted—

First National Securities v. Hegerty [1985]– forge wife's signature to mortgage severs the joint tenancy

"(5) In considering whether or not to allow an amendment proposed under this section, the court or the comptroller shall have regard to any relevant principles applicable under the European Patent Convention."

Relief for partially valid patent

3-003   **3.**—(1) In section 63 of the 1977 Act (relief for infringement of partially valid patent), after subsection (3) there is inserted—

"(4) The court or the comptroller may also grant relief under this section in the case of a European patent (UK) on condition that the claims of the patent are limited to its or his satisfaction by the European Patent Office at the request of the proprietor."

Relief for partially valid patent

3-004   **4.**—In section 72 of the 1977 Act (power to revoke patents on application), in subsection (4), "under section 75 below" is omitted and after that subsection there is inserted—

"(4A) The reference in subsection (4) above to the specification being amended is to its being amended under section 75 below and also, in the case of a European patent (UK), to its being amended under any provision of the European Patent Convention under which the claims of the patent may be limited by amendment at the request of the proprietor."

Restrictions on applications abroad by United Kingdom residents

3-005   **7.**—(1) In section 23 of the 1977 Act (restrictions on applications abroad by United Kingdom residents), in subsection (1), after "an invention" there is inserted "if subsection (1A) below applies to that application,".

(2) After that subsection there is inserted—

"(1A) This subsection applies to an application if–

(a) the application contains information which relates to military technology or for any other reason publication of the information might be prejudicial to national security; or

(b) the application contains information the publication of which might be prejudicial to the safety of the public."

Co-ownership

3-006   **9.**—In section 36 of the 1977 Act (co-ownership), in subsection (3), after "others"there is inserted—

"(a) amend the specification of the patent or apply for such an amendment to be allowed or for the patent to be revoked, or (b)".

Compensation of employees for certain inventions

3-007   **10.**—(1) In section 40 of the 1977 Act (compensation of employees for certain inventions), for subsection (1) there is substituted—

"(1) Where it appears to the court or the comptroller on an application made by an employee within the prescribed period that–

(a) the employee has made an invention belonging to the employer for which a patent has been granted,

(b) having regard among other things to the size and nature of the employer's undertaking, the invention or the patent for it (or the combination of both) is of outstanding benefit to the employer, and

(c) by reason of those facts it is just that the employee should be awarded compensation to be paid by the employer,

the court or the comptroller may award him such compensation of an amount determined under section 41 below."

(2) In subsection (2)(c) of that section, for "the patent" there is substituted "the invention or the patent for it (or both)".

(3) In section 41 of that Act (amount of compensation), for subsection (1) there is substituted—

"(1) An award of compensation to an employee under section 40(1) or (2) above shall be such as will secure for the employee a fair share (having regard to all the circumstances) of the benefit which the employer has derived, or may reasonably be expected to derive, from any of the following–

(a) the invention in question;

(b) the patent for the invention;

(c) the assignment, assignation or grant of–

(i) the property or any right in the invention, or

(ii) the property in, or any right in or under, an application for the patent,

to a person connected with the employer."

(4) In subsections (4) and (5) of that section, the words "a patent for" are omitted.

(5) In subsection (5)(a) of that section, after "the patent" there is inserted "for it".

(6) In section 43 of that Act (provisions supplementing sections 39 to 42), in subsection (5)—

(a) for "a patent" there is substituted "an invention or patent";

(b) for "the patent", in both places, there is substituted "it".

(7) After subsection (5) of that section there is inserted—

"(5A) For the purposes of sections 40 and 41 above the benefit derived or expected to be derived by an employer from an invention shall not include any benefit derived or expected to be derived from the invention after the patent for it has expired or has been surrendered or revoked."

(8) This section, and the entry in Schedule 3 corresponding to subsection (4), apply in relation to an invention the patent for which is applied for on or after the commencement of this section. In this subsection "patent" has the meaning given by section 43(4) of the 1977 Act.

Enforcement of damages

11.—In section 61 of the 1977 Act (proceedings for infringement of a patent), **3-008** after subsection (6) there is inserted—

"(7) If the comptroller awards any sum by way of damages on a reference under subsection (3) above, then–

(a) in England and Wales, the sum shall be recoverable, if a county court so orders, by execution issued from the county court or otherwise as if it were payable under an order of that court;

(b) in Scotland, payment of the sum may be enforced in like manner as an extract registered decree arbitral bearing a warrant for execution issued by the sheriff court of any sheriffdom in Scotland;

(c) in Northern Ireland, payment of the sum may be enforced as if it were a money judgment."

Threats of infringement proceedings

3-009   **12.**—(1) Section 70 of the 1977 Act (remedy for groundless threats of infringement proceedings) is amended as follows.

(2) For subsection (2) there is substituted –

"(2) In any such proceedings the claimant or pursuer shall, subject to subsection (2A) below, be entitled to the relief claimed if he proves that the threats were so made and satisfies the court that he is a person aggrieved by them.

"(2A) If the defendant or defender proves that the acts in respect of which proceedings were threatened constitute or, if done, would constitute an infringement of a patent –

(a) the claimant or pursuer shall be entitled to the relief claimed only if he shows that the patent alleged to be infringed is invalid in a relevant respect;

(b) even if the claimant or pursuer does show that the patent is invalid in a relevant respect, he shall not be entitled to the relief claimed if the defendant or defender proves that at the time of making the threats he did not know, and had no reason to suspect, that the patent was invalid in that respect."

(3) For subsection (4) there is substituted—

"(4) Proceedings may not be brought under this section for –

(a) a threat to bring proceedings for an infringement alleged to consist of making or importing a product for disposal or of using a process, or

(b) a threat, made to a person who has made or imported a product for disposal or used a process, to bring proceedings for an infringement alleged to consist of doing anything else in relation to that product or process."

(4) For subsection (5) there is substituted—

"(5) For the purposes of this section a person does not threaten another person with proceedings for infringement of a patent if he merely –

(a) provides factual information about the patent,

(b) makes enquiries of the other person for the sole purpose of discovering whether, or by whom, the patent has been infringed as mentioned in subsection (4)(a) above, or

(c) makes an assertion about the patent for the purpose of any enquiries so made."

(5) After subsection (5) there is inserted—

"(6) In proceedings under this section for threats made by one person (A) to another (B) in respect of an alleged infringement of a patent for an invention, it shall be a defence for A to prove that he used his best endeavours, without success, to discover –

(a) where the invention is a product, the identity of the person (if any) who made or (in the case of an imported product) imported it for disposal;

(b) where the invention is a process and the alleged infringement consists of offering it for use, the identity of a person who used the process;

(c) where the invention is a process and the alleged infringement is an act falling within section 60(1)(c) above, the identity of the person who used the process to produce the product in question;

and that he notified B accordingly, before or at the time of making the threats, identifying the endeavours used."

Opinions by Patent Office as to validity or infringement

13.—(1) After section 74 of the 1977 Act there is inserted—   **3-010**

"Opinions by Patent Office

74A Opinions as to validity or infringement

(1) The proprietor of a patent or any other person may request the comptroller to issue an opinion –
   (a) as to whether a particular act constitutes, or (if done) would constitute, an infringement of the patent;
   (b) as to whether, or to what extent, the invention in question is not patentable because the condition in section 1(1)(a) or (b) above is not satisfied.

(2) Subsection (1) above applies even if the patent has expired or has been surrendered.

(3) The comptroller shall issue an opinion if requested to do so under subsection (1) above, but shall not do so –
   (a) in such circumstances as may be prescribed, or
   (b) if for any reason he considers it inappropriate in all the circumstances to do so.

(4) An opinion under this section shall not be binding for any purposes.

(5) An opinion under this section shall be prepared by an examiner.

(6) For the purposes of section 101 below, only the person making a request under subsection (1) above shall be regarded as a party to a proceeding before the comptroller in relation to that request.

74B Reviews of opinions under section 74A

(1) Rules may make provision for a review before the comptroller, on an application by the proprietor or an exclusive licensee of the patent in question, of an opinion under section 74A above.

(2) The rules may, in particular –
   (a) prescribe the circumstances in which, and the period within which, an application may be made;
   (b) provide that, in prescribed circumstances, proceedings for a review may not be brought or continued where other proceedings have been brought;
   (c) make provision under which, in prescribed circumstances, proceedings on a review are to be treated for prescribed purposes as if they were proceedings under section 61(1)(c) or (e), 71(1) or 72(1)(a) above;
   (d) provide for there to be a right of appeal against a decision made on a review only in prescribed cases."

(2) In section 74 of that Act (proceedings in which validity of patent may be put in issue), in subsection (8), after "the validity of a patent is not put in issue merely because" there is inserted "(a)" and at the end there is inserted "or
   (b) its validity is being considered in connection with an opinion under section 74A below or a review of such an opinion."

(3) In section 32(2) of that Act (rules about the register of patents), after paragraph (b) there is inserted –

Re 88 Berkeley Rd NW9 [1971] sufficient by registered post, even not read.

"(ba) the entering on the register of notices concerning opinions issued, or to be issued, under section 74A below;".

SCHEDULES

Section 5

Schedule 1

AMENDMENTS RELATING TO INTERNATIONAL OBLIGATIONS

3-011 2. In section 77 (effect of European patent (UK)), in subsection (5)(a), after "restored" there is inserted "or is revoked by the Board of Appeal and is subsequently restored by the Enlarged Board of Appeal".

3-012 3. (1) Section 78 (effect of filing an application for a European patent (UK)) is amended as follows.

(2) In subsection (5A), at the end there is inserted "; and the occurrence of any event mentioned in subsection (5)(b) shall not prevent matter contained in an application for a European patent (UK) becoming part of the state of the art by virtue of section 2(3) above as regards other inventions where the event occurs before the publication of that application."

(3) For subsection (6) there is substituted–

"(6) Where, between subsections (1) to (3) above ceasing to apply to an application for a European patent (UK) and the re-establishment of the rights of the applicant, a person–

(a) begins in good faith to do an act which would constitute an infringement of the rights conferred by publication of the application if those subsections then applied, or

(b) makes in good faith effective and serious preparations to do such an act,

he shall have the right to continue to do the act or, as the case may be, to do the act, notwithstanding subsections (1) to (3) applying again and notwithstanding the grant of the patent.

(6A) Subsections (5) and (6) of section 20B above have effect for the purposes of subsection (6) above as they have effect for the purposes of that section and as if the references to subsection (4) of that section were references to subsection (6) above.

(6B) Subject to subsection (6A) above, the right conferred by subsection (6) above does not extend to granting a licence to another person to do the act in question.

(6C) Subsections (6) to (6B) above apply in relation to the use of a patented invention for the services of the Crown as they apply in relation to an infringement of the rights conferred by publication of the application (or, as the case may be, infringement of the patent).

"Patented invention" has the same meaning as in section 55 above."

3-013 9. (1) Section 130 (interpretation) is amended as follows.

(2) In subsection (1)–

(a) in the definition of "application for a European patent (UK)" and "international application for a patent (UK)", after "and" there is inserted "(subject to subsection (4A) below)";

(b) at the end of the definition of "designate" there is inserted "and includes a reference to a country being treated as designated in pursuance of the convention or treaty".

(3) After subsection (4) there is inserted–

"(4A) An international application for a patent is not, by reason of being treated by virtue of the European Patent Convention as an application for a European patent (UK), to be treated also as an international application for a patent (UK)."

(4) After subsection (5) there is inserted–

"(5A) References in this Act to the amendment of a patent or its specification (whether under this Act or by the European Patent Office) include, in particular, limitation of the claims (as interpreted by the description and any drawings referred to in the description or claims)."

Section 15

Schedule 2

MINOR AND CONSEQUENTIAL AMENDMENTS

3-014 2. In section 1 (patentable inventions), in subsection (1)(d), after "subsections (2) and (3)" there is inserted "or section 4A".

3-015 3. In section 2 (novelty), subsection (6) is omitted.

3-016 5. In section 12 (reference before grant of foreign or convention patent of questions about entitlement etc), in subsection (6)—

(a) in paragraph (a), after "application is withdrawn" there is inserted "whether before or";

(b) in paragraph (c), for "but after" there is substituted "or the".

6. In section 16(1) (publication of application), after "section 22 below" there is inserted "and to any prescribed restrictions". **3-017**

7. In section 20B (inserted by the Regulatory Reform Order) (effect of reinstatement of applications), after subsection (6) there is inserted— **3-018**

"(6A) The above provisions apply in relation to the use of a patented invention for the services of the Crown as they apply in relation to infringement of the rights conferred by publication of the application for a patent (or, as the case may be, infringement of the patent). "Patented invention" has the same meaning as in section 55 below."

8. (1) Section 22 (information prejudicial to defence of realm or safety of public) is amended as follows. **3-019**

(2) In the heading, for "defence of realm" there is substituted "national security".

(3) In subsections (1) and (5)(a), (c) and (d), for "the defence of the realm" there is substituted "national security".

(4) In subsection (6)—

(a) in paragraph (a), for the words from "inspect and authorise" to "in connection with it" there is substituted –

"(i) inspect the application and any documents sent to the comptroller in connection with it;

(ii) authorise a government body with responsibility for the production of atomic energy or for research into matters connected with its production or use, or a person appointed by such a government body, to inspect the application and any documents sent to the comptroller in connection with it;";

(b) for the words from "that Authority" to the end there is substituted "a government body or a person appointed by a government body carries out an inspection which the body or person is authorised to carry out under paragraph (a) above, the body or (as the case may be) the person shall report on the inspection to the Secretary of State as soon as practicable."

10. (1) Section 38 (effect of transfer of patent under section 37) is amended as follows. **3-020**

(2) In subsection (3), after "new proprietor or proprietors" there is inserted "or, as the case may be, the new applicant".

(3) In subsection (5), after "proprietors of the patent" there is inserted "or, as the case may be, the new applicant".

13. Section 60(4) (meaning of infringement: Community Patent Convention) is omitted. **3-021**

14. In section 61 (proceedings for infringement of patent), in subsection (4)(b), for "plaintiff" there is substituted "claimant". **3-022**

15. In section 62(2) (discretion to refuse damages etc for infringement committed while fees unpaid), for "any further period specified under"there is substituted "the further period specified in". **3-023**

16. In section 63 (relief for infringement of partially valid patent), in subsection (2), for "plaintiff" there is substituted "claimant". **3-024**

17. In section 70 (remedy for groundless threats of infringement proceedings), in subsection (3)(c), for "plaintiff" there is substituted "claimant" **3-025**

18. In section 72(1) (power to revoke patents on application), "on the application of any person" is omitted and after the first mention of "invention" there is inserted "on the application of any person (including the proprietor of the patent)". **3-026**

19. In section 75 (amendment of patent in infringement or revocation proceedings), in subsection (1), for "is" there is substituted "may be". **3-027**

22. In sections 103 and 105 (legal privilege), in the definition of "the relevant conventions" in subsection (2),"the Community Patent Convention" is omitted. **3-028**

26. (1) Section 123 (rules) is amended as follows. **3-029**

(2) In subsection (2), for paragraph (i) there is substituted –

"(i) giving effect to an inventor's rights to be mentioned conferred by section 13, and providing for an inventor's waiver of any such right to be subject to acceptance by the comptroller;".

(3) After that subsection there is inserted –

"(2A) The comptroller may set out in directions any forms the use of which is required by rules; and any such directions shall be published in the prescribed manner."

(4) Subsections (4) and (5) are omitted.

27. In section 130(1) (interpretation)— **3-030**

(a) the definition of "Community patent"and the "and" preceding it are omitted;

(b) in the definition of "relevant convention court", "the Community Patent Convention" is omitted.

The Regulatory Reform (Patents) Order 2004 (Draft)

Whereas:

(a) the Secretary of State for Trade and Industry ("the Secretary of State") has consulted—

    (i) such organisations as appear to her to be representative of interests substantially affected by her proposals for this Order,

    (ii) the Comptroller-General of Patents, Designs and Trade Marks,

    (iii) the Law Commission,

    (iv) the National Assembly for Wales, and

    (v) such other persons as she considers appropriate;

(b) following the consultation mentioned in recital (a) the Secretary of State considered it appropriate to proceed with the making of this Order;

(c) a document containing the Secretary of State's proposals was laid before Parliament as required by section 6 of the Regulatory Reform Act 2001 and the period for Parliamentary consideration under section 8 of that Act has expired;

(d) the Secretary of State has had regard to the representations made during that period and in particular to the Sixth Report of Session 2003-2004 of the Delegated Powers and Regulatory Reform Committee of the House of Lords and the Second Report of Session 2003-2004 of the Regulatory Reform Committee of the House of Commons;

(e) a draft of this Order was laid before Parliament with a statement giving details of those representations [and the changes to the Secretary of State's proposals in the light of them];

(f) (f) the draft was approved by resolution of each House of Parliament;

(g) the Secretary of State is of the opinion that this Order does not remove any necessary protection or prevent any person from continuing to exercise any right or freedom which he might reasonably expect to continue to exercise; and

(h) this Order creates burdens affecting persons in the carrying on of certain activities, and the Secretary of State is of the opinion that—

    (i) the provisions of this Order, taken as a whole, strike a fair balance between the public interest and the interests of the persons affected by the burdens being created, and

    (ii) the extent to which this Order removes or reduces one or more burdens, or has other beneficial effects for persons affected by the burdens imposed by the existing law, makes it desirable for this Order to be made;

Now therefore the Secretary of State, in exercise of the powers conferred by section 1 of the Regulatory Reform Act 2001, hereby makes the following Order:—

Amendment of the Patents Act 1977

2. The Patents Act 1977(a) shall be amended as follows. **4-001**

3. In section 5(2) of that Act (priority date) for the words from "each having" **4-002** to "date of filing the application in suit" there shall be substituted "the application in suit has a date of filing during the period allowed under subsection (2A)(a) or (b) below" and after that subsection there shall be inserted—
"(2A) The periods are—
    (a) the period of twelve months immediately following the date of filing of the earlier specified relevant application, or if there is more than one, of the earliest of them; and
    (b) where the comptroller has given permission under subsection (2B) below for a late declaration to be made under subsection (2) above, the period commencing immediately after the end of the period allowed under paragraph (a) above and ending at the end of the prescribed period.
(2B) The applicant may make a request to the comptroller for permission to make a late declaration under subsection (2) above.
(2C) The comptroller shall grant a request made under subsection (2B) above if, and only if—
    (a) the request complies with the relevant requirements of rules; and
    (b) the comptroller is satisfied that the applicant's failure to file the application in suit within the period allowed under subsection (2A)(a) above was unintentional."

4. (1) Section 14 of that Act (making of application) shall be amended as **4-003** follows.
(2) Subsection (1)(b) and the word "and" immediately preceding it shall cease to have effect.
(3) After subsection (1) there shall be inserted—
    "(1A) Where an application for a patent is made, the fee prescribed for the purposes of this subsection ("the application fee") shall be paid not later than the end of the period prescribed for the purposes of section 15(10) below."
(4) After subsection (9) there shall be inserted—
    "(10) Subsection (9) above does not affect the power of the comptroller under section 117(1) below to correct an error or mistake in a withdrawal of an application for a patent."

5. For section 15 of that Act (date of filing application) there shall be substitu- **4-004** ted—
    "15 Date of filing application
    (1) Subject to the following provisions of this Act, the date of filing an application for a patent shall be taken to be the earliest date on which documents filed at the Patent Office to initiate the application satisfy the following conditions—
        (a) the documents indicate that a patent is sought;
        (b) the documents identify the person applying for a patent or contain information sufficient to enable that person to be contacted by the Patent Office; and

nduct(3) .
Re Dennis [1986] = Bankruptcy is sufficient to sever under Bank Act 1914.

    (c) the documents contain either—
        (i) something which is or appears to be a description of the invention for which a patent is sought; or
        (ii) a reference, complying with the relevant requirements of rules, to an earlier relevant application made by the applicant or a predecessor in title of his.

(2) It is immaterial for the purposes of subsection (1)(c)(i) above—
    (a) whether the thing is in, or is accompanied by a translation into, a language accepted by the Patent Office in accordance with rules;
    (b) whether the thing otherwise complies with the other provisions of this Act and with any relevant rules.

(3) Where documents filed at the Patent Office to initiate an application for a patent satisfy one or more of the conditions specified in subsection (1) above, but do not satisfy all those conditions, the comptroller shall as soon as practicable after the filing of those documents notify the applicant of what else must be filed in order for the application to have a date of filing.

(4) Where documents filed at the Patent Office to initiate an application for a patent satisfy all the conditions specified in subsection (1) above, the comptroller shall as soon as practicable after the filing of the last of those documents notify the applicant of—
    (a) the date of filing the application, and
    (b) the requirements that must be complied with, and the periods within which they are required by this Act or rules to be complied with, if the application is not to be treated as having been withdrawn.

(5) Subsection (6) below applies where—
    (a) an application has a date of filing by virtue of subsection (1) above;
    (b) within the prescribed period the applicant files at the Patent Office—
        (i) a drawing, or
        (ii) part of the description of the invention for which a patent is sought, and
    (c) that drawing or that part of the description was missing from the application at the date of filing.

(6) Unless the applicant withdraws the drawing or the part of the description filed under subsection (5)(b) above ("the missing part") before the end of the prescribed period—
    (a) the missing part shall be treated as included in the application; and
    (b) the date of filing the application shall be the date on which the missing part is filed at the Patent Office.

(7) Subsection (6)(b) above does not apply if—
    (a) on or before the date which is the date of filing the application by virtue of subsection (1) above a declaration is made under section 5(2) above in or in connection with the application;
    (b) the applicant makes a request for subsection (6)(b) above not to apply; and
    (c) the request complies with the relevant requirements of rules and is made within the prescribed period.

(8) Subsections (6) and (7) above do not affect the power of the comptroller under section 117(1) below to correct an error or mistake.

(9) Where, after an application for a patent has been filed and before the patent is granted—

(a) a new application is filed by the original applicant or his successor in title in accordance with rules in respect of any part of the matter contained in the earlier application, and

(b) the conditions mentioned in subsection (1) above are satisfied in relation to the new application (without the new application contravening section 76 below),

the new application shall be treated as having, as its date of filing, the date of filing the earlier application.

(10) Where there is a date of filing an application by virtue of this section, the application shall be treated as having been withdrawn at the end of the prescribed period, unless before the end of that period the applicant—

(a) files at the Patent Office one or more claims, the abstract and (where a reference to an earlier relevant application has been filed as mentioned in subsection (1)(c)(ii) above)—

(i) a description of the invention for which a patent is sought, and

(ii) a copy of the application referred to, complying with the relevant requirements of rules;

(b) pays the application fee; and

(c) makes a request for a search under section 17 below and pays the search fee.

(11) In this section "relevant application" has the meaning given by section 5(5) above.

"15A Preliminary examination

(1) The comptroller shall refer an application for a patent to an examiner for a preliminary examination if—

(a) the application has a date of filing;

(b) the application has not been withdrawn or treated as withdrawn; and

(c) the application fee has been paid.

(2) On a preliminary examination of an application the examiner shall—

(a) determine whether the application complies with those requirements of this Act and the rules which are designated by the rules as formal requirements for the purposes of this Act; and

(b) determine whether any requirements under section 13(2) or 15(10) above remain to be complied with.

(3) The examiner shall report to the comptroller his determinations under subsection (2) above.

(4) If on the preliminary examination of an application it is found that—

(a) any drawing referred to in the application, or

(b) part of the description of the invention for which the patent is sought,

is missing from the application, then the examiner shall include this finding in his report under subsection (3) above.

(5) Subsections (6) to (8) below apply if a report is made to the comptroller under subsection (3) above that not all the formal requirements have been complied with.

(6) The comptroller shall specify a period during which the applicant shall have the opportunity—

    (a) to make observations on the report, and

    (b) to amend the application so as to comply with those requirements (subject to section 76 below).

(7) The comptroller may refuse the application if the applicant fails to amend the application as mentioned in subsection (6)(b) above before the end of the period specified by the comptroller under that subsection.

(8) Subsection (7) above does not apply if—

    (a) the applicant makes observations as mentioned in subsection (6)(a) above before the end of the period specified by the comptroller under that subsection, and

    (b) as a result of the observations, the comptroller is satisfied that the formal requirements have been complied with.

(9) If a report is made to the comptroller under subsection (3) above—

    (a) that any requirement of section 13(2) or 15(10) above has not been complied with; or

    (b) that a drawing or part of the description of the invention has been found to be missing,

then the comptroller shall notify the applicant accordingly."

4-005   6. (1) Section 17 of that Act (preliminary examination and search) shall be amended as follows.

(2) For the heading there shall be substituted "Search".

(3) For subsection (1) there shall be substituted—

"(1) The comptroller shall refer an application for a patent to an examiner for a search if, and only if—

(a) the comptroller has referred the application to an examiner for a preliminary examination under section 15A(1) above;

(b) the application has not been withdrawn or treated as withdrawn;

(c) before the end of the prescribed period—

    (i) the applicant makes a request to the Patent Office in the prescribed form for a search; and

    (ii) the fee prescribed for the search ("the search fee") is paid;

(d) the application includes—

    (i) a description of the invention for which a patent is sought; and

    (ii) one or more claims; and

(e) the description and each of the claims comply with the requirements of rules as to language."

(4) Subsections (2) and (3) shall cease to have effect.

4-006   7. (1) Section 18 of that Act (substantive examination and grant or refusal of patent) shall be amended as follows.

(2) In subsection (1) the words "preliminary examination and" shall be omitted.

(3) In subsection (2) after the words "any examination" there shall be inserted "carried out under section 15A above".

(4) In subsection (4) for the words "section 17" there shall be substituted "section 15A".

4-007   8. After section 20 of that Act there shall be inserted—

"20A Reinstatement of applications

(1) Subsection (2) below applies where an application for a patent is refused, or is treated as having been refused or withdrawn, as a direct consequence of a failure by the applicant to comply with a requirement of this Act or rules within a period which is—

    (a) set out in this Act or rules, or

    (b) specified by the comptroller.

(2) Subject to subsection (3) below, the comptroller shall reinstate the application if, and only if—

    (a) the applicant requests him to do so;

    (b) the request complies with the relevant requirements of rules; and

    (c) he is satisfied that the failure to comply referred to in subsection (1) above was unintentional.

(3) The comptroller shall not reinstate the application if—

    an extension remains available under this Act or rules for the period referred to in subsection (1) above; or

    the period referred to in subsection (1) above is set out or specified—

        (i) in relation to any proceedings before the comptroller;

        (ii) for the purposes of section 5(2A)(b) above; or

        (iii) for the purposes of a request under this section or section 117B below.

(4) Where the application was made by two or more persons jointly, a request under subsection (2) above may, with the leave of the comptroller, be made by one or more of those persons without joining the others.

(5) If the application has been published under section 16 above, then the comptroller shall publish notice of a request under subsection (2) above in the prescribed manner.

(6) If an application is reinstated under this section the applicant shall comply with the requirement referred to in subsection (1) above within the further period specified by the comptroller.

(7) The further period specified under subsection (6) above shall not be less than two months.

(8) If the applicant fails to comply with subsection (6) above the application shall be treated as having been withdrawn on the expiry of the period specified under that subsection.

"20B Effect of reinstatement under section 20A

(1) The effect of reinstatement of an application under section 20A above is as follows.

(2) Anything done under or in relation to the application during the period between termination and reinstatement shall be treated as valid.

(3) If the application has been published under section 16 above before its termination anything done during that period which would have constituted an infringement of the rights conferred by publication of the application if the termination had not occurred shall be treated as an infringement of those rights—

    (a) if done at a time when it was possible for the period referred to in section 20A(1) above to be extended, or

    (b) if it was a continuation or repetition of an earlier act infringing those rights.

(4) If the application has been published under section 16 above before its termination and, after the termination and before publication of notice of the request for its reinstatement, a person—

(a) began in good faith to do an act which would have constituted an infringement of the rights conferred by publication of the application if the termination had not taken place, or

(b) made in good faith effective and serious preparations to do such an act,

he has the right to continue to do the act or, as the case may be, to do the act, notwithstanding the reinstatement of the application and the grant of the patent; but this right does not extend to granting a licence to another person to do the act.

(5) If the act was done, or the preparations were made, in the course of a business, the person entitled to the right conferred by subsection (4) above may—

(a) authorise the doing of that act by any partners of his for the time being in that business, and

(b) assign that right, or transmit it on death (or in the case of a body corporate on its dissolution), to any person who acquires that part of the business in the course of which the act was done or the preparations were made.

(6) Where a product is disposed of to another in exercise of a right conferred by subsection (4) or (5) above, that other and any person claiming through him may deal with the product in the same way as if it had been disposed of by the applicant.

(7) In this section "termination", in relation to an application, means—

(a) the refusal of the application, or

(b) the application being treated as having been refused or withdrawn."

4-008   9. (1) For the heading "*Security and safety*" **appearing before section 22 of that Act there shall be substituted** "*National security*".

(2) Section 22 of that Act (information prejudicial to defence of realm or safety of public) shall be amended as follows.

(3) In the heading the words "or safety of public" shall be omitted.

(4) For subsection (1) there shall be substituted—

"(1) This subsection applies to an application for a patent if—

(a) it is to be filed at the Patent Office under this Act or a treaty or international convention to which the United Kingdom is a party, and

(b) one (or more) of the conditions in subsection (1A) below is met in respect of it.

(1A) The conditions are—

(a) that the application is required to be made in a secure manner, by virtue of an agreement between the applicant and a government department or person acting on behalf of a government department;

(b) that—

(i) the Schedule to the Regulatory Reform (Patents) Order 2004 applies to the application; and

(ii) the applicant or the inventor of the invention for which a patent is sought (or, if there is more than one applicant or inventor, any of them) is resident in the United Kingdom;

(c) that the application is to be filed with the written permission of a government of a country outside the United Kingdom in pursuance of arrangements with the government of the United Kingdom under which the application may be published only if the foreign government has permitted publication.

(1B) An application to which subsection (1) above applies must be filed in the prescribed manner.

(1C) No information contained in an application to which subsection (1) above applies may be published or communicated to any person in the relevant period, without the authority of the comptroller.

(1D) The relevant period is the period—

(a) starting on the date of filing the application, and

(b) ending when the comptroller gives directions under subsection (1E) below in respect of the application or notifies the applicant under subsection (1G) below that he has decided not to give any such directions.

(1E) The comptroller may give directions in respect of an application to which subsection (1) above applies prohibiting or restricting—

(a) the publication of information contained in the application;

(b) the communication to a specified person or description of persons of information contained in the application.

(1F) Subsection (1E) above applies whether or not the application is filed in the manner prescribed for the purposes of subsection (1B) above.

(1G) If an application to which subsection (1) above applies is filed in the manner prescribed for the purposes of subsection (1B) above the comptroller must, within the period of six weeks starting on the date of filing the application—

(a) give directions under subsection (1E) above, or

(b) notify the applicant that he has decided not to give any such directions.

(1H) Subsection (1K) below applies if the conditions in subsection (1I) below or the conditions in subsection (1J) below are met.

(1I) The conditions are that—

(a) the Secretary of State notifies the comptroller that the publication of information about a matter might be prejudicial to the defence of the realm;

(b) the Schedule to the Regulatory Reform (Patents) Order 2004 does not apply to the application; and

(c) it appears to the comptroller that an application filed at the Patent Office under this Act or a treaty or international convention to which the United Kingdom is a party contains information about such a matter.

(1J) The conditions are that the Secretary of State notifies the comptroller that—

(a) the Schedule to the Regulatory Reform (Patents) Order 2004 applies to an application, and

(b) neither the applicant nor the inventor of the invention for which a patent is sought (or, if there is more than one applicant or inventor, none of them) is resident in the United Kingdom.

(1K) The comptroller may give directions in respect of the application prohibiting or restricting—

(a) the publication of information contained in the application;

(b) the communication to a specified person or description of persons of any such information."

(5) Subsection (2) shall cease to have effect.

(6) In subsection (3) for the words "so communicated" there shall be substituted "communicated in contravention of the directions".

(7) In subsection (5)—

(a) in paragraphs (a), (c) and (d), the words "or the safety of the public" shall be omitted;

(b) paragraph (b) shall be omitted.

(8) In subsection (6)(a) for the words from ", inspect and authorise" to "in connection with it there shall be substituted "—

(i) inspect the application and any documents sent to the comptroller in connection with it;

(ii) authorise a government body with responsibility for the production or use of atomic energy or for research into matters connected with its production or use, or a person appointed by such a government body, to inspect the application and any documents sent to the comptroller in connection with it;".

(9) In subsection (6) for the words from "that Authority" to the end of that subsection there shall be substituted "a government body or a person appointed by a government body carries out an inspection which the body or person is authorised to carry out under paragraph (a) above, the body or (as the case may be) the person shall report on the inspection to the Secretary of State as soon as practicable."

(10) After subsection (8) there shall be inserted—

"(8A) This subsection applies to a person if he knows or ought reasonably to have known that an application for a patent is one to which subsection (1) above applies and—

(a) he files the application or causes it to be filed other than in the manner prescribed for the purposes of subsection (1B) above, or

(b) he publishes or communicates information contained in the application in contravention of subsection (1C) above.

(8B) A person to whom subsection (8A) above applies is liable—

(a) on summary conviction, to a fine not exceeding the prescribed sum; or

(b) on conviction on indictment, to imprisonment for a term not exceeding two years or a fine, or both."

4-009   10. (1) Section 23 of that Act (restrictions on applications abroad by United Kingdom residents) shall be amended as follows.

(2) In subsection (1) for the words from "unless" to the end of the subsection there shall be substituted "if the condition set out in subsection (1A) below, the condition set out in subsection (1B) below or the condition set out in subsection (1C) below is met."

(3) After subsection (1) there shall be inserted—

"(1A) The condition is that—
>   (a) an application for a patent for the same invention has been filed at the Patent Office;
>   (b) section 22(1) above applies to the application by virtue of section 22(1A)(a) or (b) above;
>   (c) the comptroller has power under section 22(1E) above to give directions in respect of the application; and
>   (d) the applicant has not been notified under section 22(1G)(b) above that the comptroller has decided not to give directions under section 22(1E) above.

(1B) The condition is that—
>   (a) an application for a patent for the same invention has been filed at the Patent Office;
>   (b) directions have been given in respect of the application under section 22(1E) or (1K) above; and
>   (c) the directions have not been revoked.

(1C) The condition is that—
>   (a) an application for a patent for the same invention has not been filed at the Patent Office; and
>   (b) if an application for a patent for the same invention were to be filed at the Patent Office, section 22(1) above would apply to the application by virtue of section 22(1A)(a) or (b) above."

(4) In subsection (3) at the beginning insert "Subject to subsection (3A) below,".

(5) After subsection (3) there shall be inserted—

"(3A) A person is liable under subsection (3) above only if he knows or ought reasonably to have known that filing the application, or causing the application to be filed, would contravene this section."

11. After section 23 of that Act there shall be inserted— **4-010**

"23A Guidance by the comptroller

(1) If requested to do so by a person proposing to file, or cause to be filed, an application for a patent at the Patent Office, the comptroller shall give guidance to the person on whether section 22(1) above applies to the application by virtue of section 22(1A)(b) above.

(2) If requested to do so by a person proposing to file, or cause to be filed, an application outside the United Kingdom for a patent or other protection for an invention, the comptroller shall give guidance to the person on whether section 22(1) above would apply to the application by virtue of section 22(1A)(b) above, if the application were to be filed at the Patent Office as an application for a patent."

12. In section 28 of that Act (restoration of lapsed patents) for subsection (3) **4-011** there shall be substituted—

"(3) If the comptroller is satisfied that the failure of the proprietor of the patent—
>   (a) to pay the renewal fee within the prescribed period; or
>   (b) to pay that fee and any prescribed additional fee within the period of six months immediately following the end of that period,

was unintentional, the comptroller shall by order restore the patent on payment of any unpaid renewal fee and any prescribed additional fee."

4-012   13. (1) Section 30 of that Act (nature of, and transactions in, patents and applications for patents) shall be amended as follows.

(2) In subsection (6)—

(a) for the words "the parties to the transaction" there shall be substituted "the assignor or mortgagor";

(b) the words "or in the case of a body corporate" to the end of the subsection shall be omitted.

(3) After subsection (6) there shall be inserted—

"(6A) If a transaction mentioned in subsection (6) above is by a body corporate, references in that subsection to such a transaction being signed by or on behalf of the assignor or mortgagor shall be taken to include references to its being under the seal of the body corporate."

4-013   14. In section 72(1)(d) of that Act (power to revoke patents on application) for the words "section 15(4)" there shall be substituted "section 15(9)".

4-014   19. In section 97(1)(c) of that Act (appeals from the comptroller) for the words "subsection (1) or (2)" there shall be substituted "subsection (1E) or (1K)".

Copyright, Designs and Patents Act 1988

CHAPTER 48

BE IT ENACTED by the Queen's most Excellent Majesty, by and with the advice and consent of the Lords Spiritual and Temporal, and Commons, in this present Parliament assembled, and by the authority of the same, as follows:—

PART I

COPYRIGHT

CHAPTER I

SUBSISTENCE, OWNERSHIP AND DURATION OF COPYRIGHT

Introductory

Copyright and copyright works

5-001   1.—(1) Copyright is a property right which subsists in accordance with this Part in the following descriptions of work—

(a) original literary, dramatic, musical or artistic works,

(b) sound recordings, films [or broadcasts][1] and

---

[1] Words substituted subject to the savings specified in SI 2003/2498 reg 32 by SI 2003/2498 Pt II reg 5 (2)

(c) the typographical arrangement of published editions.

(2) In this Part "copyright work" means a work of any of those descriptions in which copyright subsists.

(3) Copyright does not subsist in a work unless the requirements of this Part with respect to qualification for copyright protection are met (see section 153 and the provisions referred to there).

Rights subsisting in copyright works

2.—(1) The owner of the copyright in a work of any description has the 5-002 exclusive right to do the acts specified in Chapter II as the acts restricted by the copyright in a work of that description.

(2) In relation to certain descriptions of copyright work the following rights conferred by Chapter IV (moral rights) subsist in favour of the author, director or commissioner of the work, whether or not he is the owner of the copyright—

(a) section 77 (right to be identified as author or director),

(b) section 80 (right to object to derogatory treatment of work), and

(c) section 85 (right to privacy of certain photographs and films).

Descriptions of work and related provisions

Literary, dramatic and musical works

3.—(1) In this Part— 5-003

"literary work" means any work, other than a dramatic or musical work,
which is written, spoken or sung, and accordingly includes—
(a) a table or compilation [other than a database]^1, [...]^2
(b) a computer program; [...]^3
[(c) preparatory design material for a computer program; [and]^4]^5
[(d) a database;]^6
"dramatic work" includes a work of dance or mime; and
"musical work" means a work consisting of music, exclusive of any words
or action intended to be sung, spoken or performed with the music.

(2) Copyright does not subsist in a literary, dramatic or musical work unless and until it is recorded, in writing or otherwise; and references in this Part to the time at which such a work is made are to the time at which it is so recorded.

(3) It is immaterial for the purposes of subsection (2) whether the work is recorded by or with the permission of the author; and where it is not recorded by the author, nothing in that subsection affects the question whether copyright subsists in the record as distinct from the work recorded.

[Databases

3A.—(1) In this Part "database" means a collection of independent works, 5-004 data or other materials which—

(a) are arranged in a systematic or methodical way, and

(b) are individually accessible by electronic or other means.

---

^{1} Words inserted by SI 1997/3032 Pt II reg 5 (a)
^{2} Word repealed by SI 1992/3233 reg 3
^{3} Word repealed by SI 1997/3032 Pt II reg 5 (b)
^{4} Word inserted by SI 1997/3032 Pt II reg 5 (c)
^{5} Words inserted by SI 1992/3233 reg 3
^{6} Inserted by SI 1997/3032 Pt II reg 5 (c)

(2) For the purposes of this Part a literary work consisting of a database is original if, and only if, by reason of the selection or arrangement of the contents of the database the database constitutes the author's own intellectual creation.][1]

Artistic works

5-005   **4.**—(1) In this Part "artistic work" means —
  (a) a graphic work, photograph, sculpture or collage, irrespective of artistic quality,
  (b) a work of architecture being a building or a model for a building, or
  (c) a work of artistic craftsmanship.
(2) In this Part—
  "building" includes any fixed structure, and a part of a building or fixed structure;
  "graphic work" includes—
    (a) any painting, drawing, diagram, map, chart or plan, and
    (b) any engraving, etching, lithograph, woodcut or similar work;

  "photograph" means a recording of light or other radiation on any medium on which an image is produced or from which an image may by any means be produced, and which is not part of a film;
  "sculpture" includes a cast or model made for purposes of sculpture.

[Sound recordings

5-006   **5A.**—(1) In this Part "sound recording" means—
  (a) a recording of sounds, from which the sounds may be reproduced, or
  (b) a recording of the whole or any part of a literary, dramatic or musical work, from which sounds reproducing the work or part may be produced,
 regardless of the medium on which the recording is made or the method by which the sounds are reproduced or produced.
(2) Copyright does not subsist in a sound recording which is, or to the extent that it is, a copy taken from a previous sound recording.][2]

[Films

5-007   **5B.**—(1) In this Part "film" means a recording on any medium from which a moving image may by any means be produced.
(2) The sound track accompanying a film shall be treated as part of the film for the purposes of this Part.
(3) Without prejudice to the generality of subsection (2), where that subsection applies—
  (a) references in this Part to showing a film include playing the film sound track to accompany the film, and
  (b) references to playing a sound recording do not include playing the film sound track to accompany the film.
(4) Copyright does not subsist in a film which is, or to the extent that it is, a copy taken from a previous film.
(5) Nothing in this section affects any copyright subsisting in a film sound track as a sound recording.][3]

---

[1] Inserted by SI 1997/3032 Pt II reg 6
[2] Substituted by SI 1995/3297 Pt II reg 9 (1)
[3] Substituted by SI 1995/3297 Pt II reg 9 (1)

Broadcasts

6.—[(1) In this Part a "broadcast" means an electronic transmission of visual **5-008** images, sounds or other information which—

    (a) is transmitted for simultaneous reception by members of the public and is capable of being lawfully received by them, or

    (b) is transmitted at a time determined solely by the person making the transmission for presentation to members of the public,

and which is not excepted by subsection (1A); and references to broadcasting shall be construed accordingly.

(1A) Excepted from the definition of "broadcast" is any internet transmission unless it is—

    (a) a transmission taking place simultaneously on the internet and by other means,

    (b) a concurrent transmission of a live event, or

    (c) a transmission of recorded moving images or sounds forming part of a programme service offered by the person responsible for making the transmission, being a service in which programmes are transmitted at scheduled times determined by that person.][1]

(2) An encrypted transmission shall be regarded as capable of being lawfully received by members of the public only if decoding equipment has been made available to members of the public by or with the authority of the person making the transmission or the person providing the contents of the transmission.

(3) References in this Part to the person making a broadcast [or a transmission which is a broadcast][2] are—

    (a) to the person transmitting the programme, if he has responsibility to any extent for its contents, and

    (b) to any person providing the programme who makes with the person transmitting it the arrangements necessary for its transmission;

and references in this Part to a programme, in the context of broadcasting, are to any item included in a broadcast.

[(4) For the purposes of this Part, the place from which a [wireless][3] broadcast is made is the place where, under the control and responsibility of the person making the broadcast, the programme-carrying signals are introduced into an uninterrupted chain of communication (including, in the case of a satellite transmission, the chain leading to the satellite and down towards the earth).][4]

[(4A) Subsections (3) and (4) have effect subject to section 6A (safeguards in case of certain satellite broadcasts).][5]

(5) References in this Part to the reception of a broadcast include reception of a broadcast relayed by means of a telecommunications system.

[(5A) The relaying of a broadcast by reception and immediate re-transmission shall be regarded for the purposes of this Part as a separate act of broadcasting from the making of the broadcast which is so re-transmitted.][6]

(6) Copyright does not subsist in a broadcast which infringes, or to the extent that it infringes, the copyright in another broadcast [...][7].

---

[1] Substituted by SI 2003/2498 Pt 2 reg 4 (a)
[2] Words substituted by SI 2003/2498 Pt II reg 4 (b)
[3] Word inserted by SI 2003/2498 Pt II reg 4 (c)
[4] Substituted by SI 1996/2967 Pt II reg 5
[5] Inserted by SI 1996/2967 Pt II reg 6 (1)
[6] Inserted by SI 2003/2498 Pt II reg 4 (d)
[7] Words repealed SI 2003/2498 Sch 2 para 1

[Safeguards in case of certain satellite broadcasts

5-009   **6A.**—(1) This section applies where the place from which a broadcast by way of satellite transmission is made is located in a country other than an EEA State and the law of that country fails to provide at least the following level of protection—

(a) exclusive rights in relation to [wireless][1] broadcasting equivalent to those conferred by section 20 ([infringement by communication to the public][2]) on the authors of literary, dramatic, musical and artistic works, films and broadcasts;

(b) a right in relation to live [wireless][3] broadcasting equivalent to that conferred on a performer by section 182(1)(b) (consent required for live broadcast of performance); and

(c) a right for authors of sound recordings and performers to share in a single equitable remuneration in respect of the [wireless][4] broadcasting of sound recordings.

(2) Where the place from which the programme-carrying signals are transmitted to the satellite ("the uplink station") is located in an EEA State—

(a) that place shall be treated as the place from which the broadcast is made, and

(b) the person operating the uplink station shall be treated as the person making the broadcast.

(3) Where the uplink station is not located in an EEA State but a person who is established in an EEA State has commissioned the making of the broadcast—

(a) that person shall be treated as the person making the broadcast, and

(b) the place in which he has his principal establishment in the European Economic Area shall be treated as the place from which the broadcast is made.][5]

Published editions

5-010   **8.**—(1) In this Part "published edition", in the context of copyright in the typographical arrangement of a published edition, means a published edition of the whole or any part of one or more literary, dramatic or musical works.

(2) Copyright does not subsist in the typographical arrangement of a published edition if, or to the extent that, it reproduces the typographical arrangement of a previous edition.

Authorship and ownership of copyright

Authorship of work

5-011   **9.**—(1) In this Part "author", in relation to a work, means the person who creates it.

(2) That person shall be taken to be—

[(aa) in the case of a sound recording, the producer;

(ab) in the case of a film, the producer and the principal director;][6]

---

[1] Word inserted by SI 2003/2498 Pt II reg 5 (3) (a) (i)
[2] Words substituted by SI 2003/2498 Pt II reg 5 (3) (a) (ii)
[3] Word inserted by SI 2003/2498 Pt II reg 5 (3) (b)
[4] Word inserted by SI 2003/2498 Pt II Reg 5 (3) (b)
[5] Inserted by SI 1996/2967 Pt II reg 6 (2)
[6] Substituted by SI 1996/2967 Pt II reg 18 (1)

(b) in the case of a broadcast, the person making the broadcast (see section 6(3)) or, in the case of a broadcast which relays another broadcast by reception and immediate re-transmission, the person making that other broadcast;

(d) in the case of the typographical arrangement of a published edition, the publisher.

(3) In the case of a literary, dramatic, musical or artistic work which is computer-generated, the author shall be taken to be the person by whom the arrangements necessary for the creation of the work are undertaken.

(4) For the purposes of this Part a work is of "unknown authorship" if the identity of the author is unknown or, in the case of a work of joint authorship, if the identity of none of the authors is known.

(5) For the purposes of this Part the identity of an author shall be regarded as unknown if it is not possible for a person to ascertain his identity by reasonable inquiry; but if his identity is once known it shall not subsequently be regarded as unknown.

Works of joint authorship

10.—(1) In this Part a "work of joint authorship" means a work produced by **5-012** the collaboration of two or more authors in which the contribution of each author is not distinct from that of the other author or authors.

[(1A) A film shall be treated as a work of joint authorship unless the producer and the principal director are the same person.][1]

(2) A broadcast shall be treated as a work of joint authorship in any case where more than one person is to be taken as making the broadcast (see section 6(3)).

(3) References in this Part to the author of a work shall, except as otherwise provided, be construed in relation to a work of joint authorship as references to all the authors of the work.

First ownership of copyright

11.—(1) The author of a work is the first owner of any copyright in it, subject **5-013** to the following provisions.

(2) Where a literary, dramatic, musical or artistic work [, or a film,][2] is made by an employee in the course of his employment, his employer is the first owner of any copyright in the work subject to any agreement to the contrary.

(3) This section does not apply to Crown copyright or Parliamentary copyright (see sections 163 and 165) or to copyright which subsists by virtue of section 168 (copyright of certain international organisations).

Duration of copyright

[Duration of copyright in literary, dramatic, musical or artistic works

12.—(1) The following provisions have effect with respect to the duration of **5-014** copyright in a literary, dramatic, musical or artistic work.

(2) Copyright expires at the end of the period of 70 years from the end of the calendar year in which the author dies, subject as follows.

(3) If the work is of unknown authorship, copyright expires—

---

[1] Inserted by SI 1996/2967 Pt II reg 18 (2)
[2] Words inserted by SI 1996/2967 Pt II reg 18 (3)

(a) at the end of the period of 70 years from the end of the calendar year in which the work was made, or

(b) if during that period the work is made available to the public, at the end of the period of 70 years from the end of the calendar year in which it is first so made available,

subject as follows.

(4) Subsection (2) applies if the identity of the author becomes known before the end of the period specified in paragraph (a) or (b) of subsection (3).

(5) For the purposes of subsection (3) making available to the public includes—

(a) in the case of a literary, dramatic or musical work—
    (i) performance in public, or
    [(ii) communication to the public;][1]

(b) in the case of an artistic work—
    (i) exhibition in public,
    (ii) a film including the work being shown in public, or
    [(iii) communication to the public;][2]

but in determining generally for the purposes of that subsection whether a work has been made available to the public no account shall be taken of any unauthorised act.

(6) Where the country of origin of the work is not an EEA state and the author of the work is not a national of an EEA state, the duration of copyright is that to which the work is entitled in the country of origin, provided that does not exceed the period which would apply under subsections (2) to (5).

(7) If the work is computer-generated the above provisions do not apply and copyright expires at the end of the period of 50 years from the end of the calendar year in which the work was made.

(8) The provisions of this section are adapted as follows in relation to a work of joint authorship—

(a) the reference in subsection (2) to the death of the author shall be construed—
    (i) if the identity of all the authors is known, as a reference to the death of the last of them to die, and
    (ii) if the identity of one or more of the authors is known and the identity of one or more others is not, as a reference to the death of the last whose identity is known;

(b) the reference in subsection (4) to the identity of the author becoming known shall be construed as a reference to the identity of any of the authors becoming known;

(c) the reference in subsection (6) to the author not being a national of an EEA state shall be construed as a reference to none of the authors being a national of an EEA state.

(9) This section does not apply to Crown copyright or Parliamentary copyright (see [sections 163 to 166A][3]) or to copyright which subsists by virtue of section 168 (copyright of certain international organisations).][4]

---

[1] Substituted by SI 2003/2498 Sch 1 (1) para 4 (1)
[2] Substituted by SI 2003/2498 Sch 1 (1) para 4 (2)
[3] Words substituted by Scotland Act 1998 c.46 Sch 8 para 25 (2)
[4] Substituted by SI 1995/3297 Pt II reg 5 (1)

[Duration of copyright in sound recordings

13A.—(1) The following provisions have effect with respect to the duration of **5-015** copyright in a sound recording.

[(2) Subject to subsections (4) and (5), copyright expires–

    (a) at the end of the period of 50 years from the end of the calendar year in which the recording is made, or

    (b) if during that period the recording is published, 50 years from the end of the calendar year in which it is first published, or

    (c) if during that period the recording is not published but is made available to the public by being played in public or communicated to the public, 50 years from the end of the calendar year in which it is first so made available,

but in determining whether a sound recording has been published, played in public or communicated to the public, no account shall be taken of any unauthorised act.][1]

(4) Where the author of a sound recording is not a national of an EEA state, the duration of copyright is that to which the sound recording is entitled in the country of which the author is a national, provided that does not exceed the period which would apply under [subsection (2)][2].

(5) If or to the extent that the application of subsection (4) would be at variance with an international obligation to which the United Kingdom became subject prior to 29th October 1993, the duration of copyright shall be as specified in [subsection (2)][3].][4]

[Duration of copyright in films

13B.—(1) The following provisions have effect with respect to the duration of **5-016** copyright in a film.

(2) Copyright expires at the end of the period of 70 years from the end of the calendar year in which the death occurs of the last to die of the following persons—

    (a) the principal director,

    (b) the author of the screenplay,

    (c) the author of the dialogue, or

    (d) the composer of music specially created for and used in the film;

subject as follows.

(3) If the identity of one or more of the persons referred to in subsection (2)(a) to (d) is known and the identity of one or more others is not, the reference in that subsection to the death of the last of them to die shall be construed as a reference to the death of the last whose identity is known.

(4) If the identity of the persons referred to in subsection (2)(a) to (d) is unknown, copyright expires at—

    (a) the end of the period of 70 years from the end of the calendar year in which the film was made, or

    (b) if during that period the film is made available to the public, at the end of the period of 70 years from the end of the calendar year in which it is first so made available.

---

[1] Substituted by SI 2003/2498 Pt II reg 29 (a)
[2] Words substituted by SI 2003/2498 Pt II reg 29 (c)
[3] Words substituted by SI 2003/2498 Pt II reg 29 (c)
[4] Inserted by SI 1995/3297 Pt II reg 6 (1)

(5) Subsections (2) and (3) apply if the identity of any of those persons becomes known before the end of the period specified in paragraph (a) or (b) of subsection (4).

(6) For the purposes of subsection (4) making available to the public includes—

    (a) showing in public, or

    [(b) communicating to the public;][1]

but in determining generally for the purposes of that subsection whether a film has been made available to the public no account shall be taken of any unauthorised act.

(7) Where the country of origin is not an EEA state and the author of the film is not a national of an EEA state, the duration of copyright is that to which the work is entitled in the country of origin, provided that does not exceed the period which would apply under subsections (2) to (6).

(8) In relation to a film of which there are joint authors, the reference in subsection (7) to the author not being a national of an EEA shall be construed as a reference to none of the authors being a national of an EEA state.

(9) If in any case there is no person falling within paragraphs (a) to (d) of subsection (2), the above provisions do not apply and copyright expires at the end of the period of 50 years from the end of the calendar year in which the film was made.

(10) For the purposes of this section the identity of any of the persons referred to in subsection (2)(a) to (d) shall be regarded as unknown if it is not possible for a person to ascertain his identity by reasonable inquiry; but if the identity of any such person is once known it shall not subsequently be regarded as unknown.][2]

[Duration of copyright in broadcasts [...]][3]

5-017   **14.**—(1) The following provisions have effect with respect to the duration of copyright in a broadcast [...][4].

(2) Copyright in a broadcast [...][5] expires at the end of the period of 50 years from the end of the calendar year in which the broadcast was made [...][6], subject as follows.

(3) Where the author of the broadcast [...][7] is not a national of an EEA state, the duration of copyright in the broadcast [...][8] is that to which it is entitled in the country of which the author is a national, provided that does not exceed the period which would apply under subsection (2).

(4) If or to the extent that the application of subsection (3) would be at variance with an international obligation to which the United Kingdom became subject prior to 29th October 1993, the duration of copyright shall be as specified in subsection (2).

(5) Copyright in a repeat broadcast [...][9] expires at the same time as the copyright in the original broadcast [...][10]; and accordingly no copyright arises in

---

[1] Substituted by SI 2003/2498 Sch 1 (1) para 4 (3)
[2] Inserted by SI 1995/3297 Pt II reg 6 (1)
[3] Words repealed by SI 2003/2498 Sch 2 para 1
[4] Words repealed by SI 2003/2498 Sch 2 para 1
[5] Words repealed by SI 2003/2498 Sch 2 para 1
[6] Words repealed by SI 2003/2498 Sch 2 para 1
[7] Words repealed by SI 2003/2498 Sch 2 para 1
[8] Words repealed by SI 2003/2498 Sch 2 para 1
[9] Words repealed by SI 2003/2498 Sch 2 para 1
[10] Words repealed by SI 2003/2498 Sch 2 para 1

respect of a repeat broadcast [...]¹ which is broadcast [...]² after the expiry of the copyright in the original broadcast [...]³.

(6) A repeat broadcast [...]⁴ means one which is a repeat [...]⁵ of a broadcast previously made [...]⁶.]⁷

Duration of copyright in typographical arrangement of published editions

15. Copyright in the typographical arrangement of a published edition **5-018** expires at the end of the period of 25 years from the end of the calendar year in which the edition was first published.

[Meaning of country of origin

15A.—(1) For the purposes of the provisions of this Part relating to the **5-019** duration of copyright the country of origin of a work shall be determined as follows.

(2) If the work is first published in a Berne Convention country and is not simultaneously published elsewhere, the country of origin is that country.

(3) If the work is first published simultaneously in two or more countries only one of which is a Berne Convention country, the country of origin is that country.

(4) If the work is first published simultaneously in two or more countries of which two or more are Berne Convention countries, then—

    (a) if any of those countries is an EEA state, the country of origin is that country; and

    (b) if none of those countries is an EEA state, the country of origin is the Berne Convention country which grants the shorter or shortest period of copyright protection.

(5) If the work is unpublished or is first published in a country which is not a Berne Convention country (and is not simultaneously published in a Berne Convention country), the country of origin is—

    (a) if the work is a film and the maker of the film has his headquarters in, or is domiciled or resident in a Berne Convention country, that country;

    (b) if the work is—

        (i) a work of architecture constructed in a Berne Convention country, or

        (ii) an artistic work incorporated in a building or other structure situated in a Berne Convention country,

    that country;

    (c) in any other case, the country of which the author of the work is a national.

(6) In this section—

    (a) a "Berne Convention country" means a country which is a party to any Act of the International Convention for the Protection of Literary and Artistic Works signed at Berne on 9th September 1886; and

---

¹ Words repealed by SI 2003/2498 Sch 2 para 1
² Words repealed by SI 2003/2498 Sch 2 para 1
³ Words repealed by SI 2003/2498 Sch 2 para 1
⁴ Words repealed by SI 2003/2498 Sch 2 para 1
⁵ Words repealed by SI 2003/2498 Sch 2 para 1
⁶ Words repealed by SI 2003/2498 Sch 2 para 1
⁷ Substituted by SI 1995/3297 Pt II reg 7 (1)

(b) references to simultaneous publication are to publication within 30 days of first publication.]¹

CHAPTER II

RIGHTS OF COPYRIGHT OWNER

The acts restricted by copyright

The acts restricted by copyright in a work

5-020   **16.**—(1) The owner of the copyright in a work has, in accordance with the following provisions of this Chapter, the exclusive right to do the following acts in the United Kingdom—

(a) to copy the work (see section 17);

(b) to issue copies of the work to the public (see section 18);

[(ba) to rent or lend the work to the public (see section 18A);]²

(c) to perform, show or play the work in public (see section 19);

[(d) to communicate the work to the public (see section 20);]³

(e) to make an adaptation of the work or do any of the above in relation to an adaptation (see section 21);

and those acts are referred to in this Part as the "acts restricted by the copyright".

(2) Copyright in a work is infringed by a person who without the licence of the copyright owner does, or authorises another to do, any of the acts restricted by the copyright.

(3) References in this Part to the doing of an act restricted by the copyright in a work are to the doing of it—

(a) in relation to the work as a whole or any substantial part of it, and

(b) either directly or indirectly;

and it is immaterial whether any intervening acts themselves infringe copyright.

(4) This Chapter has effect subject to—

(a) the provisions of Chapter III (acts permitted in relation to copyright works), and

(b) the provisions of Chapter VII (provisions with respect to copyright licensing).

Infringement of copyright by copying

5-021   **17.**—(1) The copying of the work is an act restricted by the copyright in every description of copyright work; and references in this Part to copying and copies shall be construed as follows.

(2) Copying in relation to a literary, dramatic, musical or artistic work means reproducing the work in any material form.

This includes storing the work in any medium by electronic means.

(3) In relation to an artistic work copying includes the making of a copy in three dimensions of a two-dimensional work and the making of a copy in two dimensions of a three-dimensional work.

---

¹ Inserted by SI 1995/3297 Pt II reg 8 (1)
² Inserted by SI 1996/2967 Pt II reg 10 (1)
³ Substituted by SI 2003/2498 Pt II reg 6 (2)

(4) Copying in relation to a film [or broadcast][1] includes making a photograph of the whole or any substantial part of any image forming part of the film [or broadcast][2].

(5) Copying in relation to the typographical arrangement of a published edition means making a facsimile copy of the arrangement.

(6) Copying in relation to any description of work includes the making of copies which are transient or are incidental to some other use of the work.

Infringement by issue of copies to the public

18.—(1) The issue to the public of copies of the work is an act restricted by the copyright in every description of copyright work.   **5-022**

[(2) References in this Part to the issue to the public of copies of a work are to-

(a) the act of putting into circulation in the EEA copies not previously put into circulation in the EEA by or with the consent of the copyright owner, or

(b) the act of putting into circulation outside the EEA copies not previously put into circulation in the EEA or elsewhere.

(3) Reference in this Part to the issue to the public of copies of a work do not include-

(a) any subsequent distribution, sale, hiring or loan of copies previously put into circulation (but see section 18A: infringement by rental or lending), or

(b) any subsequent importation of such copies into the United Kingdom or another EEA state,

except so far as paragraph (a) of subsection (2) applies to putting into circulation in the EEA copies previously put into circulation outside the EEA.][3]

[(4) References in this Part to the issue of copies of a work include the issue of the original.][4]

[Infringement by rental or lending of work to the public

18A.—(1) The rental or lending of copies of the work to the public is an act restricted by the copyright in-   **5-023**

(a) a literary, dramatic or musical work,

(b) an artistic work, other than-

(i) a work of architecture in the form of a building or a model for a building, or

(ii) a work of applied art, or

(c) a film or a sound recording.

(2) In this Part, subject to the following provisions of this section-

(a) "rental" means making a copy of the work available for use, on terms that it will or may be returned, for direct or indirect economic or commercial advantage, and

(b) "lending" means making a copy of the work available for use, on terms that it will or may be returned, otherwise than for direct or indirect economic or commercial advantage, through an establishment which is accessible to the public.

(3) The expressions "rental" and "lending" do not include-

---

[1] Words substituted by SI 2003/2498 Pt II reg 5 (5)
[2] Words substituted by SI 2003/2498 Pt II reg 5 (5)
[3] Substituted by SI 1996/2967 Pt II reg 9 (2)
[4] Inserted by SI 1996/2967 Pt II reg 9 (3)

(a) making available for the purpose of public performance, playing or showing in public, [or communication to the public][1];

(b) making available for the purpose of exhibition in public; or

(c) making available for on-the-spot reference use.

(4) The expression "lending" does not include making available between establishments which are accessible to the public.

(5) Where lending by an establishment accessible to the public gives rise to a payment the amount of which does not go beyond what is necessary to cover the operating costs of the establishment, there is no direct or indirect economic or commercial advantage for the purposes of this section.

(6) References in this Part to the rental or lending of copies of a work include the rental or lending of the original.][2]

Infringement by performance, showing or playing of work in public

5-024   **19.**—(1) The performance of the work in public is an act restricted by the copyright in a literary, dramatic or musical work.

(2) In this Part "performance", in relation to a work—

(a) includes delivery in the case of lectures, addresses, speeches and sermons, and

(b) in general, includes any mode of visual or acoustic presentation, including presentation by means of a sound recording, film [or broadcast][3] of the work.

(3) The playing or showing of the work in public is an act restricted by the copyright in a sound recording, film [or broadcast][4].

(4) Where copyright in a work is infringed by its being performed, played or shown in public by means of apparatus for receiving visual images or sounds conveyed by electronic means, the person by whom the visual images or sounds are sent, and in the case of a performance the performers, shall not be regarded as responsible for the infringement.

[Infringement by communication to the public

5-025   **20.**—(1) The communication to the public of the work is an act restricted by the copyright in–

(a) a literary, dramatic, musical or artistic work,

(b) a sound recording or film, or

(c) a broadcast.

(2) References in this Part to communication to the public are to communication to the public by electronic transmission, and in relation to a work include–

(a) the broadcasting of the work;

(b) the making available to the public of the work by electronic transmission in such a way that members of the public may access it from a place and at a time individually chosen by them.][5]

Infringement by making adaptation or act done in relation to adaptation

5-026   **21.**—(1) The making of an adaptation of the work is an act restricted by the copyright in a literary, dramatic or musical work.

---

[1] Words substituted by SI 2003/2498 Sch 1 (1) para 6 (2) (a)

[2] Inserted by SI 1996/2967 Pt II reg 10 (2)

[3] Words substituted by SI 2003/2498 Sch 1 (1) para 3 (1) (b)

[4] Words substituted by SI 2003/2498 Sch 1 (1) para 3 (1) (c)

[5] Substituted by SI 2003/2498 Pt II reg 6 (1)

For this purpose an adaptation is made when it is recorded, in writing or otherwise.

(2) The doing of any of the acts specified in sections 17 to 20, or subsection (1) above, in relation to an adaptation of the work is also an act restricted by the copyright in a literary, dramatic or musical work.

For this purpose it is immaterial whether the adaptation has been recorded, in writing or otherwise, at the time the act is done.

(3) In this Part "adaptation" —

    (a) in relation to a literary [work,][1] [other than a computer program or a database, or in relation to a][2] dramatic work, means—

        (i) a translation of the work;

        (ii) a version of a dramatic work in which it is converted into a non-dramatic work or, as the case may be, of a non-dramatic work in which it is converted into a dramatic work;

        (iii) a version of the work in which the story or action is conveyed wholly or mainly by means of pictures in a form suitable for reproduction in a book, or in a newspaper, magazine or similar periodical;

    [(ab) in relation to a computer program, means an arrangement or altered version of the program or a translation of it;][3]

    [(ac) in relation to a database, means an arrangement or altered version of the database or a translation of it;][4]

    (b) in relation to a musical work, means an arrangement or transcription of the work.

(4) In relation to a computer program a "translation" includes a version of the program in which it is converted into or out of a computer language or code or into a different computer language or code [...][5].

(5) No inference shall be drawn from this section as to what does or does not amount to copying a work.

Secondary infringement of copyright

Secondary infringement: importing infringing copy

22. The copyright in a work is infringed by a person who, without the licence **5-027** of the copyright owner, imports into the United Kingdom, otherwise than for his private and domestic use, an article which is, and which he knows or has reason to believe is, an infringing copy of the work.

Secondary infringement: possessing or dealing with infringing copy

23. The copyright in a work is infringed by a person who, without the licence **5-028** of the copyright owner—

    (a) possesses in the course of a business,

    (b) sells or lets for hire, or offers or exposes for sale or hire,

    (c) in the course of a business exhibits in public or distributes, or

    (d) distributes otherwise than in the course of a business to such an extent as to affect prejudicially the owner of the copyright,

---

[1] Words inserted by SI 1992/3233 reg 5 (1)

[2] Words substituted by SI 1997/3032 Pt II reg 7 (a)

[3] Inserted by SI 1992/3233 reg 5 (2)

[4] Inserted by SI 1997/3032 Pt II reg 7 (b)

[5] Words repealed by SI 1992/3233 reg 5 (3)

an article which is, and which he knows or has reason to believe is, an infringing copy of the work.

Secondary infringement: providing means for making infringing copies

5-029   **24.**—(1) Copyright in a work is infringed by a person who, without the licence of the copyright owner—

    (a) makes,

    (b) imports into the United Kingdom,

    (c) possesses in the course of a business, or

    (d) sells or lets for hire, or offers or exposes for sale or hire,

an article specifically designed or adapted for making copies of that work, knowing or having reason to believe that it is to be used to make infringing copies.

(2) Copyright in a work is infringed by a person who without the licence of the copyright owner transmits the work by means of a telecommunications system (otherwise than by [communication to the public][1]), knowing or having reason to believe that infringing copies of the work will be made by means of the reception of the transmission in the United Kingdom or elsewhere.

Secondary infringement: permitting use of premises for infringing performance

5-030   **25.**—(1) Where the copyright in a literary, dramatic or musical work is infringed by a performance at a place of public entertainment, any person who gave permission for that place to be used for the performance is also liable for the infringement unless when he gave permission he believed on reasonable grounds that the performance would not infringe copyright.

(2) In this section "place of public entertainment" includes premises which are occupied mainly for other purposes but are from time to time made available for hire for the purposes of public entertainment.

Secondary infringement: provision of apparatus for infringing performance, &c

5-031   **26.**—(1) Where copyright in a work is infringed by a public performance of the work, or by the playing or showing of the work in public, by means of apparatus for—

    (a) playing sound recordings,

    (b) showing films, or

    (c) receiving visual images or sounds conveyed by electronic means,

the following persons are also liable for the infringement.

(2) A person who supplied the apparatus, or any substantial part of it, is liable for the infringement if when he supplied the apparatus or part—

    (a) he knew or had reason to believe that the apparatus was likely to be so used as to infringe copyright, or

    (b) in the case of apparatus whose normal use involves a public performance, playing or showing, he did not believe on reasonable grounds that it would not be so used as to infringe copyright.

(3) An occupier of premises who gave permission for the apparatus to be brought onto the premises is liable for the infringement if when he gave permission he knew or had reason to believe that the apparatus was likely to be so used as to infringe copyright.

---

[1] Words substituted by SI 2003/2498 Sch 1 (1) para 5 (a)

(4) A person who supplied a copy of a sound recording or film used to infringe copyright is liable for the infringement if when he supplied it he knew or had reason to believe that what he supplied, or a copy made directly or indirectly from it, was likely to be so used as to infringe copyright.

Infringing copies

Meaning of "infringing copy"

27.—(1) In this Part "infringing copy", in relation to a copyright work, shall **5-032** be construed in accordance with this section.

(2) An article is an infringing copy if its making constituted an infringement of the copyright in the work in question.

(3) [...][1] An article is also an infringing copy if—

(a) it has been or is proposed to be imported into the United Kingdom, and

(b) its making in the United Kingdom would have constituted an infringement of the copyright in the work in question, or a breach of an exclusive licence agreement relating to that work.

(4) Where in any proceedings the question arises whether an article is an infringing copy and it is shown—

(a) that the article is a copy of the work, and

(b) that copyright subsists in the work or has subsisted at any time,

it shall be presumed until the contrary is proved that the article was made at a time when copyright subsisted in the work.

(5) Nothing in subsection (3) shall be construed as applying to an article which may lawfully be imported into the United Kingdom by virtue of any enforceable Community right within the meaning of section 2(1) of the European Communities Act 1972.

(6) In this Part "infringing copy" includes a copy falling to be treated as an infringing copy by virtue of any of the following provisions—

[section 31A(6) and (9) (making a single accessible copy for personal use),
section 31B(9) and (10) (multiple copies for visually impaired persons),
section 31C(2) (intermediate copies held by approved bodies),][2]
section 32(5) (copies made for purposes of instruction or examination),
section 35(3) (recordings made by educational establishments for educational purposes),
section 36(5) (reprographic copying by educational establishments for purposes of instruction),
section 37(3)(b) (copies made by librarian or archivist in reliance on false declaration),
section 56(2) (further copies, adaptations, &c. of work in electronic form retained on transfer of principal copy),
section 63(2) (copies made for purpose of advertising artistic work for sale),
section 68(4) (copies made for purpose of broadcast [...][3]),
[section 70(2) (recording for the purposes of time-shifting),
section 71(2) (photographs of broadcasts), or][4]

---

[1] Words repealed by SI 1996/2967 Pt II reg 9 (4)
[2] Words inserted by Copyright (Visually Impaired Persons) Act 2002 c.33 s 7 (1)
[3] Words repealed by SI 2003/2498 Sch 2 para 1
[4] Words inserted by SI 2003/2498 Pt II reg 20 (3)

any provision of an order under section 141 (statutory licence for certain reprographic copying by educational establishments).

CHAPTER III

ACTS PERMITTED IN RELATION TO COPYRIGHT WORKS

Introductory

Introductory provisions

5-033   **28.**—(1) The provisions of this Chapter specify acts which may be done in relation to copyright works notwithstanding the subsistence of copyright; they relate only to the question of infringement of copyright and do not affect any other right or obligation restricting the doing of any of the specified acts.

(2) Where it is provided by this Chapter that an act does not infringe copyright, or may be done without infringing copyright, and no particular description of copyright work is mentioned, the act in question does not infringe the copyright in a work of any description.

(3) No inference shall be drawn from the description of any act which may by virtue of this Chapter be done without infringing copyright as to the scope of the acts restricted by the copyright in any description of work.

(4) The provisions of this Chapter are to be construed independently of each other, so that the fact that an act does not fall within one provision does not mean that it is not covered by another provision.

General

[Making of temporary copies

5-034   **28A** Copyright in a literary work, other than a computer program or a database, or in a dramatic, musical or artistic work, the typographical arrangement of a published edition, a sound recording or a film, is not infringed by the making of a temporary copy which is transient or incidental, which is an integral and essential part of a technological process and the sole purpose of which is to enable–

    (a) a transmission of the work in a network between third parties by an intermediary; or

    (b) a lawful use of the work;

and which has no independent economic significance.][1]

Research and private study

5-035   **29.**—[(1) Fair dealing with a literary [work, other than a database, or a][2] dramatic, musical or artistic work for the purposes of research for a non-commercial purpose does not infringe any copyright in the work provided that it is accompanied by a sufficient acknowledgement.][3]

[(1A) Fair dealing with a database for the purposes of research or private study does not infringe any copyright in the database provided that the source is indicated.][4]

---

[1] Inserted by SI 2003/2498 Pt II reg 8 (1)
[2] Words inserted by SI 1997/3032 Pt II reg 8 (1)
[3] Substituted by SI 2003/2498 Pt II reg 9 (a)
[4] Inserted by SI 1997/3032 Pt II reg 8 (2)

[(1B) No acknowledgement is required in connection with fair dealing for the purposes mentioned in subsection (1) where this would be impossible for reasons of practicality or otherwise.

(1C) Fair dealing with a literary, dramatic, musical or artistic work for the purposes of private study does not infringe any copyright in the work.][1]

(2) Fair dealing with the typographical arrangement of a published edition for the purposes [of research or private study][2] does not infringe any copyright in the arrangement.

(3) Copying by a person other than the researcher or student himself is not fair dealing if—

(a) in the case of a librarian, or a person acting on behalf of a librarian, he does anything which regulations under section 40 would not permit to be done under section 38 or 39 (articles or parts of published works: restriction on multiple copies of same material), or

(b) in any other case, the person doing the copying knows or has reason to believe that it will result in copies of substantially the same material being provided to more than one person at substantially the same time and for substantially the same purpose.

[(4) It is not fair dealing—

(a) to convert a computer program expressed in a low level language into a version expressed in a higher level language, or

(b) incidentally in the course of so converting the program, to copy it,

(these acts being permitted if done in accordance with section 50B (decompilation)).][3]

[(4A) It is not fair dealing to observe, study or test the functioning of a computer program in order to determine the ideas and principles which underlie any element of the program (these acts being permitted if done in accordance with section 50BA (observing, studying and testing)).][4]

Criticism, review and news reporting

30.—(1) Fair dealing with a work for the purpose of criticism or review, of **5-036** that or another work or of a performance of a work, does not infringe any copyright in the work provided that it is accompanied by a sufficient acknowledgement [and provided that the work has been made available to the public][5].

[(1A) For the purposes of subsection (1) a work has been made available to the public if it has been made available by any means, including–

(a) the issue of copies to the public;

(b) making the work available by means of an electronic retrieval system;

(c) the rental or lending of copies of the work to the public;

(d) the performance, exhibition, playing or showing of the work in public;

(e) the communication to the public of the work,

but in determining generally for the purposes of that subsection whether a work has been made available to the public no account shall be taken of any unauthorised act.][6]

(2) Fair dealing with a work (other than a photograph) for the purpose of reporting current events does not infringe any copyright in the work provided

---

[1] Inserted by SI 2003/2498 Pt II reg 9 (b)

[2] Words substituted by SI 2003/2498 Pt II reg 9 (c)

[3] Inserted by SI 1992/3233 reg 7

[4] Inserted by SI 2003/2498 Pt II reg 9 (d)

[5] Words inserted by SI 2003/2498 Pt II reg 10 (1) (a)

[6] Inserted by SI 2003/2498 Pt II reg 10 (1) (b)

that (subject to subsection (3)) it is accompanied by a sufficient acknowledgement.

(3) No acknowledgement is required in connection with the reporting of current events by means of a sound recording, film [or broadcast where this would be impossible for reasons of practicality or otherwise][1].

Incidental inclusion of copyright material

5-037   **31.**—(1) Copyright in a work is not infringed by its incidental inclusion in an artistic work, sound recording, film [or broadcast][2].

(2) Nor is the copyright infringed by the issue to the public of copies, or the playing, showing [or communication to the public][3], of anything whose making was, by virtue of subsection (1), not an infringement of the copyright.

(3) A musical work, words spoken or sung with music, or so much of a sound recording [or broadcast][4] as includes a musical work or such words, shall not be regarded as incidentally included in another work if it is deliberately included.

[Visual impairment

Making a single accessible copy for personal use

5-038   **31A**—(1) If a visually impaired person has lawful possession or lawful use of a copy ("the master copy") of the whole or part of—

(a) a literary, dramatic, musical or artistic work; or
(b) a published edition,

which is not accessible to him because of the impairment, it is not an infringement of copyright in the work, or in the typographical arrangement of the published edition, for an accessible copy of the master copy to be made for his personal use.

(2) Subsection (1) does not apply—

(a) if the master copy is of a musical work, or part of a musical work, and the making of an accessible copy would involve recording a performance of the work or part of it; or
(b) if the master copy is of a database, or part of a database, and the making of an accessible copy would infringe copyright in the database.

(3) Subsection (1) does not apply in relation to the making of an accessible copy for a particular visually impaired person if, or to the extent that, copies of the copyright work are commercially available, by or with the authority of the copyright owner, in a form that is accessible to that person.

(4) An accessible copy made under this section must be accompanied by—

(a) a statement that it is made under this section; and
(b) a sufficient acknowledgement.

(5) If a person makes an accessible copy on behalf of a visually impaired person under this section and charges for it, the sum charged must not exceed the cost of making and supplying the copy.

(6) If a person holds an accessible copy made under subsection (1) when he is not entitled to have it made under that subsection, the copy is to be treated as an infringing copy, unless he is a person falling within subsection (7)(b).

---

[1] Words substituted by SI 2003/2498 Pt II reg 10 (1) (c)
[2] Words substituted by SI 2003/2498 Sch 1 (1) para 3 (1) (d)
[3] Words substituted by SI 2003/2498 Sch 1 (1) para 6 (2) (b)
[4] Words substituted by SI 2003/2498 Sch 1 (1) para 3 (1) (e)

(7) A person who holds an accessible copy made under subsection (1) may transfer it to—

    (a) a visually impaired person entitled to have the accessible copy made under subsection (1); or

    (b) a person who has lawful possession of the master copy and intends to transfer the accessible copy to a person falling within paragraph (a).

(8) The transfer by a person ("V") of an accessible copy made under subsection (1) to another person ("T") is an infringement of copyright by V unless V has reasonable grounds for believing that T is a person falling within subsection (7)(a) or (b).

(9) If an accessible copy which would be an infringing copy but for this section is subsequently dealt with—

    (a) it is to be treated as an infringing copy for the purposes of that dealing; and

    (b) if that dealing infringes copyright, is to be treated as an infringing copy for all subsequent purposes.

(10) In subsection (9), "dealt with" means sold or let for hire or offered or exposed for sale or hire or [communicated to the public.][1]

[Multiple copies for visually impaired persons

31B—(1) If an approved body has lawful possession of a copy ("the master **5-039** copy") of the whole or part of—

    (a) a commercially published literary, dramatic, musical or artistic work; or

    (b) a commercially published edition,

it is not an infringement of copyright in the work, or in the typographical arrangement of the published edition, for the body to make, or supply, accessible copies for the personal use of visually impaired persons to whom the master copy is not accessible because of their impairment.

(2) Subsection (1) does not apply—

    (a) if the master copy is of a musical work, or part of a musical work, and the making of an accessible copy would involve recording a performance of the work or part of it; or

    (b) if the master copy is of a database, or part of a database, and the making of an accessible copy would infringe copyright in the database.

(3) Subsection (1) does not apply in relation to the making of an accessible copy if, or to the extent that, copies of the copyright work are commercially available, by or with the authority of the copyright owner, in a form that is accessible to the same or substantially the same degree.

(4) Subsection (1) does not apply in relation to the supply of an accessible copy to a particular visually impaired person if, or to the extent that, copies of the copyright work are commercially available, by or with the authority of the copyright owner, in a form that is accessible to that person.

(5) An accessible copy made under this section must be accompanied by—

    (a) a statement that it is made under this section; and

    (b) a sufficient acknowledgement.

(6) If an approved body charges for supplying a copy made under this section, the sum charged must not exceed the cost of making and supplying the copy.

---

[1] Inserted by Copyright (Visually Impaired Persons) Act 2002 c.33 s 1

(7) An approved body making copies under this section must, if it is an educational establishment, ensure that the copies will be used only for its educational purposes.

(8) If the master copy is in copy-protected electronic form, any accessible copy made of it under this section must, so far as it is reasonably practicable to do so, incorporate the same, or equally effective, copy protection (unless the copyright owner agrees otherwise).

(9) If an approved body continues to hold an accessible copy made under subsection (1) when it would no longer be entitled to make or supply such a copy under that subsection, the copy is to be treated as an infringing copy.

(10) If an accessible copy which would be an infringing copy but for this section is subsequently dealt with—

> (a) it is to be treated as an infringing copy for the purposes of that dealing; and
> (b) if that dealing infringes copyright, is to be treated as an infringing copy for all subsequent purposes.

(11) In subsection (10), "dealt with" means sold or let for hire or offered or exposed for sale or hire or [communicated to the public][1].

(12) "Approved body" means an educational establishment or a body that is not conducted for profit.

(13) "Supplying" includes lending.][2]

[Intermediate copies and records

5-040   **31C**—(1) An approved body entitled to make accessible copies under section 31B may hold an intermediate copy of the master copy which is necessarily created during the production of the accessible copies, but only—

> (a) if and so long as the approved body continues to be entitled to make accessible copies of that master copy; and
> (b) for the purposes of the production of further accessible copies.

(2) An intermediate copy which is held in breach of subsection (1) is to be treated as an infringing copy.

(3) An approved body may lend or transfer the intermediate copy to another approved body which is entitled to make accessible copies of the work or published edition under section 31B.

(4) The loan or transfer by an approved body ("A") of an intermediate copy to another person ("B") is an infringement of copyright by A unless A has reasonable grounds for believing that B—

> (a) is another approved body which is entitled to make accessible copies of the work or published edition under section 31B; and
> (b) will use the intermediate copy only for the purposes of the production of further accessible copies.

(5) If an approved body charges for lending or transferring the intermediate copy, the sum charged must not exceed the cost of the loan or transfer.

(6) An approved body must—

> (a) keep records of accessible copies made under section 31B and of the persons to whom they are supplied;
> (b) keep records of any intermediate copy lent or transferred under this section and of the persons to whom it is lent or transferred; and
> (c) allow the copyright owner or a person acting for him, on giving reasonable notice, to inspect the records at any reasonable time.

---

[1] Words substituted by Copyright (Visually Impaired Persons) Act 2002 c.33 s 2
[2] Inserted by Copyright (Visually Impaired Persons) Act 2002 c.33 s 2

(7) Within a reasonable time of making an accessible copy under section 31B, or lending or transferring an intermediate copy under this section, the approved body must—

    (a) notify each relevant representative body; or

    (b) if there is no such body, notify the copyright owner.

(8) A relevant representative body is a body which—

    (a) represents particular copyright owners, or owners of copyright in the type of copyright work concerned; and

    (b) has given notice to the Secretary of State of the copyright owners, or the classes of copyright owner, represented by it.

(9) The requirement to notify the copyright owner under subsection (7)(b) does not apply if it is not reasonably possible for the approved body to ascertain the name and address of the copyright owner.][1]

[Licensing schemes

31D—(1) Section 31B does not apply to the making of an accessible copy in a **5-041** particular form if—

    (a) a licensing scheme operated by a licensing body is in force under which licences may be granted by the licensing body permitting the making and supply of copies of the copyright work in that form;

    (b) the scheme is not unreasonably restrictive; and

    (c) the scheme and any modification made to it have been notified to the Secretary of State by the licensing body.

(2) A scheme is unreasonably restrictive if it includes a term or condition which—

    (a) purports to prevent or limit the steps that may be taken under section 31B or 31C; or

    (b) has that effect.

(3) But subsection (2) does not apply if—

    (a) the copyright work is no longer published by or with the authority of the copyright owner; and

    (b) there are reasonable grounds for preventing or restricting the making of accessible copies of the work.

(4) If section 31B or 31C is displaced by a licensing scheme, sections 119 to 122 apply in relation to the scheme as if it were one to which those sections applied as a result of section 117.][2]

[Limitations, etc. following infringement of copyright

31E—(1) The Secretary of State may make an order under this section if it **5-042** appears to him that the making of copies—

    (a) under section 31B; or

    (b) under a licence granted under a licensing scheme that has been notified under section 31D,

has led to infringement of copyright on a scale which, in the Secretary of State's opinion, would not have occurred if section 31B had not been in force, or the licence had not been granted.

(2) The order may prohibit one or more named approved bodies, or one or more specified categories of approved body, from—

    (a) acting under section 31B; or

    (b) acting under a licence of a description specified in the order.

---

[1] Inserted by Copyright (Visually Impaired Persons) Act 2002 c.33 s 3
[2] Inserted by Copyright (Visually Impaired Persons) Act 2002 c.33 s 4

(3) The order may disapply—

    (a) the provisions of section 31B; or

    (b) the provisions of a licence, or a licensing scheme, of a description specified in the order,

in respect of the making of copies of a description so specified.

(4) If the Secretary of State proposes to make an order he must, before making it, consult—

    (a) such bodies representing copyright owners as he thinks fit; and

    (b) such bodies representing visually impaired persons as he thinks fit.

(5) If the Secretary of State proposes to make an order which includes a prohibition he must, before making it, consult—

    (a) if the proposed order is to apply to one or more named approved bodies, that body or those bodies;

    (b) if it is to apply to one or more specified categories of approved body, to such bodies representing approved bodies of that category or those categories as he thinks fit.

(6) An approved body which is prohibited by an order from acting under a licence may not apply to the Copyright Tribunal under section 121(1) in respect of a refusal or failure by a licensing body to grant such a licence.][1]

[Definitions and other supplementary provision for sections 31A to 31E

5-043   **31F**—(1) This section supplements sections 31A to 31E and includes definitions.

(2) A copy of a copyright work (other than an accessible copy made under section 31A or 31B) is to be taken to be accessible to a visually impaired person only if it is as accessible to him as it would be if he were not visually impaired.

(3) "Accessible copy", in relation to a copyright work, means a version which provides for a visually impaired person improved access to the work.

(4) An accessible copy may include facilities for navigating around the version of the copyright work but may not include—

    (a) changes that are not necessary to overcome problems caused by visual impairment; or

    (b) changes which infringe the right (provided by section 80) not to have the work subjected to derogatory treatment.

(5) "Approved body" has the meaning given in section 31B(12).

(6) "Lending", in relation to a copy, means making it available for use, otherwise than for direct or indirect economic or commercial advantage, on terms that it will or may be returned.

(7) For the purposes of subsection (6), a loan is not to be treated as being for direct or indirect economic or commercial advantage if a charge is made for the loan which does not exceed the cost of making and supplying the copy.

(8) The definition of "lending" in section 18A does not apply for the purposes of sections 31B and 31C.

(9) "Visually impaired person" means a person—

    (a) who is blind;

    (b) who has an impairment of visual function which cannot be improved, by the use of corrective lenses, to a level that would normally be acceptable for reading without a special level or kind of light;

    (c) who is unable, through physical disability, to hold or manipulate a book; or

---

[1] Inserted by Copyright (Visually Impaired Persons) Act 2002 c.33 s 5

(d) who is unable, through physical disability, to focus or move his eyes to the extent that would normally be acceptable for reading.

(10) The Secretary of State may by regulations prescribe—

(a) the form in which; or

(b) the procedure in accordance with which,

any notice required under section 31C(7) or (8), or 31D(1), must be given.

(11) Any power to make regulations or orders is exercisable by statutory instrument subject to annulment in pursuance of a resolution of either House of Parliament.][1]

Education

Things done for purposes of instruction or examination

32.—[(1) Copyright in a literary, dramatic, musical or artistic work is not **5-044** infringed by its being copied in the course of instruction or of preparation for instruction, provided the copying–

(a) is done by a person giving or receiving instruction,

(b) is not done by means of a reprographic process, and

(c) is accompanied by a sufficient acknowledgement,

and provided that the instruction is for a non-commercial purpose.

(2) Copyright in a sound recording, film or broadcast is not infringed by its being copied by making a film or film sound-track in the course of instruction, or of preparation for instruction, in the making of films or film sound-tracks, provided the copying–

(a) is done by a person giving or receiving instruction, and

(b) is accompanied by a sufficient acknowledgement,

and provided that the instruction is for a non-commercial purpose.

(2A) Copyright in a literary, dramatic, musical or artistic work which has been made available to the public is not infringed by its being copied in the course of instruction or of preparation for instruction, provided the copying–

(a) is fair dealing with the work,

(b) is done by a person giving or receiving instruction,

(c) is not done by means of a reprographic process, and

(d) is accompanied by a sufficient acknowledgement.

(2B) The provisions of section 30(1A) (works made available to the public) apply for the purposes of subsection (2A) as they apply for the purposes of section 30(1).][2]

(3) Copyright is not infringed by anything done for the purposes of an examination by way of setting the questions, communicating the questions to the candidates or answering the questions [, provided that the questions are accompanied by a sufficient acknowledgement][3].

[(3A) No acknowledgement is required in connection with copying as mentioned in subsection (1), (2) or (2A), or in connection with anything done for the purposes mentioned in subsection (3), where this would be impossible for reasons of practicality or otherwise.][4]

(4) Subsection (3) does not extend to the making of a reprographic copy of a musical work for use by an examination candidate in performing the work.

---

[1] Inserted by Copyright (Visually Impaired Persons) Act 2002 c.33 s 1

[2] Substituted by SI 2003/2498 Pt II reg 11 (1) (a)

[3] Words inserted by SI 2003/2498 Pt II reg 11 (1) (b)

[4] Inserted by SI 2003/2498 Pt II reg 11 (1) (c)

(5) Where a copy which would otherwise be an infringing copy is made in accordance with this section but is subsequently dealt with, it shall be treated as an infringing copy for the purpose of that dealing, and if that dealing infringes copyright for all subsequent purposes.

[For this purpose "dealt with" means—

   (a) sold or let for hire, offered or exposed for sale or hire; or

   (b) communicated to the public, unless that communication, by virtue of subsection (3), is not an infringement of copyright.][1]

Anthologies for educational use

5-045   **33.**—(1) The inclusion of a short passage from a published literary or dramatic work in a collection which—

   (a) is intended for use in educational establishments and is so described in its title, and in any advertisements issued by or on behalf of the publisher, and

   (b) consists mainly of material in which no copyright subsists,

does not infringe the copyright in the work if the work itself is not intended for use in such establishments and the inclusion is accompanied by a sufficient acknowledgement.

(2) Subsection (1) does not authorise the inclusion of more than two excerpts from copyright works by the same author in collections published by the same publisher over any period of five years.

(3) In relation to any given passage the reference in subsection (2) to excerpts from works by the same author—

   (a) shall be taken to include excerpts from works by him in collaboration with another, and

   (b) if the passage in question is from such a work, shall be taken to include excerpts from works by any of the authors, whether alone or in collaboration with another.

(4) References in this section to the use of a work in an educational establishment are to any use for the educational purposes of such an establishment.

Performing, playing or showing work in course of activities of educational establishment

5-046   **34.**—(1) The performance of a literary, dramatic or musical work before an audience consisting of teachers and pupils at an educational establishment and other persons directly connected with the activities of the establishment—

   (a) by a teacher or pupil in the course of the activities of the establishment, or

   (b) at the establishment by any person for the purposes of instruction,

is not a public performance for the purposes of infringement of copyright.

(2) The playing or showing of a sound recording, film [or broadcast][2] before such an audience at an educational establishment for the purposes of instruction is not a playing or showing of the work in public for the purposes of infringement of copyright.

(3) A person is not for this purpose directly connected with the activities of the educational establishment simply because he is the parent of a pupil at the establishment.

---

[1] Words substituted by SI 2003/2498 Pt II reg 11 (1) (d)

[2] Words substituted by SI 2003/2498 Sch 1 (1) para 3 (1) (f)

Recording by educational establishments of broadcasts [...]¹

35.—(1) A recording of a broadcast [...]² or a copy of such a recording, may **5-047** be made by or on behalf of an educational establishment for the educational purposes of that establishment without thereby infringing the copyright in the broadcast [...]³ or in any work included in it [, provided that it is accompanied by a sufficient acknowledgement of the broadcast and that the educational purposes are non-commercial]⁴.

[(1A) Copyright is not infringed where a recording of a broadcast or a copy of such a recording, whose making was by virtue of subsection (1) not an infringement of copyright, is communicated to the public by a person situated within the premises of an educational establishment provided that the communication cannot be received by any person situated outside the premises of that establishment.]⁵

(2) This section does not apply if or to the extent that there is a licensing scheme certified for the purposes of this section under section 143 providing for the grant of licences.

(3) Where a copy which would otherwise be an infringing copy is made in accordance with this section but is subsequently dealt with, it shall be treated as an infringing copy for the purposes of that dealing, and if that dealing infringes copyright for all subsequent purposes.

For this purpose "dealt with" means sold or let for hire [,offered or exposed for sale or hire, or communicated from within the premises of an educational establishment to any person situated outside those premises]⁶.

Reprographic copying by educational establishments of passages from published works

36.—(1) Reprographic copies of passages from published literary, dramatic **5-048** or musical works may, to the extent permitted by this section, be made by or on behalf of an educational establishment for the purposes of instruction without infringing any copyright in the work, [provided that they are accompanied by a sufficient acknowledgement and the instruction is for a non-commercial purpose]⁷.

[(1A) No acknowledgement is required in connection with the making of copies as mentioned in subsection (1) where this would be impossible for reasons of practicality or otherwise.

(1B) Reprographic copies of passages from published editions may, to the extent permitted by this section, be made by or on behalf of an educational establishment for the purposes of instruction without infringing any copyright in the typographical arrangement of the edition.]⁸

(2) Not more than one per cent. of any work may be copied by or on behalf of an establishment by virtue of this section in any quarter, that is, in any period 1st January to 31st March, 1st April to 30th June, 1st July to 30th September or 1st October to 31st December.

---

¹ Words repealed by SI 2003/2498 Sch 2 para 1
² Words repealed by SI 2003/2498 Sch 2 para 1
³ Words repealed by SI 2003/2498 Sch 2 para 1
⁴ Words inserted by SI 2003/2498 Pt II reg 12 (1) (a)
⁵ Inserted by SI 2003/2498 Pt II reg 12 (1) (b)
⁶ Words substituted by SI 2003/2498 Pt II reg 12 (1) (c)
⁷ Words substituted by SI 2003/2498 Pt II reg 13 (a)
⁸ Inserted by SI 2003/2498 Pt II reg 13 (b)

(3) Copying is not authorised by this section if, or to the extent that, licences are available authorising the copying in question and the person making the copies knew or ought to have been aware of that fact.

(4) The terms of a licence granted to an educational establishment authorising the reprographic copying for the purposes of instruction of passages from published [...][1] works are of no effect so far as they purport to restrict the proportion of a work which may be copied (whether on payment or free of charge) to less than that which would be permitted under this section.

(5) Where a copy which would otherwise be an infringing copy is made in accordance with this section but is subsequently dealt with, it shall be treated as an infringing copy for the purposes of that dealing, and if that dealing infringes copyright for all subsequent purposes.

For this purpose "dealt with" means sold or let for hire [, offered or exposed for sale or hire or communicated to the public][2].

[Lending of copies by educational establishments

5-049   **36A.** Copyright in a work is not infringed by the lending of copies of the work by an educational establishment.][3]

Libraries and archives

Libraries and archives: introductory

5-050   **37.**—(1) In sections 38 to 43 (copying by librarians and archivists)—
  (a) references in any provision to a prescribed library or archive are to a library or archive of a description prescribed for the purposes of that provision by regulations made by the Secretary of State; and
  (b) references in any provision to the prescribed conditions are to the conditions so prescribed.

(2) The regulations may provide that, where a librarian or archivist is required to be satisfied as to any matter before making or supplying a copy of a work—
  (a) he may rely on a signed declaration as to that matter by the person requesting the copy, unless he is aware that it is false in a material particular, and
  (b) in such cases as may be prescribed, he shall not make or supply a copy in the absence of a signed declaration in such form as may be prescribed.

(3) Where a person requesting a copy makes a declaration which is false in a material particular and is supplied with a copy which would have been an infringing copy if made by him—
  (a) he is liable for infringement of copyright as if he had made the copy himself, and
  (b) the copy shall be treated as an infringing copy.

(4) The regulations may make different provision for different descriptions of libraries or archives and for different purposes.

(5) Regulations shall be made by statutory instrument which shall be subject to annulment in pursuance of a resolution of either House of Parliament.

---

[1] Words repealed by SI 2003/2498 Sch 2 para 1
[2] Words substituted by SI 2003/2498 Pt II reg 13 (c)
[3] Inserted by SI 1996/2967 Pt II reg 11 (1)

(6) References in this section, and in sections 38 to 43, to the librarian or archivist include a person acting on his behalf.

Copying by librarians: articles in periodicals

38.—(1) The librarian of a prescribed library may, if the prescribed **5-051** conditions are complied with, make and supply a copy of an article in a periodical without infringing any copyright in the text, in any illustrations accompanying the text or in the typographical arrangement.

(2) The prescribed conditions shall include the following—

[(a) that copies are supplied only to persons satisfying the librarian that they require them for the purposes of–

    (i) research for a non-commercial purpose, or

    (ii) private study,

and will not use them for any other purpose;][1]

(b) that no person is furnished with more than one copy of the same article or with copies of more than one article contained in the same issue of a periodical; and

(c) that persons to whom copies are supplied are required to pay for them a sum not less than the cost (including a contribution to the general expenses of the library) attributable to their production.

Copying by librarians: parts of published works

39.—(1) The librarian of a prescribed library may, if the prescribed **5-052** conditions are complied with, make and supply from a published edition a copy of part of a literary, dramatic or musical work (other than an article in a periodical) without infringing any copyright in the work, in any illustrations accompanying the work or in the typographical arrangement.

(2) The prescribed conditions shall include the following—

[(a) that copies are supplied only to persons satisfying the librarian that they require them for the purposes of–

    (i) research for a non-commercial purpose, or

    (ii) private study,

and will not use them for any other purpose;][2]

(b) that no person is furnished with more than one copy of the same material or with a copy of more than a reasonable proportion of any work; and

(c) that persons to whom copies are supplied are required to pay for them a sum not less than the cost (including a contribution to the general expenses of the library) attributable to their production.

Restriction on production of multiple copies of the same material

40.—(1) Regulations for the purposes of sections 38 and 39 (copying by **5-053** librarian of article or part of published work) shall contain provision to the effect that a copy shall be supplied only to a person satisfying the librarian that his requirement is not related to any similar requirement of another person.

(2) The regulations may provide—

(a) that requirements shall be regarded as similar if the requirements are for copies of substantially the same material at substantially the same time and for substantially the same purpose; and

---

[1] Substituted by SI 2003/2498 Pt II reg 14 (1)
[2] Substituted by SI 2003/2498 Pt II reg 14 (1)

(b) that requirements of persons shall be regarded as related if those persons receive instruction to which the material is relevant at the same time and place.

[Lending of copies by libraries or archives

5-054   **40A.**—(1) Copyright in a work of any description is not infringed by the lending of a book by a public library if the book is within the public lending right scheme.

For this purpose-

(a) "the public lending right scheme" means the scheme in force under section 1 of the Public Lending Right Act 1979, and

(b) a book is within the public lending right scheme if it is a book within the meaning of the provisions of the scheme relating to eligibility, whether or not it is in fact eligible.

(2) Copyright in a work is not infringed by the lending of copies of the work by a prescribed library or archive (other than a public library) which is not conducted for profit.][1]

Copying by librarians: supply of copies to other libraries

5-055   **41.**—(1) The librarian of a prescribed library may, if the prescribed conditions are complied with, make and supply to another prescribed library a copy of—

(a) an article in a periodical, or

(b) the whole or part of a published edition of a literary, dramatic or musical work,

without infringing any copyright in the text of the article or, as the case may be, in the work, in any illustrations accompanying it or in the typographical arrangement.

(2) Subsection (1)(b) does not apply if at the time the copy is made the librarian making it knows, or could by reasonable inquiry ascertain, the name and address of a person entitled to authorise the making of the copy.

Copying by librarians or archivists: replacement copies of works

5-056   **42.**—(1) The librarian or archivist of a prescribed library or archive may, if the prescribed conditions are complied with, make a copy from any item in the permanent collection of the library or archive—

(a) in order to preserve or replace that item by placing the copy in its permanent collection in addition to or in place of it, or

(b) in order to replace in the permanent collection of another prescribed library or archive an item which has been lost, destroyed or damaged,

without infringing the copyright in any literary, dramatic or musical work, in any illustrations accompanying such a work or, in the case of a published edition, in the typographical arrangement.

(2) The prescribed conditions shall include provision for restricting the making of copies to cases where it is not reasonably practicable to purchase a copy of the item in question to fulfil that purpose.

Copying by librarians or archivists: certain unpublished works

5-057   **43.**—(1) The librarian or archivist of a prescribed library or archive may, if the prescribed conditions are complied with, make and supply a copy of the

---

[1] Inserted by SI 1996/2967 Pt II reg 11 (2)

whole or part of a literary, dramatic or musical work from a document in the library or archive without infringing any copyright in the work or any illustrations accompanying it.

(2) This section does not apply if—

(a) the work had been published before the document was deposited in the library or archive, or

(b) the copyright owner has prohibited copying of the work,

and at the time the copy is made the librarian or archivist making it is, or ought to be, aware of that fact.

(3) The prescribed conditions shall include the following—

[(a) that copies are supplied only to persons satisfying the librarian or archivist that they require them for the purposes of–

(i) research for a non-commercial purpose, or

(ii) private study,

and will not use them for any other purpose;][1]

(b) that no person is furnished with more than one copy of the same material; and

(c) that persons to whom copies are supplied are required to pay for them a sum not less than the cost (including a contribution to the general expenses of the library or archive) attributable to their production.

Copy of work required to be made as condition of export

44. If an article of cultural or historical importance or interest cannot **5-058** lawfully be exported from the United Kingdom unless a copy of it is made and deposited in an appropriate library or archive, it is not an infringement of copyright to make that copy.

[Legal deposit libraries

44A—(1) Copyright is not infringed by the copying of a work from the **5-059** internet by a deposit library or person acting on its behalf if–

(a) the work is of a description prescribed by regulations under section 10(5) of the 2003 Act,

(b) its publication on the internet, or a person publishing it there, is connected with the United Kingdom in a manner so prescribed, and

(c) the copying is done in accordance with any conditions so prescribed.

(2) Copyright is not infringed by the doing of anything in relation to relevant material permitted to be done under regulations under section 7 of the 2003 Act.

(3) The Secretary of State may by regulations make provision excluding, in relation to prescribed activities done in relation to relevant material, the application of such of the provisions of this Chapter as are prescribed.

(4) Regulations under subsection (3) may in particular make provision prescribing activities–

(a) done for a prescribed purpose,

(b) done by prescribed descriptions of reader,

(c) done in relation to prescribed descriptions of relevant material,

(d) done other than in accordance with prescribed conditions.

(5) Regulations under this section may make different provision for different purposes.

---

[1] Substituted by SI 2003/2498 Pt II reg 14 (2)

(6) Regulations under this section shall be made by statutory instrument which shall be subject to annulment in pursuance of a resolution of either House of Parliament.

(7) In this section–

    (a) "the 2003 Act" means the Legal Deposit Libraries Act 2003;

    (b) "deposit library", "reader" and "relevant material" have the same meaning as in section 7 of the 2003 Act;

    (c) "prescribed" means prescribed by regulations made by the Secretary of State.][1]

Public administration

Parliamentary and judicial proceedings

5-060   **45.**—(1) Copyright is not infringed by anything done for the purposes of parliamentary or judicial proceedings.

(2) Copyright is not infringed by anything done for the purposes of reporting such proceedings; but this shall not be construed as authorising the copying of a work which is itself a published report of the proceedings.

Royal Commissions and statutory inquiries

5-061   **46.**—(1) Copyright is not infringed by anything done for the purposes of the proceedings of a Royal Commission or statutory inquiry.

(2) Copyright is not infringed by anything done for the purpose of reporting any such proceedings held in public; but this shall not be construed as authorising the copying of a work which is itself a published report of the proceedings.

(3) Copyright in a work is not infringed by the issue to the public of copies of the report of a Royal Commission or statutory inquiry containing the work or material from it.

(4) In this section—

    "Royal Commission" includes a Commission appointed for Northern Ireland by the Secretary of State in pursuance of the prerogative powers of Her Majesty delegated to him under section 7(2) of the Northern Ireland Constitution Act 1973; and

    "statutory inquiry" means an inquiry held or investigation conducted in pursuance of a duty imposed or power conferred by or under an enactment.

Material open to public inspection or on official register

5-062   **47.**—(1) Where material is open to public inspection pursuant to a statutory requirement, or is on a statutory register, any copyright in the material as a literary work is not infringed by the copying of so much of the material as contains factual information of any description, by or with the authority of the appropriate person, for a purpose which does not involve the issuing of copies to the public.

(2) Where material is open to public inspection pursuant to a statutory requirement, copyright is not infringed by the copying or issuing to the public of copies of the material, by or with the authority of the appropriate person, for the purpose of enabling the material to be inspected at a more convenient time or place or otherwise facilitating the exercise of any right for the purpose of which the requirement is imposed.

---

[1] Inserted by Legal Deposit Libraries Act 2003 c.28 s 8 (1)

(3) Where material which is open to public inspection pursuant to a statutory requirement, or which is on a statutory register, contains information about matters of general scientific, technical, commercial or economic interest, copyright is not infringed by the copying or issuing to the public of copies of the material, by or with the authority of the appropriate person, for the purpose of disseminating that information.

(4) The Secretary of State may be order provide that subsection (1), (2) or (3) shall, in such cases as may be specified in the order, apply only to copies marked in such manner as may be so specified.

(5) The Secretary of State may be order provide that subsections (1) to (3) apply, to such extent and with such modifications as may be specified in the order—

    (a) to material made open to public inspection by—
        (i) an international organisation specified in the order, or
        (ii) a person so specified who has functions in the United Kingdom under an international agreement to which the United Kingdom is party, or
    (b) to a register maintained by an international organisation specified in the order,

as they apply in relation to material open to public inspection pursuant to a statutory requirement or to a statutory register.

    (6) In this section—
    "appropriate person" means the person required to make the material open to public inspection or, as the case may be, the person maintaining the register;
    "statutory register" means a register maintained in pursuance of a statutory requirement; and
    "statutory requirement" means a requirement imposed by provision made by or under an enactment.

(7) An order under this section shall be made by statutory instrument which shall be subject to annulment in pursuance of a resolution of either House of Parliament.

Material communicated to the Crown in the course of public business

48.—(1) This section applies where a literary, dramatic, musical or artistic **5-063** work has in the course of public business been communicated to the Crown for any purpose, by or with the licence of the copyright owner and a document or other material thing recording or embodying the work is owned by or in the custody or control of the Crown.

(2) The Crown may, for the purpose for which the work was communicated to it, or any related purpose which could reasonably have been anticipated by the copyright owner, copy the work and issue copies of the work to the public without infringing any copyright in the work.

(3) The Crown may not copy a work, or issue copies of a work to the public, by virtue of this section if the work has previously been published otherwise than by virtue of this section.

(4) In subsection (1) "public business" includes any activity carried on by the Crown.

(5) This section has effect subject to any agreement to the contrary between the Crown and the copyright owner.

[(6) In this section "the Crown" includes a health service body, as defined in section 60(7) of the National Health Service and Community Care Act 1990, [[a

Primary Care Trust established under section 16A of the National Health Service Act 1977,][1] the Commission for Health Improvement][2] and a National Health Service trust established under Part I of that Act or the National Health Service (Scotland) Act 1978 [and an NHS foundation trust][3]; and the reference in subsection (1) above to public business shall be construed accordingly.][4]

Public records

5-064   **49.** Material which is comprised in public records within the meaning of the Public Records Act 1958, the Public Records (Scotland) Act 1937 or the Public Records Act (Northern Ireland) 1923 [, or in Welsh public records (as defined in the Government of Wales Act 1998),][5] which are open to public inspection in pursuance of that Act, may be copied, and a copy may be supplied to any person, by or with the authority of any officer appointed under that Act, without infringement of copyright.

Acts done under statutory authority

5-065   **50.**—(1) Where the doing of a particular act is specifically authorised by an Act of Parliament, whenever passed, then, unless the Act provides otherwise, the doing of that act does not infringe copyright.

(2) Subsection (1) applies in relation to an enactment contained in Northern Ireland legislation as it applies in relation to an Act of Parliament.

(3) Nothing in this section shall be construed as excluding any defence of statutory authority otherwise available under or by virtue of any enactment.

[Computer programs: lawful users

Back up copies

5-066   **50A.**—(1) It is not an infringement of copyright for a lawful user of a copy of a computer program to make any back up copy of it which it is necessary for him to have for the purposes of his lawful use.

(2) For the purposes of this section and sections 50B[, 50BA][6] and 50C a person is a lawful user of a computer program if (whether under a licence to do any acts restricted by the copyright in the program or otherwise), he has a right to use the program.

(3) Where an act is permitted under this section, it is irrelevant whether or not there exists any term or condition in an agreement which purports to prohibit or restrict the act (such terms being, by virtue of section 296A, void).

Decompilation

5-067   **50B.**—(1) It is not an infringement of copyright for a lawful user of a copy of a computer program expressed in a low level language—

    (a) to convert it into a version expressed in a higher level language, or

    (b) incidentally in the course of so converting the program, to copy it,

(that is, to "decompile" it), provided that the conditions in subsection (2) are met.

---

[1] Words inserted by SI 2000/90 Sch 1 para 22
[2] Words inserted by SI 1999/2795 art 3
[3] Words inserted by Health and Social Care (Community Health and Standards) Act 2003 c.43 Sch 4 para 72
[4] Inserted by National Health Service and Community Care Act 1990 c.19 s 60 (2) Sch 8 para 3
[5] Words inserted by Government of Wales Act 1998 c.38 Sch 12 para 27
[6] Word inserted by SI 2003/2498 Pt II reg 15 (2)

(2) The conditions are that—

    (a) it is necessary to decompile the program to obtain the information necessary to create an independent program which can be operated with the program decompiled or with another program ("the permitted objective"); and

    (b) the information so obtained is not used for any purpose other than the permitted objective.

(3) In particular, the conditions in subsection (2) are not met if the lawful user—

    (a) has readily available to him the information necessary to achieve the permitted objective;

    (b) does not confine the decompiling to such acts as are necessary to achieve the permitted objective;

    (c) supplies the information obtained by the decompiling to any person to whom it is not necessary to supply it in order to achieve the permitted objective; or

    (d) uses the information to create a program which is substantially similar in its expression to the program decompiled or to do any act restricted by copyright.

(4) Where an act is permitted under this section, it is irrelevant whether or not there exists any term or condition in an agreement which purports to prohibit or restrict the act (such terms being, by virtue of section 296A, void).

[Observing, studying and testing of computer programs

50BA—(1) It is not an infringement of copyright for a lawful user of a copy **5-068** of a computer program to observe, study or test the functioning of the program in order to determine the ideas and principles which underlie any element of the program if he does so while performing any of the acts of loading, displaying, running, transmitting or storing the program which he is entitled to do.

(2) Where an act is permitted under this section, it is irrelevant whether or not there exists any term or condition in an agreement which purports to prohibit or restrict the act (such terms being, by virtue of section 296A, void).][1]

Other acts permitted to lawful users

50C.—(1) It is not an infringement of copyright for a lawful user of a copy of **5-069** a computer program to copy or adapt it, provided that the copying or adapting—

    (a) is necessary for his lawful use; and

    (b) is not prohibited under any term or condition of an agreement regulating the circumstances in which his use is lawful.

(2) It may, in particular, be necessary for the lawful use of a computer program to copy it or adapt it for the purpose of correcting errors in it.

(3) This section does not apply to any copying or adapting permitted under [sections 50A, 50B or 50BA][2].[3]

---

[1] Inserted by SI 2003/2498 Pt II reg 15 (1)
[2] Words substituted by SI 2003/2498 Pt II reg 15 (3)
[3] Inserted by SI 1992/3233 reg 8

[Databases: permitted acts

Acts permitted in relation to databases

5-070   **50D.**—(1) It is not an infringement of copyright in a database for a person who has a right to use the database or any part of the database, (whether under a licence to do any of the acts restricted by the copyright in the database or otherwise) to do, in the exercise of that right, anything which is necessary for the purposes of access to and use of the contents of the database or of that part of the database.

(2) Where an act which would otherwise infringe copyright in a database is permitted under this section, it is irrelevant whether or not there exists any term or condition in any agreement which purports to prohibit or restrict the act (such terms being, by virtue of section 296B, void).][1]

Designs

Design documents and models

5-071   **51.**—(1) It is not an infringement of any copyright in a design document or model recording or embodying a design for anything other than an artistic work or a typeface to make an article to the design or to copy an article made to the design.

(2) Nor is it an infringement of the copyright to issue to the public, or include in a film [or communicate to the public][2], anything the making of which was, by virtue of subsection (1), not an infringement of that copyright.

(3) In this section—

"design" means the design of any aspect of the shape or configuration (whether internal or external) of the whole or part of an article, other than surface decoration; and

"design document" means any record of a design, whether in the form of a drawing, a written description, a photograph, data stored in a computer or otherwise.

Effect of exploitation of design derived from artistic work

5-072   **52.**—(1) This section applies where an artistic work has been exploited, by or with the licence of the copyright owner, by—

(a) making by an industrial process articles falling to be treated for the purposes of this Part as copies of the work, and

(b) marketing such articles, in the United Kingdom or elsewhere.

(2) After the end of the period of 25 years from the end of the calendar year in which such articles are first marketed, the work may be copied by making articles of any description, or doing anything for the purpose of making articles of any description, and anything may be done in relation to articles so made, without infringing copyright in the work.

(3) Where only part of an artistic work is exploited as mentioned in subsection (1), subsection (2) applies only in relation to that part.

(4) The Secretary of State may by order make provision—

(a) as to the circumstances in which an article, or any description of article, is to be regarded for the purposes of this section as made by an industrial process;

---

[1] Inserted by SI 1997/3032 Pt II reg 9
[2] Words substituted by SI 2003/2498 Sch 1 (1) para 8 (3)

(b) excluding from the operation of this section such articles of a primarily literary or artistic character as he thinks fit.

(5) An order shall be made by statutory instrument which shall be subject to annulment in pursuance of a resolution of either House of Parliament.

(6) In this section—

(a) references to articles do not include films; and
(b) references to the marketing of an article are to its being sold or let for hire or offered or exposed for sale or hire.

Things done in reliance on registration of design

53.—(1) The copyright in an artistic work is not infringed by anything **5-073** done—

(a) in pursuance of an assignment or licence made or granted by a person registered under the Registered Designs Act 1949 as the proprietor of a corresponding design, and
(b) in good faith in reliance on the registration and without notice of any proceedings for the cancellation [or invalidation][1] of the registration or for rectifying the relevant entry in the register of designs;

and this is so notwithstanding that the person registered as the proprietor was not the proprietor of the design for the purposes of the 1949 Act.

(2) In subsection (1) a "corresponding design", in relation to an artistic work, means a design within the meaning of the 1949 Act which if applied to an article would produce something which would be treated for the purposes of this Part as a copy of the artistic work.

Typefaces

Use of typeface in ordinary course of printing

54.—(1) It is not an infringement of copyright in an artistic work consisting **5-074** of the design of a typeface—

(a) to use the typeface in the ordinary course of typing, composing text, typesetting or printing,
(b) to possess an article for the purpose of such use, or
(c) to do anything in relation to material produced by such use;

and this is so notwithstanding that an article is used which is an infringing copy of the work.

(2) However, the following provisions of this Part apply in relation to persons making, importing or dealing with articles specifically designed or adapted for producing material in a particular typeface, or possessing such articles for the purpose of dealing with them, as if the production of material as mentioned in subsection (1) did infringe copyright in the artistic work consisting of the design of the typeface—

section 24 (secondary infringement: making, importing, possessing or dealing with article for making infringing copy),
sections 99 and 100 (order for delivery up and right of seizure),
section 107(2) (offence of making or possessing such an article), and
section 108 (order for delivery up in criminal proceedings).

(3) The references in subsection (2) to "dealing with" an article are to selling, letting for hire, or offering or exposing for sale or hire, exhibiting in public, or distributing.

---

[1] Words inserted by SI 2001/3949 Sch 1 para 16

Articles for producing material in particular typeface

5-075   **55.**—(1) This section applies to the copyright in an artistic work consisting of the design of a typeface where articles specifically designed or adapted for producing material in that typeface have been marketed by or with the licence of the copyright owner.

(2) After the period of 25 years from the end of the calendar year in which the first such articles are marketed, the work may be copied by making further such articles, or doing anything for the purpose of making such articles, and anything may be done in relation to articles so made, without infringing copyright in the work.

(3) In subsection (1) "marketed" means sold, let for hire or offered or exposed for sale or hire, in the United Kingdom or elsewhere.

Works in electronic form

Transfers of copies of works in electronic form

5-076   **56.**—(1) This section applies where a copy of a work in electronic form has been purchased on terms which, expressly or impliedly or by virtue of any rule of law, allow the purchaser to copy the work, or to adapt it or make copies of an adaptation, in connection with his use of it.

(2) If there are no express terms—

> (a) prohibiting the transfer of the copy by the purchaser, imposing obligations which continue after a transfer, prohibiting the assignment of any licence or terminating any licence on a transfer, or
>
> (b) providing for the terms on which a transferee may do the things which the purchaser was permitted to do,

anything which the purchaser was allowed to do may also be done without infringement of copyright by a transferee; but any copy, adaptation or copy of an adaptation made by the purchaser which is not also transferred shall be treated as an infringing copy for all purposes after the transfer.

(3) The same applies where the original purchased copy is no longer usable and what is transferred is a further copy used in its place.

(4) The above provisions also apply on a subsequent transfer, with the substitution for references in subsection (2) to the purchaser of references to the subsequent transferor.

Miscellaneous: literary, dramatic, musical and artistic works

Anonymous or pseudonymous works: acts permitted on assumptions as to expiry of copyright or death of author

5-077   **57.**—(1) Copyright in a literary, dramatic, musical or artistic work is not infringed by an act done at a time when, or in pursuance of arrangements made at a time when—

> (a) it is not possible by reasonable inquiry to ascertain the identity of the author, and
> (b) it is reasonable to assume—
>> (i) that copyright has expired, or

      (ii) that the author died [70 years]¹ or more before the beginning of the calendar year in which the act is done or the arrangements are made.

(2) Subsection (1)(b)(ii) does not apply in relation to—

    (a) a work in which Crown copyright subsists, or

    (b) a work in which copyright originally vested in an international organisation by virtue of section 168 and in respect of which an Order under that section specifies a copyright period longer than [70 years]².

(3) In relation to a work of joint authorship—

    (a) the reference in subsection (1) to its being possible to ascertain the identity of the author shall be construed as a reference to its being possible to ascertain the identity of any of the authors, and

    (b) the reference in subsection (1)(b)(ii) to the author having died shall be construed as a reference to all the authors having died.

Use of notes or recordings of spoken words in certain cases

58.—(1) Where a record of spoken words is made, in writing or otherwise, **5-078** for the purpose—

    (a) of reporting current events, or

    (b) of [communicating to the public]³ the whole or part of the work,

it is not an infringement of any copyright in the words as a literary work to use the record or material taken from it (or to copy the record, or any such material, and use the copy) for that purpose, provided the following conditions are met.

(2) The conditions are that—

    (a) the record is a direct record of the spoken words and is not taken from a previous record or from a broadcast [...]⁴;

    (b) the making of the record was not prohibited by the speaker and, where copyright already subsisted in the work, did not infringe copyright;

    (c) the use made of the record or material taken from it is not of a kind prohibited by or on behalf of the speaker or copyright owner before the record was made; and

    (d) the use is by or with the authority of a person who is lawfully in possession of the record.

Public reading or recitation

59.—(1) The reading or recitation in public by one person of a reasonable **5-079** extract from a published literary or dramatic work does not infringe any copyright in the work if it is accompanied by a sufficient acknowledgement.

(2) Copyright in a work is not infringed by the making of a sound recording, or the [communication to the public]⁵, of a reading or recitation which by virtue of subsection (1) does not infringe copyright in the work, provided that the recording [or communication to the public]⁶ consists mainly of material in relation to which it is not necessary to rely on that subsection.

---

¹ Words substituted by SI 1995/3297 Pt II reg 5 (2)
² Words substituted by SI 1995/3297 Pt II reg 5 (2)
³ Words substituted by SI 2003/2498 Sch 1 (1) para 12 (a)
⁴ Words repealed by SI 2003/2498 Sch 2 para 1
⁵ Words substituted by SI 2003/2498 Sch 1 (1) para 5 (b)
⁶ Words substituted by SI 2003/2498 Sch 1 (1) para 9 (1) (a)

Abstracts of scientific or technical articles

5-080   **60.**—(1) Where an article on a scientific or technical subject is published in a periodical accompanied by an abstract indicating the contents of the article, it is not an infringement of copyright in the abstract, or in the article, to copy the abstract or issue copies of it to the public.

(2) This section does not apply if or to the extent that there is a licensing scheme certified for the purposes of this section under section 143 providing for the grant of licences.

Recordings of folksongs

5-081   **61.**—(1) A sound recording of a performance of a song may be made for the purpose of including it in an archive maintained by a designated body without infringing any copyright in the words as a literary work or in the accompanying musical work, provided the conditions in subsection (2) below are met.

(2) The conditions are that—
   (a) the words are unpublished and of unknown authorship at the time the recording is made,
   (b) the making of the recording does not infringe any other copyright, and
   (c) its making is not prohibited by any performer.

(3) Copies of a sound recording made in reliance on subsection (1) and included in an archive maintained by a designated body may, if the prescribed conditions are met, be made and supplied by the archivist without infringing copyright in the recording or the works included in it.

(4) The prescribed conditions shall include the following—
   [(a) that copies are only supplied to persons satisfying the archivist that they require them for the purposes of–
      (i) research for a non-commercial purpose, or
      (ii) private study,
   and will not use them for any other purpose, and][1]
   (b) that no person is furnished with more than one copy of the same recording.

(5) In this section—
   (a) "designated" means designated for the purposes of this section by order of the Secretary of State, who shall not designate a body unless satisfied that it is not established or conducted for profit,
   (b) "prescribed" means prescribed for the purposes of this section by order of the Secretary of State, and
   (c) references to the archivist include a person acting on his behalf.

(6) An order under this section shall be made by statutory instrument which shall be subject to annulment in pursuance of a resolution of either House of Parliament.

Representation of certain artistic works on public display

5-082   **62.**—(1) This section applies to—
   (a) buildings, and
   (b) sculptures, models for buildings and works of artistic craftsmanship, if permanently situated in public place or in premises open to the public.

(2) The copyright in such a work is not infringed by—
   (a) making a graphic work representing it,
   (b) making a photograph or film of it, or

---

[1] Substituted by SI 2003/2498 Pt II reg 16

(c) [making a broadcast of]¹ a visual image of it.

(3) Nor is the copyright infringed by the issue to the public of copies, or the [communication to the public]², of anything whose making was, by virtue of this section, not an infringement of the copyright.

Advertisement of sale of artistic work

63.—(1) It is not an infringement of copyright in an artistic work to copy it, **5-083** or to issue copies to the public, for the purpose of advertising the sale of the work.

(2) Where a copy which would otherwise be an infringing copy is made in accordance with this section but is subsequently dealt with for any other purpose, it shall be treated as an infringing copy for the purposes of that dealing, and if that dealing infringes copyright for all subsequent purposes.

For this purpose "dealt with" means sold or let for hire, offered or exposed for sale or hire, exhibited in public [,distributed or communicated to the public]³.

Making of subsequent works by same artist

64. Where the author of an artistic work is not the copyright owner, he does **5-084** not infringe the copyright by copying the work in making another artistic work, provided he does not repeat or imitate the main design of the earlier work.

Reconstruction of buildings

65. Anything done for the purposes of reconstructing a building does not **5-085** infringe any copyright—
  (a) in the building, or
  (b) in any drawings or plans in accordance with which the building was, by or with the licence of the copyright owner, constructed.

[Miscellaneous: lending of works and playing of sound recordings

Lending to public of copies of certain works

66.—(1) The Secretary of State may by order provide that in such cases as **5-086** may be specified in the order the lending to the public of copies of literary, dramatic, musical or artistic works, sound recordings or films shall be treated as licensed by the copyright owner subject only to the payment of such reasonable royalty or other payment as may be agreed or determined in default of agreement by the Copyright Tribunal.

(2) No such order shall apply if, or to the extent that, there is a licensing scheme certified for the purposes of this section under section 143 providing for the grant of licences.

(3) An order may make different provision for different cases and may specify cases by reference to any factor relating to the work, the copies lent, the lender or the circumstances of the lending.

(4) An order shall be made by statutory instrument; and no order shall be made unless a draft of it has been laid before and approved by a resolution of each House of Parliament.

¹ Words substituted by SI 2003/2498 Sch 1 (1) para 14
² Words substituted by SI 2003/2498 Sch 1 (1) para 5 (c)
³ Words substituted by SI 2003/2498 Pt II reg 17

(5) Nothing in this section affects any liability under section 23 (secondary infringement: possessing or dealing with infringing copy) in respect of the lending of infringing copies.][1]

[Miscellaneous: films and sound recordings

Films: acts permitted on assumptions as to expiry of copyright, &c

5-087   **66A.**—(1) Copyright in a film is not infringed by an act done at a time when, or in pursuance of arrangements made at a time when—

(a) it is not possible by reasonable inquiry to ascertain the identity of any of the persons referred to in section 13B(2)(a) to (d) (persons by reference to whose life the copyright period is ascertained), and

(b) it is reasonable to assume—

(i) that copyright has expired, or

(ii) that the last to die of those persons died 70 years or more before the beginning of the calendar year in which the act is done or the arrangements are made.

(2) Subsection (1)(b)(ii) does not apply in relation to—

(a) a film in which Crown copyright subsists, or

(b) a film in which copyright originally vested in an international organisation by virtue of section 168 and in respect of which an Order under that section specifies a copyright period longer than 70 years.][2]

Miscellaneous: sound recordings, films and computer programs

Playing of sound recordings for purposes of club, society, &c

5-088   **67.**—(1) It is not an infringement of the copyright in a sound recording to play it as part of the activities of, or for the benefit of, a club, society or other organisation if the following conditions are met.

(2) The conditions are—

(a) that the organisation is not established or conducted for profit and its main objects are charitable or are otherwise concerned with the advancement of religion, education or social welfare,

[(b) that the sound recording is played by a person who is acting primarily and directly for the benefit of the organisation and who is not acting with a view to gain,

(c) that the proceeds of any charge for admission to the place where the recording is to be heard are applied solely for the purposes of the organisation, and

(d) that the proceeds from any goods or services sold by, or on behalf of, the organisation –

(i) in the place where the sound recording is heard, and

(ii) on the occasion when the sound recording is played, are applied solely for the purposes of the organisation.][3]

---

[1] Substituted by SI 1996/2967 Pt II reg 11 (3)
[2] Inserted by SI 1995/3297 Pt II reg 6 (2)
[3] Substituted by SI 2003/2498 Pt II reg 18 (1)

Miscellaneous: broadcasts [...][1]

Incidental recording for purposes of broadcast [...][2]

68.—(1) This section applies where by virtue of a licence or assignment of **5-089** copyright a person is authorised to broadcast [...][3]—

    (a) a literary, dramatic or musical work, or an adaptation of such a work,

    (b) an artistic work, or

    (c) a sound recording or film.

(2) He shall by virtue of this section be treated as licensed by the owner of the copyright in the work to do or authorise any of the following for the purposes of the broadcast [...][4]—

    (a) in the case of a literary, dramatic or musical work, or an adaptation of such a work, to make a sound recording or film of the work or adaptation;

    (b) in the case of an artistic work, to take a photograph or make a film of the work;

    (c) in the case of a sound recording or film, to make a copy of it.

(3) That licence is subject to the condition that the recording, film, photograph or copy in question—

    (a) shall not be used for any other purpose, and

    (b) shall be destroyed within 28 days of being first used for broadcasting the work [...][5].

(4) A recording, film, photograph or copy made in accordance with this section shall be treated as an infringing copy—

    (a) for the purposes of any use in breach of the condition mentioned in subsection (3)(a), and

    (b) for all purposes after that condition or the condition mentioned in subsection (3)(b) is broken.

Recording for purposes of supervision and control of broadcasts and [other services][6]

69.—(1) Copyright is not infringed by the making or use by the British Broad- **5-090** casting Corporation, for the purpose of maintaining supervision and control over programmes broadcast by them, of recordings of those programmes.

[(2) Copyright is not infringed by anything done in pursuance of—

    [(a) section 167(1) of the Broadcasting Act 1990, section 115(4) or (6) or 117 of the Broadcasting Act 1996 or paragraph 20 of Schedule 12 to the Communications Act 2003;][7]

    (b) a condition which, [by virtue of section 334(1) of the Communications Act 2003][8], is included in a licence granted under Part I or III of that Act or Part I or II of the Broadcasting Act 1996; [...][9]

    (c) a direction given under section 109(2) of the Broadcasting Act 1990 (power of [OFCOM][10] to require production of recordings etc.)

---

[1] Words repealed by SI 2003/2498 Sch 2 para 1
[2] Words repealed by SI 2003/2498 Sch 2 para 1
[3] Words repealed by SI 2003/2498 Sch 2 para 1
[4] Words repealed by SI 2003/2498 Sch 2 para 1
[5] Words repealed by SI 2003/2498 Sch 2 para 1
[6] Words substituted by SI 2003/2498 Sch 1 (1) para 2 (1)
[7] Substituted by Communications Act 2003 c.21 Sch 17 para 91 (2) (a)
[8] Words substituted by Communications Act 2003 c.21 Sch 17 para 91 (2) (b)
[9] Word repealed by Communications Act 2003 c.21 Sch 19 para 1
[10] Word substituted by Communications Act 2003 c.21 Sch 17 para 91 (2) (c)

[(d) section 334(3) of the Communications Act 2003.][1] [2]

[(3) Copyright is not infringed by the use by OFCOM in connection with the performance of any of their functions under the Broadcasting Act 1990, the Broadcasting Act 1996 or the Communications Act 2003 of—

(a) any recording, script or transcript which is provided to them under or by virtue of any provision of those Acts; or

(b) any existing material which is transferred to them by a scheme made under section 30 of the Communications Act 2003.

(4) In subsection (3), 'existing material' means—

(a) any recording, script or transcript which was provided to the Independent Television Commission or the Radio Authority under or by virtue of any provision of the Broadcasting Act 1990 or the Broadcasting Act 1996; and

(b) any recording or transcript which was provided to the Broadcasting Standards Commission under section 115(4) or (6) or 116(5) of the Broadcasting Act 1996.][3]

Recording for purposes of time-shifting

5-091   **70.**—[(1) The making [in domestic premises][4] for private and domestic use of a recording of a broadcast [...][5] solely for the purpose of enabling it to be viewed or listened to at a more convenient time does not infringe any copyright in the broadcast [...][6] or in any work included in it.

[(2) Where a copy which would otherwise be an infringing copy is made in accordance with this section but is subsequently dealt with—

(a) it shall be treated as an infringing copy for the purposes of that dealing; and

(b) if that dealing infringes copyright, it shall be treated as an infringing copy for all subsequent purposes.

(3) In subsection (2), "dealt with" means sold or let for hire, offered or exposed for sale or hire or communicated to the public.][7] [8]

[Photographs of broadcasts

5-092   **71.**—(1) The making in domestic premises for private and domestic use of a photograph of the whole or any part of an image forming part of a broadcast, or a copy of such a photograph, does not infringe any copyright in the broadcast or in any film included in it.

(2) Where a copy which would otherwise be an infringing copy is made in accordance with this section but is subsequently dealt with—

(a) it shall be treated as an infringing copy for the purposes of that dealing; and

(b) if that dealing infringes copyright, it shall be treated as an infringing copy for all subsequent purposes.

(3) In subsection (2), "dealt with" means sold or let for hire, offered or exposed for sale or hire or communicated to the public.][9]

---

[1] Inserted by Communications Act 2003 c.21 Sch 17 para 91 (2) (d)
[2] Substituted by Broadcasting Act 1996 c.55 Sch 10 (III) para 31
[3] Substituted by Communications Act 2003 c.21 Sch 17 para 91 (3)
[4] Words inserted by SI 2003/2498 Pt II reg 19 (2)
[5] Words repealed by SI 2003/2498 Sch 2 para 1
[6] Words repealed by SI 2003/2498 Sch 2 para 1
[7] Words inserted by SI 2003/2498 Pt II reg 19 (2)
[8] Existing text of s 70 renumbered as s 70 (1) by SI 2003/2498 Pt II reg 19 (1)
[9] Substituted by SI 2003/2498 Pt II reg 20 (1)

Free public showing or playing of broadcast [...][1]

72.—(1) The showing or playing in public of a broadcast [...][2] to an audience **5-093** who have not paid for admission to the place where the broadcast [...][3] is to be seen or heard does not infringe any copyright in—

[(a) the broadcast;

(b) any sound recording (except so far as it is an excepted sound recording) included in it; or

(c) any film included in it.][4]

[(1A) For the purposes of this Part an "excepted sound recording" is a sound recording–

(a) whose author is not the author of the broadcast in which it is included; and

(b) which is a recording of music with or without words spoken or sung.

(1B) Where by virtue of subsection (1) the copyright in a broadcast shown or played in public is not infringed, copyright in any excepted sound recording included in it is not infringed if the playing or showing of that broadcast in public–

(a) forms part of the activities of an organisation that is not established or conducted for profit; or

(b) is necessary for the purposes of–

(i) repairing equipment for the reception of broadcasts;

(ii) demonstrating that a repair to such equipment has been carried out; or

(iii) demonstrating such equipment which is being sold or let for hire or offered or exposed for sale or hire.][5]

(2) The audience shall be treated as having paid for admission to a place—

(a) if they have paid for admission to a place of which that place forms part; or

(b) if goods or services are supplied at that place (or a place of which it forms part)—

(i) at prices which are substantially attributable to the facilities afforded for seeing or hearing the broadcast [...][6], or

(ii) at prices exceeding those usually charged there and which are partly attributable to those facilities.

(3) The following shall not be regarded as having paid for admission to a place—

(a) persons admitted as residents or inmates of the place;

(b) persons admitted as members of a club or society where the payment is only for membership of the club or society and the provision of facilities for seeing or hearing broadcasts [...][7] is only incidental to the main purposes of the club or society.

(4) Where the making of the broadcast [...][8] was an infringement of the copyright in a sound recording or film, the fact that it was heard or seen in public

---

[1] Words repealed by SI 2003/2498 Sch 2 para 1
[2] Words repealed by SI 2003/2498 Sch 2 para 1
[3] Words repealed by SI 2003/2498 Sch 2 para 1
[4] Substituted by SI 2003/2498 Pt II reg 21 (1) (a)
[5] Inserted by SI 2003/2498 Pt II reg 21 (1) (b)
[6] Words repealed by SI 2003/2498 Sch 2 para 1
[7] Words repealed by SI 2003/2498 Sch 2 para 1
[8] Words repealed by SI 2003/2498 Sch 2 para 1

by the reception of the broadcast [...][1] shall be taken into account in assessing the damages for that infringement.

[Reception and re-transmission of [wireless broadcast by cable][2]

5-094   **73.**—(1) This section applies where a [wireless][3] broadcast made from a place in the United Kingdom is [received and immediately re-transmitted by cable][4].

(2) The copyright in the broadcast is not infringed—
>   (a) if the [re-transmission by cable][5] is in pursuance of a relevant require-
>   ment, or
>   (b) if and to the extent that the broadcast is made for reception in the area
>   in which [it is re-transmitted by cable][6] and forms part of a qualifying
>   service.

(3) The copyright in any work included in the broadcast is not infringed if and to the extent that the broadcast is made for reception in the area in which [it is re-transmitted by cable][7]; but where the making of the broadcast was an infringement of the copyright in the work, the fact that the broadcast was re-transmitted [by cable][8] shall be taken into account in assessing the damages for that infringement.

(4) Where—
>   (a) the [re-transmission by cable][9] is in pursuance of a relevant requirement,
>   but
>   (b) to any extent, the area in which the [re-transmission by cable takes
>   place][10] ("the cable area") falls outside the area for reception in which
>   the broadcast is made ("the broadcast area"),

the [re-transmission by cable][11] (to the extent that it is provided for so much of the cable area as falls outside the broadcast area) of any work included in the broadcast shall, subject to subsection (5), be treated as licensed by the owner of the copyright in the work, subject only to the payment to him by the person making the broadcast of such reasonable royalty or other payment in respect of the [re-transmission by cable of the broadcast][12] as may be agreed or determined in default of agreement by the Copyright Tribunal.

(5) Subsection (4) does not apply if, or to the extent that, the [re-transmission of the work by cable][13] is (apart from that subsection licensed by the owner of the copyright in the work.

(6) In this section "qualifying service" means, subject to subsection (8), any of the following services—
>   (a) a regional or national Channel 3 service,
>   (b) Channel 4, Channel 5 and S4C,
>   [(c) the public teletext service,
>   (d) S4C Digital, and][14]

---

[1] Words repealed by SI 2003/2498 Sch 2 para 1
[2] Words substituted by SI 2003/2498 Pt II reg 22 (1) (a)
[3] Word inserted by SI 2003/2498 Pt II reg 22 (1) (b)
[4] Words substituted by SI 2003/2498 Pt II reg 22 (1) (b)
[5] Words substituted by SI 2003/2498 Pt II reg 22 (1) (c)
[6] Words substituted by SI 2003/2498 Pt II reg 22 (1) (d)
[7] Words substituted by SI 2003/2498 Pt II reg 22 (1) (d)
[8] Words substituted by SI 2003/2498 Pt II reg 22 (1) (e)
[9] Words substituted by SI 2003/2498 Pt II reg 22 (1) (f) (i)
[10] Words substituted by SI 2003/2498 Pt II reg 22 (1) (f) (ii)
[11] Words substituted by SI 2003/2498 Pt II reg 22 (1) (f) (iii)
[12] Words substituted by SI 2003/2498 Pt II reg 22 (1) (f) (iv)
[13] Words substituted by SI 2003/2498 Pt II reg 22 (1) (g)
[14] Substituted by Communications Act 2003 c.21 Sch 17 para 92 (2) (a)

(e) the television broadcasting services and teletext service of the British Broadcasting Corporation;

[and expressions used in this subsection have the same meanings as in Part 3 of the Communications Act 2003.][1]

[(7) In this section 'relevant requirement' means a requirement imposed by a general condition (within the meaning of Chapter 1 of Part 2 of the Communications Act 2003) the setting of which is authorised under section 64 of that Act (must-carry obligations).][2]

(8) The Secretary of State may by order amend subsection (6) so as to add any service to, or remove any service from, the definition of "qualifying service".

(9) The Secretary of State may also by order—

(a) provide that in specified cases subsection (3) is to apply in relation to broadcasts of a specified description which are not made as mentioned in that subsection, or

(b) exclude the application of that subsection in relation to broadcasts of a specified description made as mentioned in that subsection.

(10) Where the Secretary of State exercises the power conferred by subsection (9)(b) in relation to broadcasts of any description, the order may also provide for subsection (4) to apply, subject to such modifications as may be specified in the order, in relation to broadcasts of that description.

(11) An order under this section may contain such transitional provision as appears to the Secretary of State to be appropriate.

(12) An order under this section shall be made by statutory instrument which shall be subject to annulment in pursuance of a resolution of either House of Parliament.

[(13) In this section references to re-transmission by cable include the transmission of microwave energy between terrestrial fixed points.][3]][4]

[Royalty or other sum payable in pursuance of section 73(4)

73A.—(1) An application to settle the royalty or other sum payable in **5-095** pursuance of subsection (4) of section 73 (reception and re-transmission of [wireless broadcast by cable][5]) may be made to the Copyright Tribunal by the copyright owner or the person making the broadcast.

(2) The Tribunal shall consider the matter and make such order as it may determine to be reasonable in the circumstances.

(3) Either party may subsequently apply to the Tribunal to vary the order, and the Tribunal shall consider the matter and make such order confirming or varying the original order as it may determine to be reasonable in the circumstances.

(4) An application under subsection (3) shall not, except with the special leave of the Tribunal, be made within twelve months from the date of the original order or of the order on a previous application under that subsection.

(5) An order under subsection (3) has effect from the date on which it is made or such later date as may be specified by the Tribunal.][6]

---

[1] Words substituted by Communications Act 2003 c.21 Sch 17 para 92 (2) (b)
[2] Substituted by Communications Act 2003 c.21 Sch 17 para 92 (3)
[3] Inserted by SI 2003/2498 Pt II reg 22 (1) (h)
[4] Substituted by Broadcasting Act 1996 c.55 Sch 9 para 1
[5] Words substituted by SI 2003/2498 Pt II reg 22 (2)
[6] Inserted by Broadcasting Act 1996 c.55 Sch 9 para 1

Provision of subtitled copies of broadcast [...][1]

5-096 **74.**—(1) A designated body may, for the purpose of providing people who are deaf or hard of hearing, or physically or mentally handicapped in other ways, with copies which are sub-titled or otherwise modified for their special needs, make copies of [...][2] broadcasts [...][3] and issue [or lend][4] copies to the public, without infringing any copyright in the broadcasts [...][5] or works included in them.

(2) A "designated body" means a body designated for the purposes of this section by order of the Secretary of State, who shall not designate a body unless he is satisfied that it is not established or conducted for profit.

(3) An order under this section shall be made by statutory instrument which shall be subject to annulment in pursuance of a resolution of either House of Parliament.

(4) This section does not apply if, or to the extent that, there is a licensing scheme certified for the purposes of this section under section 143 providing for the grant of licences.

Recording for archival purposes

5-097 **75.**—(1) A recording of a broadcast [...][6] of a designated class, or a copy of such a recording, may be made for the purpose of being placed in an archive maintained by a designated body without thereby infringing any copyright in the broadcast [...][7] or in any work included in it.

(2) In subsection (1) "designated" means designated for the purposes of this section by order of the Secretary of State, who shall not designate a body unless he is satisfied that it is not established or conducted for profit.

(3) An order under this section shall be made by statutory instrument which shall be subject to annulment in pursuance of a resolution of either House of Parliament.

Adaptations

Adaptations

5-098 **76.** An act which by virtue of this Chapter may be done without infringing copyright in a literary, dramatic or musical work does not, where that work is an adaptation, infringe any copyright in the work from which the adaptation was made.

---

[1] Words repealed by SI 2003/2498 Sch 2 para 1
[2] Word repealed by SI 2003/2498 Sch 2 para 1
[3] Words repealed by SI 2003/2498 Sch 2 para 1
[4] Words inserted by SI 2003/2498 Pt II reg 23 (1)
[5] Words repealed by SI 2003/2498 Sch 2 para 1
[6] Words repealed by SI 2003/2498 Sch 2 para 1
[7] Words repealed by SI 2003/2498 Sch 2 para 1

CHAPTER IV

MORAL RIGHTS

Right to be identified as author or director

Right to be identified as author or director

77.—(1) The author of a copyright literary, dramatic, musical or artistic **5-099** work, and the director of a copyright film, has the right to be identified as the author or director of the work in the circumstances mentioned in this section; but the right is not infringed unless it has been asserted in accordance with section 78.

(2) The author of a literary work (other than words intended to be sung or spoken with music) or a dramatic work has the right to be identified whenever—

    (a) the work is published commercially, performed in public [or communicated to the public][1]; or

    (b) copies of a film or sound recording including the work are issued to the public;

and that right includes the right to be identified whenever any of those events occur in relation to an adaptation of the work as the author of the work from which the adaptation was made.

(3) The author of a musical work, or a literary work consisting of words intended to be sung or spoken with music, has the right to be identified whenever—

    (a) the work is published commercially;

    (b) copies of a sound recording of the work are issued to the public; or

    (c) a film of which the sound-track includes the work is shown in public or copies of such a film are issued to the public;

and that right includes the right to be identified whenever any of those events occur in relation to an adaptation of the work as the author of the work from which the adaptation was made.

(4) The author of an artistic work has the right to be identified whenever—

    (a) the work is published commercially or exhibited in public, or a visual image of it is [communicated to the public][2];

    (b) a film including a visual image of the work is shown in public or copies of such a film are issued to the public; or

    (c) in the case of a work of architecture in the form of a building or a model for a building, a sculpture or a work of artistic craftsmanship, copies of a graphic work representing it, or of a photograph of it, are issued to the public.

(5) The author of a work of architecture in the form of a building also has the right to be identified on the building as constructed or, where more than one building is constructed to the design, on the first to be constructed.

(6) The director of a film has the right to be identified whenever the film is shown in public [or communicated to the public][3] or copies of the film are issued to the public.

(7) The right of the author or director under this section is—

---

[1] Words substituted by SI 2003/2498 Sch 1 (1) para 8 (1) (a)

[2] Words substituted by SI 2003/2498 Sch 1 (1) para 8 (2) (a)

[3] Words substituted by SI 2003/2498 Sch 1 (1) para 8 (1) (b)

(a) in the case of commercial publication or the issue to the public of copies of a film or sound recording, to be identified in or on each copy or, if that is not appropriate, in some other manner likely to bring his identity to the notice of a person acquiring a copy,

(b) in the case of identification on a building, to be identified by appropriate means visible to persons entering or approaching the building, and

(c) in any other case, to be identified in a manner likely to bring his identity to the attention of a person seeing or hearing the performance, exhibition, showing [or communication to the public][1] in question;

and the identification must in each case be clear and reasonably prominent.

(8) If the author or director in asserting his right to be identified specifies a pseudonym, initials or some other particular form of identification, that form shall be used; otherwise any reasonable form of identification may be used.

(9) This section has effect subject to section 79 (exceptions to right).

Requirement that right be asserted

5-100　**78.**—(1) A person does not infringe the right conferred by section 77 (right to be identified as author or director) by doing any of the acts mentioned in that section unless the right has been asserted in accordance with the following provisions so as to bind him in relation to that act.

(2) The right may be asserted generally, or in relation to any specified act or description of acts—

(a) on an assignment of copyright in the work, by including in the instrument effecting the assignment a statement that the author or director asserts in relation to that work his right to be identified, or

(b) by instrument in writing signed by the author or director.

(3) The right may also be asserted in relation to the public exhibition of an artistic work—

(a) by securing that when the author or other first owner of copyright parts with possession of the original, or of a copy made by him or under his direction or control, the author is identified on the original or copy, or on a frame, mount or other thing to which it is attached, or

(b) by including in a licence by which the author or other first owner of copyright authorises the making of copies of the work a statement signed by or on behalf of the person granting the licence that the author asserts his right to be identified in the event of the public exhibition of a copy made in pursuance of the licence.

(4) The persons bound by an assertion of the right under subsection (2) or (3) are—

(a) in the case of an assertion under subsection (2)(a), the assignee and anyone claiming through him, whether or not he has notice of the assertion;

(b) in the case of an assertion under subsection (2)(b), anyone to whose notice the assertion is brought;

(c) in the case of an assertion under subsection (3)(a), anyone into whose hands that original or copy comes, whether or not the identification is still present or visible;

(d) in the case of an assertion under subsection (3)(b), the licensee and anyone into whose hands a copy made in pursuance of the licence comes, whether or not he has notice of the assertion.

---

[1] Words substituted by SI 2003/2498 Sch 1 (1) para 9 (1) (b)

(5) In an action for infringement of the right the court shall, in considering remedies, take into account any delay in asserting the right.

Exceptions to right

79.—(1) The right conferred by section 77 (right to be identified as author or director) is subject to the following exceptions. **5-101**

(2) The right does not apply in relation to the following descriptions of work—

    (a) a computer program;

    (b) the design of a typeface;

    (c) any computer-generated work.

(3) The right does not apply to anything done by or with the authority of the copyright owner where copyright in the work originally [vested in the author's or director's employer by virtue of section 11(2) (works produced in the course of employment).][1]

(4) The right is not infringed by an act which by virtue of any of the following provisions would not infringe copyright in the work—

    (a) section 30 (fair dealing for certain purposes), so far as it relates to the reporting of current events by means of a sound recording, film [or broadcast][2];

    (b) section 31 (incidental inclusion of work in an artistic work, sound recording, film [or broadcast][3]);

    (c) section 32(3) (examination questions);

    (d) section 45 (parliamentary and judicial proceedings);

    (e) section 46(1) or (2) (Royal Commissions and statutory inquiries);

    (f) section 51 (use of design documents and models);

    (g) section 52 (effect of exploitation of design derived from artistic work);

    (h) [section 57 or 66A (acts permitted on assumptions as to expiry of copyright, &c)][4].

(5) The right does not apply in relation to any work made for the purpose of reporting current events.

(6) The right does not apply in relation to the publication in—

    (a) a newspaper, magazine or similar periodical, or

    (b) an encyclopaedia, dictionary, yearbook or other collective work of reference,

of a literary, dramatic, musical or artistic work made for the purposes of such publication or made available with the consent of the author for the purposes of such publication.

(7) The right does not apply in relation to—

    (a) a work in which Crown copyright or Parliamentary copyright subsists, or

    (b) a work in which copyright originally vested in an international organisation by virtue of section 168,

unless the author or director has previously been identified as such in or on published copies of the work.

---

[1] Words substituted by SI 2003/2498 Sch 1 (1) para 18 (1)

[2] Words substituted by SI 2003/2498 Sch 1 (1) para 3 (1) (g)

[3] Words substituted by SI 2003/2498 Sch 1 (1) para 3 (1) (h)

[4] Words substituted by SI 1995/3297 Pt II reg 6 (3)

Right to object to derogatory treatment of work

5-102   **80.**—(1) The author of a copyright literary, dramatic, musical or artistic work, and the director of a copyright film, has the right in the circumstances mentioned in this section not to have his work subjected to derogatory treatment.

(2) For the purposes of this section—

    (a) "treatment" of a work means any addition to, deletion from or alteration to or adaptation of the work, other than—

        (i) a translation of a literary or dramatic work, or

        (ii) an arrangement or transcription of a musical work involving no more than a change of key or register;

  and

    (b) the treatment of a work is derogatory if it amounts to distortion or mutilation of the work or is otherwise prejudicial to the honour or reputation of the author or director;

and in the following provisions of this section references to a derogatory treatment of a work shall be construed accordingly.

(3) In the case of a literary, dramatic or musical work the right is infringed by a person who—

    (a) publishes commercially, performs in public [or communicates to the public][1] a derogatory treatment of the work; or

    (b) issues to the public copies of a film or sound recording of, or including, a derogatory treatment of the work.

(4) In the case of an artistic work the right is infringed by a person who—

    (a) publishes commercially or exhibits in public a derogatory treatment of the work, [or communicates to the public][2] a visual image of a derogatory treatment of the work,

    (b) shows in public a film including a visual image of a derogatory treatment of the work or issues to the public copies of such a film, or

    (c) in the case of—

        (i) a work of architecture in the form of a model for a building,

        (ii) a sculpture, or

        (iii) a work of artistic craftsmanship,

  issues to the public copies of a graphic work representing, or of a photograph of, a derogatory treatment of the work.

(5) Subsection (4) does not apply to a work of architecture in the form of a building; but where the author of such a work is identified on the building and it is the subject of derogatory treatment he has the right to require the identification to be removed.

(6) In the case of a film, the right is infringed by a person who—

    (a) shows in public [or communicates to the public][3] a derogatory treatment of the film; or

    (b) issues to the public copies of a derogatory treatment of the film [...][4]

(7) The right conferred by this section extends to the treatment of parts of a work resulting from a previous treatment by a person other than the author or

---

[1] Words substituted by SI 2003/2498 Sch 1 (1) para 10 (1) (a)
[2] Words substituted by SI 2003/2498 Sch 1 (1) para 13 (2)
[3] Words substituted by SI 2003/2498 Sch 1 (1) para 10 (1) (b)
[4] Words repealed by SI 1995/3297 Pt II reg 9 (2)

director, if those parts are attributed to, or are likely to be regarded as the work of, the author or director.

(8) This section has effect subject to sections 81 and 82 (exceptions to and qualifications of right).

Exceptions to right

81.—(1) The right conferred by section 80 (right to object to derogatory **5-103** treatment of work) is subject to the following exceptions.

(2) The right does not apply to a computer program or to any computer-generated work.

(3) The right does not apply in relation to any work made for the purpose of reporting current events.

(4) The right does not apply in relation to the publication in—
  (a) a newspaper, magazine or similar periodical, or
  (b) an encyclopaedia, dictionary, yearbook or other collective work of reference,

of a literary, dramatic, musical or artistic work made for the purposes of such publication or made available with the consent of the author for the purposes of such publication.
Nor does the right apply in relation to any subsequent exploitation elsewhere of such a work without any modification of the published version.

(5) The right is not infringed by an act which by virtue of [section 57 or 66A (acts permitted on assumptions as to expiry of copyright, &c)][1] would not infringe copyright.

(6) The right is not infringed by anything done for the purpose of—
  (a) avoiding the commission of an offence,
  (b) complying with a duty imposed by or under an enactment, or
  (c) in the case of the British Broadcasting Corporation, avoiding the inclusion in a programme broadcast by them of anything which offends against good taste or decency or which is likely to encourage or incite to crime or to lead to disorder or to be offensive to public feeling,

provided, where the author or director is identified at the time of the relevant act or has previously been identified in or on published copies of the work, that there is a sufficient disclaimer.

Qualification of right in certain cases

82.—(1) This section applies to—   **5-104**
  (a) works in which copyright originally vested in the author's [or director's][2] employer by virtue of section 11(2) (works produced in course of employment) [...][3],
  (b) works in which Crown copyright or Parliamentary copyright subsists, and
  (c) works in which copyright originally vested in an international organisation by virtue of section 168.

(2) The right conferred by section 80 (right to object to derogatory treatment of work) does not apply to anything done in relation to such a work by or with the authority of the copyright owner unless the author or director—
  (a) is identified at the time of the relevant act, or
  (b) has previously been identified in or on published copies of the work;

---

[1] Words substituted by SI 1995/3297 Pt II reg 6 (3)
[2] Words inserted by SI 2003/2498 Sch 1 (1) para 18 (2)
[3] Words repealed by SI 2003/2498 Sch 2 para 1

and where in such a case the right does apply, it is not infringed if there is a sufficient disclaimer.

Infringement of right by possessing or dealing with infringing article

5-105   **83.**—(1) The right conferred by section 80 (right to object to derogatory treatment of work) is also infringed by a person who—

(a) possesses in the course of a business, or

(b) sells or lets for hire, or offers or exposes for sale or hire, or

(c) in the course of a business exhibits in public or distributes, or

(d) distributes otherwise than in the course of a business so as to affect pre-judicially the honour or reputation of the author or director,

an article which is, and which he knows or has reason to believe is, an infringing article.

(2) An "infringing article" means a work or a copy of a work which—

(a) has been subjected to derogatory treatment within the meaning of section 80, and

(b) has been or is likely to be the subject of any of the acts mentioned in that section in circumstances infringing that right.

False attribution of work

False attribution of work

5-106   **84.**—(1) A person has the right in the circumstances mentioned in this section—

(a) not to have a literary, dramatic, musical or artistic work falsely attributed to him as author, and

(b) not to have a film falsely attributed to him as director;

and in this section an "attribution", in relation to such a work, means a statement (express or implied) as to who is the author or director.

(2) The right is infringed by a person who—

(a) issues to the public copies of a work of any of those descriptions in or on which there is a false attribution, or

(b) exhibits in public an artistic work, or a copy of an artistic work, in or on which there is a false attribution.

(3) The right is also infringed by a person who—

(a) in the case of a literary, dramatic or musical work, performs the work in public [or communicates it to the public][1] as being the work of a person, or

(b) in the case of a film, shows it in public [or communicates it to the public][2] as being directed by a person,

knowing or having reason to believe that the attribution is false.

(4) The right is also infringed by the issue to the public or public display of material containing a false attribution in connection with any of the acts mentioned in subsection (2) or (3).

(5) The right is also infringed by a person who in the course of a business—

(a) possesses or deals with a copy of a work of any of the descriptions mentioned in subsection (1) in or on which there is a false attribution, or

---

[1] Words substituted by SI 2003/2498 Sch 1 (1) para 10 (2) (a)
[2] Words substituted by SI 2003/2498 Sch 1 (1) para 10 (2) (b)

(b) in the case of an artistic work, possesses or deals with the work itself when there is a false attribution in or on it,

knowing or having reason to believe that there is such an attribution and that it is false.

(6) In the case of an artistic work the right is also infringed by a person who in the course of a business—

(a) deals with a work which has been altered after the author parted with possession of it as being the unaltered work of the author, or

(b) deals with a copy of such a work as being a copy of the unaltered work of the author,

knowing or having reason to believe that that is not the case.

(7) References in this section to dealing are to selling or letting for hire, offering or exposing for sale or hire, exhibiting in public, or distributing.

(8) This section applies where, contrary to the fact—

(a) a literary, dramatic or musical work is falsely represented as being an adaptation of the work of a person, or

(b) a copy of an artistic work is falsely represented as being a copy made by the author of the artistic work,

as it applies where the work is falsely attributed to a person as author.

Right to privacy of certain photographs and films

Right to privacy of certain photographs and films

85.—(1) A person who for private and domestic purposes commissions the **5-107** taking of a photograph or the making a film has, where copyright subsists in the resulting work, the right not to have—

(a) copies of the work issued to the public,

(b) the work exhibited or shown in in public, or

(c) the work [communicated to the public][1];

and, except as mentioned in subsection (2), a person who does or authorises the doing of any of those acts infringes that right.

(2) The right is not infringed by an act which by virtue of any of the following provisions would not infringe copyright in the work—

(a) section 31 (incidental inclusion of work in an artistic work, film [or broadcast][2]);

(b) section 45 (parliamentary and judicial proceedings);

(c) section 46 (Royal Commissions and statutory inquiries);

(d) section 50 (acts done under statutory authority);

(e) [section 57 or 66A (acts permitted on assumptions as to expiry of copyright, &c)][3].

Supplementary

Duration of rights

86.—(1) The rights conferred by section 77 (right to be identified as author **5-108** or director), section 80 (right to object to derogatory treatment of work) and section 85 (right to privacy of certain photographs and films) continue to subsist so long as copyright subsists in the work.

---

[1] Words substituted by SI 2003/2498 Sch 1 (1) para 8 (2) (b)

[2] Words substituted by SI 2003/2498 Sch 1 (1) para 3 (1) (i)

[3] Words substituted by SI 1995/3297 Pt II reg 6 (3)

(2) The right conferred by section 84 (false attribution) continues to subsist until 20 years after a person's death.

Consent and waiver of rights

5-109 **87.**—(1) It is not an infringement of any of the rights conferred by this Chapter to do any act to which the person entitled to the right has consented.

(2) Any of those rights may be waived by instrument in writing signed by the person giving up the right.

(3) A waiver—

    (a) may relate to a specific work, to works of a specified description or to works generally, and may relate to existing or future works, and

    (b) may be conditional or unconditional and may be expressed to be subject to revocation;

and if made in favour of the owner or prospective owner of the copyright in the work or works to which it relates, it shall be presumed to extend to his licensees and successors in title unless a contrary intention is expressed.

(4) Nothing in this Chapter shall be construed as excluding the operation of the general law of contract or estoppel in relation to an informal waiver or other transaction in relation to any of the rights mentioned in subsection (1).

Application of provisions to joint works

5-110 **88.**—(1) The right conferred by section 77 (right to be identified as author or director) is, in the case of a work of joint authorship, a right of each joint author to be identified as a joint author and must be asserted in accordance with section 78 by each joint author in relation to himself.

(2) The right conferred by section 80 (right to object to derogatory treatment of work) is, in the case of a work of joint authorship, a right of each joint author and his right is satisfied if he consents to the treatment in question.

(3) A waiver under section 87 of those rights by one joint author does not affect the rights of the other joint authors.

(4) The right conferred by section 84 (false attribution) is infringed, in the circumstances mentioned in that section—

    (a) by any false statement as to the authorship of a work of joint authorship, and

    (b) by the false attribution of joint authorship in relation to a work of sole authorship;

and such a false attribution infringes the right of every person to whom authorship of any description is, whether rightly or wrongly, attributed.

(5) The above provisions also apply (with any necessary adaptations) in relation to a film which was, or is alleged to have been, jointly directed, as they apply to a work which is, or is alleged to be, a work of joint authorship.

A film is "jointly directed" if it is made by the collaboration of two or more directors and the contribution of each director is not distinct from that of the other director or directors.

(6) The right conferred by section 85 (right to privacy of certain photographs and films) is, in the case of a work made in pursuance of a joint commission, a right of each person who commissioned the making of the work, so that—

    (a) the right of each is satisfied if he consents to the act in question, and

    (b) a waiver under section 87 by one of them does not affect the rights of the others.

Application of provisions to parts of works

89.—(1) The rights conferred by section 77 (right to be identified as author **5-111** or director) and section 85 (right to privacy of certain photographs and films) apply in relation to the whole or any substantial part of a work.

(2) The rights conferred by section 80 (right to object to derogatory treatment of work) and section 84 (false attribution) apply in relation to the whole or any part of a work.

CHAPTER V

DEALINGS WITH RIGHTS IN COPYRIGHT WORKS

Copyright

Assignment and licences

90.—(1) Copyright is transmissible by assignment, by testamentary disposi- **5-112** tion or by operation of law, as personal or moveable property.

(2) An assignment or other transmission of copyright may be partial, that is, limited so as to apply—

(a) to one or more, but not all, of the things the copyright owner has the exclusive right to do;

(b) to part, but not the whole, of the period for which the copyright is to subsist.

(3) An assignment of copyright is not effective unless it is in writing signed by or on behalf of the assignor.

(4) A licence granted by a copyright owner is binding on every successor in title to his interest in the copyright, except a purchaser in good faith for valuable consideration and without notice (actual or constructive) of the licence or a person deriving title from such a purchaser; and references in this Part to doing anything with, or without, the licence of the copyright owner shall be construed accordingly.

Prospective ownership of copyright

91.—(1) Where by an agreement made in relation to future copyright, and **5-113** signed by or on behalf of the prospective owner of the copyright, the prospective owner purports to assign the future copyright (wholly or partially) to another person, then if, on the copyright coming into existence, the assignee or another person claiming under him would be entitled as against all other persons to require the copyright to be vested in him, the copyright shall vest in the assignee or his successor in title by virtue of this subsection.

(2) In this Part—

"future copyright" means copyright which will or may come into existence in respect of a future work or class of works or on the occurrence of a future event; and

"prospective owner" shall be construed accordingly, and includes a person who is prospectively entitled to copyright by virtue of such an agreement as is mentioned in subsection (1).

(3) A licence granted by a prospective owner of copyright is binding on every successor in title to his interest (or prospective interest) in the right, except a purchaser in good faith for valuable consideration and without notice (actual or constructive) of the licence or a person deriving title from such a purchaser; and

references in this Part to doing anything with, or without, the licence of the copyright owner shall be construed accordingly.

Exclusive licences

5-114   **92.**—(1) In this Part an "exclusive licence" means a licence in writing signed by or on behalf of the copyright owner authorising the licensee to the exclusion of all other persons, including the person granting the licence, to exercise a right which would otherwise be exercisable exclusively by the copyright owner.

(2) The licensee under an exclusive licence has the same rights against a successor in title who is bound by the licence as he has against the person granting the licence.

Copyright to pass under will with unpublished work

5-115   **93.** Where under a bequest (whether specific or general) a person is entitled, beneficially or otherwise, to—

> (a) an original document or other material thing recording or embodying a literary, dramatic, musical or artistic work which was not published before the death of the testator, or
>
> (b) an original material thing containing a sound recording or film which was not published before the death of the testator,

the bequest shall, unless a contrary intention is indicated in the testator's will or a codicil to it, be construed as including the copyright in the work in so far as the testator was the owner of the copyright immediately before his death.

[Presumption of transfer of rental right in case of film production agreement

5-116 ˈ   **93A.**—(1) Where an agreement concerning film production is concluded between an author and a film producer, the author shall be presumed, unless the agreement provides to the contrary, to have transferred to the film producer any rental right in relation to the film arising by virtue of the inclusion of a copy of the author's work in the film.

(2) In this section "author" means an author, or prospective author, of a literary, dramatic, musical or artistic work.

(3) Subsection (1) does not apply to any rental right in relation to the film arising by virtue of the inclusion in the film of the screenplay, the dialogue or music specifically created for and used in the film.

(4) Where this section applies, the absence of signature by or on behalf of the author does not exclude the operation of section 91(1) (effect of purported assignment of future copyright).

(5) The reference in subsection (1) to an agreement concluded between an author and a film producer includes any agreement having effect between those persons, whether made by them directly or through intermediaries.

(6) Section 93B (right to equitable remuneration on transfer of rental right) applies where there is a presumed transfer by virtue of this section as in the case of an actual transfer.][1]

---

[1] Inserted by SI 1996/2967 Pt II reg 12

[Right to equitable remuneration where rental right transferred

93B.—(1) Where an author to whom this section applies has transferred his **5-117** rental right concerning a sound recording or a film to the producer of the sound recording or film, he retains the right to equitable remuneration for the rental.

The authors to whom this section applies are-

(a) the author of a literary, dramatic, musical or artistic work, and

(b) the principal director of a film.

(2) The right to equitable remuneration under this section may not be assigned by the author except to a collecting society for the purpose of enabling it to enforce the right on his behalf.

The right is, however, transmissible by testamentary disposition or by operation of law as personal or moveable property; and it may be assigned or further transmitted by any person into whose hands it passes.

(3) Equitable remuneration under this section is payable by the person for the time being entitled to the rental right, that is, the person to whom the right was transferred or any successor in title of his.

(4) The amount payable by way of equitable remuneration is as agreed by or on behalf of the persons by and to whom it is payable, subject to section 93C (reference of amount to Copyright Tribunal).

(5) An agreement is of no effect in so far as it purports to exclude or restrict the right to equitable remuneration under this section.

(6) References in this section to the transfer of rental right by one person to another include any arrangement having that effect, whether made by them directly or through intermediaries.

(7) In this section a "collecting society" means a society or other organisation which has as its main object, or one of its main objects, the exercise of the right to equitable remuneration under this section on behalf of more than one author.][1]

[Equitable remuneration reference of amount to Copyright Tribunal

93C.—(1) In default of agreement as to the amount payable by way of **5-118** equitable remuneration under section 93B, the person by or to whom it is payable may apply to the Copyright Tribunal to determine the amount payable.

(2) A person to or by whom equitable remuneration is payable under that section may also apply to the Copyright Tribunal-

(a) to vary any agreement as to the amount payable, or

(b) to vary any previous determination of the Tribunal as to that matter;

but except with the special leave of the Tribunal no such application may be made within twelve months from the date of a previous determination.

An order made on an application under this subsection has effect from the date on which it is made or such later date as may be specified by the Tribunal.

(3) On an application under this section the Tribunal shall consider the matter and make such order as to the method of calculating and paying equitable remuneration as it may determine to be reasonable in the circumstances, taking into account the importance of the contribution of the author to the film or sound recording.

(4) Remuneration shall not be considered inequitable merely because it was paid by way of a single payment or at the time of the transfer of the rental right.

---

[1] Inserted by SI 1996/2967 Pt II reg 14 (1)

(5) An agreement is of no effect in so far as it purports to prevent a person questioning the amount of equitable remuneration or to restrict the powers of the Copyright Tribunal under this section.][1]][2]

Moral rights

Moral rights not assignable

5-119   **94.** The rights conferred by Chapter IV (moral rights) are not assignable.

Transmission of moral rights on death

5-120   **95.**—(1) On the death of a person entitled to the right conferred by section 77 (right to identification of author or director), section 80 (right to object to derogatory treatment of work) or section 85 (right to privacy of certain photographs and films)—

> (a) the right passes to such person as he may be testamentary disposition specifically direct,
>
> (b) if there is no such direction but the copyright in the work in question forms part of his estate, the right passes to the person to whom the copyright passes, and
>
> (c) if or to the extent that the right does not pass under paragraph (a) or (b) it is exercisable by his personal representatives.

(2) Where copyright forming part of a person's estate passes in part to one person and in part to another, as for example where a bequest is limited so as to apply—

> (a) to one or more, but not all, of the things the copyright owner has the exclusive right to do or authorise, or
>
> (b) to part, but not the whole, of the period for which the copyright is to subsist,

any right which passes with the copyright by virtue of subsection (1) is correspondingly divided.

(3) Where by virtue of subsection (1)(a) or (b) a right becomes exercisable by more than one person—

> (a) it may, in the case of the right conferred by section 77 (right to identification of author or director), be asserted by any of them;
>
> (b) it is, in the case of the right conferred by section 80 (right to object to derogatory treatment of work) or section 85 (right to privacy of certain photographs and films), a right exercisable by each of them and is satisfied in relation to any of them if he consents to the treatment or act in question; and
>
> (c) any waiver of the right in accordance with section 87 by one of them does not affect the rights of the others.

(4) A consent or waiver previously given or made binds any person to whom a right passes by virtue of subsection (1).

(5) Any infringement after a person's death of the right conferred by section 84 (false attribution) is actionable by his personal representatives.

(6) Any damages recovered by personal representatives by virtue of this section in respect of an infringement after a person's death shall devolve as part of his estate as if the right of action had subsisted and been vested in him immediately before his death.

---

[1] Inserted by SI 1996/2967 Pt II reg 14 (1)
[2] Inserted by SI 1996/2967 Pt II reg 14 (1)

CHAPTER VI

REMEDIES FOR INFRINGEMENT

Rights and remedies of copyright owner

Infringement actionable by copyright owner

96.—(1) An infringement of copyright is actionable by the copyright owner.   **5-121**
(2) In an action for infringement of copyright all such relief by way of damages, injunctions, accounts or otherwise is available to the plaintiff as is available in respect of the infringement of any other property right.
(3) This section has effect subject to the following provisions of this Chapter.

Provisions as to damages in infringement action

97.—(1) Where in an action for infringement of copyright it is shown that at **5-122** the time of the infringement the defendant did not know, and had no reason to believe, that copyright subsisted in the work to which the action relates, the plaintiff is not entitled to damages against him, but without prejudice to any other remedy.
(2) The court may in an action for infringement of copyright having regard to all the circumstances, and in particular to—
    (a) the flagrancy of the infringement, and
    (b) any benefit accruing to the defendant by reason of the infringement,
award such additional damages as the justice of the case may require.

[Injunctions against service providers

97A—(1) The High Court (in Scotland, the Court of Session) shall have **5-123** power to grant an injunction against a service provider, where that service provider has actual knowledge of another person using their service to infringe copyright.
(2) In determining whether a service provider has actual knowledge for the purpose of this section, a court shall take into account all matters which appear to it in the particular circumstances to be relevant and, amongst other things, shall have regard to–
    (a) whether a service provider has received a notice through a means of contact made available in accordance with regulation 6(1)(c) of the Electronic Commerce (EC Directive) Regulations 2002 (SI 2002/2013); and
    (b) the extent to which any notice includes–
        (i) the full name and address of the sender of the notice;
        (ii) details of the infringement in question.
(3) In this section "service provider" has the meaning given to it by regulation 2 of the Electronic Commerce (EC Directive) Regulations 2002.][1]

Undertaking to take licence of right in infringement proceedings

98.—(1) If in proceedings for infringement of copyright in respect of which a **5-124** licence is available as of right under section 144 (powers exercisable in conse-quence of report of [Competition Commission][2]) the defendant undertakes to

---

[1] Inserted by SI 2003/2498 Pt II reg 27 (1)
[2] Words substituted by SI 1999/506 Pt II art 23

take a licence on such terms as may be agreed or, in default of agreement, settled by the Copyright Tribunal under that section—

    (a) no injunction shall be granted against him,

    (b) no order for delivery up shall be made under section 99, and

    (c) the amount recoverable against him by way of damages or on an account of profits shall not exceed double the amount which would have been payable by him as licensee if such a licence on those terms had been granted before the earliest infringement.

(2) An undertaking may be given at any time before final order in the proceedings, without any admission of liability.

(3) Nothing in this section affects the remedies available in respect of an infringement committed before licences of right were available.

Order for delivery up

5-125   **99.**—(1) Where a person—

    (a) has an infringing copy of a work in his possession, custody or control in the course of a business, or

    (b) has in his possession, custody or control an article specifically designed or adapted for making copies of a particular copyright work, knowing or having reason to believe that it has been or is to be used to make infringing copies,

the owner of the copyright in the work may apply to the court for an order that the infringing copy or article be delivered up to him or to such other person as the court may direct.

(2) An application shall not be made after the end of the period specified in section 113 (period after which remedy of delivery up not available); and no order shall be made unless the court also makes, or it appears to the court that there are grounds for making, an order under section 114 (order as to disposal of infringing copy or other article).

(3) A person to whom an infringing copy or other article is delivered up in pursuance of an order under this section shall, if an order under section 114 is not made, retain it pending the making of an order, or the decision not to make an order, under that section.

(4) Nothing in this section affects any other power of the court.

Right to seize infringing copies and other articles

5-126   **100.**—(1) An infringing copy of a work which is found exposed or otherwise immediately available for sale or hire, and in respect of which the copyright owner would be entitled to apply for an order under section 99, may be seized and detained by him or a person authorised by him.

The right to seize and detain is exercisable subject to the following conditions and is subject to any decision of the court under section 114.

(2) Before anything is seized under this section notice of the time and place of the proposed seizure must be given to a local police station.

(3) A person may for the purpose of exercising the right conferred by this section enter premises to which the public have access but may not seize anything in the possession, custody or control of a person at a permanent or regular place of business of his, and may not use any force.

(4) At the time when anything is seized under this section there shall be left at the place where it was seized a notice in the prescribed form containing the prescribed particulars as to the person by whom or on whose authority the seizure is made and the grounds on which it is made.

(5) In this section—

"premises" includes land, buildings, moveable structures, vehicles, vessels, aircraft and hovercraft; and

"prescribed" means prescribed by order of the Secretary of State.

(6) An order of the Secretary of State under this section shall be made by statutory instrument which shall be subject to annulment in pursuance of a resolution of either House of Parliament.

Rights and remedies of exclusive licensee

Rights and remedies of exclusive licensee

101.—(1) An exclusive licensee has, except against the copyright owner, the **5-127** same rights and remedies in respect of matters occurring after the grant of the licence as if the licence had been an assignment.

(2) His rights and remedies are concurrent with those of the copyright owner; and references in the relevant provisions of this Part to the copyright owner shall be construed accordingly.

(3) In an action brought by an exclusive licensee by virtue of this section a defendant may avail himself of any defence which would have been available to him if the action had been brought by the copyright owner.

[Certain infringements actionable by a non-exclusive licensee

101A—(1) A non-exclusive licensee may bring an action for infringement of **5-128** copyright if –

(a) the infringing act was directly connected to a prior licensed act of the licensee; and

(b) the licence –

(i) is in writing and is signed by or on behalf of the copyright owner; and

(ii) expressly grants the non-exclusive licensee a right of action under this section.

(2) In an action brought under this section, the non-exclusive licensee shall have the same rights and remedies available to him as the copyright owner would have had if he had brought the action.

(3) The rights granted under this section are concurrent with those of the copyright owner and references in the relevant provisions of this Part to the copyright owner shall be construed accordingly.

(4) In an action brought by a non-exclusive licensee by virtue of this section a defendant may avail himself of any defence which would have been available to him if the action had been brought by the copyright owner.

(5) Subsections (1) to (4) of section 102 shall apply to a non-exclusive licensee who has a right of action by virtue of this section as it applies to an exclusive licensee.

(6) In this section a "non-exclusive licensee" means the holder of a licence authorising the licensee to exercise a right which remains exercisable by the copyright owner.][1]

Exercise of concurrent rights

102.—(1) Where an action for infringement of copyright brought by the **5-129** copyright owner or an exclusive licensee relates (wholly or partly) to an infringe-

---

[1] Inserted by SI 2003/2498 Pt II reg 28

ment in respect of which they have concurrent rights of action, the copyright owner or, as the case may be, the exclusive licensee may not, without the leave of the court, proceed with the action unless the other is either joined as a plaintiff or added as a defendant.

(2) A copyright owner or exclusive licensee who is added as a defendant in pursuance of subsection (1) is not liable for any costs in the action unless he takes part in the proceedings.

(3) The above provisions do not affect the granting of interlocutory relief on an application by a copyright owner or exclusive licensee alone.

(4) Where an action for infringement of copyright is brought which relates (wholly or partly) to an infringement in respect of which the copyright owner and an exclusive licensee have or had concurrent rights of action—

    (a) the court shall in assessing damages take into account—
        (i) the terms of the licence, and
        (ii) any pecuniary remedy already awarded or available to either of them in respect of the infringement;
    (b) no account of profits shall be directed if an award of damages has been made, or an account of profits has been directed, in favour of the other of them in respect of the infringement; and
    (c) the court shall if an account of profits is directed apportion the profits between them as the court considers just, subject to any agreement between them;

and these provisions apply whether or not the copyright owner and the exclusive licensee are both parties to the action.

(5) The copyright owner shall notify any exclusive licensee having concurrent rights before applying for an order under section 99 (order for delivery up) or exercising the right conferred by section 100 (right of seizure); and the court may on the application of the licensee make such order under section 99 or, as the case may be, prohibiting or permitting the exercise by the copyright owner of the right conferred by section 100, as it thinks fit having regard to the terms of the licence.

Remedies for infringement of moral rights

Remedies for infringement of moral rights

5-130   **103.**—(1) An infringement of a right conferred by Chapter IV (moral rights) is actionable as a breach of statutory duty owed to the person entitled to the right.

(2) In proceedings for infringement of the right conferred by section 80 (right to object to derogatory treatment of work) the court may, if it thinks it is an adequate remedy in the circumstances, grant an injunction on terms prohibiting the doing of any act unless a disclaimer is made, in such terms and in such manner as may be approved by the court, dissociating the author or director from the treatment of the work.

Presumptions

Presumptions relevant to literary, dramatic, musical and artistic works

5-131   **104.**—(1) The following presumptions apply in proceedings brought by virtue of this Chapter with respect to a literary, dramatic, musical or artistic work.

(2) Where a name purporting to be that of the author appeared on copies of the work as published or on the work when it was made, the person whose name appeared shall be presumed, until the contrary is proved—

(a) to be the author of the work;

(b) to have made it in circumstances not falling within section 11(2), 163, 165 or 168 (works produced in course of employment, Crown copyright, Parliamentary copyright or copyright of certain international organisations).

(3) In the case of a work alleged to be a work of joint authorship, subsection (2) applies in relation to each person alleged to be one of the authors.

(4) Where no name purporting to be that of the author appeared as mentioned in subsection (2) but—

(a) the work qualifies for copyright protection by virtue of section 155 (qualification by reference to country of first publication), and

(b) a name purporting to be that of the publisher appeared on copies of the work as first published,

the person whose name appeared shall be presumed, until the contrary is proved, to have been the owner of the copyright at the time of publication.

(5) If the author of the work is dead or the identity of the author cannot be ascertained by reasonable inquiry, it shall be presumed, in the absence of evidence to the contrary—

(a) that the work is an original work, and

(b) that the plaintiff's allegations as to what was the first publication of the work and as to the country of first publication are correct.

Presumptions relevant to sound recordings and films

105.—(1) In proceedings brought by virtue of this Chapter with respect to a **5-132** sound recording, where copies of the recording as issued to the public bear a label or other mark stating—

(a) that a named person was the owner of copyright in the recording at the date of issue of the copies, or

(b) that the recording was first published in a specified year or in a specified country,

the label or mark shall be admissible as evidence of the facts stated and shall be presumed to be correct until the contrary is proved.

(2) In proceedings brought by virtue of this Chapter with respect to a film, where copies of the film as issued to the public bear a statement—

(a) that a named person was the [director or producer][1] of the film,

[(aa) that a named person was the principal director, the author of the screenplay, the author of the dialogue or the composer of music specifically created for and used in the film,][2]

(b) that a named person was the owner of copyright in the film at the date of issue of the copies, or

(c) that the film was first published in a specified year or in a specified country,

the statement shall be admissible as evidence of the facts stated and shall be presumed to be correct until the contrary is proved.

(3) In proceedings brought by virtue of this Chapter with respect to a computer program, where copies of the program are issued to the public in electronic form bearing a statement—

---

[1] Words substituted by SI 1996/2967 Pt II reg 18 (4) (a)

[2] Inserted by SI 1995/3297 Pt II reg 6 (4)

(a) that a named person was the owner of copyright in the program at the date of issue of the copies, or

(b) that the program was first published in a specified country or that copies of it were first issued to the public in electronic form in a specified year,

the statement shall be admissible as evidence of the facts stated and shall be presumed to be correct until the contrary is proved.

(4) The above presumptions apply equally in proceedings relating to an infringement alleged to have occurred before the date on which the copies were issued to the public.

(5) In proceedings brought by virtue of this Chapter with respect to a film, where the film as shown in public [or communicated to the public][1] bears a statement—

(a) that a named person was the [director or producer][2] of the film, or

[(aa) that a named person was the principal director of the film, the author of the screenplay, the author of the dialogue or the composer of music specifically created for and used in the film, or,][3]

(b) that a named person was the owner of copyright in the film immediately after it was made,

the statement shall be admissible as evidence of the facts stated and shall be presumed to be correct until the contrary is proved.

This presumption applies equally in proceedings relating to an infringement alleged to have occurred before the date on which the film was shown in public [or communicated to the public][4].

[(6) For the purposes of this section, a statement that a person was the director of a film shall be taken, unless a contrary indication appears, as meaning that he was the principal director of the film.][5]

Presumptions relevant to works subject to Crown copyright

5-133   **106.** In proceedings brought by virtue of this Chapter with respect to a literary, dramatic or musical work in which Crown copyright subsists, where there appears on printed copies of the work a statement of the year in which the work was first published commercially, that statement shall be admissible as evidence of the fact stated and shall be presumed to be correct in the absence of evidence to the contrary.

Offences

Criminal liability for making or dealing with infringing articles, &c

5-134   **107.**—(1) A person commits an offence who, without the licence of the copyright owner—

(a) makes for sale or hire, or

(b) imports into the United Kingdom otherwise than for his private and domestic use, or

(c) possesses in the course of a business with a view to committing any act infringing the copyright, or

(d) in the course of a business—

---

[1] Words substituted by SI 2003/2498 Sch 1 (1) para 8 (1) (c)
[2] Words substituted by SI 1996/2967 Pt II reg 18 (4) (a)
[3] Inserted by SI 1996/2967 Pt II reg 18 (4) (b)
[4] Words by SI 2003/2498 Sch 1 (1) para 8 (1) (c)
[5] Inserted by SI 1996/2967 Pt II reg 18 (4) (c)

      (i) sells or lets for hire, or

      (ii) offers or exposes for sale or hire, or

      (iii) exhibits in public, or

      (iv) distributes, or

   (e) distributes otherwise than in the course of a business to such an extent as to affect prejudicially the owner of the copyright,

an article which is, and which he knows or has reason to believe is, an infringing copy of a copyright work.

   (2) A person commits an offence who—

   (a) makes an article specifically designed or adapted for making copies of a particular copyright work, or

   (b) has such an article in his possession,

knowing or having reason to believe that it is to be used to make infringing copies for sale or hire or for use in the course of a business.

   [(2A) A person who infringes copyright in a work by communicating the work to the public –

   (a) in the course of a business, or

   (b) otherwise than in the course of a business to such an extent as to affect prejudicially the owner of the copyright,

commits an offence if he knows or has reason to believe that, by doing so, he is infringing copyright in that work.][1]

   (3) Where copyright is infringed (otherwise than by reception of a [communication to the public][2])—

   (a) by the public performance of a literary, dramatic or musical work, or

   (b) by the playing or showing in public of a sound recording or film,

any person who caused the work to be so performed, played or shown is guilty of an offence if he knew or had reason to believe that copyright would be infringed.

   (4) A person guilty of an offence under subsection (1)(a), (b), (d)(iv) or (e) is liable—

   (a) on summary conviction to imprisonment for a term not exceeding six months or a fine not exceeding the statutory maximum, or both;

   (b) on conviction on indictment to a fine or imprisonment for a term not exceeding [ten][3] years, or both.

   [(4A) A person guilty of an offence under subsection (2A) is liable –

   (a) on summary conviction to imprisonment for a term not exceeding three months or a fine not exceeding the statutory maximum, or both;

   (b) on conviction on indictment to a fine or imprisonment for a term not exceeding two years, or both.][4]

   (5) A person guilty of any other offence under this section is liable on summary conviction to imprisonment for a term not exceeding six months or a fine not exceeding level 5 on the standard scale, or both.

   (6) Sections 104 to 106 (presumptions as to various matters connected with copyright) do not apply to proceedings for an offence under this section; but without prejudice to their application in proceedings for an order under section 108 below.

---

[1] Inserted by SI 2003/2498 Pt II reg 26 (1) (a)

[2] Words substituted by SI 2003/2498 Sch 1 (1) para 9 (2)

[3] Word substituted by Copyright, etc. and Trade Marks (Offences and Enforcement) Act 2002 c.25 s 1 (2)

[4] Inserted by SI 2003/2498 Pt II reg 26 (1) (b)

Order for delivery up in criminal proceedings

5-135   **108.**—(1) The court before which proceedings are brought against a person for an offence under section 107 may, if satisfied that at the time of his arrest or charge—

(a) he had in his possession, custody or control in the course of a business an infringing copy of a copyright work, or

(b) he had in his possession, custody or control an article specifically designed or adapted for making copies of a particular copyright work, knowing or having reason to believe that it had been or was to be used to make infringing copies,

order that the infringing copy or article be delivered up to the copyright owner or to such other person as the court may direct.

(2) For this purpose a person shall be treated as charged with an offence—

(a) in England, Wales and Northern Ireland, when he is orally charged or is served with a summons or indictment;

(b) in Scotland, when he is cautioned, charged or served with a complaint or indictment.

(3) An order may be made by the court of its own motion or on the application of the prosecutor (or, in Scotland, the Lord Advocate or procurator-fiscal), and may be made whether or not the person is convicted of the offence, but shall not be made—

(a) after the end of the period specified in section 113 (period after which remedy of delivery up not available), or

(b) if it appears to the court unlikely that any order will be made under section 114 (order as to disposal of infringing copy or other article).

(4) An appeal lies from an order made under this section by a magistrates' court—

(a) in England and Wales, to the Crown Court, and

(b) in Northern Ireland, to the county court;

and in Scotland, where an order has been made under this section, the person from whose possession, custody or control the infringing copy or article has been removed may, without prejudice to any other form of appeal under any rule of law, appeal against that order in the same manner as against sentence.

(5) A person to whom an infringing copy or other article is delivered up in pursuance of an order under this section shall retain it pending the making of an order, or the decision not to make an order, under section 114.

(6) Nothing in this section affects the powers of the court under [section 143 of the Powers of Criminal Courts (Sentencing) Act 2000][1], [Part II of the Proceeds of Crime (Scotland) Act 1995][2] or Article 7 of the Criminal Justice (Northern Ireland) Order 1980 (general provisions as to forfeiture in criminal proceedings).

Search warrants

5-136   **109.**—(1) Where a justice of the peace (in Scotland, a sheriff or justice of the peace) is satisfied by information on oath given by a constable (in Scotland, by evidence on oath) that there are reasonable grounds for believing—

(a) that an offence under [section 107(1), (2) or (2A)][3] has been or is about to be committed in any premises, and

---

[1] Words substituted by Powers of Criminal Courts (Sentencing) Act 2000 c.6 Sch 9 para 115

[2] Words substituted by Criminal Procedure (Consequential Provisions) (Scotland) Act 1995 c.40 Sch 4 para 70 (2)

[3] Words substituted by SI 2003/2498 Pt II reg 26 (2) (i)

(b) that evidence that such an offence has been or is about to be committed is in those premises,

he may issue a warrant authorising a constable to enter and search the premises, using such reasonable force as is necessary.

(2) The power conferred by subsection (1) does not, in England and Wales, extend to authorising a search for material of the kinds mentioned in section 9(2) of the Police and Criminal Evidence Act 1984 (certain classes of personal or confidential material).

(3) A warrant under this section—
    (a) may authorise persons to accompany any constable executing the warrant, and
    (b) remains in force for 28 days from the date of its issue.

(4) In executing a warrant issued under this section a constable may seize an article if he reasonably believes that it is evidence that any offence under [section 107(1), (2) or (2A)][1] has been or is about to be committed.

(5) In this section "premises" includes land, buildings, [fixed or][2] moveable structures, vehicles, vessels, aircraft and hovercraft.

Offence by body corporate: liability of officers

110.—(1) Where an offence under section 107 committed by a body **5-137** corporate is proved to have been committed with the consent or connivance of a director, manager, secretary or other similar officer of the body, or a person purporting to act in any such capacity, he as well as the body corporate is guilty of the offence and liable to be proceeded against and punished accordingly.

(2) In relation to a body corporate whose affairs are managed by its members "director" means a member of the body corporate.

Provision for preventing importation of infringing copies

Infringing copies may be treated as prohibited goods

111.—(1) The owner of the copyright in a published literary, dramatic or **5-138** musical work may give notice in writing to the Commissioners of Customs and Excise—
    (a) that he is the owner of the copyright in the work, and
    (b) that he requests the Commissioners, for a period specified in the notice, to treat as prohibited goods printed copies of the work which are infringing copies.

(2) The period specified in a notice under subsection (1) shall not exceed five years and shall not extend beyond the period for which copyright is to subsist.

(3) The owner of the copyright in a sound recording or film may give notice in writing to the Commissioners of Customs and Excise—
    (a) that he is the owner of the copyright in the work,
    (b) that infringing copies of the work are expected to arrive in the United Kingdom at a time and a place specified in the notice, and
    (c) that he requests the Commissioners to treat the copies as prohibited goods.

[(3A) The Commissioners may treat as prohibited goods only infringing copies of works which arrive in the United Kingdom—

---

[1] Words substituted by SI 2003/2498 Pt II reg 26 (2) (ii)
[2] Words inserted by Copyright, etc. and Trade Marks (Offences and Enforcement) Act 2002 c.25 s 2 (2) (c)

(a) from outside the European Economic Area, or

(b) from within that Area but not having been entered for free circulation.

(3B) This section does not apply to goods entered, or expected to be entered, for free circulation, export, re-export or for a suspensive procedure in respect of which an application may be made under Article 3(1) of Council Regulation (EC) No. 3295/94 laying down measures to prohibit the release for free circulation, export, re-export or entry for a suspensive procedure of counterfeit and pirated goods.][1]

(4) When a notice is in force under this section the importation of goods to which the notice relates, otherwise than by a person for his private and domestic use, [subject to subsections (3A) and (3B), is prohibited][2]; but a person is not by reason of the prohibition liable to any penalty other than forfeiture of the goods.

Supplementary

Period after which remedy of delivery up not available

5-139   **113.**—(1) An application for an order under section 99 (order for delivery up in civil proceedings) may not be made after the end of the period of six years from the date on which the infringing copy or article in question was made, subject to the following provisions.

(2) If during the whole or any part of that period the copyright owner—

(a) is under a disability, or

(b) is prevented by fraud or concealment from discovering the facts entitling him to apply for an order,

an application may be made at any time before the end of the period of six years from the date on which he ceased to be under a disability or, as the case may be, could with reasonable diligence have discovered those facts.

(3) In subsection (2) "disability"—

(a) in England and Wales, has the same meaning as in the Limitation Act 1980;

(b) in Scotland, means legal disability within the meaning of the Prescription and Limitation (Scotland) Act 1973;

(c) in Northern Ireland, has the same meaning as in the Statute of Limitations (Northern Ireland) 1958.

(4) An order under section 108 (order for delivery up in criminal proceedings) shall not, in any case, be made after the end of the period of six years from the date on which the infringing copy or article in question was made.

Order as to disposal of infringing copy or other article

5-140   **114.**—(1) An application may be made to the court for an order that an infringing copy or other article delivered up in pursuance of an order under section 99 or 108, or seized and detained in pursuance of the right conferred by section 100, shall be—

(a) forfeited to the copyright owner, or

(b) destroyed or otherwise dealt with as the court may think fit,

or for a decision that no such order should be made.

(2) In considering what order (if any) should be made, the court shall consider whether other remedies available in an action for infringement of

---

[1] Inserted by SI 1995/1445 reg 2 (2)

[2] Words substituted by SI 1995/1445 reg 2 (3)

copyright would be adequate to compensate the copyright owner and to protect his interests.

(3) Provision shall be made by rules of court as to the service of notice on persons having an interest in the copy or other articles, and any such person is entitled—

(a) to appear in proceedings for an order under this section, whether or not he was served with notice, and

(b) to appeal against any order made, whether or not he appeared;

and an order shall not take effect until the end of the period within which notice of an appeal may be given or, if before the end of that period notice of appeal is duly given, until the final determination or abandonment of the proceedings on the appeal.

(4) Where there is more than one person interested in a copy or other article, the court shall make such order as it thinks just and may (in particular) direct that the article be sold, or otherwise dealt with, and the proceeds divided.

(5) If the court decides that no order should be made under this section, the person in whose possession, custody or control the copy or other article was before being delivered up or seized is entitled to its return.

(6) References in this section to a person having an interest in a copy or other article include any person in whose favour an order could be made in respect of it under this section or under section 204 or 231 of this Act or [section 19 of the Trade Marks Act 1994][1] (which make similar provision in relation to infringement of rights in performances, design right and trade marks).

[Forfeiture of infringing copies, etc.: England and Wales or Northern Ireland

114A—(1) In England and Wales or Northern Ireland where there have come **5-141** into the possession of any person in connection with the investigation or prosecution of a relevant offence—

(a) infringing copies of a copyright work, or

(b) articles specifically designed or adapted for making copies of a particular copyright work,

that person may apply under this section for an order for the forfeiture of the infringing copies or articles.

(2) For the purposes of this section "relevant offence" means—

(a) an offence under [section 107(1), (2) or (2A)][2] (criminal liability for making or dealing with infringing articles, etc.),

(b) an offence under the Trade Descriptions Act 1968 (c. 29), or

(c) an offence involving dishonesty or deception.

(3) An application under this section may be made—

(a) where proceedings have been brought in any court for a relevant offence relating to some or all of the infringing copies or articles, to that court, or

(b) where no application for the forfeiture of the infringing copies or articles has been made under paragraph (a), by way of complaint to a magistrates' court.

(4) On an application under this section, the court shall make an order for the forfeiture of any infringing copies or articles only if it is satisfied that a relevant offence has been committed in relation to the infringing copies or articles.

---

[1] Words substituted by Trade Marks Act 1994 c.26 Sch 4 para 8 (2)

[2] Words substituted by SI 2003/2498 Pt II reg 26 (2) (iii)

(5) A court may infer for the purposes of this section that such an offence has been committed in relation to any infringing copies or articles if it is satisfied that such an offence has been committed in relation to infringing copies or articles which are representative of the infringing copies or articles in question (whether by reason of being of the same design or part of the same consignment or batch or otherwise).

(6) Any person aggrieved by an order made under this section by a magistrates' court, or by a decision of such a court not to make such an order, may appeal against that order or decision—

    (a) in England and Wales, to the Crown Court, or

    (b) in Northern Ireland, to the county court.

(7) An order under this section may contain such provision as appears to the court to be appropriate for delaying the coming into force of the order pending the making and determination of any appeal (including any application under section 111 of the Magistrates' Courts Act 1980 (c. 43) or Article 146 of the Magistrates' Courts (Northern Ireland) Order 1981 (S.I. 1981/1675 (N.I. 26)) (statement of case)).

(8) Subject to subsection (9), where any infringing copies or articles are forfeited under this section they shall be destroyed in accordance with such directions as the court may give.

(9) On making an order under this section the court may direct that the infringing copies or articles to which the order relates shall (instead of being destroyed) be forfeited to the owner of the copyright in question or dealt with in such other way as the court considers appropriate.][1]

[Forfeiture of infringing copies, etc.: Scotland

5-142   **114B**—(1) In Scotland the court may make an order under this section for the forfeiture of any—

    (a) infringing copies of a copyright work, or

    (b) articles specifically designed or adapted for making copies of a particular copyright work.

(2) An order under this section may be made—

    (a) on an application by the procurator-fiscal made in the manner specified in section 134 of the Criminal Procedure (Scotland) Act 1995 (c. 46), or

    (b) where a person is convicted of a relevant offence, in addition to any other penalty which the court may impose.

(3) On an application under subsection (2)(a), the court shall make an order for the forfeiture of any infringing copies or articles only if it is satisfied that a relevant offence has been committed in relation to the infringing copies or articles.

(4) The court may infer for the purposes of this section that such an offence has been committed in relation to any infringing copies or articles if it is satisfied that such an offence has been committed in relation to infringing copies or articles which are representative of the infringing copies or articles in question (whether by reason of being of the same design or part of the same consignment or batch or otherwise).

(5) The procurator-fiscal making the application under subsection (2)(a) shall serve on any person appearing to him to be the owner of, or otherwise to have an interest in, the infringing copies or articles to which the application relates a copy of the application, together with a notice giving him the opportu-

---

[1] Inserted by Copyright, etc. and Trade Marks (Offences and Enforcement) Act 2002 c.25 s 3

nity to appear at the hearing of the application to show cause why the infringing copies or articles should not be forfeited.

(6) Service under subsection (5) shall be carried out, and such service may be proved, in the manner specified for citation of an accused in summary proceedings under the Criminal Procedure (Scotland) Act 1995.

(7) Any person upon whom notice is served under subsection (5) and any other person claiming to be the owner of, or otherwise to have an interest in, infringing copies or articles to which an application under this section relates shall be entitled to appear at the hearing of the application to show cause why the infringing copies or articles should not be forfeited.

(8) The court shall not make an order following an application under subsection (2)(a)—

    (a) if any person on whom notice is served under subsection (5) does not appear, unless service of the notice on that person is proved, or

    (b) if no notice under subsection (5) has been served, unless the court is satisfied that in the circumstances it was reasonable not to serve such notice.

(9) Where an order for the forfeiture of any infringing copies or articles is made following an application under subsection (2)(a), any person who appeared, or was entitled to appear, to show cause why infringing copies or articles should not be forfeited may, within 21 days of the making of the order, appeal to the High Court by Bill of Suspension.

(10) Section 182(5)(a) to (e) of the Criminal Procedure (Scotland) Act 1995 (c. 46) shall apply to an appeal under subsection (9) as it applies to a stated case under Part 2 of that Act.

(11) An order following an application under subsection (2)(a) shall not take effect—

    (a) until the end of the period of 21 days beginning with the day after the day on which the order is made, or

    (b) if an appeal is made under subsection (9) above within that period, until the appeal is determined or abandoned.

(12) An order under subsection (2)(b) shall not take effect—

    (a) until the end of the period within which an appeal against the order could be brought under the Criminal Procedure (Scotland) Act 1995, or

    (b) if an appeal is made within that period, until the appeal is determined or abandoned.

(13) Subject to subsection (14), infringing copies or articles forfeited under this section shall be destroyed in accordance with such directions as the court may give.

(14) On making an order under this section the court may direct that the infringing copies or articles to which the order relates shall (instead of being destroyed) be forfeited to the owner of the copyright in question or dealt with in such other way as the court considers appropriate.

(15) For the purposes of this section—

    "relevant offence" means an offence under [section 107(1), (2) or (2A)][1] (criminal liability for making or dealing with infringing articles, etc.), or under the Trade Descriptions Act 1968 (c. 29) or any offence involving dishonesty or deception;

    "the court" means—

---

[1] Words substituted by SI 2003/2498 Pt II reg 26 (2) (iv)

(a) in relation to an order made on an application under subsection (2)(a), the sheriff, and

(b) in relation to an order made under subsection (2)(b), the court which imposed the penalty.][1]

Jurisdiction of county court and sheriff court

5-143 **115.**—(1) In England, Wales and Northern Ireland a county court may entertain proceedings under—

section 99 (order for delivery up of infringing copy or other article),

section 102(5) (order as to exercise of rights by copyright owner where exclusive licensee has concurrent rights), or

section 114 (order as to disposal of infringing copy or other article),

[save that, in Northern Ireland, a county court may entertain such proceedings only][2] where the value of the infringing copies and other articles in question does not exceed the county court limit for actions in tort.

(2) In Scotland proceedings for an order under any of those provisions may be brought in the sheriff court.

(3) Nothing in this section shall be construed as affecting the jurisdiction of the High Court or, in Scotland, the Court of Session.

CHAPTER VII

COPYRIGHT LICENSING

Licensing schemes and licensing bodies

Licensing schemes and licensing bodies

5-144 **116.**—(1) In this Part a "licensing scheme" means a scheme setting out—

(a) the classes of case in which the operator of the scheme, or the person on whose behalf he acts, is willing to grant copyright licences, and

(b) the terms on which licences would be granted in those classes of case;

and for this purpose a "scheme" includes anything in the nature of a scheme, whether described as a scheme or as a tariff or by any other name.

(2) In this Chapter a "licensing body" means a society or other organisation which has as its main object, or one of its main objects, the negotiation or granting, either as owner or prospective owner of copyright or as agent for him, of copyright licences, and whose objects include the granting of licences covering works of more than one author.

(3) In this section "copyright licences" means licences to do, or authorise the doing of, any of the acts restricted by copyright.

(4) References in this Chapter to licences or licensing schemes covering works of more than one author do not include licences or schemes covering only—

(a) a single collective work or collective works of which the authors are the same, or

(b) works made by, or by employees of or commissioned by, a single individual, firm, company or group of companies.

---

[1] Inserted by Copyright, etc. and Trade Marks (Offences and Enforcement) Act 2002 c.25 s 3
[2] Words inserted by SI 1991/724 Sch 1 Pt I para 1

For this purpose a group of companies means a holding company and its subsidiaries, within the meaning of section 736 of the Companies Act 1985.

References and applications with respect to licensing schemes

[Licensing schemes to which following sections apply

117. Sections 118 to 123 (references and applications with respect to licensing **5-145** schemes) apply to licensing schemes which are operated by licensing bodies and cover works of more than one author, so far as they relate to licences for-

(a) copying the work,

(b) rental or lending of copies of the work to the public,

(c) performing, showing or playing the work in public, or

[(d) communicating the work to the public;]¹

and references in those sections to a licensing scheme shall be construed accordingly.]²

Reference of proposed licensing scheme to tribunal

118.—(1) The terms of a licensing scheme proposed to be operated by a **5-146** licensing body may be referred to the Copyright Tribunal by an organisation claiming to be representative of persons claiming that they require licences in cases of a description to which the scheme would apply, either generally or in relation to any description of case.

(2) The Tribunal shall first decide whether to entertain the reference, and may decline to do so on the ground that the reference is premature.

(3) If the Tribunal decides to entertain the reference it shall consider the matter referred and make such order, either confirming or varying the proposed scheme, either generally or so far as it relates to cases of the description to which the reference relates, as the Tribunal may determine to be reasonable in the circumstances.

(4) The order may be made so as to be in force indefinitely or for such period as the Tribunal may determine.

Reference of licensing scheme to tribunal

119.—(1) If while a licensing scheme is in operation a dispute arises between **5-147** the operator of the scheme and—

(a) a person claiming that he requires a licence in a case of a description to which the scheme applies, or

(b) an organisation claiming to be representative of such persons,

that person or organisation may refer the scheme to the Copyright Tribunal in so far as it relates to cases of that description.

(2) A scheme which has been referred to the Tribunal under this section shall remain in operation until proceedings on the reference are concluded.

(3) The Tribunal shall consider the matter in dispute and make such order, either confirming or varying the scheme so far as it relates to cases of the description to which the reference relates, as the Tribunal may determine to be reasonable in the circumstances.

(4) The order may be made so as to be in force indefinitely or for such period as the Tribunal may determine.

¹ Substituted by SI 2003/2498 Sch 1 Pt I para 4 (4)
² Substituted by SI 1996/2967 Pt II reg 15 (2)

Further reference of scheme to tribunal

5-148   **120.**—(1) Where the Copyright Tribunal has on a previous reference of a licensing scheme under [section 118, 119 or 128A][1], or under this section, made an order with respect to the scheme, then, while the order remains in force—

(a) the operator of the scheme,

(b) a person claiming that he requires a licence in a case of the description to which the order applies, or

(c) an organisation claiming to be representative of such persons,

may refer the scheme again to the Tribunal so far as it relates to cases of that description.

(2) A licensing scheme shall not, except with the special leave of the Tribunal, be referred again to the Tribunal in respect of the same description of cases—

(a) within twelve months from the date of the order on the previous reference, or

(b) if the order was made so as to be in force for 15 months or less, until the last three months before the expiry of the order.

(3) A scheme which has been referred to the Tribunal under this section shall remain in operation until proceedings on the reference are concluded.

(4) The Tribunal shall consider the matter in dispute and make such order, either confirming, varying or further varying the scheme so far as it relates to cases of the description to which the reference relates, as the Tribunal may determine to be reasonable in the circumstances.

(5) The order may be made so as to be in force indefinitely or for such period as the Tribunal may determine.

Application for grant of licence in connection with licensing scheme

5-149   **121.**—(1) A person who claims, in a case covered by a licensing scheme, that the operator of the scheme has refused to grant him or procure the grant to him of a licence in accordance with the scheme, or has failed to do so within a reasonable time after being asked, may apply to the Copyright Tribunal.

(2) A person who claims, in a case excluded from a licensing scheme, that the operator of the scheme either—

(a) has refused to grant him a licence or procure the grant to him of a licence, or has failed to do so within a reasonable time of being asked, and that in the circumstances it is unreasonable that a licence should not be granted, or

(b) proposes terms for a licence which are unreasonable,

may apply to the Copyright Tribunal.

(3) A case shall be regarded as excluded from a licensing scheme for the purposes of subsection (2) if—

(a) the scheme provides for the grant of licences subject to terms excepting matters from the licence and the case falls within such an exception, or

(b) the case is so similar to those in which licences are granted under the scheme that it is unreasonable that it should not be dealt with in the same way.

(4) If the Tribunal is satisfied that the claim is well-founded, it shall make an order declaring that, in respect of the matters specified in the order, the applicant is entitled to a licence on such terms as the Tribunal may determine to be

---

[1] Words substituted by SI 2003/2498 Pt II reg 21 (4)

applicable in accordance with the scheme or, as the case may be, to be reasonable in the circumstances.

(5) The order may be made so as to be in force indefinitely or for such period as the Tribunal may determine.

Application for review of order as to entitlement to licence

122.—(1) Where the Copyright Tribunal has made an order under section **5-150** 121 that a person is entitled to a licence under a licensing scheme, the operator of the scheme or the original applicant may apply to the Tribunal to review its order.

(2) An application shall not be made, except with the special leave of the Tribunal—

    (a) within twelve months from the date of the order, or of the decision on a previous application under this section, or

    (b) if the order was made so as to be in force for 15 months or less, or as a result of the decision on a previous application under this section is due to expire within 15 months of that decision, until the last three months before the expiry date.

(3) The Tribunal shall on an application for review confirm or vary its order as the Tribunal may determine to be reasonable having regard to the terms applicable in accordance with the licensing scheme or, as the case may be, the circumstances of the case.

Effect of order of tribunal as to licensing scheme

123.—(1) A licensing scheme which has been confirmed or varied by the **5-151** Copyright Tribunal—

    (a) under section 118 (reference of terms of proposed scheme), or

    (b) under section 119 or 120 (reference of existing scheme to Tribunal),

shall be in force or, as the case may be, remain in operation, so far as it relates to the description of case in respect of which the order was made, so long as the order remains in force.

(2) While the order is in force a person who in a case of a class to which the order applies—

    (a) pays to the operator of the scheme any charges payable under the scheme in respect of a licence covering the case in question or, if the amount cannot be ascertained, gives an undertaking to the operator to pay them when ascertained, and

    (b) complies with the other terms applicable to such a licence under the scheme,

shall be in the same position as regards infringement of copyright as if he had at all material times been the holder of a licence granted by the owner of the copyright in question in accordance with the scheme.

(3) The Tribunal may direct that the order, so far as it varies the amount of charges payable, has effect from a date before that on which it is made, but not earlier than the date on which the reference was made or, if later, on which the scheme came into operation.

If such a direction is made—

    (a) any necessary repayments, or further payments, shall be made in respect of charges already paid, and

    (b) the reference in subsection (2)(a) to the charges payable under the scheme shall be construed as a reference to the charges so payable by virtue of the order.

No such direction may be made where subsection (4) below applies.

(4) An order of the Tribunal under section 119 or 120 made with respect to a scheme which is certified for any purpose under section 143 has effect, so far as it varies the scheme by reducing the charges payable for licences, from the date on which the reference was made to the Tribunal.

(5) Where the Tribunal has made an order under section 121 (order as to entitlement to licence under licensing scheme) and the order remains in force, the person in whose favour the order is made shall if he—

> (a) pays to the operator of the scheme any charges payable in accordance with the order or, if the amount cannot be ascertained, gives an undertaking to pay the charges when ascertained, and
>
> (b) complies with the other terms specified in the order,

be in the same position as regards infringement of copyright as if he had at all material times been the holder of a licence granted by the owner of the copyright in question on the terms specified in the order.

References and applications with respect to licensing by licensing bodies

[Licences to which following sections apply

5-152   **124.** Sections 125 to 128 (references and applications with respect to licensing by licensing bodies) apply to licences which are granted by a licensing body otherwise than in pursuance of a licensing scheme and cover works of more than one author, so far as they authorise-

> (a) copying the work,
>
> (b) rental or lending of copies of the work to the public,
>
> (c) performing, showing or playing the work in public, or
>
> [(d) communicating the work to the public;][1]

and references in those sections to a licence shall be construed accordingly.][2]

Reference to tribunal of proposed licence

5-153   **125.**—(1) The terms on which a licensing body proposes to grant a licence may be referred to the Copyright Tribunal by the prospective licensee.

(2) The Tribunal shall first decide whether to entertain the reference, and may decline to do so on the ground that the reference is premature.

(3) If the Tribunal decides to entertain the reference it shall consider the terms of the proposed licence and make such order, either confirming or varying the terms, as it may determine to be reasonable in the circumstances.

(4) The order may be made so as to be in force indefinitely or for such period as the Tribunal may determine.

Reference to tribunal of expiring licence

5-154   **126.**—(1) A licensee under a licence which is due to expire, by effluxion of time or as a result of notice given by the licensing body, may apply to the Copyright Tribunal on the ground that it is unreasonable in the circumstances that the licence should cease to be in force.

(2) Such an application may not be made until the last three months before the licence is due to expire.

---

[1] Substituted by SI 2003/2498 Sch 1 Pt I para 4 (4)
[2] Substituted by SI 1996/2967 Pt II reg 15 (3)

(3) A licence in respect of which a reference has been made to the Tribunal shall remain in operation until proceedings on the reference are concluded.

(4) If the Tribunal finds the application well-founded, it shall make an order declaring that the licensee shall continue to be entitled to the benefit of the licence on such terms as the Tribunal may determine to be reasonable in the circumstances.

(5) An order of the Tribunal under this section may be made so as to be in force indefinitely or for such period as the Tribunal may determine.

Application for review of order as to licence

127.—(1) Where the Copyright Tribunal has made an order under [section **5-155** 125, 126 or 128B (where that order did not relate to a licensing scheme)][1], the licensing body or the person entitled to the benefit of the order may apply to the Tribunal to review its order.

(2) An application shall not be made, except with the special leave of the Tribunal—

    (a) within twelve months from the date of the order or of the decision on a previous application under this section, or

    (b) if the order was made so as to be in force for 15 months or less, or as a result of the decision on a previous application under this section is due to expire within 15 months of that decision, until the last three months before the expiry date.

(3) The Tribunal shall on an application for review confirm or vary its order as the Tribunal may determine to be reasonable in the circumstances.

Effect of order of tribunal as to licence

128.—(1) Where the Copyright Tribunal has made an order under section **5-156** 125 or 126 and the order remains in force, the person entitled to the benefit of the order shall if he—

    (a) pays to the licensing body any charges payable in accordance with the order or, if the amount cannot be ascertained, gives an undertaking to pay the charges when ascertained, and

    (b) complies with the other terms specified in the order,

be in the same position as regards infringement of copyright as if he had at all material times been the holder of a licence granted by the owner of the copyright in question on the terms specified in the order.

(2) The benefit of the order may be assigned—

    (a) in the case of an order under section 125, if assignment is not prohibited under the terms of the Tribunal's order; and

    (b) in the case of an order under section 126, if assignment was not prohibited under the terms of the original licence.

(3) The Tribunal may direct that an order under section 125 or 126, or an order under section 127 varying such an order, so far as it varies the amount of charges payable, has effect from a date before that on which it is made, but not earlier than the date on which the reference or application was made or, if later, on which the licence was granted or, as the case may be, was due to expire.

If such a direction is made—

    (a) any necessary repayments, or further payments, shall be made in respect of charges already paid, and

---

[1] Words substituted by SI 2003/2498 Pt II reg 21 (5)

(b) the reference in subsection (1)(a) to the charges payable in accordance with the order shall be construed, where the order is varied by a later order, as a reference to the charges so payable by virtue of the later order.

[Notification of licence or licensing scheme for excepted sound recordings

5-157 **128A**—(1) This section only applies to a proposed licence or licensing scheme that will authorise the playing in public of excepted sound recordings included in broadcasts, in circumstances where by reason of the exclusion of excepted sound recordings from section 72(1), the playing in public of such recordings would otherwise infringe the copyright in them.

(2) A licensing body must notify the Secretary of State of the details of any proposed licence or licensing scheme for excepted sound recordings before it comes into operation.

(3) A licence or licensing scheme, which has been notified under subsection (2), may not be operated by the licensing body until 28 days have elapsed since that notification.

(4) Subject to subsection (5), the Secretary of State shall take into account the matters set out in subsection (6) and then either –
  (a) refer the licence or licensing scheme to the Copyright Tribunal for a determination of whether the licence or licensing scheme is reasonable in the circumstances, or
  (b) notify the licensing body that he does not intend to refer the licence or licensing scheme to the Tribunal.

(5) If the Secretary of State becomes aware –
  (a) that a licensing body has failed to notify him of a licence or licensing scheme under subsection (2) before it comes into operation; or
  (b) that a licence or licensing scheme has been operated within 28 days of a notification under subsection (2),
subsection (4) does not apply, but the Secretary of State may at any time refer the licence or licensing scheme to the Tribunal for a determination of whether the licence or licensing scheme is reasonable in the circumstances, or may notify the licensing body that he does not intend to refer it to the Tribunal.

(6) The matters referred to in subsection (4) are –
  (a) whether the terms and conditions of the proposed licence or licensing scheme have taken into account the factors set out in subsection (7);
  (b) any written representations received by the Secretary of State;
  (c) previous determinations of the Tribunal;
  (d) the availability of other schemes, or the granting of other licences, to other persons in similar circumstances, and the terms of those schemes or licences; and
  (e) the extent to which the licensing body has consulted any person who would be affected by the proposed licence or licensing scheme, or organisations representing such persons, and the steps, if any, it has taken as a result.

(7) The factors referred to in subsection (6) are –
  (a) the extent to which the broadcasts to be shown or played by a potential licensee in circumstances mentioned in subsection (1) are likely to include excepted sound recordings;
  (b) the size and the nature of the audience that a licence or licensing scheme would permit to hear the excepted sound recordings;

(c) what commercial benefit a potential licensee is likely to obtain from playing the excepted sound recordings; and

(d) the extent to which the owners of copyright in the excepted sound recordings will receive equitable remuneration, from sources other than the proposed licence or licensing scheme, for the inclusion of their recordings in the broadcasts to be shown or played in public by a potential licensee.

(8) A proposed licence or licensing scheme that must be notified to the Secretary of State under subsection (2) may only be referred to the Tribunal under section 118 or 125 before such notification takes place.

(9) A proposed licensing scheme that has been notified to the Secretary of State under subsection (2) may only be referred to the Tribunal under section 119 after the Secretary of State has notified the licensing body that he does not intend to refer the licensing scheme to the Tribunal.

(10) If a reference made to the Tribunal under section 118 or 125 is permitted under subsection (8) then–

(a) the reference shall not be considered premature only because the licence or licensing scheme has not been notified to the Secretary of State under subsection (2); and

(b) where the Tribunal decides to entertain the reference, subsection (2) to (5) shall not apply.

(11) Nothing in this section shall be taken to prejudice any right to make a reference or application to the Tribunal under sections 120 to 122, 126 or 127.

(12) This section applies to modifications to an existing licence or licensing scheme as it applies to a proposed licence or licensing scheme.

(13) In this section and in section 128B, any reference to a "licence" means a licence granted by a licensing body otherwise than in pursuance of a licensing scheme and which covers works of more than one author.][1]

[References to the Tribunal by the Secretary of State under section 128A

128B—(1) The Copyright Tribunal may make appropriate enquiries to **5-158** establish whether a licence or licensing scheme referred to it by the Secretary of State under section 128A(4)(a) or (5) is reasonable in the circumstances.

(2) When considering the matter referred, and after concluding any such enquiries, the Tribunal shall take into account–

(a) whether the terms and conditions of the proposed licence or licensing scheme have taken into account the factors set out in section 128A(7); and

(b) any other factors it considers relevant,

and shall then make an order under subsection (3).

(3) The Tribunal shall make such order–

(a) in the case of a licensing scheme, either confirming or varying the proposed scheme, either generally or so far as it relates to cases of any description; or

(b) in the case of a licence, either confirming or varying the proposed licence, as the Tribunal may determine to be reasonable in the circumstances.

(4) The Tribunal may direct that the order, so far as it reduces the amount of charges payable, has effect from a date before that on which it is made.

If such a direction is made, any necessary repayments to a licensee shall be made in respect of charges already paid.

---

[1] Inserted by SI 2003/2498 Pt II reg 21 (3)

(5) The Tribunal may award simple interest on repayments, at such rate and for such period, ending not later than the date of the order, as it thinks fit.][1]

Factors to be taken into account in certain classes of case

General considerations: unreasonable discrimination

5-159 **129.** In determining what is reasonable on a reference or application under this Chapter relating to a licensing scheme or licence, the Copyright Tribunal shall have regard to—

> (a) the availability of other schemes, or the granting of other licences, to other persons in similar circumstances, and
>
> (b) the terms of those schemes or licences,

and shall exercise its powers so as to secure that there is no unreasonable discrimination between licensees, or prospective licensees, under the scheme or licence to which the reference or application relates and licensees under other schemes operated by, or other licences granted by, the same person.

Licences for reprographic copying

5-160 **130.** Where a reference or application is made to the Copyright Tribunal under this Chapter relating to the licensing of reprographic copying of published literary, dramatic, musical or artistic works, or the typographical arrangement of published editions, the Tribunal shall have regard to—

> (a) the extent to which published editions of the works in question are otherwise available,
>
> (b) the proportion of the work to be copied, and
>
> (c) the nature of the use to which the copies are likely to be put.

Licences for educational establishments in respect of works included in broadcasts [...][2]

5-161 **131.**—(1) This section applies to references or applications under this Chapter relating to licences for the recording by or on behalf of educational establishments of broadcasts [...][3] which include copyright works, or the making of copies of such recordings, for educational purposes.

(2) The Copyright Tribunal shall, in considering what charges (if any) should be paid for a licence, have regard to the extent to which the owners of copyright in the works included in the broadcast [...][4] have already received, or are entitled to receive, payment in respect of their inclusion.

Mention of specific matters not to exclude other relevant considerations

5-162 **135.** The mention in sections 129 to 134 of specific matters to which the Copyright Tribunal is to have regard in certain classes of case does not affect the Tribunal's general obligation in any case to have regard to all relevant considerations.

---

[1] Inserted by SI 2003/2498 Pt II reg 21 (3)
[2] Words repealed by SI 2003/2498 Sch 2 para 1
[3] Words repealed by SI 2003/2498 Sch 2 para 1
[4] Words repealed by SI 2003/2498 Sch 2 para 1

[Use as of right of sound recordings in broadcasts [...]][1]

[Circumstances in which right available

135A.—(1) Section 135C applies to the inclusion in a broadcast [...]² of any **5-163** sound recordings if—

    (a) a licence to include those recordings in the broadcast [...]³ could be granted by a licensing body or such a body could procure the grant of a licence to do so,

    (b) the condition in subsection (2) or (3) applies, and

    (c) the person including those recordings in the broadcast [...]⁴ has complied with section 135B.

(2) Where the person including the recordings in the broadcast [...]⁵ does not hold a licence to do so, the condition is that the licensing body refuses to grant, or procure the grant of, such a licence, being a licence—

    (a) whose terms as to payment for including the recordings in the broadcast [...]⁶ would be acceptable to him or comply with an order of the Copyright Tribunal under section 135D relating to such a licence or any scheme under which it would be granted, and

    (b) allowing unlimited needletime or such needletime as he has demanded.

(3) Where he holds a licence to include the recordings in the broadcast [...]⁷, the condition is that the terms of the licence limit needletime and the licensing body refuses to substitute or procure the substitution of terms allowing unlimited needletime or such needletime as he has demanded, or refuses to do so on terms that fall within subsection (2)(a).

(4) The references in subsection (2) to refusing to grant, or procure the grant of, a licence, and in subsection (3) to refusing to substitute or procure the substitution of terms, include failing to do so within a reasonable time of being asked.

(5) In the group of sections from this section to section 135G—

    ["broadcast" does not include any broadcast which is a transmission of the kind specified in section 6(1A)(b) or (c);]⁸

    "needletime" means the time in any period (whether determined as a number of hours in the period or a proportion of the period, or otherwise) in which any recordings may be included in a broadcast [...]⁹;

    "sound recording" does not include a film sound track when accompanying a film.

(6) In sections 135B to 135G, "terms of payment" means terms as to payment for including sound recordings in a broadcast [...]¹⁰.]¹¹

---

¹ Words repealed by SI 2003/2498 Sch 2 para 1
² Words repealed by SI 2003/2498 Sch 2 para 1
³ Words repealed by SI 2003/2498 Sch 2 para 1
⁴ Words repealed by SI 2003/2498 Sch 2 para 1
⁵ Words repealed by SI 2003/2498 Sch 2 para 1
⁶ Words repealed by SI 2003/2498 Sch 2 para 1
⁷ Words repealed by SI 2003/2498 Sch 2 para 1
⁸ Inserted by SI 2003/2498 Sch 1 Pt I para 15 (1)
⁹ Words repealed by SI 2003/2498 Sch 2 para 1
¹⁰ Words repealed by SI 2003/2498 Sch 2 para 1
¹¹ Inserted by Broadcasting Act 1990 c.42 s 175 (1)

[Notice of intention to exercise right

5-164 **135B.**—(1) A person intending to avail himself of the right conferred by section 135C must—

(a) give notice to the licensing body of his intention to exercise the right, asking the body to propose terms of payment, and

(b) after receiving the proposal or the expiry of a reasonable period, give reasonable notice to the licensing body of the date on which he proposes to begin exercising that right, and the terms of payment in accordance with which he intends to do so.

(2) Where he has a licence to include the recordings in a broadcast [...][1], the date specified in a notice under subsection (1)(b) must not be sooner than the date of expiry of that licence except in a case falling within section 135A(3).

(3) Before the person intending to avail himself of the right begins to exercise it, he must—

(a) give reasonable notice to the Copyright Tribunal of his intention to exercise the right, and of the date on which he proposes to begin to do so, and

(b) apply to the Tribunal under section 135D to settle the terms of payment.][2]

[Conditions for exercise of right

5-165 **135C.**—(1) A person who, on or after the date specified in a notice under section 135B(1)(b), includes in a broadcast [...][3] any sound recordings in circumstances in which this section applies, and who—

(a) complies with any reasonable condition, notice of which has been given to him by the licensing body, as to inclusion in the broadcast [...][4] of those recordings,

(b) provides that body with such information about their inclusion in the broadcast [...][5] as it may reasonably require, and

(c) makes the payments to the licensing body that are required by this section,

shall be in the same position as regards infringement of copyright as if he had at all material times been the holder of a licence granted by the owner of the copyright in question.

(2) Payments are to be made at not less than quarterly intervals in arrears.

(3) The amount of any payment is that determined in accordance with any order of the Copyright Tribunal under section 135D or, if no such order has been made—

(a) in accordance with any proposal for terms of payment made by the licensing body pursuant to a request under section 135B, or

(b) where no proposal has been so made or the amount determined in accordance with the proposal so made is unreasonably high, in accordance with the terms of payment notified to the licensing body under section 135B(1)(b).

---

[1] Words repealed by SI 2003/2498 Sch 2 para 1
[2] Inserted by Broadcasting Act 1990 c.42 s 175 (1)
[3] Words repealed by SI 2003/2498 Sch 2 para 1
[4] Words repealed by SI 2003/2498 Sch 2 para 1
[5] Words repealed by SI 2003/2498 Sch 2 para 1

(4) Where this section applies to the inclusion in a broadcast [...]^1 of any sound recordings, it does so in place of any licence.]^2

[Applications to settle payments

135D.—(1) On an application to settle the terms of payment, the Copyright **5-166** Tribunal shall consider the matter and make such order as it may determine to be reasonable in the circumstances.

(2) An order under subsection (1) has effect from the date the applicant begins to exercise the right conferred by section 135C and any necessary repayments, or further payments, shall be made in respect of amounts that have fallen due.]^3

[References etc. about conditions, information and other terms

135E.—(1) A person exercising the right conferred by section 135C, or who **5-167** has given notice to the Copyright Tribunal of his intention to do so, may refer to the Tribunal—

    (a) any question whether any condition as to the inclusion in a broadcast [...]^4 of sound recordings, notice of which has been given to him by the licensing body in question, is a reasonable condition, or

    (b) any question whether any information is information which the licensing body can reasonably require him to provide.

(2) On a reference under this section, the Tribunal shall consider the matter and make such order as it may determine to be reasonable in the circumstances.]^5

[Application for review of order

135F.—(1) A person exercising the right conferred by section 135C or the **5-168** licensing body may apply to the Copyright Tribunal to review any order under section 135D or 135E.

(2) An application shall not be made, except with the special leave of the Tribunal—

    (a) within twelve months from the date of the order, or of the decision on a previous application under this section, or

    (b) if the order was made so as to be in force for fifteen months or less, or as a result of a decision on a previous application is due to expire within fifteen months of that decision, until the last three months before the expiry date.

(3) On the application the Tribunal shall consider the matter and make such order confirming or varying the original order as it may determine to be reasonable in the circumstances.

(4) An order under this section has effect from the date on which it is made or such later date as may be specified by the Tribunal.]^6

---

^{1} Words repealed by SI 2003/2498 Sch 2 para 1
^{2} Inserted by Broadcasting Act 1990 c.42 s 175 (1)
^{3} Inserted by Broadcasting Act 1990 c.42 s 175 (1)
^{4} Words repealed by SI 2003/2498 Sch 2 para 1
^{5} Inserted by Broadcasting Act 1990 c.42 s 175 (1)
^{6} Inserted by Broadcasting Act 1990 c.42 s 175 (1)

[Factors to be taken into account

5-169　**135G.**—(1) In determining what is reasonable on an application or reference under section 135D or 135E, or on reviewing any order under section 135F, the Copyright Tribunal shall—

    (a) have regard to the terms of any orders which it has made in the case of persons in similar circumstances exercising the right conferred by section 135C, and

    (b) exercise its powers so as to secure that there is no unreasonable discrimination between persons exercising that right against the same licensing body.

(2) In settling the terms of payment under section 135D, the Tribunal shall not be guided by any order it has made under any enactment other than that section.

(3) Section 134 (factors to be taken into account: retransmissions) applies on an application or reference under sections 135D to 135F as it applies on an application or reference relating to a licence.][1]

[Power to amend sections 135A to 135G

5-170　**135H.**—(1) The Secretary of State may by order, subject to such transitional provision as appears to him to be appropriate, amend sections 135A to 135G so as—

    (a) to include in any reference to sound recordings any works of a description specified in the order; or

    (b) to exclude from any reference to a broadcast [...][2] any broadcast [...][3] of a description so specified.

(2) An order shall be made by statutory instrument; and no order shall be made unless a draft of it has been laid before and approved by resolution of each House of Parliament.][4][5]

[Royalty or other sum payable for lending of certain works][6]

[Royalty or other sum payable for lending of certain works

5-171　**142.**—(1) An application to settle the royalty or other sum payable in pursuance of section 66 (lending of copies of certain copyright works) may be made to the Copyright Tribunal by the copyright owner or the person claiming to be treated as licensed by him.

(2) The Tribunal shall consider the matter and make such order as it may determine to be reasonable in the circumstances.

(3) Either party may subsequently apply to the Tribunal to vary the order, and the Tribunal shall consider the matter and make such order confirming or varying the original order as it may determine to be reasonable in the circumstances.

(4) An application under subsection (3) shall not, except with the special leave of the Tribunal, be made within twelve months from the date of the original order or of the order on a previous application under that subsection.

---

[1] Inserted by Broadcasting Act 1990 c.42 s 175 (1)
[2] Words repealed by SI 2003/2498 Sch 2 para 1
[3] Words repealed by SI 2003/2498 Sch 2 para 1
[4] Inserted by Broadcasting Act 1996 c.55 Pt VII s 139 (1)
[5] Inserted by Broadcasting Act 1990 c.42 s 175 (1)
[6] Substituted by SI 1996/2967 Pt II reg 13 (2)

(5) An order under subsection (3) has effect from the date on which it is made or such later date as may be specified by the Tribunal.]^1

Certification of licensing schemes

Powers exercisable in consequence of competition report

Powers exercisable in consequence of report of Monopolies and Mergers Commission

144.—[(1) Subsection (1A) applies where whatever needs to be remedied, **5-172** mitigated or prevented by the Secretary of State, the Office of Fair Trading or (as the case may be) the Competition Commission under section 12(5) of the Competition Act 1980 or section 41(2), 55(2), 66(6), 75(2), 83(2), 138(2), 147(2) or 160(2) of, or paragraph 5(2) or 10(2) of Schedule 7 to, the Enterprise Act 2002 (powers to take remedial action following references to the Commission in connection with public bodies and certain other persons, mergers or market investigations) consists of or includes—

    (a) conditions in licences granted by the owner of copyright in a work restricting the use of the work by the licensee or the right of the copyright owner to grant other licences; or

    (b) a refusal of a copyright owner to grant licences on reasonable terms.

(1A) The powers conferred by Schedule 8 to the Enterprise Act 2002 include power to cancel or modify those conditions and, instead or in addition, to provide that licences in respect of the copyright shall be available as of right.

(2) The references to anything permitted by Schedule 8 to the Enterprise Act 2002 in section 12(5A) of the Competition Act 1980 and in sections 75(4)(a), 83(4)(a), 84(2)(a), 89(1), 160(4)(a), 161(3)(a) and 164(1) of, and paragraphs 5, 10 and 11 of Schedule 7 to, the Act of 2002 shall be construed accordingly.]^2

(3) [The Secretary of State, the Office of Fair Trading or (as the case may be) the Competition Commission]^3 shall only exercise the powers available by virtue of this section if he [or it]^4 is satisfied that to do so does not contravene any Convention relating to copyright to which the United Kingdom is a party.

(4) The terms of a licence available by virtue of this section shall, in default of agreement, be settled by the Copyright Tribunal on an application by the person requiring the licence; and terms so settled shall authorise the licensee to do everything in respect of which a licence is so available.

(5) Where the terms of a licence are settled by the Tribunal, the licence has effect from the date on which the application to the Tribunal was made.

[Compulsory collective administration of certain rights

[Collective exercise of certain rights in relation to cable re-transmission

144A.—(1) This section applies to the right of the owner of copyright in a **5-173** literary, dramatic, musical or artistic work, sound recording or film to grant or refuse authorisation for cable re-transmission of a [wireless]^5 broadcast from another EEA member state in which the work is included.

---

^{1} Substituted by SI 1996/2967 Pt II reg 13 (2)
^{2} Substituted by Enterprise Act 2002 c.40 Sch 25 para 18 (2)
^{3} Words substituted by Enterprise Act 2002 c.40 Sch 25 para 18 (3) (a)
^{4} Words inserted by Enterprise Act 2002 c.40 Sch 25 para 18 (3) (b)
^{5} Word inserted by SI 2003/2498 Pt II reg 5 (6)

That right is referred to below as "cable re-transmission right".

(2) Cable re-transmission right may be exercised against a cable operator only through a licensing body.

(3) Where a copyright owner has not transferred management of his cable re-transmission right to a licensing body, the licensing body which manages rights of the same category shall be deemed to be mandated to manage his right.

Where more than one licensing body manages rights of that category, he may choose which of them is deemed to be mandated to manage his right.

(4) A copyright owner to whom subsection (3) applies has the same rights and obligations resulting from any relevant agreement between the cable operator and the licensing body as have copyright owners who have transferred management of their cable re-transmission right to that licensing body.

(5) Any rights to which a copyright owner may be entitled by virtue of subsection (4) must be claimed within the period of three years beginning with the date of the cable re-transmission concerned.

(6) This section does not affect any rights exercisable by the maker of the broadcast, whether in relation to the broadcast or a work included in it.

[(7) In this section–

"cable operator" means a person responsible for cable re-transmission of a wireless broadcast; and

"cable re-transmission" means the reception and immediate re-transmission by cable, including the transmission of microwave energy between terrestrial fixed points, of a wireless broadcast.][1]][2]][3]

CHAPTER VIII

THE COPYRIGHT TRIBUNAL

The Tribunal

The Copyright Tribunal

5-174   **145.**—(1) The Tribunal established under section 23 of the Copyright Act 1956 is renamed the Copyright Tribunal.

(2) The Tribunal shall consist of a chairman and two deputy chairmen appointed by the Lord Chancellor, after consultation with the [Secretary of State][4], and not less than two or more than eight ordinary members appointed by the Secretary of State.

(3) A person is not eligible for appointment as chairman or deputy chairman [unless—][5]

[(a) he has a 7 year general qualification, within the meaning of section 71 of the Courts and Legal Services Act 1990;

(b) he is an advocate or solicitor in Scotland of at least 7 years' standing;

(c) he is a member of the Bar of Northern Ireland or solicitor of the Supreme Court of Northern Ireland of at least 7 years' standing; or

(d) he has held judicial office.][6]

---

[1] Substituted by SI 2003/2498 Sch 1 (1) para 15 (2)
[2] Inserted by SI 1996/2967 Pt II reg 7
[3] Inserted by SI 1996/2967 Pt II reg 7
[4] Words substituted by SI 1999/678 art 7 (4)
[5] Word substituted by Courts and Legal Services Act 1990 c.41 s 71 (2) Sch 10 para 73
[6] Words substituted by Courts and Legal Services Act 1990 c.41 s 71 (2) Sch 10 para 73

Membership of the Tribunal

146.—(1) The members of the Copyright Tribunal shall hold and vacate **5-175** office in accordance with their terms of appointment, subject to the following provisions.

(2) A member of the Tribunal may resign his office by notice in writing to the Secretary of State or, in the case of the chairman or a deputy chairman, to the Lord Chancellor.

(3) The Secretary of State or, in the case of the chairman or a deputy chairman, the Lord Chancellor may by notice in writing to the member concerned remove him from office if—

(a) he has become bankrupt or made an arrangement with his creditors or, in Scotland, his estate has been sequestrated or he has executed a trust deed for his creditors or entered into a composition contract, or

(b) he is incapacitated by physical or mental illness,

or if he is in the opinion of the Secretary of State or, as the case may be, the Lord Chancellor otherwise unable or unfit to perform his duties as member.

[(3A) A person who is the chairman or a deputy chairman of the Tribunal shall vacate his office on the day on which he attains the age of 70 years; but this subsection is subject to section 26(4) to (6) of the Judicial Pensions and Retirement Act 1993 (power to authorise continuance in office up to the age of 75 years).][1]

(4) If a member of the Tribunal is by reason of illness, absence or other reasonable cause for the time being unable to perform the duties of his office, either generally or in relation to particular proceedings, a person may be appointed to discharge his duties for a period not exceeding six months at one time or, as the case may be, in relation to those proceedings.

(5) The appointment shall be made—

(a) in the case of the chairman or deputy chairman, by the Lord Chancellor, who shall appoint a person who would be eligible for appointment to that office, and

(b) in the case of an ordinary member, by the Secretary of State;

and a person so appointed shall have during the period of his appointment, or in relation to the proceedings in question, the same powers as the person in whose place he is appointed.

(6) The Lord Chancellor shall consult the Lord Advocate before exercising his powers under this section.

Jurisdiction and procedure

Jurisdiction of the Tribunal

149. [The Copyright Tribunal has jurisdiction under this Part][2] to hear and **5-176** determine proceedings under—

[(za) section 73 (determination of royalty or other remuneration to be paid with respect to re-transmission of broadcast including work);][3]

[(zb) section 93C (application to determine amount of equitable remuneration under section 93B;][4]

(a) section 118, 119, or 120 (reference of licensing scheme);

---

[1] Inserted by Judicial Pensions and Retirement Act 1993 c.8 Sch 6 para 49

[2] Words substituted by SI 1996/2967 Pt II reg 24 (2) (a)

[3] Inserted by Broadcasting Act 1996 c.55 Sch 9 para 3

[4] Inserted by SI 1996/2967 Pt II reg 14 (2)

(b) section 121 or 122 (application with respect to entitlement to licence under licensing scheme);

(c) section 125, 126 or 127 (reference or application with respect to licensing by licensing body);

[[(ca) section 128B (reference by the Secretary of State under section 128A);][1]

(cc) section 135D or 135E (application or reference with respect to use as of right of sound recordings in broadcasts [...][2]);][3]

(d) section 139 (appeal against order as to coverage of licensing scheme or licence);

(e) section 142 (application to settle royalty or other sum payable for [lending of certain works][4]);

(f) section 144(4) (application to settle terms of copyright licence available as of right) [...][5]

Appeals

Appeal to the court on point of law

5-177   **152.**—(1) An appeal lies on any point of law arising from a decision of the Copyright Tribunal to the High Court or, in the case of proceedings of the Tribunal in Scotland, to the Court of Session.

(2) Provision shall be made by rules under section 150 limiting the time within which an appeal may be brought.

(3) Provision may be made by rules under that section—

(a) for suspending, or authorising or requiring the Tribunal to suspend, the operation of orders of the Tribunal in cases where its decision is appealed against;

(b) for modifying in relation to an order of the Tribunal whose operation is suspended the operation of any provision of this Act as to the effect of the order;

(c) for the publication of notices or the taking of other steps for securing that persons affected by the suspension of an order of the Tribunal will be informed of its suspension.

CHAPTER IX

QUALIFICATION FOR AND EXTENT OF COPYRIGHT
PROTECTION

Qualification for copyright protection

Qualification for copyright protection

5-178   **153.**—(1) Copyright does not subsist in a work unless the qualification requirements of this Chapter are satisfied as regards—

(a) the author (see section 154), or

(b) the country in which the work was first published (see section 155), or

---

[1] Inserted by SI 2003/2498 Pt II reg 21 (6)
[2] Words repealed by SI 2003/2498 Sch 2 Pt II para 1
[3] Inserted by Broadcasting Act 1990 c.42 s 175 (2)
[4] Words substituted by SI 1996/2967 Pt II reg 13 (3)
[5] Repealed by SI 1996/2967 Pt II reg 24 (2) (b)

(c) in the case of a broadcast [...][1], the country from which the broadcast was made [...][2] (see section 156).

(2) Subsection (1) does not apply in relation to Crown copyright or Parliamentary copyright (see [sections 163 to 166A][3]) or to copyright subsisting by virtue of section 168 (copyright of certain international organisations).

(3) If the qualification requirements of this Chapter, or section 163, 165 or 168, are once satisfied in respect of a work, copyright does not cease to subsist by reason of any subsequent event.

Qualification by reference to author

154.—(1) A work qualifies for copyright protection if the author was at the material time a qualifying person, that is— **5-179**

    (a) a British citizen, a [British overseas territories citizen][4], a British National (Overseas), a British Overseas citizen, a British subject or a British protected person within the meaning of the British Nationality Act 1981, or

    (b) an individual domiciled or resident in the United Kingdom or another country to which the relevant provisions of this Part extend, or

    (c) a body incorporated under the law of a part of the United Kingdom or of another country to which the relevant provisions of this Part extend.

(2) Where, or so far as, provision is made by Order under section 159 (application of this Part to countries to which it does not extend), a work also qualifies for copyright protection if at the material time the author was a citizen or subject of, an individual domiciled or resident in, or a body incorporated under the law of, a country to which the Order relates.

(3) A work of joint authorship qualifies for copyright protection if at the material time any of the authors satisfies the requirements of subsection (1) or (2); but where a work qualifies for copyright protection only under this section, only those authors who satisfy those requirements shall be taken into account for the purposes of—

    section 11(1) and (2) (first ownership of copyright; entitlement of author or author's employer),

    [section 12 (duration of copyright), and section 9(4) (meaning of "unknown authorship") so far as it applies for the purposes of section 12][5], and

    section 57 (anonymous or pseudonymous works: acts permitted on assumptions as to expiry of copyright or death of author).

(4) The material time in relation to a literary, dramatic, musical or artistic work is—

    (a) in the case of an unpublished work, when the work was made or, if the making of the work extended over a period, a substantial part of that period;

    (b) in the case of a published work, when the work was first published or, if the author had died before that time, immediately before his death.

(5) The material time in relation to other descriptions of work is as follows—

    (a) in the case of a sound recording or film, when it was made;

    (b) in the case of a broadcast, when the broadcast was made;

---

[1] Words repealed by SI 2003/2498 Sch 2 para 1
[2] Words repealed by SI 2003/2498 Sch 2 para 1
[3] Words substituted by Scotland Act 1998 c.46 Sch 8 para 25 (3)
[4] Words substituted by British Overseas Territories Act 2002 c.8 s 2 (3)
[5] Substituted by SI 1995/3297 Pt II reg 5 (3)

(d) in the case of the typographical arrangement of a published edition, when the edition was first published.

Qualification by reference to country of first publication

5-180   **155.**—(1) A literary, dramatic, musical or artistic work, a sound recording or film, or the typographical arrangement of a published edition, qualifies for copyright protection if it is first published—

(a) in the United Kingdom, or

(b) in another country to which the relevant provisions of this Part extend.

(2) Where, or so far as, provision is made by Order under section 159 (application of this Part to countries to which it does not extend), such a work also qualifies for copyright protection if it is first published in a country to which the Order relates.

(3) For the purposes of this section, publication in one country shall not be regarded as other than the first publication by reason of simultaneous publication elsewhere; and for this purpose publication elsewhere within the previous 30 days shall be treated as simultaneous.

Qualification by reference to place of transmission

5-181   **156.**—(1) A broadcast qualifies for copyright protection if it is made from [...][1] a place in—

(a) the United Kingdom, or

(b) another country to which the relevant provisions of this Part extend.

(2) Where, or so far as, provision is made by Order under section 159 (application of this Part to countries to which it does not extend), a broadcast [...][2] also qualifies for copyright protection if it is made from [...][3] a place in a country to which the Order relates.

Extent and application of this Part

Countries to which this Part extends

5-182   **157.**—(1) This Part extends to England and Wales, Scotland and Northern Ireland.

(2) Her Majesty may by Order in Council direct that this Part shall extend, subject to such exceptions and modifications as may be specified in the Order, to—

(a) any of the Channel Islands,

(b) the Isle of Man, or

(c) any colony.

(3) That power includes power to extend, subject to such exceptions and modifications as may be specified in the Order, any Order in Council made under the following provisions of this Chapter.

(4) The legislature of a country to which this Part has been extended may modify or add to the provisions of this Part, in their operation as part of the law of that country, as the legislature may consider necessary to adapt the provisions to the circumstances of that country—

(a) as regards procedure and remedies, or

---

[1] Words repealed by SI 2003/2498 Sch 2 para 1
[2] Words repealed by SI 2003/2498 Sch 2 para 1
[3] Words repealed by SI 2003/2498 Sch 2 para 1

(b) as regards works qualifying for copyright protection by virtue of a connection with that country.

(5) Nothing in this section shall be construed as restricting the extent of paragraph 36 of Schedule 1 (transitional provisions: dependent territories where the Copyright Act 1956 or the Copyright Act 1911 remains in force) in relation to the law of a dependent territory to which this Part does not extend.

Countries ceasing to be colonies

158.—(1) The following provisions apply where a country to which this Part **5-183** has been extended ceases to be a colony of the United Kingdom.

(2) As from the date on which it ceases to be a colony it shall cease to be regarded as a country to which this Part extends for the purposes of—

(a) section 160(2)(a) (denial of copyright protection to citizens of countries not giving adequate protection to British works), and

(b) sections 163 and 165 (Crown and Parliamentary copyright).

(3) But it shall continue to be treated as a country to which this Part extends for the purposes of sections 154 to 156 (qualification for copyright protection) until—

(a) an Order in Council is made in respect of that country under section 159 (application of this Part to countries to which it does not extend), or

(b) an Order in Council is made declaring that it shall cease to be so treated by reason of the fact that the provisions of this Part as part of the law of that country have been repealed or amended.

(4) A statutory instrument containing an Order in Council under subsection (3)(b) shall be subject to annulment in pursuance of a resolution of either House of Parliament.

Application of this Part to countries to which it does not extend

159.—(1) Her Majesty may be Order in Council make provision for applying **5-184** in relation to a country to which this Part does not extend any of the provisions of this Part specified in the Order, so as to secure that those provisions—

(a) apply in relation to persons who are citizens or subjects of that country or are domiciled or resident there, as they apply to persons who are British citizens or are domiciled or resident in the United Kingdom, or

(b) apply in relation to bodies incorporated under the law of that country as they apply in relation to bodies incorporated under the law of a part of the United Kingdom, or

(c) apply in relation to works first published in that country as they apply in relation to works first published in the United Kingdom, or

(d) apply in relation to broadcasts made from [...][1] that country as they apply in relation to broadcasts made from [...][2] the United Kingdom.

(2) An Order may make provision for all or any of the matters mentioned in subsection (1) and may—

(a) apply any provisions of this Part subject to such exceptions and modifications as are specified in the Order; and

(b) direct that any provisions of this Part apply either generally or in relation to such classes or works, or other classes of case, as are specified in the Order.

---

[1] Words repealed by SI 2003/2498 Sch 2 para 1
[2] Words repealed by SI 2003/2498 Sch 2 para 1

(3) Except in the case of a Convention country or another member State of the European Economic Community, Her Majesty shall not make an Order in Council under this section in relation to a country unless satisfied that provision has been or will be made under the law of that country, in respect of the class of works to which the Order relates, giving adequate protection to the owners of copyright under this Part.

(4) In subsection (3) "Convention country" means a country which is a party to a Convention relating to copyright to which the United Kingdom is also a party.

(5) A statutory instrument containing an Order in Council under this section shall be subject to annulment in pursuance of a resolution of either House of Parliament.

Denial of copyright protection to citizens of countries not giving adequate protection to British works

5-185   **160.**—(1) If it appears to Her Majesty that the law of a country fails to give adequate protection to British works to which this section applies, or to one or more classes of such works, Her Majesty may make provision by Order in Council in accordance with this section restricting the rights conferred by this Part in relation to works of authors connected with that country.

(2) An Order in Council under this section shall designate the country concerned and provide that, for the purposes specified in the Order, works first published after a date specified in the Order shall not be treated as qualifying for copyright protection by virtue of such publication if at that time the authors are—

    (a) citizens or subjects of that country (not domiciled or resident in the United Kingdom or another country to which the relevant provisions of this Part extend), or

    (b) bodies incorporated under the law of that country;

and the Order may make such provision for all the purposes of this Part or for such purposes as are specified in the Order, and either generally or in relation to such class of cases as are specified in the Order, having regard to the nature and extent of that failure referred to in subsection (1).

(3) This section applies to literary, dramatic, musical and artistic works, sound recordings and films; and "British works" means works of which the author was a qualifying person at the material time within the meaning of section 154.

(4) A statutory instrument containing an Order in Council under this section shall be subject to annulment in pursuance of a resolution of either House of Parliament.

Supplementary

Territorial waters and the continental shelf

5-186   **161.**—(1) For the purposes of this Part the territorial waters of the United Kingdom shall be treated as part of the United Kingdom.

(2) This Part applies to things done in the United Kingdom sector of the continental shelf on a structure or vessel which is present there for purposes directly connected with the exploration of the sea bed or subsoil or the exploitation of their natural resources as it applies to things done in the United Kingdom.

(3) The United Kingdom sector of the continental shelf means the areas designated by order under section 1(7) of the Continental Shelf Act 1964.

British ships, aircraft and hovercraft

162.—(1) This Part applies to things done on a British ship, aircraft or **5-187** hovercraft as it applies to things done in the United Kingdom.

(2) In this section—

"British ship" means a ship which is a British ship for the purposes of the [Merchant Shipping Act 1995][1] otherwise than by virtue of registration in a country outside the United Kingdom;and

"British aircraft" and "British hovercraft" mean an aircraft or hovercraft registered in the United Kingdom.

CHAPTER X

MISCELLANEOUS AND GENERAL

Crown and Parliamentary copyright

Crown copyright

163.—(1) Where a work is made by Her Majesty or by an officer or servant of **5-188** the Crown in the course of his duties—

(a) the work qualifies for copyright protection notwithstanding section 153(1) (ordinary requirement as to qualification for copyright protection), and

(b) Her Majesty is the first owner of any copyright in the work.

[(1A) For the purposes of this section, works made by Her Majesty include any sound recording, film [or live broadcast][2] of the proceedings of the National Assembly for Wales (including proceedings of a committee of the Assembly or of a sub-committee of such a committee) which is made by or under the direction or control of the Assembly; but a work shall not be regarded as made by or under the direction or control of the Assembly by reason only of its being commissioned by or on behalf of the Assembly.][3]

(2) Copyright in such a work is referred to in this Part as "Crown copyright", notwithstanding that it may be, or have been, assigned to another person.

(3) Crown copyright in a literary, dramatic, musical or artistic work continues to subsist—

(a) until the end of the period of 125 years from the end of the calendar year in which the work was made, or

(b) if the work is published commercially before the end of the period of 75 years from the end of the calendar year in which it was made, until the end of the period of 50 years from the end of the calendar year in which it was first so published.

(4) In the case of a work of joint authorship where one or more but not all of the authors are persons falling within subsection (1), this section applies only in relation to those authors and the copyright subsisting by virtue of their contribution to the work.

---

[1] Words substituted by Merchant Shipping Act 1995 c.21 Sch 13 para 84 (a)
[2] Words substituted by SI 2003/2498 Sch 1 Pt II para 11 (a)
[3] Inserted by Government of Wales Act 1998 c.38 Sch 12 para 28

(5) Except as mentioned above, and subject to any express exclusion elsewhere in this Part, the provisions of this Part apply in relation to Crown copyright as to other copyright.

(6) This section does not apply to a work if, or to the extent that, Parliamentary copyright subsists in the work (see [sections 165 to 166A][1]).

Copyright in Acts and Measures

5-189   **164.**—(1) Her Majesty is entitled to copyright in every Act of Parliament [, Act of the Scottish Parliament][2] [, Act of the Northern Ireland Assembly][3] or Measure of the General Synod of the Church of England.

(2) The copyright subsists from Royal Assent until the end of the period of 50 years from the end of the calendar year in which Royal Assent was given.

(3) References in this Part to Crown copyright (except in section 163) include copyright under this section; and, except as mentioned above, the provisions of this Part apply in relation to copyright under this section as to other Crown copyright.

(4) No other copyright, or right in the nature of copyright, subsists in an Act or Measure.

Parliamentary copyright

5-190   **165.**—(1) Where a work is made by or under the direction or control of the House of Commons or the House of Lords—

    (a) the work qualifies for copyright protection notwithstanding section 153(1) (ordinary requirement as to qualification for copyright protection), and

    (b) the House by whom, or under whose direction or control, the work is made is the first owner of any copyright in the work, and if the work is made by or under the direction or control of both Houses, the two Houses are joint first owners of copyright.

(2) Copyright in such a work is referred to in this Part as "Parliamentary copyright", notwithstanding that it may be, or have been, assigned to another person.

(3) Parliamentary copyright in a literary, dramatic, musical or artistic work continues to subsist until the end of the period of 50 years from the end of the calendar year in which the work was made.

(4) For the purposes of this section, works made by or under the direction or control of the House of Commons or the House of Lords include—

    (a) any work made by an officer or employee of that House in the course of his duties, and

    (b) any sound recording, film [or live broadcast][4] of the proceedings of that House;

but a work shall not be regarded as made by or under the direction or control of either House by reason only of its being commissioned by or on behalf of that House.

(5) In the case of a work of joint authorship where one or more but not all of the authors are acting on behalf of, or under the direction or control of, the House of Commons or the House of Lords, this section applies only in relation to

---

[1] Words substituted by Scotland Act 1998 c.46 Sch 8 para 25 (4)
[2] Words inserted by Scotland Act 1998 c.46 Sch 8 para 25 (5)
[3] Words inserted by Northern Ireland Act 1998 c.47 s 99 Sch 13 para 8 (5)
[4] Words substituted by SI 2003/2498 Sch 1 Pt I para 11 (b)

those authors and the copyright subsisting by virtue of their contribution to the work.

(6) Except as mentioned above, and subject to any express exclusion elsewhere in this Part, the provisions of this Part apply in relation to Parliamentary copyright as to other copyright.

(7) The provisions of this section also apply, subject to any exceptions or modifications specified by Order in Council, to works made by or under the direction or control of any other legislative body of a country to which this Part extends; and references in this Part to "Parliamentary copyright" shall be construed accordingly.

(8) A statutory instrument containing an Order in Council under subsection (7) shall be subject to annulment in pursuance of a resolution of either House of Parliament.

Copyright in Parliamentary Bills

166.—(1) Copyright in every Bill introduced into Parliament belongs, in **5-191** accordance with the following provisions, to one or both of the Houses of Parliament.

(2) Copyright in a public Bill belongs in the first instance to the House into which the Bill is introduced, and after the Bill has been carried to the second House to both Houses jointly, and subsists from the time when the text of the Bill is handed in to the House in which it is introduced.

(3) Copyright in a private Bill belongs to both Houses jointly and subsists from the time when a copy of the Bill is first deposited in either House.

(4) Copyright in a personal Bill belongs in the first instance to the House of Lords, and after the Bill has been carried to the House of Commons to both Houses jointly, and subsists from the time when it is given a First Reading in the House of Lords.

(5) Copyright under this section ceases—
  (a) on Royal Assent, or
  (b) if the Bill does not receive Royal Assent, on the withdrawal or rejection of the Bill or the end of the Session:

Provided that, copyright in a Bill continues to subsist notwithstanding its rejection in any Session by the House of Lords if, by virtue of the Parliament Acts 1911 and 1949, it remains possible for it to be presented for Royal Assent in that Session.

(6) References in this Part to Parliamentary copyright (except in section 165) include copyright under this section; and, except as mentioned above, the provisions of this Part apply in relation to copyright under this section as to other Parliamentary copyright.

(7) No other copyright, or right in the nature of copyright, subsists in a Bill after copyright has once subsisted under this section; but without prejudice to the subsequent operation of this section in relation to a Bill which, not having passed in one Session, is reintroduced in a subsequent Session.

Houses of Parliament: supplementary provisions with respect to copyright

167.—(1) For the purposes of holding, dealing with and enforcing copyright, **5-192** and in connection with all legal proceedings relating to copyright, each House of Parliament shall be treated as having the legal capacities of a body corporate, which shall not be affected by a prorogation or dissolution.

(2) The functions of the House of Commons as owner of copyright shall be exercised by the Speaker on behalf of the House; and if so authorised by the Speaker, or in case of a vacancy in the office of Speaker, those functions may be discharged by the Chairman of Ways and Means or a Deputy Chairman.

(3) For this purpose a person who on the dissolution of Parliament was Speaker of the House of Commons, Chairman of Ways and Means or a Deputy Chairman may continue to act until the corresponding appointment is made in the next Session of Parliament.

(4) The functions of the House of Lords as owner of copyright shall be exercised by the Clerk of the Parliaments on behalf of the House; and if so authorised by him, or in case of a vacancy in the office of Clerk of the Parliaments, those functions may be discharged by the Clerk Assistant or the Reading Clerk.

(5) Legal proceedings relating to copyright—
    (a) shall be brought by or against the House of Commons in the name of "The Speaker of the House of Commons"; and
    (b) shall be brought by or against the House of Lords in the name of "The Clerk of the Parliaments".

Other miscellaneous provisions

Copyright vesting in certain international organisations

5-193   **168.**—(1) Where an original literary, dramatic, musical or artistic work—
    (a) is made by an officer or employee of, or is published by, an international organisation to which this section applies, and
    (b) does not qualify for copyright protection under section 154 (qualification by reference to author) or section 155 (qualification by reference to country of first publication),
copyright nevertheless subsists in the work by virtue of this section and the organisation is first owner of that copyright.

(2) The international organisations to which this section applies are those as to which Her Majesty has by Order in Council declared that it is expedient that this section should apply.

(3) Copyright of which an international organisation is first owner by virtue of this section continues to subsist until the end of the period of 50 years from the end of the calendar year in which the work was made or such longer period as may be specified by Her Majesty by Order in Council for the purpose of complying with the international obligations of the United Kingdom.

(4) An international organisation to which this section applies shall be deemed to have, and to have had at all material times, the legal capacities of a body corporate for the purpose of holding, dealing with and enforcing copyright and in connection with all legal proceedings relating to copyright.

(5) A statutory instrument containing an Order in Council under this section shall be subject to annulment in pursuance of a resolution of either House of Parliament.

Folklore, &c.: anonymous unpublished works

5-194   **169.**—(1) Where in the case of an unpublished literary, dramatic, musical or artistic work of unknown authorship there is evidence that the author (or, in the case of a joint work, any of the authors) was a qualifying individual by connection with a country outside the United Kingdom, it shall be presumed until the contrary is proved that he was such a qualifying individual and that copyright accordingly subsists in the work, subject to the provisions of this Part.

(2) If under the law of that country a body is appointed to protect and enforce copyright in such works, Her Majesty may by Order in Council designate that body for the purposes of this section.

(3) A body so designated shall be recognised in the United Kingdom as having authority to do in place of the copyright owner anything, other than assign copyright, which it is empowered to do under the law of that country; and it may, in particular, bring proceedings in its own name.

(4) A statutory instrument containing an Order in Council under this section shall be subject to annulment in pursuance of a resolution of either House of Parliament.

(5) In subsection (1) a "qualifying individual" means an individual who at the material time (within the meaning of section 154) was a person whose works qualified under that section for copyright protection.

(6) This section does not apply if there has been an assignment of copyright in the work by the author of which notice has been given to the designated body; and nothing in this section affects the validity of an assignment of copyright made, or licence granted, by the author or a person lawfully claiming under him.

Transitional provisions and savings

Transitional provisions and savings

170. Schedule 1 contains transitional provisions and savings relating to works **5-195** made, and acts or events occurring, before the commencement of this Part, and otherwise with respect to the operation of the provisions of this Part.

Rights and privileges under other enactments or the common law

171.—(1) Nothing in this Part affects—   **5-196**

 (a) any right or privilege of any person under any enactment (except where the enactment is expressly repealed, amended or modified by this Act);

 (b) any right or privilege of the Crown subsisting otherwise than under an enactment;

 (c) any right or privilege of either House of Parliament;

 (d) the right of the Crown or any person deriving title from the Crown to sell, use or otherwise deal with articles forfeited under the laws relating to customs and excise;

 (e) the operation of any rule of equity relating to breaches of trust or confidence.

(2) Subject to those savings, no copyright or right in the nature of copyright shall subsist otherwise than by virtue of this Part or some other enactment in that behalf.

(3) Nothing in this Part affects any rule of law preventing or restricting the enforcement of copyright, on grounds of public interest or otherwise.

(4) Nothing in this Part affects any right of action or other remedy, whether civil or criminal, available otherwise than under this Part in respect of acts infringing any of the rights conferred by Chapter IV (moral rights).

(5) The savings in subsection (1) have effect subject to section 164(4) and section 166(7) (copyright in Acts, Measures and Bills: exclusion of other rights in the nature of copyright).

Interpretation

General provisions as to construction

5-197   **172.**—(1) This Part restates and amends the law of copyright, that is, the provisions of the Copyright Act 1956, as amended.

(2) A provision of this Part which corresponds to a provision of the previous law shall not be construed as departing from the previous law merely because of a change of expression.

(3) Decisions under the previous law may be referred to for the purpose of establishing whether a provision of this Part departs from the previous law, or otherwise for establishing the true construction of this Part.

[[Meaning of EEA and related expressions

5-198   **172A.**—(1) In this Part-
    "the EEA" means the European Economic Area;
    "EEA national" means a national of an EEA state; and
    "EEA state" means a state which is a contracting party to the EEA Agreement.][1]

(2) References in this Part to a person being an EEA national shall be construed in relation to a body corporate as references to its being incorporated under the law of an EEA state.

(3) The "EEA Agreement" means the Agreement on the European Economic Area signed at Oporto on 2nd May 1992, as adjusted by the Protocol signed at Brussels on 17th March 1993.][2]

Construction of references to copyright owner

5-199   **173.**—(1) Where different persons are (whether in consequence of a partial assignment or otherwise) entitled to different aspects of copyright in a work, the copyright owner for any purpose of this Part is the person who is entitled to the aspect of copyright relevant for that purpose.

(2) Where copyright (or any aspect of copyright) is owned by more than one person jointly, references in this Part to the copyright owner are to all the owners, so that, in particular, any requirement of the licence of the copyright owner requires the licence of all of them.

Meaning of "educational establishment" and related expressions

5-200   **174.**—(1) The expression "educational establishment" in a provision of this Part means —
    (a) any school, and
    (b) any other description of educational establishment specified for the purposes of this Part, or that provision, by order of the Secretary of State.

(2) The Secretary of State may be order provide that the provisions of this Part relating to educational establishments shall apply, with such modifications and adaptations as may be specified in the order, in relation to teachers who are

---

[1] Substituted by SI 1996/2967 Pt II reg 9 (5)
[2] Inserted by SI 1995/3297 Pt II reg 11 (1)

employed by a local education authority to give instruction elsewhere to pupils who are unable to attend an educational establishment.

(3) In subsection (1)(a) "school" —

(a) in relation to England and Wales, has the same meaning as in the [Education Act 1996][1];

(b) in relation to Scotland, has the same meaning as in the Education (Scotland) Act 1962, except that it includes an approved school within the meaning of the Social Work (Scotland) Act 1968; and

(c) in relation to Northern Ireland, has the same meaning as in the Education and Libraries (Northern Ireland) Order 1986.

(4) An order under subsection (1)(b) may specify a description of educational establishment by reference to the instruments from time to time in force under any enactment specified in the order.

(5) In relation to an educational establishment the expressions "teacher" and "pupil" in this Part include, respectively, any person who gives and any person who receives instruction.

(6) References in this Part to anything being done "on behalf of" an educational establishment are to its being done for the purposes of that establishment by any person.

(7) An order under this section shall be made by statutory instrument which shall be subject to annulment in pursuance of a resolution of either House of Parliament.

Meaning of publication and commercial publication

175.—(1) In this Part "publication", in relation to a work—   **5-201**

(a) means the issue of copies to the public, and

(b) includes, in the case of a literary, dramatic, musical or artistic work, making it available to the public by means of an electronic retrieval system;

and related expressions shall be construed accordingly.

(2) In this Part "commercial publication", in relation to a literary, dramatic, musical or artistic work means—

(a) issuing copies of the work to the public at a time when copies made in advance of the receipt of orders are generally available to the public, or

(b) making the work available to the public by means of an electronic retrieval system;

and related expressions shall be construed accordingly.

(3) In the case of a work of architecture in the form of a building, or an artistic work incorporated in a building, construction of the building shall be treated as equivalent to publication of the work.

(4) The following do not constitute publication for the purposes of this Part and references to commercial publication shall be construed accordingly—

(a) in the case of a literary, dramatic or musical work—

(i) the performance of the work, or

(ii) the [communication to the public of the work][2] (otherwise than for the purposes of an electronic retrieval system);

(b) in the case of an artistic work—

(i) the exhibition of the work,

(ii) the issue to the public of copies of a graphic work representing, or of photographs of, a work of architecture in the form of a building

---

[1] Words substituted by Education Act 1996 c.56 Sch 37 (I) para 83

[2] Words substituted by SI 2003/2498 Sch 1 Pt I para 6 (1) (a)

or a model for a building, a sculpture or a work of artistic craftsmanship,
  (iii) the issue to the public of copies of a film including the work, or
  (iv) the [communication to the public of the work][1] (otherwise than
       for the purposes of an electronic retrieval system);
(c) in the case of a sound recording or film—
  (i) the work being played or shown in public, or
  (ii) the [communication to the public of the work][2].

(5) References in this Part to publication or commercial publication do not
include publication which is merely colourable and not intended to satisfy the
reasonable requirements of the public.

(6) No account shall be taken for the purposes of this section of any unauthorised act.

Requirement of signature: application in relation to body corporate

5-202   **176.**—(1) The requirement in the following provisions that an instrument be
signed by or on behalf of a person is also satisfied in the case of a body corporate
by the affixing of its seal—
  section 78(3)(b) (assertion by licensor of right to identification of author in
     case of public exhibition of copy made in pursuance of the licence),
  section 90(3) (assignment of copyright),
  section 91(1) (assignment of future copyright),
  section 92(1) (grant of exclusive licence).

(2) The requirement in the following provisions that an instrument be signed
by a person is satisfied in the case of a body corporate by signature on behalf of
the body or by the affixing of its seal—
  section 78(2)(b) (assertion by instrument in writing of right to have author
     identified),
  section 87(2) (waiver of moral rights).

Adaptation of expressions for Scotland

5-203   **177.** In the application of this Part to Scotland—
  "account of profits" means accounting and payment of profits;
  "accounts" means count, reckoning and payment;
  "assignment" means assignation;
  "costs" means expenses;
  "defendant" means defender;
  "delivery up" means delivery;
  "estoppel" means personal bar;
  "injunction" means interdict;
  "interlocutory relief" means interim remedy; and
  "plaintiff" means pursuer.

Minor definitions

5-204   **178.** In this Part—
  "article" , in the context of an article in a periodical, includes an item of
     any description;
  "business" includes a trade or profession;
  "collective work" means —
       (a) a work of joint authorship, or

---

[1] Words substituted by SI 2003/2498 Sch 1 Pt I para 6 (1) (b)
[2] Words substituted by SI 2003/2498 Sch 1 Pt I para 6 (1) (c)

(b) a work in which there are distinct contributions by different authors or in which works or parts of works of different authors are incorporated;

"computer-generated", in relation to a work, means that the work is generated by computer in circumstances such that there is no human author of the work;

"country" includes any territory;

"the Crown" includes the Crown in right of [the Scottish Administration or of][1] Her Majesty's Government in Northern Ireland or in any country outside the United Kingdom to which this Part extends;

"electronic" means actuated by electric, magnetic, electro-magnetic, electro-chemical or electro-mechanical energy, and "in electronic form" means in a form usable only by electronic means;

"employed", "employee", "employer" and "employment" refer to employment under a contract of service or of apprenticeship;

"facsimile copy" includes a copy which is reduced or enlarged in scale;

"international organisation" means an organisation the members of which include one or more states;

"judicial proceedings" includes proceedings before any court, tribunal or person having authority to decide any matter affecting a person's legal rights or liabilities;

"parliamentary proceedings" includes proceedings of the Northern Ireland Assembly [of the Scottish Parliament][2] or of the European Parliament;

["private study" does not include any study which is directly or indirectly for a commercial purpose;][3]

["producer", in relation to a sound recording or a film, means the person by whom the arrangements necessary for the making of the sound recording or film are undertaken;][4]

["public library" means a library administered by or on behalf of-

(a) in England and Wales, a library authority within the meaning of the Public Libraries and Museums Act 1964;

(b) in Scotland, a statutory library authority within the meaning of the Public Libraries (Scotland) Act 1955;

(c) in Northern Ireland, an Education and Library Board within the meaning of the Education and Libraries (Northern Ireland) Order 1986;][5]

["rental right" means the right of a copyright owner to authorise or prohibit the rental of copies of the work (see section 18A);][6]

"reprographic copy" and "reprographic copying" refer to copying by means of a reprographic process;

"reprographic process" means a process—

(a) for making facsimile copies, or

(b) involving the use of an appliance for making multiple copies,

and includes, in relation to a work held in electronic form, any copying by electronic means, but does not include the making of a film or sound recording;

---

[1] Words inserted by Scotland Act 1998 c.46 Sch 8 para 25 (7) (a)

[2] Words inserted by Scotland Act 1998 c.46 Sch 8 para 25 (7) (b)

[3] Inserted by SI 2003/2498 Sch 1 Pt I para 15 (3)

[4] Inserted by SI 1996/2967 Pt II reg 18 (5)

[5] Inserted by SI 1996/2967 Pt II reg 11 (5)

[6] Inserted by SI 1996/2967 Pt II reg 10 (3)

"sufficient acknowledgement" means an acknowledgement identifying the work in question by its title or other description, and identifying the author unless—

    (a) in the case of a published work, it is published anonymously;

    (b) in the case of an unpublished work, it is not possible for a person to ascertain the identity of the author by reasonable inquiry;

"sufficient disclaimer", in relation to an act capable of infringing the right conferred by section 80 (right to object to derogatory treatment of work), means a clear and reasonably prominent indication—

    (a) given at the time of the act, and

    (b) if the author or director is then identified, appearing along with the identification,

that the work has been subjected to treatment to which the author or director has not consented;

"telecommunications system" means a system for conveying visual images, sounds or other information by electronic means;

"typeface" includes an ornamental motif used in printing;

"unauthorised", as regards anything done in relation to a work, means done otherwise than—

    (a) by or with the licence of the copyright owner, or

    (b) if copyright does not subsist in the work, by or with the licence of the author or, in a case where section 11(2) would have applied, the author's employer or, in either case, persons lawfully claiming under him, or

    (c) in pursuance of section 48 (copying, &c. of certain material by the Crown);

["wireless broadcast" means a broadcast by means of wireless telegraphy;][1]

"wireless telegraphy" means the sending of electro-magnetic energy over paths not provided by a material substance constructed or arranged for that purpose [, but does not include the transmission of microwave energy between terrestrial fixed points][2];

"writing" includes any form of notation or code, whether by hand or otherwise and regardless of the method by which, or medium in or on which, it is recorded, and "written" shall be construed accordingly.

Index of defined expressions

5-205   **179.** The following Table shows provisions defining or otherwise explaining expressions used in this Part (other than provisions defining or explaining an expression used only in the same section)—

[accessible copy	section 31F(3)][1]
account of profits and accounts (in Scotland)	section 177
acts restricted by copyright	section 16(1)
adaptation	section 21(3)
[approved body	section 31B(12)][2]
archivist (in sections 37 to 43)	section 37(6)
article (in a periodical)	section 178

---

[1] Inserted by SI 2003/2498 Sch 1 Pt I para 15 (3)
[2] Words inserted by SI 1996/2967 Pt II reg 8

artistic work	section 4(1)
assignment (in Scotland)	section 177
author	sections 9 and 10(3)
broadcast (and related expressions)	section 6
building	section 4(2)
business	section 178 [...][3]
collective work	section 178
commencement (in Schedule 1)	paragraph 1(2) of that Schedule
commercial publication	section 175
[communication to the public	section 20][4]
computer-generated	section 178
copy and copying	section 17
copyright (generally)	section 1
copyright (in Schedule 1)	paragraph 2(2) of that Schedule
copyright owner	sections 101(2) and 173
Copyright Tribunal	section 145
copyright work	section 1(2)
costs (in Scotland)	section 177
country	section 178
[country of origin	section 15A][5]
the Crown	section 178
Crown copyright	sections 163(2) and 164(3)
[database	section 3A(1)][6]
defendant (in Scotland)	section 177
delivery up (in Scotland)	section 177
dramatic work	section 3(1)
[[EEA,][7] EEA national and EEA state	section 172A][8]
educational establishment	sections 174(1) to (4)
electronic and electronic form	section 178
employed, employee, employer and employment	section 178
[excepted sound recording	section 72(1A)][9]
exclusive licence	section 92(1)

existing works (in Schedule 1)	paragraph 1(3) of that Schedule
facsimile copy	section 178
film	[section 5B][10]
future copyright	section 91(2)
general licence (in sections 140 and 141)	section 140(7)
graphic work	section 4(2)
infringing copy	section 27
injunction (in Scotland)	section 177
interlocutory relief (in Scotland)	section 177
international organisation	section 178
issue of copies to the public	section 18(2)
joint authorship (work of)	sections 10(1) and (2)
judicial proceedings	section 178
[lawful user (in sections 50A to 50C)	section 50A(2)][11]
[lending	section 18A(2) to (6)][12]
librarian (in sections 37 to 43)	section 37(6)
licence (in sections 125 to 128)	section 124
licence of copyright owner	sections 90(4), 91(3) and 173
licensing body (in Chapter VII)	section 116(2)
licensing scheme (generally)	section 116(1)
licensing scheme (in sections 118 to 121)	section 117
literary work	section 3(1)
made (in relation to a literary, dramatic or musical work)	section 3(2)
musical work	section 3(1)
[needletime	section 135A][13]
the new copyright provisions (in Schedule 1)	paragraph 1(1) of that Schedule
the 1911 Act (in Schedule 1)	paragraph 1(1) of that Schedule
the 1956 Act (in Schedule 1)	paragraph 1(1) of that Schedule
on behalf of (in relation to an educational establishment)	section 174(5)

[original (in relation to a database)	section 3A(2).][14]
Parliamentary copyright	[sections 165(2) and (7) and 166(6) and 166A(3)][15]
parliamentary proceedings	section 178
performance	section 19(2)
photograph	section 4(2)
plaintiff (in Scotland)	section 177
prescribed conditions (in sections 38 to 43)	section 37(1)(b)
prescribed library or archive (in sections 38 to 43)	section 37(1)(a)
[private study	section 178][16]
[producer (in relation to a sound recording or film)	section 178][17]
programme (in the context of broadcasting)	section 6(3)
prospective owner (of copyright)	section 91(2)
[public library	section 178.][18]
publication and related expressions	section 175
published edition (in the context of copyright in the typographical arrangement)	section 8
pupil	section 174(5)
rental	[section 18A(2) to (6)][19]
[rental right	section 178][20]
reprographic copies and reprographic copying	section 178
reprographic process	section 178
sculpture	section 4(2)
signed	section 176
sound recording	[sections 5A and 135A][21]
sufficient acknowledgement	section 178
sufficient disclaimer	section 178
teacher	section 174(5)
telecommunications system	section 178
[terms of payment	section 135A][22]
typeface	section 178
unauthorised (as regards things done in relation to a work)	section 178
unknown (in relation to the author of a work)	section 9(5)

unknown authorship (work of)	section 9(4)
[visually impaired person	section 31F(9)][23]
[wireless broadcast	section 178][24]
wireless telegraphy	section 178
work (in Schedule 1)	paragraph 2(1) of that Schedule
work of more than one author (in Chapter VII)	section 116(4)
writing and written	section 178

[1] Inserted by Copyright (Visually Impaired Persons) Act 2002 c.33 s 7 (2)
[2] Inserted by Copyright (Visually Impaired Persons) Act 2002 c.33 s 7 (2)
[3] Repealed by SI 2003/2498 Sch 2 para 1
[4] Inserted by SI 2003/2498 Sch 1 Pt I para 15 (4)
[5] Inserted by SI 1995/3297 Pt II reg 8 (2)
[6] Inserted by SI 1997/3032 Pt II reg 11
[7] Words inserted by SI 1996/2967 Pt II reg 9 (6) (a)
[8] Inserted by SI 1995/3297 Pt II reg 11 (2)
[9] Inserted by SI 2003/2498 Pt II reg 21 (7)
[10] Words substituted by SI 1995/3297 Pt II reg 9 (5) (a)
[11] Inserted by SI 1992/3233 reg 9
[12] Inserted by SI 1996/2967 Pt II reg 10 (4)
[13] Words inserted by Broadcasting Act 1990 c.42 s 175 (3)
[14] Inserted by SI 1997/3032 Pt II Reg 11
[15] Words substituted by Scotland Act 1998 c.46 Sch 8 para 25 (8)
[16] Inserted by SI 2003/2498 Sch 1 Pt I para 15 (4)
[17] Inserted by SI 1996/2967 Pt II reg 18 (6)
[18] Inserted by SI 1996/2967 Pt II reg 11 (6)
[19] Words substituted by SI 1996/2967 Pt II reg 10 (4)
[20] Inserted by SI 1996/2967 Pt II reg 10 (4)
[21] Words substituted by SI 1995/3297 Pt II reg 9 (5) (b)
[22] Words inserted by Broadcasting Act 1990 c.42 s 175 (3)
[23] Inserted by Copyright (Visually Impaired Persons) Act 2002 c.33 s 7 (2)
[24] Inserted by SI 2003/2498 Sch 1 Pt I para 15 (4)

PART II

RIGHTS IN PERFORMANCES

Introductory

Rights conferred on performers and persons having recording rights

5-206   180.—(1) This Part confers rights—

(a) on a performer, by requiring his consent to the exploitation of his performances (see sections 181 to 184), and

(b) on a person having recording rights in relation to a performance, in relation to recordings made without his consent or that of the performer (see sections 185 to 188),

and creates offences in relation to dealing with or using illicit recordings and certain other related acts (see sections 198 and 201).

(2) In this Part—
"performance" means —

(a) a dramatic performance (which includes dance and mime),

(b) a musical performance,

(c) a reading or recitation of a literary work, or

(d) a performance of a variety act or any similar presentation,

which is, or so far as it is, a live performance given by one or more individuals;and

"recording", in relation to a performance, means a film or sound recording—

(a) made directly from the live performance,

(b) made from a broadcast of [...][1] the performance, or

(c) made, directly or indirectly, from another recording of the performance.

(3) The rights conferred by this Part apply in relation to performances taking place before the commencement of this Part; but no act done before commencement, or in pursuance of arrangements made before commencement, shall be regarded as infringing those rights.

(4) The rights conferred by this Part are independent of—

(a) any copyright in, or moral rights relating to, any work performed or any film or sound recording of, or broadcast [...][2] including, the performance, and

(b) any other right or obligation arising otherwise than under this Part.

Performers' rights

Qualifying performances

181. A performance is a qualifying performance for the purposes of the **5-207** provisions of this Part relating to performers' rights if it is given by a qualifying individual (as defined in section 206) or takes place in a qualifying country (as so defined).

[Consent required for recording, &c. of live performance

182.—(1) A performer's rights are infringed by a person who, without his **5-208** consent-

(a) makes a recording of the whole or any substantial part of a qualifying performance directly from the live performance,

(b) broadcasts live [...][3] the whole or any substantial part of a qualifying performance,

(c) makes a recording of the whole or any substantial part of a qualifying performance directly from a broadcast of [...][4] the live performance.

(3) In an action for infringement of a performer's rights brought by virtue of this section damages shall not be awarded against a defendant who shows that at the time of the infringement he believed on reasonable grounds that consent had been given.][5]

---

[1] Words repealed by SI 2003/2498 Sch 2 para 1
[2] Words repealed by SI 2003/2498 Sch 2 para 1
[3] Words repealed by SI 2003/2498 Sch 2 para 1
[4] Words repealed by SI 2003/2498 Sch 2 para 1
[5] Substituted by SI 1996/2967 Pt II reg 20 (1)

[Consent required for copying of recording

5-209   **182A.**—(1) A performer's rights are infringed by a person who, without his consent, makes [...]¹ a copy of a recording of the whole or any substantial part of a qualifying performance.

[(1A) In subsection (1), making a copy of a recording includes making a copy which is transient or is incidental to some other use of the original recording.]²

(2) It is immaterial whether the copy is made directly or indirectly.

(3) The right of a performer under this section to authorise or prohibit the making of such copies is referred to in this Part as "reproduction right".]³

[Consent required for issue of copies to public

5-210   **182B.**—(1) A performer's rights are infringed by a person who, without his consent, issues to the public copies of a recording of the whole or any substantial part of a qualifying performance.

(2) References in this Part to the issue to the public of copies of a recording are to-

    (a) the act of putting into circulation in the EEA copies not previously put into circulation in the EEA by or with the consent of the performer, or

    (b) the act of putting into circulation outside the EEA copies not previously put into circulation in the EEA or elsewhere.

(3) References in this Part to the issue to the public of copies of a recording do not include-

    (a) any subsequent distribution, sale, hiring or loan of copies previously put into circulation (but see section 182C: consent required for rental or lending), or

    (b) any subsequent importation of such copies into the United Kingdom or another EEA state,

except so far as paragraph (a) of subsection (2) applies to putting into circulation in the EEA copies previously put into circulation outside the EEA.

(4) References in this Part to the issue of copies of a recording of a performance include the issue of the original recording of the live performance.

(5) The right of a performer under this section to authorise or prohibit the issue of copies to the public is referred to in this Part as "distribution right".]⁴

[Consent required for rental or lending of copies to public

5-211   **182C.**—(1) A performer's rights are infringed by a person who, without his consent, rents or lends to the public copies of a recording of the whole or any substantial part of a qualifying performance.

(2) In this Part, subject to the following provisions of this section-

    (a) "rental" means making a copy of a recording available for use, on terms that it will or may be returned, for direct or indirect economic or commercial advantage, and

    (b) "lending" means making a copy of a recording available for use, on terms that it will or may be returned, otherwise than for direct or indirect economic or commercial advantage, through an establishment which is accessible to the public.

(3) The expressions "rental" and "lending" do not include-

---

¹ Words repealed by SI 2003/2498 Sch 2 para 1
² Inserted by SI 2003/2498 Pt II reg 8 (3)
³ Inserted by SI 1996/2967 Pt II reg 20 (2)
⁴ Inserted by SI 1996/2967 Pt II reg 20 (2)

(a) making available for the purpose of public performance, playing or showing in public [or communication to the public]¹;

(b) making available for the purpose of exhibition in public; or

(c) making available for on-the-spot reference use.

(4) The expression "lending" does not include making available between establishments which are accessible to the public.

(5) Where lending by an establishment accessible to the public gives rise to a payment the amount of which does not go beyond what is necessary to cover the operating costs of the establishment, there is no direct or indirect economic or commercial advantage for the purposes of this section.

(6) References in this Part to the rental or lending of copies of a recording of a performance include the rental or lending of the original recording of the live performance.

(7) In this Part-

"rental right" means the right of a performer under this section to authorise or prohibit the rental of copies to the public, and

"lending right" means the right of a performer under this section to authorise or prohibit the lending of copies to the public.]²

[Consent required for making available to the public

182CA—(1) A performer's rights are infringed by a person who, without his **5-212** consent, makes available to the public a recording of the whole or any substantial part of a qualifying performance by electronic transmission in such a way that members of the public may access the recording from a place and at a time individually chosen by them.

(2) The right of a performer under this section to authorise or prohibit the making available to the public of a recording is referred to in this Part as "making available right".]³

[Right to equitable remuneration for exploitation of sound recording

182D.—(1) Where a commercially published sound recording of the whole **5-213** or any substantial part of a qualifying performance-

(a) is played in public, or

[(b) is communicated to the public otherwise than by its being made available to the public in the way mentioned in section 182CA(1),]⁴

the performer is entitled to equitable remuneration from the owner of the copyright in the sound recording.

(2) The right to equitable remuneration under this section may not be assigned by the performer except to a collecting society for the purpose of enabling it to enforce the right on his behalf.

The right is, however, transmissible by testamentary disposition or by operation of law as personal or moveable property; and it may be assigned or further transmitted by any person into whose hands it passes.

(3) The amount payable by way of equitable remuneration is as agreed by or on behalf of the persons by and to whom it is payable, subject to the following provisions.

---

¹ Words substituted by SI 2003/2498 Sch 1 Pt I para 6 (2) (c)

² Inserted by SI 1996/2967 Pt II reg 20 (2)

³ Inserted by SI 2003/2498 Pt II reg 7 (1)

⁴ Substituted by SI 2003/2498 Pt II reg 7 (2)

(4) In default of agreement as to the amount payable by way of equitable remuneration, the person by or to whom it is payable may apply to the Copyright Tribunal to determine the amount payable.

(5) A person to or by whom equitable remuneration is payable may also apply to the Copyright Tribunal-

(a) to vary any agreement as to the amount payable, or

(b) to vary any previous determination of the Tribunal as to that matter;

but except with the special leave of the Tribunal no such application may be made within twelve months from the date of a previous determination.

An order made on an application under this subsection has effect from the date on which it is made or such later date as may be specified by the Tribunal.

(6) On an application under this section the Tribunal shall consider the matter and make such order as to the method of calculating and paying equitable remuneration as it may determine to be reasonable in the circumstances, taking into account the importance of the contribution of the performer to the sound recording.

(7) An agreement is of no effect in so far as it purports-

(a) to exclude or restrict the right to equitable remuneration under this section, or

(b) to prevent a person questioning the amount of equitable remuneration or to restrict the powers of the Copyright Tribunal under this section.][1]

Infringement of performer's rights by use of recording made without consent

5-214   **183.** A performer's rights are infringed by a person who, without his consent—

(a) shows or plays in public the whole or any substantial part of a qualifying performance, or

(b) [communicates to the public][2] the whole or any substantial part of a qualifying performance,

by means of a recording which was, and which that person knows or has reason to believe was, made without the performer's consent.

Infringement of performer's rights by importing, possessing or dealing with illicit recording

5-215   **184.**—(1) A performer's rights are infringed by a person who, without his consent—

(a) imports into the United Kingdom otherwise than for his private and domestic use, or

(b) in the course of a business possesses, sells or lets for hire, offers or exposes for sale or hire, or distributes,

a recording of a qualifying performance which is, and which that person knows or has reason to believe is, an illicit recording.

(2) Where in an action for infringement of a performer's rights brought by virtue of this section a defendant shows that the illicit recording was innocently acquired by him or a predecessor in title of his, the only remedy available against him in respect of the infringement is damages not exceeding a reasonable payment in respect of the act complained of.

---

[1] Inserted by SI 1996/2967 Pt II reg 20 (2)

[2] Words substituted by SI 2003/2498 Sch 1 Pt I para 13 (1) (a)

(3) In subsection (2) "innocently acquired" means that the person acquiring the recording did not know and had no reason to believe that it was an illicit recording.

Rights of person having recording rights

Exclusive recording contracts and persons having recording rights

185.—(1) In this Part an "exclusive recording contract" means a contract **5-216** between a performer and another person under which that person is entitled to the exclusion of all other persons (including the performer) to make recordings of one or more of his performances with a view to their commercial exploitation.

(2) References in this Part to a "person having recording rights", in relation to a performance, are (subject to subsection (3)) to a person—
> (a) who is party to and has the benefit of an exclusive recording contract to which the performance is subject, or
> (b) to whom the benefit of such a contract has been assigned,

and who is a qualifying person.

(3) If a performance is subject to an exclusive recording contract but the person mentioned in subsection (2) is not a qualifying person, references in this Part to a "person having recording rights" in relation to the performance are to any person—
> (a) who is licensed by such a person to make recordings of the performance with a view to their commercial exploitation, or
> (b) to whom the benefit of such a licence has been assigned,

and who is a qualifying person.

(4) In this section "with a view to commercial exploitation" means with a view to the recordings being sold or let for hire, or shown or played in public.

Consent required for recording of performance subject to exclusive contract

186.—(1) A person infringes the rights of a person having recording rights in **5-217** relation to a performance who, without his consent or that of the performer, makes a recording of the whole or any substantial part of the performance [...][1].

(2) In an action for infringement of those rights brought by virtue of this section damages shall not be awarded against a defendant who shows that at the time of the infringement he believed on reasonable grounds that consent had been given.

Infringement of recording rights by use of recording made without consent

187.—(1) A person infringes the rights of a person having recording rights in **5-218** relation to a performance who, without his consent or, in the case of a qualifying performance, that of the performer—
> (a) shows or plays in public the whole or any substantial part of the performance, or
> (b) [communicates to the public][2] the whole or any substantial part of the performance,

by means of a recording which was, and which that person knows or has reason to believe was, made without the appropriate consent.

(2) The reference in subsection (1) to "the appropriate consent" is to the consent of—

[1] Words repealed by SI 2003/2498 Sch 2 para 1
[2] Words substituted by SI 2003/2498 Sch 1 Pt I para 13 (1) (b)

    (a) the performer, or

    (b) the person who at the time the consent was given had recording rights in relation to the performance (or, if there was more than one such person, of all of them).

Infringement of recording rights by importing, possessing or dealing with illicit recording

5-219   **188.**—(1) A person infringes the rights of a person having recording rights in relation to a performance who, without his consent or, in the case of a qualifying performance, that of the performer—

    (a) imports into the United Kingdom otherwise than for his private and domestic use, or

    (b) in the course of a business possesses, sells or lets for hire, offers or exposes for sale or hire, or distributes,

a recording of the performance which is, and which that person knows or has reason to believe is, an illicit recording.

    (2) Where in an action for infringement of those rights brought by virtue of this section a defendant shows that the illicit recording was innocently acquired by him or a predecessor in title of his, the only remedy available against him in respect of the infringement is damages not exceeding a reasonable payment in respect of the act complained of.

    (3) In subsection (2) "innocently acquired" means that the person acquiring the recording did not know and had no reason to believe that it was an illicit recording.

Exceptions to rights conferred

Acts permitted notwithstanding rights conferred by this Part

5-220   **189.** The provisions of Schedule 2 specify acts which may be done notwithstanding the rights conferred by this Part, being acts which correspond broadly to certain of those specified in Chapter III of Part I (acts permitted notwithstanding copyright).

Power of tribunal to give consent on behalf of performer in certain cases

5-221   **190.**—[(1) The Copyright Tribunal may, on the application of a person wishing to make a copy of a recording of a performance, give consent in a case where the identity or whereabouts of the person entitled to the reproduction right cannot be ascertained by reasonable inquiry.][1]

    (2) Consent given by the Tribunal has effect as consent of [the person entitled to the reproduction right][2] for the purposes of—

    (a) the provisions of this Part relating to performers' rights, and

    (b) section 198(3)(a) (criminal liability: sufficient consent in relation to qualifying performances),

and may be given subject to any conditions specified in the Tribunal's order.

    (3) The Tribunal shall not give consent under subsection (1)(a) except after the service or publication of such notices as may be required by rules made under section 150 (general procedural rules) or as the Tribunal may in any particular case direct.

    (5) In any case the Tribunal shall take into account the following factors—

---

[1] Substituted by SI 1996/2967 Pt II reg 23 (2)
[2] Words substituted by SI 1996/2967 Pt II reg 23 (3)

(a) whether the original recording was made with the performer's consent and is lawfully in the possession or control of the person proposing to make the further recording;

(b) whether the making of the further recording is consistent with the obligations of the parties to the arrangements under which, or is otherwise consistent with the purposes for which, the original recording was made.

(6) Where the Tribunal gives consent under this section it shall, in default of agreement between the applicant and [the person entitled to the reproduction right]¹, make such order as it thinks fit as to the payment to be made to [that person]² in consideration of consent being given.

[Duration of rights]³

[Duration of rights

191.—(1) The following provisions have effect with respect to the duration of **5-222**
the rights conferred by this Part.

(2) The rights conferred by this Part in relation to a performance expire—

(a) at the end of the period of 50 years from the end of the calendar year in which the performance takes place, or

(b) if during that period a recording of the performance is released, 50 years from the end of the calendar year in which it is released,

subject as follows.

(3) For the purposes of subsection (2) a recording is "released" when it is first published, played or shown in public [or communicated to the public]⁴; but in determining whether a recording has been released no account shall be taken of any unauthorised act.

(4) Where a performer is not a national of an EEA state, the duration of the rights conferred by this Part in relation to his performance is that to which the performance is entitled in the country of which he is a national, provided that does not exceed the period which would apply under subsections (2) and (3).

(5) If or to the extent that the application of subsection (4) would be at variance with an international obligation to which the United Kingdom became subject prior to 29th October 1993, the duration of the rights conferred by this Part shall be as specified in subsections (2) and (3).]⁵

[Performers' property rights

[Performers' property rights

191A.—(1) The following rights conferred by this Part on a performer-   **5-223**
reproduction right (section 182A),
distribution right (section 182B),
rental right and lending right (section 182C),
[making available right (section 182CA),]⁶
are property rights ("a performer's property rights").

---

¹ Words substituted by SI 1996/2967 Pt II reg 23 (5) (a)
² Words substituted by SI 1996/2967 Pt II reg 23 (5) (b)
³ Substituted by SI 1996/2967 Pt II reg 21 (5) (a)
⁴ Words substituted by SI 2003/2498 Sch 1 (1) para 8 (1) (d)
⁵ Substituted by SI 1995/3297 Pt II reg 10
⁶ Words inserted by SI 2003/2498 Pt II reg 7 (3)

(2) References in this Part to the consent of the performer shall be construed in relation to a performer's property rights as references to the consent of the rights owner.

(3) Where different persons are (whether in consequence of a partial assignment or otherwise) entitled to different aspects of a performer's property rights in relation to a performance, the rights owner for any purpose of this Part is the person who is entitled to the aspect of those rights relevant for that purpose.

(4) Where a performer's property rights (or any aspect of them) is owned by more than one person jointly, references in this Part to the rights owner are to all the owners, so that, in particular, any requirement of the licence of the rights owner requires the licence of all of them.][1]

[Assignment and licences

5-224   **191B.**—(1) A performer's property rights are transmissible by assignment, by testamentary disposition or by operation of law, as personal or moveable property.

(2) An assignment or other transmission of a performer's property rights may be partial, that is, limited so as to apply-

   (a) to one or more, but not all, of the things requiring the consent of the rights owner;

   (b) to part, but not the whole, of the period for which the rights are to subsist.

(3) An assignment of a performer's property rights is not effective unless it is in writing signed by or on behalf of the assignor.

(4) A licence granted by the owner of a performer's property rights is binding on every successor in title to his interest in the rights, except a purchaser in good faith for valuable consideration and without notice (actual or constructive) of the licence or a person deriving title from such a purchaser; and references in this Part to doing anything with, or without, the licence of the rights owner shall be construed accordingly.][2]

[Prospective ownership of a performer's property rights

5-225   **191C.**—(1) This section applies where by an agreement made in relation to a future recording of a performance, and signed by or on behalf of the performer, the performer purports to assign his performer's property rights (wholly or partially) to another person.

(2) If on the rights coming into existence the assignee or another person claiming under him would be entitled as against all other persons to require the rights to be vested in him, they shall vest in the assignee or his successor in title by virtue of this subsection.

(3) A licence granted by a prospective owner of a performer's property rights is binding on every successor in title to his interest (or prospective interest) in the rights, except a purchaser in good faith for valuable consideration and without notice (actual or constructive) of the licence or a person deriving title from such a purchaser.

References in this Part to doing anything with, or without, the licence of the rights owner shall be construed accordingly.

---

[1] Inserted by SI 1996/2967 Pt II reg 21 (1)
[2] Inserted by SI 1996/2967 Pt II reg 21 (1)

(4) In subsection (3) "prospective owner" in relation to a performer's property rights means a person who is prospectively entitled to those rights by virtue of such an agreement as is mentioned in subsection (1).][1]

[Exclusive licences

191D.—(1) In this Part an "exclusive licence" means a licence in writing **5-226** signed by or on behalf of the owner of a performer's property rights authorising the licensee to the exclusion of all other persons, including the person granting the licence, to do anything requiring the consent of the rights owner.

(2) The licensee under an exclusive licence has the same rights against a successor in title who is bound by the licence as he has against the person granting the licence.][2]

[Performer's property right to pass under will with unpublished original recording

191E. Where under a bequest (whether general or specific) a person is **5-227** entitled beneficially or otherwise to any material thing containing an original recording of a performance which was not published before the death of the testator, the bequest shall, unless a contrary intention is indicated in the testator's will or a codicil to it, be construed as including any performer's rights in relation to the recording to which the testator was entitled immediately before his death.][3]

[Presumption of transfer of rental right in case of film production agreement

191F.—(1) Where an agreement concerning film production is concluded **5-228** between a performer and a film producer, the performer shall be presumed, unless the agreement provides to the contrary, to have transferred to the film producer any rental right in relation to the film arising from the inclusion of a recording of his performance in the film.

(2) Where this section applies, the absence of signature by or on behalf of the performer does not exclude the operation of section 191C (effect of purported assignment of future rights).

(3) The reference in subsection (1) to an agreement concluded between a performer and a film producer includes any agreement having effect between those persons, whether made by them directly or through intermediaries.

(4) Section 191G (right to equitable remuneration on transfer of rental right) applies where there is a presumed transfer by virtue of this section as in the case of an actual transfer.][4]

[Right to equitable remuneration where rental right transferred

191G.—(1) Where a performer has transferred his rental right concerning a **5-229** sound recording or a film to the producer of the sound recording or film, he retains the right to equitable remuneration for the rental.

The reference above to the transfer of rental right by one person to another includes any arrangement having that effect, whether made by them directly or through intermediaries.

---

[1] Inserted by SI 1996/2967 Pt II reg 21 (1)
[2] Inserted by SI 1996/2967 Pt II reg 21 (1)
[3] Inserted by SI 1996/2967 Pt II reg 21 (1)
[4] Inserted by SI 1996/2967 Pt II reg 21 (1)

(2) The right to equitable remuneration under this section may not be assigned by the performer except to a collecting society for the purpose of enabling it to enforce the right on his behalf.

The right is, however, transmissible by testamentary disposition or by operation of law as personal or moveable property; and it may be assigned or further transmitted by any person into whose hands it passes.

(3) Equitable remuneration under this section is payable by the person for the time being entitled to the rental right, that is, the person to whom the right was transferred or any successor in title of his.

(4) The amount payable by way of equitable remuneration is as agreed by or on behalf of the persons by and to whom it is payable, subject to section 191H (reference of amount to Copyright Tribunal).

(5) An agreement is of no effect in so far as it purports to exclude or restrict the right to equitable remuneration under this section.

(6) In this section a "collecting society" means a society or other organisation which has as its main object, or one of its main objects, the exercise of the right to equitable remuneration on behalf of more than one performer.][1]

[Equitable remuneration: reference of amount to Copyright Tribunal

5-230   **191H.**—(1) In default of agreement as to the amount payable by way of equitable remuneration under section 191G, the person by or to whom it is payable may apply to the Copyright Tribunal to determine the amount payable.

(2) A person to or by whom equitable remuneration is payable may also apply to the Copyright Tribunal-

    (a) to vary any agreement as to the amount payable, or

    (b) to vary any previous determination of the Tribunal as to that matter;

but except with the special leave of the Tribunal no such application may be made within twelve months from the date of a previous determination.

An order made on an application under this subsection has effect from the date on which it is made or such later date as may be specified by the Tribunal.

(3) On an application under this section the Tribunal shall consider the matter and make such order as to the method of calculating and paying equitable remuneration as it may determine to be reasonable in the circumstances, taking into account the importance of the contribution of the performer to the film or sound recording.

(4) Remuneration shall not be considered inequitable merely because it was paid by way of a single payment or at the time of the transfer of the rental right.

(5) An agreement is of no effect in so far as it purports to prevent a person questioning the amount of equitable remuneration or to restrict the powers of the Copyright Tribunal under this section.][2]

[Infringement actionable by rights owner

5-231   **191I.**—(1) An infringement of a performer's property rights is actionable by the rights owner.

(2) In an action for infringement of a performer's property rights all such relief by way of damages, injunctions, accounts or otherwise is available to the plaintiff as is available in respect of the infringement of any other property right.

(3) This section has effect subject to the following provisions of this Part.][3]

---

[1] Inserted by SI 1996/2967 Pt II reg 21 (1)
[2] Inserted by SI 1996/2967 Pt II reg 21 (1)
[3] Inserted by SI 1996/2967 Pt II reg 21 (1)

[Provisions as to damages in infringement action

191J.—(1) Where in an action for infringement of a performer's property 5-232
rights it is shown hat at the time of the infringement the defendant did not know,
and had no reason to believe, that the rights subsisted in the recording to which
the action relates, the plaintiff is not entitled to damages against him, but without
prejudice to any other remedy.

(2) The court may in an action for infringement of a performer's property
rights having regard to all the circumstances, and in particular to-

    (a) the flagrancy of the infringement, and

    (b) any benefit accruing to the defendant by reason of the infringement,

award such additional damages as the justice of the case may require.][1]

[Injunctions against service providers

191JA—(1) The High Court (in Scotland, the Court of Session) shall have 5-233
power to grant an injunction against a service provider, where that service
provider has actual knowledge of another person using their service to infringe a
performer's property right.

(2) In determining whether a service provider has actual knowledge for the
purpose of this section, a court shall take into account all matters which appear
to it in the particular circumstances to be relevant and, amongst other things,
shall have regard to–

    (a) whether a service provider has received a notice through a means of
        contact made available in accordance with regulation 6(1)(c) of the
        Electronic Commerce (EC Directive) Regulations 2002 (SI 2002/2013);
        and

    (b) the extent to which any notice includes–

        (i) the full name and address of the sender of the notice;

        (ii) details of the infringement in question.

(3) In this section "service provider" has the meaning given to it by
regulation 2 of the Electronic Commerce (EC Directive) Regulations 2002.

(4) Section 177 applies in respect of this section as it applies in respect of Part
1.][2]

[Undertaking to take licence of right in infringement proceedings

191K.—(1) If in proceedings for infringement of a performer's property 5-234
rights in respect of which a licence is available as of right under paragraph 17 of
Schedule 2A (powers exercisable in consequence of competition report) the
defendant undertakes to take a licence on such terms as may be agreed or, in
default of agreement, settled by the Copyright Tribunal under that paragraph-

    (a) no injunction shall be granted against him,

    (b) no order for delivery up shall be made under section 195, and

    (c) the amount recoverable against him by way of damages or on an
        account of profits shall not exceed double the amount which would have
        been payable by him as licensee if such a licence on those terms had
        been granted before the earliest infringement.

(2) An undertaking may be given at any time before final order in the proceedings, without any admission of liability.

---

[1] Inserted by SI 1996/2967 Pt II reg 21 (1)
[2] Inserted by SI 2003/2498 Pt II reg 27 (2)

(3) Nothing in this section affects the remedies available in respect of an infringement committed before licences of right were available.][1]

[Rights and remedies for exclusive licensee

5-235   **191L.**—(1) An exclusive licensee has, except against the owner of a performer's property rights, the same rights and remedies in respect of matters occurring after the grant of the licence as if the licence had been an assignment.

(2) His rights and remedies are concurrent with those of the rights owner; and references in the relevant provisions of this Part to the rights owner shall be construed accordingly.

(3) In an action brought by an exclusive licensee by virtue of this section a defendant may avail himself of any defence which would have been available to him if the action had been brought by the rights owner.][2]

[Exercise of concurrent rights

5-236   **191M.**—(1) Where an action for infringement of a performer's property rights brought by the rights owner or an exclusive licensee relates (wholly or partly) to an infringement in respect of which they have concurrent rights of action, the rights owner or, as the case may be, the exclusive licensee may not, without the leave of the court, proceed with the action unless the other is either joined as plaintiff or added as a defendant.

(2) A rights owner or exclusive licensee who is added as a defendant in pursuance of subsection (1) is not liable for any costs in the action unless he takes part in the proceedings.

(3) The above provisions do not affect the granting of interlocutory relief on an application by the rights owner or exclusive licensee alone.

(4) Where an action for infringement of a performer's property rights is brought which relates (wholly or partly) to an infringement in respect of which the rights owner and an exclusive licensee have or had concurrent rights of action-

> (a) the court shall in assessing damages take into account-
>> (i) the terms of the licence, and
>> (ii) any pecuniary remedy already awarded or available to either of them in respect of the infringement;
> (b) no account of profits shall be directed if an award of damages has been made, or an account of profits has been directed, in favour of the other of them in respect of the infringement; and
> (c) the court shall if an account of profits is directed apportion the profits between them as the court considers just, subject to any agreement between them;

and these provisions apply whether or not the rights owner and the exclusive licensee are both parties to the action.

(5) The owner of a performer's property rights shall notify any exclusive licensee having concurrent rights before applying for an order under section 195 (order for delivery up) or exercising the right conferred by section 196 (right of seizure); and the court may on the application of the licensee make such order under section 195 or, as the case may be, prohibiting or permitting the exercise by the rights owner of the right conferred by section 196, as it thinks fit having regard to the terms of the licence.][3]][4]

---

[1] Inserted by SI 1996/2967 Pt II reg 21 (1)
[2] Inserted by SI 1996/2967 Pt II reg 21 (1)
[3] Inserted by SI 1996/2967 Pt II reg 21 (1)
[4] Inserted by SI 1996/2967 Pt II reg 21 (1)

[Non-property rights

[Performers' non-property rights

192A.—(1) the rights conferred on a performer by-   **5-237**
    section 182 (consent required for recording, &c. of live performance),
    section 183 (infringement of performer's rights by use of recording made
        without consent), and
    section 184 (infringement of performer's rights importing, possessing or
        dealing with illicit recording),
are not assignable or transmissible, except to the following extent. They are
referred to in this Part as "a performer's non-property rights".

(2) On the death of a person entitled to any such right-
    (a) the right passes to such person as he may by testamentary disposition
        specifically direct, and
    (b) if or to the extent that there is no such direction, the right is exercisable
        by his personal representatives.

(3) References in this Part to the performer, in the context of the person
having any such right, shall be construed as references to the person for the time
being entitled to exercise those rights.

(4) Where by virtue of subsection (2)(a) a right becomes exercisable by more
than one person, it is exercisable by each of them independently of the other or
others.

(5) Any damages recovered by personal representatives by virtue of this
section in respect of an infringement after a person's death shall devolve as part of
his estate as if the right of action had subsisted and been vested in him immediately before his death.

Transmissibility of rights of person having recording rights

192B.—(1) The rights conferred by this Part on a person having recording **5-238**
rights are not assignable or transmissible.

(2) This does not affect section 185(2)(b) or (3)(b), so far as those provisions
confer rights under this Part on a person to whom the benefit of a contract or
licence is assigned.][1][2]

Duration and transmission of rights; consent

Consent

193.—(1) Consent for the purposes of this Part [by a person having a perfor- **5-239**
mer's non-property rights, or by a person having recording rights,][3] may be given
in relation to a specific performance, a specified description of performances or
performances generally, and may relate to past or future performances.

(2) A person having recording rights in a performance is bound by any
consent given by a person through whom he derives his rights under the exclusive
recording contract or licence in question, in the same way as if the consent had
been given by him.

[1] Substituted by SI 1996/2967 Pt II reg 21 (2)
[2] Substituted by SI 1996/2967 Pt II reg 21 (2)
[3] Words inserted by SI 1996/2967 Pt II reg 21 (3) (a)

(3) Where [a performer's non-property right]¹ passes to another person, any consent binding on the person previously entitled binds the person to whom the right passes in the same way as if the consent had been given by him.

Infringement actionable as breach of statutory duty

5-240   **194.** [An infringement of
    (a) a performer's non-property rights, or
    (b) any right conferred by this Part on a person having recording rights,
is actionable by the person entitled to the right as a breach of statutory duty.]²

Delivery up or seizure of illicit recordings

Order for delivery up

5-241   **195.**—(1) Where a person has in his possession, custody or control in the course of a business an illicit recording of a performance, a person having performer's rights or recording rights in relation to the performance under this Part may apply to the court for an order that the recording be delivered up to him or to such other person as the court may direct.

(2) An application shall not be made after the end of the period specified in section 203; and no order shall be made unless the court also makes, or it appears to the court that there are grounds for making, an order under section 204 (order as to disposal of illicit recording).

(3) A person to whom a recording is delivered up in pursuance of an order under this section shall, if an order under section 204 is not made, retain it pending the making of an order, or the decision not to make an order, under that section.

(4) Nothing in this section affects any other power of the court.

Right to seize illicit recordings

5-242   **196.**—(1) An illicit recording of a performance which is found exposed or otherwise immediately available for sale or hire, and in respect of which a person would be entitled to apply for an order under section 195, may be seized and detained by him or a person authorised by him.

The right to seize and detain is exercisable subject to the following conditions and is subject to any decision of the court under section 204 (order as to disposal of illicit recording).

(2) Before anything is seized under this section notice of the time and place of the proposed seizure must be given to a local police station.

(3) A person may for the purpose of exercising the right conferred by this section enter premises to which the public have access but may not seize anything in the possession, custody or control of a person at a permanent or regular place of business of his and may not use any force.

(4) At the time when anything is seized under this section there shall be left at the place where it was seized a notice in the prescribed form containing the prescribed particulars as to the person by whom or on whose authority the seizure is made and the grounds on which it is made.

(5) In this section—

---

¹ Words substituted by SI 1996/2967 Pt II reg 21 (3) (b)
² Words substituted by SI 1996/2967 Pt II reg 21 (4)

"premises" includes land, buildings, fixed or moveable structures, vehicles, vessels, aircraft and hovercraft; and

"prescribed" means prescribed by order of the Secretary of State.

(6) An order of the Secretary of State under this section shall be made by statutory instrument which shall be subject to annulment in pursuance of a resolution of either House of Parliament.

Meaning of "illicit recording"

197.—(1) In this Part "illicit recording", in relation to a performance, shall be construed in accordance with this section.   **5-243**

(2) For the purposes of a performer's rights, a recording of the whole or any substantial part of a performance of his is an illicit recording if it is made, otherwise than for private purposes, without his consent.

(3) For the purposes of the rights of a person having recording rights, a recording of the whole or any substantial part of a performance subject to the exclusive recording contract is an illicit recording if it is made, otherwise than for private purposes, without his consent or that of the performer.

(4) For the purposes of sections 198 and 199 (offences and orders for delivery up in criminal proceedings), a recording is an illicit recording if it is an illicit recording for the purposes mentioned in subsection (2) or subsection (3).

(5) In this Part "illicit recording" includes a recording falling to be treated as an illicit recording by virtue of any of the following provisions of Schedule 2—

paragraph 4(3) (recordings made for purposes of instruction or examination),

paragraph 6(2) (recordings made by educational establishments for educational purposes),

paragraph 12(2) (recordings of performance in electronic form retained on transfer of principal recording), [...][1]

paragraph 16(3) (recordings made for purposes of broadcast [...][2]),

[paragraph 17A(2) (recording for the purposes of time-shifting), or

paragraph 17B(2) (photographs of broadcasts),][3]

but otherwise does not include a recording made in accordance with any of the provisions of that Schedule.

(6) It is immaterial for the purposes of this section where the recording was made

Offences

Criminal liability for making, dealing with or using illicit recordings

198.—(1) A person commits an offence who without sufficient consent—   **5-244**

(a) makes for sale or hire, or

(b) imports into the United Kingdom otherwise than for his private and domestic use, or

(c) possesses in the course of a business with a view to committing any act infringing the rights conferred by this Part, or

(d) in the course of a business—

   (i) sells or lets for hire, or

   (ii) offers or exposes for sale or hire, or

---

[1] Word repealed by SI 2003/2498 Sch 2 para 1

[2] Words repealed by SI 2003/2498 Sch 2 para 1

[3] Inserted by SI 2003/2498 Pt II reg 20 (4)

(iii) distributes,

a recording which is, and which he knows or has reason to believe is, an illicit recording.

[(1A) A person who infringes a performer's making available right—

(a) in the course of a business, or

(b) otherwise than in the course of a business to such an extent as to affect prejudicially the owner of the making available right,

commits an offence if he knows or has reason to believe that, by doing so, he is infringing the making available right in the recording.][1]

(2) A person commits an offence who causes a recording of a performance made without sufficient consent to be—

(a) shown or played in public, or

[(b) communicated to the public,][2]

thereby infringing any of the rights conferred by this Part, if he knows or has reason to believe that those rights are thereby infringed.

(3) In subsections (1) and (2) "sufficient consent" means —

(a) in the case of a qualifying performance, the consent of the performer, and

(b) in the case of a non-qualifying performance subject to an exclusive recording contract—

(i) for the purposes of subsection (1)(a) (making of recording), the consent of the performer or the person having recording rights, and

(ii) for the purposes of subsection (1)(b), (c) and (d) and subsection (2) (dealing with or using recording), the consent of the person having recording rights.

The references in this subsection to the person having recording rights are to the person having those rights at the time the consent is given or, if there is more than one such person, to all of them.

(4) No offence is committed under subsection (1) or (2) by the commission of an act which by virtue of any provision of Schedule 2 may be done without infringing the rights conferred by this Part.

(5) A person guilty of an offence under subsection (1)(a), (b) or (d)(iii) is liable—

(a) on summary conviction to imprisonment for a term not exceeding six months or a fine not exceeding the statutory maximum, or both;

(b) on conviction on indictment to a fine or imprisonment for a term not exceeding [ten][3] years, or both.

[(5A) A person guilty of an offence under subsection (1A) is liable—

(a) on summary conviction to imprisonment for a term not exceeding three months or a fine not exceeding the statutory maximum, or both;

(b) on conviction on indictment to a fine or imprisonment for a term not exceeding two years, or both.][4]

(6) A person guilty of any other offence under this section is liable on summary conviction to a fine not exceeding level 5 on the standard scale or imprisonment for a term not exceeding six months, or both.

---

[1] Inserted by SI 2003/2498 Pt II reg 26 (3) (a)

[2] Substituted by SI 2003/2498 Sch 1 Pt I para 4 (5)

[3] Word substituted by Copyright, etc. and Trade Marks (Offences and Enforcement) Act 2002 c.25 s 1 (3)

[4] Inserted by SI 2003/2498 Pt II reg 26 (3) (b)

Order for delivery up in criminal proceedings

199.—(1) The court before which proceedings are brought against a person **5-245** for an offence under section 198 may, if satisfied that at the time of his arrest or charge he had in his possession, custody or control in the course of a business an illicit recording of a performance, order that it be delivered up to a person having performers' rights or recording rights in relation to the performance or to such other person as the court may direct.

(2) For this purpose a person shall be treated as charged with an offence—
- (a) in England, Wales and Northern Ireland, when he is orally charged or is served with a summons or indictment;
- (b) in Scotland, when he is cautioned, charged or served with a complaint or indictment.

(3) An order may be made by the court of its own motion or on the application of the prosecutor (or, in Scotland, the Lord Advocate or procurator-fiscal), and may be made whether or not the person is convicted of the offence, but shall not be made—
- (a) after the end of the period specified in section 203 (period after which remedy of delivery up not available), or
- (b) if it appears to the court unlikely that any order will be made under section 204 (order as to disposal of illicit recording).

(4) An appeal lies from an order made under this section by a magistrates' court—
- (a) in England and Wales, to the Crown Court, and
- (b) in Northern Ireland, to the county court;

and in Scotland, where an order has been made under this section, the person from whose possession, custody or control the illicit recording has been removed may, without prejudice to any other form of appeal under any rule of law, appeal against that order in the same manner as against sentence.

(5) A person to whom an illicit recording is delivered up in pursuance of an order under this section shall retain it pending the making of an order, or the decision not to make an order, under section 204.

(6) Nothing in in this section affects the powers of the court under [section 143 of the Powers of Criminal Courts (Sentencing) Act 2000][1], [Part II of the Proceeds of Crime (Scotland) Act 1995][2] or Article 7 of the Criminal Justice (Northern Ireland) Order 1980 (general provisions as to forfeiture in criminal proceedings).

Search warrants

200.—(1) Where a justice of the peace (in Scotland, a sheriff or justice of the **5-246** peace) is satisfied by information on oath given by a constable (in Scotland, by evidence on oath) that there are reasonable grounds for believing—
- (a) that an offence under [section 198(1) or (1A)][3] (offences of making, importing [,possessing, selling etc.][4] or distributing illicit recordings) has been or is about to be committed in any premises, and
- (b) that evidence that such an offence has been or is about to be committed is in those premises,

---

[1] Words substituted by Powers of Criminal Courts (Sentencing) Act 2000 c.6 Sch 9 para 116

[2] Words substituted by Criminal Procedure (Consequential Provisions) (Scotland) Act 1995 c.40 Sch 4 para 70 (3)

[3] Words substituted by SI 2003/2498 Pt II reg 26 (4) (a)

[4] Words inserted by Copyright, etc. and Trade Marks (Offences and Enforcement) Act 2002 c.25 s 2 (3) (a) (ii)

he may issue a warrant authorising a constable to enter and search the premises, using such reasonable force as is necessary.

(2) The power conferred by subsection (1) does not, in England and Wales, extend to authorising a search for material of the kinds mentioned in section 9(2) of the Police and Criminal Evidence Act 1984 (certain classes of personal or confidential material).

(3) A warrant under subsection (1)—

    (a) may authorise persons to accompany any constable executing the warrant, and

    (b) remains in force for 28 days from the date of its issue.

[(3A) In executing a warrant issued under subsection (1) a constable may seize an article if he reasonably believes that it is evidence that any offence under [section 198(1) or (1A)]¹ has been or is about to be committed.]²

(4) In this section "premises" includes land, buildings, fixed or moveable structures, vehicles, vessels, aircraft and hovercraft.

False representation of authority to give consent

5-247   **201.**—(1) It is an offence for a person to represent falsely that he is authorised by any person to give consent for the purposes of this Part in relation to a performance, unless he believes on reasonable grounds that he is so authorised.

(2) A person guilty of an offence under this section is liable on summary conviction to imprisonment for a term not exceeding six months or a fine not exceeding level 5 on the standard scale or both.

Supplementary provisions with respect to delivery up and seizure

Period after which remedy of delivery up not available

5-248   **203.**—(1) An application for an order under section 195 (order for delivery up in civil proceedings) may not be made after the end of the period of six years from the date on which the illicit recording in question was made, subject to the following provisions.

(2) If during the whole or any part of that period a person entitled to apply for an order—

    (a) is under a disability, or

    (b) is prevented by fraud or concealment from discovering the facts entitling him to apply,

an application may be made by him at any time before the end of the period of six years from the date on which he ceased to be under a disability or, as the case may be, could with reasonable diligence have discovered those facts.

(3) In subsection (2) "disability" —

    (a) in England and Wales, has the same meaning as in the Limitation Act 1980;

    (b) in Scotland, means legal disability within the meaning of the Prescription and Limitations (Scotland) Act 1973;

    (c) in Northern Ireland, has the same meaning as in the Statute of Limitation (Northern Ireland) 1958.

---

¹ Words substituted by SI 2003/2498 Pt II reg 26 (4) (b)
² Inserted by Copyright, etc. and Trade Marks (Offences and Enforcement) Act 2002 c.25 s 2 (3) (b)

(4) An order under section 199 (order for delivery up in criminal proceedings) shall not, in any case, be made after the end of the period of six years from the date on which the illicit recording in question was made.

Order as to disposal of illicit recording

204.—(1) An application may be made to the court for an order than an illicit recording of a performance delivered up in pursuance of an order under section 195 or 199, or seized and detained in pursuance of the right conferred by section 196, shall be— **5-249**

    (a) forfeited to such person having performer's rights or recording rights in relation to the performance as the court may direct, or

    (b) destroyed or otherwise dealt with as the court may think fit,

or for a decision that no such order should be made.

(2) In considering what order (if any) should be made, the court shall consider whether other remedies available in an action for infringement of the rights conferred by this Part would be adequate to compensate the person or persons entitled to the rights and to protect their interests.

(3) Provision shall be made by rules of court as to the service of notice on persons having an interest in the recording, and any such person is entitled—

    (a) to appear in proceedings for an order under this section, whether or not he was served with notice, and

    (b) to appeal against any order made, whether or not he appeared;

and an order shall not take effect until the end of the period within which notice of an appeal may be given or, if before the end of that period notice of appeal is duly given, until the final determination or abandonment of the proceedings on the appeal.

(4) Where there is more than one person interested in a recording, the court shall make such order as it thinks just and may (in particular) direct that the recording be sold, or otherwise dealt with, and the proceeds divided.

(5) If the court decides that no order should be made under this section, the person in whose possession, custody or control the recording was before being delivered up or seized is entitled to its return.

(6) References in this section to a person having an interest in a recording include any person in whose favour an order could be made in respect of the recording under this section or under section 114 or 231 of this Act or [section 19 of the Trade Marks Act 1994][1] (which make similar provision in relation to infringement of copyright, design right and trade marks).

[Forfeiture of illicit recordings: England and Wales or Northern Ireland

204A—(1) In England and Wales or Northern Ireland where illicit recordings of a performance have come into the possession of any person in connection with the investigation or prosecution of a relevant offence, that person may apply under this section for an order for the forfeiture of the illicit recordings. **5-250**

(2) For the purposes of this section "relevant offence" means—

    (a) an offence under [section 198(1) or (1A)][2] (criminal liability for making or dealing with illicit recordings),

    (b) an offence under the Trade Descriptions Act 1968 (c. 29), or

    (c) an offence involving dishonesty or deception.

(3) An application under this section may be made—

---

[1] Words substituted by Trade Marks Act 1994 c.26 Sch 4 para 8 (2)
[2] Words substituted by SI 2003/2498 Pt II reg 26 (4) (c)

2. trustee

(a) where proceedings have been brought in any court for a relevant offence relating to some or all of the illicit recordings, to that court, or

(b) where no application for the forfeiture of the illicit recordings has been made under paragraph (a), by way of complaint to a magistrates' court.

(4) On an application under this section, the court shall make an order for the forfeiture of any illicit recordings only if it is satisfied that a relevant offence has been committed in relation to the illicit recordings.

(5) A court may infer for the purposes of this section that such an offence has been committed in relation to any illicit recordings if it is satisfied that such an offence has been committed in relation to illicit recordings which are representative of the illicit recordings in question (whether by reason of being part of the same consignment or batch or otherwise).

(6) Any person aggrieved by an order made under this section by a magistrates' court, or by a decision of such a court not to make such an order, may appeal against that order or decision—

(a) in England and Wales, to the Crown Court, or

(b) in Northern Ireland, to the county court.

(7) An order under this section may contain such provision as appears to the court to be appropriate for delaying the coming into force of the order pending the making and determination of any appeal (including any application under section 111 of the Magistrates' Courts Act 1980 (c. 43) or Article 146 of the Magistrates' Courts (Northern Ireland) Order 1981 (S.I. 1987/1675 (N.I. 26)) (statement of case)).

(8) Subject to subsection (9), where any illicit recordings are forfeited under this section they shall be destroyed in accordance with such directions as the court may give.

(9) On making an order under this section the court may direct that the illicit recordings to which the order relates shall (instead of being destroyed) be forfeited to the person having the performers' rights or recording rights in question or dealt with in such other way as the court considers appropriate.][1]

[Forfeiture: Scotland

5-251 **204B**—(1) In Scotland the court may make an order under this section for the forfeiture of any illicit recordings.

(2) An order under this section may be made—

(a) on an application by the procurator-fiscal made in the manner specified in section 134 of the Criminal Procedure (Scotland) Act 1995 (c. 46), or

(b) where a person is convicted of a relevant offence, in addition to any other penalty which the court may impose.

(3) On an application under subsection (2)(a), the court shall make an order for the forfeiture of any illicit recordings only if it is satisfied that a relevant offence has been committed in relation to the illicit recordings.

(4) The court may infer for the purposes of this section that such an offence has been committed in relation to any illicit recordings if it is satisfied that such an offence has been committed in relation to illicit recordings which are representative of the illicit recordings in question (whether by reason of being part of the same consignment or batch or otherwise).

(5) The procurator-fiscal making the application under subsection (2)(a) shall serve on any person appearing to him to be the owner of, or otherwise to have an interest in, the illicit recordings to which the application relates a copy of

---

[1] Inserted by Copyright, etc. and Trade Marks (Offences and Enforcement) Act 2002 c.25 s 4

the application, together with a notice giving him the opportunity to appear at the hearing of the application to show cause why the illicit recordings should not be forfeited.

(6) Service under subsection (5) shall be carried out, and such service may be proved, in the manner specified for citation of an accused in summary proceedings under the Criminal Procedure (Scotland) Act 1995.

(7) Any person upon whom notice is served under subsection (5) and any other person claiming to be the owner of, or otherwise to have an interest in, illicit recordings to which an application under this section relates shall be entitled to appear at the hearing of the application to show cause why the illicit recordings should not be forfeited.

(8) The court shall not make an order following an application under subsection (2)(a)—

    (a) if any person on whom notice is served under subsection (5) does not appear, unless service of the notice on that person is proved, or

    (b) if no notice under subsection (5) has been served, unless the court is satisfied that in the circumstances it was reasonable not to serve such notice.

(9) Where an order for the forfeiture of any illicit recordings is made following an application under subsection (2)(a), any person who appeared, or was entitled to appear, to show cause why the illicit recordings should not be forfeited may, within 21 days of the making of the order, appeal to the High Court by Bill of Suspension.

(10) Section 182(5)(a) to (e) of the Criminal Procedure (Scotland) Act 1995 shall apply to an appeal under subsection (9) as it applies to a stated case under Part 2 of that Act.

(11) An order following an application under subsection (2)(a) shall not take effect—

    (a) until the end of the period of 21 days beginning with the day after the day on which the order is made, or

    (b) if an appeal is made under subsection (9) above within that period, until the appeal is determined or abandoned.

(12) An order under subsection (2)(b) shall not take effect—

    (a) until the end of the period within which an appeal against the order could be brought under the Criminal Procedure (Scotland) Act 1995 (c. 46), or

    (b) if an appeal is made within that period, until the appeal is determined or abandoned.

(13) Subject to subsection (14), illicit recordings forfeited under this section shall be destroyed in accordance with such directions as the court may give.

(14) On making an order under this section the court may direct that the illicit recordings to which the order relates shall (instead of being destroyed) be forfeited to the person having the performers' rights or recording rights in question or dealt with in such other way as the court considers appropriate.

(15) For the purposes of this section—

    "relevant offence" means an offence under [section 198(1) or (1A)][1] (criminal liability for making or dealing with illicit recordings), or under the Trade Descriptions Act 1968 (c. 29) or any offence involving dishonesty or deception;

    "the court" means—

---

[1] Words substituted by SI 2003/2498 Pt II reg 26 (4) (d)

(a) in relation to an order made on an application under subsection (2)(a), the sheriff, and

(b) in relation to an order made under subsection (2)(b), the court which imposed the penalty.][1]

[Licensing of performers' property rights

Licensing of performers' property rights

5-252   **205A.** The provisions of Schedule 2A have effect with respect to the licensing of performers' property rights.][2]

[Jurisdiction of Copyright Tribunal

Jurisdiction of Copyright Tribunal

5-253   **205B**—(1) The Copyright Tribunal has jurisdiction under this Part to hear and determine proceedings under-

(a) section 182D (amount of equitable remuneration for exploitation of commercial sound recording);

(b) section 190 (application to give consent on behalf of owner of reproduction right);

(c) section 191H (amount of equitable remuneration on transfer of rental right);

[(cc) paragraph 19 of Schedule 2 (determination of royalty or other remuneration to be paid with respect to re-transmission of broadcast including performance or recording);][3]

(d) paragraph 3, 4 or 5 of Schedule 2A (reference of licensing scheme);

(e) paragraph 6 or 7 of that Schedule (application with respect to licence under licensing scheme);

(f) paragraph 10, 11 or 12 of that Schedule (reference or application with respect to licensing by licensing body);

(g) paragraph 15 of that Schedule (application to settle royalty for certain lending);

(h) paragraph 17 of that Schedule (application to settle terms of licence available as of right).

(2) The provisions of Chapter VIII of Part I (general provisions relating to the Copyright Tribunal) apply in relation to the Tribunal when exercising any jurisdiction under this Part.

(3) Provision shall be made by rules under section 150 prohibiting the Tribunal from entertaining a reference under paragraph 3, 4 or 5 of Schedule 2A (reference of licensing scheme) by a representative organisation unless the Tribunal is satisfied that the organisation is reasonably representative of the class of persons which it claims to represent.][4]

---

[1] Inserted by Copyright, etc. and Trade Marks (Offences and Enforcement) Act 2002 c.25 s 4
[2] Inserted by SI 1996/2967 Pt II reg 22 (1)
[3] Inserted by Broadcasting Act 1996 c.55 Sch 9 para 4
[4] Inserted by SI 1996/2967 Pt II reg 24 (1)

Qualification for protection and extent

Qualifying countries, individuals and persons

206.—(1) In this Part—   **5-254**
"qualifying country" means —
    (a) the United Kingdom,
    (b) another member State of the European Economic Community, or
    (c) to the extent that an Order under section 208 so provides, a country designated under that section as enjoying reciprocal protection;

"qualifying individual" means a citizen or subject of, or an individual resident in, a qualifying country; and
"qualifying person" means a qualifying individual or a body corporate or other body having legal personality which—
    (a) is formed under the law of a part of the United Kingdom or another qualifying country, and
    (b) has in any qualifying country a place of business at which substantial business activity is carried on.

(2) The reference in the definition of "qualifying individual" to a person's being a citizen or subject of a qualifying country shall be construed —
    (a) in relation to the United Kingdom, as a reference to his being a British citizen, and
    (b) in relation to a colony of the United Kingdom, as a reference to his being a British Dependent Territories' citizen by connection with that colony.
(3) In determining for the purpose of the definition of "qualifying person" whether substantial business activity is carried on at a place of business in any country, no account shall be taken of dealings in goods which are at all material times outside that country.

Countries to which this Part extends

207. This Part extends to England and Wales, Scotland and Northern **5-255**
Ireland.

Countries enjoying reciprocal protection

208.—(1) Her Majesty may by Order in Council designate as enjoying **5-256**
reciprocal protection under this Part—
    (a) a Convention country, or
    (b) a country as to which Her Majesty is satisfied that provision has been or will be made under its law giving adequate protection for British performances.
(2) A "Convention country" means a country which is a party to a Convention relating to performers' rights to which the United Kingdom is also a party.
(3) A "British performance" means a performance—
    (a) given by an individual who is a British citizen or resident in the United Kingdom, or
    (b) taking place in the United Kingdom.

(4) If the law of that country provides adequate protection only for certain descriptions of performance, an Order under subsection (1)(b) designating that country shall contain provision limiting to a corresponding extent the protection afforded by this Part in relation to performances connected with that country.

(5) The power conferred by subsection (1)(b) is exercisable in relation to any of the Channel Islands, the Isle of Man or any colony of the United Kingdom, as in relation to a foreign country.

(6) A statutory instrument containing an Order in Council under this section shall be subject to annulment in pursuance of a resolution of either House of Parliament.

Territorial waters and the continental shelf

5-257   **209.**—(1) For the purposes of this Part the territorial waters of the United Kingdom shall be treated as part of the United Kingdom.

(2) This Part applies to things done in the United Kingdom sector of the continental shelf on a structure or vessel which is present there for purposes directly connected with the exploration of the sea bed or subsoil or the exploitation of their natural resources as it applies to things done in the United Kingdom.

(3) The United Kingdom sector of the continental shelf means the areas designated by order under section 1(7) of the Continental Shelf Act 1964.

British ships, aircraft and hovercraft

5-258   **210.**—(1) This Part applies to things done on a British ship, aircraft or hovercraft as it applies to things done in the United Kingdom.

(2) In this section—
> "British ship" means a ship which is a British ship for the purposes of the [Merchant Shipping Act 1995][1] otherwise than by virtue of registration in a country outside the United Kingdom; and
> "British aircraft" and "British hovercraft" mean an aircraft or hovercraft registered in the United Kingdom.

Interpretation

Expressions having same meaning as in copyright provisions

5-259   **211.**—(1) The following expression have the same meaning in this Part as in Part I (copyright)—
> broadcast,
> business,
> [communication to the public,][2]
> country,
> defendant (in Scotland),
> delivery up (in Scotland),
> [EEA national,][3]
> film,
> [injunction (in Scotland)][4]
> literary work,
> published,

---

[1] Words substituted by Merchant Shipping Act 1995 c.21 Sch 13 para 84 (b)
[2] Words inserted by SI 2003/2498 Sch 1 Pt I para 15 (5) (a) (i)
[3] Words inserted by SI 1995/3297 Pt II reg 11 (3)
[4] Words inserted by SI 2003/2498 Sch 1 Pt I para 15 (5) (a) (i)

[sound recording, and][1]

[wireless broadcast.][2]

(2) The provisions of [section 6(3) to (5A) and 19(4)][3] (supplementary provisions relating to broadcasting [...][4]) apply for the purposes of this Part, and in relation to an infringement of the rights conferred by this Part, as they apply for the purposes of Part I and in relation to an infringement of copyright.

Index of defined expressions

212. The following Table shows provisions defining or otherwise explaining **5-260** expressions used in this Part (other than provisions defining or explaining an expression used only in the same section)—

broadcast (and related expressions)	section 211 (and section 6)
business	section 211(1) (and section 178) [...][1]
[communication to the public	section 211(1) (and section 20)][2]
[consent of performer (in relation to performer's property rights)	section 191A(2)][3]
country	section 211(1) (and section 178)
defendant (in Scotland)	section 211(1) (and section 177)
delivery up (in Scotland)	section 211(1) (and section 177)
[distribution right	section 182B(5)][4]
[EEA national	section 211(1) (and section 172A)][5]
exclusive recording contract	section 185(1)
film	section 211(1) (and [section 5B][6])
illicit recording	section 197
[injunction (in Scotland)	section 211(1) (and section 177)][7]
[lending right	section 182C(7)][8]
literary work	section 211(1) (and section 3(1))
[making available right	section 182CA][9]
performance	section 180(2)
[performer's non-property rights	section 192A(1)
performer's property rights	section 191A(1)][10]
published	section 211(1) (and section 175)
qualifying country	section 206(1)
qualifying individual	section 206(1) and (2)
qualifying performance	section 181

---

[1] Words substituted by SI 2003/2498 Sch 1 (1) para 15 (5) (a) (ii)
[2] Words inserted by SI 2003/2498 Sch 1 Pt I para 15 (5) (a) (i)
[3] Words substituted by SI 2003/2498 Sch 1 Pt I para 15 (5) (b)
[4] Words repealed by SI 2003/2498 Sch 2 para 1

City of London Building Society v. Flegg [1988]

qualifying person	section 206(1) and (3)
recording (of a performance)	section 180(2)
recording rights (person having)	section 185(2) and (3)
[rental right	section 182C(7)
reproduction right	section 182A(3)][11]
[rights owner (in relation to perfor-mer's property rights)	section 191A(3) and (4)][12]
sound recording	section 211(1) (and [section 5A][13]).

[1] Words repealed by SI 2003/2498 Sch 2 para 1
[2] Words inserted by SI 2003/2498 Sch 1 Pt I para 15 (6)
[3] Words inserted by SI 1996/2967 Pt II reg 21 (6)
[4] Words inserted by SI 1996/2967 Pt II reg 20 (4)
[5] Words inserted by SI 1995/3297 Pt II reg 11 (4)
[6] Words substituted by SI 1995/3297 Pt II reg 9 (6) (a)
[7] Words inserted by SI 2003/2498 Sch 1 Pt I para 15 (6)
[8] Words inserted by SI 1996/2967 Pt II reg 20 (4)
[9] Words inserted by SI 2003/2498 Sch 1 Pt I para 15 (6)
[10] Words inserted by SI 1996/2967 Pt II reg 21 (6)
[11] Words inserted by SI 1996/2967 Pt II reg 20 (4)
[12] Words inserted by SI 1996/2967 Pt II reg 21 (6)
[13] Words substituted by SI 1995/3297 Pt II reg 9 (6) (b)

PART III

DESIGN RIGHT

CHAPTER I

DESIGN RIGHT IN ORIGINAL DESIGNS

Introductory

Design right

5-261   **213.**—(1) Design right is a property right which subsists in accordance with this Part in an original design.

(2) In this Part "design" means the design of any aspect of the shape or configuration (whether internal or external) of the whole or part of an article.

(3) Design right does not subsist in—

    (a) a method or principle of construction,

    (b) features of shape or configuration of an article which—

        (i) enable the article to be connected to, or placed in, around or against, another article so that either article may perform its function, or

        (ii) are dependent upon the appearance of another article of which the article is intended by the designer to form an integral part, or

    (c) surface decoration.

(4) A design is not "original" for the purposes of this Part if it is commonplace in the design field in question at the time of its creation.

(5) Design right subsists in a design only if the design qualifies for design right protection by reference to—

    (a) the designer or the person by whom the design was commissioned or the designer employed (see sections 218 and 219), or

    (b) the person by whom and country in which articles made to the design were first marketed (see section 220),

or in accordance with any Order under section 221 (power to make further provision with respect to qualification).

[(5A) Design right does not subsist in a design which consists of or contains a controlled representation within the meaning of the Olympic Symbol etc. (protection) Act 1995.][1]

(6) Design right does not subsist unless and until the design has been recorded in a design document or an article has been made to the design.

(7) Design right does not subsist in a design which was so recorded, or to which an article was made, before the commencement of this Part.

The designer

214.—(1) In this Part the "designer", in relation to a design, means the **5-262** person who creates it.

(2) In the case of a computer-generated design the person by whom the arrangements necessary for the creation of the design are undertaken shall be taken to be the designer.

Ownership of design right

215.—(1) The designer is the first owner of any design right in a design **5-263** which is not created in pursuance of a commission or in the course of employment.

(2) Where a design is created in pursuance of a commission, the person commissioning the design is the first owner of any design right in it.

(3) Where, in a case not falling within subsection (2) a design is created by an employee in the course of his employment, his employer is the first owner of any design right in the design.

(4) If a design qualifies for design right protection by virtue of section 220 (qualification by reference to first marketing of articles made to the design), the above rules do not apply and the person by whom the articles in question are marketed is the first owner of the design right.

Duration of design right

216.—(1) Design right expires—   **5-264**

    (a) fifteen years from the end of the calendar year in which the design was first recorded in a design document or an article was first made to the design, whichever first occurred, or

    (b) if articles made to the design are made available for sale or hire within five years from the end of that calendar year, ten years from the end of the calendar year in which that first occurred.

(2) The reference in subsection (1) to articles being made available for sale or hire is to their being made so available anywhere in the world by or with the licence of the design right owner.

---

[1] Inserted by Olympic Symbol etc. (Protection) Act 1995 c.32 s 14 (1)

Qualification for design right protection

Qualifying individuals and qualifying persons

5-265 **217.**—(1) In this Part—

"qualifying individual" means a citizen or subject of, or an individual habitually resident in, a qualifying country; and

"qualifying person" means a qualifying individual or a body corporate or other body having legal personality which—

(a) is formed under the law of a part of the United Kingdom or another qualifying country, and

(b) has in any qualifying country a place of business at which substantial business activity is carried on.

(2) References in this Part to a qualifying person include the Crown and the government of any other qualifying country.

(3) In this section "qualifying country" means —

(a) the United Kingdom,

(b) a country to which this Part extends by virtue of an Order under section 255,

(c) another member State of the European Economic Community, or

(d) to the extent that an Order under section 256 so provides, a country designated under that section as enjoying reciprocal protection.

(4) The reference in the definition of "qualifying individual" to a person's being a citizen or subject of a qualifying country shall be construed —

(a) in relation to the United Kingdom, as a reference to his being a British citizen, and

(b) in relation to a colony of the United Kingdom, as a reference to his being a British Dependent Territories' citizen by connection with that colony.

(5) In determining for the purpose of the definition of "qualifying person" whether substantial business activity is carried on at a place of business in any country, no account shall be taken of dealings in goods which are at all material times outside that country.

Qualification by reference to designer

5-266 **218.**—(1) This section applies to a design which is not created in pursuance of a commission or in the course of employment.

(2) A design to which this section applies qualifies for design right protection if the designer is a qualifying individual or, in the case of a computer-generated design, a qualifying person.

(3) A joint design to which this section applies qualifies for design right protection if any of the designers is a qualifying individual or, as the case may be, a qualifying person.

(4) Where a joint design qualifies for design right protection under this section, only those designers who are qualifying individuals or qualifying persons are entitled to design right under section 215(1) (first ownership of design right: entitlement of designer).

Qualification by reference to commissioner or employer

219.—(1) A design qualifies for design right protection if it is created in **5-267** pursuance of a commission from, or in the course of employment with, a qualifying person.

(2) In the case of a joint commission or joint employment a design qualifies for design right protection if any of the commissioners or employers is a qualifying person.

(3) Where a design which is jointly commissioned or created in the course of joint employment qualifies for design right protection under this section, only those commissioners or employers who are qualifying persons are entitled to design right under section 215(2) or (3) (first ownership of design right: entitlement of commissioner or employer).

Qualification by reference to first marketing

220.—(1) A design which does not qualify for design right protection under **5-268** section 218 or 219 (qualification by reference to designer, commissioner or employer) qualifies for design right protection if the first marketing of articles made to the design—

(a) is by a qualifying person who is exclusively authorised to put such articles on the market in the United Kingdom, and

(b) takes place in the United Kingdom, another country to which this Part extends by virtue of an Order under section 255, or another member State of the European Economic Community.

(2) If the first marketing of articles made to the design is done jointly by two or more persons, the design qualifies for design right protection if any of those persons meets the requirements specified in subsection (1)(a).

(3) In such a case only the persons who meet those requirements are entitled to design right under section 215(4) (first ownership of design right: entitlement of first marketer of articles made to the design).

(4) In subsection (1)(a) "exclusively authorised" refers—

(a) to authorisation by the person who would have been first owner of design right as designer, commissioner of the design or employer of the designer if he had been a qualifying person, or by a person lawfully claiming under such a person, and

(b) to exclusivity capable of being enforced by legal proceedings in the United Kingdom.

Power to make further provision as to qualification

221.—(1) Her Majesty may, with a view to fulfilling an international **5-269** obligation of the United Kingdom, by Order in Council provide that a design qualifies for design right protection if such requirements as are specified in the Order are met.

(2) An Order may make different provision for different descriptions of design or article; and may make such consequential modifications of the operation of sections 215 (ownership of design right) and sections 218 to 220 (other means of qualification) as appear to Her Majesty to be appropriate.

(3) A statutory instrument containing an Order in Council under this section shall be subject to annulment in pursuance of a resolution of either House of Parliament.

Dealings with design right

Assignment and licences

5-270   **222.**—(1) Design right is transmissible by assignment, by testamentary disposition or by operation of law, as personal or moveable property.

(2) An assignment or other transmission of design right may be partial, that is, limited so as to apply—

   (a) to one or more, but not all, of the things the design right owner has the exclusive right to do;

   (b) to part, but not the whole, of the period for which the right is to subsist.

(3) An assignment of design right is not effective unless it is in writing signed by or on behalf of the assignor.

(4) A licence granted by the owner of design right is binding on every successor in title to his interest in the right, except a purchaser in good faith for valuable consideration and without notice (actual or constructive) of the licence or a person deriving title from such a purchaser; and references in this Part to doing anything with, or without, the licence of the design right owner shall be construed accordingly.

Prospective ownership of design right

5-271   **223.**—(1) Where by an agreement made in relation to future design right, and signed by or on behalf of the prospective owner of the design right, the prospective owner purports to assign the future design right (wholly or partially) to another person, then if, on the right coming into existence, the assignee or another person claiming under him would be entitled as against all other persons to require the right to be vested in him, the right shall vest in him by virtue of this section.

(2) In this section—

   "future design right" means design right which will or may come into existence in respect of a future design or class of designs or on the occurrence of a future event; and

   "prospective owner" shall be construed accordingly, and includes a person who is prospectively entitled to design right by virtue of such an agreement as is mentioned in subsection (1).

(3) A licence granted by a prospective owner of design right is binding on every successor in title to his interest (or prospective interest) in the right, except a purchaser in good faith for valuable consideration and without notice (actual or constructive) of the licence or a person deriving title from such a purchaser; and references in this Part to doing anything with, or without, the licence of the design right owner shall be construed accordingly.

Assignment of right in registered design presumed to carry with it design right

5-272   **224.** Where a design consisting of a design in which design right subsists is registered under the Registered Designs Act 1949 and the proprietor of the registered design is also the design right owner, an assignment of the right in the registered design shall be taken to be also an assignment of the design right, unless a contrary intention appears.

Exclusive licences

225.—(1) In this Part an "exclusive licence" means a licence in writing signed **5-273** by or on behalf of the design right owner authorising the licensee to the exclusion of all other persons, including the person granting the licence, to exercise a right which would otherwise be exercisable exclusively by the design right owner.

(2) The licensee under an exclusive licence has the same rights against any successor in title who is bound by the licence as he has against the person granting the licence.

CHAPTER II

RIGHTS OF DESIGN RIGHT OWNER AND REMEDIES

Infringement of design right

Primary infringement of design right

226.—(1) The owner of design right in a design has the exclusive right to **5-274** reproduce the design for commercial purposes—
- (a) by making articles to that design, or
- (b) by making a design document recording the design for the purpose of enabling such articles to be made.

(2) Reproduction of a design by making articles to the design means copying the design so as to produce articles exactly or substantially to that design, and references in this Part to making articles to a design shall be construed according-ly.

(3) Design right is infringed by a person who without the licence of the design right owner does, or authorises another to do, anything which by virtue of this section is the exclusive right of the design right owner.

(4) For the purposes of this section reproduction may be direct or indirect, and it is immaterial whether any intervening acts themselves infringe the design right.

(5) This section has effect subject to the provisions of Chapter III (exceptions to rights of design right owner).

Secondary infringement: importing or dealing with infringing article

227.—(1) Design right is infringed by a person who, without the licence of **5-275** the design right owner—
- (a) imports into the United Kingdom for commercial purposes, or
- (b) has in his possession for commercial purposes, or
- (c) sells, lets for hire, or offers or exposes for sale or hire, in the course of a business,

an article which is, and which he knows or has reason to believe is, an infringing article.

(2) This section has effect subject to the provisions of Chapter III (exceptions to rights of design right owner).

Meaning of "infringing article"

228.—(1) In this Part "infringing article", in relation to a design, shall be **5-276** construed in accordance with this section.

(2) An article is an infringing article if its making to that design was an infringement of design right in the design.

(3) An article is also an infringing article if—

   (a) it has been or is proposed to be imported into the United Kingdom, and

   (b) its making to that design in the United Kingdom would have been an infringement of design right in the design or a breach of an exclusive licence agreement relating to the design.

(4) Where it is shown that an article is made to a design in which design right subsists or has subsisted at any time, it shall be presumed until the contrary is proved that the article was made at a time when design right subsisted.

(5) Nothing in subsection (3) shall be construed as applying to an article which may lawfully be imported into the United Kingdom by virtue of any enforceable Community right within the meaning of section 2(1) of the European Communities Act 1972.

(6) The expression "infringing article" does not include a design document, notwithstanding that its making was or would have been an infringement of design right.

Remedies for infringement

Rights and remedies of design right owner

5-277   **229.**—(1) An infringement of design right is actionable by the design right owner.

(2) In an action for infringement of design right all such relief by way of damages, injunctions, accounts or otherwise is available to the plaintiff as is available in respect of the infringement of any other property right.

(3) The court may in an action for infringement of design right, having regard to all the circumstances and in particular to—

   (a) the flagrancy of the infringement, and

   (b) any benefit accruing to the defendant by reason of the infringement,

award such additional damages as the justice of the case may require.

(4) This section has effect subject to section 233 (innocent infringement).

Order for delivery up

5-278   **230.**—(1) Where a person—

   (a) has in his possession, custody or control for commercial purposes an infringing article, or

   (b) has in his possession, custody or control anything specifically designed or adapted for making articles to a particular design, knowing or having reason to believe that it has been or is to be used to make an infringing article,

the owner of the design right in the design in question may apply to the court for an order that the infringing article or other thing be delivered up to him or to such other person as the court may direct.

(2) An application shall not be made after the end of the period specified in the following provisions of this section; and no order shall be made unless the court also makes, or it appears to the court that there are grounds for making, an order under section 231 (order as to disposal of infringing article, &c.).

(3) An application for an order under this section may not be made after the end of the period of six years from the date on which the article or thing in question was made, subject to subsection (4).

(4) If during the whole or any part of that period the design right owner—

    (a) is under a disability, or

    (b) is prevented by fraud or concealment from discovering the facts entitling him to apply for an order,

an application may be made at any time before the end of the period of six years from the date on which he ceased to be under a disability or, as the case may be, could with reasonable diligence have discovered those facts.

(5) In subsection (4) "disability" —

    (a) in England and Wales, has the same meaning as in the Limitation Act 1980;

    (b) in Scotland, means legal disability within the meaning of the Prescription and Limitation (Scotland) Act 1973;

    (c) in Northern Ireland, has the same meaning as in the Statute of Limitations (Northern Ireland) 1958.

(6) A person to whom an infringing article or other thing is delivered up in pursuance of an order under this section shall, if an order under section 231 is not made, retain it pending the making of an order, or the decision not to make an order, under that section.

(7) Nothing in this section affects any other power of the court.

Order as to disposal of infringing articles, &c

231.—(1) An application may be made to the court for an order that an **5-279** infringing article or other thing delivered up in pursuance of an order under section 230 shall be—

    (a) forfeited to the design right owner, or

    (b) destroyed or otherwise dealt with as the court may think fit,

or for a decision that no such order should be made.

(2) In considering what order (if any) should be made, the court shall consider whether other remedies available in an action for infringement of design right would be adequate to compensate the design right owner and to protect his interests.

(3) Provision shall be made by rules of court as to the service of notice on persons having an interest in the article or other thing, and any such person is entitled—

    (a) to appear in proceedings for an order under this section, whether or not he was served with notice, and

    (b) to appeal against any order made, whether or not he appeared;

and an order shall not take effect until the end of the period within which notice of an appeal may be given or, if before the end of that period notice of appeal is duly given, until the final determination or abandonment of the proceedings on the appeal.

(4) Where there is more than one person interested in an article or other thing, the court shall make such order as it thinks just and may (in particular) direct that the thing be sold, or otherwise dealt with, and the proceeds divided.

(5) If the court decides that no order should be made under this section, the person in whose possession, custody or control the article or other thing was before being delivered up or seized is entitled to its return.

(6) References in this section to a person having an interest in an article or other thing include any person in whose favour an order could be made in respect

of it under this section or under section 114 or 204 of this Act or [section 19 of the Trade Marks Act 1994][1] (which make similar provision in relation to infringement of copyright, rights in performances and trade marks).

Innocent infringement

5-280   **233.**—(1) Where in an action for infringement of design right brought by virtue of section 226 (primary infringement) it is shown that at the time of the infringement the defendant did not know, and had no reason to believe, that design right subsisted in the design to which the action relates, the plaintiff is not entitled to damages against him, but without prejudice to any other remedy.

(2) Where in an action for infringement of design right brought by virtue of section 227 (secondary infringement) a defendant shows that the infringing article was innocently acquired by him or a predecessor in title of his, the only remedy available against him in respect of the infringement is damages not exceeding a reasonable royalty in respect of the act complained of.

(3) In subsection (2) "innocently acquired" means that the person acquiring the article did not know and had no reason to believe that it was an infringing article.

Rights and remedies of exclusive licensee

5-281   **234.**—(1) An exclusive licensee has, except against the design right owner, the same rights and remedies in respect of matters occurring after the grant of the licence as if the licence had been an assignment.

(2) His rights and remedies are concurrent with those of the design right owner; and references in the relevant provisions of this Part to the design right owner shall be construed accordingly.

(3) In an action brought by an exclusive licensee by virtue of this section a defendant may avail himself of any defence which would have been available to him if the action had been brought by the design right owner.

Exercise of concurrent rights

5-282   **235.**—(1) Where an action for infringement of design right brought by the design right owner or an exclusive licensee relates (wholly or partly) to an infringement in respect of which they have concurrent rights of action, the design right owner or, as the case may be, the exclusive licensee may not, without the leave of the court, proceed with the action unless the other is either joined as a plaintiff or added as a defendant.

(2) A design right owner or exclusive licensee who is added as a defendant in pursuance of subsection (1) is not liable for any costs in the action unless he takes part in the proceedings.

(3) The above provisions do not affect the granting of interlocutory relief on the application of the design right owner or an exclusive licensee.

(4) Where an action for infringement of design right is brought which relates (wholly or partly) to an infringement in respect of which the design right owner and an exclusive licensee have concurrent rights of action—

    (a) the court shall, in assessing damages, take into account—
        (i) the terms of the licence, and
        (ii) any pecuniary remedy already awarded or available to either of
           them in respect of the infringement;

---

[1] Words substituted by Trade Marks Act 1994 c.26 Sch 4 para 8 (2)

    (b) no account of profits shall be directed if an award of damages has been made, or an account of profits has been directed, in favour of the other of them in respect of the infringement; and

    (c) the court shall if an account of profits is directed apportion the profits between them as the court considers just, subject to any agreement between them;

and these provisions apply whether or not the design right owner and the exclusive licensee are both parties to the action.

(5) The design right owner shall notify any exclusive licensee having concurrent rights before applying for an order under section 230 (order for delivery up of infringing article, &c.); and the court may on the application of the licensee make such order under that section as it thinks fit having regard to the terms of the licence.

CHAPTER III

EXCEPTIONS TO RIGHTS OF DESIGN RIGHT OWNERS

Infringement of copyright

Infringement of copyright

236. Where copyright subsists in a work which consists of or includes a **5-283** design in which design right subsists, it is not an infringement of design right in the design to do anything which is an infringement of the copyright in that work.

Availability of licences of right

Licences available in last five years of design right

237.—(1) Any person is entitled as of right to a licence to do in the last five **5-284** years of the design right term anything which would otherwise infringe the design right.

(2) The terms of the licence shall, in default of agreement, be settled by the comptroller.

(3) The Secretary of State may if it appears to him necessary in order to—

    (a) comply with an international obligation of the United Kingdom, or

    (b) secure or maintain reciprocal protection for British designs in other countries,

by order exclude from the operation of subsection (1) designs of a description specified in the order or designs applied to articles of a description so specified.

(4) An order shall be made by statutory instrument; and no order shall be made unless a draft of it has been laid before and approved by a resolution of each House of Parliament.

Powers exercisable for protection of the public interest

238.—[(1) Subsection (1A) applies where whatever needs to be remedied, **5-285** mitigated or prevented by the Secretary of State, the Competition Commission or (as the case may be) the Office of Fair Trading under section 12(5) of the Competition Act 1980 or section 41(2), 55(2), 66(6), 75(2), 83(2), 138(2), 147(2) or 160(2) of, or paragraph 5(2) or 10(2) of Schedule 7 to, the Enterprise Act 2002 (powers to take remedial action following references to the Commission in connection with public bodies and certain other persons, mergers or market investigations etc.) consists of or includes—

    (a) conditions in licences granted by a design right owner restricting the use of the design by the licensee or the right of the design right owner to grant other licences, or

    (b) a refusal of a design right owner to grant licences on reasonable terms.

(1A) The powers conferred by Schedule 8 to the Enterprise Act 2002 include power to cancel or modify those conditions and, instead or in addition, to provide that licences in respect of the design right shall be available as of right.

(2) The references to anything permitted by Schedule 8 to the Enterprise Act 2002 in section 12(5A) of the Competition Act 1980 and in sections 75(4)(a), 83(4)(a), 84(2)(a), 89(1), 160(4)(a), 161(3)(a) and 164(1) of, and paragraphs 5, 10 and 11 of Schedule 7 to, the Act of 2002 shall be construed accordingly.][1]

(3) The terms of a licence available by virtue of this section shall, in default of agreement, be settled by the comptroller.

Undertaking to take licence of right in infringement proceedings

5-286   **239.**—(1) If in proceedings for infringement of design right in a design in respect of which a licence is available as of right under section 237 or 238 the defendant undertakes to take a licence on such terms as may be agreed or, in default of agreement, settled by the comptroller under that section—

    (a) no injunction shall be granted against him,

    (b) no order for delivery up shall be made under section 230, and

    (c) the amount recoverable against him by way of damages or on an account of profits shall not exceed double the amount which would have been payable by him as licensee if such a licence on those terms had been granted before the earliest infringement.

(2) An undertaking may be given at any time before final order in the proceedings, without any admission of liability.

(3) Nothing in this section affects the remedies available in respect of an infringement committed before licences of right were available.

Crown use of designs

Crown use of designs

5-287   **240.**—(1) A government department, or a person authorised in writing by a government department, may without the licence of the design right owner—

    (a) do anything for the purpose of supplying articles for the services of the Crown, or

    (b) dispose of articles no longer required for the services of the Crown;

and nothing done by virtue of this section infringes the design right.

(2) References in this Part to "the services of the Crown" are to—

    (a) the defence of the realm,

    (b) foreign defence purposes, and

    (c) health service purposes.

(3) The reference to the supply of articles for "foreign defence purposes" is to their supply—

    (a) for the defence of a country outside the realm in pursuance of an agreement or arrangement to which the government of that country and Her Majesty's Government in the United Kingdom are parties; or

---

[1] Substituted by Enterprise Act 2002 c.40 Sch 25 para 18 (4)

(b) for use by armed forces operating in pursuance of a resolution of the United Nations or one of its organs.

(4) The reference to the supply of articles for "health service purposes" are to their supply for the purpose of providing—

[(za) primary medical services or primary dental services under Part 1 of the National Health Service Act 1977 [or primary medical services under Part 1 of the National Health Service (Scotland) Act 1978,][1]][2]

(a) pharmaceutical services, general medical services or general dental services under—

(i) Part II of the National Health Service Act 1977 [(in the case of pharmaceutical services)][3],

(ii) Part II of the National Health Service (Scotland) Act 1978 [(in the case of pharmaceutical services or general dental services)][4], or

(iii) the corresponding provisions of the law in force in Northern Ireland; or

(b) personal medical services [or personal dental services][5] in accordance with arrangements made under—

(i) [...][6]

(ii) section 17C of the 1978 Act [(in the case of personal dental services)][7], or

(iii) the corresponding provisions of the law in force in Northern Ireland.

(5) In this Part—

"Crown use", in relation to a design, means the doing of anything by virtue of this section which would otherwise be an infringement of design right in the design; and

"the government department concerned", in relation to such use, means the government department by whom or on whose authority the act was done.

(6) The authority of a government department in respect of Crown use of a design may be given to a person either before or after the use and whether or not he is authorised, directly or indirectly, by the design right owner to do anything in relation to the design.

(7) A person acquiring anything sold in the exercise of powers conferred by this section, and any person claiming under him, may deal with it in the same manner as if the design right were held on behalf of the Crown.

Crown use: compensation for loss of profit

243.—(1) Where Crown use is made of a design, the government **5-288** department concerned shall pay—

(a) to the design right owner, or

---

[1] Words inserted by Health and Social Care (Community Health and Standards) Act 2003 c.43 Sch 11 para 52 (a)

[2] Substituted by National Health Service (Primary Care) Act 1997 c.46 Sch 2 Pt I para 63

[3] Words inserted by Health and Social Care (Community Health and Standards) Act 2003 c.43 Sch 11 para 52 (b)

[4] Words inserted by SI 2004/957 Sch 1 para 52 (c)

[5] Words inserted by National Health Service (Primary Care) Act 1997 c.46 Sch 2 Pt I para 63

[6] Words repealed by Health and Social Care (Community Health and Standards) Act 2003 c.43 Sch 11 para 52 (c)

[7] Words inserted by SI 2004/957 Sch 1 para 52 (c)

(b) if there is an exclusive licence in force in respect of the design, to the exclusive licensee,

compensation for any loss resulting from his not being awarded a contract to supply the articles made to the design.

(2) Compensation is payable only to the extent that such a contract could have been fulfilled from his existing manufacturing capacity; but is payable notwithstanding the existence of circumstances rendering him ineligible for the award of such a contract.

(3) In determining the loss, regard shall be had to the profit which would have been made on such a contract and to the extent to which any manufacturing capacity was under-used.

(4) No compensation is payable in respect of any failure to secure contracts for the supply of articles made to the design otherwise than for the services of the Crown.

(5) The amount payable shall, if not agreed between the design right owner or licensee and the government department concerned with the approval of the Treasury, be determined by the court on a reference under section 252; and it is in addition to any amount payable under section 241 or 242.

(6) In the application of this section to Northern Ireland, the reference in subsection (5) to the Treasury shall, where the government department concerned is a Northern Ireland department, be construed as a reference to the Department of Finance and Personnel.

[(7) In the application of this section to Scotland, where the government department referred to in subsection (5) is any part of the Scottish Administration, the words "with the approval of the Treasury" in that subsection are omitted.][1]

General

Power to provide for further exceptions

5-289

245.—(1) The Secretary of State may if it appears to him necessary in order to—

(a) comply with an international obligation of the United Kingdom, or

(b) secure or maintain reciprocal protection for British designs in other countries,

by order provide that acts of a description specified in the order do not infringe design right.

(2) An order may make different provision for different descriptions of design or article.

(3) An order shall be made by statutory instrument and no order shall be made unless a draft of it has been laid before and approved by a resolution of each House of Parliament.

---

[1] Inserted by SI 1999/1820 Sch 2 (I) para 93 (3)

CHAPTER IV

JURISDICTION OF THE COMPTROLLER AND THE COURT

Jurisdiction of the comptroller

Jurisdiction to decide matters relating to design right

246.—(1) A party to a dispute as to any of the following matters may **5-290** refer the dispute to the comptroller for his decision—
  (a) the subsistence of design right,
  (b) the term of design right, or
  (c) the identity of the person in whom design right first vested;
and the comptroller's decision on the reference is binding on the parties to the dispute.
  (2) No other court or tribunal shall decide any such matter except—
  (a) on a reference or appeal from the comptroller,
  (b) in infringement or other proceedings in which the issue arises incidentally, or
  (c) in proceedings brought with the agreement of the parties or the leave of the comptroller.
  (3) The comptroller has jurisdiction to decide any incidental question of fact or law arising in the course of a reference under this section.

Application to settle terms of licence of right

247.—(1) A person requiring a licence which is available as of right by **5-291** virtue of—
  (a) section 237 (licences available in last five years of design right), or
  (b) an order under section 238 (licences made available in the public interest),
may apply to the comptroller to settle the terms of the licence.
  (2) No application for the settlement of the terms of a licence available by virtue of section 237 may be made earlier than one year before the earliest date on which the licence may take effect under that section.
  (3) The terms of a licence settled by the comptroller shall authorise the licensee to do—
  (a) in the case of licence available by virtue of section 237, everything which would be an infringement of the design right in the absence of a licence;
  (b) in the case of a licence available by virtue of section 238, everything in respect of which a licence is so available.
  (4) In settling the terms of a licence the comptroller shall have regard to such factors as may be prescribed by the Secretary of State by order made by statutory instrument.
  (5) No such order shall be made unless a draft of it has been laid before and approved by a resolution of each House of Parliament.
  (6) Where the terms of a licence are settled by the comptroller, the licence has effect—
  (a) in the case of an application in respect of a licence available by virtue of section 237 made before the earliest date on which the licence may take effect under that section, from that date;

(b) in any other case, from the date on which the application to the comptroller was made.

Settlement of terms where design right owner unknown

5-292

248.—(1) This section applies where a person making an application under section 247 (settlement of terms of licence of right) is unable on reasonable inquiry to discover the identity of the design right owner.

(2) The comptroller may in settling the terms of the licence order that the licence shall be free of any obligation as to royalties or other payments.

(3) If such an order is made the design right owner may apply to the comptroller to vary the terms of the licence with effect from the date on which his application is made.

(4) If the terms of a licence are settled by the comptroller and it is subsequently established that a licence was not available as of right, the licensee shall not be liable in damages for, or for an account of profits in respect of, anything done before he was aware of any claim by the design right owner that a licence was not available.

Appeals as to terms of licence of right

5-293

249.—(1) An appeal lies from any decision of the comptroller under section 247 or 248 (settlement of terms of licence of right) to the Appeal Tribunal constituted under section 28 of the Registered Designs Act 1949.

(2) Section 28 of that Act applies to appeals from the comptroller under this section as it applies to appeals from the registrar under that Act; but rules made under that section may make different provision for appeals under this section.

Jurisdiction of the court

References and appeals on design right matters

5-294

251.—(1) In any proceedings before him under section 246 (reference of matter relating to design right), the comptroller may at any time order the whole proceedings or any question or issue (whether of fact or law) to be referred, on such terms as he may direct, to the High Court or, in Scotland, the Court of Session.

(2) The comptroller shall make such an order if the parties to the proceedings agree that he should do so.

(3) On a reference under this section the court may exercise any power available to the comptroller by virtue of this Part as respects the matter referred to it and, following its determination, may refer any matter back to the comptroller.

(4) An appeal lies from any decision of the comptroller in proceedings before him under section 246 (decisions on matters relating to design right) to the High Court or, in Scotland, the Court of Session.

CHAPTER V

MISCELLANEOUS AND GENERAL

Miscellaneous

Remedy for groundless threats of infringement proceedings

253.—(1) Where a person threatens another person with proceedings **5-295** for infringement of design right, a person aggrieved by the threats may bring an action against him claiming—
(a) a declaration to the effect that the threats are unjustifiable;
(b) an injunction against the continuance of the threats;
(c) damages in respect of any loss which he has sustained by the threats.

(2) If the plaintiff proves that the threats were made and that he is a person aggrieved by them, he is entitled to the relief claimed unless the defendant shows that the acts in respect of which proceedings were threatened did constitute, or if done would have constituted, an infringement of the design right concerned.

(3) Proceedings may not be brought under this section in respect of a threat to bring proceedings for an infringement alleged to consist of making or importing anything.

(4) Mere notification that a design is protected by design right does not constitute a threat of proceedings for the purposes of this section.

Licensee under licence of right not to claim connection with design right owner

254.—(1) A person who has a licence in respect of a design by virtue of **5-296** section 237 or 238 (licences of right) shall not, without the consent of the design right owner—
(a) apply to goods which he is marketing, or proposes to market, in reliance on that licence a trade description indicating that he is the licensee of the design right owner, or
(b) use any such trade description in an advertisement in relation to such goods.

(2) A contravention of subsection (1) is actionable by the design right owner.

(3) In this section "trade description",the reference to applying a trade description to goods and "advertisement" have the same meaning as in the Trade Descriptions Act 1968.

Extent of operation of this Part

Countries to which this Part extends

255.—(1) This Part extends to England and Wales, Scotland and **5-297** Northern Ireland.

(2) Her Majesty may by Order in Council direct that this Part shall extend, subject to such exceptions and modifications as may be specified in the Order, to—
(a) any of the Channel Islands,
(b) the Isle of Man, or

(c) any colony.

(3) That power includes power to extend, subject to such exceptions and modifications as may be specified in the Order, any Order in Council made under section 221 (further provision as to qualification for design right protection) or section 256 (countries enjoying reciprocal protection).

(4) The legislature of a country to which this Part has been extended may modify or add to the provisions of this Part, in their operation as part of the law of that country, as the legislature may consider necessary to adapt the provisions to the circumstances of that country; but not so as to deny design right protection in a case where it would otherwise exist.

(5) Where a country to which this Part extends ceases to be a colony of the United Kingdom, it shall continue to be treated as such a country for the purposes of this Part until—

(a) an Order in Council is made under section 256 designating it as a country enjoying reciprocal protection, or

(b) an Order in Council is made declaring that it shall cease to be so treated by reason of the fact that the provisions of this Part as part of the law of that country have been amended or repealed.

(6) A statutory instrument containing an Order in Council under subsection (5)(b) shall be subject to annulment in pursuance of a resolution of either House of Parliament.

Countries enjoying reciprocal protection

5-298

256.—(1) Her Majesty may, if it appears to Her that the law of a country provides adequate protection for British designs, by Order in Council designate that country as one enjoying reciprocal protection under this Part.

(2) If the law of a country provides adequate protection only for certain classes of British design, or only for designs applied to certain classes of article, any Order designating that country shall contain provision limiting, to a corresponding extent, the protection afforded by this Part in relation to designs connected with that country.

(3) An Order under this section shall be subject to annulment in pursuance of a resolution of either House of Parliament.

Interpretation

Construction of references to design right owner

5-299

258.—(1) Where different persons are (whether in consequence of a partial assignment or otherwise) entitled to different aspects of design right in a work, the design right owner for any purpose of this Part is the person who is entitled to the right in the respect relevant for that purpose.

(2) Where design right (or any aspect of design right) is owned by more than one person jointly, references in this Part to the design right owner are to all the owners, so that, in particular, any requirement of the licence of the design right owner requires the licence of all of them.

Joint designs

5-300

259.—(1) In this Part a "joint design" means a design produced by the collaboration of two or more designers in which the contribution of each is not distinct from that of the other or others.

(2) References in this Part to the designer of a design shall, except as otherwise provided, be construed in relation to a joint design as references to all the designers of the design.

Application of provisions to articles in kit form

260.—(1) The provisions of this Part apply in relation to a kit, that is, a **5-301** complete or substantially complete set of components intended to be assembled into an article, as they apply in relation to the assembled article.

(2) Subsection (1) does not affect the question whether design right subsists in any aspect of the design of the components of a kit as opposed to the design of the assembled article.

Adaptation of expressions in relation to Scotland

262. In the application of this Part to Scotland—   **5-302**
    "account of profits" means accounting and payment of profits;
    "accounts" means count, reckoning and payment;
    "assignment" means assignation;
    "costs" means expenses;
    "defendant" means defender;
    "delivery up" means delivery;
    "injunction" means interdict;
    "interlocutory relief" means interim remedy; and
    "plaintiff" means pursuer.

Minor definitions

263.—(1) In this Part—   **5-303**
    "British design" means a design which qualifies for design right protection by reason of a connection with the United Kingdom of the designer or the person by whom the design is commissioned or the designer is employed;
    "business" includes a trade or profession;
    "commission" means a commission for money or money's worth;
    "the comptroller" means the Comptroller-General of Patents, Designs and Trade Marks;
    "computer-generated", in relation to a design, means that the design is generated by computer in circumstances such that there is no human designer,
    "country" includes any territory;
    "the Crown" includes the Crown in right of Her Majesty's Government in Northern Ireland [and the Crown in right of the Scottish Administration][1];
    "design document" means any record of a design, whether in the form of a drawing, a written description, a photograph, data stored in a computer or otherwise;
    "employee", "employment" and "employer" refer to employment under a contract of service or of apprenticeship;
    "government department" includes a Northern Ireland department [and any part of the Scottish Administration][2].

(2) References in this Part to "marketing", in relation to an article, are to its being sold or let for hire, or offered or exposed for sale or hire, in the

---

[1] Words inserted by SI 1999/1820 Sch 2 (I) para 93 (4) (a)
[2] Words inserted by SI 1999/1820 Sch 2 (I) para 93 (4) (b)

course of a business, and related expressions shall be construed accordingly; but no account shall be taken for the purposes of this Part of marketing which is merely colourable and not intended to satisfy the reasonable requirements of the public.

(3) References in this Part to an act being done in relation to an article for "commercial purposes" are to its being done with a view to the article in question being sold or hired in the course of a business.

Index of defined expressions

5-304

264. The following Table shows provisions defining or otherwise explaining expressions used in this Part (other than provisions defining or explaining an expression used only in the same section)—

account of profits and accounts (in Scotland)	section 262
assignment (in Scotland)	section 262
British designs	section 263(1)
business	section 263(1)
commercial purposes	section 263(3)
commission	section 263(1)
the comptroller	section 263(1)
computer-generated	section 263(1)
costs (in Scotland)	section 262
country	section 263(1)
the Crown	section 263(1)
Crown use	sections 240(5) and 244(2)
defendant (in Scotland)	section 262
delivery up (in Scotland)	section 262
design	section 213(2)
design document	section 263(1)
designer	sections 214 and 259(2)
design right	section 213(1)
design right owner	sections 234(2) and 258
employee, employment and employer	section 263(1)
exclusive licence	section 225(1)
government department	section 263(1)
government department concerned (in relation to Crown use)	section 240(5)

infringing article	section 228
injunction (in Scotland)	section 262
interlocutory relief (in Scotland)	section 262
joint design	section 259(1)
licence (of the design right owner)	sections 222(4), 223(3) and 258
making articles to a design	section 226(2)
marketing (and related expressions)	section 263(2)
original	section 213(4)
plaintiff (in Scotland)	section 262
qualifying individual	section 217(1)
qualifying person	sections 217(1) and (2)
signed	section 261

PART VI

PATENTS

Patents county courts

Patents county courts: special jurisdiction

287.—(1) The Lord Chancellor may by order made by statutory **5-305** instrument designate any county court as a patents county court and confer on it jurisdiction (its "special jurisdiction") to hear and determine such descriptions of proceedings—

(a) relating to patents or designs, or

(b) ancillary to, or arising out of the same subject matter as, proceedings relating to patents or designs,

as may be specified in the order.

(2) The special jurisdiction of a patents county court is exercisable throughout England and Wales, but rules of court may provide for a matter pending in one such court to be heard and determined in another or partly in that and partly in another.

(3) A patents county court may entertain proceedings within its special jurisdiction notwithstanding that no pecuniary remedy is sought.

(4) An order under this section providing for the discontinuance of any of the special jurisdiction of a patents county court may make provision as to proceedings pending in the court when the order comes into operation.

(5) Nothing in this section shall be construed as affecting the ordinary jurisdiction of a county court.

Transfer of proceedings between High Court and patents county court

5-306   **289.**—(1) No order shall be made under section 41 of the County Courts Act 1984 (power of High Court to order proceedings to be transferred from the county court) in respect of proceedings within the special jurisdiction of a patents county court.

(2) In considering in relation to proceedings within the special jurisdiction of a patents county court whether an order should be made under section 40 or 42 of the County Courts Act 1984 (transfer of proceedings from or to the High Court), the court shall have regard to the financial position of the parties and may order the transfer of the proceedings to a patents county court or, as the case may be, refrain from ordering their transfer to the High Court notwithstanding that the proceedings are likely to raise an important question of fact or law.

PART VII

MISCELLANEOUS AND GENERAL

[Circumvention of protection measures][1]

[Circumvention of technical devices applied to computer programs

5-307   **296.**—(1) This section applies where–
(a) a technical device has been applied to a computer program; and
(b) a person (A) knowing or having reason to believe that it will be used to make infringing copies–
(i) manufactures for sale or hire, imports, distributes, sells or lets for hire, offers or exposes for sale or hire, advertises for sale or hire or has in his possession for commercial purposes any means the sole intended purpose of which is to facilitate the unauthorised removal or circumvention of the technical device; or
(ii) publishes information intended to enable or assist persons to remove or circumvent the technical device.

(2) The following persons have the same rights against A as a copyright owner has in respect of an infringement of copyright–
(a) a person–
(i) issuing to the public copies of, or
(ii) communicating to the public,
the computer program to which the technical device has been applied;
(b) the copyright owner or his exclusive licensee, if he is not the person specified in paragraph (a);
(c) the owner or exclusive licensee of any intellectual property right in the technical device applied to the computer program.

(3) The rights conferred by subsection (2) are concurrent, and sections 101(3) and 102(1) to (4) apply, in proceedings under this section, in relation to persons with concurrent rights as they apply, in proceedings mentioned in those provisions, in relation to a copyright owner and exclusive licensee with concurrent rights.

---

[1] Substituted by SI 2003/2498 Pt II reg 24 (1)

(4) Further, the persons in subsection (2) have the same rights under section 99 or 100 (delivery up or seizure of certain articles) in relation to any such means as is referred to in subsection (1) which a person has in his possession, custody or control with the intention that it should be used to facilitate the unauthorised removal or circumvention of any technical device which has been applied to a computer program, as a copyright owner has in relation to an infringing copy.

(5) The rights conferred by subsection (4) are concurrent, and section 102(5) shall apply, as respects anything done undersection 99 or 100 by virtue of subsection (4), in relation to persons with concurrent rights as it applies, as respects anything done under section 99 or 100, in relation to a copyright owner and exclusive licensee with concurrent rights.

(6) In this section references to a technical device in relation to a computer program are to any device intended to prevent or restrict acts that are not authorised by the copyright owner of that computer program and are restricted by copyright.

(7) The following provisions apply in relation to proceedings under this section as in relation to proceedings under Part 1 (copyright)–
- (a) sections 104 to 106 of this Act (presumptions as to certain matters relating to copyright); and
- (b) section 72 of the Supreme Court Act 1981, section 15 of the Law Reform (Miscellaneous Provisions) (Scotland) Act 1985 and section 94A of the Judicature (Northern Ireland) Act 1978 (withdrawal of privilege against self-incrimination in certain proceedings relating to intellectual property);

and section 114 of this Act applies, with the necessary modifications, in relation to the disposal of anything delivered up or seized by virtue of subsection (4).

(8) Expressions used in this section which are defined for the purposes of Part 1 of this Act (copyright) have the same meaning as in that Part.][1]

[Circumvention of technological measures

296ZA—(1) This section applies where–   **5-308**
- (a) effective technological measures have been applied to a copyright work other than a computer program; and
- (b) a person (B) does anything which circumvents those measures knowing, or with reasonable grounds to know, that he is pursuing that objective.

(2) This section does not apply where a person, for the purposes of research into cryptography, does anything which circumvents effective technological measures unless in so doing, or in issuing information derived from that research, he affects prejudicially the rights of the copyright owner.

(3) The following persons have the same rights against B as a copyright owner has in respect of an infringement of copyright–
- (a) a person–
    - (i) issuing to the public copies of, or
    - (ii) communicating to the public,
    the work to which effective technological measures have been applied; and

---

[1] Substituted by SI 2003/2498 Pt II reg 24 (1)

(b) the copyright owner or his exclusive licensee, if he is not the person specified in paragraph (a).

(4) The rights conferred by subsection (3) are concurrent, and sections 101(3) and 102(1) to (4) apply, in proceedings under this section, in relation to persons with concurrent rights as they apply, in proceedings mentioned in those provisions, in relation to a copyright owner and exclusive licensee with concurrent rights.

(5) The following provisions apply in relation to proceedings under this section as in relation to proceedings under Part 1 (copyright)–

(a) sections 104 to 106 of this Act (presumptions as to certain matters relating to copyright); and

(b) section 72 of the Supreme Court Act 1981, section 15 of the Law Reform (Miscellaneous Provisions) (Scotland) Act 1985 and section 94A of the Judicature (Northern Ireland) Act 1978 (withdrawal of privilege against self-incrimination in certain proceedings relating to intellectual property).

(6) Subsections (1) to (4) and (5)(b) and any other provision of this Act as it has effect for the purposes of those subsections apply, with any necessary adaptations, to rights in performances, publication right and database right.

(7) The provisions of regulation 22 (presumptions relevant to database right) of the Copyright and Rights in Databases Regulations 1997 (SI 1997/3032) apply in proceedings brought by virtue of this section in relation to database right.][1]

[Devices and services designed to circumvent technological measures

5-309   **296ZB**—(1) A person commits an offence if he–

(a) manufactures for sale or hire, or

(b) imports otherwise than for his private and domestic use, or

(c) in the course of a business–

(i) sells or lets for hire, or

(ii) offers or exposes for sale or hire, or

(iii) advertises for sale or hire, or

(iv) possesses, or

(v) distributes, or

(d) distributes otherwise than in the course of a business to such an extent as to affect prejudicially the copyright owner,

any device, product or component which is primarily designed, produced, or adapted for the purpose of enabling or facilitating the circumvention of effective technological measures.

(2) A person commits an offence if he provides, promotes, advertises or markets–

(a) in the course of a business, or

(b) otherwise than in the course of a business to such an extent as to affect prejudicially the copyright owner,

a service the purpose of which is to enable or facilitate the circumvention of effective technological measures.

(3) Subsections (1) and (2) do not make unlawful anything done by, or on behalf of, law enforcement agencies or any of the intelligence services–

(a) in the interests of national security; or

---

[1] Substituted by SI 2003/2498 Pt II reg 24 (1)

(b) for the purpose of the prevention or detection of crime, the investigation of an offence, or the conduct of a prosecution,

and in this subsection "intelligence services" has the meaning given in section 81 of the Regulation of Investigatory Powers Act 2000.

(4) A person guilty of an offence under subsection (1) or (2) is liable –

(a) on summary conviction, to imprisonment for a term not exceeding three months, or to a fine not exceeding the statutory maximum, or both;

(b) on conviction on indictment to a fine or imprisonment for a term not exceeding two years, or both.

(5) It is a defence to any prosecution for an offence under this section for the defendant to prove that he did not know, and had no reasonable ground for believing, that –

(a) the device, product or component; or

(b) the service,

enabled or facilitated the circumvention of effective technological measures.][1]

[Devices and services designed to circumvent technological measures: search warrants and forfeiture

296ZC—(1) The provisions of sections 297B (search warrants), 297C (forfeiture of unauthorised decoders: England and Wales or Northern Ireland) and 297D (forfeiture of unauthorised decoders: Scotland) apply to offences under section 296ZB with the following modifications. **5-310**

(2) In section 297B the reference to an offence under section 297A(1) shall be construed as a reference to an offence under section 296ZB(1) or (2).

(3) In sections 297C(2)(a) and 297D(15) the references to an offence under section 297A(1) shall be construed as a reference to an offence under section 296ZB(1).

(4) In sections 297C and 297D references to unauthorised decoders shall be construed as references to devices, products or components for the purpose of circumventing effective technological measures.][2]

[Rights and remedies in respect of devices and services designed to circumvent technological measures

296ZD—(1) This section applies where – **5-311**

(a) effective technological measures have been applied to a copyright work other than a computer program; and

(b) a person (C) manufactures, imports, distributes, sells or lets for hire, offers or exposes for sale or hire, advertises for sale or hire, or has in his possession for commercial purposes any device, product or component, or provides services which –

(i) are promoted, advertised or marketed for the purpose of the circumvention of, or

(ii) have only a limited commercially significant purpose or use other than to circumvent, or

(iii) are primarily designed, produced, adapted or performed for the purpose of enabling or facilitating the circumvention of,

those measures.

---

[1] Substituted by SI 2003/2498 Pt II reg 24 (1)
[2] Substituted by SI 2003/2498 Pt II reg 24 (1)

(2) The following persons have the same rights against C as a copyright owner has in respect of an infringement of copyright –

    (a) a person –

        (i) issuing to the public copies of, or

        (ii) communicating to the public,

the work to which effective technological measures have been applied;

    (b) the copyright owner or his exclusive licensee, if he is not the person specified in paragraph (a); and

    (c) the owner or exclusive licensee of any intellectual property right in the effective technological measures applied to the work.

(3) The rights conferred by subsection (2) are concurrent, and sections 101(3) and 102(1) to (4) apply, in proceedings under this section, in relation to persons with concurrent rights as they apply, in proceedings mentioned in those provisions, in relation to a copyright owner and exclusive licensee with concurrent rights.

(4) Further, the persons in subsection (2) have the same rights under section 99 or 100 (delivery up or seizure of certain articles) in relation to any such device, product or component which a person has in his possession, custody or control with the intention that it should be used to circumvent effective technological measures, as a copyright owner has in relation to any infringing copy.

(5) The rights conferred by subsection (4) are concurrent, and section 102(5) shall apply, as respects anything done under section 99 or 100 by virtue of subsection (4), in relation to persons with concurrent rights as it applies, as respects anything done under section 99 or 100, in relation to a copyright owner and exclusive licensee with concurrent rights.

(6) The following provisions apply in relation to proceedings under this section as in relation to proceedings under Part 1 (copyright)–

    (a) sections 104 to 106 of this Act (presumptions as to certain matters relating to copyright); and

    (b) section 72 of the Supreme Court Act 1981, section 15 of the Law Reform (Miscellaneous Provisions) (Scotland) Act 1985 and section 94A of the Judicature (Northern Ireland) Act 1978 (withdrawal of privilege against self-incrimination in certain proceedings relating to intellectual property);

and section 114 of this Act applies, with the necessary modifications, in relation to the disposal of anything delivered up or seized by virtue of subsection (4).

(7) In section 97(1) (innocent infringement of copyright) as it applies to proceedings for infringement of the rights conferred by this section, the reference to the defendant not knowing or having reason to believe that copyright subsisted in the work shall be construed as a reference to his not knowing or having reason to believe that his acts enabled or facilitated an infringement of copyright.

(8) Subsections (1) to (5), (6)(b) and (7) and any other provision of this Act as it has effect for the purposes of those subsections apply, with any necessary adaptations, to rights in performances, publication right and database right.

(9) The provisions of regulation 22 (presumptions relevant to database right) of the Copyright and Rights in Databases Regulations 1997 (SI 1997/

3032) apply in proceedings brought by virtue of this section in relation to database right.][1]

[Remedy where effective technological measures prevent permitted acts

296ZE—(1) In this section–   5-312
  "permitted act" means an act which may be done in relation to copyright works, notwithstanding the subsistence of copyright, by virtue of a provision of this Act listed in Part 1 of Schedule 5A;
  "voluntary measure or agreement" means–
  (a) any measure taken voluntarily by a copyright owner, his exclusive licensee or a person issuing copies of, or communicating to the public, a work other than a computer program, or
  (b) any agreement between a copyright owner, his exclusive licensee or a person issuing copies of, or communicating to the public, a work other than a computer program and another party,

the effect of which is to enable a person to carry out a permitted act.

(2) Where the application of any effective technological measure to a copyright work other than a computer program prevents a person from carrying out a permitted act in relation to that work then that person or a person being a representative of a class of persons prevented from carrying out a permitted act may issue a notice of complaint to the Secretary of State.

(3) Following receipt of a notice of complaint, the Secretary of State may give to the owner of that copyright work or an exclusive licensee such directions as appear to the Secretary of State to be requisite or expedient for the purpose of–
  (a) establishing whether any voluntary measure or agreement relevant to the copyright work the subject of the complaint subsists; or
  (b) (where it is established there is no subsisting voluntary measure or agreement) ensuring that the owner or exclusive licensee of that copyright work makes available to the complainant the means of carrying out the permitted act the subject of the complaint to the extent necessary to so benefit from that permitted act.

(4) The Secretary of State may also give directions–
  (a) as to the form and manner in which a notice of complaint in subsection (2) may be delivered to him;
  (b) as to the form and manner in which evidence of any voluntary measure or agreement may be delivered to him; and
  (c) generally as to the procedure to be followed in relation to a complaint made under this section;
and shall publish directions given under this subsection in such manner as in his opinion will secure adequate publicity for them.

(5) It shall be the duty of any person to whom a direction is given under subsection (3)(a) or (b) to give effect to that direction.

(6) The obligation to comply with a direction given under subsection (3)(b) is a duty owed to the complainant or, where the complaint is made by

---

[1] Substituted by SI 2003/2498 Pt II reg 24 (1)

a representative of a class of persons, to that representative and to each person in the class represented; and a breach of the duty is actionable accordingly (subject to the defences and other incidents applying to actions for breach of statutory duty).

(7) Any direction under this section may be varied or revoked by a subsequent direction under this section.

(8) Any direction given under this section shall be in writing.

(9) This section does not apply to copyright works made available to the public on agreed contractual terms in such a way that members of the public may access them from a place and at a time individually chosen by them.

(10) This section applies only where a complainant has lawful access to the protected copyright work, or where the complainant is a representative of a class of persons, where the class of persons have lawful access to the work.

(11) Subsections (1) to (10) apply with any necessary adaptations to –

(a) rights in performances, and in this context the expression "permitted act" refers to an act that may be done by virtue of a provision of this Act listed in Part 2 of Schedule 5A;

(b) database right, and in this context the expression "permitted act" refers to an act that may be done by virtue of a provision of this Act listed in Part 3 of Schedule 5A; and

(c) publication right.][1]

[Interpretation of sections 296ZA to 296ZE

5-313   **296ZF**—(1) In sections 296ZA to 296ZE, "technological measures" are any technology, device or component which is designed, in the normal course of its operation, to protect a copyright work other than a computer program.

(2) Such measures are "effective" if the use of the work is controlled by the copyright owner through –

(a) an access control or protection process such as encryption, scrambling or other transformation of the work, or

(b) a copy control mechanism,

which achieves the intended protection.

(3) In this section, the reference to –

(a) protection of a work is to the prevention or restriction of acts that are not authorised by the copyright owner of that work and are restricted by copyright; and

(b) use of a work does not extend to any use of the work that is outside the scope of the acts restricted by copyright.

(4) Expressions used in sections 296ZA to 296ZE which are defined for the purposes of Part 1 of this Act (copyright) have the same meaning as in that Part.][2]

---

[1] Substituted by SI 2003/2498 Pt II reg 24 (1)
[2] Substituted by SI 2003/2498 Pt II reg 24 (1)

[Electronic rights management information

296ZG—(1) This section applies where a person (D), knowingly and **5-314** without authority, removes or alters electronic rights management information which—

(a) is associated with a copy of a copyright work, or

(b) appears in connection with the communication to the public of a copyright work, and

where D knows, or has reason to believe, that by so doing he is inducing, enabling, facilitating or concealing an infringement of copyright.

(2) This section also applies where a person (E), knowingly and without authority, distributes, imports for distribution or communicates to the public copies of a copyright work from which electronic rights management information—

(a) associated with the copies, or

(b) appearing in connection with the communication to the public of the work,

has been removed or altered without authority and where E knows, or has reason to believe, that by so doing he is inducing, enabling, facilitating or concealing an infringement of copyright.

(3) A person issuing to the public copies of, or communicating, the work to the public, has the same rights against D and E as a copyright owner has in respect of an infringement of copyright.

(4) The copyright owner or his exclusive licensee, if he is not the person issuing to the public copies of, or communicating, the work to the public, also has the same rights against D and E as he has in respect of an infringement of copyright.

(5) The rights conferred by subsections (3) and (4) are concurrent, and sections 101(3) and 102(1) to (4) apply, in proceedings under this section, in relation to persons with concurrent rights as they apply, in proceedings mentioned in those provisions, in relation to a copyright owner and exclusive licensee with concurrent rights.

(6) The following provisions apply in relation to proceedings under this section as in relation to proceedings under Part 1 (copyright)–

(a) sections 104 to 106 of this Act (presumptions as to certain matters relating to copyright); and

(b) section 72 of the Supreme Court Act 1981, section 15 of the Law Reform (Miscellaneous Provisions) (Scotland) Act 1985 and section 94A of the Judicature (Northern Ireland) Act 1978 (withdrawal of privilege against self-incrimination in certain proceedings relating to intellectual property).

(7) In this section–

(a) expressions which are defined for the purposes of Part 1 of this Act (copyright) have the same meaning as in that Part; and

(b) "rights management information" means any information provided by the copyright owner or the holder of any right under copyright which identifies the work, the author, the copyright owner or the holder of any intellectual property rights, or information about the terms and conditions of use of the work, and any numbers or codes that represent such information.

(8) Subsections (1) to (5) and (6)(b), and any other provision of this Act as it has effect for the purposes of those subsections, apply, with any necessary adaptations, to rights in performances, publication right and database right.

(9) The provisions of regulation 22 (presumptions relevant to database right) of the Copyright and Rights in Databases Regulations 1997 (SI 1997/3032) apply in proceedings brought by virtue of this section in relation to database right.][1]][2]

[Computer programs

Avoidance of certain terms

5-315   **296A.**—(1) Where a person has the use of a computer program under an agreement, any term or condition in the agreement shall be void in so far as it purports to prohibit or restrict—

> (a) the making of any back up copy of the program which it is necessary for him to have for the purposes of the agreed use;
> (b) where the conditions in section 50B(2) are met, the decompiling of the program; or
> [(c) the observing, studying or testing of the functioning of the program in accordance with section 50BA.][3]

(2) In this section, decompile, in relation to a computer program, has the same meaning as in section 50B.][4]

[Databases

Avoidance of certain terms relating to databases

5-316   **296B.** Where under an agreement a person has a right to use a database or part of a database, any term or condition in the agreement shall be void in so far as it purports to prohibit or restrict the performance of any act which would but for section 50D infringe the copyright in the database.][5]

Fraudulent reception of transmissions

Offence of fraudulently receiving programmes

5-317   **297.**—(1) A person who dishonestly receives a programme included in a broadcasting [...][6] service provided from a place in the United Kingdom with intent to avoid payment of any charge applicable to the reception of the programme commits an offence and is liable on summary conviction to a fine not exceeding level 5 on the standard scale.

(2) Where an offence under this section committed by a body corporate is proved to have been committed with the consent or connivance of a director, manager, secretary or other similar officer of the body, or a person purporting to act in any such capacity, he as well as the body

---

[1] Inserted by SI 2003/2498 Pt II reg 25
[2] Inserted by SI 2003/2498 Pt II reg 25
[3] Substituted by SI 2003/2498 Pt II reg 15 (4)
[4] Inserted by SI 1992/3233 reg 11
[5] Inserted by SI 1997/3032 Pt II reg 10
[6] Words repealed by SI 2003/2498 Sch 2 para 1

corporate is guilty of the offence and liable to be proceeded against and punished accordingly.

In relation to a body corporate whose affairs are managed by its members "director" means a member of the body corporate.

[Unauthorised decoders

297A—(1) A person commits an offence if he –   **5-318**

(a) makes, imports, distributes, sells or lets for hire or offers or exposes for sale or hire any unauthorised decoder;

(b) has in his possession for commercial purposes any unauthorised decoder;

(c) instals, maintains or replaces for commercial purposes any unauthorised decoder; or

(d) advertises any unauthorised decoder for sale or hire or otherwise promotes any unauthorised decoder by means of commercial communications.

(2) A person guilty of an offence under subsection (1) is liable –

[(a) on summary conviction, to imprisonment for a term not exceeding six months, or to a fine not exceeding the statutory maximum, or to both;][1]

(b) on conviction on indictment, to imprisonment for a term not exceeding [ten][2] years, or to a fine, or to both.

(3) It is a defence to any prosecution for an offence under this section for the defendant to prove that he did not know, and had no reasonable ground for believing, that the decoder was an unauthorised decoder.

(4) In this section –

"apparatus" includes any device, component or electronic data (including software);

"conditional access technology" means any technical measure or arrangement whereby access to encrypted transmissions in an intelligible form is made conditional on prior individual authorisation;

"decoder" means any apparatus which is designed or adapted to enable (whether on its own or with any other apparatus) an encrypted transmission to be decoded;

"encrypted" includes subjected to scrambling or the operation of cryptographic envelopes, electronic locks, passwords or any other analogous application;

"transmission" means –

(a) any programme included in a broadcasting [...][3] service which is provided from a place in the United Kingdom or any other member State; or

(b) an information society service (within the meaning of Directive 98/34/EC of the European Parliament and of the Council of 22nd June 1998, as amended by Directive 98/48/EC of the European Parliament and of the Council of 20th

---

[1] Substituted by Copyright, etc. and Trade Marks (Offences and Enforcement) Act 2002 c.25 s 1 (4) (a)

[2] Word substituted by Copyright, etc. and Trade Marks (Offences and Enforcement) Act 2002 c.25 s 1 (4) (b)

[3] Words repealed by SI 2003/2498 Sch 2 para 1

July 1998) which is provided from a place in the United Kingdom or any other member State; and

"unauthorised", in relation to a decoder, means that the decoder is designed or adapted to enable an encrypted transmission, or any service of which it forms part, to be accessed in an intelligible form without payment of the fee (however imposed) which the person making the transmission, or on whose behalf it is made, charges for accessing the transmission or service (whether by the circumvention of any conditional access technology related to the transmission or service or by any other means).][1]

[Search warrants

5-319
297B—(1) Where a justice of the peace (in Scotland, a sheriff or justice of the peace) is satisfied by information on oath given by a constable (in Scotland, by evidence on oath) that there are reasonable grounds for believing—

(a) that an offence under section 297A(1) has been or is about to be committed in any premises, and
(b) that evidence that such an offence has been or is about to be committed is in those premises,

he may issue a warrant authorising a constable to enter and search the premises, using such reasonable force as is necessary.

(2) The power conferred by subsection (1) does not, in England and Wales, extend to authorising a search for material of the kinds mentioned in section 9(2) of the Police and Criminal Evidence Act 1984 (c. 60) (certain classes of personal or confidential material).

(3) A warrant under subsection (1)—

(a) may authorise persons to accompany any constable executing the warrant, and
(b) remains in force for 28 days from the date of its issue.

(4) In executing a warrant issued under subsection (1) a constable may seize an article if he reasonably believes that it is evidence that any offence under section 297A(1) has been or is about to be committed.

(5) In this section "premises" includes land, buildings, fixed or moveable structures, vehicles, vessels, aircraft and hovercraft.][2]

[Forfeiture of unauthorised decoders: England and Wales or Northern Ireland

5-320
297C—(1) In England and Wales or Northern Ireland where unauthorised decoders have come into the possession of any person in connection with the investigation or prosecution of a relevant offence, that person may apply under this section for an order for the forfeiture of the unauthorised decoders.

(2) For the purposes of this section "relevant offence" means—

(a) an offence under section 297A(1) (criminal liability for making, importing, etc. unauthorised decoders),
(b) an offence under the Trade Descriptions Act 1968, or
(c) an offence involving dishonesty or deception.

(3) An application under this section may be made—

---

[1] Substituted by SI 2000/1175 reg 2 (2)
[2] Inserted by Copyright, etc. and Trade Marks (Offences and Enforcement) Act 2002 c.25 s 2 (4)

(a) where proceedings have been brought in any court for a relevant offence relating to some or all of the unauthorised decoders, to that court, or

(b) where no application for the forfeiture of the unauthorised decoders has been made under paragraph (a), by way of complaint to a magistrates' court.

(4) On an application under this section, the court shall make an order for the forfeiture of any unauthorised decoders only if it is satisfied that a relevant offence has been committed in relation to the unauthorised decoders.

(5) A court may infer for the purposes of this section that such an offence has been committed in relation to any unauthorised decoders if it is satisfied that such an offence has been committed in relation to unauthorised decoders which are representative of the unauthorised decoders in question (whether by reason of being of the same design or part of the same consignment or batch or otherwise).

(6) Any person aggrieved by an order made under this section by a magistrates' court, or by a decision of such a court not to make such an order, may appeal against that order or decision—

(a) in England and Wales, to the Crown Court, or

(b) in Northern Ireland, to the county court.

(7) An order under this section may contain such provision as appears to the court to be appropriate for delaying the coming into force of the order pending the making and determination of any appeal (including any application under section 111 of the Magistrates' Courts Act 1980 (c. 43) or Article 146 of the Magistrates' Courts (Northern Ireland) Order 1981 (S.I. 1981/1675 (N.I. 26)) (statement of case)).

(8) Subject to subsection (9), where any unauthorised decoders are forfeited under this section they shall be destroyed in accordance with such directions as the court may give.

(9) On making an order under this section the court may direct that the unauthorised decoders to which the order relates shall (instead of being destroyed) be forfeited to a person who has rights or remedies under section 298 in relation to the unauthorised decoders in question, or dealt with in such other way as the court considers appropriate.][1]

[Forfeiture of unauthorised decoders: Scotland

297D—(1) In Scotland the court may make an order under this section **5-321** for the forfeiture of unauthorised decoders.

(2) An order under this section may be made—

(a) on an application by the procurator-fiscal made in the manner specified in section 134 of the Criminal Procedure (Scotland) Act 1995 (c. 46), or

(b) where a person is convicted of a relevant offence, in addition to any other penalty which the court may impose.

(3) On an application under subsection (2)(a), the court shall make an order for the forfeiture of any unauthorised decoders only if it is satisfied that a relevant offence has been committed in relation to the unauthorised decoders.

(4) The court may infer for the purposes of this section that such an offence has been committed in relation to any unauthorised decoders if it is

---

[1] Inserted by Copyright, etc. and Trade Marks (Offences and Enforcement) Act 2002 c.25 s 5

satisfied that such an offence has been committed in relation to unauthorised decoders which are representative of the unauthorised decoders in question (whether by reason of being of the same design or part of the same consignment or batch or otherwise).

(5) The procurator-fiscal making the application under subsection (2)(a) shall serve on any person appearing to him to be the owner of, or otherwise to have an interest in, the unauthorised decoders to which the application relates a copy of the application, together with a notice giving him the opportunity to appear at the hearing of the application to show cause why the unauthorised decoders should not be forfeited.

(6) Service under subsection (5) shall be carried out, and such service may be proved, in the manner specified for citation of an accused in summary proceedings under the Criminal Procedure (Scotland) Act 1995 (c. 46).

(7) Any person upon whom notice is served under subsection (5) and any other person claiming to be the owner of, or otherwise to have an interest in, unauthorised decoders to which an application under this section relates shall be entitled to appear at the hearing of the application to show cause why the unauthorised decoders should not be forfeited.

(8) The court shall not make an order following an application under subsection (2)(a)—

(a) if any person on whom notice is served under subsection (5) does not appear, unless service of the notice on that person is proved, or

(b) if no notice under subsection (5) has been served, unless the court is satisfied that in the circumstances it was reasonable not to serve such notice.

(9) Where an order for the forfeiture of any unauthorised decoders is made following an application under subsection (2)(a), any person who appeared, or was entitled to appear, to show cause why the unauthorised decoders should not be forfeited may, within 21 days of the making of the order, appeal to the High Court by Bill of Suspension.

(10) Section 182(5)(a) to (e) of the Criminal Procedure (Scotland) Act 1995 shall apply to an appeal under subsection (9) as it applies to a stated case under Part 2 of that Act.

(11) An order following an application under subsection (2)(a) shall not take effect—

(a) until the end of the period of 21 days beginning with the day after the day on which the order is made, or

(b) if an appeal is made under subsection (9) above within that period, until the appeal is determined or abandoned.

(12) An order under subsection (2)(b) shall not take effect—

(a) until the end of the period within which an appeal against the order could be brought under the Criminal Procedure (Scotland) Act 1995 (c. 46), or

(b) if an appeal is made within that period, until the appeal is determined or abandoned.

(13) Subject to subsection (14), where any unauthorised decoders are forfeited under this section they shall be destroyed in accordance with such directions as the court may give.

(14) On making an order under this section the court may direct that the unauthorised decoders to which the order relates shall (instead of being

destroyed) be forfeited to a person who has rights or remedies under section 298 in relation to the unauthorised decoders in question, or dealt with in such other way as the court considers appropriate.

(15) For the purposes of this section—

"relevant offence" means an offence under section 297A(1) (criminal liability for making, importing, etc. unauthorised decoders), or under the Trade Descriptions Act 1968 (c. 29) or any offence involving dishonesty or deception;

"the court" means—

(a) in relation to an order made on an application under subsection (2)(a), the sheriff, and

(b) in relation to an order made under subsection (2)(b), the court which imposed the penalty.][1]

[Rights and remedies in respect of apparatus, &c. for unauthorised reception of transmissions

298.—(1) A person who – 5-322

(a) makes charges for the reception of programmes included in a broadcasting [...][2] service provided from a place in the United Kingdom or any other member State,

(b) sends encrypted transmissions of any other description from a place in the United Kingdom or any other member State, or

(c) provides conditional access services from a place in the United Kingdom or any other member State,

is entitled to the following rights and remedies.

(2) He has the same rights and remedies against a person –

(a) who –

(i) makes, imports, distributes, sells or lets for hire, offers or exposes for sale or hire, or advertises for sale or hire,

(ii) has in his possession for commercial purposes, or

(iii) instals, maintains or replaces for commercial purposes,

any apparatus designed or adapted to enable or assist persons to access the programmes or other transmissions or circumvent conditional access technology related to the programmes or other transmissions when they are not entitled to do so, or

(b) who publishes or otherwise promotes by means of commercial communications any information which is calculated to enable or assist persons to access the programmes or other transmissions or circumvent conditional access technology related to the programmes or other transmissions when they are not entitled to do so,

as a copyright owner has in respect of an infringement of copyright.

(3) Further, he has the same rights under section 99 or 100 (delivery up or seizure of certain articles) in relation to any such apparatus as a copyright owner has in relation to an infringing copy.

(4) Section 72 of the Supreme Court Act 1981, section 15 of the Law Reform (Miscellaneous Provisions) (Scotland) Act 1985 and section 94A of the Judicature (Northern Ireland) Act 1978 (withdrawal of privilege against self-incrimination in certain proceedings relating to intellectual

---

[1] Inserted by Copyright, etc. and Trade Marks (Offences and Enforcement) Act 2002 c.25 s 5

[2] Words repealed by SI 2003/2498 Sch 2 para 1

property) apply to proceedings under this section as to proceedings under Part I of this Act (copyright).

(5) In section 97(1) (innocent infringement of copyright) as it applies to proceedings for infringement of the rights conferred by this section, the reference to the defendant not knowing or having reason to believe that copyright subsisted in the work shall be construed as a reference to his not knowing or having reason to believe that his acts infringed the rights conferred by this section.

(6) Section 114 applies, with the necessary modifications, in relation to the disposal of anything delivered up or seized by virtue of subsection (3) above.

(7) In this section "apparatus", "conditional access technology" and "encrypted" have the same meanings as in section 297A, "transmission" includes transmissions as defined in that section and "conditional access services" means services comprising the provision of conditional access technology.][1]

Supplementary provisions as to fraudulent reception

5-323   **299.**—(1) Her Majesty may by Order in Council—

  (a) provide that section 297 applies in relation to programmes included in services provided from a country or territory outside the United Kingdom, and

  (b) provide that section 298 applies in relation to such programmes and to encrypted transmissions sent from such a country or territory.

(3) A statutory instrument containing an Order in Council under subsection (1) shall be subject to annulment in pursuance of a resolution of either House of Parliament.

(4) Where sections 297 and 298 apply in relation to a broadcasting service [...][2], they also apply to any service run for the person providing that service, or a person providing programmes for that service, which consists wholly or mainly in the sending by means of a telecommunications system of sounds or visual images, or both.

(5) In sections 297[, 297A][3] and 298, and this section, "programme" [and "broadcasting"][4], and related expressions, have the same meaning as in Part I (copyright).

Provisions for the benefit of the Hospital for Sick Children

Provisions for the benefit of the Hospital for Sick Children

5-324   **301.** The provisions of Schedule 6 have effect for conferring on trustees for the benefit of the Hospital for Sick Children, Great Ormond Street, London, a right to a royalty in respect of the public performance, commercial publication [or communication to the public][5] of the play "Peter Pan" by Sir James Matthew Barrie, or of any adaptation of that work, notwithstanding that copyright in the work expired on 31st December 1987.

---

[1] Substituted by SI 2000/1175 reg 2 (3)
[2] Words repealed by SI 2003/2498 Sch 2 para 1
[3] Words inserted by Broadcasting Act 1990 c.42 s 179 (2) (b)
[4] Words substituted by SI 2003/2498 Sch 1 Pt I para 3 (3)
[5] Words substituted by SI 2003/2498 Sch 1 Pt I para 6 (2) (d)

SCHEDULES

COPYRIGHT: TRANSITIONAL PROVISIONS AND SAVINGS

Introductory

1.—(1) In this Schedule—   **5-325**
"the 1911 Act" means the Copyright Act 1911,
"the 1956 Act" means the Copyright Act 1956, and
"the new copyright provisions" means the provisions of this Act relating to copyright,
that is, Part I (including this Schedule) and Schedules 3, 7 and 8 so far as they
make amendments or repeals consequential on the provisions of Part I.

(2) References in this Schedule to "commencement", without more, are to the date on
which the new copyright provisions come into force.

(3) References in this Schedule to "existing works" are to works made before commencement; and for this purpose a work of which the making extended over a period shall be taken to
have been made when its making was completed.

2.—(1) In relation to the 1956 Act, references in this Schedule to a work include any work **5-326**
or other subject-matter within the meaning of that Act.

(2) In relation to the 1911 Act—
(a) references in this Schedule to copyright include the right conferred by section 24 of
that Act in substitution for a right subsisting immediately before the commencement
of that Act;
(b) references in this Schedule to copyright in a sound recording are to the copyright
under that Act in records embodying the recording; and
(c) references in this Schedule to copyright in a film are to any copyright under that
Act in the film (so far as it constituted a dramatic work for the purposes of that Act)
or in photographs forming part of the film.

General principles: continuity of the law

3. The new copyright provisions apply in relation to things existing at commencement as **5-327**
they apply in relation to things coming into existence after commencement, subject to any
express provision to the contrary.

4.—(1) The provisions of this paragraph have effect for securing the continuity of the law **5-328**
so far as the new copyright provisions re-enact (with or without modification) earlier
provisions.

(2) A reference in an enactment, instrument or other document to copyright, or to a work
or other subject-matter in which copyright subsists, which apart from this Act would be
construed as referring to copyright under the 1956 Act shall be construed, so far as may be
required for continuing its effect, as being, or as the case may require, including, a reference to
copyright under this Act or to works in which copyright subsists under this Act.

(3) Anything done (including subordinate legislation made), or having effect as done,
under or for the purposes of a provision repealed by this Act has effect as if done under or for
the purposes of the corresponding provision of the new copyright provisions.

(4) References (expressed or implied) in this Act or any other enactment, instrument or
document to any of the new copyright provisions shall, so far as the context permits, be
construed as including, in relation to times, circumstances and purposes before commencement, a reference to corresponding earlier provisions.

(5) A reference (express or implied) in an enactment, instrument or other document to a
provision repealed by this Act shall be construed, so far as may be required for continuing its
effect, as a reference to the corresponding provisions of this Act.

(6) The provisions of this paragraph have effect subject to any specific transitional
provision or saving and to any express amendment made by this Act.

Subsistence of copyright

5.—(1) Copyright subsists in an existing work after commencement only if copyright subsisted in it immediately before commencement.

(2) Sub-paragraph (1) does not prevent an existing work qualifying for copyright protection after commencement—

    (a) under section 155 (qualification by virtue of first publication), or

    (b) by virtue of an Order under section 159 (application of Part I to countries to which it does not extend).

7.—

5-330

(1) No copyright subsists in a film, as such, made before 1st June 1957.

(2) Where a film made before that date was an original dramatic work within the meaning of the 1911 Act, the new copyright provisions have effect in relation to the film as if it was an original dramatic work within the meaning of Part I.

(3) The new copyright provisions have effect in relation to photographs forming part of a film made before 1st June 1957 as they have effect in relation to photographs not forming part of a film.

5-331

8.—(1) A film sound-track to which section 13(9) of the 1956 Act applied before commencement (film to be taken to include sounds in associated sound-track) shall be treated for the purposes of the new copyright provisions not as part of the film, but as a sound recording.

(2) However—

    (a) copyright subsists in the sound recording only if copyright subsisted in the film immediately before commencement, and it continues to subsist until copyright in the film expires;

    (b) the author and first owner of copyright in the film shall be treated as having been author and first owner of the copyright in the sound recording; and

    (c) anything done before commencement under or in relation to the copyright in the film continues to have effect in relation to the sound recording as in relation to the film.

5-332

[**9.** No copyright subsists in—

    (a) a wireless broadcast made before 1st June 1957, or

    (b) a broadcast by cable made before 1st January 1985;

and any such broadcast shall be disregarded for the purposes of section 14(5) (duration of copyright in repeats).][1]

Authorship of work

5-333

10. The question who was the author of an existing work shall be determined in accordance with the new copyright provisions for the purposes of the rights conferred by Chapter IV of Part I (moral rights), and for all other purposes shall be determined in accordance with the law in force at the time the work was made.

First ownership of copyright

5-334

11.—(1) The question who was first owner of copyright in an existing work shall be determined in accordance with the law in force at the time the work was made.

(2) Where before commencement a person commissioned the making of a work in circumstances falling within—

    (a) section 4(3) of the 1956 Act or paragraph (a) of the proviso to section 5(1) of the 1911 Act (photographs, portraits and engravings), or

    (b) the proviso to section 12(4) of the 1956 Act (sound recordings),

those provisions apply to determine first ownership of copyright in any work made in pursuance of the commission after commencement.

Duration of copyright in existing works

5-335 [1] Substituted by SI 2003/2498 Sch 1 Pt I para 16 (a)

12.—(1) The following provisions have effect with respect to the duration of copyright in existing works.

The question which provision applies to a work shall be determined by reference to the facts immediately before commencement; and expressions used in this paragraph which were defined for the purposes of the 1956 Act have the same meaning as in that Act.

(2) Copyright in the following descriptions of work continues to subsist until the date on which it would have expired under the 1956 Act—

(a) literary, dramatic or musical works in relation to which the period of 50 years mentioned in the proviso to section 2(3) of the 1956 Act (duration of copyright in works made available to the public after the death of the author) has begun to run;

(b) engravings in relation to which the period of 50 years mentioned in the proviso to section 3(4) of the 1956 Act (duration of copyright in works published after the death of the author) has begun to run;

(c) published photographs and photographs taken before 1st June 1957;

(d) published sound recordings and sound recordings made before 1st June 1957;

(e) published films and films falling within section 13(3)(a) of the 1956 Act (films registered under former enactments relating to registration of films).

(3) Copyright in anonymous or pseudonymous literary, dramatic, musical or artistic works (other than photographs) continues to subsist—

(a) if the work is published, until the date on which it would have expired in accordance with the 1956 Act, and

(b) if the work is unpublished, until the end of the period of 50 years from the end of the calendar year in which the new copyright provisions come into force or, if during that period the work is first made available to the public within the meaning of [section 12(3)][1] (duration of copyright in works of unknown authorship), the date on which copyright expires in accordance with that provision;

unless, in any case, the identity of the author becomes known before that date, in which case [section 12(2)][2] applies (general rule: life of the author [plus 70][3] years).

(4) Copyright in the following descriptions of work continues to subsist until the end of the period of 50 years from the end of the calendar year in which the new copyright provisions come into force—

(a) literary, dramatic and musical works of which the author has died and in relation to which none of the acts mentioned in paragraphs(a)to(e) of the proviso to section 2(3) of the 1956 Act has been done;

(b) unpublished engravings of which the author has died;

(c) unpublished photographs taken on or after 1st June 1957.

(5) Copyright in the following descriptions of work continues to subsist until the end of the period of 50 years from the end of the calendar year in which the new copyright provisions come into force—

(a) unpublished sound recordings made on or after 1st June 1957;

(b) films not falling within sub-paragraph (2)(e) above,

unless the recording or film is published before the end of that period in which case copyright in it shall continue until the end of the period of 50 years from the end of the calendar year in which the recording or film is published.

(6) Copyright in any other description of existing work continues to subsist until the date on which copyright in that description of work expires in accordance with sections 12 to 15 of this Act.

(7) The above provisions do not apply to works subject to Crown or Parliamentary copyright (see paragraphs 41 to 43 below).

Perpetual copyright under the Copyright Act 1775

13.—(1) The rights conferred on universities and colleges by the Copyright Act 1775 shall **5-336** continue to subsist until the end of the period of 50 years from the end of the calendar year in which the new copyright provisions come into force and shall then expire.

(2) The provisions of the following Chapters of Part I—

Chapter III (acts permitted in relation to copyright works),

Chapter VI (remedies for infringement),

---

[1] Words substituted by SI 2003/2498 Sch 1 Pt I para 18 (3) (a)

[2] Words substituted by SI 2003/2498 Sch 1 Pt I para 18 (3) (b)

[3] Words substituted by SI 2003/2498 Sch 1 Pt I para 18 (3) (c)

Chapter VII (provisions with respect to copyright licensing), and
Chapter VIII (the Copyright Tribunal),
apply in relation to those rights as they apply in relation to copyright under this Act.

Acts infringing copyright

5-337   **14.**—(1) The provisions of Chapters II and III of Part I as to the acts constituting an infringement of copyright apply only in relation to acts done after commencement; the provisions of the 1956 Act continue to apply in relation to acts done before commencement.

(2) So much of section 18(2) as extends the restricted act of issuing copies to the public to include the rental to the public of copies of sound recordings, films or computer programs does not apply in relation to a copy of a sound recording, film or computer program acquired by any person before commencement for the purpose of renting it to the public.

(3) For the purposes of section 27 (meaning of "infringing copy") the question whether the making of an article constituted an infringement of copyright, or would have done if the article had been made in the United Kingdom, shall be determined—

    (a) in relation to an article made on or after 1st June 1957 and before commencement, by reference to the 1956 Act, and

    (b) in relation to an article made before 1st June 1957, by reference to the 1911 Act.

(4) For the purposes of the application of sections 31(2), 51(2) and 62(3) (subsequent exploitation of things whose making was, by virtue of an earlier provision of the section, not an infringement of copyright) to things made before commencement, it shall be assumed that the new copyright provisions were in force at all material times.

(5) Section 55 (articles for producing material in a particular typeface) applies where articles have been marketed as mentioned in subsection (1) before commencement with the substitution for the period mentioned in subsection (2) of the period of 25 years from the end of the calendar year in which the new copyright provisions come into force.

(6) Section 56 (transfer of copies, adaptations, &c. of work in electronic form) does not apply in relation to a copy purchased before commencement.

(7) In section 65 (reconstruction of buildings) the reference to the owner of the copyright in the drawings or plans is, in relation to buildings constructed before commencement, to the person who at the time of the construction was the owner of the copyright in the drawings or plans under the 1956 Act, the 1911 Act or any enactment repealed by the 1911 Act.

5-338   **15.**—(1) Section 57 (anonymous or pseudonymous works: acts permitted on assumptions as to expiry of copyright or death of author) has effect in relation to existing works subject to the following provisions.

(2) Subsection (1)(b)(i) (assumption as to expiry of copyright) does not apply in relation to—

    (a) photographs, or

    (b) the rights mentioned in paragraph 13 above (rights conferred by the Copyright Act 1775).

5-339   **16.** The following provisions of section 7 of the 1956 Act continue to apply in relation to existing works—

    (a) subsection (6) (copying of unpublished works from manuscript or copy in library, museum or other institution);

    (b) subsection (7) (publication of work containing material to which subsection (6) applies), except (duty to give notice of intended publication) paragraph (a);

    (c) subsection (8) (subsequent broadcasting, performance, &c. of material published in accordance with subsection (7));

and subsection (9)(d) (illustrations) continues to apply for the purposes of those provisions.

5-340   **17.** Where in the case of a dramatic or musical work made before 1st July 1912, the right conferred by the 1911 Act did not include the sole right to perform the work in public, the acts restricted by the copyright shall be treated as not including—

    (a) performing the work in public,

    [(b) communicating the work to the public, or][1]

    (c) doing any of the above in relation to an adaptation of the work;

---

[1] Substituted by SI 2003/2498 Sch 1 (1) para 4 (6)

and where the right conferred by the 1911 Act consisted only of the sole right to perform the work in public, the acts restricted by the copyright shall be treated as consisting only of those acts.

18. Where a work made before 1st July 1912 consists of an essay, article or portion forming part of and first published in a review, magazine or other periodical or work of a like nature, the copyright is subject to any right of publishing the essay, article, or portion in a separate form to which the author was entitled at the commencement of the 1911 Act, or would if that Act had not been passed, have become entitled under section 18 of the Copyright Act 1842. **5-341**

Designs

20.—(1) Where section 10 of the 1956 Act (effect of industrial application of design corresponding to artistic work) applied in relation to an artistic work at any time before commencement, section 52(2) of this Act applies with the substitution for the period of 25 years mentioned there of the relevant period of 15 years as defined in section 10(3) of the 1956 Act. **5-342**

(2) Except as provided in sub-paragraph (1), section 52 applies only where articles are marketed as mentioned in subsection (1)(b) after commencement.

Moral rights

22.—(1) No act done before commencement is actionable by virtue of any provision of Chapter IV of Part I (moral rights). **5-343**

(2) Section 43 of the 1956 Act (false attribution of authorship) continues to apply in relation to acts done before commencement.

23.—(1) The following provisions have effect with respect to the rights conferred by— **5-344**
    (a) section 77 (right to be identified as author or director), and
    (b) section 80 (right to object to derogatory treatment of work).
(2) The rights do not apply—
    (a) in relation to a literary, dramatic, musical and artistic work of which the author died before commencement; or
    (b) in relation to a film made before commencement.
(3) The rights in relation to an existing literary, dramatic, musical or artistic work do not apply—
    (a) where copyright first vested in the author, to anything which by virtue of an assignment of copyright made or licence granted before commencement may be done without infringing copyright;
    (b) where copyright first vested in a person other than the author, to anything done by or with the licence of the copyright owner.
(4) The rights do not apply to anything done in relation to a record made in pursuance of section 8 of the 1956 Act (statutory recording licence).

24. The right conferred by section 85 (right to privacy of certain photographs and films) does not apply to photographs taken or films made before commencement. **5-345**

Assignments and licences

25.—(1) Any document made or event occurring before commencement which had any operation— **5-346**
    (a) affecting the ownership of the copyright in an existing work, or
    (b) creating, transferring or terminating an interest, right or licence in respect of the copyright in an existing work,
has the corresponding operation in relation to copyright in the work under this Act.
(2) Expressions used in such a document shall be construed in accordance with their effect immediately before commencement.

—(1) Section 91(1) of this Act (assignment of future copyright: statutory vesting of legal interest on copyright coming into existence) does not apply in relation to an agreement made before 1st June 1957.

(2) The repeal by this Act of section 37(2) of the 1956 Act (assignment of future copyright: devolution of right where assignee dies before copyright comes into existence) does not affect the operation of that provision in relation to an agreement made before commencement.

5-348   27.—(1) Where the author of a literary, dramatic, musical or artistic work was the first owner of the copyright in it, no assignment of the copyright and no grant of any interest in it, made by him (otherwise than by will) after the passing of the 1911 Act and before 1st June 1957, shall be operative to vest in the assignee or grantee any rights with respect to the copyright in the work beyond the expiration of 25 years from the death of the author.

(2) The reversionary interest in the copyright expectant on the termination of that period may after commencement be assigned by the author during his life but in the absence of any assignment shall, on his death, devolve on his legal personal representatives as part of his estate.

(3) Nothing in this paragraph affects—

(a) an assignment of the reversionary interest by a person to whom it has been assigned,

(b) an assignment of the reversionary interest after the death of the author by his personal representatives or any person becoming entitled to it, or

(c) any assignment of the copyright after the reversionary interest has fallen in.

(4) Nothing in this paragraph applies to the assignment of the copyright in a collective work or a licence to publish a work or part of a work as part of a collective work.

(5) In sub-paragraph (4) "collective work" means —

(a) any encyclopedia, dictionary, yearbook, or similar work;

(b) a newspaper, review, magazine, or similar periodical; and

(c) any work written in distinct parts by different authors, or in which works or parts of works of different authors are incorporated.

5-349   28.—(1) This paragraph applies where copyright subsists in a literary, dramatic, musical or artistic work made before 1st July 1912 in relation to which the author, before the commencement of the 1911 Act, made such an assignment or grant as was mentioned in paragraph (a) of the proviso to section 24(1) of that Act (assignment or grant of copyright or performing right for full term of the right under the previous law).

(2) If before commencement any event has occurred or notice has been given which by virtue of paragraph 38 of Schedule 7 to the 1956 Act had any operation in relation to copyright in the work under that Act, the event or notice has the corresponding operation in relation to copyright under this Act.

(3) Any right which immediately before commencement would by virtue of paragraph 38(3) of that Schedule have been exercisable in relation to the work, or copyright in it, is exercisable in relation to the work or copyright in it under this Act.

(4) If in accordance with paragraph 38(4) of that Schedule copyright would, on a date after the commencement of the 1956 Act, have reverted to the author or his personal representatives and that date falls after the commencement of the new copyright provisions—

(a) the copyright in the work shall revert to the author or his personal representatives, as the case may be, and

(b) any interest of any other person in the copyright which subsists on that date by virtue of any document made before the commencement of the 1911 Act shall thereupon determine.

5-350   29. Section 92(2) of this Act (rights of exclusive licensee against successors in title of person granting licence) does not apply in relation to an exclusive licence granted before commencement.

Bequests

5-351   30.—(1) Section 93 of this Act (copyright to pass under will with original document or other material thing embodying unpublished work)—

(a) does not apply where the testator died before 1st June 1957, and

(b) where the testator died on or after that date and before commencement, applies only in relation to an original document embodying a work.

(2) In the case of an author who died before 1st June 1957, the ownership after his death of a manuscript of his, where such ownership has been acquired under a testamentary disposition made by him and the manuscript is of a work which has not been published or performed in public, is prima facie proof of the copyright being with the owner of the manuscript.

Remedies for infringement

31.—(1) Sections 96 and 97 of this Act (remedies for infringement) apply only in relation **5-352** to an infringement of copyright committed after commencement; section 17 of the 1956 Act continues to apply in relation to infringements committed before commencement.

(2) Sections 99 and 100 of this Act (delivery up or seizure of infringing copies, &c.) apply to infringing copies and other articles made before or after commencement; section 18 of the 1956 Act, and section 7 of the 1911 Act, (conversion damages, &c.), do not apply after commencement except for the purposes of proceedings begun commencement.

(3) Sections 101 to 102 of this Act (rights and remedies of exclusive licensee) apply where sections 96 to 100 of this Act apply; section 19 of the 1956 Act continues to apply where section 17 or 18 of that Act applies.

(4) Sections 104 to 106 of this Act (presumptions) apply only in proceedings brought by virtue of this Act; section 20 of the 1956 Act continues to apply in proceedings brought by virtue of that Act.

32. Sections 101 and 102 of this Act (rights and remedies of exclusive licensee) do not **5-353** apply to a licence granted before 1st June 1957.

33.—(1) The provisions of section 107 of this Act (criminal liability for making or dealing **5-354** with infringing articles, &c.) apply only in relation to acts done after commencement; section 21 of the 1956 Act (penalties and summary proceedings in respect of dealings which infringe copyright) continues to apply in relation to acts done before commencement.

(2) Section 109 of this Act (search warrants) applies in relation to offences committed before commencement in relation to which section 21A or 21B of the 1956 Act applied; sections 21A and 21B continue to apply in relation to warrants issued before commencement.

Copyright Tribunal: proceedings pending on commencement

Qualification for copyright protection

35. Every work in which copyright subsisted under the 1956 Act immediately before com- **5-355** mencement shall be deemed to satisfy the requirements of Part I of this Act as to qualification for copyright protection.

Section 189   Schedule 2

RIGHTS IN PERFORMANCES: PERMITTED ACTS

Introductory

1.—(1) The provisions of this Schedule specify acts which may be done in relation to a per- **5-356** formance or recording notwithstanding the rights conferred by Part II; they relate only to the question of infringement of those rights and do not affect any other right or obligation restricting the doing of any of the specified acts.

(2) No inference shall be drawn from the description of any act which may by virtue of this Schedule be done without infringing the rights conferred by Part II as to the scope of those rights.

(3) The provisions of this Schedule are to be construed independently of each other, so that the fact that an act does not fall within one provision does not mean that it is not covered by another provision.

[Making of temporary copies

5-357   [**1A.** The rights conferred by Part 2 are not infringed by the making of a temporary copy of a recording of a performance which is transient or incidental, which is an integral and essential part of a technological process and the sole purpose of which is to enable –

(a) a transmission of the recording in a network between third parties by an intermediary; or

(b) a lawful use of the recording;

and which has no independent economic significance.][1]][2]

Criticism, reviews and news reporting

5-358   **2.**—[(1) Fair dealing with a performance or recording for the purpose of criticism or review, of that or another performance or recording, or of a work, does not infringe any of the rights conferred by Part 2 provided that the performance or recording has been made available to the public.

(1A) Fair dealing with a performance or recording for the purpose of reporting current events does not infringe any of the rights conferred by Part 2.][3]

(2) Expressions used in this paragraph have the same meaning as in section 30.

Incidental inclusion of performance or recording

5-359   **3.**—(1) The rights conferred by Part II are not infringed by the incidental inclusion of a performance or recording in a sound recording, film [or broadcast][4].

(2) Nor are those rights infringed by anything done in relation to copies of, or the playing, showing [or communication to the public][5] of, anything whose making was, by virtue of sub-paragraph (1), not an infringement of those rights.

(3) A performance or recording so far as it consists of music, or words spoken or sung with music, shall not be regarded as incidentally included in a sound recording [or broadcast][6] if it is deliberately included.

(4) Expressions used in this paragraph have the same meaning as in section 31.

Things done for purposes of instruction or examination

5-360   **4.**—(1) The rights conferred by Part II are not infringed by the copying of a recording of a performance in the course of instruction, or of preparation for instruction, in the making of films or film sound-tracks, provided the copying is done by a person giving or receiving instruction [and the instruction is for a non-commercial purpose][7].

(2) The rights conferred by Part II are not infringed—

(a) by the copying of a recording of a performance for the purposes of setting or answering the questions in an examination, or

(b) by anything done for the purposes of an examination by way of communicating the questions to the candidates.

(3) Where a recording which would otherwise be an illicit recording is made in accordance with this paragraph but is subsequently dealt with, it shall be treated as an illicit recording for the purposes of that dealing, and if that dealing infringes any right conferred by Part II for all subsequent purposes.

[For this purpose "dealt with" means –

(a) sold or let for hire, offered or exposed for sale or hire; or

(b) communicated to the public, unless that communication, by virtue of sub-paragraph (2)(b), is not an infringement of the rights conferred by Part 2.][8]

(4) Expressions used in this paragraph have the same meaning as in section 32.

---

[1] Inserted by SI 2003/2498 Pt II reg 8 (2)
[2] Inserted by SI 2003/2498 Pt II reg 8 (2)
[3] Substituted by SI 2003/2498 Pt II reg 10 (2)
[4] Words substituted by SI 2003/2498 Sch 1 (1) para 3 (1) (l)
[5] Words substituted by SI 2003/2498 Sch 1 (1) para 6 (2) (e)
[6] Words substituted by SI 2003/2498 Sch 1 (1) para 3 (1) (m)
[7] Words inserted by SI 2003/2498 Pt II reg 11 (2) (a)
[8] Words substituted by SI 2003/2498 Pt II reg 11 (2) (b)

Playing or showing sound recording, film [or broadcast]¹ at educational establishment

5.—(1) The playing or showing of a sound recording, film [or broadcast]² at an educational **5-361** establishment for the purposes of instruction before an audience consisting of teachers and pupils at the establishment and other persons directly connected with the activities of the establishment is not a playing or showing of a performance in public for the purposes of infringement of the rights conferred by Part II.

(2) A person is not for this purpose directly connected with the activities of the educational establishment simply because he is the parent of a pupil at the establishment.

(3) Expressions used in this paragraph have the same meaning as in section 34 and any provision made under section 174(2) with respect to the application of that section also applies for the purposes of this paragraph.

Recording of broadcasts [...]³ by educational establishments

6.—(1) A recording of a broadcast [...]⁴, or a copy of such a recording, may be made by or **5-362** on behalf of an educational establishment for the educational purposes of that establishment without thereby infringing any of the rights conferred by Part II in relation to any performance or recording included in it [, provided that the educational purposes are non-commercial]⁵.

[(1A) The rights conferred by Part 2 are not infringed where a recording of a broadcast or a copy of such a recording, whose making was by virtue of sub-paragraph (1) not an infringement of such rights, is communicated to the public by a person situated within the premises of an educational establishment provided that the communication cannot be received by any person situated outside the premises of that establishment.

(1B) This paragraph does not apply if or to the extent that there is a licensing scheme certified for the purposes of this paragraph under paragraph 16 of Schedule 2A providing for the grant of licences.]⁶

(2) Where a recording which would otherwise be an illicit recording is made in accordance with this paragraph but is subsequently dealt with, it shall be treated as an illicit recording for the purposes of that dealing, and if that dealing infringes any right conferred by Part II for all subsequent purposes.

For this purpose "dealt with" means sold or let for hire [, offered or exposed for sale or hire, or communicated from within the premises of an educational establishment to any person situated outside those premises.]⁷

(3) Expressions used in this paragraph have the same meaning as in section 35 and any provision made under section 174(2) with respect to the application of that section also applies for the purposes of this paragraph.

[Lending of copies by educational establishments

6A.—(1) The rights conferred by Part II are not infringed by the lending of copies of a **5-363** recording of a performance by an educational establishment.

(2) Expressions used in this paragraph have the same meaning as in section 36A; and any provision with respect to the application of that section made under section 174(2) (instruction given elsewhere than an educational establishment) applies also for the purposes of this paragraph.]⁸

[Lending of copies by libraries or archives

6B.—(1) The rights conferred by Part II are not infringed by the lending of copies of a **5-364** recording of a performance by a prescribed library or archive (other than a public library) which is not conducted for profit.

---

¹ Words substituted by SI 2003/2498 Sch 1 (1) para 2 (2)
² Words substituted by SI 2003/2498 Sch 1 (1) para 3 (1) (n)
³ Words repealed by SI 2003/2498 Sch 2 para 1
⁴ Words repealed by SI 2003/2498 Sch 2 para 1
⁵ Words inserted by SI 2003/2498 Pt II reg 12 (2) (a)
⁶ Inserted by SI 2003/2498 Pt II Reg 12 (2) (b)
⁷ Words by SI 2003/2498 Pt II reg 12 (2) (c)
⁸ Inserted by SI 1996/2967 Pt II reg 20 (3)

(2) Expressions used in this paragraph have the same meaning as in section 40A(2); and any provision under section 37 prescribing libraries or archives for the purposes of that section applies also for the purposes of this paragraph.][1]

Copy of work required to be made as condition of export

5-365   7.—(1) If an article of cultural or historical importance or interest cannot lawfully be exported from the United Kingdom unless a copy of it is made and deposited in an appropriate library or archive, it is not an infringement of any right conferred by Part II to make that copy.

(2) Expressions used in this paragraph have the same meaning as in section 44.

Parliamentary and judicial proceedings

5-366   8.—(1) The rights conferred by Part II are not infringed by anything done for the purposes of parliamentary or judicial proceedings or for the purpose of reporting such proceedings.

(2) Expressions used in this paragraph have the same meaning as in section 45.

Royal Commissions and statutory inquiries

5-367   9.—(1) The rights conferred by Part II are not infringed by anything done for the purposes of the proceedings of a Royal Commission or statutory inquiry or for the purpose of reporting any such proceedings held in public.

(2) Expressions used in this paragraph have the same meaning as in section 46.

Public records

5-368   10.—(1) Material which is comprised in public records within the meaning of the Public Records Act 1958, the Public Records (Scotland) Act 1937 or the Public Records Act (Northern Ireland) 1923 [, or in Welsh public records (as defined in the Government of Wales Act 1998),][2] which are open to public inspection in pursuance of that Act, may be copied, and a copy may be supplied to any person, by or with the authority of any officer appointed under that Act, without infringing any right conferred by Part II.

(2) Expressions used in this paragraph have the same meaning as in section 49.

Acts done under statutory authority

5-369   11.—(1) Where the doing of a particular act is specifically authorised by an Act of Parliament, whenever passed, then, unless the Act provides otherwise, the doing of that act does not infringe the rights conferred by Part II.

(2) Sub-paragraph (1) applies in relation to an enactment contained in Northern Ireland legislation as it applies to an Act of Parliament.

(3) Nothing in this paragraph shall be construed as excluding any defence of statutory authority otherwise available under or by virtue of any enactment.

(4) Expressions used in this paragraph have the same meaning as in section 50.

Transfer of copies of works in electronic form

5-370 [1] Inserted by SI 1996/2967 Pt II reg 20 (3)
[2] Words inserted by Government of Wales Act 1998 c.38 Sch 12 para 29

—(1) This paragraph applies where a recording of a performance in electronic form has been purchased on terms which, expressly or impliedly or by virtue of any rule of law, allow the purchaser to make further recordings in connection with his use of the recording.

(2) If there are no express terms—

    (a) prohibiting the transfer of the recording by the purchaser, imposing obligations which continue after a transfer, prohibiting the assignment of any consent or terminating any consent on a transfer, or

    (b) providing for the terms on which a transferee may do the things which the purchaser was permitted to do,

anything which the purchaser was allowed to do may also be done by a transferee without infringement of the rights conferred by this Part, but any recording made by the purchaser which is not also transferred shall be treated as an illicit recording for all purposes after the transfer.

(3) The same applies where the original purchased recording is no longer usable and what is transferred is a further copy used in its place.

(4) The above provisions also apply on a subsequent transfer, with the substitution for references in sub-paragraph (2) to the purchaser of references to the subsequent transferor.

(5) This paragraph does not apply in relation to a recording purchased before the commencement of Part II.

(6) Expressions used in this paragraph have the same meaning as in section 56.

Use of recordings of spoken works in certain cases

13.—(1) Where a recording of the reading or recitation of a literary work is made for the **5-371** purpose—

    (a) of reporting current events, or

    (b) of [communicating to the public][1] the whole or part of the reading or recitation,

it is not an infringement of the rights conferred by Part II to use the recording (or to copy the recording and use the copy) for that purpose, provided the following conditions are met.

(2) The conditions are that—

    (a) the recording is a direct recording of the reading or recitation and is not taken from a previous recording or from a broadcast [...][2];

    (b) the making of the recording was not prohibited by or on behalf of the person giving the reading or recitation;

    (c) the use made of the recording is not of a kind prohibited by or on behalf of that person before the recording was made; and

    (d) the use is by or with the authority of a person who is lawfully in possession of the recording.

(3) Expressions used in this paragraph have the same meaning as in section 58.

Recordings of folksongs

14.—(1) A recording of a performance of a song may be made for the purpose of **5-372** including it in an archive maintained by a designated body without infringing any of the rights conferred by Part II, provided the conditions in sub-paragraph (2) below are met.

(2) The conditions are that—

    (a) the words are unpublished and of unknown authorship at the time the recording is made,

    (b) the making of the recording does not infringe any copyright, and

    (c) its making is not prohibited by any performer.

(3) Copies of a recording made in reliance on sub-paragraph (1) and included in an archive maintained by a designated body may, if the prescribed conditions are met, be made and supplied by the archivist without infringing any of the rights conferred by Part II.

(4) In this paragraph—

    "designated body" means a body designated for the purposes of section 61, and

    "the prescribed conditions" means the conditions prescribed for the purposes of subsection (3) of that section;

and other expressions used in this paragraph have the same meaning as in that section.

---

[1] Words substituted by SI 2003/2498 Sch 1 (1) para 12 (b)
[2] Words repealed by SI 2003/2498 Sch 2 para 1

[Lending of certain recordings

5-373

14A.—(1) The Secretary of State may by order provide that in such cases as may be specified in the order the lending to the public of copies of films or sound recordings shall be treated as licensed by the performer subject only to the payment of such reasonable royalty or other payment as may be agreed or determined in default of agreement by the Copyright Tribunal.

(2) No such order shall apply if, or to the extent that, there is a licensing scheme certified for the purposes of this paragraph under paragraph 16 of Schedule 2A providing for the grant of licences.

(3) An order may make different provision for different cases and may specify cases by reference to any factor relating to the work, the copies lent, the lender or the circumstances of the lending.

(4) An order shall be made by statutory instrument; and no order shall be made unless a draft of it has been laid before and approved by a resolution of each House of Parliament.

(5) Nothing in this section affects any liability under section 184(1)(b) (secondary infringement: possessing or dealing with illicit recording) in respect of the lending of illicit recordings.

(6) Expressions used in this paragraph have the same meaning as in section 66.][1]

Playing of sound recordings for purposes of club, society, &c

5-374

15.—(1) It is not an infringement of any right conferred by Part II to play a sound recording as part of the activities of, or for the benefit of, a club, society or other organisation if the following conditions are met.

(2) The conditions are—

    (a) that the organisation is not established or conducted for profit and its main objects are charitable or are otherwise concerned with the advancement of religion, education or social welfare,

    [(b) that the sound recording is played by a person who is acting primarily and directly for the benefit of the organisation and who is not acting with a view to gain,

    (c) that the proceeds of any charge for admission to the place where the recording is to be heard are applied solely for the purposes of the organisation, and

    (d) that the proceeds from any goods or services sold by, or on behalf of, the organisation—

        (i) in the place where the sound recording is heard, and

        (ii) on the occasion when the sound recording is played,

    are applied solely for the purposes of the organisation.][2]

(3) Expressions used in this paragraph have the same meaning as in section 67.

Incidental recording for purposes of broadcast [...][3]

5-375

16.—(1) A person who proposes to broadcast a recording of a performance [...][4] in circumstances not infringing the rights conferred by Part II shall be treated as having consent for the purposes of that Part for the making of a further recording for the purposes of the broadcast [...][5].

(2) That consent is subject to the condition that the further recording—

    (a) shall not be used for any other purpose, and

    (b) shall be destroyed within 28 days of being first used for broadcasting the performance [...][6].

(3) A recording made in accordance with this paragraph shall be treated as an illicit recording—

---

[1] Inserted by SI 1996/2967 Pt II reg 20 (3)
[2] Substituted by SI 2003/2498 Pt II reg 18 (2)
[3] Words repealed by SI 2003/2498 Sch 2 para 1
[4] Words repealed by SI 2003/2498 Sch 2 para 1
[5] Words repealed by SI 2003/2498 Sch 2 para 1
[6] Words repealed by SI 2003/2498 Sch 2 para 1

(a) for the purposes of any use in breach of the condition mentioned in sub-paragraph (2)(a), and

(b) for all purposes after that condition or the condition mentioned in sub-paragraph (2)(b) is broken.

(4) Expressions used in this paragraph have the same meaning as in section 68.

Recordings for purposes of supervision and control of broadcasts and [other services]¹

17.—(1) The rights conferred by Part II are not infringed by the making or use by the British Broadcasting Corporation, for the purpose of maintaining supervision and control over programmes broadcast by them, of recordings of those programmes. **5-376**

[(2) The rights conferred by Part II are not infringed by anything done in pursuance of—

[(a) section 167(1) of the Broadcasting Act 1990, section 115(4) or (6) or 117 of the Broadcasting Act 1996 or paragraph 20 of Schedule 12 to the Communications Act 2003;]²

(b) a condition which, [by virtue of section 334(1) of the Communications Act 2003]³, is included in a licence granted under Part I or III of that Act or Part I or II of the Broadcasting Act 1996; [...]⁴

(c) a direction given under section 109(2) of the Broadcasting Act 1990 (power of [OFCOM]⁵ to require production of recordings etc)[;]⁶

[(d) section 334(3) of the Communications Act 2003.]⁷]⁸

[(3) The rights conferred by Part 2 are not infringed by the use by OFCOM in connection with the performance of any of their functions under the Broadcasting Act 1990, the Broadcasting Act 1996 or the Communications Act 2003 of—

(a) any recording, script or transcript which is provided to them under or by virtue of any provision of those Acts; or

(b) any existing material which is transferred to them by a scheme made under section 30 of the Communications Act 2003.

(4) In subsection (3), "existing material" means—

(a) any recording, script or transcript which was provided to the Independent Television Commission or the Radio Authority under or by virtue of any provision of the Broadcasting Act 1990 or the Broadcasting Act 1996; and

(b) any recording or transcript which was provided to the Broadcasting Standards Commission under section 115(4) or (6) or 116(5) of the Broadcasting Act 1996.]⁹

[Recording for the purposes of time-shifting

[**17A.**—(1) The making in domestic premises for private and domestic use of a recording of a broadcast solely for the purpose of enabling it to be viewed or listened to at a more convenient time does not infringe any right conferred by Part 2 in relation to a performance or recording included in the broadcast. **5-377**

(2) Where a recording which would otherwise be an illicit recording is made in accordance with this paragraph but is subsequently dealt with–

(a) it shall be treated as an illicit recording for the purposes of that dealing; and

(b) if that dealing infringes any right conferred by Part 2, it shall be treated as an illicit recording for all subsequent purposes.

(3) In sub-paragraph (2), "dealt with" means sold or let for hire, offered or exposed for sale or hire or communicated to the public.

(4) Expressions used in this paragraph have the same meaning as in section 70.]¹⁰]¹¹

---

¹ Words substituted by SI 2003/2498 Sch 1 (1) para 2 (1)
² Substituted by Communications Act 2003 c.21 Sch 17 para 93 (2) (a)
³ Words substituted by Communications Act 2003 c.21 Sch 17 para 93 (2) (b)
⁴ Word repealed by Communications Act 2003 c.21 Sch 19 para 1
⁵ Word substituted by Communications Act 2003 c.21 Sch 17 para 93 (2) (c)
⁶ Inserted by Communications Act 2003 c.21 Sch 17 para 93 (2) (d)
⁷ Inserted by Communications Act 2003 c.21 Sch 17 para 93 (2) (d)
⁸ Substituted by Broadcasting Act 1996 c.55 Sch 10 (III) para 32
⁹ Substituted by Communications Act 2003 c.21 Sch 17 para 93 (3)
¹⁰ Inserted by SI 2003/2498 Pt II reg 19 (3)
¹¹ Inserted by SI 2003/2498 Pt II reg 19 (3)

[Photographs of broadcasts

5-378   **[17B.**—(1) The making in domestic premises for private and domestic use of a photograph of the whole or any part of an image forming part of a broadcast, or a copy of such a photograph, does not infringe any right conferred by Part 2 in relation to a performance or recording included in the broadcast.

(2) Where a recording which would otherwise be an illicit recording is made in accordance with this paragraph but is subsequently dealt with–

     (a) it shall be treated as an illicit recording for the purposes of that dealing; and

     (b) if that dealing infringes any right conferred by Part 2, it shall be treated as an illicit recording for all subsequent purposes.

(3) In sub-paragraph (2), "dealt with" means sold or let for hire, offered or exposed for sale or hire or communicated to the public.

(4) Expressions used in this paragraph have the same meaning as in section 71.][1]][2]

Free public showing or playing of broadcast [...][3]

5-379   **18.**—(1) The showing or playing in public of a broadcast [...][4] to an audience who have not paid for admission to the place where the broadcast [...][5] is to be seen or heard does not infringe any right conferred by Part II in relation to a performance or recording included in—

     (a) the broadcast [...][6], or

     (b) any sound recording [(except so far as it is an excepted sound recording)][7] or film which is played or shown in public by reception of the broadcast [...][8].

[(1A) The showing or playing in public of a broadcast to an audience who have not paid for admission to the place where the broadcast is to be seen or heard does not infringe any right conferred by Part 2 in relation to a performance or recording included in any excepted sound recording which is played in public by reception of the broadcast, if the playing or showing of that broadcast in public–

     (a) forms part of the activities of an organisation that is not established or conducted for profit; or

     (b) is necessary for the purposes of–

        (i) repairing equipment for the reception of broadcasts;

        (ii) demonstrating that a repair to such equipment has been carried out; or

        (iii) demonstrating such equipment which is being sold or let for hire or offered or exposed for sale or hire.][9]

(2) The audience shall be treated as having paid for admission to a place—

     (a) if they have paid for admission to a place of which that place forms part; or

     (b) if goods or services are supplied at that place (or a place of which it forms part)—

        (i) at prices which are substantially attributable to the facilities afforded for seeing or hearing the broadcast [...][10], or

        (ii) at prices exceeding those usually charged there and which are partly attributable to those facilities.

(3) The following shall not be regarded as having paid for admission to a place—

     (a) persons admitted as residents or inmates of the place;

     (b) persons admitted as members of a club or society where the payment is only for membership of the club or society and the provision of facilities for seeing or hearing broadcasts [...][11] is only incidental to the main purposes of the club or society.

(4) Where the making of the broadcast [...][12] was an infringement of the rights conferred by Part II in relation to a performance or recording, the fact that it was heard or seen in public

---

[1] Inserted by SI 2003/2498 Pt II reg 20 (2)

[2] Inserted by SI 2003/2498 Pt II reg 20 (2)

[3] Words repealed by SI 2003/2498 Sch 2 para 1

[4] Words repealed by SI 2003/2498 Sch 2 para 1

[5] Words repealed by SI 2003/2498 Sch 2 para 1

[6] Words repealed by SI 2003/2498 Sch 2 para 1

[7] Words inserted by SI 2003/2498 Pt II reg 21 (2) (a)

[8] Words repealed by SI 2003/2498 Sch 2 para 1

[9] Inserted by SI 2003/2498 Pt II reg 21 (2) (b)

[10] Words repealed by SI 2003/2498 Sch 2 para 1

[11] Words repealed by SI 2003/2498 Sch 2 para 1

[12] Words repealed by SI 2003/2498 Sch 2 para 1

by the reception of the broadcast [...][1] shall be taken into account in assessing the damages for that infringement.

(5) Expressions used in this paragraph have the same meaning as in section 72.

[Reception and re-transmission of][2] [wireless broadcast by cable][3]

19.—(1) This paragraph applies where a [wireless][4] broadcast made from a place in the **5-380** United Kingdom is [received and immediately re-transmitted by cable][5].

(2) The rights conferred by Part II in relation to a performance or recording included in the broadcast are not infringed if and to the extent that the broadcast is made for reception in the area in which [it is re-transmitted by cable][6]; but where the making of the broadcast was an infringement of those rights, the fact that the broadcast was re-transmitted [by cable][7] shall be taken into account in assessing the damages for that infringement.

(3) Where—

    (a) the [re-transmission by cable][8] is in pursuance of a relevant requirement, but

    (b) to any extent, the area in which the [re-transmission by cable takes place][9] ("the cable area") falls outside the area for reception in which the broadcast is made ("the broadcast area"),

the [re-transmission by cable][10] (to the extent that it is provided for so much of the cable area as falls outside the broadcast area) of any performance or recording included in the broadcast shall, subject to sub-paragraph (4), be treated as licensed by the owner of the rights conferred by Part II in relation to the performance or recording, subject only to the payment to him by the person making the broadcast of such reasonable royalty or other payment in respect of the [re-transmission by cable of the broadcast][11] as may be agreed or determined in default of agreement by the Copyright Tribunal.

(4) Sub-paragraph (3) does not apply if, or to the extent that, the [re-transmission of the performance or recording by cable][12] is (apart from that sub-paragraph) licensed by the owner of the rights conferred by Part II in relation to the performance or recording.

(5) The Secretary of State may by order—

    (a) provide that in specified cases sub-paragraph (2) is to apply in relation to broadcasts of a specified description which are not made as mentioned in that sub-paragraph, or

    (b) exclude the application of that sub-paragraph in relation to broadcasts of a specified description made as mentioned in that sub-paragraph.

(6) Where the Secretary of State exercises the power conferred by sub-paragraph (5)(b) in relation to broadcasts of any description, the order may also provide for sub-paragraph (3) to apply, subject to such modifications as may be specified in the order, in relation to broadcasts of that description.

(7) An order under this paragraph may contain such transitional provision as appears to the Secretary of State to be appropriate.

(8) An order under this paragraph shall be made by statutory instrument which shall be subject to annulment in pursuance of a resolution of either House of Parliament.

(9) Expressions used in this paragraph have the same meaning as in section 73.][13]

[**19A.**—(1) An application to settle the royalty or other sum payable in pursuance of sub- **5-381** paragraph (3) of paragraph 19 may be made to the Copyright Tribunal by the owner of the rights conferred by Part II or the person making the broadcast.

---

[1] Words repealed by SI 2003/2498 Sch 2 para 1
[2] Substituted by Broadcasting Act 1996 c.55 Sch 9 para 5
[3] Words substituted by SI 2003/2498 Pt II reg 22 (3) (a)
[4] Word inserted by SI 2003/2498 Pt II reg 22 (3) (b) (i)
[5] Words substituted by SI 2003/2498 Pt II reg 22 (3) (b) (ii)
[6] Words substituted by SI 2003/2498 Pt II reg 22 (3) (c) (i)
[7] Words substituted by SI 2003/2498 Pt II reg 22 (3) (c) (ii)
[8] Word substituted by SI 2003/2498 Pt II reg 22 (3) (d) (i)
[9] Words substituted by SI 2003/2498 Pt II reg 22 (3) (d) (ii)
[10] Words substituted by SI 2003/2498 Pt II reg 22 (3) (d) (iii)
[11] Words substituted by SI 2003/2498 Pt II reg 22 (3) (d) (iv)
[12] Words substituted by SI 2003/2498 Pt II reg 22 (3) (e)
[13] Substituted by Broadcasting Act 1996 c.55 Sch 9 para 5

(2) The Tribunal shall consider the matter and make such order as it may determine to be reasonable in the circumstances.

(3) Either party may subsequently apply to the Tribunal to vary the order, and the Tribunal shall consider the matter and make such order confirming or varying the original order as it may determine to be reasonable in the circumstances.

(4) An application under sub-paragraph (3) shall not, except with the special leave of the Tribunal, be made within twelve months from the date of the original order or of the order on a previous application under that sub-paragraph.

(5) An order under sub-paragraph (3) has effect from the date on which it is made or such later date as may be specified by the Tribunal.][1]

Provision of sub-titled copies of broadcast [...][2]

5-382   **20.**—(1) A designated body may, for the purpose of providing people who are deaf or hard of hearing, or physically or mentally handicapped in other ways, with copies which are sub-titled or otherwise modified for their special needs, make recordings of [broadcasts and copies of such recordings, and issue or lend copies to the public,][3] without infringing any right conferred by Part II in relation to a performance or recording included in the broadcast [...][4].

[(1A) This paragraph does not apply if, or to the extent that, there is a licensing scheme certified for the purposes of this paragraph under paragraph 16 of Schedule 2A providing for the grant of licences.][5]

(2) In this paragraph "designated body" means a body designated for the purposes of section 74 and other expressions used in this paragraph have the same meaning as in that section.

Recording of broadcast [...][6] for archival purposes

5-383   **21.**—(1) A recording of a broadcast [...][7] of a designated class, or a copy of such a recording, may be made for the purpose of being placed in an archive maintained by a designated body without thereby infringing any right conferred by Part II in relation to a performance or recording included in the broadcast [...][8].

(2) In this paragraph "designated class" and "designated body" means a class or body designated for the purposes of section 75 and other expressions used in this paragraph have the same meaning as in that section.

Schedule 2A

[Licensing of Performers' Property Rights

[Licensing schemes and licensing bodies

5-384   **1.**—(1) In Part II a "licensing scheme" means a scheme setting out-

    (a) the classes of case in which the operator of the scheme, or the person on whose behalf he acts, is willing to grant performers' property right licences, and

    (b) the terms on which licences would be granted in those classes of case;

and for this purpose a "scheme" includes anything in the nature of a scheme, whether described as a scheme or as a tariff or by any other name.

(2) In Part II a "licensing body" means a society or other organisation which has as its main object, or one of its main objects, the negotiating or granting, whether as owner or prospective owner of a performer's property rights or as agent for him, of performers' property right licences, and whose objects include the granting of licences covering the performances of more than one performer.

---

[1] Inserted by Broadcasting Act 1996 c.55 Sch 9 para 6
[2] Words repealed by SI 2003/2498 Sch 2 para 1
[3] Words substituted by SI 2003/2498 Pt II reg 23 (2) (a)
[4] Words repealed by SI 2003/2498 Sch 2 para 1
[5] Inserted by SI 2003/2498 Pt II reg 23 (2) (b)
[6] Words repealed by SI 2003/2498 Sch 2 para 1
[7] Words repealed by SI 2003/2498 Sch 2 para 1
[8] Words repealed by SI 2003/2498 Sch 2 para 1

(3) In this paragraph "performers' property right licences" means licences to do, or authorise the doing of, any of the things for which consent is required under [section 182A, 182B, 182C or 182CA][1].

(4) References in this Part to licences or licensing schemes covering the performances of more than one performer do not include licences or schemes covering only-

    (a) performances recorded in a single recording,

    (b) performances recorded in more than one recording where-

        (i) the performers giving the performances are the same, or

        (ii) the recordings are made by, or by employees of or commissioned by, a single individual, firm, company or group of companies.

For purpose a group of companies means a holding company and its subsidiaries within the meaning of section 736 of the Companies Act 1985.][2]

[References and applications with respect to licensing schemes

2. Paragraphs 3 to 8 (references and applications with respect to licensing schemes) apply to licensing schemes operated by licensing bodies in relation to a performer's property rights which cover the performances of more than one performer, so far as they relate to licences for- **5-385**

    (a) copying a recording of the whole or any substantial part of a qualifying performance, [...][3]

    [(aa) making such a recording available to the public in the way mentioned in section 182CA(1), or][4]

    (b) renting or lending copies of a recording to the public;

and in those paragraphs "licensing scheme" means a licensing scheme of any of those descriptions.][5]

[Reference of proposed licensing scheme to tribunal

3.—(1) The terms of a licensing scheme proposed to be operated by a licensing body may be referred to the Copyright Tribunal by an organisation claiming to be representative of persons claiming that they require licences in cases of a description to which the scheme would apply, either generally or in relation to any description of case. **5-386**

(2) The Tribunal shall first decide whether to entertain the reference, and may decline to do so on the ground that the reference is premature.

(3) If the Tribunal decides to entertain the reference it shall consider the matter referred and make such order, either confirming or varying the proposed scheme, either generally or so far as it relates to cases of the description to which the reference relates, as the Tribunal may determine to be e in the circumstances.

(4) The order may be made so as to be in force indefinitely or for such period as the Tribunal may determine.][6]

[Reference of licensing scheme to tribunal

4.—(1) If while a licensing scheme is in operation a dispute arises between the operator of the scheme and- **5-387**

    (a) a person claiming that he requires a licence in a case of a description to which the scheme applies, or

    (b) an organisation claiming to be representative of such persons,

that person or organisation may refer the scheme to the Copyright Tribunal in so far as it relates to cases of that description.

(2) A scheme which has been referred to the Tribunal under this paragraph shall remain in operation until proceedings on the reference are concluded.

(3) The Tribunal shall consider the matter in dispute and make such order, either confirming or varying the scheme so far as it relates to cases of the description to which the reference relates, as the Tribunal may determine to be reasonable in the circumstances.

(4) The order may be made so as to be in force indefinitely or for such period as the Tribunal may determine.][7]

---

[1] Words substituted by SI 2003/2498 Pt II reg 7 (4) (a)

[2] Inserted by SI 1996/2967 Pt II reg 22 (2)

[3] Word repealed by SI 2003/2498 Sch 2 para 1

[4] Inserted by SI 2003/2498 Pt II reg 7 (4) (b)

[5] Inserted by SI 1996/2967 Pt II reg 22 (2)

[6] Inserted by SI 1996/2967 Pt II reg 22 (2)

[7] Inserted by SI 1996/2967 Pt II reg 22 (2)

[Further reference of scheme to tribunal

5-388

5.—(1) Where the Copyright Tribunal has on a previous reference of a licensing scheme under paragraph 3 or 4, or under this paragraph, made an order with respect to the scheme, then, while the order remains in force-

(a) the operator of the scheme,

(b) a person claiming that he requires a licence in a case of the description to which the order applies, or

(c) an organisation claiming to be representative of such persons,

may refer the scheme again to the Tribunal so far as it relates to cases of that description.

(2) A licensing scheme shall not, except with the special leave of the Tribunal, be referred again to the Tribunal in respect of the same description of cases-

(a) within twelve months from the date of the order on the previous reference, or

(b) if the order was made so as to be in force for 15 months or less, until the last three months before the expiry of the order.

(3) A scheme which has been referred to the Tribunal under this paragraph shall remain in operation until proceedings on the reference are concluded.

(4) The Tribunal shall consider the matter in dispute and make such order, either confirming, varying or further varying the scheme so far as it relates to cases of the description to which the reference relates, as the Tribunal may determine to be reasonable in the circumstances.

(5) The order may be made so as to be in force indefinitely or for such period as the Tribunal may determine.][1]

[Application for grant of licence in connection with licensing scheme

5-389

6.—(1) A person who claims, in a case covered by a licensing scheme, that the operator of the scheme has refused to grant him or procure the grant to him of a licence in accordance with the scheme, or has failed to do so within a reasonable time after being asked, may apply to the Copyright Tribunal.

(2) A person who claims, in a case excluded from a licensing scheme, that the operator of the scheme either-

(a) has refused to grant him a licence or procure the grant to him of a licence, or has failed to do so within a reasonable time of being asked, and that in the circumstances it is unreasonable that a licence should not be granted, or

(b) proposes terms for a licence which are unreasonable,

may apply to the Copyright Tribunal.

(3) A case shall be regarded as excluded from a licensing scheme for the purposes of sub-paragraph (2) if-

(a) the scheme provides for the grant of licences subject to terms excepting matters from the licence and the case falls within such an exception, or

(b) the case is so similar to those in which licences are granted under the scheme that it is unreasonable that it should not be dealt with in the same way.

(4) If the Tribunal is satisfied that the claim is well-founded, it shall make an order declaring that, in respect of the matters specified in the order, the applicant is entitled to a licence on such terms as the Tribunal may determine to be applicable in accordance with the scheme or, as the case may be, to be reasonable in the circumstances.

(5) The order may be made so as to be in force indefinitely or for such period as the Tribunal may determine.][2]

[Application for review of order as to entitlement to licence

5-390

7.—(1) Where the Copyright Tribunal has made an order under paragraph 6 that a person is entitled to a licence under a licensing scheme, the operator of the scheme or the original applicant may apply to the Tribunal to review its order.

(2) An application shall not be made, except with the special leave of the Tribunal-

(a) within twelve months from the date of the order, or of the decision on a previous application under this paragraph, or

(b) if the order was made so as to be in force for 15 months or less, or as a result of the decision on a previous application under this paragraph is due to expire within 15 months of that decision, until the last three months before the expiry date.

---

[1] Inserted by SI 1996/2967 Pt II reg 22 (2)

[2] Inserted by SI 1996/2967 Pt II reg 22 (2)

(3) The Tribunal shall on an application for review confirm or vary its order as the Tribunal may determine to be reasonable having regard to the terms applicable in accordance with the licensing scheme or, as the case may be, the circumstances of the case.][1]

[Effect of order of tribunal as to licensing scheme

8.—(1) A licensing scheme which has been confirmed or varied by the Copyright **5-391** Tribunal-
    (a) under paragraph 3 (reference of terms of proposed scheme), or
    (b) under paragraph 4 or 5 (reference of existing scheme to Tribunal),
shall be in force or, as the case may be, remain in operation, so far as it relates to the description of case in respect of which the order was made, so long as the order remains in force.

(2) While the order is in force a person who in a case of a class to which the order applies-
    (a) pays to the operator of the scheme any charges payable under the scheme in respect of a licence covering the case in question or, if the amount cannot be ascertained, gives an undertaking to the operator to pay them when ascertained, and
    (b) complies with the other terms applicable to such a licence under the scheme,
shall be in the same position as regards infringement of performers' property rights as if he had at all material times been the holder of a licence granted by the rights owner in question in accordance with the scheme.

(3) The Tribunal may direct that the order, so far as it varies the amount of charges payable, has effect from a date before that on which it is made, but not earlier than the date on which the reference was made or, if later, on which the scheme came into operation.
If such a direction is made-
    (a) any necessary repayments, or further payments, shall be made in respect of charges already paid, and
    (b) the reference in sub-paragraph (2)(a) to the charges payable under the scheme shall be construed as a reference to the charges so payable by virtue of the order.
No such direction may be made where sub-paragraph (4) below applies.

(4) An order of the Tribunal under paragraph 4 or 5 made with respect to a scheme which is certified for any purpose under paragraph 16 has effect, so far as it varies the scheme by reducing the charges payable for licences, from the date on which the reference was made to the Tribunal.

(5) Where the Tribunal has made an order under paragraph 6 (order as to entitlement to licence under licensing scheme) and the order remains in force, the person in whose favour the order is made shall if he-
    (a) pays to the operator of the scheme any charges payable in accordance with the order or, if the amount cannot be ascertained, gives an undertaking to pay the charges when ascertained, and
    (b) complies with the other terms specified in the order,
be in the same position as regards infringement of performers' property rights as if he had at all material times been the holder of a licence granted by the rights owner in question on the terms specified in the order.][2]

[References and applications with respect to licensing by licensing bodies

9. Paragraphs 10 to 13 (references and applications with respect to licensing by licensing **5-392** bodies) apply to licences relating to a performer's property rights which cover the performance of more than one performer granted by a licensing body otherwise than in pursuance of a licensing scheme, so far as the licences authorise-
    (a) copying a recording of the whole or any substantial part of a qualifying performance, [...][3]
    [(aa) making such a recording available to the public in the way mentioned in section 182CA(1), or][4]
    (b) renting or lending copies of a recording to the public;
and references in those paragraphs to a licence shall be construed accordingly.][5]

[Reference to tribunal of proposed licence

[1] Inserted by SI 1996/2967 Pt II reg 22 (2)
[2] Inserted by SI 1996/2967 Pt II reg 22 (2)
[3] Word repealed by SI 2003/2498 Sch 2 para 1
[4] Inserted by SI 2003/2498 Pt II reg 7 (4) (b)
[5] Inserted by SI 1996/2967 Pt II reg 22 (2)

5-393

—(1) The terms on which a licensing body proposes to grant a licence may be referred to the Copyright Tribunal by the prospective licensee.

(2) The Tribunal shall first decide whether to entertain the reference, and may decline to do so on the ground that the reference is premature.

(3) If the Tribunal decides to entertain the reference it shall consider the terms of the proposed licence and make such order, either confirming or varying the terms as it may determine to be reasonable in the circumstances.

(4) The order may be made so as to be in force indefinitely or for such period as the Tribunal may determine.][1]

[Reference to tribunal of expiring licence

5-394

11.—(1) A licensee under a licence which is due to expire, by effluxion of time or as a result of notice given by the licensing body, may apply to the Copyright Tribunal on the ground that it is unreasonable in the circumstances that the licence should cease to be in force.

(2) Such an application may not be made until the last three months before the licence is due to expire.

(3) A licence in respect of which a reference has been made to the Tribunal shall remain in operation until proceedings on the reference are concluded.

(4) If the Tribunal finds the application well-founded, it shall make an order declaring that the licensee shall continue to be entitled to the benefit of the licence on such terms as the Tribunal may determine to be reasonable in the circumstances.

(5) An order of the Tribunal under this paragraph may be made so as to be in force indefinitely or for such period as the Tribunal may determine.][2]

[Application for review of order as to licence

5-395

12.—(1) Where the Copyright Tribunal has made an order under paragraph 10 or 11, the licensing body or the person entitled to the benefit of the order may apply to the Tribunal to review its order.

(2) An application shall not be made, except with the special leave of the Tribunal-

    (a) within twelve months from the date of the order or of the decision on a previous application under this paragraph, or

    (b) if the order was made so as to be in force for 15 months or less, or as a result of the decision on a previous application under this paragraph is due to expire within 15 months of that decision, until the last three months before the expiry date.

(3) The Tribunal shall on an application for review confirm or vary its order as the Tribunal may determine to be reasonable in the circumstances.][3]

[Effect of order of tribunal as to licence

5-396

13.—(1) Where the Copyright Tribunal has made an order under paragraph 10 or 11 and the order remains in force, the person entitled to the benefit of the order shall if he-

    (a) pays to the licensing body any charges payable in accordance with the order or, if the amount cannot be ascertained, gives an undertaking to pay the charges when ascertained, and

    (b) complies with the other terms specified in the order,

be in the same position as regards infringement of performers' property rights as if he had at all material times been the holder of a licence granted by the rights owner in question on the terms specified in the order.

(2) The benefit of the order may be assigned-

    (a) in the case of an order under paragraph 10, if assignment is not prohibited under the terms of the Tribunal's order; and

    (b) in the case of an order under paragraph 11, if assignment was not prohibited under the terms of the original licence.

(3) The Tribunal may direct that an order under paragraph 10 or 11, or an order under paragraph 12 varying such an order, so far as it varies the amount of charges payable, has effect from a date before that on which it is made, but not earlier than the date on which the reference or application was made or, if later, on which the licence was granted or, as the case may be, was due to expire.

If such a direction is made-

---

[1] Inserted by SI 1996/2967 Pt II reg 22 (2)
[2] Inserted by SI 1996/2967 Pt II reg 22 (2)
[3] Inserted by SI 1996/2967 Pt II reg 22 (2)

(a) any necessary repayments, or further payments, shall be made in respect of charges already paid, and

(b) the reference in sub-paragraph (1)(a) to the charges payable in accordance with the order shall be construed, where the order is varied by a later order, as a reference to the charges so payable by virtue of the later order.]¹

[General considerations: unreasonable discrimination

14.—(1) In determining what is reasonable on a reference or application under this Schedule relating to a licensing scheme or licence, the Copyright Tribunal shall have regard to-
    (a) the availability of other schemes, or the granting of other licences, to other persons in similar circumstances, and
    (b) the terms of those schemes or licences,
and shall exercise its powers so as to secure that there is no unreasonable discrimination between licensees, or prospective licensees, under the scheme or licence to which the reference or application relates and licensees under other schemes operated by, or other licences granted by, the same person.

(2) This does not affect the Tribunal's general obligation in any case to have regard to all relevant circumstances.]²

5-397

[Application to settle royalty or other sum payable for lending

15.—(1) An application to settle the royalty or other sum payable in pursuance of paragraph 14A of Schedule 2 (lending of certain recordings) may be made to the Copyright Tribunal by the owner of a performer's property rights or the person claiming to be treated as licensed by him.

(2) The Tribunal shall consider the matter and make such order as it may determine to be reasonable in the circumstances.

(3) Either party may subsequently apply to the Tribunal to vary the order, and the Tribunal shall consider the matter and make such order confirming or varying the original order as it may determine to be reasonable in the circumstances.

(4) An application under sub-paragraph (3) shall not, except with the special leave of the Tribunal, be made within twelve months from the date of the original order or of the order on a previous application under that sub-paragraph.

(5) An order under sub-paragraph (3) has effect from the date on which it is made or such later date as may be specified by the Tribunal.]³

5-398

[Certification of licensing schemes

16.—(1) A person operating or proposing to operate a licensing scheme may apply to the Secretary of State to certify the scheme for the purposes of [paragraph 6, 14A or 20 of Schedule 2 (recording of broadcasts by educational establishments, lending of certain recordings, provision of sub-titled copies of broadcast)]⁴.

(2) The Secretary of State shall by order made by statutory instrument certify the scheme if he is satisfied that it-
    (a) enables the works to which it relates to be identified with sufficient certainty by persons likely to require licences, and
    (b) sets out clearly the charges (if any) payable and the other terms on which licences will be granted.

(3) The scheme shall be scheduled to the order and the certification shall come into operation for the purposes of [the relevant paragraph of Schedule 2]⁵
    (a) on such date, not less than eight weeks after the order is made, as may be specified in the order, or
    (b) if the scheme is the subject of a reference under paragraph 3 (reference of proposed scheme), any later date on which the order of the Copyright Tribunal under that paragraph comes into force or the reference is withdrawn.

(4) A variation of the scheme is not effective unless a corresponding amendment of the order is made; and the Secretary of State shall make such an amendment in the case of a

5-399

---

¹ Inserted by SI 1996/2967 Pt II reg 22 (2)
² Inserted by SI 1996/2967 Pt II reg 22 (2)
³ Inserted by SI 1996/2967 Pt II reg 22 (2)
⁴ Words substituted by SI 2003/2498 Sch 1 Pt I para 17 (a)
⁵ Words substituted by SI 2003/2498 Sch 1 Pt I para 17 (b)

variation ordered by the Copyright Tribunal on a reference under paragraph 3, 4 or 5, and may do so in any other case if he thinks fit.

(5) The order shall be revoked if the scheme ceases to be operated and may be revoked if it appears to the Secretary of State that it is no longer being operated according to its terms.][1]

[Powers exercisable in consequence of competition report

5-400

17.—(1) Sub-paragraph (1A) applies where whatever needs to be remedied, mitigated or prevented by the Secretary of State, the Competition Commission or (as the case may be) the Office of Fair Trading under section 12(5) of the Competition Act 1980 or section 41(2), 55(2), 66(6), 75(2), 83(2), 138(2), 147(2) or 160(2) of, or paragraph 5(2) or 10(2) of Schedule 7 to, the Enterprise Act 2002 (powers to take remedial action following references to the Commission in connection with public bodies and certain other persons, mergers or market investigations etc.) consists of or includes—

    (a) conditions in licences granted by the owner of a performer's property rights restricting the use to which a recording may be put by the licensee or the right of the owner to grant other licenses, or

    (b) a refusal of an owner of a performer's property rights to grant licences on reasonable terms.

(1A) The powers conferred by Schedule 8 to the Enterprise Act 2002 include power to cancel or modify those conditions and, instead or in addition, to provide that licences in respect of the performer's property rights shall be available as of right.

(2) The references to anything permitted by Schedule 8 to the Enterprise Act 2002 in section 12(5A) of the Competition Act 1980 and in sections 75(4)(a), 83(4)(a), 84(2)(a), 89(1), 160(4)(a), 161(3)(a) and 164(1) of, and paragraphs 5, 10 and 11 of Schedule 7 to, the Act of 2002 shall be construed accordingly.][2]

(3) [The Secretary of State, the Competition Commission or (as the case may be) the Office of Fair Trading][3] shall only exercise the powers available by virtue of this paragraph if he [or it][4] is satisfied that do so does not contravene any Convention relating to performers' rights to which the United kingdom is a party.

(4) The terms of a licence available by virtue of this paragraph shall, in default of agreement, be settled by the Copyright Tribunal on an application by the person requiring the licence; and terms so settled shall authorise the licensee to do everything in respect of which a licence is so available.

(5) Where the terms of a licence are settled by the Tribunal, the licence has effect from the date on which the application to the Tribunal was made.][5]

---

[1] Inserted by SI 1996/2967 Pt II reg 22 (2)
[2] Substituted by Enterprise Act 2002 c.40 Sch 25 para 18 (5) (a)
[3] Words substituted by Enterprise Act 2002 c.40 Sch 25 para 18 (5) (b) (i)
[4] Words inserted by Enterprise Act 2002 c.40 Sch 25 para 18 (5) (b) (ii)
[5] Inserted by SI 1996/2967 Pt II reg 22 (2)

Trade Marks Act 1994

CHAPTER 26

BE IT ENACTED by the Queen's most Excellent Majesty, by and with the advice and consent of the Lords Spiritual and Temporal, and Commons, in this present Parliament assembled, and by the authority of the same, as follows:—

PART I

REGISTERED TRADE MARKS

Introductory

Trade marks

1.—(1) In this Act a "trade mark" means any sign capable of being represented **6-001** graphically which is capable of distinguishing goods or services of one undertaking from those of other undertakings.

A trade mark may, in particular, consist of words (including personal names), designs, letters, numerals or the shape of goods or their packaging.

(2) References in this Act to a trade mark include, unless the context otherwise requires, references to a collective mark (see section 49) or certification mark (see section 50).

Registered trade marks

2.—(1) A registered trade mark is a property right obtained by the registration **6-002** of the trade mark under this Act and the proprietor of a registered trade mark has the rights and remedies provided by this Act.

(2) No proceedings he to prevent or recover damages for the infringement of an unregistered trade mark as such; but nothing in this Act affects the law relating to passing off.

Grounds for refusal of registration

Absolute grounds for refusal of registration

3.—(1) The following shall not be registered— **6-003**
  (a) signs which do not satisfy the requirements of section 1(1).
  (b) trade marks which are devoid of any distinctive character.
  (c) trade marks which consist exclusively of signs or indications which may serve, in trade, to designate the kind, quality, quantity, intended purpose, value, geographical origin, the time of production of goods or of rendering of services, or other characteristics of goods or services,
  (d) trade marks which consist exclusively of signs or indications which have become customary in the current language or in the bona fide and established practices of the trade:
  Provided that, a trade mark shall not be refused registration by virtue of paragraph (b), (c) or (d) above if, before the date of application for registra-

tion, it has in fact acquired a distinctive character as a result of the use made of it.

(2) A sign shall not be registered as a trade mark if it consists exclusively of—
    (a) the shape which results from the nature of the goods themselves,
    (b) the shape of goods which is necessary to obtain a technical result, or
    (c) the shape which gives substantial value to the goods.

(3) A trade mark shall not be registered if it is—
    (a) contrary to public policy or to accepted principles of morality, or
    (b) of such a nature as to deceive the public (for instance as to the nature, quality or geographical origin of the goods or service).

(4) A trade mark shall not be registered if or to the extent that its use is prohibited in the United Kingdom by any enactment or rule of law or by any provision of Community law.

(5) A trade mark shall not be registered in the cases specified, or referred to, in section 4 (specially protected emblems).

(6) A trade mark shall not be registered if or to the extent that the application is made in bad faith.

Specially protected emblems

6-004   **4.**—(1) A trade mark which consists of or contains—
    (a) the Royal arms, or any of the principal armorial bearings of the Royal arms, or any insignia or device so nearly resembling the Royal arms or any such armorial bearing as to be likely to be mistaken for them or it,
    (b) a representation of the Royal crown or any of the Royal flags,
    (c) a representation of Her Majesty or any member of the Royal family, or any colourable imitation thereof, or
    (d) words, letters or devices likely to lead persons to think that the applicant either has or recently has had Royal patronage or authorisation,
shall not be registered unless it appears to the registrar that consent has been given by or on behalf of Her Majesty or, as the case may be, the relevant member of the Royal family.

(2) A trade mark which consists of or contains a representation of—
    (a) the national flag of the United Kingdom (commonly known as the Union Jack), or
    (b) the flag of England, Wales, Scotland, Northern Ireland or the Isle of Man,
shall not be registered if it appears to the registrar that the use of the trade mark would be misleading or grossly offensive.
Provision may be made by rules identifying the flags to which paragraph (b) applies.

(3) A trade mark shall not be registered in the cases specified in—
section 57 (national emblems, &c. of Convention countries), or section 58 (emblems, &c. of certain international organisations).

(4) Provision may be made by rules prohibiting in such cases as may be prescribed the registration of a trade mark which consists of or contains—
    (a) arms to which a person is entitled by virtue of a grant of arms by the Crown, or
    (b) insignia so nearly resembling such arms as to be likely to be mistaken for them,
unless it appears to the registrar that consent has been given by or on behalf of that person.

Where such a mark is registered, nothing in this Act shall be construed as authorising its use in any way contrary to the laws of arms.

Relative grounds for refusal of registration

5.—(1) A trade mark shall not be registered if it is identical with an earlier **6-005** trade mark and the goods or services for which the trade mark is applied for are identical with the goods or services for which the earlier trade mark is protected.

(2) A trade mark shall not be registered if because—

    (a) it is identical with an earlier trade mark and is to be registered for goods or services similar to those for which the earlier trade mark is protected, or

    (b) it is similar to an earlier trade mark and is to be registered for goods or services identical with or similar to those for which the earlier trade mark is protected,

there exists a likelihood of confusion of the part of the public, which includes the likelihood of association with the earlier trade mark.

(3) A trade mark which—

    (a) is identical with or similar to an earlier trade mark, [...]¹

    (b) [...]²

shall not be registered if, or to the extent that, the earlier trade mark has a reputation in the United Kingdom (or, in the case of a Community trade mark, in the European Community) and the use of the later mark without due cause would take unfair advantage of, or be detrimental to, the distinctive character or the repute of the earlier trade mark.

(4) A trade mark shall not be registered if, or to the extent that, its use in the United Kingdom is liable to be prevented—

    (a) by virtue of any rule of law (in particular, the law of passing off) protecting an unregistered trade mark or other sign used in the course of trade, or

    (b) by virtue of an earlier right other than those referred to in subsections (1) to (3) or paragraph (a) above, in particular by virtue of the law of copyright, design right or registered designs.

A person thus entitled to prevent the use of a trade mark is referred to in this Act as the proprietor of an "earlier right" in relation to the trade mark.

(5) Nothing in this section prevents the registration of a trade mark where the proprietor of the earlier trade mark or other earlier right consents to the registration.

Meaning of "earlier trade mark"

6.—(1) In this Act an "earlier trade mark" means — **6-006**

    (a) a registered trade mark, international trade mark (UK) or Community trade mark which has a date of application for registration earlier than that of the trade mark in question, taking account (where appropriate) of the priorities claimed in respect of the trade marks,

    (b) a Community trade mark which has a valid claim to seniority from an earlier registered trade mark or international trade mark (UK), or

    (c) a trade mark which, at the date of application for registration of the trade mark in question or (where appropriate) of the priority claimed in

---

¹ Word repealed by SI 2004/946 reg 7 (1)

² Repealed by SI 2004/946 reg 7 (1)

respect of the application, was entitled to protection under the Parts Convention [or the WTO agreement][1] as a well known trade mark.

(2) References in this Act to an earlier trade mark include a trade mark in respect of which an application for registration has been made and which, if registered, would be an earlier trade mark by virtue of subsection (1)(a) or (b), subject to its being so registered.

(3) A trade mark within subsection (1)(a) or (b) whose registration expires shall continue to be taken into account in determining the registrability of a later mark for a period of one year after the expiry unless the registrar is satisfied that there was no bona fide use of the mark during the two years immediately preceding the expiry.

[Raising of relative grounds in opposition proceedings in case of non-use

6-007   **6A.**—(1) This section applies where—

    (a) an application for registration of a trade mark has been published,

    (b) there is an earlier trade mark in relation to which the conditions set out in section 5(1), (2) or (3) obtain, and

    (c) the registration procedure for the earlier trade mark was completed before the start of the period of five years ending with the date of publication.

(2) In opposition proceedings, the registrar shall not refuse to register the trade mark by reason of the earlier trade mark unless the use conditions are met.

(3) The use conditions are met if—

    (a) within the period of five years ending with the date of publication of the application the earlier trade mark has been put to genuine use in the United Kingdom by the proprietor or with his consent in relation to the goods or services for which it is registered, or

    (b) the earlier trade mark has not been so used, but there are proper reasons for non-use.

(4) For these purposes—

    (a) use of a trade mark includes use in a form differing in elements which do not alter the distinctive character of the mark in the form in which it was registered, and

    (b) use in the United Kingdom includes affixing the trade mark to goods or to the packaging of goods in the United Kingdom solely for export purposes.

(5) In relation to a Community trade mark, any reference in subsection (3) or (4) to the United Kingdom shall be construed as a reference to the European Community.

(6) Where an earlier trade mark satisfies the use conditions in respect of some only of the goods or services for which it is registered, it shall be treated for the purposes of this section as if it were registered only in respect of those goods or services.

(7) Nothing in this section affects—

    (a) the refusal of registration on the grounds mentioned in section 3 (absolute grounds for refusal) or section 5(4)(relative grounds of refusal on the basis of an earlier right), or

---

[1] Words inserted by SI 1999/1899 Pt IV reg 13 (1)

(b) the making of an application for a declaration of invalidity under section 47(2) (application on relative grounds where no consent to registration).][1]

Raising of relative grounds in case of honest concurrent use

7.—(1) This section applies where on an application for the registration of a **6-008** trade mark it appears to the registrar—

(a) that there is an earlier trade mark in relation to which the conditions set out in section 5(1), (2) or (3) obtain, or

(b) that there is an earlier right in relation to which the condition set out in section 5(4) is satisfied,

but the applicant shows to the satisfaction of the registrar that there has been honest concurrent use of the trade mark for which registration is sought.

(2) In that case the registrar shall not refuse the application by reason of the earlier trade mark or other earlier right unless objection on that ground is raised in opposition proceedings by the proprietor of that earlier trade mark or other earlier right.

(3) For the purposes of this section "honest concurrent use" means such use in the United Kingdom, by the applicant or with his consent, as would formerly have amounted to honest concurrent use for the purposes of section 12(2) of the Trade Marks Act 1938.

(4) Nothing in this section affects—

(a) the refusal of registration on the grounds mentioned in section 3 (absolute grounds for refusal), or

(b) the making of an application for a declaration of invalidity under section 47(2) (application on relative grounds where no consent to registration).

(5) This section does not apply when there is an order in force under section 8 below.

Power to require that relative grounds be raised in opposition proceedings

8.—(1) The Secretary of State may by order provide that in any case a trade **6-009** mark shall not be refused registration on a ground mentioned in section 5 (relative grounds for refusal) unless objection on that ground is raised in opposition proceedings by the proprietor of the earlier trade mark or other earlier right.

(2) The order may make such consequential provision as appears to the Secretary of State appropriate—

(a) with respect to the carrying out by the registrar of searches of earlier trade marks, and

(b) as to the persons by whom an application for a declaration of invalidity may be made on the grounds specified in section 47(2) (relative grounds).

(3) An order making such provision as is mentioned in subsection (2)(a) may direct that so much of section 37 (examination of application) as requires a search to be carried out shall cease to have effect.

(4) An order making such provision as is mentioned in subsection (2)(b) may provide that so much of section 47(3) as provides that any person may make an application for a declaration of invalidity shall have effect subject to the provisions of the order.

---

[1] Inserted by SI 2004/946 reg 4

(5) An order under this section shall be made by statutory instrument, and no order shall be made unless a draft of it has been laid before and approved by a resolution of each House of Parliament.

No such draft of an order making such provision as is mentioned in subsection (1) shall be laid before Parliament until after the end of the period of ten years beginning with the day on which applications for Community trade marks may first be filed in pursuance of the Community Trade Mark Regulation.

(6) An order under this section may contain such transitional provisions as appear to the Secretary of State to be appropriate.

Effects of registered trade mark

Rights conferred by registered trade mark

6-010   **9.**—(1) The proprietor of a registered trade mark has exclusive rights in the trade mark which are infringed by use of the trade mark in the United Kingdom without his consent.

The acts amounting to infringement, if done without the consent of the proprietor, are specified in section 10.

(2) References in this Act to the infringement of a registered trade mark are to any such infringement of the rights of the proprietor.

(3) The rights of the proprietor have effect from the date of registration (which in accordance with section 40(3) is the date of filing of the application for registration):

Provided that—

    (a) no infringement proceedings may be begun before the date on which the trade mark is in fact registered; and

    (b) no offence under section 92 (unauthorised use of trade mark, &c. in relation to goods) is committed by anything done before the date of publication of the registration.

Infringement of registered trade mark

6-011   **10.**—(1) A person infringes a registered trade mark if he uses in the course of trade a sign which is identical with the trade mark in relation to goods or services which are identical with those for which it is registered.

(2) A person infringes a registered trade mark if he uses in the course of trade a sign where because—

    (a) the sign is identical with the trade mark and is used in relation to goods or services similar to those for which the trade mark is registered, or

    (b) the sign is similar to the trade mark and is used in relation to goods or services identical with or similar to those for which the trade mark is registered,

there exists a likelihood of confusion on the part of the public, which includes the likelihood of association with the trade mark.

(3) A person infringes a registered trade mark if he uses in the course of trade[, in relation to goods or services,][1] a sign which—

    (a) is identical with or similar to the trade mark, [...][2]

---

[1] Words inserted by SI 2004/946 reg 7 (2) (a)

[2] Word repealed by SI 2004/946 reg 7 (2) (b)

(b) [...]¹

where the trade mark has a reputation in the United Kingdom and the use of the sign, being without due cause, takes unfair advantage of, or is detrimental to, the distinctive character or the repute of the trade mark.

(4) For the purposes of this section a person uses a sign if, in particular, he—

(a) affixes it to goods or the packaging thereof;

(b) offers or exposes goods for sale, puts them on the market or stocks them for those purposes under the sign, or offers or supplies services under the sign;

(c) imports or exports goods under the sign; or

(d) uses the sign on business papers or in advertising.

(5) A person who applies a registered trade mark to material intended to be used for labelling or packaging goods, as a business paper, or for advertising goods or services, shall be treated as a party to any use of the material which infringes the registered trade mark if when he applied the mark he knew or had reason to believe that the application of the mark was not duly authorised by the proprietor or a licensee.

(6) Nothing in the preceding provisions of this section shall be construed as preventing the use of a registered trade mark by any person for the purpose of identifying goods or services as those of the proprietor or a licensee.

But any such use otherwise than in accordance with honest practices in industrial or commercial matters shall be treated as infringing the registered trade mark if the use without due cause takes unfair advantage of, or is detrimental to, the distinctive character or repute of the trade mark.

Limits on effect of registered trade mark

11.—(1) A registered trade mark is not infringed by the use of another **6-012** registered trade mark in relation to goods or services for which the latter is registered (but see section 47(6) (effect of declaration of invalidity of registration)).

(2) A registered trade mark is not infringed by—

(a) the use by a person of his own name or address,

(b) the use of indications concerning the kind, quality, quantity, intended purpose, value, geographical origin, the time of production of goods or of rendering of services, or other characteristics of goods or services, or

(c) the use of the trade mark where it is necessary to indicate the intended purpose of a product or service (in particular, as accessories or spare parts),

provided the use is in accordance with honest practices in industrial or commercial matters.

(3) A registered trade mark is not infringed by the use in the course of trade in a particular locality of an earlier right which applies only in that locality.

For this purpose an "earlier right" means an unregistered trade mark or other sign continuously used in relation to goods or services by a person or a predecessor in title of his from a date prior to whichever is the earlier of—

(a) the use of the first-mentioned trade mark in relation to those goods or services by the proprietor or a predecessor in title of his, or

(b) the registration of the first-mentioned trade mark in respect of those goods or services in the name of the proprietor or a predecessor in title of his;

---

¹ Repealed by SI 2004/946 reg 7 (2) (b)

and an earlier right shall be regarded as applying in a locality if, or to the extent that, its use in that locality is protected by virtue of any rule of law (in particular, the law of passing off).

Exhaustion of rights conferred by registered trade mark

6-013   **12.**—(1) A registered trade mark is not infringed by the use of the trade mark in relation to goods which have been put on the market in the European Economic Area under that trade mark by the proprietor or with his consent.

(2) Subsection (1) does not apply where there exist legitimate reasons for the proprietor to oppose further dealings in the goods (in particular, where the condition of the goods has been changed or impaired after they have been put on the market).

Registration subject to disclaimer or limitation

6-014   **13.**—(1) An applicant for registration of a trade mark, or the proprietor of a registered trade mark, may—

(a) disclaim any right to the exclusive use of any specified element of the trade mark, or

(b) agree that the rights conferred by the registration shall be subject to a specified territorial or other limitation;

and where the registration of a trade mark is subject to a disclaimer or limitation, the rights conferred by section 9 (rights conferred by registered trade mark) are restricted accordingly.

(2) Provision shall be made by rules as to the publication and entry in the register of a disclaimer or limitation.

Infringement proceedings

Action for infringement

6-015   **14.**—(1) An infringement of a registered trade mark is actionable by the proprietor of the trade mark.

(2) In an action for infringement all such relief by way of damages, injunctions, accounts or otherwise is available to him as is available in respect of the infringement of any other property right.

Order for erasure &c. of offending sign

6-016   **15.**—(1) Where a person is found to have infringed a registered trade mark, the court may make an order requiring him—

(a) to cause the offending sign to be erased, removed or obliterated from any infringing goods, material or articles in his possession, custody or control, or

(b) if it is not reasonably practicable for the offending sign to be erased, removed or obliterated, to secure the destruction of the infringing goods, material or articles in question.

(2) If an order under subsection (1) is not complied with, or it appears to the court likely that such an order would not be complied with, the court may order that the infringing goods, material or articles be delivered to such person as the court may direct for erasure, removal or obliteration of the sign, or for destruction, as the case may be.

Order for delivery up of infringing goods, material or articles

16.—(1) The proprietor of a registered trade mark may apply to the court for **6-017** an order for the delivery up to him, or such other person as the court may direct, of any infringing goods, material or articles which a person has in his possession, custody or control in the course of a business.

(2) An application shall not be made after the end of the period specified in section 18 (period after which remedy of delivery up not available), and no order shall be made unless the court also makes, or it appears to the court that there are grounds for making, an order under section 19 (order as to disposal of infringing goods, &c.).

(3) A person to whom any infringing goods, material or articles are delivered up in pursuance of an order under this section shall, if an order under section 19 is not made, retain them pending the making of an order, or the decision not to make an order, under that section.

(4) Nothing in this section affects any other power of the court.

Meaning of "infringing goods, material or articles"

17.—(1) In this Act the expressions "infringing goods", "infringing material" **6-018** and "infringing articles" shall be construed as follows

(2) Goods are "infringing goods", in relation to a registered trade mark, if they or their packaging bear a sign identical or similar to that mark and—

 (a) the application of the sign to the goods or their packaging was an infringement of the registered trade mark, or

 (b) the goods are proposed to be imported into the United Kingdom and the application of the sign in the United Kingdom to them or their packaging would be an infringement of the registered trade mark, or

 (c) the sign has otherwise been used in relation to the goods in such a way as to infringe the registered trade mark.

(3) Nothing in subsection (2) shall be construed as affecting the importation of goods which may lawfully be imported into the United Kingdom by virtue of an enforceable Community right.

(4) Material is "infringing material", in relation to a registered trade mark if it bears a sign identical or similar to that mark and either—

 (a) it is used for labelling or packaging goods, as a business paper, or for advertising goods or services, in such a way as to infringe the registered trade mark, or

 (b) it is intended to be so used and such use would infringe the registered trade mark.

(5) "Infringing articles", in relation to a registered trade mark, means articles—

 (a) which are specifically designed or adapted for making copies of a sign identical or similar to that mark, and

 (b) which a person has in his possession, custody or control, knowing or having reason to believe that they have been or are to be used to produce infringing goods or material.

Period after which remedy of delivery up not available

18.—(1) An application for an order under section 16 (order for delivery up **6-019** of infringing goods, material or articles) may not be made after the end of the period of six years from—

(a) in the case of infringing goods, the date on which the trade mark was applied to the goods or their packaging,

(b) in the case of infringing material, the date on which the trade mark was applied to the material, or

(c) in the case of infringing articles, the date on which they were made,

except as mentioned in the following provisions.

(2) If during the whole or part of that period the proprietor of the registered trade mark—

(a) is under a disability, or

(b) is prevented by fraud or concealment from discovering the facts entitling him to apply for an order.

an application may be made at any time before the end of the period of six years from the date on which he ceased to be under a disability or, as the case may be, could with reasonable diligence have discovered those facts.

(3) In subsection (2) "disability"—

(a) in England and Wales, has the same meaning as in the Limitation Act 1980;

(b) in Scotland, means legal disability within the meaning of the Prescription and Limitation (Scotland) Act 1973,

(c) in Northern Ireland, has the same meaning as in the Limitation (Northern Ireland) Order 1989.

Order as to disposal of infringing goods, material or articles

6-020   **19.**—(1) Where infringing goods, material or articles have been delivered up in pursuance of an order under section 16, an application may be made to the court—

(a) for an order that they be destroyed or forfeited to such person as the court may think fit, or

(b) for a decision that no such order should be made.

(2) In considering what order (if any) should be made, the court shall consider whether other remedies available in an action for infringement of the registered trade mark would be adequate to compensate the proprietor and any licensee and protect their interests.

(3) Provision shall be made by rules of court as to the service of notice on persons having an interest in the goods, material or articles, and any such person is entitled—

(a) to appear in proceedings for an order under this section, whether or not he was served with notice, and

(b) to appeal against any order made, whether or not he appeared;

and an order shall not take effect until the end of the period within which notice of an appeal may be given or, if before the end of that period notice of appeal is duly given, until the final determination or abandonment of the proceedings on the appeal.

(4) Where there is more than one person interested in the goods, material or articles, the court shall make such order as it thinks just.

(5) If the court decides that no order should be made under this section, the person in whose possession, custody or control the goods, material or articles were before being delivered up is entitled to their return.

(6) References in this section to a person having an interest in goods, material or articles include any person in whose favour an order could be made under this section or under section 114, 204 or 231 of the Copyright, Designs and

Patents Act 1988 (which make similar provision in relation to infringement of copyright, rights in performances and design right).

Jurisdiction of sheriff court or county court in Northern Ireland

20. Proceedings for an order under section 16 (order for delivery up of **6-021** infringing goods, material or articles) or section 19 (order as to disposal of infringing goods, &c.) may be brought—

(a) in the sheriff court in Scotland, or

(b) in a county court in Northern Ireland.

This does not affect the jurisdiction of the Court of Session or the High Court in Northern Ireland.

Remedy for groundless threats of infringement proceedings

21.—(1) Where a person threatens another with proceedings for infringement **6-022** of a registered trade mark other than—

(a) the application of the mark to goods or their packaging,

(b) the importation of goods to which, or to the packaging of which, the mark has been applied, or

(c) the supply of services under the mark,

any person aggrieved may bring proceedings for relief under this section.

(2) The relief which may be applied for is any of the following—

(a) a declaration that the threats are unjustifiable,

(b) an injunction against the continuance of the threats,

(c) damages in respect of any loss he has sustained by the threats;

and the plaintiff is entitled to such relief unless the defendant shows that the acts in respect of which proceedings were threatened constitute (or if done would constitute) an infringement of the registered trade mark concerned.

(3) If that is shown by the defendant, the plaintiff is nevertheless entitled to relief if he shows that the registration of the trade mark is invalid or liable to be revoked in a relevant respect.

(4) The mere notification that a trade mark is registered, or that an application for registration has been made, does not constitute a threat of proceedings for the purposes of this section

Registered trade mark as object of property

Nature of registered trade mark

22. A registered trade mark is personal property (in Scotland, incorporeal **6-023** moveable property).

Co-ownership of registered trade mark

23.—(1) Where a registered trade mark is granted to two or more persons **6-024** jointly, each of them is entitled, subject to an agreement to the contrary, to an equal undivided share in the registered trade mark.

(2) The following provisions apply where two or more persons are co-proprietors of a registered trade mark, by virtue of subsection (1) or otherwise.

(3) Subject to any agreement to the contrary, each co-proprietor is entitled, by himself or his agents, to do for his own benefit and without the consent of or the need to account to the other or others, any act which would otherwise amount to an infringement of the registered trade mark

(4) One co-proprietor may not without the consent of the other or others—

(a) grant a licence to use the registered trade mark, or

(b) assign or charge his share in the registered trade mark (or, in Scotland, cause or permit security to be granted over it).

(5) Infringement proceedings may be brought by any co-proprietor, but he may not, without the leave of the court, proceed with the action unless the other, or each of the others, is either joined as a plaintiff or added as a defendant.

A co-proprietor who is thus added as a defendant shall not be made liable for any costs in the action unless he takes part in the proceedings.

Nothing in this subsection affects the granting of interlocutory relief on the application of a single co-proprietor.

(6) Nothing in this section affects the mutual rights and obligations of trustees or personal representatives, or their rights and obligations as such.

Assignment, &c. of registered trade mark

6-025   **24.**—(1) A registered trade mark is transmissible by assignment, testamentary disposition or operation of law in the same way as other personal or moveable property.

It is so transmissible either in connection with the goodwill of a business or independently.

(2) An assignment or other transmission of a registered trade mark may be partial, that is, limited so as to apply—

(a) in relation to some but not all of the goods or services for which the trade mark is registered, or

(b) in relation to use of the trade mark in a particular manner or a particular locality.

(3) An assignment of a registered trade mark, or an assent relating to a registered trade mark, is not effective unless it is in writing signed by or on behalf of the assignor or, as the case may be, a personal representative.

Except in Scotland, this requirement may be satisfied in a case where the assignor or personal representative is a body corporate by the affixing of its seal.

(4) The above provisions apply to assignment by way of security as in relation to any other assignment.

(5) A registered trade mark may be the subject of a charge (in Scotland, security) in the same way as other personal or moveable property.

(6) Nothing in this Act shall be construed as affecting the assignment or other transmission of an unregistered trade mark as part of the goodwill of a business.

Registration of transactions affecting registered trade mark

6-026   **25.**—(1) On application being made to the registrar by—

(a) a person claiming to be entitled to an interest in or under a registered trade mark by virtue of a registrable transaction, or

(b) any other person claiming to be affected by such a transaction,

the prescribed particulars of the transaction shall be entered in the register.

(2) The following are registrable transactions—

(a) an assignment of a registered trade mark or any right in it;

(b) the grant of a licence under a registered trade mark;

(c) the granting of any security interest (whether fixed or floating) over a registered trade mark or any right in or under it;

(d) the making by personal representatives of an assent in relation to a registered trade mark or any right in or under it;

(e) an order of a court or other competent authority transferring a registered trade mark or any right in or under it.

(3) Until an application has been made for registration of the prescribed particulars of a registrable transaction—

(a) the transaction is ineffective as against a person acquiring a conflicting interest in or under the registered trade mark in ignorance of it, and

(b) a person claiming to be a licensee by virtue of the transaction does not have the protection of section 30 or 31 (rights and remedies of licensee in relation to infringement).

(4) Where a person becomes the proprietor or a licensee of a registered trade mark by virtue of a registrable transaction, then unless

(a) an application for registration of the prescribed particulars of the transaction is made before the end of the period of six months beginning with its date, or

(b) the court is satisfied that it was not practicable for such an application to be made before the end of that period and that an application was made as soon as practicable thereafter,

he is not entitled to damages or an account of profits in respect of any infringement of the registered trade mark occurring after the date of the transaction and before the prescribed particulars of the transaction are registered.

(5) Provision may be made by rules as to—

(a) the amendment of registered particulars relating to a licence so as to reflect any alteration of the terms of the licence, and

(b) the removal of such particulars from the register—

(i) where it appears from the registered particulars that the licence was granted for a fixed period and that period has expired, or

(ii) where no such period is indicated and, after such period as may be prescribed, the registrar has notified the parties of his intention to remove the particulars from the register.

(6) Provision may also be made by rules as to the amendment or removal from the register of particulars relating to a security interest on the application of, or with the consent of, the person entitled to the benefit of that interest.

Trusts and equities

26.—(1) No notice of any trust (express, implied or constructive) shall be 6-027 entered in the register; and the registrar shall not be affected by any such notice.

(2) Subject to the provisions of this Act, equities (in Scotland, rights) in respect of a registered trade mark may be enforced in like manner as in respect of other personal or moveable property.

Application for registration of trade mark as an object of property

27.—(1) The provisions of sections 22 to 26 (which relate to a registered trade 6-028 mark as an object of property) apply, with the necessary modifications, in relation to an application for the registration of a trade mark as in relation to a registered trade mark.

(2) In section 23 (co-ownership of registered trade mark) as it applies in relation to an application for registration the reference in subsection (1) to the granting of the registration shall be construed as a reference to the making of the application.

(3) In section 25 (registration of transactions affecting registered trade marks) as it applies in relation to a transaction affecting an application for the registration of a trade mark, the references to the entry of particulars in the

register, and to the making of an application to register particulars, shall be construed as references to the giving of notice to the registrar of those particulars.

Licensing of registered trade mark

6-029   **28.**—(1) A licence to use a registered trade mark may be general or limited.

A limited licence may, in particular, apply—

(a) in relation to some but not all of the goods or services for which the trade mark is registered, or

(b) in relation to use of the trade mark in a particular manner or a particular locality.

(2) A licence is not effective unless it is in writing signed by or on behalf of the grantor.

Except in Scotland, this requirement may be satisfied in a case where the grantor is a body corporate by the affixing of its seal.

(3) Unless the licence provides otherwise, it is binding on a successor in title to the grantor's interest.

References in this Act to doing anything with, or without, the consent of the proprietor of a registered trade mark shall be construed accordingly.

(4) Where the licence so provides, a sub-licence may be granted by the licensee; and references in this Act to a licence or licensee include a sub-licence or sub-licensee.

Exclusive licences

6-030   **29.**—(1) In this Act an "exclusive licence" means a licence (whether general or limited) authorising the licensee to the exclusion of all other persons, including the person granting the licence, to use a registered trade mark in the manner authorised by the licence.

The expression "exclusive licensee" shall be construed accordingly

(2) An exclusive licensee has the same rights against a successor in title who is bound by the licence as he has against the person granting the licence.

General provisions as to rights of licensees in case of infringement

6-031   **30.**—(1) This section has effect with respect to the rights of a licensee in relation to infringement of a registered trade mark.

The provisions of this section do not apply where or to the extent that, by virtue of section 31(1) below (exclusive licensee having rights and remedies of assignee), the licensee has a right to bring proceedings in his own name.

(2) A licensee is entitled, unless his licence, or any licence through which his interest is derived, provides otherwise, to call on the proprietor of the registered trade mark to take infringement proceedings in respect of any matter which affects his interests.

(3) If the proprietor—

(a) refuses to do so, or

(b) fails to do so within two months after being called upon.

the licensee may bring the proceedings in his own name as if he were the proprietor.

(4) Where infringement proceedings are brought by a licensee by virtue of this section the licensee may not, without the leave of the court, proceed with the

action unless the proprietor is either joined as a plaintiff or added as a defendant.

This does not affect the granting of interlocutory relief on an application by a licensee alone.

(5) A proprietor who is added as a defendant as mentioned in subsection (4) shall not be made liable for any costs in the action unless he takes part in the proceedings.

(6) In infringement proceedings brought by the proprietor of a registered trade mark any loss suffered or likely to be suffered by licensees shall be taken into account; and the court may give such directions as it thinks fit as to the extent to which the plaintiff is to hold the proceeds of any pecuniary remedy on behalf of licensees.

(7) The provisions of this section apply in relation to an exclusive licensee if or to the extent that he has, by virtue of section 31(1), the rights and remedies of an assignee as if he were the proprietor of the registered trade mark.

Exclusive licensee having rights and remedies of assignee

31.—(1) An exclusive licence may provide that the licensee shall have, to such **6-032** extent as may be provided by the licence, the same rights and remedies in respect of matters occurring after the grant of the licence as if the licence had been an assignment.

Where or to the extent that such provision is made, the licensee is entitled, subject to the provisions of the licence and to the following provisions of this section, to bring infringement proceedings, against any person other than the proprietor, in his own name.

(2) Any such rights and remedies of an exclusive licensee are concurrent with those of the proprietor of the registered trade mark, and references to the proprietor of a registered trade mark in the provisions of this Act relating to infringement shall be construed accordingly.

(3) In an action brought by an exclusive licensee by virtue of this section a defendant may avail himself of any defence which would have been available to him if the action had been brought by the proprietor of the registered trade mark.

(4) Where proceedings for infringement of a registered trade mark brought by the proprietor or an exclusive licensee relate wholly or partly to an infringement in respect of which they have concurrent rights of action, the proprietor or, as the case may be, the exclusive licensee may not, without the leave of the court, proceed with the action unless the other is either joined as a plaintiff or added as a defendant.

This does not affect the granting of interlocutory relief on an application by a proprietor or exclusive licensee alone.

(5) A person who is added as a defendant as mentioned in subsection (4) shall not be made liable for any costs in the action unless he takes part in the proceedings.

(6) Where an action for infringement of a registered trade mark is brought which relates wholly or partly to an infringement in respect of which the proprietor and an exclusive licensee have or had concurrent rights of action—

    (a) the court shall in assessing damages take into account—

        (i) the terms of the licence, and

        (ii) any pecuniary remedy already awarded or available to either of them in respect of the infringement;

(b) no account of profits shall be directed if an award of damages has been made, or an account of profits has been directed, in favour of the other of them in respect of the infringement; and

(c) the court shall if an account of profits is directed apportion the profits between them as the court considers just, subject to any agreement between them.

The provisions of this subsection apply whether or not the proprietor and the exclusive licensee are both parties to the action, and if they are not both parties the court may give such directions as it thinks fit as to the extent to which the party to the proceedings is to hold the proceeds of any pecuniary remedy on behalf of the other.

(7) The proprietor of a registered trade mark shall notify any exclusive licensee who has a concurrent right of action before applying for an order under section 16 (order for delivery up), and the court may on the application of the licensee make such order under that section as it thinks fit having regard to the terms of the licence.

(8) The provisions of subsections (4) to (7) above have effect subject to any agreement to the contrary between the exclusive licensee and the proprietor.

Application for registered trade mark

Application for registration

6-033   **32.**—(1) An application for registration of a trade mark shall be made to the registrar.

(2) The application shall contain—

(a) a request for registration of a trade mark,

(b) the name and address of the applicant,

(c) a statement of the goods or services in relation to which it is sought to register the trade mark, and

(d) a representation of the trade mark.

(3) The application shall state that the trade mark is being used, by the applicant or with his consent, in relation to those goods or services, or that he has a bona fide intention that it should be so used.

(4) The application shall be subject to the payment of the application fee and such class fees as may be appropriate

Date of filing

6-034   **33.**—(1) The date of filing of an application for registration of a trade mark is the date on which documents containing everything required by section 32(2) are furnished to the registrar by the applicant.

If the documents are furnished on different days, the date of filing is the last of those days.

(2) References in this Act to the date of application for registration are to the date of filing of the application.

Classification of trade marks

6-035   **34.**—(1) Goods and services shall be classified for the purposes of the registration of trade marks according to a prescribed system of classification.

(2) Any question arising as to the class within which any goods or services fall shall be determined by the registrar, whose decision shall be final.

Priority

Claim to priority of Convention application

35.—(1) A person who has duly filed an application for protection of a trade **6-036** mark in a Convention country (a "Convention application"), or his successor in title, has a right to priority, for the purposes of registering the same trade mark under this Act for some or all of the same goods or services, for a period of six months from the date of filing of the first such application.

(2) If the application for registration under this Act is made within that six-month period—

(a) the relevant date for the purposes of establishing which rights take precedence shall be the date of filing of the first Convention application, and

(b) the registrability of the trade mark shall not be affected by any use of the mark in the United Kingdom in the period between that date and the date of the application under this Act.

(3) Any filing which in a Convention country is equivalent to a regular national filing, under its domestic legislation or an international agreement, shall be treated as giving rise to the right of priority.

A "regular national filing" means a filing which is adequate to establish the date on which the application was filed in that country, whatever may be the subsequent fate of the application.

(4) A subsequent application concerning the same subject as the first Convention application, filed in the same Convention country, shall be considered the first Convention application (of which the filing date is the starting date of the period of priority), if at the time of the subsequent application—

(a) the previous application has been withdrawn, abandoned or refused, without having been laid open to public inspection and without leaving any rights outstanding, and

(b) it has not yet served as a basis for claiming a right of priority.

The previous application may not thereafter serve as a basis for claiming a right of priority.

(5) Provision may be made by rules as to the manner of claiming a right to priority on the basis of a Convention application.

(6) A right to priority arising as a result of a Convention application may be assigned or otherwise transmitted, either with the application or independently.

The reference in subsection (1) to the applicant's "successor in title" shall be construed accordingly.

Claim to priority from other relevant overseas application

36.—(1) Her Majesty may by Order in Council make provision for **6-037** conferring on a person who has duly filed an application for protection of a trade mark in—

(a) any of the Channel Islands or a colony, or

(b) a country or territory in relation to which Her Majesty's Government in the United Kingdom have entered into a treaty, convention, arrangement or engagement for the reciprocal protection of trade marks,

a right to priority, for the purpose of registering the same trade mark under this Act for some or all of the same goods or services, for a specified period from the date of filing of that application.

(2) An Order in Council under this section may make provision corresponding to that made by section 35 in relation to Convention countries or such other
provision as appears to Her Majesty to be appropriate.

(3) A statutory instrument containing an Order in Council under this
section shall be subject to annulment in pursuance of a resolution of either House
of Parliament.

Registration procedure

Examination of application

6-038   **37.**—(1) The registrar shall examine whether an application for registration
of a trade mark satisfies the requirements of this Act (including any requirements
imposed by rules)

(2) For that purpose he shall carry out a search, to such extent as he
considers necessary, of earlier trade marks.

(3) If it appears to the registrar that the requirements for registration are not
met, he shall inform the applicant and give him an opportunity, within such
period as the registrar may specify, to make representations or to amend the
application.

(4) If the applicant fails to satisfy the registrar that those requirements are
met, or to amend the application so as to meet them, or fails to respond before the
end of the specified period, the registrar shall refuse to accept the application.

(5) If it appears to the registrar that the requirements for registration are met,
he shall accept the application.

Publication, opposition proceedings and observations

6-039   **38.**—(1) When an application for registration has been accepted, the
registrar shall cause the application to be published in the prescribed manner

(2) Any person may, within the prescribed time from the date of the publication of the application, give notice to the registrar of opposition to the
registration.

The notice shall be given in writing in the prescribed manner, and shall
include a statement of the grounds of opposition.

(3) Where an application has been published, any person may, at any time
before the registration of the trade mark, make observations in writing to the
registrar as to whether the trade mark should be registered; and the registrar shall
inform the applicant of any such observations.

A person who makes observations does not thereby become a party to the proceedings on the application.

Withdrawal, restriction or amendment of application

6-040   **39.**—(1) The applicant may at any time withdraw his application or restrict
the goods or services covered by the application.

If the application has been published, the withdrawal or restriction shall also
be published.

(2) In other respects, an application may be amended, at the request of the
applicant, only by correcting—

    (a) the name or address of the applicant,

    (b) errors of wording or of copying, or

    (c) obvious mistakes,

and then only where the correction does not substantially affect the identity of the trade mark or extend the goods or services covered by the application

(3) Provision shall be made by rules for the publication of any amendment which affects the representation of the trade mark, or the goods or services covered by the application, and for the making of objections by any person claiming to be affected by it.

Registration

40.—(1) Where an application has been accepted and—   **6-041**

(a) no notice of opposition is given within the period referred to in section 38(2), or

(b) all opposition proceedings are withdrawn or decided in favour of the applicant,

the registrar shall register the trade mark, unless it appears to him having regard to matters coming to his notice [since the application was accepted that the registration requirements (other than those mentioned in section 5(1), (2) or (3)) were not met at that time.][1]

(2) A trade mark shall not be registered unless any fee prescribed for the registration is paid within the prescribed period.

If the fee is not paid within that period, the application shall be deemed to be withdrawn.

(3) A trade mark when registered shall be registered as of the date of filing of the application for registration, and that date shall be deemed for the purposes of this Act to be the date of registration.

(4) On the registration of a trade mark the registrar shall publish the registration in the prescribed manner and issue to the applicant a certificate of registration.

Registration: supplementary provisions

41.—(1) Provision may be made by rules as to—   **6-042**

(a) the division of an application for the registration of a trade mark into several applications;

(b) the merging of separate applications or registrations;

(c) the registration of a series of trade marks.

(2) A series of trade marks means a number of trade marks which resemble each other as to their material particulars and differ only as to matters of a non-distinctive character not substantially affecting the identity of the trade mark.

(3) Rules under this section may include provision as to—

(a) the circumstances in which, and conditions subject to which, division, merger or registration of a series is permitted, and

(b) the purposes for which an application to which the rules apply is to be treated as a single application and those for which it is to be treated as a number of separate applications.

Duration, renewal and alteration of registered trade mark

Duration of registration

42.—(1) A trade mark shall be registered for a period of ten years from the   **6-043** date of registration.

---

[1] Words substituted by SI 2004/946 reg 5

(2) Registration may be renewed in accordance with section 43 for further periods of ten years.

Renewal of registration

6-044   **43.**—(1) The registration of a trade mark may be renewed at the request of the proprietor, subject to payment of a renewal fee.

(2) Provision shall be made by rules for the registrar to inform the proprietor of a registered trade mark, before the expiry of the registration, of the date of expiry and the manner in which the registration may be renewed.

(3) A request for renewal must be made, and the renewal fee paid, before the expiry of the registration.

Failing this, the request may be made and the fee paid within such further period (of not less than six months) as may be prescribed, in which case an additional renewal fee must also be paid within that period.

(4) Renewal shall take effect from the expiry of the previous registration.

(5) If the registration is not renewed in accordance with the above provisions, the registrar shall remove the trade mark from the register.

Provision may be made by rules for the restoration of the registration of a trade mark which has been removed from the register, subject to such condition (if any) as may be prescribed.

(6) The renewal or restoration of the registration of a trade mark shall be published in the prescribed manner.

Alteration of registered trade mark

6-045   **44.**—(1) A registered trade mark shall not be altered in the register, during the period of registration or on renewal.

(2) Nevertheless, the registrar may, at the request of the proprietor, allow the alteration of a registered trade mark where the mark includes the proprietor's name or address and the alteration is limited to alteration of that name or address and does not substantially affect the identity of the mark.

(3) Provision shall be made by rules for the publication of any such alteration and the making of objections by any person claiming to be affected by it.

Surrender, revocation and invalidity

Surrender of registered trade mark

6-046   **45.**—(1) A registered trade mark may be surrendered by the proprietor in respect of some or all of the goods or services for which it is registered.

(2) Provision may be made by rules—

(a) as to the manner and effect of a surrender, and

(b) for protecting the interests of other persons having a right in the registered trade mark.

Revocation of registration

6-047   **46.**—(1) The registration of a trade mark may be revoked on any of the following grounds—

(a) that within the period of five years following the date of completion of the registration procedure it has not been put to genuine use in the United Kingdom, by the proprietor or with his consent, in relation to the goods or services for which it is registered, and there are no proper reasons for non-use;

(b) that such use has been suspended for an uninterrupted period of five years, and there are no proper reasons for non-use;

(c) that, in consequence of acts or inactivity of the proprietor, it has become the common name in the trade for a product or service for which it is registered;

(d) that in consequence of the use made of it by the proprietor or with his consent in relation to the goods or services for which it is registered, it is liable to mislead the public, particularly as to the nature, quality or geographical origin of those goods or services.

(2) For the purposes of subsection (1) use of a trade mark includes use in a form differing in elements which do not alter the distinctive character of the mark in the form in which it was registered, and use in the United Kingdom includes affixing the trade mark to goods or to the packaging of goods in the United Kingdom solely for export purposes.

(3) The registration of a trade mark shall not be revoked on the ground mentioned in subsection (1)(a) or (b) if such use as is referred to in that paragraph is commenced or resumed after the expiry of the five year period and before the application for revocation is made:

Provided that, any such commencement or resumption of use after the expiry of the five year period but within the period of three months before the making of the application shall be disregarded unless preparation for the commencement or resumption began before the proprietor became aware that the application might be made.

(4) An application for revocation may be made by any person, and may be made either to the registrar or to the court, except that—

(a) if proceedings concerning the trade mark in question are pending in the court, the application must be made to the court; and

(b) if in any other case the application is made to the registrar, he may at any stage of the proceedings refer the application to the court.

(5) Where grounds for revocation exist in respect of only some of the goods or services for which the trade mark is registered, revocation shall relate to those goods or services only.

(6) Where the registration of a trade mark is revoked to any extent, the rights of the proprietor shall be deemed to have ceased to that extent as from—

(a) the date of the application for revocation, or

(b) if the registrar or court is satisfied that the grounds for revocation existed at an earlier date, that date.

Grounds for invalidity of registration

47.—(1) The registration of a trade mark may be declared invalid on the **6-048** ground that the trade mark was registered in breach of section 3 or any of the provisions referred to in that section (absolute grounds for refusal of registration).

Where the trade mark was registered in breach of subsection (1)(b), (c) or (d) of that section, it shall not be declared invalid if, in consequence of the use which has been made of it, it has after registration acquired a distinctive character in relation to the goods or services for which it is registered.

(2) The registration of a trade mark may be declared invalid on the ground—

(a) that there is an earlier trade mark in relation to which the conditions set out in section 5(1), (2) or (3) obtain, or

(b) that there is an earlier right in relation to which the condition set out in section 5(4) is satisfied, unless the proprietor of that earlier trade mark or other earlier right has consented to the registration.

[(2A) But the registration of a trade mark may not be declared invalid on the ground that there is an earlier trade mark unless—

    (a) the registration procedure for the earlier trade mark was completed within the period of five years ending with the date of the application for the declaration,

    (b) the registration procedure for the earlier trade mark was not completed before that date, or

    (c) the use conditions are met.

(2B) The use conditions are met if—

    (a) within the period of five years ending with the date of the application for the declaration the earlier trade mark has been put to genuine use in the United Kingdom by the proprietor or with his consent in relation to the goods or services for which it is registered, or

    (b) it has not been so used, but there are proper reasons for non-use.

(2C) For these purposes—

    (a) use of a trade mark includes use in a form differing in elements which do not alter the distinctive character of the mark in the form in which it was registered, and

    (b) use in the United Kingdom includes affixing the trade mark to goods or to the packaging of goods in the United Kingdom solely for export purposes.

(2D) In relation to a Community trade mark, any reference in subsection (2B) or (2C) to the United Kingdom shall be construed as a reference to the European Community.

(2E) Where an earlier trade mark satisfies the use conditions in respect of some only of the goods or services for which it is registered, it shall be treated for the purposes of this section as if it were registered only in respect of those goods or services.][1]

(3) An application for a declaration of invalidity may be made by any person, and may be made either to the registrar or to the court, except that—

    (a) if proceedings concerning the trade mark in question are pending in the court, the application must be made to the court; and

    (b) if in any other case the application is made to the registrar, he may at any stage of the proceedings refer the application to the court.

(4) In the case of bad faith in the registration of a trade mark, the registrar himself may apply to the court for a declaration of the invalidity of the registration.

(5) Where the grounds of invalidity exist in respect of only some of the goods or services for which the trade mark is registered, the trade mark shall be declared invalid as regards those goods or services only.

(6) Where the registration of a trade mark is declared invalid to any extent, the registration shall to that extent be deemed never to have been made.

Provided that this shall not affect transactions past and closed.

Effect of acquiescence

6-049   **48.**—(1) Where the proprietor of an earlier trade mark or other earlier right has acquiesced for a continuous period of five years in the use of a registered trade mark in the United Kingdom, being aware of that use, there shall cease to be any entitlement on the basis of that earlier trade mark or other right—

---

[1] Inserted by SI 2004/946 reg 6

(a) to apply for a declaration that the registration of the later trade mark is invalid, or

(b) to oppose the use of the later trade mark in relation to the goods or services in relation to which it has been so used.

unless the registration of the later trade mark was applied for in bad faith.

(2) Where subsection (1) applies, the proprietor of the later trade mark is not entitled to oppose the use of the earlier trade mark or, as the case may be, the exploitation of the earlier right, notwithstanding that the earlier trade mark or right may no longer be invoked against his later trade mark.

Collective marks

Collective marks

49.—(1) A collective mark is a mark distinguishing the goods or services of **6-050** members of the association which is the proprietor of the mark from those of other undertakings.

(2) The provisions of this Act apply to collective marks subject to the provisions of Schedule 1.

Certification marks

Certification marks

50.—(1) A certification mark is a mark indicating that the goods or services **6-051** in connection with which it is used are certified by the proprietor of the mark in respect of origin, material, mode of manufacture of goods or performance of services, quality, accuracy or other characteristics.

(2) The provisions of this Act apply to certification marks subject to the provisions of Schedule 2.

PART II

COMMUNITY TRADE MARKS AND INTERNATIONAL MATTERS

Community trade marks

Meaning of "Community trade mark"

51. In this Act—   6-052

"Community trade mark" has the meaning given by Article 1(1) of the Community Trade Mark Regulation, and

"the Community Trade Mark Regulation" means Council Regulation (EC) No. 40/94 of 20th December 1993 on the Community trade mark.

Power to make provision in connection with Community Trade Mark Regulation

52.—(1) The Secretary of State may by regulation make such provision as he **6-053** considers appropriate in connection with the operation of the Community Trade Mark Regulation.

(2) Provision may, in particular, be made with respect to—

(a) the making of applications for Community trade marks by way of the Patent Office;

(b) the procedures for determining a posteriori the invalidity, or liability to revocation, of the registration of a trade mark from which a Community trade mark claims seniority.

(c) the conversion of a Community trade mark, or an application for a Community trade mark, into an application for registration under this Act;

(d) the designation of courts in the United Kingdom having jurisdiction over proceedings arising out of the Community Trade Mark Regulation.

(3) Without prejudice to the generality of subsection (1), provision may be made by regulations under this section—

(a) applying in relation to a Community trade mark the provisions of—

(i) section 21 (remedy for groundless threats of infringement proceedings);

(ii) sections 89 to 91 (importation of infringing goods, material or articles); and

(iii) sections 92, 93, 95 and 96 (offences); and

(b) making in relation to the list of professional representatives maintained in pursuance of Article 89 of the Community Trade Mark Regulation and persons on that list, provision corresponding to that made by, or capable of being made under, sections 84 to 88 in relation to the register of trade mark agents and registered trade mark agents.

(4) Regulations under this section shall be made by statutory instrument which shall be subject to annulment in pursuance of a resolution of either House of Parliament.

The Madrid Protocol international registration

The Madrid Protocol

6-054   **53.** In this Act—

"the Madrid Protocol" means the Protocol relating to the Madrid Agreement concerning the International Registration of Marks, adopted at Madrid on 27th June 1989;

"the International Bureau" has the meaning given by Article 2(1) of that Protocol, and

"international trade mark (UK)" means a trade mark which is entitled to protection in the United Kingdom under that Protocol.

Power to make provision giving effect to Madrid Protocol

6-055   **54.**—(1) The Secretary of State may by order make such provision as he thinks fit for giving effect in the United Kingdom to the provisions of the Madrid Protocol.

(2) Provision may, in particular, be made with respect to—

(a) the making of application for international registrations by way of the Patent Office as office of origin;

(b) the procedures to be followed where the basic United Kingdom application or registration fails or ceases to be in force;

   (c) the procedures to be followed where the Patent Office receives from the International Bureau a request for extension of protection to the United Kingdom;

   (d) the effects of a successful request for extension of protection to the United Kingdom;

   (e) the transformation of an application for an international registration, or an international registration, into a national application for registration,

   (f) the communication of information to the International Bureau.

   (g) the payment of fees and amounts prescribed in respect of application for international registrations, extensions of protection and renewals.

(3) Without prejudice to the generality of subsection (1), provision may be made by regulations under this section applying in relation to an international trade mark (UK) the provisions of—

   (a) section 21 (remedy for groundless threats of infringement proceedings);

   (b) sections 89 to 91 (importation of infringing goods, material or articles); and

   (c) sections 92, 93, 95 and 96 (offences).

(4) An order under this section shall be made by statutory instrument which shall be subject to annulment in pursuance of a resolution of either House of Parliament.

The Paris Convention: supplementary provisions

The Paris Convention

   55.—(1) In this Act—   **6-056**

   (a) "the Paris Convention" means the Paris Convention for the Protection of Industrial Property of March 20th 1883, as revised or amended from time to time, [...][1]

   [(aa) "the WTO agreement" means the Agreement establishing the World Trade Organisation signed at Marrakesh on 15th April 1994, and][2]

   (b) a "Convention country" means a country, other than the United Kingdom, which is a party to that Convention.

(2) The Secretary of State may by order make such amendments of this Act, and rules made under this Act, as appear to him appropriate in consequence of any revision or amendment of the Parts Convention [or the WTO agreement][3] after the passing of this Act.

(3) Any such order shall be made by statutory instrument which shall be subject to annulment in pursuance of a resolution of either House of Parliament.

Protection of well-known trade marks Article 6bis

   56.—(1) References in this Act to a trade mark which is entitled to protection **6-057** under the Paris Convention [or the WTO agreement][4] as a well known trade mark are to a mark which is well-known in the United Kingdom as being the mark of a person who—

   (a) is a national of a Convention country, or

---

[1] Word repealed by SI 1999/1899 Pt IV reg 13 (2)
[2] Words inserted by SI 1999/1899 Pt IV reg 13 (2)
[3] Words inserted by SI 1999/1899 Pt IV reg 13 (3)
[4] Words inserted by SI 1999/1899 Pt IV reg 13 (4)

(b) is domiciled in, or has a real and effective industrial or commercial establishment in, a Convention country.

whether or not that person carries on business, or has any goodwill, in the United Kingdom.

References to the proprietor of such a mark shall be construed accordingly.

(2) The proprietor of a trade mark which is entitled to protection under the Paris Convention [or the WTO agreement][1] as a well known trade mark is entitled to restrain by injunction the use in the United Kingdom of a trade mark which, or the essential part of which, is identical or similar to his mark, in relation to identical or similar goods or services, where the use is likely to cause confusion.

This right is subject to section 48 (effect of acquiescence by proprietor of earlier trade mark).

(3) Nothing in subsection (2) affects the continuation of any bona fide use of a trade mark begun before the commencement of this section

National emblems, &c. of Convention countries: Article 6ter

6-058 57.—(1) A trade mark which consists of or contains the flag of a Convention country shall not be registered without the authorisation of the competent authorities of that country, unless it appears to the registrar that use of the flag in the manner proposed is permitted without such authorisation.

(2) A trade mark which consists of or contains the armorial bearings or any other state emblem of a Convention country which is protected under the Paris Convention [or the WTO agreement][2] shall not be registered without the authorisation of the competent authorities of that country.

(3) A trade mark which consists of or contains an official sign or hallmark adopted by a Convention country and indicating control and warranty shall not, where the sign or hallmark is protected under the Paris Convention [or the WTO agreement][3], be registered in relation to goods or services of the same, or a similar kind, as those in relation to which it indicates control and warranty, without the authorisation of the competent authorities of the country concerned.

(4) The provisions of this section as to national flags and other state emblems, and official signs or hallmarks, apply equally to anything which from a heraldic point of view imitates any such flag or other emblem, or sign or hallmark.

(5) Nothing in this section prevents the registration of a trade mark on the application of a national of a country who is authorised to make use of a state emblem, or official sign or hallmark, of that country, notwithstanding that it is similar to that of another country.

(6) Where by virtue of this section the authorisation of the competent authorities of a Convention country is or would be required for the registration of a trade mark, those authorities are entitled to restrain by injunction any use of the mark in the United Kingdom without their authorisation.

Emblems, &c. of certain international organisations: Article 6ter

6-059 58.—(1) This section applies to—
(a) the armorial bearings, flags or other emblems, and
(b) the abbreviations and names,

---

[1] Words inserted by SI 1999/1899 Pt IV reg 13 (4)
[2] Words inserted by SI 1999/1899 Pt IV reg 13 (5)
[3] Words inserted by SI 1999/1899 Pt IV reg 13 (5)

of international intergovernmental organisations of which one or more Convention countries are members.

(2) A trade mark which consists of or contains any such emblem, abbreviation or name which is protected under the Paris Convention [or the WTO agreement][1] shall not be registered without the authorisation of the international organisation concerned, unless it appears to the registrar that the use of the emblem, abbreviation or name in the manner proposed—

(a) is not such as to suggest to the public that a connection exists between the organisation and the trade mark, or

(b) is not likely to mislead the public as to the existence of a connection between the user and the organisation.

(3) The provisions of this section as to emblems of an international organisation apply equally to anything which from a heraldic point of view imitates any such emblem.

(4) Where by virtue of this section the authorisation of an international organisation is or would be required for the registration of a trade mark, that organisation is entitled to restrain by injunction any use of the mark in the United Kingdom without its authorisation.

(5) Nothing in this section affects the rights of a person whose bona fide use of the trade mark in question began before 4th January 1962 (when the relevant provisions of the Paris Convention entered into force in relation to the United Kingdom).

Notification under Article 6ter of the Convention

59.—(1) For the purposes of section 57 state emblems of a Convention **6-060** country (other than the national flag), and official signs or hallmarks, shall be regarded as protected under the Paris Convention only if, or to the extent that—

(a) the country in question has notified the United Kingdom in accordance with Article 6ter(3) of the Convention that it desires to protect that emblem, sign or hallmark,

(b) the notification remains in force, and

(c) the United Kingdom has not objected to it in accordance with Article 6ter(4) or any such objection has been withdrawn.

(2) For the purposes of section 58 the emblems, abbreviations and names of an international organisation shall be regarded as protected under the Paris Convention only if, or to the extent that—

(a) the organisation in question has notified the United Kingdom in accordance with Article 6ter(3) of the Convention that it desires to protect that emblem, abbreviation or name,

(b) the notification remains in force, and

(c) the United Kingdom has not objected to it in accordance with Article 6ter(4) or any such objection has been withdrawn.

(3) Notification under Article 6ter(3) of the Paris Convention shall have effect only in relation to applications for registration made more than two months after the receipt of the notification.

(4) The registrar shall keep and make available for public inspection by any person, at all reasonable hours and free of charge, a list of—

(a) the state emblems and official signs or hallmarks, and

(b) the emblems, abbreviations and names of international organisations,

which are for the time being protected under the Paris Convention by virtue of notification under Article 6ter(3).

---

[1] Words inserted by SI 1999/1899 Pt IV reg 13 (6)

[(5) Any reference in this section to Article 6ter of the Paris Convention shall be construed as including a reference to that Article as applied by the WTO agreement.][1]

Acts of agent or representative: Article 6septies

6-061   **60.**—(1) The following provisions apply where an application for registration of a trade mark is made by a person who is an agent or representative of a person who is the proprietor of the mark in a Convention country.

(2) If the proprietor opposes the application, registration shall be refused.

(3) If the application (not being so opposed) is granted, the proprietor may—

   (a) apply for a declaration of the invalidity of the registration, or

   (b) apply for the rectification of the register so as to substitute his name as the proprietor of the registered trade mark.

(4) The proprietor may (notwithstanding the rights conferred by this Act in relation to a registered trade mark) by injunction restrain any use of the trade mark in the United Kingdom which is not authorised by him.

(5) Subsections (2), (3) and (4) do not apply if, or to the extent that, the agent or representative justifies his action.

(6) An application under subsection (3)(a) or (b) must be made within three years of the proprietor becoming aware of the registration; and no injunction shall be granted under subsection (4) in respect of a use in which the proprietor has acquiesced for a continuous period of three years or more.

PART III

ADMINISTRATIVE AND OTHER SUPPLEMENTARY PROVISIONS

The registrar

The register

6-062   **62.** In this Act "the registrar" means the Comptroller-General of Patents, Designs and Trade Marks

The registrar

The register

6-063   **63.**—(1) The registrar shall maintain a register of trade marks.

References in this Act to "the register" are to that register; and references to registration (in particular, in the expression "registered trade mark") are, unless the context otherwise requires, to registration in that register.

(2) There shall be entered in the register in accordance with this Act—

   (a) registered trade marks.

   (b) such particulars as may be prescribed of registrable transactions affecting a registered trade mark, and

   (c) such other matters relating to registered trade marks as may be prescribed.

(3) The register shall be kept in such manner as may be prescribed, and provision shall in particular be made for—

---

[1] Inserted by SI 1999/1899 Pt IV reg 13 (7)

(a) public inspection of the register, and
(b) the supply of certified or uncertified copies, or extracts, of entries in the register.

Rectification or correction of the register

64.—(1) Any person having a sufficient interest may apply for the rectification **6-064** of an error or omission in the register.

Provided that an application for rectification may not be made in respect of a matter affecting the validity of the registration of a trade mark.

(2) An application for rectification may be made either to the registrar or to the court, except that—

(a) if proceedings concerning the trade mark in question are pending in the court, the application must be made to the court; and

(b) if in any other case the application is made to the registrar, he may at any stage of the proceedings refer the application to the court.

(3) Except where the registrar or the court directs otherwise, the effect of rectification of the register is that the error or omission in question shall be deemed never to have been made.

(4) The registrar may, on request made in the prescribed manner by the proprietor of a registered trade mark, or a licensee, enter any change in his name or address as recorded in the register.

(5) The registrar may remove from the register matter appearing to him to have ceased to have effect.

Powers and duties of the registrar

Exclusion of liability in respect of official acts

70.—(1) The registrar shall not be taken to warrant the validity of the registra- **6-065** tion of a trade mark under this Act or under any treaty, convention, arrangement or engagement to which the United Kingdom is a party.

(2) The registrar is not subject to any liability by reason of, or in connection with, any examination required or authorised by this Act, or any such treaty, convention, arrangement or engagement, or any report or other proceedings consequent on such examination.

(3) No proceedings lie against an officer of the registrar in respect of any matter for which, by virtue of this section, the registrar is not liable.

Legal proceedings and appeals

Registration to be prima facie evidence of validity

72. In all legal proceedings relating to a registered trade mark (including pro- **6-066** ceedings for rectification of the register) the registration of a person as proprietor of a trade mark shall be prima facie evidence of the validity of the original registration and of any subsequent assignment or other transmission of it.

Certificate of validity of contested registration

73.—(1) If in proceedings before the court the validity of the registration of a **6-067** trade mark is contested and it is found by the court that the trade mark is validly registered, the court may give a certificate to that effect.

(2) If the court gives such a certificate and in subsequent proceedings—

(a) the validity of the registration is again questioned, and

(b) the proprietor obtains a final order or judgment in his favour,

he is entitled to his costs as between solicitor and client unless the court directs otherwise.

This subsection does not extend to the costs of an appeal in any such proceedings.

Registrar's appearance in proceedings involving the register

6-068   **74.**—(1) In proceedings before the court involving an application for—

(a) the revocation of the registration of a trade mark,

(b) a declaration of the invalidity of the registration of a trade mark, or

(c) the rectification of the register,

the registrar is entitled to appear and be heard, and shall appear if so directed by the court.

(2) Unless otherwise directed by the court, the registrar may instead of appearing submit to the court a statement in writing signed by him, giving particulars of

(a) any proceedings before him in relation to the matter in issue,

(b) the grounds of any decision given by him affecting it,

(c) the practice of the Patent Office in like cases, or

(d) such matters relevant to the issues and within his knowledge as registrar as he thinks fit;

and the statement shall be deemed to form part of the evidence in the proceedings.

(3) Anything which the registrar is or may be authorised or required to do under this section may be done on his behalf by a duly authorised officer.

The court

6-069   **75.** In this Act, unless the context otherwise requires, "the court" means —

(a) in England and Wales and Northern Ireland, the High Court, and

(b) in Scotland, the Court of Session.

Appeals from the registrar

6-070   **76.**—(1) An appeal lies from any decision of the registrar under this Act, except as otherwise expressly provided by rules.

For this purpose "decision" includes any act of the registrar in exercise of a discretion vested in him by or under this Act.

(2) Any such appeal may be brought either to an appointed person or to the court

(3) Where an appeal is made to an appointed person, he may refer the appeal to the court if—

(a) it appears to him that a point of general legal importance is involved.

(b) the registrar requests that it be so referred, or

(c) such a request is made by any party to the proceedings before the registrar in which the decision appealed against was made.

Before doing so the appointed person shall give the appellant and any other party to the appeal an opportunity to make representations as to whether the appeal should be referred to the court.

(4) Where an appeal is made to an appointed person and he does not refer it to the court, he shall hear and determine the appeal and his decision shall be final.

(5) The provisions of sections 68 and 69 (costs and security for costs; evidence) apply in relation to proceedings before an appointed person as in relation to proceedings before the registrar.

Persons appointed to hear and determine appeals

77.—(1) For the purposes of section 76 an "appointed person" means a **6-071** person appointed by the Lord Chancellor to hear and decide appeals under this Act.

Rules, fees, hours of business, &c

The trade marks journal

81. Provision shall be made by rules for the publication by the registrar of a **6-072** journal containing particulars of any application for the registration of a trade mark (including a representation of the mark) and such other information relating to trade marks as the registrar thinks fit.

Importation of infringing goods, material or articles

Infringing goods, material or articles may be treated as prohibited goods

89.—(1) The proprietor of a registered trade mark, or a licensee, may give **6-073** notice in writing to the Commissioners of Customs and Excise—
  (a) that he is the proprietor or, as the case may be, a licensee of the registered trade mark,
  (b) that, at a time and place specified in the notice, goods which are, in relation to that registered trade mark, infringing goods, material or articles are expected to arrive in the United Kingdom—
    (i) from outside the European Economic Area, or
    (ii) from within that Area but not having been entered for free circulation, and
  (c) that he requests the Commissioners to treat them as prohibited goods.

(2) When a notice is in force under this section the importation of the goods to which the notice relates, otherwise than by a person for his private and domestic use, is prohibited; but a person is not by reason of the prohibition liable to any penalty other than forfeiture of the goods.

[(3) This section does not apply to goods entered, or expected to be entered, for free circulation, export, re-export or for a suspensive procedure in respect of which an application may be made under Article 3(1) of Council Regulation (EC) No. 3295/94 laying down measures to prohibit the release for free circulation, export, re-export or entry for a suspensive procedure of counterfeit and pirated goods.]¹

Offences

Unauthorised use of trade mark, &c. in relation to goods

92.—(1) A person commits an offence who with a view to gain for himself or **6-074** another, or with intent to cause loss to another, and without the consent of the proprietor—

---
¹ Substituted by SI 1995/1444 reg 2

    (a) applies to goods or their packaging a sign identical to, or likely to be mistaken form, a registered trade mark, or

    (b) sells or lets for hire, offers or exposes for sale or hire or distributes goods which bear, or the packaging of which bears, such a sign, or

    (c) has in his possession, custody or control in the course of a business any such goods with a view to the doing of anything, by himself or another, which would be an offence under paragraph (b).

(2) A person commits an offence who with a view to gain for himself or another, or with intent to cause loss to another, and without the consent of the proprietor—

    (a) applies a sign identical to, or likely to be mistaken for, a registered trade mark to material intended to be used—

        (i) for labelling or packaging goods,

        (ii) as a business paper in relation to goods, or

        (iii) for advertising goods, or

    (b) uses in the course of a business material bearing such a sign for labelling or packaging goods, as a business paper in relation to goods, or for advertising goods, or

    (c) has in his possession, custody or control in the course of a business any such material with a view to the doing of anything, by himself or another, which would be an offence under paragraph (b).

(3) A person commits an offence who with a view to gain for himself or another, or with intent to cause loss to another, and without the consent of the proprietor—

    (a) makes an article specifically designed or adapted for making copies of a sign identical to, or likely to be mistaken for, a registered trade mark, or

    (b) has such an article in his possession, custody or control in the course of a business,

knowing or having reason to believe that it has been, or is to be, used to produce goods, or material for labelling or packaging goods, as a business paper in relation to goods, or for advertising goods.

(4) A person does not commit an offence under this section unless—

    (a) the goods are goods in respect of which the trade mark is registered, or

    (b) the trade mark has a reputation in the United Kingdom and the use of the sign takes or would take unfair advantage of, or is or would be detrimental to, the distinctive character or the repute of the trade mark.

(5) It is a defence for a person charged with an offence under this section to show that he believed on reasonable grounds that the use of the sign in the manner in which it was used, or was to be used, was not an infringement of the registered trade mark.

(6) A person guilty of an offence under this section is liable—

    (a) on summary conviction to imprisonment for a term not exceeding six months or a fine not exceeding the statutory maximum, or both;

    (b) on conviction on indictment to a fine or imprisonment for a term not exceeding ten years, or both.

[Search warrants

6-075   **92A**—(1) Where a justice of the peace (in Scotland, a sheriff or justice of the peace) is satisfied by information on oath given by a constable (in Scotland, by evidence on oath) that there are reasonable grounds for believing—

(a) that an offence under section 92 (unauthorised use of trade mark, etc. in relation to goods) has been or is about to be committed in any premises, and

(b) that evidence that such an offence has been or is about to be committed is in those premises,

he may issue a warrant authorising a constable to enter and search the premises, using such reasonable force as is necessary.

(2) The power conferred by subsection (1) does not, in England and Wales, extend to authorising a search for material of the kinds mentioned in section 9(2) of the Police and Criminal Evidence Act 1984 (c. 60) (certain classes of personal or confidential material).

(3) A warrant under subsection (1)—

(a) may authorise persons to accompany any constable executing the warrant, and

(b) remains in force for 28 days from the date of its issue.

(4) In executing a warrant issued under subsection (1) a constable may seize an article if he reasonably believes that it is evidence that any offence under section 92 has been or is about to be committed.

(5) In this section "premises" includes land, buildings, fixed or moveable structures, vehicles, vessels, aircraft and hovercraft.][1]

Enforcement function of local weights and measures authority

93.—(1) It is the duty of every local weights and measures authority to **6-076** enforce within their area the provisions of section 92 (unauthorised use of trade mark, &c. in relation to goods).

(2) The following provisions of the Trade Descriptions Act 1968 apply in relation to the enforcement of that section as in relation to the enforcement of that Act—

section 27 (power to make test purchases),

section 28 (power to enter premises and inspect and seize goods and documents),

section 29 (obstruction of authorised officers), and

section 33 (compensation for loss, &c. of goods seized).

(3) Subsection (1) above does not apply in relation to the enforcement of section 92 in Northern Ireland, but it is the duty of the Department of Economic Development to enforce that section in Northern Ireland.

For that purpose the provisions of the Trade Descriptions Act 1968 specified in subsection (2) apply as if for the references to a local weights and measures authority and any officer of such an authority there were substituted references to that Department and any of its officers.

(4) Any enactment which authorises the disclosure of information for the purpose of facilitating the enforcement of the Trade Descriptions Act 1968 shall apply as if section 92 above were contained in that Act and as if the functions of any person in relation to the enforcement of that section were functions under that Act.

(5) Nothing in this section shall be construed as authorising a local weights and measures authority to bring proceedings in Scotland for an offence.

---

[1] Inserted by Copyright, etc. and Trade Marks (Offences and Enforcement) Act 2002 c.25 s 6

Falsification of register, &c

6-077   **94.**—(1) It is an offence for a person to make, or cause to be made, a false entry in the register of trade marks, knowing or having reason to believe that it is false.

(2) It is an offence for a person—

(a) to make or cause to be made anything falsely purporting to be a copy of an entry in the register, or

(b) to produce or tender or cause to be produced or tendered in evidence any such thing,

knowing or having reason to believe that it is false.

(3) A person guilty of an offence under this section is liable—

(a) on conviction on indictment, to imprisonment for a term not exceeding two years or a fine, or both;

(b) on summary conviction, to imprisonment for a term not exceeding six months or a fine not exceeding the statutory maximum, or both.

Falsely representing trade mark as registered

6-078   **95.**—(1) It is an offence for a person—

(a) falsely to represent that a mark is a registered trade mark, or

(b) to make a false representation as to the goods or services for which a trade mark is registered

knowing or having reason to believe that the representation is false.

(2) For the purposes of this section, the use in the United Kingdom in relation to a trade mark—

(a) of the word "registered", or

(b) of any other word or symbol importing a reference (express or implied) to registration,

shall be deemed to be a representation as to registration under this Act unless it is shown that the reference is to registration elsewhere than in the United Kingdom and that the trade mark is in fact so registered for the goods or services in question.

(3) A person guilty of an offence under this section is liable on summary conviction to a fine not exceeding level 3 on the standard scale.

Forfeiture of counterfeit goods, &c

Forfeiture; England and Wales or Northern Ireland

6-079   **97.**—(1) In England and Wales or Northern Ireland where there has come into the possession of any person in connection with the investigation or prosecution of a relevant offence—

(a) goods which, or the packaging of which, bears a sign identical to or likely to be mistaken for a registered trade mark,

(b) material bearing such a sign and intended to be used for labelling or packaging goods, as a business paper in relation to goods, or for advertising goods, or

(c) articles specifically designed or adapted for making copies of such a sign,

that person may apply under this section for an order for the forfeiture of the goods, material or articles.

(2) An application under this section may be made—

(a) where proceedings have been brought in any court for a relevant offence relating to some or all of the goods, material or articles, to that court;

(b) where no application for the forfeiture of the goods, material or articles has been made under paragraph (a), by way of complaint to a magistrates'court.

(3) On an application under this section the court shall make an order for the forfeiture of any goods, material or articles only if it is satisfied that a relevant offence has been committed in relation to the goods, material or articles.

(4) A court may infer for the purposes of this section that such an offence has been committed in relation to any goods, material or articles if it is satisfied that such an offence has been committed in relation to goods, material or articles which are representative of them (whether by reason of being of the same design or part of the same consignment or batch or otherwise).

(5) Any person aggrieved by an order made under this section by a magistrates court, or by a decision of such a court not to make such an order, may appeal against that order or decision—

(a) in England and Wales, to the Crown Court;

(b) in Northern Ireland, to the county court,

and an order so made may contain such provision as appears to the court to be appropriate for delaying the coming into force of the order pending the making and determination of any appeal (including any application under section 111 of the Magistrates' Courts Act 1980 or Article 146 of the Magistrates' Courts (Northern Ireland) Order 1981 (statement of case))

(6) Subject to subsection (7), where any goods, material or articles are forfeited under this section they shall be destroyed in accordance with such directions as the court may give.

(7) On making an order under this section the court may, if it considers it appropriate to do so, direct that the goods, material or articles to which the order relates shall (instead of being destroyed) be released, to such person as the court may specify, on condition that that person—

(a) causes the offending sign to be erased, removed or obliterated, and

(b) complies with any order to pay costs which has been made against him in the proceedings for the order for forfeiture.

(8) For the purposes of this section a "relevant offence" means an offence under section 92 above (unauthorised use of trade mark, &c. in relation to goods) or under the Trade Descriptions Act 1968 or any offence involving dishonesty or deception.

Forfeiture; Scotland

98.—(1) In Scotland the court may make an order for the forfeiture of any—   **6-080**

(a) goods which bear, or the packaging of which bears, a sign identical to or likely to be mistaken for a registered trade mark,

(b) material bearing such a sign and intended to be used for labelling or packaging goods, as a.business paper in relation to goods, or for advertising goods, or

(c) articles specifically designed or adapted for making copies of such a sign.

(2) An order under this section may be made—

(a) on an application by the procurator-fiscal made in the manner specified in [section 134 of the Criminal Procedure (Scotland) Act 1995][1], or

(b) where a person is convicted of a relevant offence, in addition to any other penalty which the court may impose.

(3) On an application under subsection (2)(a), the court shall make an order for the forfeiture of any goods, material or articles only if it is satisfied that a relevant offence has been committed in relation to the goods, material or articles.

(4) The court may infer for the purposes of this section that such an offence has been committed in relation to any goods, material or articles if it is satisfied that such an offence has been committed in relation to goods, material or articles which are representative of them (whether by reason of being of the same design or part of the same consignment or batch or otherwise).

(5) The procurator-fiscal making the application under subsection (2)(a) shall serve on any person appearing to him to be the owner of, or otherwise to have an interest in, the goods, material or articles to which the application relates a copy of the application, together with a notice giving him the opportunity to appear at the hearing of the application to show cause why the goods, material or articles should not be forfeited.

(6) Service under subsection (5) shall be carried out, and such service may be proved, in the manner specified for citation of an accused in summary proceedings under the [Criminal Procedure (Scotland) Act 1995][2].

(7) Any person upon whom notice is served under subsection (5) and any other person claiming to be the owner of, or otherwise to have an interest in, goods, material or articles to which an application under this section relates shall be entitled to appear at the hearing of the application to show cause why the goods, material or articles should not be forfeited.

(8) The court shall not make an order following an application under subsection (2)(a)—

(a) if any person on whom notice is served under subsection (5) does not appear, unless service of the notice on that person is proved; or

(b) if no notice under subsection (5) has been served, unless the court is satisfied that in the circumstances it was reasonable not to serve such notice.

(9) Where an order for the forfeiture of any goods, material or articles is made following an application under subsection (2)(a) any person who appeared, or was entitled to appear, to show cause why goods, material or articles should not be forfeited may, within 21 days of the making of the order, appeal to the High Court by Bill of suspension; and [section 182(5)(a) to (e) of the Criminal Procedure (Scotland) Act 1995][3] shall apply to an appeal under this subsection as it applies to a stated case under Part II of that Act.

(10) An order following an application under subsection (2)(a) shall not take effect—

(a) until the end of the period of 21 days beginning with the day after the day on which the order is made; or

---

[1] Words substituted by Criminal Procedure (Consequential Provisions) (Scotland) Act 1995 c.40 Sch 4 para 92 (3) (a)

[2] Words substituted by Criminal Procedure (Consequential Provisions) (Scotland) Act 1995 c.40 Sch 4 para 92 (3) (b)

[3] Words substituted by Criminal Procedure (Consequential Provisions) (Scotland) Act 1995 c.40 Sch 4 para 92 (3) (c)

(b) if an appeal is made under subsection (9) above within that period, until the appeal is determined or abandoned

(11) An order under subsection (2)(b) shall not take effect—

(a) until the end of the period within which an appeal against the order could be brought under the [Criminal Procedure (Scotland) Act 1995][1]; or

(b) if an appeal is made within that period, until the appeal is determined or abandoned.

(12) Subject to subsection (13), goods, material or articles forfeited under this section shall be destroyed in accordance with such directions as the court may give.

(13) On making an order under this section the court may if it considers it appropriate to do so, direct that the goods, material or articles to which the order relates shall (instead of being destroyed) be released, to such person as the court may specify, on condition that that person causes the offending sign to be erased, removed or obliterated

(14) For the purposes of this section—

"relevant offence" means an offence under section 92 (unauthorised use of trade mark, &c. in relation to goods) or under the Trade Descriptions Act 1968 or any offence involving dishonesty or deception,

"the court" means —

(a) in relation to an order made on an application under subsection (2)(a), the sheriff, and

(b) in relation to an order made unless subsection (2)(b), the court which imposed the penalty.

PART IV

MISCELLANEOUS AND GENERAL PROVISIONS

Miscellaneous

Unauthorised use of Royal arms. &c

99.—(1) A person shall not without the authority of Her Majesty use in **6-081** connection with any business the Royal arms (or arms so closely resembling the Royal arms as to be calculated to deceive) in such manner as to be calculated to lead to the belief that he is duly authorised to use the Royal arms.

(2) A person shall not without the authority of Her Majesty or of a member of the Royal family use in connection with any business any device, emblem or title in such a manner as to be calculated to lead to the belief that he is employed by, or supplies goods or services to Her Majesty or that member of the Royal family.

(3) A person who contravenes subsection (1) commits an offence and is liable on summary conviction to a fine not exceeding level 2 on the standard scale.

(4) Contravention of subsection (1) or (2) may be restrained by injunction in proceedings brought by—

(a) any person who is authorised to use the arms, device, emblem or title in question, or

---

[1] Words substituted by Criminal Procedure (Consequential Provisions) (Scotland) Act 1995 c.40 Sch 4 para 92 (3) (d)

(b) any person authorised by the Lord Chamberlain to take such proceedings

(5) Nothing in this section affects any right of the proprietor of a trade mark
containing any such arms, device, emblem or title to use that trade mark.

Burden of proving use of trade mark

6-082   **100.** If in any civil proceedings under this Act a question arises as to the use
to which a registered trade mark has been put, if is for the proprietor to show
what use has been made of it.

Interpretation

Adaptation of expressions for Scotland

6-083   **102.** In the application of this Act to Scotland—
"account of profits" means accounting and payment of profits.
"accounts" means count, reckoning and payment.
"assignment" means assignation;
"costs" means expenses;
"declaration" means declarator;
"defendant" means defender;
"delivery up" means delivery;
"injunction" means interdict;
"interlocutory relief" means interim remedy; and
"plaintiff" means pursuer.

Minor definitions

6-084   **103.**—(1) In this Act—
"business" includes a trade or profession;
"director", in relation to a body corporate whose affairs are managed by its
members, means any member of the body;
"infringement proceedings", in relation to a registered trade mark,
includes proceedings under section 16 (order for delivery up of
infringing goods, &c.);
"publish" means make available to the public, and references to publication—
(a) in relation to an application for registration, are to publication
under section 38(1), and
(b) in relation to registration, are to publication under section 40(4);

"statutory provisions" includes provisions of subordinate legislation within
the meaning of the Interpretation Act 1978;
"trade" includes any business or profession..

(2) References in this Act to use (or any particular description of use) of a
trade mark, or of a sign identical with, similar to, or likely to be mistaken for a
trade mark, include use (or that description of use) otherwise than by means of a
graphic representation.

(3) References in this Act to a Community instrument include references to
any instrument amending or replacing that instrument

Index of defined expressions

104. In this Act the expressions listed below are defined by or otherwise fall **6-085** to be construed in accordance with the provisions indicated—

account of profits and accounts (in Scotland)	section 102
appointed person (for purposes of section 76)	section 77
assignment (in Scotland)	section 102
business	section 103(1)
certification mark	section 50(1)
collective mark	section 49(1)
commencement (of this Act)	section 109(2)
Community trade mark	section 51
Community Trade Mark Regulation	section 51
Convention country	section 55(1)(b)
costs (in Scotland)	section 102
the court	section 75
date of application	section 33(2)
date of filing	section 33(1)
date of registration	section 40(3)
defendant (in Scotland)	section 102
delivery up (in Scotland)	section 102
director	section 103(1)
earlier right	section 5(4)
earlier trade mark	section 6
exclusive licence and licensee	section 29(1)
infringement (of registered trade mark)	section 9(1) and (2) and 10
infringement proceedings	section 103(1)
infringing articles	section 17
infringing goods	section 17
infringing material	section 17
injunction (in Scotland)	section 102
interlocutory relief (in Scotland)	section 102
the International Bureau	section 53
International trade mark (UK)	section 53
Madrid Protocol	section 53

Paris Convention	section 55(1)(a)
plaintiff (in Scotland)	section 102
prescribed	section 78(1)(b)
protected under the Paris Convention	
—well-known trade marks	section 56(1)
—state emblems and official signs or hallmarks	section 57(1)
—emblems, &c. of international organisations	section 58(2)
publish and references to publication	section 103(1)
register, registered (and related expressions)	section 63(1)
registered trade mark agent	section 83(1)
registrable transaction	section 25(2)
the registrar	section 62
rules	section 78
statutory provisions	section 103(1)
trade	section 103(1)
trade mark	
—generally	section 1(1)
—includes collective mark or certification mark	section 1(2)
United Kingdom (references include Isle of Man)	section 108(2)
use (of trade mark or sign)	section 103(2)
well-known trade mark (under Paris Convention)	section 56(1)

Other general provisions

Territorial waters and the continental shelf

6-086   **107.**—(1) For the purposes of this Act the territorial waters of the United Kingdom shall be treated as part of the United Kingdom.

(2) This Act applies to things done in the United Kingdom sector of the continental shelf on a structure or vessel which is present there for purposes directly connected with the exploration of the sea bed or subsoil or the exploitation of their natural resources as it applies to things done in the United Kingdom.

(3) The United Kingdom sector of the continental shelf means the areas designated by order under section 1(7) of the Continental Shelf Act 1964.

Extent

6-087   **108.**—(1) This Act extends to England and Wales, Scotland and Northern Ireland.

(2) This Act also extends to the Isle of Man, subject to such exceptions and modifications as Her Majesty may specify by Order in Council, and subject to

any such Order references in this Act to the United Kingdom shall be construed as including the Isle of Man.

SCHEDULES

Schedule 1

COLLECTIVE MARKS

General

1. The provisions of this Act apply to collective marks subject to the following provisions.   **6-088**

Signs of which a collective mark may consist

2. In relation to a collective mark the reference in section 1(1) (signs of which a trade mark may   **6-089**
consist) to distinguishing goods or services of one undertaking from those of other undertakings shall
be construed as a reference to distinguishing goods or services of members of the association which
is the proprietor of the mark from those of other undertakings.

Indication of geographical origin

3.—(1) Notwithstanding section 3(1)(c), a collective mark may be registered which consists of   **6-090**
signs or indications which may serve, in trade, to designate the geographical origin of the goods or
services.

(2) However, the proprietor of such a mark is not entitled to prohibit the use of the signs or indications in accordance with honest practices in industrial or commercial matters (in particular, by a
person who is entitled to use a geographical name).

Mark not to be misleading as to character or significance

4.—(1) A collective mark shall not be registered if the public is liable to be misled as regards the   **6-091**
character or significance of the mark, in particular if it is likely to be taken to be something other than
a collective mark.

(2) The registrar may accordingly require that a mark in respect of which application is made for
registration include some indication that it is a collective mark.

Notwithstanding section 39(2), an application may be amended so as to comply with any such
requirement.

Regulations governing use of collective mark

5.—(1) An applicant for registration of a collective mark must fine with the registrar regulations   **6-092**
governing the use of the mark.

(2) The regulations must specify the persons authorised to use the mark, the conditions of
membership of the association and, where they exist, the conditions of use of the mark, including any
sanctions against misuse.

Further requirements with which the regulations have to comply may be imposed by rules.

Approval of regulations by registrar

6.—(1) A collective mark shall not be registered unless the regulations governing the use of the   **6-093**
mark—

(a) comply with paragraph 5(2) and any further requirements imposed by rules, and

(b) are not contrary to public policy or to accepted principles of morality

(2) Before the end of the prescribed period after the date of the application for registration of a collective mark, the applicant must file the regulations with the registrar and pay the prescribed fee.

If he does not do so, the application shall be deemed to be withdrawn.

6-094   **7.**—(1) The registrar shall consider whether the requirements mentioned in paragraph 6(1) are met.

(2) If it appears to the registrar that those requirements are not met, he shall the applicant and give him an opportunity, within such period as the registrar may specify, to make representations or to file amended regulations.

(3) If the applicant fails to satisfy the registrar that those requirements are not, or to file regulations amended so as to meet them, or fails to respond before the end of the specified period, the registrar shall refuse the application.

(4) If it appears to the registrar that those requirements, and the other requirements for registration, are met, he shall accept the application and shall proceed in accordance with section 38 (publication, opposition proceedings and observations).

6-095   **8.** The regulations shall be published and notice of opposition may be given, and observations may be made, relating to the matters mentioned in paragraph 6(1).

This is in addition to any other grounds on which the application may be opposed or observations made.

Regulations to be open to inspection

6-096   **9.** The regulations governing the use of a registered collective mark shall be open to public inspection in the same way as the register.

Amendment of regulations

6-097   **10.**—(1) An amendment of the regulations governing the use of a registered collective mark is not effective unless and until the amended regulations are filed with the registrar and accepted by him.

(2) Before accepting any amended regulations the registrar may in any case where it appears to him expedient to do so cause them to be published.

(3) If he does so, notice of opposition may be given, and observations may be made, relating to the matters mentioned in paragraph 6(1).

Infringement rights of authorised users

6-098   **11.** The following provisions apply in relation to an authorised user of a registered collective mark as in relation to a licensee of a trade mark—

(a) section 10(5) (definition of infringement: unauthorised application of mark to certain material);

(b) section 19(2) (order as to disposal of infringing goods, material or articles adequacy of other remedies);

(c) section 89 (prohibition of importation of infringing goods, material or articles request to Commissioners of Customs and Excise).

6-099   **12.**—(1) The following provisions (which correspond to the provisions of section 30 general provisions as to rights of licensees in case of infringement) have effect as regards the rights of an authorised user in relation to infringement of a registered collective mark.

(2) An authorised user is entitled, subject to any agreement to the contrary between him and the proprietor, to call on the proprietor to take infringement proceedings in respect of any matter which affects his interests.

(3) If the proprietor—

(a) refuses to do so, or

(b) fails to do so within two months after being called upon,

the authorised user may bring the proceedings in his own name as if he were the proprietor.

(4) Where infringement proceedings are brought by virtue of this paragraph, the authorised user may not, without the leave of the court, proceed with the action unless the proprietor is either joined as a plaintiff or added as a defendant.

This does not affect the granting of interlocutory relief on an application by an authorised user alone.

(5) A proprietor who is added as a defendant as mentioned in sub-paragraph (4) shall not be made liable for any costs in the action unless he takes part in the proceedings.

(6) In infringement proceedings brought by the proprietor of a registered collective mark any loss suffered or likely to be suffered by authorised users shall be taken into account; and the court may give such directions as it thinks fit as to the extent to which the plaintiff is to hold the proceeds of any pecuniary remedy on behalf of such users.

Grounds for revocation of registration

13. Apart from the grounds of revocation provided for in section 46, the registration of a **6-100** collective mark may be revoked on the ground

> (a) that the manner in which the mark has been used by the proprietor has caused it to become liable to mislead the public in the manner referred to in paragraph 4(1); or
>
> (b) that the proprietor has failed to observe, or to secure the observance of, the regulations governing the use of the mark, or
>
> (c) that an amendment of the regulations has been made so that the regulations
>
> > (i) no longer comply with paragraph 5(2) and any further conditions imposed by rules, or
> >
> > (ii) are contrary to public policy or to accepted principles of morality.

Grounds for invalidity of registration

14. Apart from the grounds of invalidity provided for in section 47, the registration of a collective **6-101** mark may be declared invalid on the ground that the mark was registered in breach of the provisions of paragraph 4(1) or 6(1)

Section 50   Schedule 2

CERTIFICATION MARKS

General

1. The provisions of this Act apply to certification marks subject to the following provisions.   **6-102**

Signs of which a certification mark may consist

2. In relation to a certification mark the reference in section 1(1) (signs of which a trade mark **6-103** may consist) to distinguishing goods or services of one undertaking from those of other undertakings shall be construed as a reference to distinguishing goods or services which are certified from those which are not.

Indication of geographical origin

3.—(1) Notwithstanding section 3(1)(c) a certification mark may be registered which consists of **6-104** signs or indications which may serve, in trade, to designate the geographical origin of the goods or services.

(2) However, the proprietor of such a mark is not entitled to prohibit the use of the signs or indications in accordance with honest practices in industrial or commercial matters (in particular, by a person who is entitled to use a geographical name).

Nature of proprietor's business

4. A certification mark shall not be registered if the proprietor carries on a business involving **6-105** the supply of goods or services of the kind certified.

Mark not to be misleading as to character or significance

6-106

—(1) A certification mark shall not be registered if the public is liable to be misled as regards the character or significance of the mark, in particular if it is likely to be taken to be something other than a certification mark.

(2) The registrar may accordingly require that a mark in respect of which application is made for registration include some indication that it is a certification mark.

Notwithstanding section 39(2); an application may be amended so as to comply with any such requirement.

Regulations governing use of certification mark

6-107   **6.**—(1) An applicant for registration of a certification mark must file with the registrar regulations governing the use of the mark.

(2) The regulations must indicate who is authorised to use the mark, the characteristics to be certified by the mark, how the certifying body is to test those characteristics and to supervise the use of the mark, the fees (if any) to be paid in connection with the operation of the mark and the procedures for resolving disputes.

Further requirements with which the regulations have to comply may be imposed by rules.

Approval of regulations, &c

6-108   **7.**—(1) A certification mark shall not be registered unless—
  (a) the regulations governing the use of the mark—
      (i) comply with paragraph 6(2) and any further requirements imposed by rules, and
      (ii) are not contrary to public policy or to accepted principles of morality, and
  (b) the applicant is competent to certify the goods or services for which the mark is to be registered.

(2) Before the end of the prescribed period after the date of the application for registration of a certification mark, the applicant must file the regulations with the registrar and pay the prescribed fee.

If he does not do so, the application shall be deemed to be withdrawn.

8.—

6-109   (1) The registrar shall consider whether the requirements mentioned in paragraph 7(1) are met.

(2) If it appears to the registrar that those requirements are not met, he shall inform the applicant and give him an opportunity, within such period as the registrar may specify, to make representations or to file amended regulations.

(3) If the applicant fails to satisfy the registrar that those requirements are met, or to file regulations amended so as to meet them, or fails to respond before the end of the specified period, the registrar shall refuse the application.

(4) If it appears to the registrar that those requirements, and the other requirements for registration, are met, he shall accept the application and shall proceed in accordance with section 38 (publication, opposition proceedings and observations).

6-110   **9.** The regulations shall be published and notice of opposition may be given, and observations may be made, relating to the matters mentioned in paragraph 7(1)

This is in addition to any other grounds on which the application may be opposed or observations made.

Regulations to be open to inspection

6-111   **10.** The regulations governing the use of a registered certification mark shall be open to public inspection in the same way as the register.

Amendment of regulations

6-112   **11.**—(1) An amendment of the regulations governing the use of a registered certification mark is not effective unless and until the amended regulations art filed with the registrar and accepted by him.

(2) Before accepting any amended regulations the registrar may in any case where it appears to him expedient to do so cause them to be published.

(3) If he does so, notice of opposition may be given, and observations may be made, relating to the matters mentioned in paragraph 7(1).

Consent to assignment of registered certification mark

12. The assignment or other transmission of a registered certification mark is not effective **6-113** without the consent of the registrar.

Infringement rights of authorised users

13. The following provisions apply in relation to an authorised user of a registered certification **6-114** mark as in relation to a licensee of a trade mark—

    (a) section 10(5) (definition of infringement unauthorised application of mark to certain material);

    (b) section 19(2) (order as to disposal of infringing goods, material or articles: adequacy of other remedies);

    (c) section 89 (prohibition of importation of infringing goods, material or articles request to Commissioners of Customs and Excise).

14. In infringement proceedings brought by the proprietor of a registered certification mark any **6-115** loss suffered or likely to be suffered by authorised users shall be taken into account, and the court may give such directions as it thinks fit as to the extent to which the plaintiff is to told the proceeds of any pecuniary remedy on behalf of such users.

Grounds for revocation of registration

15. Apart from the grounds of revocation provided for in section 46, the registration of a certifica- **6-116** tion mark may be revoked on the ground—

    (a) that the proprietor has begun to carry on such a business as is mentioned in paragraph 4.

    (b) that the manner in which the mark has been used by the proprietor has caused it to become liable to mislead the public in the manner referred to in paragraph 5(1),

    (c) that the proprietor has failed to observe, or to secure the observance of, the regulations governing the use of the mark,

    (d) that an amendment of the regulations has been made so that the regulations—

        (i) no longer comply with paragraph 6(2) and any further conditions imposed by rules, or

        (ii) are contrary to public policy or to accepted principles of morality, or

    (e) that the proprietor is no longer competent to certify the goods or services for which the mark is registered.

Grounds for invalidity of registration

16. Apart from the grounds of invalidity provided for in section 47, the registration of a certifica- **6-117** tion mark may be declared invalid on the ground that the mark was registered in breach of the provisions of paragraph 4, 5(1) or 7(1)

Trade Marks (Amendment) Rules 2001

(S.I. 3832)

Rule 7(2)   Schedule 4

[CLASSIFICATION OF GOODS AND SERVICES

[Goods

[**Class 1** Chemicals used in industry, science and photography, as well as in **7-001** agriculture, horticulture and forestry; unprocessed artificial resins, unprocessed plastics; manures; fire extinguishing compositions; tempering and soldering preparations; chemical substances for preserving foodstuffs; tanning substances; adhesives used in industry.][1]

7-002   [**Class 2** Paints, varnishes, lacquers; preservatives against rust and against deterioration of wood; colorants; mordants; raw natural resins; metals in foil and powder form for painters, decorators, printers and artists.][2]

7-003   [**Class 3** Bleaching preparations and other substances for laundry use; cleaning, polishing, scouring and abrasive preparations; soaps; perfumery, essential oils, cosmetics, hair lotions; dentifrices.][3]

7-004   [**Class 4** Industrial oils and greases; lubricants; dust absorbing, wetting and binding compositions; fuels (including motor spirit) and illuminants; candles and wicks for lighting.][4]

7-005   [**Class 5** Pharmaceutical and veterinary preparations; sanitary preparations for medical purposes; dietetic substances adapted for medical use, food for babies; plasters, materials for dressings; material for stopping teeth, dental wax; disinfectants; preparations for destroying vermin; fungicides, herbicides.][5]

7-006   [**Class 6** Common metals and their alloys; metal building materials; transportable buildings of metal; materials of metal for railway tracks; non-electric cables and wires of common metal; ironmongery, small items of metal hardware; pipes and tubes of metal; safes; goods of common metal not included in other classes; ores.][6]

7-007   [**Class 7** Machines and machine tools; motors and engines (except for land vehicles); machine coupling and transmission components (except for land vehicles); agricultural implements other than hand-operated; incubators for eggs.][7]

7-008   [**Class 8** Hand tools and implements (hand-operated); cutlery; side arms; razors.][8]

7-009   [**Class 9** Scientific, nautical, surveying, photographic, cinematographic, optical, weighing, measuring, signalling, checking (supervision), life-saving and teaching apparatus and instruments; apparatus and instruments for conducting, switching, transforming, accumulating, regulating or controlling electricity; apparatus for recording, transmission or reproduction of sound or images; magnetic data carriers, recording discs; automatic vending machines and mechanisms for coin-operated apparatus; cash registers, calculating machines, data processing equipment and computers; fire-extinguishing apparatus.][9]

7-010   [**Class 10** Surgical, medical, dental and veterinary apparatus and instruments, artificial limbs, eyes and teeth; orthopedic articles; suture materials.][10]

---

[1] Inserted by SI 2001/3832 reg 8
[2] Inserted by SI 2001/3832 reg 8
[3] Inserted by SI 2001/3832 reg 8
[4] Inserted by SI 2001/3832 reg 8
[5] Inserted by SI 2001/3832 reg 8
[6] Inserted by SI 2001/3832 reg 8
[7] Inserted by SI 2001/3832 reg 8
[8] Inserted by SI 2001/3832 reg 8
[9] Inserted by SI 2001/3832 reg 8
[10] Inserted by SI 2001/3832 reg 8

[**Class 11** Apparatus for lighting, heating, steam generating, cooking, refriger- **7-011** ating, drying, ventilating, water supply and sanitary purposes.][1]

[**Class 12** Vehicles; apparatus for locomotion by land, air or water.][2] **7-012**

[**Class 13** Firearms; ammunition and projectiles; explosives; fireworks.][3] **7-013**

[**Class 14** Precious metals and their alloys and goods in precious metals or **7-014** coated therewith, not included in other classes; jewellery, precious stones; horological and chronometric instruments.][4]

[**Class 15** Musical instruments.][5] **7-015**

[**Class 16** Paper, cardboard and goods made from these materials, not **7-016** included in other classes; printed matter; bookbinding material; photographs; stationery; adhesives for stationery or household purposes; artists' materials; paint brushes; typewriters and office requisites (except furniture); instructional and teaching material (except apparatus); plastic materials for packaging (not included in other classes); printers' type; printing blocks.][6]

[**Class 17** Rubber, gutta-percha, gum, asbestos, mica and goods made from **7-017** these materials and not included in other classes; plastics in extruded form for use in manufacture; packing, stopping and insulating materials; flexible pipes, not of metal.][7]

[**Class 18** Leather and imitations of leather, and goods made of these **7-018** materials and not included in other classes; animal skins, hides; trunks and travelling bags; umbrellas, parasols and walking sticks; whips, harness and saddlery.][8]

[**Class 19** Building materials (non-metallic); non-metallic rigid pipes for **7-019** building; asphalt, pitch and bitumen; non-metallic transportable buildings; monuments, not of metal.][9]

[**Class 20** Furniture, mirrors, picture frames; goods (not included in other **7-020** classes) of wood, cork, reed, cane, wicker, horn, bone, ivory, whalebone, shell, amber, mother-of-pearl, meerschaum and substitutes for all these materials, or of plastics.][10]

[**Class 21** Household or kitchen utensils and containers (not of precious **7-021** metal or coated therewith); combs and sponges; brushes (except paint brushes); brush-making materials; articles for cleaning purposes; steelwool; unworked or semi-worked glass (except glass used in building); glassware, porcelain and earthenware not included in other classes.][11]

---

[1] Inserted by SI 2001/3832 reg 8
[2] Inserted by SI 2001/3832 reg 8
[3] Inserted by SI 2001/3832 reg 8
[4] Inserted by SI 2001/3832 reg 8
[5] Inserted by SI 2001/3832 reg 8
[6] Inserted by SI 2001/3832 reg 8
[7] Inserted by SI 2001/3832 reg 8
[8] Inserted by SI 2001/3832 reg 8
[9] Inserted by SI 2001/3832 reg 8
[10] Inserted by SI 2001/3832 reg 8
[11] Inserted by SI 2001/3832 reg 8

7-022 [**Class 22** Ropes, string, nets, tents, awnings, tarpaulins, sails, sacks and bags (not included in other classes); padding and stuffing materials (except of rubber or plastics); raw fibrous textile materials.][1]

7-023 [**Class 23** Yarns and threads, for textile use.][2]

7-024 [**Class 24** Textiles and textile goods, not included in other classes; bed and table covers.][3]

7-025 [**Class 25** Clothing, footwear, headgear.][4]

7-026 [**Class 26** Lace and embroidery, ribbons and braid; buttons, hooks and eyes, pins and needles; artificial flowers.][5]

7-027 [**Class 27** Carpets, rugs, mats and matting, linoleum and other materials for covering existing floors; wall hangings (non-textile).][6]

7-028 [**Class 28** Games and playthings; gymnastic and sporting articles not included in other classes; decorations for Christmas trees.][7]

7-029 [**Class 29** Meat, fish, poultry and game; meat extracts; preserved, dried and cooked fruits and vegetables; jellies, jams, compotes; eggs, milk and milk products; edible oils and fats.][8]

7-030 [**Class 30** Coffee, tea, cocoa, sugar, rice, tapioca, sago, artificial coffee; flour and preparations made from cereals, bread, pastry and confectionery, ices; honey, treacle; yeast, baking-powder; salt, mustard; vinegar, sauces (condiments); spices; ice.][9]

7-031 [**Class 31** Agricultural, horticultural and forestry products and grains not included in other classes; live animals; fresh fruits and vegetables; seeds, natural plants and flowers; foodstuffs for animals; malt.][10]

7-032 [**Class 32** Beers; mineral and aerated waters and other non-alcoholic drinks; fruit drinks and fruit juices; syrups and other preparations for making beverages.][11]

7-033 [**Class 33** Alcoholic beverages (except beers).][12]

7-034 [**Class 34** Tobacco; smokers' articles; matches.][13]][14]

[Services

7-035 [**Class 35** Advertising; business management; business administration; office functions.][15]

---

[1] Inserted by SI 2001/3832 reg 8
[2] Inserted by SI 2001/3832 reg 8
[3] Inserted by SI 2001/3832 reg 8
[4] Inserted by SI 2001/3832 reg 8
[5] Inserted by SI 2001/3832 reg 8
[6] Inserted by SI 2001/3832 reg 8
[7] Inserted by SI 2001/3832 reg 8
[8] Inserted by SI 2001/3832 reg 8
[9] Inserted by SI 2001/3832 reg 8
[10] Inserted by SI 2001/3832 reg 8
[11] Inserted by SI 2001/3832 reg 8
[12] Inserted by SI 2001/3832 reg 8
[13] Inserted by SI 2001/3832 reg 8
[14] Inserted by SI 2001/3832 reg 8
[15] Inserted by SI 2001/3832 reg 8

[**Class 36** Insurance; financial affairs; monetary affairs; real estate affairs.][1] **7-036**

[**Class 37** Building construction; repair; installation services.][2] **7-037**

[**Class 38** Telecommunications.][3] **7-038**

[**Class 39** Transport; packaging and storage of goods; travel arrangement.][4] **7-039**

[**Class 40** Treatment of materials.][5] **7-040**

[**Class 41** Education; providing of training; entertainment; sporting and cultural activities.][6] **7-041**

[**Class 42** Scientific and technological services and research and design relating thereto; industrial analysis and research services; design and development of computer hardware and software; legal services.][7] **7-042**

[**Class 43** Services for providing food and drink; temporary accommodation.][8] **7-043**

[**Class 44** Medical services; veterinary services; hygienic and beauty care for human beings or animals; agriculture, horticulture and forestry services.][9] **7-044**

[**Class 45** Personal and social services rendered by others to meet the needs of individuals; security services for the protection of property and individuals.][10]][11]][12] **7-045**

---

[1] Inserted by SI 2001/3832 reg 8
[2] Inserted by SI 2001/3832 reg 8
[3] Inserted by SI 2001/3832 reg 8
[4] Inserted by SI 2001/3832 reg 8
[5] Inserted by SI 2001/3832 reg 8
[6] Inserted by SI 2001/3832 reg 8
[7] Inserted by SI 2001/3832 reg 8
[8] Inserted by SI 2001/3832 reg 8
[9] Inserted by SI 2001/3832 reg 8
[10] Inserted by SI 2001/3832 reg 8
[11] Inserted by SI 2001/3832 reg 8
[12] Inserted by SI 2001/3832 reg 8

Plant Varieties Act 1997

CHAPTER 66

*BE IT ENACTED by the Queen's most Excellent Majesty, by and with the advice
and consent of the Lords Spiritual and Temporal, and Commons, in this present
Parliament assembled, and by the authority of the same, as follows:—*

PART I

PLANT VARIETIES

Preliminary

Plant breeders' rights

8-001   **1.**—(1) Rights, to be known as plant breeders' rights, may be granted in
accordance with this Part of this Act.

(2) Plant breeders' rights may subsist in varieties of all plant genera and
species.

(3) For the purposes of this Act, "variety" means a plant grouping within a
single botanical taxon of the lowest known rank, which grouping, irrespective of
whether the conditions for the grant of plant breeders' rights (which are laid down
in section 4 below) are met, can be—

> (a) defined by the expression of the characteristics resulting from a given
> genotype or combination of genotypes,
> (b) distinguished from any other plant grouping by the expression of at
> least one of those characteristics, and
> (c) considered as a unit with regard to its suitability for being propagated
> unchanged.

The Plant Variety Rights Office

8-002   **2.**—(1) The office known as the Plant Variety Rights Office shall continue in
being for the purposes of this Part of this Act under the immediate control of an
officer appointed by the Ministers and known as the Controller of Plant Variety
Rights ("the Controller").

(2) Schedule 1 to this Act (which makes further provision about the Plant
Variety Rights Office) shall have effect.

Grant of plant breeders' rights

Grant on application

8-003   **3.**—(1) Subject to this Part of this Act, plant breeders' rights shall be granted
to an applicant by the Controller on being satisfied that the conditions laid down
in section 4 below are met.

(2) The Controller may by notice require an applicant for the grant of plant
breeders' rights to provide him, within such time as may be specified in the
notice, with such information, documents, plant or other material, facilities or

test or trial results relevant to the carrying out of his function under subsection (1) above as may be so specified.

(3) If an applicant fails to comply with a notice under subsection (2) above within the period specified in the notice, the Controller may refuse the application.

Conditions for the grant of rights

4.—(1) The conditions which must be met in relation to an application for **8-004** the grant of plant breeders' rights are—

(a) that the variety to which the application relates is a qualifying variety, and

(b) that the person by whom the application is made is the person entitled to the grant of plant breeders' rights in respect of the variety to which it relates.

(2) For the purposes of subsection (1) above, a variety is a qualifying variety if it is—

(a) distinct,

(b) uniform,

(c) stable, and

(d) new;

and Part I of Schedule 2 to this Act has effect for the purpose of determining whether these criteria are met.

(3) Subject to subsections (4) and (5) below, the person entitled to the grant of plant breeders' rights in respect of a variety is the person who breeds it, or discovers and develops it, or his successor in title.

(4) If a person breeds a variety, or discovers and develops it, in the course of his employment, then, subject to agreement to the contrary, his employer, or his employer's successor in title, is the person entitled to the grant of plant breeders' rights in respect of it.

(5) Part II of Schedule 2 to this Act shall have effect as respects priorities between two or more persons who have independently bred, or discovered and developed, a variety.

(6) In this section and Schedule 2 to this Act, references to the discovery of a variety are to the discovery of a variety, whether growing in the wild or occurring as a genetic variant, whether artificially induced or not.

Rights in relation to application period

5.—(1) If an application for plant breeders' rights is granted, the holder of **8-005** the rights shall be entitled to reasonable compensation for anything done during the application period which, if done after the grant of the rights, would constitute an infringement of them.

(2) In subsection (1) above, "application period", in relation to a grant of plant breeders' rights, means the period—

(a) beginning with the day on which details of the application for the grant of the rights are published in the gazette, and

(b) ending with the grant of the rights.

Scope of plant breeders' rights

Protected variety

8-006   **6.**—(1) Plant breeders' rights shall have effect to entitle the holder to prevent anyone doing any of the following acts as respects the propagating material of the protected variety without his authority, namely—

(a) production or reproduction (multiplication),

(b) conditioning for the purpose of propagation,

(c) offering for sale,

(d) selling or other marketing,

(e) exporting,

(f) importing,

(g) stocking for any of the purposes mentioned in paragraphs (a) to (f) above, and

(h) any other act prescribed for the purposes of this provision.

(2) The holder of plant breeders' rights may give authority for the purposes of subsection (1) above with or without conditions or limitations.

(3) The rights conferred on the holder of plant breeders' rights by subsections (1) and (2) above shall also apply as respects harvested material obtained through the unauthorised use of propagating material of the protected variety, unless he has had a reasonable opportunity before the harvested material is obtained to exercise his rights in relation to the unauthorised use of the propagating material.

(4) In the case of a variety of a prescribed description, the rights conferred on the holder of plant breeders' rights by subsections (1) and (2) above shall also apply as respects any product which—

(a) is made directly from harvested material in relation to which subsection (3) above applies, and

(b) is of a prescribed description,

unless subsection (5) below applies.

(5) This subsection applies if, before the product was made, any act mentioned in subsection (1) above was done as respects the harvested material from which the product was made and either—

(a) the act was done with the authority of the holder of the plant breeders' rights, or

(b) the holder of those rights had a reasonable opportunity to exercise them in relation to the doing of the act.

(6) In this section—

(a) "prescribed" means prescribed by regulations made by the Ministers, and

(b) references to harvested material include entire plants and parts of plants.

Dependent varieties

8-007   **7.**—(1) The holder of plant breeders' rights shall have, in relation to any variety which is dependent on the protected variety, the same rights as he has under section 6 above in relation to the protected variety.

(2) For the purposes of this section, one variety is dependent on another if—

(a) its nature is such that repeated production of the variety is not possible without repeated use of the other variety, or

(b) it is essentially derived from the other variety and the other variety is not itself essentially derived from a third variety.

(3) For the purposes of subsection (2) above, a variety shall be deemed to be essentially derived from another variety ("the initial variety") if—

    (a) it is predominantly derived from—

        (i) the initial variety, or

        (ii) a variety that is itself predominantly derived from the initial variety,

while retaining the expression of the essential characteristics resulting from the genotype or combination of genotypes of the initial variety,

    (b) it is clearly distinguishable from the initial variety by one or more characteristics which are capable of a precise description, and

    (c) except for the differences which result from the act of derivation, it conforms to the initial variety in the expression of the essential characteristics that result from the genotype or combination of genotypes of the initial variety.

(4) For the purposes of subsection (3) above, derivation may, for example, be by—

    (a) the selection of—

        (i) a natural or induced mutant,

        (ii) a somaclonal variant, or

        (iii) a variant individual from plants of the initial variety,

    (b) backcrossing, or

    (c) transformation by genetic engineering.

(5) Subsection (1) above shall not apply where the existence of the dependent variety was common knowledge immediately before the coming into force of this Act.

Exceptions

General exceptions

8. Plant breeders' rights shall not extend to any act done—   **8-008**

    (a) for private and non-commercial purposes,

    (b) for experimental purposes, or

    (c) for the purpose of breeding another variety.

Farm saved seed

9.—(1) Subject to subsection (2) below, plant breeders' rights shall not extend **8-009** to the use by a farmer for propagating purposes in the field, on his own holding, of the product of the harvest which he has obtained by planting on his own holding propagating material of—

    (a) the protected variety, or

    (b) a variety which is essentially derived from the protected variety.

(2) Subsection (1) above only applies if the material is of a variety which is of a species or group specified for the purposes of this subsection by order made by the Ministers.

(3) If a farmer's use of material is excepted from plant breeders' rights by subsection (1) above, he shall, at the time of the use, become liable to pay the holder of the rights equitable remuneration, which shall be sensibly lower than the amount charged for the production of propagating material of the same variety in the same area with the holder's authority.

(4) Subsection (3) above shall not apply to a farmer who is considered to be a small farmer for the purposes of Article 14(3) third indent of the Council Regulation.

(5) Subsection (3) above shall not apply if—

    (a) before the day on which this Part of this Act comes into force, the farmer has, in relation to the variety concerned, engaged in use of the kind to which subsection (1) above applies, and

    (b) no remuneration was payable in respect of that use.

(6) The Ministers may by order provide that, on such date after 30th June 2001 as may be specified in the order, subsection (5) above shall cease to have effect in relation to a variety so specified, or varieties of a species or group so specified.

(7) The Ministers may by regulations—

    (a) make provision enabling—

        (i) holders of plant breeders' rights to require farmers or seed processors, and

        (ii) farmers or seed processors to require holders of plant breeders' rights,

    to supply such information as may be specified in the regulations, being information the supply of which the Ministers consider necessary for the purposes of this section,

    (b) make provision restricting the circumstances in which the product of a harvest of a variety which is subject to plant breeders' rights may be moved, for the purpose of being processed for planting, from the holding on which it was obtained, and

    (c) make provision for the purpose of enabling the Ministers to monitor the operation of any provision of this section or regulations under this section.

(8) Regulations under subsection (7)(a) above may include provision imposing obligations of confidence in relation to information supplied by virtue of the regulations.

(9) Subsections (3) and (4) of section 7 above shall apply for the purposes of subsection (1)(b) above as they apply for the purposes of subsection (2) of that section.

(10) For the purposes of subsection (3) above, remuneration shall be taken to be sensibly lower if it would be taken to be sensibly lower within the meaning of Article 14(3) fourth indent of the Council Regulation.

(11) In this section, references to a farmer's own holding are to any land which he actually exploits for plant growing, whether as his property or otherwise managed under his own responsibility and on his own account.

(12) The Ministers may by order amend this section as they think fit for the purpose of securing that it corresponds with the provisions for the time being of the law relating to Community plant variety rights about farm saved seed.

Exhaustion of rights

8-010   **10.**—(1) Plant breeders' rights shall not extend to any act concerning material of a variety if the material—

    (a) has been sold or otherwise marketed in the United Kingdom by, or with the consent of, the holder of the rights, or

    (b) is derived from material which has been so sold or otherwise marketed.

(2) Subsection (1) above shall not apply where the act involves—

(a) further propagation of the variety, or

(b) the export of material which enables propagation of the variety to a non-qualifying country, otherwise than for the purposes of final consumption.

(3) For the purposes of subsection (2)(b) above, a non-qualifying country is one which does not provide for the protection of varieties of the genus or species to which the variety belongs.

(4) In this section, "material", in relation to a variety, means —

(a) any kind of propagating material of the variety,

(b) harvested material of the variety, including entire plants and parts of plants, and

(c) any product made directly from material falling within paragraph (b) above.

Duration and transmission of plant breeders' rights

Duration

11.—(1) A grant of plant breeders' rights shall have effect— **8-011**

(a) in the case of potatoes, trees and vines, for 30 years from the date of the grant, and

(b) in other cases, for 25 years from that date.

(2) The Ministers may by regulations provide that, in relation to varieties of a species or group specified in the regulations, subsection (1) above shall have effect with the substitution in paragraph (a) or (b), as the case may be, of such longer period, not exceeding—

(a) in the case of paragraph (a), 35 years, and

(b) in the case of paragraph (b), 30 years,

as may be so specified.

(3) The period for which a grant of plant breeders' rights has effect shall not be affected by the fact it becomes impossible to invoke the rights—

(a) because of Article 92(2) of the Council Regulation (effect of subsequent grant of Community plant variety right), or

(b) because of suspension under section 23 below.

Transmission

12. Plant breeders' rights shall be assignable like other kinds of proprietary **8-012** rights, but in any case rights under section 6 above and rights under section 7 above may not be assigned separately.

Remedies for infringement

Remedies for infringement

13.—(1) Plant breeders' rights shall be actionable at the suit of the holder of **8-013** the rights.

(2) In any proceedings for the infringement of plant breeders' rights, all such relief by way of damages, injunction, interdict, account or otherwise shall be available as is available in any corresponding proceedings in respect of infringements of other proprietary rights.

Presumptions in proceedings relating to harvested material

8-014   **14.**—(1) This section applies to any proceedings for the infringement of plant breeders' rights as respects harvested material.

(2) If, in any, proceedings to which this section applies, the holder of the plant breeders' rights proves, in relation to any of the material to which the proceedings relate—

(a) that it has been the subject of an information notice given to the defendant by or on behalf of the holder, and

(b) that the defendant has not, within the prescribed time after the service of the notice, supplied the holder with the information about it requested in the notice,

then, as regards the material in relation to which the holder proves that to be the case, the presumptions mentioned in subsection (3) below shall apply, unless the contrary is proved or the defendant shows that he had a reasonable excuse for not supplying the information.

(3) The presumptions are—

(a) that the material was obtained through unauthorised use of propagating material, and

(b) that the holder did not have a reasonable opportunity before the material was obtained to exercise his rights in relation to the unauthorised use of the propagating material.

(4) The reference in subsection (2) above to an information notice is to a notice which—

(a) is in the prescribed form,

(b) specifies the material to which it relates,

(c) contains, in relation to that material, a request for the supply of the prescribed, but no other, information, and

(d) contains such other particulars as may be prescribed.

(5) In this section, "prescribed" means prescribed by regulations made by the Ministers.

Presumptions in proceedings relating to products made from harvested material

8-015   **15.**—(1) This section applies to any proceedings for the infringement of plant breeders' rights as respects any product made directly from harvested material.

(2) If, in any proceedings to which this section applies, the holder of the plant breeders' rights proves, in relation to any product to which the proceedings relate—

(a) that it has been the subject of an information notice given to the defendant by or on behalf of the holder, and

(b) that the defendant has not, within the prescribed time after the service of the notice, supplied the holder with the information about it requested in the notice,

then, as regards the product in relation to which the holder proves that to be the case, the presumptions mentioned in subsection (3) below shall apply, unless the contrary is proved or the defendant shows that he had a reasonable excuse for not supplying the information.

(3) The presumptions are—

(a) that the harvested material from which the product was made was obtained through unauthorised use of propagating material,

(b) that the holder did not have a reasonable opportunity before the harvested material was obtained to exercise his rights in relation to the unauthorised use of the propagating material, and

(c) that no relevant act was done, before the product was made, as respects the harvested material from which it was made.

(4) An act is relevant for the purposes of subsection (3)(c) above if it is mentioned in section 6(1) above and is—

(a) done with the authority of the holder, or

(b) one in relation to the doing of which he has a reasonable opportunity to exercise his rights.

(5) The reference in subsection (2) above to an information notice is to a notice which—

(a) is in the prescribed form,

(b) specifies the product to which it relates,

(c) contains, in relation to that product, a request for the supply of the prescribed, but no other, information, and

(d) contains such other particulars as may be prescribed.

(6) In this section, "prescribed" means prescribed by regulations made by the Ministers.

Duties of holder of plant breeders' rights

Maintenance of protected variety

16.—(1) The holder of any plant breeders' rights shall ensure that, **8-016** throughout the period for which the grant of the rights has effect, he is in a position to produce to the Controller propagating material which is capable of producing the protected variety.

(2) The holder of any plant breeders' rights shall give to the Controller, within such time as he may specify, all such information and facilities as he may request for the purpose of satisfying himself that the holder is fulfilling his duty under subsection (1) above.

(3) The facilities to be given under subsection (2) above include facilities for the inspection by or on behalf of the Controller of the measures taken for the preservation of the protected variety.

Compulsory licences

17.—(1) Subject to subsections (2) and (3) below, if the Controller is satisfied **8-017** on application that the holder of any plant breeders' rights—

(a) has unreasonably refused to grant a licence to the applicant, or

(b) has imposed or put forward unreasonable terms in granting, or offering to grant, a licence to the applicant,

he may grant to the applicant in the form of a licence under this section any such rights as might have been granted by the holder.

(2) The Controller shall not grant an application for a licence under this section unless he is satisfied—

(a) that it is necessary to do so for the purpose of securing that the variety to which the application relates—

(i) is available to the public at reasonable prices,

(ii) is widely distributed, or

(iii) is maintained in quality,

(b) that the applicant is financially and otherwise in a position to exploit in a competent and businesslike manner the rights to be conferred on him, and

(c) that the applicant intends so to exploit those rights.

(3) A licence under this section shall not be an exclusive licence.

(4) A licence under this section shall be on such terms as the Controller thinks fit and, in particular, may include—

(a) terms as to the remuneration payable to the holder of the plant breeders' rights, and

(b) terms obliging the holder of the plant breeders' rights to make propagating material available to the holder of the licence.

(5) In deciding on what terms to grant an application for a licence under this section, the Controller shall have regard to the desirability of securing—

(a) that the variety to which the application relates—

(i) is available to the public at reasonable prices,

(ii) is widely distributed, and

(iii) is maintained in quality, and

(b) that there is reasonable remuneration for the holder of the plant breeders' rights to which the application relates.

(6) An application for a licence under this section may be granted whether or not the holder of the plant breeders' rights to which the application relates has granted licences to the applicant or any other person.

(7) If and so far as any agreement purports to bind any person not to apply for a licence under this section, it shall be void.

(8) If—

(a) a licence under this section is granted as respects a variety of a species or group in relation to which a period is specified for the purposes of this provision by regulations made by the Ministers, and

(b) the grant takes place before a period of that length has passed since the date of grant of the plant breeders' rights to which the licence relates,

the licence shall not have effect until a period of that length has passed since that date.

(9) The Controller may, at any time, on the application of any person, extend, limit or in any other respect vary a licence under this section, or revoke it.

Naming of protected varieties

Selection and registration of names

8-018   **18.**—(1) The Ministers may by regulations—

(a) make provision for the selection of names for varieties which are the subject of applications for the grant of plant breeders' rights,

(b) make provision about change of name in relation to varieties in respect of which plant breeders' rights have been granted, and

(c) make provision for the keeping of a register of the names of varieties in respect of which plant breeders' rights have been granted.

(2) Regulations under subsection (1) above may, in particular—

(a) make provision enabling the Controller to require an applicant for the grant of plant breeders' rights to select a name for the variety to which the application relates,

(b) make provision enabling the Controller to require the holder of plant breeders' rights to select a different name for the protected variety,

(c) prescribe classes of variety for the purposes of the regulations,

(d) prescribe grounds on which the registration of a proposed name may be refused,

(e) prescribe the circumstances in which representations may be made regarding any decision as to the name to be registered in respect of any variety,

(f) make provision enabling the Controller—

    (i) to refuse an application for the grant of plant breeders' rights, or

    (ii) to terminate the period for which a grant of plant breeders' rights has effect,

if the applicant or holder fails to comply with a requirement imposed under the regulations,

(g) make provision for the publication or service of notices of decisions which the Controller proposes to take, and

(h) prescribe the times at which, and the circumstances in which, the register may be inspected by members of the public.

(3) The Controller shall publish notice of all entries made in the register, including alterations, corrections and erasures—

(a) in the gazette, and

(b) in such other manner as appears to the Controller to be convenient for the publication of these to all concerned.

(4) For the purposes of subsection (1) above, the variety in respect of which plant breeders' rights are granted is the protected variety.

Duty to use registered name

19.—(1) Where a name is registered under section 18 above in respect of a **8-019** variety, a person may not use any other name in selling, offering for sale or otherwise marketing propagating material of the variety.

(2) Subsection (1) above shall have effect in relation to any variety from the date on which plant breeders' rights in respect of that variety are granted, and shall continue to apply after the period for which the grant of those rights has effect.

(3) Subsection (1) above shall not preclude the use of any trade mark or trade name (whether registered under the Trade Marks Act 1994 or not) if—

(a) that mark or name and the registered name are juxtaposed, and

(b) the registered name is easily recognisable.

(4) A person who contravenes subsection (1) above shall be liable on summary conviction to a fine not exceeding level 3 on the standard scale.

(5) In any proceedings for an offence under subsection (4) above, it shall be a defence to prove that the accused took all reasonable precautions against committing the offence and had not at the time of the offence any reason to suspect that he was committing an offence.

Improper use of registered name

20.—(1) If any person uses the registered name of a protected variety in **8-020** offering for sale, selling or otherwise marketing material of a different variety within the same class, the use of the name shall be a wrong actionable in proceedings by the holder of the rights.

(2) Subsection (1) above shall also apply to the use of a name so nearly resembling the registered name as to be likely to deceive or cause confusion.

(3) In any proceedings under this section, it shall be a defence to a claim for damages to prove that the defendant took all reasonable precautions against committing the wrong and had not, when using the name, any reason to suspect that it was wrongful.

(4) In this section—

"class" means a class prescribed for the purposes of regulations under section 18(1) above,

"registered name", in relation to a protected variety, means the name registered in respect of it under section 18 above.

Termination and suspension of plant breeders' rights

Nullity

8-021   **21.**—(1) The Controller shall declare the grant of plant breeders' rights null and void if it is established—

(a) that when the rights were granted the protected variety did not meet the criterion specified in paragraph (a) or (d) of section 4(2) above,

(b) where the grant of the rights was essentially based upon information and documents furnished by the applicant, that when the rights were granted the protected variety did not meet the criterion specified in paragraph (b) or (c) of that provision, or

(c) that the person to whom the rights were granted was not the person entitled to the grant of the rights and the rights have not subsequently been transferred to him, or his successor in title.

(2) If, because of paragraph 6 of Schedule 2 to this Act, priority is established for an application for the grant of plant breeders' rights after such rights have been granted in pursuance of an application against which priority is established, subsection (1)(c) above shall only apply to the grant if the Controller decides that the application for which priority is established should be granted.

(3) Where the grant of plant breeders' rights is declared null and void under this section, it shall be deemed never to have had effect.

Cancellation

8-022   **22.**—(1) The Controller may terminate the period for which a grant of plant breeders' rights has effect if—

(a) he is satisfied that the protected variety no longer meets the criterion specified in paragraph (b) or (c) of section 4(2) above,

(b) it appears to him that the holder of the rights is no longer in a position to provide him with the propagating material mentioned in section 16(1) above,

(c) he is satisfied that the holder of the rights has failed to comply with a request under section 16(2) above, or

(d) on application by the holder of the rights, he is satisfied that the rights may properly be surrendered.

(2) Before determining an application under subsection (1)(d) above, the Controller shall—

(a) give notice of the application in the manner prescribed by regulations made by the Ministers, and

(b) follow the procedure so prescribed for hearing any person on whom the right to object is conferred by such regulations.

(3) If the Controller is satisfied, not only that the protected variety no longer meets the criterion specified in paragraph (b) or (c) of section 4(2) above, but also that it ceased to do so at some earlier date, he may make the termination retrospective to that date.

Suspension

23.—(1) The Controller may suspend the exercise of any plant breeders' **8-023** rights if, on application by the holder of a licence under section 17 above, he is satisfied that the holder of the rights is in breach of any obligation imposed on him by the licence.

(2) The Controller shall terminate a suspension under subsection (1) above if, on application by the holder of the plant breeders' rights concerned, he is satisfied that the holder is no longer in breach of the obligation whose breach led to the suspension.

(3) Subsection (1) above is without prejudice to the remedies available to the holder of a licence under section 17 above by the taking of proceedings in any court.

Proceedings before the Controller

Appeals to the Tribunal

26.—(1) An appeal shall lie to the Tribunal against the following decisions of **8-024** the Controller—

  (a) a decision to allow or refuse an application for the grant of plant breeders' rights,

  (b) any decision preliminary to the determination of such an application as to the conditions laid down in section 4 above,

  (c) a decision to allow or refuse an application under section 17(1) or (9) above,

  (d) any decision under section 21 or 22(1)(a), (b) or (c) above,

  (e) a decision to refuse an application under section 22(1)(d) above, and

  (f) a decision to allow or refuse an application under section 23(1) or (2) above.

(2) The Ministers may by regulations confer a right of appeal to the Tribunal against—

  (a) a decision of the Controller to refuse an application under section 25(3)(a) above, or

  (b) any decision of the Controller under regulations made under section 18 above or section 28 or 29 below.

False information and representations as to rights

False information

31.—(1) If any information to which this section applies is false in a material **8-025** particular and the person giving the information knows that it is false or gives it recklessly, he shall be guilty of an offence and liable on summary conviction to a fine not exceeding level 3 on the standard scale.

(2) The information to which this section applies is—

  (a) information given in an application to the Controller for a decision against which an appeal lies to the Tribunal,

   (b) information given by or on behalf of the applicant in connection with such an application, and

   (c) information given in pursuance of a request under section 16(2) above.

False representations as to rights

8-026   **32.**—(1) If, in relation to any variety, a person falsely represents that he is entitled to exercise plant breeders' rights, or any rights derived from such rights, and he knows that the representation is false, or makes it recklessly, he shall be guilty of an offence and liable on summary conviction to a fine not exceeding level 3 on the standard scale.

   (2) It is immaterial for the purposes of subsection (1) above whether or not the variety to which the representation relates is the subject of plant breeders' rights.

Miscellaneous

Disclosure of information obtained under section 14 or 15

8-027   **34.**—(1) If the holder of plant breeders' rights obtains information pursuant to a notice given for the purposes of section 14 or 15 above, he shall owe an obligation of confidence in respect of the information to the person who supplied it.

   (2) Subsection (1) above shall not have effect to restrict disclosure of information—

   (a) for the purposes of, or in connection with, establishing whether plant breeders' rights have been infringed, or

   (b) for the purposes of, or in connection with, any proceedings for the infringement of plant breeders' rights.

Reference collections of plant material

8-028   **35.**—(1) The Controller may establish and maintain reference collections of plant material.

   (2) The Controller may by means of grants of such amounts as he may determine defray or contribute towards the expenses incurred by any other person in maintaining any reference collection of plant material.

General

Application of Part I to the Crown

8-029   **39.**—(1) If—

   (a) any servant or agent of the Crown infringes any plant breeders' rights or makes himself liable to civil proceedings under section 20 above, and

   (b) the infringement or wrong is committed with the authority of the Crown,

civil proceedings in respect of the infringement or wrong shall lie against the Crown.

   (2) Except as provided by subsection (1) above, no proceedings shall lie against the Crown by virtue of the Crown Proceedings Act 1947 in respect of the infringement of plant breeders' rights or any wrong under section 20 above.

   (3) This section shall have effect as if contained in Part I of the Crown Proceedings Act 1947.

Application of Part I to existing rights

40.—(1) Subject to the following provisions of this section, this Part of this **8-030** Act applies in relation to existing rights as it applies in relation to plant breeders' rights granted under this Part of this Act.

(2) Section 5 above shall not apply in relation to existing rights.

(3) Section 11 above shall only apply to existing rights if the effect is to extend the period for which the rights are exercisable.

(4) In this section, "existing rights" means plant breeders' rights granted under Part I of the Plant Varieties and Seeds Act 1964 which are exercisable on the coming into force of this Part of this Act.

PART III

MISCELLANEOUS AND GENERAL

Miscellaneous

General

Extent

53.—(1) This Act, except section 47 above, extends to Northern Ireland. **8-031**

(2) Her Majesty may by Order in Council direct that any of the provisions of this Act shall, subject to such modifications as appear to Her Majesty to be appropriate, extend to any of the Channel Islands or the Isle of Man.

(3) An Order in Council under subsection (2) above may contain such transitional and consequential provisions as appear to Her Majesty to be expedient.

SCHEDULES

Section 4   Schedule 2

CONDITIONS FOR THE GRANT OF PLANT BREEDERS' RIGHTS

PART I

CRITERIA FOR GRANT OF RIGHTS

Distinctness

1. The variety shall be deemed to be distinct if it is clearly distinguishable by one or more character- **8-032** istics which are capable of a precise description from any other variety whose existence is a matter of common knowledge at the time of the application.

Uniformity

2. The variety shall be deemed to be uniform if, subject to the variation that may be expected **8-033** from the particular features of its propagation, it is sufficiently uniform in those characteristics which are included in the examination for distinctness.

8-034   3. The variety shall be deemed to be stable if those characteristics which are included in the examination for distinctness, as well as any others used for the variety description, remain unchanged after repeated propagation or, in the case of a particular cycle of propagation, at the end of each such cycle.

Novelty

8-035   4.—(1) The variety shall be deemed to be new if sub-paragraphs (2) and (3) below apply.

(2) This sub-paragraph applies if no sale or other disposal of propagating or harvested material of the variety for the purposes of exploiting the variety has, with the consent of the applicant, taken place in the United Kingdom earlier than one year before the date of the application.

(3) This sub-paragraph applies if no sale or other disposal of propagating or harvested material of the variety for the purposes of exploiting the variety has, with the consent of the applicant, taken place elsewhere than in the United Kingdom earlier than 4 years, or, in the case of trees or vines, 6 years, before the date of the application.

(4) For the purposes of sub-paragraphs (2) and (3) above, there shall be disregarded any sale or other disposal to which sub-paragraph (5), (6), (8) or (9) below applies.

(5) This sub-paragraph applies to any sale or other disposal of a stock of material of the variety to a person who at the time of the sale or other disposal is, or who subsequently becomes, the person entitled to the grant of plant breeders' rights in respect of the variety.

(6) This sub-paragraph applies to—

(a) any sale or other disposal of propagating material of the variety to a person as part of qualifying arrangements, and

(b) any sale or other disposal to the applicant, by a person who uses propagating material of the variety under any such arrangements, of the material produced directly or indirectly from the use.

(7) For the purposes of sub-paragraph (6) above, qualifying arrangements are arrangements under which—

(a) a person uses propagating material of the variety under the applicant's control for the purpose of increasing the applicant's stock, or of carrying out tests or trials, and

(b) the whole of the material produced, directly or indirectly, from the material becomes or remains the property of the applicant.

(8) This sub-paragraph applies to any sale or other disposal of material of the variety, other than propagating material, produced in the course of—

(a) the breeding of the variety,

(b) increasing the applicant's stock of material of the variety, or

(c) carrying out tests or trials of the variety,

which does not involve identifying the variety from which the material is produced.

(9) This sub-paragraph applies to any disposal of material of the variety, otherwise than by way of sale, at an exhibition or for the purposes of display at an exhibition.

(10) For the purposes of sub-paragraphs (2) and (3) above, any sale or other disposal of propagating or harvested material of a variety for the purposes of exploiting the variety shall, if the variety is related to another variety, be treated as being also a sale or other disposal of propagating or harvested material of the other variety for the purposes of exploiting that variety.

(11) For the purposes of sub-paragraph (10) above, a variety is related to another if its nature is such that repeated production of the variety is not possible without repeated use of the other variety.

PART II

PRIORITIES BETWEEN APPLICANTS FOR RIGHTS

8-036   5.—(1) If a variety is bred, or discovered and developed, by two or more persons independently, the first of those persons, and any successors in title of theirs, to apply for the grant of plant breeders' rights in respect of it shall be the person entitled to the grant.

(2) As between persons making applications for the grant of plant breeders' rights in respect of the same variety on the same date, the one who was first in a position to make an application for the grant of plant breeders' rights in respect of that variety, or who would have been first in that position if this Part of this Act had always been in force, shall be the person entitled to the grant.

6.—(1) If the following conditions are met, an application for the grant of plant breeders' rights **8-037** shall be treated for the purposes of paragraphs 1, 4 and 5 above as made, not on the date on which it is in fact made, but on the earlier date mentioned in sub-paragraph (7) below.

(2) The first condition is that, in the 12 months immediately preceding the application under this Part of this Act, the applicant has duly made a parallel application under the law of—

(a) the European Community,

(b) any other intergovernmental organisation, or any State, which is, and was at the time of the application, a member of the Union as defined by Article 1(xi) of the Convention, or

(c) any country or territory which is, and was at the time of the application, designated for the purposes of this provision by order made by the Ministers.

(3) The second condition is that the applicant has not duly made such a parallel application earlier than 12 months before the application under this Part of this Act.

(4) The third condition is that the application under this Part of this Act includes a claim to priority under this paragraph by reference to the parallel application.

(5) The fourth condition is that the application by reference to which priority is claimed has not been withdrawn or refused when the application under this Part of this Act is made.

(6) The fifth condition is that, within 3 months from the date of the application under this Part of this Act, the applicant submits to the Controller a copy of the documents constituting the parallel application, certified as a true copy by the authority to whom it is made.

(7) The earlier date referred to in sub-paragraph (1) above is the date of the parallel application mentioned in sub-paragraph (2) above.

(8) If more than one parallel application has been duly made as mentioned in sub-paragraph (2) above, the references in sub-paragraphs (4) to (7) above to the parallel application shall be construed as references to the earlier, or earliest, of the applications.

(9) In this paragraph—

(a) "the Convention" means the International Convention for the Protection of New Varieties of Plants done on 2nd December 1961 and revised at Geneva on 10th November 1972, 23rd October 1978 and 19th March 1991, and

(b) references to a parallel application, in relation to an application for the grant of plant breeders' rights, are to an application for the grant of plant variety rights in respect of the variety to which the application under this Part of this Act relates.

7.—(1) Any priority which an application for the grant of plant breeders' rights enjoys by virtue **8-038** of paragraph 6 above shall be forfeited if the applicant does not, before the end of the relevant period, satisfy all the requirements which are to be satisfied by an applicant before plant breeders' rights can be granted to him.

(2) For the purposes of sub-paragraph (1) above, the relevant period is the period of 2 years beginning with the day after the last day on which the applicant could have claimed priority under paragraph 6 above for his application.

(3) Where—

(a) an application for the grant of plant breeders' rights enjoys priority by virtue of paragraph 6 above, and

(b) the application by reference to which it enjoys priority is withdrawn or refused before the applicant has satisfied all the requirements which are to be satisfied by an applicant before plant breeders' rights can be granted to him,

sub-paragraph (1) above shall have effect with the substitution for "the relevant period" of "such period as the Controller may specify".

The Control of Misleading Advertisements Regulations 1988

Whereas the Secretary of State is a Minister designated for the purposes of section 2(2) of the European Communities Act 1972 in relation to measures relating to the control of advertising; And whereas a draft of these Regulations has been approved by a resolution of each House of Parliament pursuant to section 2(2) of and paragraph 2(2) of Schedule 2 to that Act; Now, therefore, the Secretary of State in exercise of the powers conferred on him by section 2(2) of that Act and of all other powers enabling him in that behalf hereby makes the following Regulations:

(S.I. 915)

Citation and commencement

9-001   **1.** These Regulations may be cited as the Control of Misleading Advertisements Regulations 1988 and shall come into force on 20th June 1988.

Interpretation

9-002   **2.**—(1) In these Regulations—

"advertisement" means any form of representation which is made in connection with a trade, business, craft or profession in order to promote the supply or transfer of goods or services, immovable property, rights or obligations;

"court", in relation to England and Wales and Northern Ireland, means the High Court, and, in relation to Scotland, the Court of Session;

"Director" means the Director General of Fair Trading;

"licensed service" means a service in respect of which a licence has been granted under Part I or III of the Broadcasting Act 1990 or under Part I or II of the Broadcasting Act 1996;

"OFCOM" means the Office of Communications established by section 1(1) of the Office of Communications Act 2002;

"products with designation of origin" are those products to which Council Regulation (EEC) No. 2081/92 of 14 July 1992 applies;

"publication"in relation to an advertisement means the dissemination of that advertisement whether to an individual person or a number of persons and whether orally or in writing or in any other way whatsoever, and "publish" shall be construed accordingly.

"S4C"and "S4C Digital" have the same meaning as in Part 3 of the Communications Act 2003;

(2) For the purposes of these Regulations an advertisement is misleading if in any way, including its presentation, it deceives or is likely to deceive the persons to whom it is addressed or whom it reaches and if, by reason of its deceptive nature, it is likely to affect their economic behaviour or, for those reasons, injures or is likely to injure a competitor of the person whose interests the advertisement seeks to promote.

(2A) For the purposes of these Regulations an advertisement is comparative if in any way, either explicitly or by implication, it identifies a competitor or goods or services offered by a competitor.

(3) In the application of these Regulations to Scotland for references to an injunction or an interim injunction there shall be substituted references to an interdict or an interim interdict respectively.

Complaints to the Director

4.—(1) Subject to paragraphs (2) and (3) below, it shall be the duty of the **9-003** Director to consider any complaint made to him that an advertisement is misleading [,or is a comparative advertisement and is not permitted under regulation 4A below][1], unless the complaint appears to the Director to be frivolous or vexatious.

(2) The Director shall not consider any complaint which these Regulations require or would require, leaving aside any question as to the frivolous or vexatious nature of the complaint, [OFCOM][2] to consider.

(3) Before considering any complaint under paragraph (1) above the Director may require the person making the complaint to satisfy him that–

(a) there have been invoked in relation to the same or substantially the same complaint about the advertisement in question such established means of dealing with such complaints as the Director may consider appropriate, having regard to all the circumstances of the particular case;

(b) a reasonable opportunity has been allowed for those means to deal with the complaint in question; and

(c) those means have not dealt with the complaint adequately.

(4) In exercising the powers conferred on him by these Regulations the Director shall have regard to–

(a) all the interests involved and in particular the public interest; and

(b) the desirability of encouraging the control, by self-regulatory bodies, of advertisements.

[Comparative Advertisements

4A—(1) A comparative advertisement shall, as far as the comparison is **9-004** concerned, be permitted only when the following conditions are met:-

(a) it is not misleading;

(b) it compares goods or services meeting the same needs or intended for the same purpose;

(c) it objectively compares one or more material, relevant, verifiable and representative features of those goods and services, which may include price;

(d) it does not create confusion in the market place between the advertiser and a competitor or between the advertiser's trade marks, trade names, other distinguishing marks, goods or services and those of a competitor;

(e) it does not discredit or denigrate the trade marks, trade names, other distinguishing marks, goods, services, activities, or circumstances of a competitor;

(f) for products with designation of origin, it relates in each case to products with the same designation;

(g) it does not take unfair advantage of the reputation of a trade mark, trade name or other distinguishing marks of a competitor or of the designation of origin of competing products;

---

[1] Words inserted by SI 2000/914 reg 4
[2] Words substituted by SI 2003/3183 Sch 1 para 2 (2)

(h) it does not present goods or services as imitations or replicas of goods or services bearing a protected trade mark or trade name.

(2) In the case of a comparative advertisement referring to a special offer, such an advertisement is not permitted unless it indicates in a clear and unequivocal way the date on which the offer ends or, where appropriate, that the special offer is subject to the availability of the goods and services, and, where the special offer has not yet begun, the date of the start of the period during which the special price or other specific conditions shall apply.

(3) The provisions of this regulations shall not be construed as –

(a) conferring a right of action in any civil proceedings in respect of any contravention of this regulation (save as provided for in these Regulations); or

(b) derogating from any right of action or other remedy (whether civil or criminal) in proceedings instituted otherwise than by virtue of these Regulations.][1]

Applications to the Court by the Director

9-005   **5.**—(1) If, having considered a complaint about an advertisement pursuant to regulation 4(1) above, he considers that the advertisement is misleading [or is a comparative advertisement and is not permitted under regulation 4A][2], the Director may, if he thinks it appropriate to do so, bring proceedings for an injunction (in which proceedings he may also apply for an interlocutory injunction) against any person appearing to him to be concerned or likely to be concerned with the publication of the advertisement.

(2) The Director shall give reasons for his decision to apply or not to apply, as the case may be, for an injunction in relation to any complaint which these Regulations require him to consider.

Functions of the Court

9-006   **6.**—(1) The court on an application by the Director may grant an injunction on such terms as it may think fit but (except where it grants an interlocutory injunction) only if the court is satisfied that the advertisement to which the application relates is misleading [or is a comparative advertisement and is not permitted under regulation 4A][3]. Before granting an injunction the court shall have regard to all the interests involved and in particular the public interest.

(2) An injunction may relate not only to a particular advertisement but to any advertisement in similar terms or likely to convey a similar impression.

(3) In considering an application for an injunction the court may, whether or not on the application of any party to the proceedings, require any person appearing to the court to be responsible for the publication of the advertisement to which the application relates to furnish the court with evidence of the accuracy of any factual claim made in the advertisement. The court shall not make such a requirement unless it appears to the court to be appropriate in the circumstances of the particular case, having regard to the legitimate interests of the person who would be the subject of or affected by the requirement and of any other person concerned with the advertisement.

(4) If such evidence is not furnished to it following a requirement made by it under paragraph (3) above or if it considers such evidence inadequate, the court may decline to consider the factual claim mentioned in that paragraph accurate.

---

[1] Inserted by SI 2000/914 reg 5
[2] Words inserted by SI 2000/914 reg 6
[3] Words inserted by SI 2000/914 reg 7 (a)

(5) The court shall not refuse to grant an injunction for lack of evidence that –

    (a) the publication of the advertisement in question has given rise to loss or damage to any person; or

    (b) the person responsible for the advertisement intended it to be misleading or failed to exercise proper care to prevent its being misleading [;or]¹

    [(c) the person responsible for the comparative advertisement intended to breach the conditions in regulation 4A(1) and (2) or failed to exercise proper care to meet the conditions in regulation 4A(1) and (2).]²

(6) An injunction may prohibit the publication or the continued or further publication of an advertisement.

Powers of the Director to obtain and disclose information and disclosure of information generally

7.—(1) For the purpose of facilitating the exercise by him of any functions **9-007** conferred on him by these Regulations, the Director may, by notice in writing signed by him or on his behalf, require any person to furnish to him such information as may be specified or described in the notice or to produce to him any documents so specified or described.

(2) A notice under paragraph (1) above may –

    (a) specify the way in which and the time within which it is to be complied with; and

    (b) be varied or revoked by a subsequent notice.

(3) Nothing in this regulation compels the production or furnishing by any person of a document or of information which he would in an action in a court be entitled to refuse to produce or furnish on grounds of legal professional privilege or, in Scotland, on the grounds of confidentiality as between client and professional legal adviser.

(4) If a person makes default in complying with a notice under paragraph (1) above the court may, on the application of the Director, make such order as the court thinks fit for requiring the default to be made good, and any such order may provide that all the costs or expenses of and incidental to the application shall be borne by the person in default or by any officers of a company or other association who are responsible for its default.

(5) Subject to any provision to the contrary made by or under any enactment, where the Director considers it appropriate to do so for the purpose of controlling misleading advertisements [or comparative advertisements which do not comply with regulation 4A]³, he may refer to any person any complaint (including any related documentation) about an advertisement or disclose to any person any information (whether or not obtained by means of the exercise of the power conferred by paragraph (1) above).

(6) For the purpose of enabling information obtained under certain enactments to be used for facilitating the performance of functions under these Regulations, the following amendments shall be made in provisions respecting disclosure of information, that is to say –

    (c) in section 41 of the Restrictive Trade Practices Act 1976 there shall be inserted –

        (i) at the end of paragraph (a) of subsection (1) the words "or the Control of Misleading Advertisements Regulations 1988";

---

¹ Words substituted by SI 2000/914 reg 7 (b)

² Inserted by SI 2000/914 reg 7 (c)

³ Words inserted by SI 2000/914 reg 8

        (ii) after the words "Fair Trading Act 1973" in paragraph (c) of subsection (1) the words "or the Control of Misleading Advertisements Regulations 1988";

    (f) in section 101 of the Telecommunications Act 1984 there shall be inserted–

        (i) after the words "the enactments" in paragraphs (b) and (d) of subsection (2) the words "or subordinate legislation";

        (ii) after the words "the enactments" in subsection (3) the words "and subordinate legislation" and after the words "Consumer Protection Act 1987" in that subsection the words "(i) the Control of Misleading Advertisements Regulations 1988";

    (g) in section 74 of the Airports Act 1986 there shall be inserted–

        (i) after the words "the enactments" in paragraphs (a) and (c) of subsection (2) the words "or subordinate legislation";

        (ii) after the words "the enactments" in subsection (3) the words "and subordinate legislation" and after the words "Consumer Protection Act 1987" in that subsection the words "(j) the Control of Misleading Advertisements Regulations 1988";

    (h) in section 42 of the Gas Act 1986 there shall be inserted–

        (i) after the words "the enactments" in paragraphs (b) and (e) of subsection (2) the words "or subordinate legislation";

        (ii) after the words "the enactments" in subsection (3) the words "and subordinate legislation" and after the words "Consumer Protection Act 1987" in that subsection the words "(k) the Control of Misleading Advertisements Regulations 1988".

(8) The Director may arrange for the dissemination in such form and manner as he considers appropriate of such information and advice concerning the operation of these Regulations as may appear to him to be expedient to give to the public and to all persons likely to be affected by these Regulations.

[[Complaints to OFCOM][1]

9-008   **8.**—[(1) It shall be the duty of OFCOM to consider any complaint made to them that any advertisement included or proposed to be included in a licensed service is misleading or is a comparative advertisement and is not permitted under regulation 4A, unless the complaint appears to OFCOM to be frivolous or vexatious.][2]

[(3) OFCOM shall give reasons for their decisions.][3]

(4) In exercising the powers [conferred on them][4] by these Regulations [OFCOM][5] shall have regard to all the interests involved and in particular the public interest.][6]

[[Control by OFCOM of misleading advertisements and comparative advertising][7]

9-009   **9.**—[(1) If, having considered a complaint about an advertisement pursuant to regulation 8(1) above, they consider that the advertisement is misleading, or is a comparative advertisement and is not permitted under regulation 4A,

---

[1] Words substituted by SI 2003/3183 Sch 1 para 3 (6)
[2] Substituted by SI 2003/3183 Sch 1 para 3 (2)
[3] Substituted by SI 2003/3183 Sch 1 para 3 (4)
[4] Words substituted by SI 2003/3183 Sch 1 para 3 (5)
[5] Words substituted by SI 2003/3183 Sch 1 para 3 (5)
[6] Substituted by Broadcasting Act 1990 c.42 Sch 20 para 51 (3)
[7] Words substituted by SI 2003/3183 Sch 1 para 4 (5)

OFCOM may, if they think it appropriate to do so, exercise in relation to the advertisement any power conferred on them by virtue of a condition included in a licence in accordance with section 325(4) of the Communications Act 2003.][1]

(2) [OFCOM may][2] require any person [appearing to them][3] to be responsible for an advertisement which [OFCOM believe][4] may be misleading [,or may be a comparative advertisement which is not permitted under regulation 4A,][5] [to furnish them][6] it with evidence as to the accuracy of any factual claim made in the advertisement. In deciding whether or not to make such a requirement [OFCOM shall have regard][7] to the legitimate interests of any person who would be the subject of or affected by the requirement.

(3) If such evidence is not [furnished to them following a requirement made by them][8] under paragraph (2) above [within a time specified][9] [by OFCOM][10] or [if they consider][11] such evidence inadequate, [OFCOM may][12] consider the factual claim inaccurate.][13]

[[Complaints about advertisements on S4C and S4C Digital][14]

10.—[(1) It shall be the duty of OFCOM to consider any complaint made to **9-010** them that any advertisement broadcast or proposed to be broadcast on S4C or S4C Digital is misleading, or is a comparative advertisement and is not permitted under regulation 4A, unless the complaint appears to OFCOM to be frivolous or vexatious.][15]

[(3) OFCOM shall give reasons for their decisions.][16]

(4) In exercising the powers conferred on them by these Regulations the [OFCOM][17] shall have regard to all the interests involved and in particular the public interest.][18]

[[Control of misleading advertisements and comparative advertisements on S4C and S4C Digital.][19]

11.—[(1) If, having considered a complaint about an advertisement pursuant **9-011** to regulation 10(1) above, they consider that the advertisement is misleading, or is a comparative advertisement and is not permitted under regulation 4A, OFCOM may, if they think it appropriate to do so, exercise in relation to the advertisement, the power conferred by paragraph 14 of Schedule 12 to the Communications Act 2003.][20]

---

[1] Substituted by SI 2003/3183 Sch 1 para 4 (2)
[2] Words substituted by SI 2003/3183 Sch 1 para 4 (3) (a)
[3] Words substituted by SI 2003/3183 Sch 1 para 4 (3) (b)
[4] Words substituted by SI 2003/3183 Sch 1 para 4 (3) (c)
[5] Words inserted by SI 2000/914 reg 10 (c)
[6] Words substituted by SI 2003/3183 Sch 1 para 4 (3) (d)
[7] Words substituted by SI 2003/3183 Sch 1 para 4 (3) (e)
[8] Words substituted by SI 2003/3183 Sch 1 para 4 (4) (a)
[9] Words inserted by SI 2000/914 reg 10 (d)
[10] Words substituted by SI 2003/3183 Sch 1 para 4 (4) (b)
[11] Words substituted by SI 2003/3183 Sch 1 para 4 (4) (c)
[12] Words substituted by SI 2003/3183 Sch 1 para 4 (4) (d)
[13] Substituted by Broadcasting Act 1990 c.42 Sch 20 para 51 (3)
[14] Words substituted by SI 2003/3183 Sch 1 para 5 (6)
[15] Substituted by SI 2003/3183 Sch 1 para 5 (2)
[16] Substituted by SI 2003/3183 Sch 1 para 5 (4)
[17] Words substituted by SI 2003/3183 Sch 1 para 5 (5)
[18] Substituted by Broadcasting Act 1990 c.42 Sch 20 para 51 (3)
[19] Words substituted by SI 2003/3183 Sch 1 para 6 (4)
[20] Substituted by SI 2003/3183 Sch 1 para 6 (2)

(2) [OFCOM][1] may require any person appearing to them to be responsible for an advertisement which [OFCOM][2] believe may be misleading [,or may be a comparative advertisement which is not permitted under regulation 4A,][3] to furnish them with evidence as to the accuracy of any factual claim made in the advertisement. In deciding whether or not to make such a requirement [OFCOM][4] shall have regard to the legitimate interests of any person who would be the subject of or affected by the requirement.

(3) If such evidence is not furnished to them following a requirement made by them under paragraph (2) above [within a time specified by][5] [OFCOM][6] or if they consider such evidence inadequate, [OFCOM][7] may consider the factual claim inaccurate.][8]

The Copyright (Industrial Process and Excluded Articles) (No. 2) Order 1989

The Secretary of State, in exercise of the powers conferred upon him by section 52(4) of the Copyright, Designs and Patents Act 1988 ("the Act"), hereby makes the following Order:—

(S.I. 1070)

10-001   **1.** This Order may be cited as the Copyright (Industrial Process and Excluded Articles) (No. 2) Order 1989 and shall come into force on 1st August 1989.

10-002   **2.** An article is to be regarded for the purposes of section 52 of the Act (limitation of copyright protection for design derived from artistic work) as made by an industrial process if—

    (a) it is one of more than fifty articles which—

        (i) all fall to be treated for the purposes of Part I of the Act as copies of a particular artistic work, but

        (ii) do not all together constitute a single set of articles as defined in section 44(1) of the Registered Designs Act 1949; or

    (b) it consists of goods manufactured in lengths or pieces, not being hand-made goods.

10-003   **3.** (1) There are excluded from the operation of section 52 of the Act—

    (a) works of sculpture, other than casts or models used or intended to be used as models or patterns to be multiplied by any industrial process;

---

[1] Words substituted by SI 2003/3183 Sch 1 para 6 (3)
[2] Words substituted by SI 2003/3183 Sch 1 para 6 (3)
[3] Words inserted by SI 2000/914 reg 12 (c)
[4] Words substituted by SI 2003/3183 Sch 1 para 6 (3)
[5] Words inserted by SI 2000/914 reg 12 (d)
[6] Words substituted by SI 2003/3183 Sch 1 para 6 (3)
[7] Words substituted by SI 2003/3183 Sch 1 para 6 (3)
[8] Substituted by Broadcasting Act 1990 c.42 Sch 20 para 51 (3)

(b) wall plaques, medals and medallions; and

(c) printed matter primarily of a literary or artistic character, including book jackets, calendars, certificates, coupons, dress-making patterns, greetings cards, labels, leaflets, maps, plans, playing cards, postcards, stamps, trade advertisements, trade forms and cards, transfers and similar articles.

(2) Nothing in article 2 of this Order shall be taken to limit the meaning of "industrial process" in paragraph (1)(a) of this article.

4. The Copyright (Industrial Designs) Rules 1957 and the Copyright **10-004** (Industrial Process and Excluded Articles) Order 1989 are hereby revoked.

The Design Right (Semiconductor Topographies) Regulations 1989

Whereas a draft of the following Regulations has been approved by resolution of each House of Parliament: Now, therefore, the Secretary of State, being designated for the purposes of section 2(2) of the European Communities Act 1972 in relation to the conferment and protection of exclusive rights in the topographies of semiconductor products, in exercise of the powers conferred on him by the said section 2(2) hereby makes the following Regulations:

(S.I. 1100)

Citation and commencement

1. These Regulations may be cited as the Design Right (Semiconductor Topo- **11-001** graphies) Regulations 1989 and shall come into force on 1st August 1989.

Interpretation

2.—(1) In these Regulations— **11-002**

"the Act" means the Copyright, Designs and Patents Act 1988;

"semiconductor product" means an article the purpose, or one of the purposes, of which is the performance of an electronic function and which consists of two or more layers, at least one of which is composed of semiconducting material and in or upon one or more of which is fixed a pattern appertaining to that or another function; and

"semiconductor topography" means a design within the meaning of section 213(2) of the Act which is a design of either of the following:

(a) the pattern fixed, or intended to be fixed, in or upon—

(i) a layer of a semiconductor product, or

(ii) a layer of material in the course of and for the purpose of the manufacture of a semiconductor product, or

(b) the arrangement of the patterns fixed, or intended to be fixed, in or upon the layers of a semiconductor product in relation to one another.

(2) Except where the context otherwise requires, these Regulations shall be construed as one with Part III of the Act (design right).

Application of Copyright, Designs and Patents Act 1988, Part III

11-003   **3.** In its application to a design which is a semiconductor topography, Part III of the Act shall have effect subject to regulations 4 to 9 below.

Qualification

11-004   **4.**—(1) Section 213(5) of the Act has effect subject to paragraphs (2) to (4) below.

(2) Part III of the Act has effect as if for section 217 of the Act there was substituted the following:

> "**217.**—
>
> (1) In this Part—
>
> "qualifying individual" means a citizen or subject of, or an individual habitually resident in, a qualifying country; and
>
> "qualifying person" means—
>
> (a) a qualifying individual,
>
> (b) a body corporate or other body having legal personality which has in any qualifying country or in Gibraltar a place of business at which substantial business activity is carried on, or
>
> (c) a person who falls within one of the additional classes set out in Part I of the ScheduleDesign Right (Semiconductor Topographies) Regulations 1989 to the .
>
> (2) References in this Part to a qualifying person include the Crown and the government of any other qualifying country.
>
> (3) In this section "qualifying country" means—
>
> (a) the United Kingdom, or
>
> (b) another member State of the European Economic Community.
>
> (4) The reference in the definition of "qualifying individual" to a person's being a citizen or subject of a qualifying country shall be construed in relation to the United Kingdom as a reference to his being a British citizen.
>
> (5) In determining for the purpose of the definition of "qualifying person" whether substantial business activity is carried on at a place of business in any country, no account shall be taken of dealings in goods which are at all material times outside that country.".

(3) Where a semiconductor topography is created in pursuance of a commission or in the course of employment and the designer of the topography is, by virtue of section 215 of the Act (as substituted by regulation 5 below), the first owner of design right in that topography, section 219 of the Act does not apply and section 218(2) to (4) of the Act shall apply to the topography as if it had not been created in pursuance of a commission or in the course of employment.

(4) Section 220 of the Act has effect subject to regulation 7 below and as if for subsection (1) there was substituted the following:

> "**220.**—
>
> (1) A design which does not qualify for design right protection under section 218 or 219 (as modified by regulation 4(3) of the Design Right (Semiconductor Topographies) Regulations 1989) or under the said regulation 4(3) qualifies for design right protection if the first marketing of articles made to the design—
>
> (a) is by a qualifying person who is exclusively authorised to put such articles on the market in every member State of the European Economic Community, and
>
> (b) takes place within the territory of any member State.";

and subsection (4) of section 220 accordingly has effect as if the words "in the United Kingdom" were omitted.

Ownership of design right

11-005   **5.** Part III of the Act has effect as if for section 215 of the Act there was substituted the following:

> "**215.**—

(1) The designer is the first owner of any design right in a design which is not created in pursuance of a commission or in the course of employment.

(2) Where a design is created in pursuance of a commission, the person commissioning the design in the first owner of any design right in it subject to any agreement in writing to the contrary.

(3) Where, in a case not falling within subsection (2) a design is created by an employee in the course of his employment, his employer is the first owner of any design right in the design subject to any agreement in writing to the contrary.

(4) If a design qualifies for design right protection by virtue of section 220 (as modified by regulation 4(4) of the Design Right (Semiconductor Topographies) Regulations 1989), the above rules do not apply and, subject to regulation 7 of the said Regulations, the person by whom the articles in question are marketed is the first owner of the design right.".

Duration of design right

6.—(1) Part III of the Act has effect as if for section 216 of the Act there was **11-006** substituted the following:

"**216.** The design right in a semiconductor topography expires—
  (a) ten years from the end of the calendar year in which the topography or articles made to the topography were first made available for sale or hire anywhere in the world by or with the licence of the design right owner, or
  (b) if neither the topography nor articles made to the topography are so made available within a period of fifteen years commencing with the earlier of the time when the topography was first recorded in a design document or the time when an article was first made to the topography, at the end of that period.".

(2) Subsection (2) of section 263 of the Act has effect as if the words "or a semi-conductor topography" were inserted after the words "in relation to an article".

(3) The substitute provision set out in paragraph (1) above has effect subject to regulation 7 below.

Confidential information

7. In determining, for the purposes of section 215(4), 216 or 220 of the Act (as **11-007** modified by these Regulations), whether there has been any marketing, or anything has been made available for sale or hire, no account shall be taken of any sale or hire, or any offer or exposure for sale or hire, which is subject to an obligation of confidence in respect of information about the semiconductor topography in question unless either—
  (a) the article or semiconductor topography sold or hired or offered or exposed for sale or hire has been sold or hired on a previous occasion (whether or not subject to an obligation of confidence), or
  (b) the obligation is imposed at the behest of the Crown, or of the government of any country outside the United Kingdom, for the protection of security in connection with the production of arms, munitions or war material.

Infringement

8.—(1) Section 226 of the Act has effect as if for subsection (1) there was sub- **11-008** stituted the following:

"**226.**—
(1) Subject to subsection (1A), the owner of design right in a design has the exclusive right to reproduce the design—
  (a) by making articles to that design, or
  (b) by making a design document recording the design for the purpose of enabling such articles to be made.
(1A) Subsection (1) does not apply to—
  (a) the reproduction of a design privately for non-commercial aims; or

(b) the reproduction of a design for the purpose of analysing or evaluating the design or analysing, evaluating or teaching the concepts, processes, systems or techniques embodied in it.".

(2) Section 227 of the Act does not apply if the article in question has previously been sold or hired within—

(a) the United Kingdom by or with the licence of the owner of design right in the semiconductor topography in question, or

(b) the territory of any other member State of the European Economic Community or the territory of Gibraltar by or with the consent of the person for the time being entitled to import it into or sell or hire it within that territory.

(3) Section 228(6) of the Act does not apply.

(4) It is not an infringement of design right in a semiconductor topography to—

(a) create another original semiconductor topography as a result of an analysis or evaluation of the first topography or of the concepts, processes, systems or techniques embodied in it, or

(b) reproduce that other topography.

(5) Anything which would be an infringement of the design right in a semiconductor topography if done in relation to the topography as a whole is an infringement of the design right in the topography if done in relation to a substantial part of the topography.

Licences of right

11-009   **9.** Section 237 of the Act does not apply.

Revocation and transitional provisions

11-010   **10.**—(1) The Semiconductor Products (Protection of Topography) Regulations 1987 are hereby revoked.

(2) Sub-paragraph (1) of paragraph 19 of Schedule 1 to the Act shall not apply in respect of a semiconductor topography created between 7th November 1987 and 31st July 1989.

(3) In its application to copyright in a semiconductor topography created before 7th November 1987, sub-paragraph (2) of the said paragraph 19 shall have effect as if the reference to sections 237 to 239 were a reference to sections 238 and 239; and subparagraph (3) of that paragraph accordingly shall not apply to such copyright.

Regulation 4(2)   [Schedule

ADDITIONAL CLASSES OF QUALIFYING PERSONS

PART I

DESCRIPTIONS OF ADDITIONAL CLASSES

11-011   **1.** British Dependent Territory citizens.

11-012   **2.** Citizens and subjects of any country specified in Part II below.

11-013   **3.** Habitual residents of any country specified in Part II below, the Isle of Man, the Channel Islands or any colony.

4. Firms and bodies corporate formed under the law of, or of any part of, the United Kingdom, Gibraltar, another member State of the European Economic Community or any country specified in Part II below with a place of business within any country so specified at which substantial business activity is carried on.

11-014

PART II

SPECIFIED COUNTRIES: CITIZENS, SUBJECTS, HABITUAL RESIDENTS, BODIES CORPORATE AND OTHER BODIES HAVING LEGAL PERSONALITY

Australia
Austria
Finland
French overseas territories (French Polynesia; French Southern and Antarctic Territories; Mayotte; New Caledonia and dependencies; Saint-Pierre and Miquelon; Wallis and Futuna Islands)
Iceland
Japan
Liechtenstein
Norway
Sweden
Switzerland
United States of America][1]

The Duration of Copyright and Rights in Performances Regulations 1995

Whereas a draft of the following Regulations has been approved by resolution of each House of Parliament: Now, therefore, the Secretary of State, being a Minister designated for the purposes of section 2(2) of the European Communities Act 1972 in relation to measures relating to the protection of copyright and rights in performances, in exercise of powers conferred by section 2(2) and (4) of the said Act of 1972, hereby makes the following Regulations:—

(S.I. 3297)

PART I

INTRODUCTORY PROVISIONS

Citation, commencement and extent

1.—(1) These Regulations may be cited as the Duration of Copyright and Rights in Performances Regulations 1995.

12-001

(2) These Regulations come into force on 1st January 1996.

(3) These Regulations extend to the whole of the United Kingdom.

Interpretation

2. In these Regulations—

12-002

---

[1] Substituted by SI 1993/2497 Sch 1 para 1

"EEA Agreement" means the Agreement on the European Economic Area signed at Oporto on 2nd May 1992, as adjusted by the Protocol signed at Brussels on 17th March 1993; and

"EEA state" means a state which is a contracting party to the EEA Agreement.

Implementation of Directive, &c

12-003   **3.** These Regulations make provision for the purpose of implementing—

(a) the main provisions of Council Directive No. 93/98/EEC of 29th October 1993 harmonizing the term of protection of copyright and certain related rights; and

(b) certain obligations of the United Kingdom created by or arising under the EEA Agreement so far as relevant to the implementation of that Directive.

Scheme of the regulations

12-004   **4.** The Copyright, Designs and Patents Act 1988 is amended in accordance with the provisions of Part II of these Regulations, subject to the savings and transitional provisions in Part III of these Regulations.

PART III

SAVINGS AND TRANSITIONAL PROVISIONS

Introductory

Introductory

12-005   **12.**—(1) References in this Part to "commencement", without more, are to the date on which these Regulations come into force.

(2) In this Part—

"the 1988 Act" means the Copyright, Designs and Patents Act 1988;

"the 1988 provisions" means the provisions of that Act as they stood immediately before commencement (including the provisions of Schedule 1 to that Act continuing the effect of earlier enactments); and

"the new provisions" means the provisions of that Act as amended by these Regulations.

(3) Expressions used in this Part which are defined for the purposes of Part I or II of the 1988 Act, in particular references to the copyright owner, have the same meaning as in that Part.

Films not protected as such

12-006   **13.** In relation to a film in which copyright does not or did not subsist as such but which is or was protected—

(a) as an original dramatic work, or

(b) by virtue of the protection of the photographs forming part of the film, references in the new provisions, and in this Part, to copyright in a film are to any copyright in the film as an original dramatic work or, as the case may be, in photographs forming part of the film.

Copyright

Copyright: interpretation

14.—(1) In the provisions of this Part relating to copyright—   **12-007**
    (a) "existing", in relation to a work, means made before commencement; and
    (b) "existing copyright work" means a work in which copyright subsisted immediately before commencement.

(2) For the purposes of those provisions a work of which the making extended over a period shall be taken to have been made when its making was completed.

(3) References in those provisions to "moral rights" are to the rights conferred by Chapter IV of Part I of the 1988 Act.

Duration of copyright: general saving

15.—(1) Copyright in an existing copyright work shall continue to subsist **12-008** until the date on which it would have expired under the 1988 provisions if that date is later than the date on which copyright would expire under the new provisions.

(2) Where paragraph (1) has effect, section 57 of the 1988 Act (anonymous or pseudonymous works: acts permitted on assumptions as to expiry of copyright or death of author) applies as it applied immediately before commencement (that is, without the amendments made by Regulation 5(2)).

Duration of copyright: application of new provisions

16. The new provisions relating to duration of copyright apply—   **12-009**
    (a) to copyright works made after commencement;
    (b) to existing works which first qualify for copyright protection after commencement;
    (c) to existing copyright works, subject to Regulation 15 (general saving for any longer period applicable under 1988 provisions); and
    (d) to existing works in which copyright expired before 31st December 1995 but which were on 1st July 1995 protected in another EEA state under legislation relating to copyright or related rights.

Extended and revived copyright

17. In the following provisions of this Part—   **12-010**
    "extended copyright" means any copyright which subsists by virtue of the new provisions after the date on which it would have expired under the 1988 provisions; and
    "revived copyright" means any copyright which subsists by virtue of the new provisions after having expired under the 1988 provisions or any earlier enactment relating to copyright.

Ownership of extended copyright

18.—(1) The person who is the owner of the copyright in a work immediately **12-011** before commencement is as from commencement the owner of any extended copyright in the work, subject as follows.

(2) If he is entitled to copyright for a period less than the whole of the copyright period under the 1988 provisions, any extended copyright is part of the reversionary interest expectant on the termination of that period.

Ownership of revived copyright

12-012   **19.**—(1) The person who was the owner of the copyright in a work immediately before it expired (the "former copyright owner") is as from commencement the owner of any revived copyright in the work, subject as follows.

(2) If the former copyright owner has died before commencement, or in the case of a legal person has ceased to exist before commencement, the revived copyright shall vest—

> (a) in the case of a film, in the principal director of the film or his personal representatives, and
>
> (b) in any other case, in the author of the work or his personal representatives.

(3) Where revived copyright vests in personal representatives by virtue of paragraph (2), it shall be held by them for the benefit of the person who would have been entitled to it had it been vested in the principal director or author immediately before his death and had devolved as part of his estate.

Prospective ownership of extended or revived copyright

12-013   **20.**—(1) Where by an agreement made before commencement in relation to extended or revived copyright, and signed by or on behalf of the prospective owner of the copyright, the prospective owner purports to assign the extended or revived copyright (wholly or partially) to another person, then if, on commencement the assignee or another person claiming under him would be entitled as against all other persons to require the copyright to be vested in him, the copyright shall vest in the assignee or his successor in title by virtue of this paragraph.

(2) A licence granted by a prospective owner of extended or revived copyright is binding on every successor in title to his interest (or prospective interest) in the right, except a purchaser in good faith for valuable consideration and without notice (actual or constructive) of the licence or a person deriving title from such a purchaser; and references in Part I of the 1988 Act to doing anything with, or without, the licence of the copyright owner shall be construed accordingly.

(3) In paragraph (2) "prospective owner" includes a person who is prospectively entitled to extended or revived copyright by virtue of such an agreement as is mentioned in paragraph (1).

Extended copyright: existing licences, agreement, &c

12-014   **21.**—(1) Any copyright licence, any term or condition of an agreement relating to the exploitation of a copyright work, or any waiver or assertion of moral rights, which—

> (a) subsists immediately before commencement in relation to an existing copyright work, and
>
> (b) is not to expire before the end of the copyright period under the 1988 provisions,

shall continue to have effect during the period of any extended copyright, subject to any agreement to the contrary.

(2) Any copyright licence, or term or condition relating to the exploitation of a copyright work, imposed by order of the Copyright Tribunal which—

> (a) subsists immediately before commencement in relation to an existing copyright work, and

(b) is not to expire before the end of the copyright period under the 1988 provisions,

shall continue to have effect during the period of any extended copyright, subject to any further order of the Tribunal.

Revived copyright: exercise of moral rights

22.—(1) The following provisions have effect with respect to the exercise of **12-015** moral rights in relation to a work in which there is revived copyright.

(2) Any waiver or assertion of moral rights which subsisted immediately before the expiry of copyright shall continue to have effect during the period of revived copyright.

(3) Moral rights are exercisable after commencement by the author of a work or, as the case may be, the director of a film in which revived copyright subsists, as with any other copyright work.

(4) Where the author or director died before commencement—

(a) the rights conferred by—

section 77 (right to identification as author or director),

section 80 (right to object to derogatory treatment of work), or

section 85 (right to privacy of certain photographs and films),

are exercisable after commencement by his personal representatives, and

(b) any infringement after commencement of the right conferred by section 84 (false attribution) is actionable by his personal representatives.

(5) Any damages recovered by personal representatives by virtue of this Regulation in respect of an infringement after a person's death shall devolve as part of his estate as if the right of action had subsisted and been vested in him immediately before his death.

(6) Nothing in these Regulations shall be construed as causing a moral right to be exercisable if, or to the extent that, the right was excluded by virtue of paragraph 23 or 24 of Schedule 1 on the commencement of the 1988 Act or would have been so excluded if copyright had not previously expired.

Revived copyright: saving for acts of exploitation when work in public domain, &c

23.—(1) No act done before commencement shall be regarded as infringing **12-016** revived copyright in a work.

(2) It is not an infringement of revived copyright in a work—

(a) to do anything after commencement in pursuance of arrangements made before 1st January 1995 at a time when copyright did not subsist in the work, or

(b) to issue to the public after commencement copies of the work made before 1st July 1995 at a time when copyright did not subsist in the work.

(3) It is not an infringement of revived copyright in a work to do anything after commencement in relation to a literary, dramatic, musical or artistic work or a film made before commencement, or made in pursuance of arrangements made before commencement, which contains a copy of that work or is an adaptation of that work if—

(a) the copy or adaptation was made before 1st July 1995 at a time when copyright did not subsist in the work in which revived copyright subsists, or

(b) the copy or adaptation was made in pursuance of arrangements made before 1st July 1995 at a time when copyright did not subsist in the work in which revived copyright subsists.

(4) It is not an infringement of revived copyright in a work to do after commencement anything which is a restricted act in relation to the work if the act is done at a time when, or is done in pursuance of arrangements made at a time when, the name and address of a person entitled to authorise the act cannot by reasonable inquiry be ascertained.

(5) In this Regulation "arrangements" means arrangements for the exploitation of the work in question.

(6) It is not an infringement of any moral right to do anything which by virtue of this Regulation is not an infringement of copyright.

Revived copyright: use as of right subject to reasonable royalty

12-017 **24.**—(1) In the case of a work in which revived copyright subsists any acts restricted by the copyright shall be treated as licensed by the copyright owner, subject only to the payment of such reasonable royalty or other remuneration as may be agreed or determined in default of agreement by the Copyright Tribunal.

(2) A person intending to avail himself of the right conferred by this Regulation must give reasonable notice of his intention to the copyright owner, stating when he intends to begin to do the acts.

(3) If he does not give such notice, his acts shall not be treated as licensed.

(4) If he does give such notice, his acts shall be treated as licensed and a reasonable royalty or other remuneration shall be payable in respect of them despite the fact that its amount is not agreed or determined until later.

(5) This Regulation does not apply if or to the extent that a licence to do the acts could be granted by a licensing body (within the meaning of section 116(2) of the 1988 Act), whether or not under a licensing scheme.

(6) No royalty or other remuneration is payable by virtue of this Regulation in respect of anything for which a royalty or other remuneration is payable under Schedule 6 to the 1988 Act.

Revived copyright: application to Copyright Tribunal

12-018 **25.**—(1) An application to settle the royalty or other remuneration payable in pursuance of Regulation 24 may be made to the Copyright Tribunal by the copyright owner or the person claiming to be treated as licensed by him.

(2) The Tribunal shall consider the matter and make such order as it may determine to be reasonable in the circumstances.

(3) Either party may subsequently apply to the Tribunal to vary the order, and the Tribunal shall consider the matter and make such order confirming or varying the original order as it may determine to be reasonable in the circumstances.

(4) An application under paragraph (3) shall not, except with the special leave of the Tribunal, be made within twelve months from the date of the original order or of the order on a previous application under that paragraph.

(5) An order under paragraph (3) has effect from the date on which it is made or such later date as may be specified by the Tribunal.

Film sound tracks: application of new provisions

12-019 **26.**—(1) The new provisions relating to the treatment of film sound tracks apply to existing sound tracks as from commencement.

(2) The owner of any copyright in a film has as from commencement corresponding rights as copyright owner in any existing sound track treated as part of the film; but without prejudice to any rights of the owner of the copyright in the sound track as a sound recording.

(3) Anything done before commencement under or in relation to the copyright in the sound recording continues to have effect and shall have effect, so far as concerns the sound track, in relation to the film as in relation to the sound recording.

(4) It is not an infringement of the copyright in the film (or of any moral right in the film) to do anything after commencement in pursuance of arrangements for the exploitation of the sound recording made before commencement.

Rights in performances

Rights in performances: interpretation

27.—(1) In the provisions of this Part relating to rights in performances— **12-020**
  (a) "existing", in relation to a performance, means given before commencement; and
  (b) "existing protected performance" means a performance in relation to which rights under Part II of the 1988 act (rights in performances) subsisted immediately before commencement.

(2) References in this Part to performers' rights are to the rights given by section 180(1)(a) of the 1988 Act and references to recording rights are to the rights given by section 180(1)(b) of that Act.

Duration of rights in performances: general saving

28. Any rights under Part II of the 1988 Act in an existing protected perfor- **12-021**
mance shall continue to subsist until the date on which they would have expired under the 1988 provisions if that date is later than the date on which the rights would expire under the new provisions.

Duration of rights in performances: application of new provisions

29. The new provisions relating to the duration of rights under Part II of the **12-022**
1988 Act apply—
  (a) to performances taking place after commencement;
  (b) to existing performances which first qualify for protection under Part II of the 1988 Act after commencement;
  (c) to existing protected performances, subject to Regulation 28 (general saving for any longer period applicable under 1988 provisions); and
  (d) to existing performances—
      (i) in which rights under Part II of the 1988 Act expired after the commencement of that Part and before 31st December 1995, or
      (ii) which were protected by earlier enactments relating to the protection of performers and in which rights under that Part did not arise by reason only that the performance was given at a date such that the rights would have ceased to subsist before the commencement of that Part,
  but which were on 1st July 1995 protected in another EEA state under legislation relating to copyright or related rights.

Extended and revived performance rights

12-023   **30.** In the following provisions of this Part—

"extended performance rights" means rights under Part II of the 1988 Act which subsist by virtue of the new provisions after the date on which they would have expired under the 1988 provisions; and

"revived performance rights" means rights under Part II of the 1988 Act which subsist by virtue of the new provisions—

(a) after having expired under the 1988 provisions, or

(b) in relation to a performance which was protected by earlier enactments relating to the protection of performers and in which rights under that Part did not arise by reason only that the performance was given at a date such that the rights would have ceased to subsist before the commencement of that Part.

References in the following provisions of this Part to "revived pre-1988 rights" are to revived performance rights within paragraph (b) of the above definition.

Entitlement to extended or revived performance rights

12-024   **31.**—(1) Any extended performance rights are exercisable as from commencement by the person who was entitled to exercise those rights immediately before commencement, that is—

(a) in the case of performers' rights, the performer or (if he has died) the person entitled by virtue of section 192(2) of the 1988 Act to exercise those rights;

(b) in the case of recording rights, the person who was within the meaning of section 185 of the 1988 Act the person having those rights.

(2) Any revived performance rights are exercisable as from commencement—

(a) in the case of rights which expired after the commencement of the 1988 Act, by the person who was entitled to exercise those rights immediately before they expired;

(b) in the case of revived pre-1988 performers' rights, by the performer or his personal representatives;

(c) in the case of revived pre-1988 recording rights, by the person who would have been the person having those rights immediately before the commencement of the 1988 Act or, if earlier, immediately before the death of the performer, applying the provisions of section 185 of that Act to the circumstances then obtaining.

(3) Any remuneration or damages received by a person's personal representatives by virtue of a right conferred on them by paragraph (1) or (2) shall devolve as part of that person's estate as if the right had subsisted and been vested in him immediately before his death.

Extended performance rights: existing consents, agreement, &c

12-025   **32.** Any consent, or any term or condition of an agreement, relating to the exploitation of an existing protected performance which—

(a) subsists immediately before commencement, and

(b) is not to expire before the end of the period for which rights under Part II of the 1988 Act subsist in relation to that performance,

shall continue to subsist during the period of any extended performance rights, subject to any agreement to the contrary.

Revived performance rights: saving for acts of exploitation when performance in public domain, &c

33.—(1) No act done before commencement shall be regarded as infringing **12-026** revived performance rights in a performance.

(2) It is not an infringement of revived performance rights in a performance—

(a) to do anything after commencement in pursuance of arrangements made before 1st January 1995 at a time when the performance was not protected, or

(b) to issue to the public after commencement a recording of a performance made before 1st July 1995 at a time when the performance was not protected.

(3) It is not an infringement of revived performance rights in a performance to do anything after commencement in relation to a sound recording or film made before commencement, or made in pursuance of arrangements made before commencement, which contains a recording of the performance if—

(a) the recording of the performance was made before 1st July 1995 at a time when the performance was not protected, or

(b) the recording of the performance was made in pursuance of arrangements made before 1st July 1995 at a time when the performance was not protected.

(4) It is not an infringement of revived performance rights in a performance to do after commencement anything at a time when, or in pursuance of arrangements made at a time when, the name and address of a person entitled to authorise the act cannot by reasonable inquiry be ascertained.

(5) In this Regulation "arrangements" means arrangements for the exploitation of the performance in question.

(6) References in this Regulation to a performance being protected are—

(a) in relation to the period after the commencement of the 1988 Act, to rights under Part II of that Act subsisting in relation to the performance, and

(b) in relation to earlier periods, to the consent of the performer being required under earlier enactments relating to the protection of performers.

Revived performance rights: use as of right subject to reasonable remuneration

34.—(1) In the case of a performance in which revived performance rights **12-027** subsist any acts which require the consent of any person under Part II of the 1988 Act (the "rights owner") shall be treated as having that consent, subject only to the payment of such reasonable remuneration as may be agreed or determined in default of agreement by the Copyright Tribunal.

(2) A person intending to avail himself of the right conferred by this Regulation must give reasonable notice of his intention to the rights owner, stating when he intends to begin to do the acts.

(3) If he does not give such notice, his acts shall not be treated as having consent.

(4) If he does give such notice, his acts shall be treated as having consent and reasonable remuneration shall be payable in respect of them despite the fact that its amount is not agreed or determined until later.

Revived performance rights: application to Copyright Tribunal

12-028   **35.**—(1) An application to settle the remuneration payable in pursuance of Regulation 34 may be made to the Copyright Tribunal by the rights owner or the person claiming to be treated as having his consent.

(2) The Tribunal shall consider the matter and make such order as it may determine to be reasonable in the circumstances.

(3) Either party may subsequently apply to the Tribunal to vary the order, and the Tribunal shall consider the matter and make such order confirming or varying the original order as it may determine to be reasonable in the circumstances.

(4) An application under paragraph (3) shall not, except with the special leave of the Tribunal, be made within twelve months from the date of the original order or of the order on a previous application under that paragraph.

(5) An order under paragraph (3) has effect from the date on which it is made or such later date as may be specified by the Tribunal.

Supplementary

Construction of references to EEA states

12-029   **36.**—(1) For the purpose of the new provisions relating to the term of copyright protection applicable to a work of which the country of origin is not an EEA state and of which the author is not a national of an EEA state—

(a) a work first published before 1st July 1995 shall be treated as published in an EEA state if it was on that date regarded under the law of the United Kingdom or another EEA state as having been published in that state;

(b) an unpublished film made before 1st July 1995 shall be treated as originating in an EEA state if it was on that date regarded under the law of the United Kingdom or another EEA state as a film whose maker had his headquarters in, or was domiciled or resident in, that state; and

(c) the author of a work made before 1st July 1995 shall be treated as an EEA national if he was on that date regarded under the law of the United Kingdom or another EEA state as a national of that state.

The references above to the law of another EEA state are to the law of that state having effect for the purposes of rights corresponding to those provided for in Part I of the 1988 Act.

(2) For the purposes of the new provisions relating to the term of protection applicable to a performance where the performer is not a national of an EEA state, the performer of a performance given before 1st July 1995 shall be treated as an EEA national if he was on that date regarded under the law of the United Kingdom or another EEA state as a national of that state.

The reference above to the law of another EEA state is to the law of that state having effect for the purposes of rights corresponding to those provided for in Part II of the 1988 Act.

(3) In this Regulation "another EEA state" means an EEA state other than the United Kingdom.

The Copyright and Related Rights Regulations 1996

Whereas a draft of the following Regulations has been approved by resolution of each House of Parliament: Now, therefore, the Secretary of State, being a Minister designated for the purposes of section 2(2) of the European Communities Act 1972 in relation to measures relating to the protection of copyright and rights in performances, in exercise of powers conferred by section 2(2) and (4) of the said Act of 1972, hereby makes the following Regulations:-

(S.I. 2967)

PART I

INTRODUCTORY PROVISIONS

Citation, commencement and extent

1.—(1) These Regulations may be cited as the Copyright and Related Rights **13-001**
Regulations 1996.
(2) These Regulations come into force on 1st December 1996.
(3) These Regulations extend to the whole of the United Kingdom.

Interpretation

2. In these Regulations- **13-002**
　"EEA Agreement" means the Agreement on the European Economic
　　Area signed at Oporto on 2nd May 1992, as adjusted by the Protocol
　　signed at Brussels on 17th March 1993; and
　"EEA state" means a state which is a contracting party to the EEA
　　Agreement.

Implementation of Directives, &c

3. These Regulations make provision for the purpose of implementing- **13-003**
　(a) Council Directive No. 92/100/EEC of 19 November 1992 on rental
　　　right and lending right and on certain rights related to copyright in the
　　　field of intellectual property;
　(b) Council Directive No. 93/83/EEC of 27 September 1993 on the coordi-
　　　nation of certain rules concerning copyright and rights related to
　　　copyright applicable to satellite broadcasting and cable retransmission;
　(c) the provisions of Council Directive No. 93/98/EEC of 29 October 1993
　　　harmonizing the term of protection of copyright and certain related
　　　rights, so far as not implemented by the Duration of Copyright and
　　　Rights in Performances Regulations 1995; and
　(d) certain obligations of the United Kingdom created by or arising under
　　　the EEA Agreement so far as relevant to the implementation of those
　　　Directives.

Scheme of the regulations

4. The Copyright, Designs, and Patents Act 1988 is amended in accordance **13-004**
with the provisions of Part II of these Regulations, subject to the savings and transitional provisions in Part III of these Regulations.

PART II

AMENDMENTS OF THE COPYRIGHT, DESIGNS AND PATENTS ACT 1988

Publication right

Publication right

13-005   **16.**—(1) A person who after the expiry of copyright protection, publishes for the first time a previously unpublished work has, in accordance with the following provisions, a property right ("publication right") equivalent to copyright.

(2) For this purpose publication includes any [making available][1] to the public, in particular—

   (a) the issue of copies to the public;

   (b) making the work available by means of an electronic retrieval system;

   (c) the rental or lending of copies of the work to the public;

   (d) the performance, exhibition or showing of the work in public; or

   [(e) communicating the work to the public.][2]

(3) No account shall be taken for this purpose of any unauthorised act.

In relation to a time when there is no copyright in the work, an unauthorised act means an act done without the consent of the owner of the physical medium in which the work is embodied or on which it is recorded.

(4) A work qualifies for publication right protection only if—

   (a) first publication is in the European Economic Area, and

   (b) the publisher of the work is at the time of first publication a national of an EEA state.

Where two or more persons jointly publish the work, it is sufficient for the purposes of paragraph (b) if any of them is a national of an EEA state.

(5) No publication right arises from the publication of a work in which Crown copyright or Parliamentary copyright subsisted.

(6) Publication right expires at the end of the period of 25 years from the end of the calendar year in which the work was first published.

(7) In this regulation a "work" means a literary, dramatic, musical or artistic work or a film.

(8) Expressions used in this regulation (other than "publication") have the same meaning as in Part I.

Application of copyright provisions to publication right

13-006   **17.**—(1) The substantive provisions of Part I relating to copyright (but not moral rights in copyright works), that is, the relevant provisions of—

   Chapter II (rights of copyright owner),

   Chapter III (acts permitted in relation to copyright works),

   Chapter V (dealings with rights in copyright works),

   Chapter VI (remedies for infringement), and

   Chapter VII (copyright licensing),

apply in relation to publication right as in relation to copyright, subject to the following exceptions and modifications.

(2) The following provisions do not apply—

---

[1] Word substituted by SI 2003/2498 Sch 1 (3) para 27 (a)
[2] Substituted by SI 2003/2498 Sch 1 (3) para 27 (b)

    (a) in Chapter III (acts permitted in relation to copyright works), sections 57, 64, 66A and 67;

    (b) in Chapter VI (remedies for infringement), sections 104 to 106;

    (c) in Chapter VII (copyright licensing), section 116(4).

(3) The following provisions have effect with the modifications indicated –

    (a) in section 107(4) and (5) (offences of making or dealing in infringing articles, &c.), the maximum punishment on summary conviction is imprisonment for a term not exceeding three months or a fine not exceeding level 5 on the standard scale, or both;

    (b) in sections 116(2), 117 and 124 for "works of more than one author" substitute "works of more than one publisher".

(4) The other relevant provisions of Part I, that is –

in Chapter I, provisions defining expressions used generally in Part I, Chapter VIII (the Copyright Tribunal),

in Chapter IX –

    section 161 (territorial waters and the continental shelf), and

    section 162 (British ships, aircraft and hovercraft), and

in Chapter X

    section 171(1) and (3) (savings for other rules of law, &c.), and

    sections 172 to 179 (general interpretation provisions),

apply, with any necessary adaptations, for the purposes of supplementing the substantive provisions of that Part as applied by this regulation.

(5) Except where the context otherwise requires, any other enactment relating to copyright (whether passed or made before or after these regulations) applies in relation to publication right as in relation to copyright.

In this paragraph "enactment" includes an enactment contained in subordinate legislation within the meaning of the Interpretation Act 1978.

Authorship of films and certain photographs

Clarification of transitional provisions relating to pre-1989 photographs

19. Any question arising, in relation to photographs which were existing **13-007** works within the meaning of Schedule 1, as to who is to be regarded as the author for the purposes of-

    (a) regulations 15 and 16 of the Duration of Copyright and Rights in Performances Regulations 1995 (duration of copyright: application of new provisions subject to general saving), or

    (b) regulation 19(2)(b) of those regulations (ownership of revived copyright),

is to be determined in accordance with section 9 as in force on the commencement of those regulations (and not, by virtue of paragraph 10 of Schedule 1, in accordance with the law in force at the time when the work was made).

PART III

TRANSITIONAL PROVISIONS AND SAVINGS

General provisions

Introductory

13-008   **25.**—(1) In this Part—
"commencement" means the commencement of these Regulations; and
"existing", in relation to a work or performance, means made or given
before commencement.

(2) For the purposes of this Part a work of which the making extended over a period shall be taken to have been made when its making was completed.

(3) In this Part a "new right" means a right arising by virtue of these Regulations, in relation to a copyright work or a qualifying performance, to authorise or prohibit an act.

The expression does not include—
(a) a right corresponding to a right which existed immediately before commencement, or
(b) a right to remuneration arising by virtue of these Regulations.

(4) Expressions used in this Part have the same meaning in relation to copyright as they have in Part I of the Copyright, Designs and Patents Act 1988, and in relation to performances as in Part II of that Act.

General rules

13-009   **26.**—(1) Subject to anything in regulations 28 to 36 (special transitional provisions and savings), these regulations apply to copyright works made, and to performances given, before or after commencement.

(2) No act done before commencement shall be regarded as an infringement of any new right, or as giving rise to any right to remuneration arising by virtue of these Regulations.

Saving for certain existing agreements

13-010   **27.**—(1) Except as otherwise expressly provided, nothing in these Regulations affects an agreement made before 19th November 1992.

(2) No act done in pursuance of any such agreement after commencement shall be regarded as an infringement of any new right.

Special provisions

Broadcasts

13-011   **28.** The provisions of—
regulation 5 (place where broadcast treated as made) and
regulation 6 (safeguards in relation to certain satellite broadcasts),
have effect in relation to broadcasts made after commencement.

Satellite broadcasting: international co-production agreements

13-012   **29.**—(1) This regulation applies to an agreement concluded before 1st January 1995—

(a) between two or more co-producers of a film, one of whom is a national of an EEA state, and

(b) the provisions of which grant to the parties exclusive rights to exploit all communication to the public of the film in separate geographical areas.

(2) Where such an agreement giving such exclusive exploitation rights in relation to the United Kingdom does not expressly or by implication address satellite broadcasting from the United Kingdom, the person to whom those exclusive rights have been granted shall not make any such broadcast without the consent of any other party to the agreement whose language-related exploitation rights would be adversely affected by that broadcast.

New rights: exercise of rights in relation to performances

30.—(1) Any new right conferred by these Regulations in relation to a   **13-013**
qualifying performance is exercisable as from commencement by the performer or (if he has died) by the person who immediately before commencement was entitled by virtue of section 192(2) to exercise the rights conferred on the performer by Part II in relation to that performance.

(2) Any remuneration or damages received by a person's personal representatives by virtue of a right conferred on them by paragraph (1) shall devolve as part of that person's estate as if the right had subsisted and been vested in him immediately before his death.

New rights: effect of pre-commencement authorisation of copying

31. Where before commencement–   **13-014**

(a) the owner or prospective owner of copyright in a literary, dramatic, musical or artistic work has authorised a person to make a copy of the work, or

(b) the owner or prospective owner of performers' rights in a performance has authorised a person to make a copy of a recording of the performance,

any new right in relation to that copy shall vest on commencement in the person so authorised, subject to any agreement to the contrary.

New rights: effect of pre-commencement film production agreement

32.—(1) Sections 93A and 191F (presumption of transfer of rental right in   **13-015**
case of production agreement) apply in relation to an agreement concluded before commencement.

As section 93A so applies, the restriction in subsection (3) of that section shall be omitted (exclusion of presumption in relation to screenplay, dialogue or music specifically created for the film).

(2) Sections 93B and 191G (right to equitable remuneration where rental right transferred) have effect accordingly, but subject to regulation 33 (right to equitable remuneration applicable to rental after 1st April 1997).

Right to equitable remuneration applicable to rental after 1st April 1997

33. No right to equitable remuneration under section 93B or 191G (right to   **13-016**
equitable remuneration where rental right transferred) arises-

(a) in respect of any rental of a sound recording or film before 1st April 1997, or

(b) in respect of any rental after that date of a sound recording or film made in pursuance of an agreement entered into before 1st July 1994, unless the author or performer (or a successor in title of his) has before 1st January 1997 notified the person by whom the remuneration would be payable that he intends to exercise that right.

Savings for existing stocks

13-017   **34.**—(1) Any new right in relation to a copyright work does not apply to a copy of the work acquired by a person before commencement for the purpose of renting or lending it to the public.

(2) Any new right in relation to a qualifying performance does not apply to a copy of a recording of the performance acquired by a person before commencement for the purpose of renting or lending it to the public.

Lending of copies by libraries or archives

13-018   **35.** Until the making of regulations under section 37 of the Copyright, Designs and Patents Act 1988 for the purposes of section 40A(2) of that Act (lending of copies by libraries or archives), the reference in section 40A(2) (and in paragraph 6B of Schedule 2) to a prescribed library or archive shall be construed as a reference to any library or archive in the United Kingdom prescribed by paragraphs 2 to 6 of Part A of Schedule 1 to the Copyright (Librarians and Archivists) (Copying of Copyright Material) Regulations 1989.

Authorship of films

13-019   **36.**—(1) Regulation 18 (authorship of films) applies as from commencement in relation to films made on or after 1st July 1994.

(2) It is not an infringement of any right which the principal director has by virtue of these Regulations to do anything after commencement in pursuance of arrangements for the exploitation of the film made before 19th November 1992.

This does not affect any right of his to equitable remuneration under section 93B.

The Copyright and Rights in Databases Regulations 1997

Whereas a draft of the following Regulations has been approved by a resolution of each House of Parliament: Now, therefore, the Secretary of State, being a Minister designated for the purposes of section 2(2) of the European Communities Act 1972 in relation to measures relating to copyright and measures relating to the prevention of unauthorised extraction of the contents of a database and of unauthorised re-utilisation of those contents, in exercise of the powers conferred by section 2(2) and (4) of that Act, hereby makes the following Regulations:—

(S.I. 3032)

PART I

INTRODUCTORY PROVISIONS

Citation, commencement and extent

1.—(1) These Regulations may be cited as the Copyright and Rights in **14-001** Databases Regulations 1997.

(2) These Regulations come into force on 1st January 1998.

(3) These Regulations extend to the whole of the United Kingdom.

Implementation of Directive

2.—(1) These Regulations make provision for the purpose of implementing— **14-002**
  (a) Council Directive No. 96/9/EC of 11 March 1996 on the legal protection of databases, [...][1]
  (b) certain obligations of the United Kingdom created by or arising under the EEA Agreement so far as relating to the implementation of that Directive[, and][2]

(2) In this Regulation "the EEA Agreement" means the Agreement on the European Economic Area signed at Oporto on 2nd May 1992, as adjusted by the Protocol signed at Brussels on 17th March 1993.

Interpretation

3. In these Regulations "the 1988 Act" means the Copyright, Designs and **14-003** Patents Act 1988.

Scheme of the Regulations

4.—(1) The 1988 Act is amended in accordance with the provisions of Part II **14-004** of these Regulations, subject to the savings and transitional provisions in Part IV of these Regulations.

(2) Part III of these Regulations has effect subject to those savings and transitional provisions.

---

[1] Word repealed by SI 2003/2501 reg 3 (a)
[2] Words substituted by SI 2003/2501 reg 3 (b)

PART III

DATABASE RIGHT

Interpretation

14-005   **12.**—(1) In this Part—

"database" has the meaning given by section 3A(1) of the 1988 Act (as inserted by Regulation 6);

"extraction", in relation to any contents of a database, means the permanent or temporary transfer of those contents to another medium by any means or in any form;

"insubstantial", in relation to part of the contents of a database, shall be construed subject to Regulation 16(2);

"investment" includes any investment, whether of financial, human or technical resources;

"jointly", in relation to the making of a database, shall be construed in accordance with Regulation 14(6);

"lawful user", in relation to a database, means any person who (whether under a licence to do any of the acts restricted by any database right in the database or otherwise) has a right to use the database;

"maker", in relation to a database, shall be construed in accordance with Regulation 14;

"re-utilisation", in relation to any contents of a database, means making those contents available to the public by any means;

"substantial", in relation to any investment, extraction or re-utilisation, means substantial in terms of quantity or quality or a combination of both.

(2) The making of a copy of a database available for use, on terms that it will or may be returned, otherwise than for direct or indirect economic or commercial advantage, through an establishment which is accessible to the public shall not be taken for the purposes of this Part to constitute extraction or re-utilisation of the contents of the database.

(3) Where the making of a copy of a database available through an establishment which is accessible to the public gives rise to a payment the amount of which does not go beyond what is necessary to cover the costs of the establishment, there is no direct or indirect economic or commercial advantage for the purposes of paragraph (2).

(4) Paragraph (2) does not apply to the making of a copy of a database available for on-the-spot reference use.

(5) Where a copy of a database has been sold within the EEA [or the Isle of Man][1] by, or with the consent of, the owner of the database right in the database, the further sale within the EEA [or the Isle of Man][2] of that copy shall not be taken for the purposes of this Part to constitute extraction or re-utilisation of the contents of the database.

Database right

14-006   **13.**—(1) A property right ("database right") subsists, in accordance with this Part, in a database if there has been a substantial investment in obtaining, verifying or presenting the contents of the database.

---

[1] Words inserted by SI 2003/2501 reg 4
[2] Words inserted by SI 2003/2501 reg 4

(2) For the purposes of paragraph (1) it is immaterial whether or not the database or any of its contents is a copyright work, within the meaning of Part I of the 1988 Act.

(3) This Regulation has effect subject to Regulation 18.

The maker of a database

14.—(1) Subject to paragraphs (2) to (4), the person who takes the initiative **14-007** in obtaining, verifying or presenting the contents of a database and assumes the risk of investing in that obtaining, verification or presentation shall be regarded as the maker of, and as having made, the database.

(2) Where a database is made by an employee in the course of his employment, his employer shall be regarded as the maker of the database, subject to any agreement to the contrary.

(3) Subject to paragraph (4), where a database is made by Her Majesty or by an officer or servant of the Crown in the course of his duties, Her Majesty shall be regarded as the maker of the database.

(4) Where a database is made by or under the direction or control of the House of Commons or the House of Lords—

(a) the House by whom, or under whose direction or control, the database is made shall be regarded as the maker of the database, and

(b) if the database is made by or under the direction or control of both Houses, the two Houses shall be regarded as the joint makers of the database.

[(4A) Where a database is made by or under the direction or control of the Scottish Parliament, the Scottish Parliamentary Corporate Body shall be regarded as the maker of the database.][1]

(5) For the purposes of this Part a database is made jointly if two or more persons acting together in collaboration take the initiative in obtaining, verifying or presenting the contents of the database and assume the risk of investing in that obtaining, verification or presentation.

(6) References in this Part to the maker of a database shall, except as otherwise provided, be construed, in relation to a database which is made jointly, as references to all the makers of the database.

First ownership of database right

15. The maker of a database is the first owner of database right in it.   **14-008**

Acts infringing database right

16.—(1) Subject to the provisions of this Part, a person infringes database **14-009** right in a database if, without the consent of the owner of the right, he extracts or re-utilises all or a substantial part of the contents of the database.

(2) For the purposes of this Part, the repeated and systematic extraction or re-utilisation of insubstantial parts of the contents of a database may amount to the extraction or re-utilisation of a substantial part of those contents.

Term of protection

17.—(1) Database right in a database expires at the end of the period of **14-010** fifteen years from the end of the calendar year in which the making of the database was completed.

---

[1] Inserted by SI 1999/1042 Sch 1 Pt II para 26

(2) Where a database is made available to the public before the end of the period referred to in paragraph (1), database right in the database shall expire fifteen years from the end of the calendar year in which the database was first made available to the public.

(3) Any substantial change to the contents of a database, including a substantial change resulting from the accumulation of successive additions, deletions or alterations, which would result in the database being considered to be a substantial new investment shall qualify the database resulting from that investment for its own term of protection.

(4) This Regulation has effect subject to Regulation 30.

Qualification for database right

14-011   **18.**—(1) Database right does not subsist in a database unless, at the material time, its maker, or if it was made jointly, one or more of its makers, was—

    (a) an individual who was a national of an EEA state or habitually resident within the EEA,

    (b) a body which was incorporated under the law of an EEA state and which, at that time, satisfied one of the conditions in paragraph (2), [...][1]

    (c) a partnership or other unincorporated body which was formed under the law of an EEA state and which, at that time, satisfied the condition in paragraph (2)(a)[,][2]

    [(d) an individual who was habitually resident within the Isle of Man,

    (e) a body which was incorporated under the law of the Isle of Man and which, at that time, satisfied one of the conditions in paragraph (2A), or

    (f) a partnership or other unincorporated body which was formed under the law of the Isle of Man and which, at that time, satisfied the condition in paragraph (2A)(a).][3]

(2) The conditions mentioned in paragraphs (1)(b) and (c) are—

    (a) that the body has its central administration or principal place of business within the EEA, or

    (b) that the body has its registered office within the EEA and the body's operations are linked on an ongoing basis with the economy of an EEA state.

[(2A) The conditions mentioned in paragraphs (1)(e) and (f) are–

    (a) that the body has its central administration or principal place of business within the Isle of Man, or

    (b) that the body has its registered office within the Isle of Man and the body's operations are linked on an ongoing basis with the economy of the Isle of Man.][4]

(3) Paragraph (1) does not apply in any case falling within Regulation 14(4).

(4) In this Regulation—

    (a) "EEA" and "EEA state" have the meaning given by section 172A of the 1988 Act;

    (b) "the material time" means the time when the database was made, or if the making extended over a period, a substantial part of that period.

---

[1] Word repealed by SI 2003/2501 reg 5 (a)
[2] Words substituted by SI 2003/2501 reg 5 (b)
[3] Inserted by SI 2003/2501 reg 5 (c)
[4] Inserted by SI 2003/2501 reg 5 (d)

Avoidance of certain terms affecting lawful users

19.—(1) A lawful user of a database which has been made available to the **14-012** public in any manner shall be entitled to extract or re-utilise insubstantial parts of the contents of the database for any purpose.

(2) Where under an agreement a person has a right to use a database, or part of a database, which has been made available to the public in any manner, any term or condition in the agreement shall be void in so far as it purports to prevent that person from extracting or re-utilising insubstantial parts of the contents of the database, or of that part of the database, for any purpose.

[Exceptions to database right

20.—(1) Database right in a database which has been made available to the **14-013** public in any manner is not infringed by fair dealing with a substantial part of its contents if—

(a) that part is extracted from the database by a person who is apart from this paragraph a lawful user of the database,

(b) it is extracted for the purpose of illustration for teaching or research and not for any commercial purpose, and

(c) the source is indicated.

(2) The provisions of Schedule 1 specify other acts which may be done in relation to a database notwithstanding the existence of database right.]¹

Acts permitted on assumption as to expiry of database right

21.—(1) Database right in a database is not infringed by the extraction or re- **14-014** utilisation of a substantial part of the contents of the database at a time when, or in pursuance of arrangements made at a time when—

(a) it is not possible by reasonable inquiry to ascertain the identity of the maker, and

(b) it is reasonable to assume that database right has expired.

(2) In the case of a database alleged to have been made jointly, paragraph (1) applies in relation to each person alleged to be one of the makers.

Presumptions relevant to database right

22.—(1) The following presumptions apply in proceedings brought by virtue **14-015** of this Part of these Regulations with respect to a database.

(2) Where a name purporting to be that of the maker appeared on copies of the database as published, or on the database when it was made, the person whose name appeared shall be presumed, until the contrary is proved—

(a) to be the maker of the database, and

(b) to have made it in circumstances not falling within Regulation 14(2) to (4).

(3) Where copies of the database as published bear a label or a mark stating—

(a) that a named person was the maker of the database, or

(b) that the database was first published in a specified year,

the label or mark shall be admissible as evidence of the facts stated and shall be presumed to be correct until the contrary is proved.

(4) In the case of a database alleged to have been made jointly, paragraphs (2) and (3), so far as is applicable, apply in relation to each person alleged to be one of the makers.

---

¹ Substituted by Legal Deposit Libraries Act 2003 c.28 s 8 (2)

Application of copyright provisions to database right

14-016   **23.** The following provisions of the 1988 Act—
sections 90 to 93 (dealing with rights in copyright works);
sections 96 to 98 (rights and remedies of copyright owner);
sections 101 and 102 (rights and remedies of exclusive licensee);
apply in relation to database right and databases in which that right subsists as they apply in relation to copyright and copyright works.

Licensing of database right

14-017   **24.** The provisions of Schedule 2 have effect with respect to the licensing of database right.

Database right: jurisdiction of Copyright Tribunal

14-018   **25.**—(1) The Copyright Tribunal has jurisdiction under this Part to hear and determine proceedings under the following provisions of Schedule 2—
(a) paragraph 3, 4 or 5 (reference of licensing scheme);
(b) paragraph 6 or 7 (application with respect to licence under licensing scheme);
(c) paragraph 10, 11 or 12 (reference or application with respect to licence by licensing body).

(2) The provisions of Chapter VIII of Part I of the 1988 Act (general provisions relating to the Copyright Tribunal) apply in relation to the Tribunal when exercising any jurisdiction under this Part.

(3) Provisions shall be made by rules under section 150 of the 1988 Act prohibiting the Tribunal from entertaining a reference under paragraph 3, 4 or 5 of Schedule 2 (reference of licensing scheme) by a representative organisation unless the Tribunal is satisfied that the organisation is reasonably representative of the class of persons which it claims to represent.

PART IV

SAVINGS AND TRANSITIONAL PROVISIONS

[Introductory

14-019   **26.** Expressions used in this Part which are defined for the purposes of Part I of the 1988 Act have the same meaning as in that Part.][1]

General rule

14-020   **27.** Subject to Regulations 28 and 29, these Regulations apply to databases made before or after [1st January 1998][2].

[General savings

14-021   **28.**—(1) Nothing in these Regulations affects any agreement made before 1st January 1998.

(2) Nothing in these Regulations affects any agreement made after 31st December 1997 and before 1st November 2003 in so far as the effect would only arise as a result of the amendment of these Regulations by the Copyright and Rights in Databases (Amendment) Regulations 2003.

---

[1] Substituted by SI 2003/2501 reg 6
[2] Words substituted by SI 2003/2501 reg 7

(3) No act done in respect of any database, in which database right subsists by virtue of the maker of the database (or one or more of its makers) falling within one of the provisions contained in Regulations 14(4) and 18(1)(a), (b) and (c),–

(a) before 1st January 1998, or

(b) after 31st December 1997, in pursuance of an agreement made before 1st January 1998,

shall be regarded as an infringement of database right in the database.

(4) No act done in respect of any database, in which database right subsists by virtue of its maker (or one or more of its makers) falling within one of the provisions contained in Regulation 18(1)(d), (e) and (f),–

(a) before 1st November 2003, or

(b) after 31st October 2003, in pursuance of an agreement made before 1st November 2003,

shall be regarded as an infringement of database right in the database.][1]

Saving for copyright in certain existing databases

29.—(1) Where a database—   **14-022**

(a) was created on or before 27th March 1996, and

(b) is a copyright work immediately before [1st January 1998][2],

copyright shall continue to subsist in the database for the remainder of its copyright term.

(2) In this Regulation "copyright term" means the period of the duration of copyright under section 12 of the 1988 Act (duration of copyright in literary, dramatic, musical or artistic works).

[Database right: term applicable to certain existing databases

30. Where–   **14-023**

(a) the making of any database is completed on or after 1st January 1983, and before 1st January 1998, and

(b) either–

(i) the database is a database in which database right subsists by virtue of the maker of the database (or one or more of its makers) falling within one of the provisions contained in Regulations 14(4) and 18(1)(a), (b) and (c) and database right begins to subsist in the database on 1st January 1998, or

(ii) the database is a database in which database right subsists by virtue of its maker (or one or more of its makers) falling within one of the provisions contained in Regulation 18(1)(d), (e) and (f) and database right begins to subsist in the database on 1st November 2003,

then database right shall subsist in the database for a period of fifteen years beginning with 1st January 1998.][3]

---

[1] Substituted by SI 2003/2501 reg 8
[2] Words substituted by SI 2003/2501 reg 9
[3] Substituted by SI 2003/2501 reg 10

Regulation 20(2)   Schedule 1

EXCEPTIONS TO DATABASE RIGHT FOR PUBLIC ADMINISTRATION

Parliamentary and judicial proceedings

14-024   1. Database right in a database is not infringed by anything done for the purposes of parliamentary or judicial proceedings or for the purposes of reporting such proceedings.

Royal Commissions and statutory inquiries

14-025   2.—(1) Database right in a database is not infringed by anything done for—
          (a) the purposes of the proceedings of a Royal Commission or statutory inquiry, or
          (b) the purpose of reporting any such proceedings held in public.
     (2) Database right in a database is not infringed by the issue to the public of copies of the report of a Royal Commission or statutory inquiry containing the contents of the database.
     (3) In this paragraph "Royal Commission" and "statutory inquiry" have the same meaning as in section 46
          of the 1988 Act.

Material open to public inspection or on official register

14-026   3.—(1) Where the contents of a database are open to public inspection pursuant to a statutory requirement, or are on a statutory register, database right in the database is not infringed by the extraction of all or a substantial part of the contents containing factual information of any description, by or with the authority of the appropriate person, for a purpose which does not involve re-utilisation of all or a substantial part of the contents.
     (2) Where the contents of a database are open to public inspection pursuant to a statutory requirement, database right in the database is not infringed by the extraction or re-utilisation of all or a substantial part of the contents, by or with the authority of the appropriate person, for the purpose of enabling the contents to be inspected at a more convenient time or place or otherwise facilitating the exercise of any right for the purpose of which the requirement is imposed.
     (3) Where the contents of a database which is open to public inspection pursuant to a statutory requirement, or which is on a statutory register, contain information about matters of general scientific, technical, commercial or economic interest, database right in the database is not infringed by the extraction or re-utilisation of all or a substantial part of the contents, by or with the authority of the appropriate person, for the purpose of disseminating that information.
     (4) In this paragraph—
          "appropriate person" means the person required to make the contents of the database open to
               public inspection or, as the case may be, the person maintaining the register;
          "statutory register" means a register maintained in pursuance of a statutory requirement; and
          "statutory requirement" means a requirement imposed by provision made by or under an
               enactment.

Material communicated to the Crown in the course of public business

14-027   4.—(1) This paragraph applies where the contents of a database have in the course of public business been communicated to the Crown for any purpose, by or with the licence of the owner of the database right and a document or other material thing recording or embodying the contents of the database is owned by or in the custody or control of the Crown.
     (2) The Crown may, for the purpose for which the contents of the database were communicated to it, or any related purpose which could reasonably have been anticipated by the owner of the database right in the database, extract or re-utilise all or a substantial part of the contents without infringing database right in the database.
     (3) The Crown may not re-utilise the contents of a database by virtue of this paragraph if the contents have previously been published otherwise than by virtue of this paragraph.
     (4) In sub-paragraph (1) "public business" includes any activity carried on by the Crown.
     (5) This paragraph has effect subject to any agreement to the contrary between the Crown and the owner of the database right in the database.

Public records

5. The contents of a database which are comprised in public records within the meaning of the   **14-028**
Public Records Act 1958, the Public Records (Scotland) Act 1937 or the Public Records Act (Northern Ireland) 1923 which are open to public inspection in pursuance of that Act, may be re-utilised by or with the authority of any officer appointed under that Act, without infringement of database right in the database.

Acts done under statutory authority

6.—(1) Where the doing of a particular act is specifically authorised by an Act of Parliament,   **14-029**
whenever passed, then, unless the Act provides otherwise, the doing of that act does not infringe database right in a database.

(2) Sub-paragraph (1) applies in relation to an enactment contained in Northern Ireland legislation as it applies in relation to an Act of Parliament.

(3) Nothing in this paragraph shall be construed as excluding any defence of statutory authority otherwise available under or by virtue of any enactment.

Regulation 24   Schedule 2

Licensing of Database Right

Licensing scheme and licensing bodies

1.—(1) In this Schedule a "licensing scheme" means a scheme setting out—   **14-030**
    (a) the classes of case in which the operator of the scheme, or the person on whose behalf he
        acts, is willing to grant database right licences, and
    (b) the terms on which licences would be granted in those classes of case;
and for this purpose a "scheme" includes anything in the nature of a scheme, whether described as a scheme or as a tariff or by any other name.

(2) In this Schedule a "licensing body" means a society or other organisation which has as its main object, or one of its main objects, the negotiating or granting, whether as owner or prospective owner of a database right or as agent for him, of database right licences, and whose objects include the granting of licences covering the databases of more than one maker.

(3) In this paragraph "database right licences" means licences to do, or authorise the doing of, any of the things for which consent is required under Regulation 16.

2. Paragraphs 3 to 8 apply to licensing schemes which are operated by licensing bodies and cover   **14-031**
databases of more than one maker so far as they relate to licences for extracting or re-utilising all or a substantial part of the contents of a database; and references in those paragraphs to a licensing scheme shall be construed accordingly.

Reference of proposed licensing scheme to tribunal

3.—(1) The terms of a licensing scheme proposed to be operated by a licensing body may be   **14-032**
referred to the Copyright Tribunal by an organisation claiming to be representative of persons claiming that they require licences in cases of a description to which the scheme would apply, either generally or in relation to any description of case.

(2) The Tribunal shall first decide whether to entertain the reference, and may decline to do so on the ground that the reference is premature.

(3) If the Tribunal decides to entertain the reference it shall consider the matter referred and make such order, either confirming or varying the proposed scheme, either generally or so far as it relates to cases of the description to which the reference relates, as the Tribunal may determine to be reasonable in the circumstances.

(4) The order may be made so as to be in force indefinitely or for such period as the Tribunal may determine.

Reference of licensing scheme to tribunal

14-033   **4.**—(1) If while a licensing scheme is in operation a dispute arises between the operator of the scheme and—

(a) a person claiming that he requires a licence in a case of a description to which the scheme applies, or

(b) an organisation claiming to be representative of such persons,

that person or organisation may refer the scheme to the Copyright Tribunal in so far as it relates to cases of that description.

(2) A scheme which has been referred to the Tribunal under this paragraph shall remain in operation until proceedings on the reference are concluded.

(3) The Tribunal shall consider the matter in dispute and make such order, either confirming or varying the scheme so far as it relates to cases of the description to which the reference relates, as the Tribunal may determine to be reasonable in the circumstances.

(4) The order may be made so as to be in force indefinitely or for such period as the Tribunal may determine.

Further reference of scheme to tribunal

14-034   **5.**—(1) Where the Copyright Tribunal has on a previous reference of a licensing scheme under paragraph 3 or 4, or under this paragraph, made an order with respect to the scheme, then, while the order remains in force—

(a) the operator of the scheme,

(b) a person claiming that he requires a licence in a case of the description to which the order applies, or

(c) an organisation claiming to be representative of such persons,

may refer the scheme again to the Tribunal so far as it relates to cases of that description.

(2) A licensing scheme shall not, except with the special leave of the Tribunal, be referred again to the Tribunal in respect of the same description of cases—

(a) within twelve months from the date of the order on the previous reference, or

(b) if the order was made so as to be in force for 15 months or less, until the last three months before the expiry of the order.

(3) A scheme which has been referred to the Tribunal under this section shall remain in operation until proceedings on the reference are concluded.

(4) The Tribunal shall consider the matter in dispute and make such order, either confirming, varying or further varying the scheme so far as it relates to cases of the description to which the reference relates, as the Tribunal may determine to be reasonable in the circumstances.

(5) The order may be made so as to be in force indefinitely or for such period as the Tribunal may determine.

Application for grant of licence in connection with licensing scheme

14-035   **6.**—(1) A person who claims, in a case covered by a licensing scheme, that the operator of the scheme has refused to grant him or procure the grant to him of a licence in accordance with the scheme, or has failed to do so within a reasonable time after being asked, may apply to the Copyright Tribunal.

(2) A person who claims, in a case excluded from a licensing scheme, that the operator of the scheme either—

(a) has refused to grant him a licence or procure the grant to him of a licence, or has failed to do so within a reasonable time of being asked, and that in the circumstances it is unreasonable that a licence should not be granted, or

(b) proposes terms for a licence which are unreasonable,

may apply to the Copyright Tribunal.

(3) A case shall be regarded as excluded from a licensing scheme for the purposes of sub-paragraph (2) if—

(a) the scheme provides for the grant of licences subject to terms excepting matters from the licence and the case falls within such an exception, or

(b) the case is so similar to those in which licences are granted under the scheme that it is unreasonable that it should not be dealt with in the same way.

(4) If the Tribunal is satisfied that the claim is well-founded, it shall make an order declaring that, in respect of the matters specified in the order, the applicant is entitled to a licence on such terms as the Tribunal may determine to be applicable in accordance with the scheme or, as the case may be, to be reasonable in the circumstances.

(5) The order may be made so as to be in force indefinitely or for such period as the Tribunal may determine.

Application for review of order as to entitlement to licence

7.—(1) Where the Copyright Tribunal has made an order under paragraph 6 that a person is entitled to a licence under a licensing scheme, the operator of the scheme or the original applicant may apply to the Tribunal to review its order.   **14-036**

(2) An application shall not be made, except with the special leave of the Tribunal—
- (a) within twelve months from the date of the order, or of the decision on a previous application under this section, or
- (b) if the order was made so as to be in force for 15 months or less, or as a result of the decision on a previous application under this section is due to expire within 15 months of that decision, until the last three months before the expiry date.

(3) The Tribunal shall on an application for review confirm or vary its order as the Tribunal may determine to be reasonable having regard to the terms applicable in accordance with the licensing scheme or, as the case may be, the circumstances of the case.

Effect of order of tribunal as to licensing scheme

8.—(1) A licensing scheme which has been confirmed or varied by the Copyright Tribunal—   **14-037**
- (a) under paragraph 3 (reference of terms of proposed scheme), or
- (b) under paragraph 4 or 5 (reference of existing scheme to Tribunal),

shall be in force or, as the case may be, remain in operation, so far as it relates to the description of case in respect of which the order was made, so long as the order remains in force.

(2) While the order is in force a person who in a case of a class to which the order applies—
- (a) pays to the operator of the scheme any charges payable under the scheme in respect of a licence covering the case in question or, if the amount cannot be ascertained, gives an undertaking to the operator to pay them when ascertained, and
- (b) complies with the other terms applicable to such a licence under the scheme,

shall be in the same position as regards infringement of database right as if he had at all material times been the holder of a licence granted by the owner of the database right in question in accordance with the scheme.

(3) The Tribunal may direct that the order, so far as it varies the amount of charges payable, has effect from a date before that on which it is made, but not earlier than the date on which the reference was made or, if later, on which the scheme came into operation.

If such a direction is made—
- (a) any necessary repayments, or further payments, shall be made in respect of charges already paid, and
- (b) the reference in sub-paragraph (2)(a) to the charges payable under the scheme shall be construed as a reference to the charges so payable by virtue of the order.

No such direction may be made where sub-paragraph (4) below applies.

(4) Where the Tribunal has made an order under paragraph 6 (order as to entitlement to licence under licensing scheme) and the order remains in force, the person in whose favour the order is made shall if he—
- (a) pays to the operator of the scheme any charges payable in accordance with the order or, if the amount cannot be ascertained, gives an undertaking to pay the charges when ascertained, and
- (b) complies with the other terms specified in the order,

be in the same position as regards infringement of database right as if he had at all material times been the holder of a licence granted by the owner of the database right in question on the terms specified in the order.

References and applications with respect to licences by licensing bodies

14-038   **9.** Paragraphs 10 to 13 (references and applications with respect to licensing by licensing bodies) apply to licences relating to database right which cover databases of more than one maker granted by a licensing body otherwise than in pursuance of a licensing scheme, so far as the licences authorise extracting or re-utilising all or a substantial part of the contents of a database; and references in those paragraphs to a licence shall be construed accordingly.

Reference to tribunal of proposed licence

14-039   **10.**—(1) The terms on which a licensing body proposes to grant a licence may be referred to the Copyright Tribunal by the prospective licensee.

(2) The Tribunal shall first decide whether to entertain the reference, and may decline to do so on the ground that the reference is premature.

(3) If the Tribunal decides to entertain the reference it shall consider the terms of the proposed licence and make such order, either confirming or varying the terms, as it may determine to be reasonable in the circumstances.

(4) The order may be made so as to be in force indefinitely or for such period as the Tribunal may determine.

Reference to tribunal of expiring licence

14-040   **11.**—(1) A licensee under a licence which is due to expire, by effluxion of time or as a result of notice given by the licensing body, may apply to the Copyright Tribunal on the ground that it is unreasonable in the circumstances that the licence should cease to be in force.

(2) Such an application may not be made until the last three months before the licence is due to expire.

(3) A licence in respect of which a reference has been made to the Tribunal shall remain in operation until proceedings on the reference are concluded.

(4) If the Tribunal finds the application well-founded, it shall make an order declaring that the licensee shall continue to be entitled to the benefit of the licence on such terms as the Tribunal may determine to be reasonable in the circumstances.

(5) An order of the Tribunal under this section may be made so as to be in force indefinitely or for such period as the Tribunal may determine.

Application for review of order as to licence

14-041   **12.**—(1) Where the Copyright Tribunal has made an order under paragraph 10 or 11, the licensing body or the person entitled to the benefit of the order may apply to the Tribunal to review its order.

(2) An application shall not be made, except with the special leave of the Tribunal—
   (a) within twelve months from the date of the order or of the decision on a previous application under this paragraph, or
   (b) if the order was made so as to be in force for 15 months or less, or as a result of the decision on a previous application under this section is due to expire within 15 months of that decision, until the last three months before the expiry date.

(3) The Tribunal shall on an application for review confirm or vary its order as the Tribunal may determine to be reasonable in the circumstances.

Effect of order of tribunal as to licence

14-042   **13.**—(1) Where the Copyright Tribunal has made an order under paragraph 10 or 11 and the order remains in force, the person entitled to the benefit of the order shall if he—
   (a) pays to the licensing body any charges payable in accordance with the order or, if the amount cannot be ascertained, gives an undertaking to pay the charges when ascertained, and
   (b) complies with the other terms specified in the order,
be in the same position as regards infringement of database right as if he had at all material times been the holder of a licence granted by the owner of the database right in question on the terms specified in the order.

(2) The benefit of the order may be assigned—

(a) in the case of an order under paragraph 10, if assignment is not prohibited under the terms of the Tribunal's order; and

(b) in the case of an order under paragraph 11, if assignment was not prohibited under the terms of the original licence.

(3) The Tribunal may direct that an order under paragraph 10 or 11, or an order under paragraph 12 varying such an order, so far as it varies the amount of charges payable, has effect from a date before that on which it is made, but not earlier than the date on which the reference or application was made or, if later, on which the licence was granted or, as the case may be, was due to expire.

If such a direction is made—

(a) any necessary repayments, or further payments, shall be made in respect of charges already paid, and

(b) the reference in sub-paragraph (1)(a) to the charges payable in accordance with the order shall be construed, where the order is varied by a later order, as a reference to the charges so payable by virtue of the later order.

General considerations: unreasonable discrimination

14. In determining what is reasonable on a reference or application under this Schedule relating **14-043**
to a licensing scheme or licence, the Copyright Tribunal shall have regard to—

(a) the availability of other schemes, or the granting of other licences, to other persons in similar circumstances, and

(b) the terms of those schemes or licences,

and shall exercise its powers so as to secure that there is no unreasonable discrimination between licensees, or prospective licensees, under the scheme or licence to which the reference or application relates and licensees under other schemes operated by, or other licences granted by, the same person.

Powers exercisable in consequence of competition report

15.—[(1) Sub-paragraph (1A) applies where whatever needs to be remedied, mitigated or **14-044**
prevented by the Secretary of State, the Office of Fair Trading or (as the case may be) the Competition Commission under section 12(5) of the Competition Act 1980 or section 41(2), 55(2), 66(6), 75(2), 83(2), 138(2), 147(2) or 160(2) of, or paragraph 5(2) or 10(2) of Schedule 7 to, the Enterprise Act 2002 (powers to take remedial action following references to the Commission in connection with public bodies and certain other persons, mergers or market investigations) or article 12(7) of, or paragraph 5(2) or 10(2) of Schedule 2 to, the Enterprise Act 2002 (Protection of Legitimate Interests) Order 2003 (power to take remedial action following references to the Commission in connection with European mergers) consists of or includes–

(a) conditions in licences granted by the owner of database right in a database restricting the use of the database by the licensee or the right of the owner of the database right to grant other licences; or

(b) a refusal of an owner of database right to grant licences on reasonable terms.

(1A) The powers conferred by Schedule 8 to the Enterprise Act 2002 include power to cancel or modify those conditions and, instead or in addition, to provide that licences in respect of the database right shall be available as of right.

(2) The references to anything permitted by Schedule 8 to the Enterprise Act 2002 in section 12(5A) of the Competition Act 1980 and in sections 75(4)(a), 83(4)(a), 84(2)(a), 89(1), 160(4)(a), 161(3)(a) and 164(1) of, and paragraphs 5, 10 and 11 of Schedule 7 to, the Act of 2002 and paragraphs 5, 10 and 11 of Schedule 2 to the Enterprise Act 2002 (Protection of Legitimate Interests) Order 2003 shall be construed accordingly.][1]

(3) The terms of a licence available by virtue of this paragraph shall, in default of agreement, be settled by the Copyright Tribunal on an application by the person requiring the licence; and terms so settled shall authorise the licensee to do everything in respect of which a licence is so available.

(4) Where the terms of a licence are settled by the Tribunal, the licence has effect from the date on which the application to the Tribunal was made.

---

[1] Substituted by SI 2003/1398 Sch 1 para 31 (2)

The Copyright and Related Rights Regulations 2003

The Secretary of State, being a Minister designated for the purposes of section 2(2) of the European Communities Act 1972, in relation to measures relating to copyright and to rights in performances and also in relation to measures relating to the prevention of unauthorised extraction of the contents of a database, and of unauthorised reutilisation of those contents, in exercise of the powers conferred on her by that section, hereby makes the following Regulations:

(S.I. 2498)

PART 1

INTRODUCTORY PROVISIONS

Citation and commencement

15-001   1. These Regulations may be cited as the Copyright and Related Rights Regulations 2003 and shall come into force on 31st October 2003.

Consequential amendments and repeals

15-002   2.—(1) Schedule 1 (consequential amendments) shall have effect.

(2) Schedule 2 (repeals) shall have effect.

PART 3

SAVINGS AND TRANSITIONAL PROVISIONS

General provisions

Introductory

15-003   30.—(1) In this Part –

"commencement" means the date upon which these regulations come into force;

"extended copyright" means any copyright in sound recordings which subsists by virtue of section 13A of the 1988 Act (as amended by regulation 29) after the date on which it would have expired under the 1988 provisions;

"prospective owner" includes a person who is prospectively entitled to extended copyright in a sound recording by virtue of such an agreement as is mentioned in regulation 37(1);

"the 1988 Act" means the Copyright, Designs and Patents Act 1988; and

"the 1988 provisions" means the provisions of the 1988 Act as they stood immediately before commencement (including the provisions of Schedule 1 to that Act continuing the effect of earlier enactments).

(2) Expressions used in this Part which are defined for the purposes of Part 1 or 2 of the 1988 Act have the same meaning as in that Part.

General rules

31.—(1) Subject to regulation 32, these Regulations apply to– **15-004**
  (a) copyright works made,
  (b) performances given,
  (c) databases, in which database right vests, made, and
  (d) works, in which publication right vests, first published,
before or after commencement.

(2) No act done before commencement shall be regarded as an infringement of any new or extended right arising by virtue of these Regulations.

Savings for certain existing agreements

32.—(1) Nothing in these Regulations affects any agreement made before **15-005** 22nd December 2002.

(2) No act done after commencement, in pursuance of an agreement made before 22nd December 2002, shall be regarded as an infringement of any new or extended right arising by virtue of these Regulations.

Special provisions

Permitted acts

33. The provisions of Chapter 3 of Part 1 (acts permitted in relation to **15-006** copyright works) and Schedule 2 (rights in performances: permitted acts) in the 1988 provisions shall continue to apply to anything done after commencement in completion of an act begun before commencement which was permitted by those provisions.

Performers' rights: making available to the public

34.—(1) Those parts of section 182D in the 1988 provisions which confer a **15-007** right to equitable remuneration in relation to the making available to the public in the way mentioned in section 182CA(1) (regulation 7) of a commercially published sound recording shall cease to apply on commencement.

(2) Any assignment made before commencement under the provisions of section 182D(2) shall, on commencement, cease to apply insofar as it relates to the new making available to the public right conferred by section 182CA (regulation 7).

Exercise of rights in relation to performances

35.—(1) The new right conferred by section 182CA (consent required for **15-008** making available to the public) (in regulation 7) is exercisable as from commencement by the performer or (if he has died) by the person who immediately before commencement was entitled by virtue of section 192A(2) to exercise the rights conferred on the performer by Part 2 in relation to that performance.

(2) Any damages received by a person's personal representatives by virtue of the right conferred by paragraph (1) shall devolve as part of that person's estate as if the right had subsisted and been vested in him immediately before his death.

Ownership of extended copyright in sound recordings

36. The person who is the owner of the copyright in a sound recording imme- **15-009** diately before commencement is as from commencement the owner of any extended copyright in that sound recording.

Prospective ownership of extended copyright in sound recordings

15-010   **37.**—(1) Where by an agreement made before commencement in relation to extended copyright in a sound recording, and signed by or on behalf of the prospective owner of the copyright, the prospective owner purports to assign the extended copyright (wholly or partially) to another person, then, if on commencement the assignee or another person claiming under him would be entitled as against all other persons to require the copyright to be vested in him, the copyright shall vest in the assignee or his successor in title by virtue of this paragraph.

(2) A licence granted by a prospective owner of extended copyright in a sound recording is binding on every successor in title to his interest (or prospective interest) in the right, except a purchaser in good faith for valuable consideration and without notice (actual or constructive) of the licence or a person deriving title from such a purchaser; and references in Part 1 of the 1988 Act to doing anything with, or without, the licence of the copyright owner shall be construed accordingly.

Extended copyright in sound recordings: existing licences, agreements, etc

15-011   **38.**—(1) Any copyright licence or any term or condition of an agreement relating to the exploitation of a sound recording which—

(a) subsists immediately before commencement in relation to an existing sound recording, and

(b) is not to expire before the end of the copyright period under the 1988 provisions,

shall continue to have effect during the period of any extended copyright in that sound recording, subject to any agreement to the contrary.

(2) Any copyright licence, or term or condition relating to the exploitation of a sound recording, imposed by order of the Copyright Tribunal which—

(a) subsists immediately before commencement in relation to an existing sound recording, and

(b) is not to expire before the end of the copyright period under the 1988 provisions,

shall continue to have effect during the period of any extended copyright, subject to any further order of the Tribunal.

Duration of copyright in sound recordings: general saving

15-012   **39.** Copyright in an existing sound recording shall continue to subsist until the date it would have expired under Regulation 15 of the Duration of Copyright and Rights in Performances Regulations 1995 (SI 1995/3297) if that date is later than the date on which copyright would expire under the provisions of section 13A of the 1988 Act as amended by regulation 29.

Sanctions and remedies

15-013   **40.**—(1) Section 296 in the 1988 provisions (devices designed to circumvent copy-protection) shall continue to apply to acts done in relation to computer programs or other works prior to commencement.

(2) Section 296 as substituted by regulation 24(1) (circumvention of technical devices applied to computer programs), and sections 296ZA (circumvention of technological measures) and 296ZD (rights and remedies in respect of devices designed to circumvent technological measures), introduced by regulation 24(1),

shall apply to acts done in relation to computer programs or other works on or after commencement.

(3) Sections 107(2A), 198(1A) and 296ZB(1) and (2) (offences) do not have effect in relation to any act committed before commencement.

CONSOLIDATED VERSION OF THE TREATY ESTABLISHING THE EUROPEAN COMMUNITY

PART ONE

PRINCIPLES

Article 2

The Community shall have as its task, by establishing a common market and **A1-001** an economic and monetary union and by implementing common policies or activities referred to in Articles 3 and 4, to promote throughout the Community a harmonious, balanced and sustainable development of economic activities, a high level of employment and of social protection, equality between men and women, sustainable and non-inflationary growth, a high degree of competitiveness and convergence of economic performance, a high level of protection and improvement of the quality of the environment, the raising of the standard of living and quality of life, and economic and social cohesion and solidarity among Member States.

Article 3

1. For the purposes set out in Article 2, the activities of the Community shall **A1-002** include, as provided in this Treaty and in accordance with the timetable set out therein:
    (a) the prohibition, as between Member States, of customs duties and quantitative restrictions on the import and export of goods, and of all other measures having equivalent effect;
    (b) a common commercial policy;
    (c) an internal market characterised by the abolition, as between Member States, of obstacles to the free movement of goods, persons, services and capital;
    (d) measures concerning the entry and movement of persons as provided for in Title IV;
    (e) a common policy in the sphere of agriculture and fisheries;
    (f) a common policy in the sphere of transport;
    (g) a system ensuring that competition in the internal market is not distorted;
    (h) the approximation of the laws of Member States to the extent required for the functioning of the common market;
    (i) the promotion of coordination between employment policies of the Member States with a view to enhancing their effectiveness by developing a coordinated strategy for employment;
    (j) a policy in the social sphere comprising a European Social Fund;
    (k) the strengthening of economic and social cohesion;
    (l) a policy in the sphere of the environment;
    (m) the strengthening of the competitiveness of Community industry;
    (n) the promotion of research and technological development;

(o) encouragement for the establishment and development of trans-European networks;

(p) a contribution to the attainment of a high level of health protection;

(q) a contribution to education and training of quality and to the flowering of the cultures of the Member States;

(r) a policy in the sphere of development cooperation;

(s) the association of the overseas countries and territories in order to increase trade and promote jointly economic and social development;

(t) a contribution to the strengthening of consumer protection;

(u) measures in the spheres of energy, civil protection and tourism.

2. In all the activities referred to in this Article, the Community shall aim to eliminate inequalities, and to promote equality, between men and women.

Article 4

A1-003   1. For the purposes set out in Article 2, the activities of the Member States and the Community shall include, as provided in this Treaty and in accordance with the timetable set out therein, the adoption of an economic policy which is based on the close coordination of Member States' economic policies, on the internal market and on the definition of common objectives, and conducted in accordance with the principle of an open market economy with free competition.

2. Concurrently with the foregoing, and as provided in this Treaty and in accordance with the timetable and the procedures set out therein, these activities shall include the irrevocable fixing of exchange rates leading to the introduction of a single currency, the ecu, and the definition and conduct of a single monetary policy and exchange-rate policy the primary objective of both of which shall be to maintain price stability and, without prejudice to this objective, to support the general economic policies in the Community, in accordance with the principle of an open market economy with free competition.

3. These activities of the Member States and the Community shall entail compliance with the following guiding principles: stable prices, sound public finances and monetary conditions and a sustainable balance of payments.

Article 5

A1-004   The Community shall act within the limits of the powers conferred upon it by this Treaty and of the objectives assigned to it therein.

In areas which do not fall within its exclusive competence, the Community shall take action, in accordance with the principle of subsidiarity, only if and in so far as the objectives of the proposed action cannot be sufficiently achieved by the Member States and can therefore, by reason of the scale or effects of the proposed action, be better achieved by the Community.

Any action by the Community shall not go beyond what is necessary to achieve the objectives of this Treaty.

Article 12

A1-005   Within the scope of application of this Treaty, and without prejudice to any special provisions contained therein, any discrimination on grounds of nationality shall be prohibited.

The Council, acting in accordance with the procedure referred to in Article 251, may adopt rules designed to prohibit such discrimination.

Article 14

1. The Community shall adopt measures with the aim of progressively estab- **A1-006** lishing the internal market over a period expiring on 31 December 1992, in accordance with the provisions of this Article and of Articles 15, 26, 47(2), 49, 80, 93 and 95 and without prejudice to the other provisions of this Treaty.

2. The internal market shall comprise an area without internal frontiers in which the free movement of goods, persons, services and capital is ensured in accordance with the provisions of this Treaty.

3. The Council, acting by a qualified majority on a proposal from the Commission, shall determine the guidelines and conditions necessary to ensure balanced progress in all the sectors concerned.

PART THREE

COMMUNITY POLICIES

TITLE I

FREE MOVEMENT OF GOODS

CHAPTER 2

PROHIBITION OF QUANTITATIVE RESTRICTIONS BETWEEN MEMBER STATES

Article 28

Quantitative restrictions on imports and all measures having equivalent effect **A1-007** shall be prohibited between Member States.

Article 29

Quantitative restrictions on exports, and all measures having equivalent **A1-008** effect, shall be prohibited between Member States.

Article 30

The provisions of Articles 28 and 29 shall not preclude prohibitions or restric- **A1-009** tions on imports, exports or goods in transit justified on grounds of public morality, public policy or public security; the protection of health and life of humans, animals or plants; the protection of national treasures possessing artistic, historic or archaeological value; or the protection of industrial and commercial property. Such prohibitions or restrictions shall not, however, constitute a means of arbitrary discrimination or a disguised restriction on trade between Member States.

TITLE VI

COMMON RULES ON COMPETITION, TAXATION AND APPROXIMATION OF LAWS

CHAPTER I

RULES ON COMPETITION

SECTION I RULES APPLYING TO UNDERTAKINGS

Article 81

A1-010 1. The following shall be prohibited as incompatible with the common market: all agreements between undertakings, decisions by associations of undertakings and concerted practices which may affect trade between Member States andwhich have as their object or effect the prevention, restriction or distortion of competition within the common market, and in particular those which:

 (a) directly or indirectly fix purchase or selling prices or any other trading conditions;

 (b) limit or control production, markets, technical development, or investment;

 (c) share markets or sources of supply;

 (d) apply dissimilar conditions to equivalent transactions with other trading parties, thereby placing them at a competitive disadvantage;

 (e) make the conclusion of contracts subject to acceptance by the other parties of supplementary obligations which, by their nature or according to commercial usage, have no connection with the subject of such contracts.

2. Any agreements or decisions prohibited pursuant to this article shall be automatically void.

3. The provisions of paragraph 1 may, however, be declared inapplicable in the case of:

 –any agreement or category of agreements between undertakings,

 –any decision or category of decisions by associations of undertakings,

 –any concerted practice or category of concerted practices,

which contributes to improving the production or distribution of goods or to promoting technical or economic progress, while allowing consumers a fair share of the resulting benefit, and which does not:

 (a) impose on the undertakings concerned restrictions which are not indispensable to the attainment of these objectives;

 (b) afford such undertakings the possibility of eliminating competition in respect of a substantial part of the products in question.

Article 82

A1-011 Any abuse by one or more undertakings of a dominant position within the common market or in a substantial part of it shall be prohibited as incompatible with the common market in so far as it may affect trade between Member States.

 Such abuse may, in particular, consist in:

 (a) directly or indirectly imposing unfair purchase or selling prices or other unfair trading conditions;

(b) limiting production, markets or technical development to the prejudice of consumers;

(c) applying dissimilar conditions to equivalent transactions with other trading parties, thereby placing them at a competitive disadvantage;

(d) making the conclusion of contracts subject to acceptance by the other parties of supplementary obligations which, by their nature or according to commercial usage, have no connection with the subject of such contracts.

PART FIVE

INSTITUTIONS OF THE COMMUNITY

TITLE I

PROVISIONS GOVERNING THE INSTITUTIONS

CHAPTER I

THE INSTITUTIONS

SECTION 4 THE COURT OF JUSTICE

Article 226

The Court of Justice and the Court of First Instance, each within its jurisdic- **A1-012** tion, shall ensure that in the interpretation and application of this Treaty the law is observed.

In addition, judicial panels may be attached to the Court of First Instance under the conditions laid down in Article 225a in order to exercise, in certain specific areas, the judicial competence laid down in this Treaty.

Article 230

The Court of Justice shall review the legality of acts adopted jointly by the **A1-013** European Parliament and the Council, of acts of the Council, of the Commission and of the ECB, other than recommendations and opinions, and of acts of the European Parliament intended to produce legal effects vis-á-vis third parties.

It shall for this purpose have jurisdiction in actions brought by a Member State, the European Parliament, the Council or the Commission on grounds of lack of competence, infringement of an essential procedural requirement, infringement of this Treaty or of any rule of law relating to its application, or misuse of powers.

The Court of Justice shall have jurisdiction under the same conditions in actions brought by the Court of Auditors and by the ECB for the purpose of protecting their prerogatives. Any natural or legal person may, under the same conditions, institute proceedings against a decision addressed to that person or against a decision which, although in the form of a regulation or a decision addressed to another person, is of direct and individual concern to the former.

The proceedings provided for in this article shall be instituted within two months of the publication of the measure, or of its notification to the plaintiff, or, in the absence thereof, of the day on which it came to the knowledge of the latter, as the case may be.

Article 232

A1-014   Should the European Parliament, the Council or the Commission, in infringement of this Treaty, fail to act, the Member States and the other institutions of the Community may bring an action before the Court of Justice to have the infringement established.

The action shall be admissible only if the institution concerned has first been called upon to act. If, within two months of being so called upon, the institution concerned has not defined its position, the action may be brought within a further period of two months.

Any natural or legal person may, under the conditions laid down in the preceding paragraphs, complain to the Court of Justice that an institution of the Community has failed to address to that person any act other than a recommendation or an opinion.

The Court of Justice shall have jurisdiction, under the same conditions, in actions or proceedings brought by the ECB in the areas falling within the latter's field of competence and in actions or proceedings brought against the latter.

Article 234

A1-015   The Court of Justice shall have jurisdiction to give preliminary rulings concerning:

(a) the interpretation of this Treaty;

(b) the validity and interpretation of acts of the institutions of the Community and of the ECB;

(c) the interpretation of the statutes of bodies established by an act of the Council, where those statutes so provide.

Where such a question is raised before any court or tribunal of a Member State, that court or tribunal may, if it considers that a decision on the question is necessary to enable it to give judgment, request the Court of Justice to give a ruling thereon.

Where any such question is raised in a case pending before a court or tribunal of a Member State against whose decisions there is no judicial remedy under national law, that court or tribunal shall bring the matter before the Court of Justice.

PART SIX

GENERAL AND FINAL PROVISIONS

Article 295

A1-016   This Treaty shall in no way prejudice the rules in Member States governing the system of property ownership.

COUNCIL REGULATION (EC) No 2100/94 of 27 July 1994 on
Community plant variety rights

Having regard to the proposal from the Commission,

Having regard to the opinion of the European Parliament,

Having regard to the opinion of the Economic and Social Committee,

Whereas plant varieties pose specific problems as regards the industrial property régime which may be applicable;

Whereas industrial property regimes for plant varieties have not been harmonized at Community level and therefore continue to be regulated by the legislation of the Member States, the content of which is not uniform;

Whereas in such circumstances it is appropriate to create a Community regime which, although co-existing with national regimes, allows for the grant of industrial property rights valid throughout the Community;

Whereas it is appropriate that the implementation and application of this Community regime should not be carried out by the authorities of the Member States but by a Community Office with legal personality, the 'Community Plant Variety Office';

Whereas the system must also have regard to developments in plant breeding techniques including biotechnology; whereas in order to stimulate the breeding and development of new varieties, there should be improved protection compared with the present situation for all plant breeders without, however, unjustifiably impairing access to protection generally or in the case of certain breeding techniques;

Whereas varieties of all botanical genera and species should be protectable;

Whereas protectable varieties must comply with internationally recognized requirements, i.e. distinctness, uniformity, stability and novelty, and also be designated by a prescribed variety denomination;

Whereas it is important to provide for a definition of a plant variety, in order to ensure the proper functioning of the system;

Whereas this definition is not intended to alter definitions which may have been established in the field of intellectual property rights, especially the patent field, nor to interfere with or exclude from application laws governing the protectability of products, including plants and plant material, or processes under such other industrial property rights;

Whereas it is however highly desirable to have a common definition in both fields; whereas therefore appropriate efforts at international level should be supported to reach such a common definition;

Whereas for the grant of Community plant variety rights an assessment of important characteristics relating to the variety is necessary; whereas, however, these characteristics need not necessarily relate to their economic importance;

Whereas the system must also clarify to whom the right to Community plant variety protection pertains; whereas in some cases it would be to several persons in common, not just to one; whereas the formal entitlement to make applications must be regulated;

Whereas the system must also define the term 'holder' used in this Regulation; whereas that term 'holder' without further specification is used in this Regulation including in its Article 29 (5), it is intended to be within the meaning of Article 13 (1) thereof;

Whereas, since the effect of a Community plant variety right should be uniform throughout the Community, commercial transactions subject to the holder's agreement must be precisely delimited; whereas the scope of protection should be extended, compared with most national systems, to certain material of the variety to take account of trade via countries outside the Community without protection; whereas, however, the introduction of the principle of exhaustion of rights must ensure that the protection is not excessive;

Whereas in order to stimulate plant breeding, the system basically confirms the internationally accepted rule of free access to protected varieties for the development therefrom, and exploitation, of new varieties;

Whereas in certain cases where the new variety, although distinct, is essentially derived from the initial variety, a certain form of dependency from the holder of the latter one should be created;

Whereas, the exercise of Community plant variety rights must be subjected to restrictions laid down in provisions adopted in the public interest;

Whereas this includes safeguarding agricultural production; whereas that purpose requires an authorization for farmers to use the product of the harvest for propagation under certain conditions;

Whereas it must be ensured that the conditions are laid down at Community level; Whereas compulsory licensing should also be provided for under certain circumstances in the public interest, which may include the need to supply the market with material offering specified features, or to maintain the incentive for continued breeding of improved varieties;

Whereas the use of prescribed variety denominations should be made obligatory;

Whereas the Community plant variety right should in principle have a life of at least 25 years and in the case of vine and tree species, at least 30 years; whereas other grounds for termination must be specified;

Whereas a Community plant variety right is an object of the holder's property and its role in relation to the non-harmonized legal provisions of the Member States, particularly of civil law, must therefore be clarified; whereas this applies also to the settlement of infringements and the enforcement of entitlement to Community plant variety rights;

Whereas, it is necessary to ensure that the full application of the principles of the Community plant variety rights system is not impaired by the effects of other systems; whereas for this purpose certain rules, in conformity with Member States' existing international commitments, are required concerning the relationship to other industrial property rights;

Whereas it is indispensable to examine whether and to what extent the conditions for the protection accorded in other industrial property systems, such as patents, should be adapted or otherwise modified for consistency with the Community plant variety rights system; whereas this, where necessary, should be laid down in balanced rules by additional Community law;

Whereas the duties and powers of the Community Plant Variety Office, including its Boards of Appeal, relating to the grant, termination or verification of Community plant variety rights and publications are as far as possible to be modelled on rules developed for other systems, as are also the Office's structure and Rules of Procedure, the collaboration with the Commission and Member States particularly through an Administrative Council, the involvement of Examination Offices in technical examination and moreover the necessary budgetary measures;

Whereas the Office should be advised and supervised by the aforementioned Administrative Council, composed of representatives of Member States and the Commission; Whereas the Treaty does not provide, for the adoption of this Regulation, powers other than those of Article 235;

Whereas this Regulation takes into account existing international conventions such as the International Convention for the Protection of New Varieties of Plants (UPOV Convention), the Convention of the Grant of European Patents (European Patent Convention) or the Agreement on trade-related aspects of intellectual property rights, including trade in counterfeit goods; whereas it consequently implements the ban on patenting plant varieties only to the extent that the European Patent Convention so requires, i.e. to plant varieties as such;

Whereas this Regulation should be re-examined for amendment as necessary in the light of future developments in the aforementioned Conventions,

HAS ADOPTED THIS REGULATION:

PART ONE

GENERAL PROVISIONS

Article 1 Community plant variety rights

A system of Community plant variety rights is hereby established as the sole **A2-001** and exclusive form of Community industrial property rights for plant varieties.

Article 2 Uniform effect of Community plant variety rights

Community plant variety rights shall have uniform effect within the territory **A2-002** of the Community and may not be granted, transferred or terminated in respect of the abovementioned territory otherwise than on a uniform basis.

Article 3 National property rights for plant varieties

This Regulation shall be without prejudice to the right of the Member States **A2-003** to grant national property rights for plant varieties, subject to the provisions of Article 92 (1).

Article 4 Community Office

For the purpose of the implementation of this Regulation a Community **A2-004** Plant Variety Office, hereinafter referred to as 'the Office', is hereby established.

PART TWO

SUBSTANTIVE LAW

CHAPTER I

CONDITIONS GOVERNING THE GRANT OF COMMUNITY PLANT VARIETY RIGHTS

Article 5 Object of Community plant variety rights

1. Varieties of all botanical genera and species, including, inter alia, hybrids **A2-005** between genera or species, may form the object of Community plant variety rights.

2. For the purpose of this Regulation, 'variety' shall be taken to mean a plant grouping within a single botanical taxon of the lowest known rank, which grouping, irrespective of whether the conditions for the grant of a plant variety right are fully met, can be:

– defined by the expression of the characteristics that results from a given genotype or combination of genotypes,

– distinguished from any other plant grouping by the expression of at least one of the said characteristics, and

– considered as a unit with regard to its suitability for being propagated unchanged.

3. A plant grouping consists of entire plants or parts of plants as far as such parts are capable of producing entire plants, both referred to hereinafter as 'variety constituents'.

4. The expression of the characteristics referred to in paragraph 2, first indent, may be either invariable or variable between variety constituents of the same kind provided that also the level of variation results from the genotype or combination of genotypes.

Article 6 Protectable varieties

A2-006 Community plant variety rights shall be granted for varieties that are:

(a) distinct;

(b) uniform;

(c) stable; and

(d) new.

Moreover, the variety must be designated by a denomination in accordance with the provisions of Article 63.

Article 7 Distinctness

A2-007 1. A variety shall be deemed to be distinct if it is clearly distinguishable by reference to the expression of the characteristics that results from a particular genotype or combination of genotypes, from any other variety whose existence is a matter of common knowledge on the date of application determined pursuant to Article 51.

2. The existence of another variety shall in particular be deemed to be a matter of common knowledge if on the date of application determined pursuant to Article 51:

(a) it was the object of a plant variety right or entered in an official register of plant varieties, in the Community or any State, or in any intergovernmental organization with relevant competence;

(b) an application for the granting of a plant variety right in its respect or for its entering in such an official register was filed, provided the application has led to the granting or entering in the meantime.

The implementing rules pursuant to Article 114 may specify further cases as examples which shall be deemed to be a matter of common knowledge.

Article 8 Uniformity

A2-008 A variety shall be deemed to be uniform if, subject to the variation that may be expected from the particular features of its propagation, it is sufficiently uniform in the expression of those characteristics which are included in the examination for distinctness, as well as any others used for the variety description.

Article 9 Stability

A2-009 A variety shall be deemed to be stable if the expression of the characteristics which are included in the examination for distinctness as well as any others used for the variety description, remain unchanged after repeated propagation or, in the case of a particular cycle of propagation, at the end of each such cycle.

Article 10 Novelty

1. A variety shall be deemed to be new if, at the date of application **A2-010** determined pursuant to Article 51, variety constituents or harvested material of the variety have not been sold or otherwise disposed of to others, by or with the consent of the breeder within the meaning of Article 11, for purposes of exploitation of the variety:

    (a) earlier than one year before the abovementioned date, within the territory of the Community;

    (b) earlier than four years or, in the case of trees or of vines, earlier than six years before the said date, outside the territory of the Community.

2. The disposal of variety constituents to an official body for statutory purposes, or to others on the basis of a contractual or other legal relationship solely for production, reproduction, multiplication, conditioning or storage, shall not be deemed to be a disposal to others within the meaning of paragraph 1, provided that the breeder preserves the exclusive right of disposal of these and other variety constituents, and no further disposal is made. However, such disposal of variety constituents shall be deemed to be a disposal in terms of paragraph 1 if these constituents are repeatedly used in the production of a hybrid variety and if there is disposal of variety constituents or harvested material of the hybrid variety.

Likewise, the disposal of variety constituents by one company or firm within the meaning of the second paragraph of Article 58 of the Treaty to another of such companies or firms shall not be deemed to be a disposal to others, if one of them belongs entirely to the other or if both belong entirely to a third such company or firm, provided no further disposal is made. This provision shall not apply in respect of cooperative societies.

3. The disposal of variety constituents or harvested material of the variety, which have been produced from plants grown for the purposes specified in Article 15 (b) and (c) and which are not used for further reproduction or multiplication, shall not be deemed to be exploitation of the variety, unless reference is made to the variety for purposes of that disposal.

Likewise, no account shall be taken of any disposal to others, if it either was due to, or in consequence of the fact that the breeder had displayed the variety at an official or officially recognized exhibition within the meaning of the Convention on International Exhibitions, or at an exhibition in a Member State which was officially recognized as equivalent by that Member State.

CHAPTER II

PERSONS ENTITLED

Article 11 Entitlement to Community plant variety rights

1. The person who bred, or discovered and developed the variety, or his **A2-011** successor in title, both – the person and his successor – referred to hereinafter as 'the breeder', shall be entitled to the Community plant variety right.

2. If two or more persons bred, or discovered and developed the variety jointly, entitlement shall be vested jointly in them or their respective successors in title. This provision shall also apply to two or more persons in cases where one or more of them discovered the variety and the other or the others developed it.

3. Entitlement shall also be invested jointly in the breeder and any other person or persons, if the breeder and the other person or persons have agreed to joint entitlement by written declaration.

4. If the breeder is an employee, the entitlement to the Community plant variety right shall be determined in accordance with the national law applicable to the employment relationship in the context of which the variety was bred, or discovered and developed.

5. Where entitlement to a Community plant variety right is vested jointly in two or more persons pursuant to paragraphs 2 to 4, one or more of them may empower the others by written declaration to such effect to claim entitlement thereto.

Article 12 Entitlement to file an application for a Community plant variety right

A2-012 1. An application for a Community plant variety right may be filed by any natural or legal person, or any body ranking as a legal person under the law applicable to that body, provided they are:

    (a) nationals of one of the Member States or nationals of a member of the Union for the Protection of New Varieties of Plants within the meaning of Article 1 (xi) of the Act of 1991 of the International Convention for the Protection of New Varieties of Plants, or are domiciled or have their seat or an establishment in such a State;

    (b) nationals of any other State who do not meet the requirements laid down in (a) in respect of domicile, seat or establishment, in so far as the Commission, after obtaining the opinion of the Administrative Council referred to in Article 36, has so decided. Such a decision may be made dependent on the other State affording protection for varieties of the same botanical taxon to nationals of all the Member States, which corresponds to the protection afforded pursuant to this Regulation; the Commission shall establish whether this condition is met.

2. An application may be filed jointly by two or more such persons.

CHAPTER III

EFFECTS OF COMMUNITY PLANT VARIETY RIGHTS

Article 13 Rights of the holder of a Community plant variety right and prohibited acts

A2-013 1. A Community plant variety right shall have the effect that the holder or holders of the Community plant variety right, hereinafter referred to as 'the holder', shall be entitled to effect the acts set out in paragraph 2.

2. Without prejudice to the provisions of Articles 15 and 16, the following acts in respect of variety constituents, or harvested material of the protected variety, both referred to hereinafter as 'material', shall require the authorization of the holder:

    (a) production or reproduction (multiplication);

    (b) conditioning for the purpose of propagation;

    (c) offering for sale;

    (d) selling or other marketing;

    (e) exporting from the Community;

    (f) importing to the Community;

(g) stocking for any of the purposes mentioned in (a) to (f).

The holder may make his authorization subject to conditions and limitations.

3. The provisions of paragraph 2 shall apply in respect of harvested material only if this was obtained through the unauthorized use of variety constituents of the protected variety, and unless the holder has had reasonable opportunity to exercise his right in relation to the said variety constituents.

4. In the implementing rules pursuant to Article 114, it may be provided that in specific cases the provisions of paragraph 2 of this Article shall also apply in respect of products obtained directly from material of the protected variety. They may apply only if such products were obtained through the unauthorized use of material of the protected variety, and unless the holder has had reasonable opportunity to exercise his right in relation to the said material. To the extent that the provisions of paragraph 2 apply to products directly obtained, they shall also be considered to be 'material'.

5. The provisions of paragraphs 1 to 4 shall also apply in relation to:

(a) varieties which are essentially derived from the variety in respect of which the Community plant variety right has been granted, where this variety is not itself an essentially derived variety;

(b) varieties which are not distinct in accordance with the provisions of Article 7 from the protected variety; and

(c) varieties whose production requires the repeated use of the protected variety.

6. For the purposes of paragraph 5 (a), a variety shall be deemed to be essentially derived from another variety, referred to hereinafter as 'the initial variety' when:

(a) it is predominantly derived from the initial variety, or from a variety that is itself predominantly derived from the initial variety;

(b) it is distinct in accordance with the provisions of Article 7 from the initial variety; and

(c) except for the differences which result from the act of derivation, it conforms essentially to the initial variety in the expression of the characteristics that results from the genotype or combination of genotypes of the initial variety.

7. The implementing rules pursuant to Article 114 may specify possible acts of derivation which come at least under the provisions of paragraph 6.

8. Without prejudice to Article 14 and 29, the exercise of the rights conferred by Community plant variety rights may not violate any provisions adopted on the grounds of public morality, public policy or public security, the protection of health and life of humans, animals or plants, the protection of the environment, the protection of industrial or commercial property, or the safeguarding of competition, of trade or of agricultural production.

Article 14 Derogation from Community plant variety right

1. Notwithstanding Article 13 (2), and for the purposes of safeguarding agri- **A2-014** cultural production, farmers are authorized to use for propagating purposes in the field, on their own holding the product of the harvest which they have obtained by planting, on their own holding, propagating material of a variety other than a hybrid or synthetic variety, which is covered by a Community plant variety right.

2. The provisions of paragraph 1 shall only apply to agricultural plant species of:

(a) Fodder plants:

            Cicer arietinum L. –Chickpea milkvetch
            Lupinus luteus L. – Yellow lupin
            Medicago sativa L. –Lucerne
            Pisum sativum L. (partim) –Field pea
            Trifolium alexandrinum L. –Berseem/Egyptian clover
            Trifolium resupinatum L. –Persian clover
            Vicia faba –Field bean
            Vicia sativa L. –Common vetch
  and, in the case of Portugal, Lolium multiflorum lam –Italian rye-grass
(b) Cereals:
            Avena sativa –Oats
            Hordeum vulgare L. –Barley
            Oryza sativa L. –Rice
            Phalaris canariensis L. –Canary grass
            Secale cereale L. –Rye
            X Triticosecale Wittm. –Triticale
            Triticium aestivum L. emend. Fiori et Paol. –Wheat
            Triticum durum Desf. –Durum wheat
            Triticum spelta L. –Spelt wheat
(c) Potatoes:
            Solanum tuberosum –Potatoes
(d) Oil and fibre plants:
            Brassica napus L. (partim) –Swede rape
            Brassica rapa L. (partim) –Turnip rape
            Linum usitatissimum –linseed with the exclusion of flax.

3. Conditions to give effect to the derogation provided for in paragraph 1 and to safeguard the legitimate interests of the breeder and of the farmer, shall be established, before the entry into force of this Regulation, in implementing rules pursuant to Article 114, on the basis of the following criteria:

– there shall be no quantitative restriction of the level of the farmer's holding to the extent necessary for the requirements of the holding,

– the product of the harvest may be processed for planting, either by the farmer himself or through services supplied to him, without prejudice to certain restrictions which Member States may establish regarding the organization of the processing of the said product of the harvest, in particular in order to ensure identity of the product entered for processing with that resulting from processing,

– small farmers shall not be required to pay any remuneration to the holder; small farmers shall be considered to be:

– in the case of those of the plant species referred to in paragraph 2 of this Article to which Council Regulation (EEC) No 1765/92 of 30 June 1992 establishing a support system for producers of certain arable crops (4) applies, farmers who do not grow plants on an area bigger than the area which would be needed to produce 92 tonnes of cereals; for the calculation of the area, Article 8 (2) of the aforesaid Regulation shall apply,

– in the case of other plant species referred to in paragraph 2 of this Article, farmers who meet comparable appropriate criteria,

– other farmers shall be required to pay an equitable remuneration to the holder, which shall be sensibly lower than the amount charged for the licensed production of propagating material of the same variety in the same area; the actual level of this equitable remuneration may be subject to variation over time, taking into account the extent to which use will be

made of the derogation provided for in paragraph 1 in respect of the variety concerned,
– monitoring compliance with the provisions of this Article or the provisions adopted pursuant to this Article shall be a matter of exclusive responsibility of holders; in organizing that monitoring, they may not provide for assistance from official bodies,
– relevant information shall be provided to the holders on their request, by farmers and by suppliers of processing services; relevant information may equally be provided by official bodies involved in the monitoring of agricultural production, if such information has been obtained through ordinary performance of their tasks, without additional burden or costs. These provisions are without prejudice, in respect of personal data, to Community and national legislation on the protection of individuals with regard to the processing and free movement of personal data.

Article 15 Limitation of the effects of Community plant variety rights

The Community plant variety rights shall not extend to: **A2-015**
(a) acts done privately and for non-commercial purposes;
(b) acts done for experimental purposes;
(c) acts done for the purpose of breeding, or discovering and developing other varieties;
(d) acts referred to in Article 13 (2) to (4), in respect of such other varieties, except where the provisions of Article 13 (5) apply, or where the other variety or the material of this variety comes under the protection of a property right which does not contain a comparable provision; and
(e) acts whose prohibition would violate the provisions laid down in Articles 13 (8), 14 or 29.

Article 16 Exhaustion of Community plant variety rights

The Community plant variety right shall not extend to acts concerning any **A2-016** material of the protected variety, or of a variety covered by the provisions of Article 13 (5), which has been disposed of to others by the holder or with his consent, in any part of the Community, or any material derived from the said material, unless such acts:
(a) involve further propagation of the variety in question, except where such propagation was intended when the material was disposed of; or
(b) involve an export of variety constituents into a third country which does not protect varieties of the plant genus or species to which the variety belongs, except where the exported materials is for final consumption purposes.

Article 17 Use of variety denominations

1. Any person who, within the territory of the Community, offers or disposes **A2-017** of to others for commercial purposes variety constituents of a protected variety, or a variety covered by the provisions of Article 13 (5), must use the variety denomination designated pursuant to Article 63; where it is used in writing, the variety denomination shall be readily distinguishable and clearly legible. If a trade mark, trade name or similar indication is associated with the designated denomination, this denomination must be easily recognizable as such.
2. Any person effecting such acts in respect of any other material of the variety, must inform of that denomination in accordance with other provisions in law or if a request is made by an authority, by the purchaser or by any other person having a legitimate interest.

3. Paragraphs 1 and 2 shall apply even after the termination of the Community plant variety right.

Article 18 Limitation of the use of variety denominations

A2-018　1. The holder may not use any right granted in respect of a designation that is identical with the variety denomination to hamper the free use of that denomination in connection with the variety, even after the termination of the Community plant variety right.

2. A third party may use a right granted in respect of a designation that is identical wih the variety denomination to hamper the free use of that denomination only if that right was granted before the variety denomination was designated pursuant to Article 63.

3. Where a variety is protected by a Community plant variety right or, in a Member State or in a Member of the International Union for the Protection of New Varieties of Plants by a national property right, neither its designated denomination or any designation which might be confused with it can be used, within the territory of the Community, in connection with another variety of the same botanical species or a species regarded as related pursuant to the publication made in accordance with Article 63 (5), or for material of such variety.

CHAPTER IV

DURATION AND TERMINATION OF COMMUNITY PLANT VARIETY RIGHTS

Article 19 Duration of Community plant variety rights

A2-019　1. The term of the Community plant variety right shall run until the end of the 25th calendar year or, in the case of varieties of vine and tree species, until the end of the 30th calendar year, following the year of grant.

2. The Council, acting by qualified majority on proposal from the Commission, may, in respect of specific genera or species, provide for an extension of these terms up to a further five years.

3. A Community plant variety right shall lapse before the expiry of the terms laid down in paragraph 1 or pursuant to paragraph 2, if the holder surrenders it by sending a written declaration to such effect to the Office, and with effect from the day following the day on which the declaration is received by the Office.

Article 20 Nullity of Community plant variety rights

A2-020　1. The Office shall declare the Community plant variety right null and void if it is established:
- (a) that the conditions laid down in Articles 7 or 10 were not complied with at the time of the Community plant variety right; or
- (b) that where the grant of the Community plant variety right has been essentially based upon information and documents furnished by the applicant, the conditions laid down in Articles 8 and 9 were not complied with at the time of the grant of the right; or
- (c) that the right has been granted to a person who is not entitled to it, unless it is transferred to the person who is so entitled.

2. Where the Community plant variety right is declared null and void, it shall be deemed not to have had, as from the outset, the effects specified in this Regulation.

Article 21 Cancellation of Community plant variety rights

1. The Office shall cancel the Community plant variety right with effect in **A2-021** futurum if it is established that the conditions laid down in Article 8 or 9 are no longer complied with. If it is established that these conditions were already no longer complied with from a point in time prior to cancellation, cancellation may be made effective as from that juncture.

2. The Office may cancel a Community plant variety right with effect in futurum if the holder, after being requested to do so, and within a time limit specified by the Office:

(a) has not fulfilled an obligation pursuant to Article 64 (3); or

(b) in the case referred to in Article 66, does not propose another suitable variety denomination; or

(c) fails to pay such fees as may be payable to keep the Community plant variety right in force; or

(d) either as the initial holder or as a successor in title as a result of a transfer pursuant to Article 23, no longer satisfies the conditions laid down in Articles 12 and 82.

CHAPTER V

COMMUNITY PLANT VARIETY RIGHTS AS OBJECTS OF PROPERTY

Article 22 Assimilation with national laws

1. Save where otherwise provided in Articles 23 to 29, a Community plant **A2-022** variety right as an object of property shall be regarded in all respects, and for the entire territory of the Community, as a corresponding property right in the Member State in which:

(a) according to the entry in the Register of Community Plant Variety Rights, the holder was domiciled or had his seat or an establishment on the relevant date; or

(b) if the conditions laid down in subparagraph (a) are not fulfilled, the first-mentioned procedural representative of the holder, as indicated in the said Register, was domiciled or had his seat or an establishment on the date of registration.

2. Where the conditions laid down in paragraph 1 are not fulfilled, the Member State referred to in paragraph 1 shall be the Member State in which the seat of the Office is located.

3. Where domiciles, seats or establishments in two or more Member States are entered in respect of the holder or the procedural representatives in the Register referred to in paragraph 1, the first-mentioned domicile or seat shall apply for the purposes of paragraph 1.

4. Where two or more persons are entered in the Register referred to in paragraph 1 as joint holders, the relevant holder for the purposes of applying paragraph 1 (a) shall be the first joint holder taken in order of entry in the Register who fulfils the conditions. Where none of the joint holders fulfils the conditions laid down in paragraph 1 (a), paragraph 2 shall be applicable.

Article 23 Transfer

1. A Community plant variety right may be the object of a transfer to one or **A2-023** more successors in title.

2. Transfer of a Community plant variety right by assignment can be made only to successors who comply with the conditions laid down in Article 12 and 82. It shall be made in writing and shall require the signature of the parties to the contract, except when it is a result of a judgement or of any other acts terminating court proceedings. Otherwise it shall be void.

3. Save as otherwise provided in Article 100, a transfer shall have no bearing on the rights acquired by third parties before the date of transfer.

4. A transfer shall not take effect for the Office and may not be cited vis-à-vis third parties unless documentary evidence thereof as provided for in the implementing rules is provided and until it has been entered in the Register of Community Plant Variety Rights. A transfer that has not yet been entered in the Register may, however, be cited vis-à-vis third parties who have acquired rights after the date of transfer but who knew of the transfer at the date on which they acquired those rights.

Article 26 The application for a Community plant variety right as an object of property

A2-024   Articles 22 to 25 shall apply to applications for Community plant variety rights. Concerning such applications, the references made in those Articles to the Register of Community Plant Variety Rights shall be regarded as references to the Register of Application for Community Plant Variety Rights.

Article 27 Contractual exploitation rights

A2-025   1. Community plant variety rights may form in full or in part the subject of contractually granted exploitation rights. Exploitation rights may be exclusive or non-exclusive.

2. The holder may invoke the rights conferred by the Community plant variety right against a person enjoying the right of exploitation who contravenes any of the conditions or limitations attached to his exploitation right pursuant to paragraph 1.

Article 28 Joint holdership

A2-026   Articles 22 to 27 shall apply mutatis mutandis in the event of joint holdership of a Community plant variety right in proportion to the respective share held, where such shares have been determined.

Article 29 Compulsory exploitation right

A2-027   1. Compulsory exploitation rights shall be granted to one or more persons by the Office, on application by that person or those persons, but only on grounds of public interest and after consulting the Administrative Council referred to in Article 36.

2. On application by a Member State, by the Commission or by an organization set up at Community level and registered by the Commission, a compulsory exploitation right may be granted, either to a category of persons satisfying specific requirements, or to anyone in one or more Member States or throughout the Community. It may be granted only on grounds of public interest and with the approval of the Administrative Council.

3. The Office shall, when granting the compulsory exploitation right, stipulate the type of acts covered and specify the reasonable conditions pertaining thereto as well as the specific requirements referred to in paragraph 2. The reasonable conditions shall take into account the interests of any holder of plant variety rights who would be affected by the grant of the compulsory exploi-

tation right. The reasonable conditions may include a possible time limitation, the payment of an appropriate royalty as equitable remuneration to the holder, and may impose certain obligations on the holder, the fulfilment of which are necessary to make use of the compulsory exploitation right.

4. On the expiry of each one-year period after the grant of the compulsory exploitation right and within the aforementioned possible time limitation, any of the parties to proceedings may request that the decision on the grant of the compulsory exploitation right be cancelled or amended. The sole grounds for such a request shall be that the circumstances determining the decision taken have in the meantime undergone change.

5. On application, the compulsory exploitation right shall be granted to the holder in respect of an essentially derived variety if the criteria set out in paragraph 1 are met. The reasonable conditions referred to in paragraph 3 shall include the payment of an appropriate royalty as equitable remuneration to the holder of the initial variety.

6. The implementing rules pursuant to Article 114 may specify certain cases as examples of public interest referred to in paragraph 1 and moreover lay down details for the implementation of the provisions of the above paragraphs.

7. Compulsory exploitation rights may not be granted by Member States in respect of a Community plant variety right.

PART FOUR

PROCEEDINGS BEFORE THE OFFICE

CHAPTER I

APPLICATIONS

Article 49 Filing of applications

1. An application for a Community plant variety right shall be filed at the **A2-028** choice of the applicant:
   (a) at the Office directly; or
   (b) at one of the sub-offices or national agencies, established or entrusted, pursuant to Article 30 (4), subject to the applicant forwarding an information on this filing to the Office directly within two weeks after filing.

Details on the manner in which the information referred to in (b) above must be forwarded, may be laid down in the implementing rules pursuant to Article 114. The omission of forwarding information on an application to the Office pursuant to (b) above, does not affect the validity of the application if the application has reached the Office within one month after filing at the sub-office or national agency.

2. Where the application is filed at one of the national agencies referred to in paragraph 1 (b), the national agency shall take all steps to forward the application to the Office within two weeks after filing. National agencies may charge the applicant a fee which shall not exceed the administrative costs of receiving and forwarding the application.

Article 50 Conditions governing applications

A2-029   1. The application for a Community plant variety right must contain at least the following:
     (a) a request for the grant of a Community plant variety right;
     (b) identification of the botanical taxon;
     (c) information identifying the applicant or, where appropriate, the joint applicants;
     (d) the name of the breeder and an assurance that, to the best of the applicants knowledge, no further persons have been involved in the breeding, or discovery and development, of the variety; if the applicant is not the breeder, or not the only breeder, he shall provide the relevant documentary evidence as to how the entitlement to the Community plant variety right came into his possession;
     (e) a provisional designation for the variety;
     (f) a technical descriptionof the variety;
     (g) the geographic origin of the variety;
     (h) the credentials of any procedural representative;
     (i) details of any previous commercialization of the variety;
     (j) details of any other application made in respect of the variety.
     2. Details of the conditions referred to in paragraph 1, including the provision of further information, may be laid down in the implementing rules pursuant to Article 114.
     3. An application shall propose a variety denomination which may accompany the application.

Article 51 Date of application

A2-030   The date of application for a Community plant variety right shall be the date on which a valid application was received by the Office pursuant to Article 49 (1) (a) or by a sub-office or national agency pursuant to Article 49 (1) (b), provided it complies with Article 50 (1) and subject to payment of the fees due pursuant to Article 83 within a time limit specified by the Office.

Article 52 The right of priority

A2-031   1. The right of priority of an application shall be determined by the date of receipt of the application. Where applications have the same date of application, the priorities thereof shall be determined according to the order in which they were received, if this can be established. Otherwise they shall have the same priority.
     2. If the applicant or his predecessor in title has already applied for a property right for the variety in a Member State or in a Member of the International Union for the Protection of New Varieties of Plants, and the date of application is within 12 months of the filing of the earlier application, the applicant shall enjoy a right of priority for the earlier application as regards the application for the Community plant variety right, provided the earlier application still exists on the date of application.
     3. The right of priority shall have the effect that the date on which the earlier application was filed shall count as the date of application for the Community plant variety right for the purposes of Articles 7, 10 and 11.
     4. Paragraphs 2 and 3 shall also apply in respect of earlier applications that were filed in another Member State, provided the conditions set out in Article 12

(1) (b), second sentence, is met regarding this State on the date of application for the Community plant variety right.

5. Any claim for a right of priority earlier than that provided for in paragraph 2 shall lapse if the applicant does not submit to the Office within three months of the date of application copies of the earlier application that have been certified by the authorities responsible for such application. If the earlier application has not been made in one of the official languages of the European Communities, the Office may require, in addition, a translation of the earlier application in one of these languages.

CHAPTER II

EXAMINATION

Article 53 Formal examination of application

1. The Office shall examine whether: A2-032
   (a) the application has effectively been filed pursuant to Article 49;
   (b) the application complies with the conditions laid down in Article 50 and the conditions laid down in the implementing rules pursuant to that Article;
   (c) where appropriate, a claim for priority complies with the provision laid down in Article 52 (2), (4) and (5); and (d) the fees due pursuant to Article 83 have been paid within a time limit specified by the Office.

2. If the application, although complying with the conditions referred to in Article 51, does not comply with other conditions laid down in Article 50, the Office shall give the applicant an opportunity to correct any deficiencies that may have been identified.

3. If the application does not comply with the conditions referred to in Article 51, the Office shall inform the applicant thereof, or, where this is not possible, publish the information pursuant to Article 89.

Article 54 Substantive examination

1. The Office shall examine whether the variety may be the object of a A2-033
Community plant variety right pursuant to Article 5, whether the variety is new pursuant to Article 10, whether the applicant is entitled to file an application pursuant to Article 12 and whether the conditions laid down in Article 82 are complied with. The Office shall also examine whether the proposed variety denomination is suitable pursuant to Article 63. For such purposes, it may avail itself of the services of other bodies.

2. The first applicant shall be deemed to be entitled to the Community plant variety right pursuant to Article 11. This shall not apply if, before a decision on the application is taken, the Office is aware, or it is shown by a final judgment delivered with regard to a claim for entitlement pursuant to Article 98 (4), that entitlement is not or is not solely vested in the first applicant. Where the identity of the sole or other person entitled has been determined, the person or persons may enter the proceedings as applicant or applicants.

Article 55 Technical examination

1. Where the Office has not discovered any impediment to the grant of a A2-034
Community plant variety right on the basis of the examination pursuant to Articles 53 and 54, it shall arrange for the technical examination relating to

compliance with the conditions laid down in Articles 7, 8 and 9 to be carried out by the competent office or offices in at least one of the Member States entrusted with responsibility for the technical examination of varieties of the species concerned by the Administrative Council, hereafter referred to as the 'Examination Office or Offices'.

2. Where no Examination Office is available, the Office may, with the consent of the Administrative Council, entrust other appropriate agencies with responsibility therefore or establish its own sub-offices for the same purposes. For the purpose of the provisions of this Chapter, such agencies or sub-offices shall be considered as Examination Offices. They may avail themselves of facilities made available by the applicant.

3. The Office shall forward to the Examination Offices copies of the application as required under the implementing rules pursuant to Article 114.

4. The Office shall determine, through general rules or through requests in individual cases, when, where and in what quantities and qualities the material for the technical examination and reference samples are to be submitted.

5. Where the applicant makes a claim for priority pursuant to Article 52 (2) or (4), he shall submit the necessary material and any further documents required within two years of the date of application pursuant to Article 51. If the earlier application is withdrawn or refused before the expiry of two years, the Office may require the applicant to submit the material or any further documents within a specified time limit.

Article 59 Objections to grant of right

A2-035 1. Any person may lodge with the Office a written objection to the grant of a Community plant variety right.

2. Objectors shall be party to the proceedings for grant of the Community plant variety right in addition to the applicant. Without prejudice to Article 88, objectors shall have access to the documents, including the results of the technical examination and the variety description as referred to in Article 57 (2).

3. Objections may be based only on the contention that:
   (a) the conditions laid down in Articles 7 to 11 are not complied with;
   (b) there is an impediment under Article 63 (3) or (4) to a proposed variety denomination.

4. Objections may be lodged:
   (a) at any time after the application and prior to a decision pursuant to Articles 61 or 62, in the case of paragraph 3 (a) hereof;
   (b) within three months of the publication of the proposed variety denomination pursuant to Article 89, in the case of objections under paragraph 3 (b) hereof.

5. The decisions on objections may be taken together with the decisions pursuant to Articles 61, 62 or 63.

Article 60 Priority of a new application in the case of objections

A2-036 Where an objection on the grounds that the conditions laid down in Article 11 are not met leads to the withdrawal or refusal of the application for a Community plant variety right and if the objector files an application for a Community plant variety right within one month following the withdrawal or within one month of the date on which the refusal becomes final in respect of the same variety, he may require that the date of the withdrawn or refused application be deemed to be the date of his application.

CHAPTER III

DECISIONS

Article 61 Refusal

1. The Office shall refuse applications for a Community plant variety right if **A2-037** and as soon as it establishes that the applicant:
  (a) has not remedied any deficiencies within the meaning of Article 53 which he was given an opportunity to correct within the time limit notified to him;
  (b) has not complied with a rule or request pursuant to Article 55 (4) or (5) within the time limit laid down, unless the Office has consented to non-submission; or
  (c) has not proposed a variety denomination which is suitable pursuant to Article 63.

2. The Office shall also refuse applications for a Community plant variety right if:
  (a) it establishes that the conditions it is required to verify pursuant to Article 54 have not been fulfilled; or
  (b) it reaches the opinion on the basis of the examination reports pursuant to Article 57, that the conditions laid down in Articles 7, 8 and 9 have not been fulfilled.

Article 62 Grant

If the Office is of the opinion that the findings of the examination are **A2-038** sufficient to decide on the application and there are no impediments pursuant to Articles 59 and 61, it shall grant the Community plant variety right. The decision shall include an official description of the variety.

Article 63 Variety denomination

1. Where a Community plant variety right is granted, the Office shall **A2-039** approve, for the variety in question, the variety denomination proposed by the applicant pursuant to Article 50 (3), if it considers, on the basis of the examination made pursuant to the second sentence of Article 54 (1), that this denomination is suitable.

2. A variety denomination is suitable, if there is no impediment pursuant to paragraphs 3 or 4 of this Article.

3. There is an impediment for the designation of a variety denomination where:
  (a) its use in the territory of the Community is precluded by the prior right of a third party;
  (b) it may commonly cause its users difficulties as regards recognition or reproduction; *Lewis v Frank Love Ltd [1961]*
  (c) it is identical or may be confused with a variety denomination under which another variety of the same or of a closely related species is entered in an official register of plant varieties or under which material of another variety has been marketed in a Member State or in a Member of the International Unit for the Protection of New Varieties of Plants, unless the other variety no longer remains in existence and its denomination has acquired no special significance;

(d) it is identical or may be confused with other designations which are commonly used for the marketing of goods or which have to be kept free under other legislation;

(e) it is liable to give offence in one of the Member States or is contrary to public policy;

(f) it is liable to mislead or to cause confusion concerning the characteristics, the value or the identity of the variety, or the identity of the breeder or any other party to proceedings.

4. There is another impediment where, in the case of a variety which has already been entered:

(a) in one of the Member States; or

(b) in a Member of the International Union for the Protection of New Varieties of Plants; or

(c) in another State for which it has been established in a Community act that varieties are evaluated there under rules which are equivalent to those laid down in the Directives on common catalogues;

in an official register of plant varieties or material thereof and has been marketed there for commercial purposes, and the proposed variety denomination differs from that which has been registered or used there, unless the latter one is the object of an impediment pursuant to paragraph 3.

5. The Office shall publish the species which it considers 'closely related' within the meaning of paragraph 3 (c).

CHAPTER IV

THE MAINTENANCE OF COMMUNITY PLANT VARIETY RIGHTS

Article 64 Technical verification

A2-040   1. The Office shall verify the continuing existence unaltered of the protected varieties.

2. For this purpose, a technical verification shall be carried out pursuant to Articles 55 and 56.

3. The holder shall be required to provide all the information necessary to assess the continuing existence unaltered of the variety to the Office and to the Examination Offices to which technical verification of the variety has been entrusted. He shall be required, in accordance with the instructions given by the Office, to submit material of the variety and to permit to verify whether appropriate measures have been taken to ensure the continuing existence unaltered of the variety.

Article 66 Amendment of the variety denomination

A2-041   1. The Office shall amend a variety denomination designated pursuant to Article 63 if it establishes that the denomination does not satisfy, or no longer satisfies, the conditions laid down in Article 63 and in the event of a prior conflicting right of a third party, if the holder agrees to the amendment or the holder or any other person required to use the variety denomination has been prohibited, by a final judgment, for this reason from using the variety denomination.

2. The Office shall give the holder an opportunity to propose an amended variety denomination and shall proceed in accordance with Article 63.

3. Objections may be lodged against the proposed amended variety denomination in accordance with Article 59 (3) (b).

CHAPTER V

APPEALS

Article 68 Persons entitled to appeal and to be parties to appeal proceedings

Any natural or legal person may appeal, subject to Article 82, against a **A2-042** decision, addressed to that person, or against a decision which, although in the form of a decision addressed to another person, is of direct and individual concern to the former. The parties to proceedings may, and the Office shall, be party to the appeal proceedings.

Article 69 Time limit and form

Notice of appeal shall be filed in writing at the Office within two months of **A2-043** the service of the decision where addressed to the appealing person, or, in the absence thereof, within two months of the publication of the decision, and a written statement setting out the grounds of appeal shall be filed within four months after the aforesaid service or publication.

Article 72 Decision on appeal

The Board of Appeal shall decide on the appeal on the basis of the examination **A2-044** carried out pursuant to Article 71. The Board of Appeal may exercise any power which lies within the competence of the Office, or it may remit the case to the competent body of the Office for further action. The latter one shall, in so far as the facts are the same, be bound by the ratio decidendi of the Board of Appeal.

Article 73 Further appeal

1. A further appeal to the Court of Justice of the European Communities **A2-045** shall lie from decisions of the Board of Appeal.

2. The further appeal may be lodged on grounds of lack of competence, infringement of an essential procedural requirement, infringement of the Treaty, of this Regulation, or of any rule of law relating to their application or misuse of power.

3. The further appeal may be made by any party to the appeal proceedings who is adversely affected by its decision, or by the Commission or the Office.

4. The further appeal shall be lodgedwith the Court of Justice within two months of service of the decision of the Board of Appeal.

5. If the Court of Justice remits the case for further action to the Board of Appeal, the Board shall, in so far as the facts are the same, be bound by the ratio decidendi of the Court of Justice.

Article 74 Direct appeal

1. A direct appeal to the Court of Justice of the European Communities may **A2-046** lie from decisions of the Office pursuant to Articles 29 and 100 (2).

2. The provisions laid down in Article 73 shall apply mutatis mutandis.

Chapter VI

Article 75 Statement of grounds on which decisions are based, right of audience

A2-047   Decisions of the Office shall be accompanied by statements of the grounds on which they are based. They shall be based only on grounds or evidence on which the parties to proceedings have had an opportunity to present their comments orally or in writing.

Article 76 Examination of the facts by the Office of its own motion

A2-048   In proceedings before it the Office shall make investigations on the facts of its own motion, to the extent that they come under the examination pursuant to Articles 54 and 55. It shall disregard facts or items of evidence which have not been submitted within the time limit set by the Office.

Article 77 Oral proceedings

A2-049   1. Oral proceedings shall be held either on the initiative of the Office itself or at the request of any of the parties to proceedings

2. Without prejudice to paragraph 3, oral proceedings before the Office shall not be public.

3. Oral proceedings before the Board of Appeal including delivery of the decision, shall be public in so far as the Board of Appeal before which the proceedings are taking place does not decide otherwise in circumstances where serious and unwarranted disadvantages could arise from admitting the public, particularly for any of the parties to the appeal proceedings.

Article 81 General principles

A2-050   1. In the absence of procedural provisions in this Regulation or in provisions adopted pursuant to this Regulation, the Office shall apply the principles of procedural law which are generally recognized in the Member States.

2. Article 48 shall apply mutatis mutandis to the staff of the Office in so far as it is involved in decisions of the kind referred to in Article 67, and to the staff of the Examination Offices, in so far as it participates in measures for the preparation of such decisions.

Chapter VIII

Registers

Article 87 Establishment of the Registers

A2-051   1. The Office shall keep a Register of Applications for Community Plant Variety Rights which shall contain the following particulars:

    (a) applications for a Community plant variety right together with a statement of the taxon and the provisional designation of the variety, the date of application and the name and address of the applicant, of the breeder and of any procedural representative concerned;

    (b) any cases of termination of proceedings concerning applications for a Community plant variety right together with the information set out in subparagraph (a);

(c) proposals for variety denominations;

(d) changes in the identity of the applicant or his procedural representative;

(e) on request, any levy of execution as referred to in Articles 24 and 26.

2. The Office shall keep a Register of Community Plant Variety Rights wherein, after grant of a Community plant variety right, the following particulars shall be entered:

(a) the species and variety denomination of the variety;

(b) the official description of the variety or a reference to documents in the Office's possession in which the official description of the variety is contained as integrating part of the Register;

(c) in the case of varieties for which material with specific components has to be used repeatedly for the production of material, a reference to such components;

(d) the name and address of the holder, of the breeder and of any procedural representative concerned;

(e) the date on which the Community plant variety right begins and ends, together with the reasons for the termination of right;

(f) on request, any contractual exclusive exploitation right or compulsory exploitation right, including the name and address of the person enjoying the right of exploitation;

(g) on request, any levy of execution as referred to in Article 24;

(h) where the holder of an initial variety and the breeder of a variety essentially derived from the initial variety both so request, the identification of the varieties as initial and essentially derived including the variety denominations and the names of the parties concerned. A request from one of the parties concerned only shall suffice if he has obtained either a non-contentious acknowledgement by the other party pursuant to Article 99 or a final decision or a final judgment pursuant to the provisions of this Regulation which contain an identification of the varieties concerned as initial and essentially derived.

3. Any other particular or any condition for the entering in both Registers may be specified in the implementing rules pursuant to Article 114.

4. The Office may of its own motion and upon consultation with the holder adapt the official variety description in respect of the number and type of characteristics or of the specified expressions of those characteristics, when necessary, in the light of the current principles governing the description of varieties of the taxon concerned, in order to render the description of the variety comparable with the descriptions of other varieties of the taxon concerned.

Article 88 Public inspection

1. The Registers mentioned in Article 87 shall be open to public inspection. **A2-052**

2. In case of a legitimate interest, the following shall be open to public inspection, in accordance with the conditions set up in the implementing rules pursuant to Article 114:

(a) documents relating to applications for grant of a Community plant variety right;

(b) documents relating to Community plant variety rights already granted;

(c) the growing of varieties for the purposes of their technical examination;

(d) the growing of varieties for the purpose of verifying their continuing existence.

3. In the case of varieties for which material with specific components has to be used repeatedly for the production of material, at the request of the applicant for a Community plant variety right, all data relating to components, including their cultivation, shall be withheld from inspection. Such a request for withholding from inspection may not be filed once the decision on the application for grant of a Community plant variety right has been taken.

4. Materials submitted or obtained in connection with examinations under Articles 55 (4), 56 and 64 may not be given to other parties by the competent authorities under this Regulation unless the person entitled gives his consent or such transfer is required in connection with the cooperation covered by this Regulation for the purposes of the examination or by virtue of legal provisions.

Article 89 Periodical publications

A2-053   The Office shall at least every two months, issue a publication containing the information entered into the Registers pursuant to Article 87 (1) and (2) (a), (d), (e), (f), (g) and (h), and not yet published. The Office shall also publish an annual report, containing information which the Office regards as expedient, but at least a list of valid Community plant variety rights, their holders, the dates of grant and expiry and the approved variety denominations. Details of these publications shall be specified by the Administrative Council.

Article 92 Cumulative protection prohibited

A2-054   1. Any variety which is the subject matter of a Community plant variety right shall not be the subject of a national plant variety right or any patent for that variety. Any rights granted contrary to the first sentence shall be ineffective.

2. Where the holder has been granted another right as referred to in paragraph 1 for the same variety prior to grant of the Community plant variety right, he shall be unable to invoke the rights conferred by such protection for the variety for as long as the Community plant variety right remains effective.

PART SIX

CIVIL LAW CLAIMS, INFRINGEMENTS, JURISDICTION

Article 94 Infringement

A2-055   1. Whosoever:
   (a) effects one of the acts set out in Article 13 (2) without being entitled to do so, in respect of a variety for which a Community plant variety right has been granted; or
   (b) omits the correct usage of a variety denomination as referred to in Article 17 (1) or omits the relevant information as referred to in Article 17 (2); or
   (c) contrary to Article 18 (3) uses the variety denomination of a variety for which a Community plant variety right has been granted or a designation that may be confused with it;

may be sued by the holder to enjoin such infringement or to pay reasonable compensation or both.

2. Whosoever acts intentionally or negligently shall moreover be liable to compensate the holder for any further damage resulting from the act in question. In cases of slight negligence, such claims may be reduced according to the degree of such slight negligence, but not however to the extent that they are less

than the advantage derived therefrom by the person who committed the infringement.

Article 95 Acts prior to grant of Community plant variety rights

The holder may require reasonable compensation from any person who has, **A2-056** in the time between publication of the application for a Community plant variety right and grant thereof, effected an act that he would be prohibited from performing subsequent thereto.

Article 98 Claiming entitlement to a Community plant variety right

1. If a Community plant variety right has been granted to a person who is **A2-057** not entitled to it under Article 11, the person entitled to it may, without prejudice to any other remedy which may be open to him under the laws of the Member States, claim to have the Community plant variety right transferred to him.

2. Where a person ist entitled to only part of a Community plant variety right, that person may, in accordance with paragraph 1, claim to be made a joint holder.

3. Claims pursuant to paragraphs 1 and 2 may be invoked only within a period of up to five years of publication of the grant of the Community plant variety right. This provision shall not apply if the holder knew, at the time it was granted to or acquired by him, that he was not entitled to such rights or that entitlement thereto was not vested solely in him.

4. The person entitled shall be eligible mutatis mutandis to pursue claims pursuant to paragraphs 1 and 2 in respect of an application for grant of a Community plant variety right filed by a person who was not entitled to it or whom the entitlement was not vested solely.

Article 99 Obtaining identification of a variety

The holder of an initial variety and the breeder of a variety essentially derived **A2-058** from the initial variety shall be entitled to obtain an acknowledgement of the identification of the varieties concerned as initial and essentially derived.

Article 101 Jurisdiction and procedure in legal actions relating to civil law claims

1. The Lugano Convention as well as the complementary provisions of this **A2-059** Article and of Articles 102 to 106 of this Regulation shall apply to proceedings relating to actions in respect of the claims referred to in Articles 94 to 100.

2. Proceedings of the type referred to in paragraph 1 shall be brought in the courts:
   - (a) of the Member State or another Contracting Party to the Lugano Convention in which the defendant is domiciled or has his seat or, in the absence of such, has an establishment; or
   - (b) if this condition is not met in any of the Member States or Contracting Parties, of the Member State in which the plaintiff is domiciled or has his seat or, in the absence of such, has an establishment; or
   - (c) if this condition is also not met in any of the Member States, of the Member States in which the seat of the Office is located.

The competent courts shall have jurisdiction in respect of infringements alleged to have been committed in any of the Member States.

3. Proceedings relating to actions in respect of claims for infringement may also be brought in the courts for the place where the harmful event occured. In such cases, the court shall have jurisdiction only in respect of infringements

alleged to have been committed in the territory of the Member State to which it belongs.

4. The legal processes and the competent courts shall be those that operate under the laws of the State determined pursuant to paragraphs 2 or 3.

Article 102 Supplementary provisions

A2-060   1. Actions for claiming entitlement pursuant to Article 98 of this Regulation shall not be considered to fall under the provisions of Article 5 (3) and (4) of the Lugano Convention.

2. Notwithstanding Article 101 of this Regulation, Articles 5 (1), 17 and 18 of the Lugano Convention shall apply.

3. For the purposes of applying Articles 101 and 102 of this Regulation, the domicile or seat of a party shall be determined pursuant to Articles 52 and 53 of the Lugano Convention.

Article 104 Entitlement to bring an action for infringement

A2-061   1. Actions for infringement may be brought by the holder. Persons enjoying exploitation rights may bring such actions unless that has been expressly excluded by agreement with the holder in the case of an exclusive exploitation right or by the Office pursuant to Articles 29 or 100 (2).

2. Any person enjoying exploitation rights shall, for the purpose of obtaining compensation for damage suffered by him, be entitled to intervene in an infringement action brought by the holder.

Article 105 Obligation of national courts or other bodies

A2-062   A national court or other body hearing an action relating to a Community plant variety right shall treat the Community plant variety right as valid.

Article 106 Stay of proceedings

A2-063   1. Where an action relates to claims pursuant to Article 98 (4) and the decision depends upon the protectability of the variety pursuant to Article 6, this decision may not be given before the Office has decided on the application for a Community plant variety right.

2. Where an action relates to a Community plant variety right that has been granted and in respect of which proceedings for revocation or cancellation pursuant to Articles 20 or 21 have been initiated, the proceedings may be stayed in so far as the decision depends upon the validity of the Community plant variety right.

Article 107 Penalties for infringement of Community plant variety rights

A2-064   Member States shall take all appropriate measures to ensure that the same provisions are made applicable to penalize infringements of Community plant variety rights as apply in the matter of infringements of corresponding national rights.

COUNCIL REGULATION (EC) No 40/94 of 20 December 1993 on the Community trade mark

THE COUNCIL OF THE EUROPEAN UNION,

Having regard to the Treaty establishing the European Community, and in particular Article 235 thereof,

Having regard to the proposal from the Commission,

Having regard to the opinion of the European Parliament,

Having regard to the opinion of the Economic and Social Committee,

Whereas it is desirable to promote throughout the Community a harmonious development of economic activities and a continuous and balanced expansion by completing an internal market which functions properly and offers conditions which are similar to those obtaining in a national market; whereas in order to create a market of this kind and make it increasingly a single market, not only must be barriers to free movement of goods and services be removed and arrangements be instituted which ensure that competition is not distorted, but, in addition, legal conditions must be created which enable undertakings to adapt their activities to the scale of the Community, whether in manufacturing and distributing goods or in providing services; whereas for those purposes, trade marks enabling the products and services of undertakings to be distinguished by identical means throughout the entire Community, regardless of frontiers, should feature amongst the legal instruments which undertakings have at their disposal;

Whereas action by the Community would appear to be necessary for the purpose of attaining the Community's said objectives; whereas such action involves the creation of Community arrangements for trade marks whereby undertakings can by means of one procedural system obtain Community trade marks to which uniform protection is given and which produce their effects throughout the entire area of the Community;

whereas the principle of the unitary character of the Community trade mark thus stated will apply unless otherwise provided for in this Regulation;

Whereas the barrier of territoriality of the rights conferred on proprietors of trade marks by the laws of the Member States cannot be removed by approximation of laws; whereas in order to open up unrestricted economic activity in the whole of the common market for the benefit of undertakings, trade marks need to be created which are governed by a uniform Community law directly applicable in all Member States;

Whereas since the Treaty has not provided the specific powers to establish such a legal instrument, Article 235 of the Treaty should be applied;

Whereas the Community law relating to trade marks nevertheless does not replace the laws of the Member States on trade marks; whereas it would not in fact appear to be justified to require undertakings to apply for registration of their trade marks as Community trade marks; whereas national trade marks continue to be necessary for those undertakings which do not want protection of their trade marks at Community level;

Whereas the rights in a Community trade mark may not be obtained otherwise than by registration, and registration is to be refused in particular if the trade mark is not distinctive, if it is unlawful or if it conflicts with earlier rights;

Whereas the protection afforded by a Community trade mark, the function of which is in particular to guarantee the trade mark as an indication of origin, is absolute in the case of identity between the mark and the sign and the goods or services; whereas the protection applies also in cases of similarity between the mark and the sign and the goods or services; whereas an interpretation should be given of the concept of similarity in relation to the likelihood of confusion; whereas the likelihood of confusion, the appreciation of which depends on numerous elements and, in particular, on the recognition of the trade mark on the market, the association which can be made with the used or registered sign, the degree of similarity between the trade mark and the sign and between the goods or services identified, constitutes the specific condition for such protection;

Whereas it follows from the principle of free flow of goods that the proprietor of a Community trade mark must not be entitled to prohibit its use by a third party in relation to goods which have been put into circulation in the Community, under the trade mark, by him or with his consent, save where there exist legitimate reasons for the proprietor to oppose further commercialization of the goods;

Whereas there is no justification for protecting Community trade marks or, as against them, any trade mark which has been registered before them, except where the trade marks are actually used;

Whereas a Community trade mark is to be regarded as an object of property which exists separately from the undertakings whose goods or services are designated by it; whereas accordingly, it must be capable of being transferred, subject to the overriding need to prevent the public being misled as a result of the transfer. It must also be capable of being charged as security in favour of a third party and of being the subject matter of licences;

Whereas administrative measures are necessary at Community level for implementing in relation to every trade mark the trade mark law created by this Regulation; whereas it is therefore essential, while retaining the Community's existing institutional structure and balance of powers, to establish an Office for Harmonization in the Internal Market (trade marks and designs) which is independent in relation to technical matters and has legal, administrative and financial autonomy; whereas to this end it is necessary and appropriate that it should be a body of the Community having legal personality and exercising the implementing powers which are conferred on it by this Regulation, and that it should operate within the framework of Community law without detracting from the competencies exercised by the Community institutions;

Whereas it is necessary to ensure that parties who are affected by decisions made by the Office are protected by the law in a manner which is suited to the special character of trade mark law; whereas to that end provision is made for an appeal to lie from decisions of the examiners and of the various divisions of the Office;

whereas if the department whose decision is contested does not rectify its decision it is to remit the appeal to a Board of Appeal of the Office, which is to decide on it; whereas decisions of the Boards of Appeal are, in turn, amenable to actions before the Court of Justice of the European Communities, which has jurisdiction to annul or to alter the contested decision;

Whereas under Council Decision 88/591/ECSC, EEC, Euratom of 24 October 1988 establishing a Court of First Instance of the European Communities, as amended by Decision 93/350/Euratom, ECSC, EEC of 8 June 1993, that Court shall exercise at the first instance the jurisdiction conferred on the Court of Justice by the Treaties establishing the Communities - with particular regard to appeals lodged under the second subparagraph of Article 173 of the EC Treaty - and by the acts adopted in implementation thereof, save as otherwise provided in an act setting up a body governed by Community law; whereas the jurisdiction which this Regulation confers on the Court of Justice to cancel and reform decisions of the appeal courts shall accordingly be exercised at the first instance by the Court in accordance with the above Decision;

Whereas in order to strengthen the protection of Community trade marks the Member States should designate, having regard to their own national system, as limited a number as possible of national courts of first and second instance having jurisdiction in matters of infringement and validity of Community trade marks;

Whereas decisions regarding the validity and infringement of Community trade marks must have effect and cover the entire area of the Community, as this is the only way of preventing inconsistent decisions on the part of the courts and the Office and of ensuring that the unitary character of Community trade marks is not undermined; whereas the rules contained in the Brussels Convention of Jurisdiction and the Enforcement of Judgments in Civil and Commercial Matters will apply to all actions at law relating to Community trade marks, save where this Regulation derogates from those rules;

Whereas contradictory judgments should be avoided in actions which involve the same acts and the same parties and which are brought on the basis of a Community trade mark and parallel national trade marks;

whereas for this purpose, when the actions are brought in the same Member State, the way in which this is to be achieved is a matter for national procedural rules, which are not prejudiced by this Regulation, whilst when the actions are brought in different Member States, provisions modelled on the rules on lis pendens and related actions of the abovementioned Brussels Convention appear appropriate;

Whereas in order to guarantee the full autonomy and independence of the Office, it is considered necessary to grant it an autonomous budget whose revenue comes principally from fees paid by the users of the system; whereas however, the Community budgetary procedure remains applicable as far as any subsidies chargeable to general budget of the European Communities are concerned; whereas moreover, the auditing of accounts should be undertaken by the Court of Auditors;

Whereas implementing measures are required for the Regulation's application, particularly as regards the adoption and amendment of fees regulations and an Implementing Regulation; whereas such measures should be adopted by the Commission, assisted by a Committee composed of representatives of the Member States, in accordance with the procedural rules laid down in Article 2, procedure III(b), of Council Decisions 87/373/EEC of 13 July 1987 laying down the procedures for the exercise of implementing powers conferred on the Commission,

HAS ADOPTED THIS REGULATION:

TITLE I

GENERAL PROVISIONS

Article 1 Community trade mark

1. A trade mark for goods or services which is registered in accordance with **A3-001** the conditions contained in this Regulation and in the manner herein provided is hereinafter referred to as a 'Community trade mark'.

2. A Community trade mark shall have a unitary character. It shall have equal effect throughout the Community: it shall not be registered, transferred or surrendered or be the subject of a decision revoking the rights of the proprietor or declaring it invalid, nor shall its use be prohibited, save in respect of the whole Community. This principle shall apply unless otherwise provided in this Regulation.

Article 2 Office

A3-002 An Office for Harmonization in the Internal Market (trade marks and designs), hereinafter referred to as 'the Office', is hereby established.

TITLE II

THE LAW RELATING TO TRADE MARKS

DEFINITION OF A COMMUNITY TRADE MARK OBTAINING A COMMUNITY TRADE MARK

Article 4 Signs of which a Community trade mark may consist

A3-003 A Community trade mark may consist of any signs capable of being represented graphically, particularly words, including personal names, designs, letters, numerals, the shape of goods or of their packaging, provided that such signs are capable of distinguishing the goods or services of one undertaking from those of other undertakings.

Article 5 Persons who can be proprietors of Community trade marks

A3-004 1. The following natural or legal persons, including authorities established under public law, may be proprietors of Community trade marks:
  (a) nationals of the Member States; or
  (b) nationals of other States which are parties to the Paris Convention for the protection of industrial property, hereinafter referred to as the 'Paris Convention', or to the Agreement establishing the World Trade Organization;
  (c) nationals of States which are not parties to the Paris Convention who are domiciled or have their seat or who have real and effective industrial or commercial establishments within the territory of the Community or of a State which is party to the Paris Convention; or
  (d) nationals, other than those referred to under subparagraph (c), of any State which is not party to the Paris Convention or to the Agreement establishing the World Trade Organization and which, according to published findings, accords to nationals of all the Member States the same protection for trade marks as it accords to its own nationals and, if nationals of the Member States are required to prove registration in the country of origin, recognizes the registration of Community trade marks as such proof.

2. With respect to the application of paragraph 1, stateless persons as defined by Article 1 of the Convention relating to the Status of Stateless Persons signed at New York on 28 September 1954, and refugees as defined by Article 1 of the Convention relating to the Status of Refugees signed at Geneva on 28 July 1951 and modified by the Protocol relating to the Status of Refugees signed at New York on 31 January 1967, shall be regarded as nationals of the country in which they have their habitual residence.

3. Persons who are nationals of a State covered by paragraph 1 (d) must prove that the trade mark for which an application for a Community trade mark has been submitted is registered in the State of origin, unless, according to published findings, the trade marks of nationals of the Member States are registered in the State of origin in question without proof of prior registration as a Community trade mark or as a national trade mark in a Member State.

Article 6 Means whereby a Community trade mark is obtained

A Community trade mark shall be obtained by registration. **A3-005**

Article 7 Absolute grounds for refusal

1. The following shall not be registered: **A3-006**
   (a) signs which do not conform to the requirements of Article 4;
   (b) trade marks which are devoid of any distinctive character;
   (c) trade marks which consist exclusively of signs or indications which may serve, in trade, to designate the kind, quality, quantity, intended purpose, value, geographical origin or the time of production of the goods or of rendering of the service, or other characteristics of the goods or service;
   (d) trade marks which consist exclusively of signs or indications which have become customary in the current language or in the bona fide and established practices of the trade;
   (e) signs which consist exclusively of:
      (i) the shape which results from the nature of the goods themselves; or
      (ii) the shape of goods which is necessary to obtain a technical result; or
      (iii) the shape which gives substantial value to the goods;
   (f) trade marks which are contrary to public policy or to accepted principles of morality;
   (g) trade marks which are of such a nature as to deceive the public, for instance as to the nature, quality or geographical origin of the goods or service;
   (h) trade marks which have not been authorized by the competent authorities and are to be refused pursuant to Article 6ter of the Paris Convention;
   (i) trade marks which include badges, emblems or escutcheons other than those covered by Article 6ter of the Paris Convention and which are of particular public interest, unless the consent of the appropriate authorities to their registration has been given.
   (j) trade marks for wines which contain or consist of a geographical indication identifying wines or for spirits which contain or consist of a geographical indication identifying spirits with respect to such wines or spirits not having that origin.
2. Paragraph 1 shall apply notwithstanding that the grounds of nonregistrability obtain in only part of the Community.
3. Paragraph 1 (b), (c) and (d) shall not apply if the trade mark has become distinctive in relation to the goods or services for which registration is requested in consequence of the use which has been made of it.

Article 8 Relative grounds for refusal

1. Upon opposition by the proprietor of an earlier trade mark, the trade **A3-007** mark applied for shall not be registered:
   (a) if it is identical with the earlier trade mark and the goods or services for which registration is applied for are identical with the goods or services for which the earlier trade mark is protected;
   (b) if because of its identity with or similarity to the earlier trade mark and the identity or similarity of the goods or services covered by the

trade marks there exists a likelihood of confusion on the part of the public in the territory in which the earlier trade mark is protected; the likelihood of confusion includes the likelihood of association with the earlier trade mark.

2. for the purposes of paragraph 1, 'Earlier trade marks' means:

(a) trade marks of the following kinds with a date of application for registration which is earlier than the date of application for registration of the Community trade mark, taking account, where appropriate, of the priorities claimed in respect of those trade marks:

    (i) Community trade marks;

    (ii) trade marks registered in a Member State, or, in the case of Belgium, the Netherlands or Luxembourg, at the Benelux Trade Mark Office;

    (iii) trade marks registered under international arrangements which have effect in a Member State;

(b) applications for the trade marks referred to in subparagraph (a), subject to their registration;

(c) trade marks which, on the date of application for registration of the Community trade mark, or, where appropriate, of the priority claimed in respect of the application for registration of the Community trade mark, are well known in a Member State, in the sense in which the words 'well known' are used in Article 6 bis of the Paris Convention.

3. Upon opposition by the proprietor of the trade mark, a trade mark shall not be registered where an agent or representative of the proprietor of the trade mark applies for registration thereof in his own name without the proprietor's consent, unless the agent or representative justifies his action.

4. Upon opposition by the proprietor of a non-registered trade mark or of another sign used in the course of trade of more than mere local significance, the trade mark applied for shall not be registered where and to the extent that, pursuant to the law of the Member State governing that sign,

(a) rights to that sign were acquired prior to the date of application for registration of the Community trade mark, or the date of the priority claimed for the application for registration of the Community trade mark;

(b) that sign confers on its proprietor the right to prohibit the use of a subsequent trade mark.

5. Furthermore, upon opposition by the proprietor of an earlier trade mark within the meaning of paragraph 2, the trade mark applied for shall not be registered where it is identical with or similar to the earlier trade mark and is to be registered for goods or services which are not similar to those for which the earlier trade mark is registered, where in the case of an earlier Community trade mark the trade mark has a reputation in the Community and, in the case of an earlier national trade mark, the trade mark has a reputation in the Member State concerned and where the use without due cause of the trade mark applied for would take unfair advantage of, or be detrimental to, the distinctive character or the repute of the earlier trade mark.

EFFECTS OF COMMUNITY TRADE MARKS

Article 9 Rights conferred by a Community trade mark

1. A Community trade mark shall confer on the proprietor exclusive rights **A3-008** therein. The proprietor shall be entitled to prevent all third parties not having his consent from using in the course of trade:
   (a) any sign which is identical with the Community trade mark in relation to goods or services which are identical with those for which the Community trade mark is registered;
   (b) any sign where, because of its identity with or similarity to the Community trade mark and the identity or similarity of the goods or services covered by the Community trade mark and the sign, there exists a likelihood of confusion on the part of the public; the likelihood of confusion includes the likelihood of association between the sign and the trade mark;
   (c) any sign which is identical with or similar to the Community trade mark in relation to goods or services which are not similar to those for which the Community trade mark is registered, where the latter has a reputation in the Community and where use of that sign without due cause takes unfair advantage of, or is detrimental to, the distinctive character or the repute of the Community trade mark.
2. The following, inter alia, may be prohibited under paragraph 1:
   (a) affixing the sign to the goods or to the packaging thereof;
   (b) offering the goods, putting them on the market or stocking them for these purposes under that sign, or offering or supplying services thereunder;
   (c) importing or exporting the goods under that sign;
   (d) using the sign on business papers and in advertising.
3. The rights conferred by a Community trade mark shall prevail against third parties from the date of publication of registration of the trade mark. Reasonable compensation may, however, be claimed in respect of matters arising after the date of publication of a Community trade mark application, which matters would, after publication of the registration of the trade mark, be prohibited by virtue of that publication. The court seized of the case may not decide upon the merits of the case until the registration has been published.

Article 10 Reproduction of Community trade marks in dictionaries

If the reproduction of a Community trade mark in a dictionary, encyclopaedia **A3-009** or similar reference work gives the impression that it constitutes the generic name of the goods or services for which the trade mark is registered, the publisher of the work shall, at the request of the proprietor of the Community trade mark, ensure that the reproduction of the trade mark at the latest in the next edition of the publication is accompanied by an indication that it is a registered trade mark.

Article 11 Prohibition on the use of a Community trade mark registered in the name of an agent or representative

Where a Community trade mark is registered in the name of the agent or **A3-010** representative of a person who is the proprietor of that trade mark, without the proprietor's authorization, the latter shall be entitled to oppose the use of his mark by his agent or representative if he has not authorized such use, unless the agent or representative justifies his action.

Article 12 Limitation of the effects of a Community trade mark

A3-011   A Community trade mark shall not entitle the proprietor to prohibit a third party from using in the course of trade:

(a) his own name or address;

(b) indications concerning the kind, quality, quantity, intended purpose, value, geographical origin, the time of production of the goods or of rendering of the service, or other characteristics of the goods or service;

(c) the trade mark where it is necessary to indicate the intended purpose of a product or service, in particular as accessories or spare parts, provided he uses them in accordance with honest practices in industrial or commercial matters.

Article 13 Exhaustion of the rights conferred by a Community trade mark

A3-012   1. A Community trade mark shall not entitle the proprietor to prohibit its use in relation to goods which have been put on the market in the Community under that trade mark by the proprietor or with his consent.

2. Paragraph 1 shall not apply where there exist legitimate reasons for the proprietor to oppose further commercialization of the goods, especially where the condition of the goods is changed or impaired after they have been put on the market.

Article 14 Complementary application of national law relating to infringement

A3-013   1. The effects of Community trade marks shall be governed solely by the provisions of this Regulation. In other respects, infringement of a Community trade mark shall be governed by the national law relating to infringement of a national trade mark in accordance with the provisions of Title X.

2. This Regulation shall not prevent actions concerning a Community trade mark being brought under the law of Member States relating in particular to civil liability and unfair competition.

3. The rules of procedure to be applied shall be determined in accordance with the provisions of Title X.

USE OF COMMUNITY TRADE MARKS

Article 15 Use of Community trade marks

A3-014   1. If, within a period of five years following registration, the proprietor has not put the Community trade mark to genuine use in the Community in connection with the goods or services in respect of which it is registered, or if such use has been suspended during an uninterrupted period of five years, the Community trade mark shall be subject to the sanctions provided for in this Regulation, unless there are proper reasons for non-use.

2. The following shall also constitute use within the meaning of paragraph 1:

(a) use of the Community trade mark in a form differing in elements which do not alter the distinctive character of the mark in the form in which it was registered;

(b) affixing of the Community trade mark to goods or to the packaging thereof in the Community solely for export purposes.

3. Use ofthe Community trade mark with the consent of the proprietor shall be deemed to constitute use by the proprietor.

COMMUNITY TRADE MARKS AS OBJECTS OF PROPERTY

Article 16 Dealing with Community trade marks as national trade marks

1. Unless Articles 17 to 24 provide otherwise, a Community trade mark as an **A3-015** object of property shall be dealt with in its entirety, and for the whole area of the Community, as a national trade mark registered in the Member State in which, according to the Register of Community trade marks,
   (a) the proprietor has his seat or his domicile on the relevant date; or
   (b) where subparagraph (a) does not apply, the proprietor has an establishment on the relevant date.

2. In cases which are not provided for by paragraph 1, the Member State referred to in that paragraph shall be the Member State in which the seat of the Office is situated.

3. If two or more persons are mentioned in the Register of Community trade marks as joint proprietors, paragraph 1 shall apply to the joint proprietor first mentioned; failing this, it shall apply to the subsequent joint proprietors in the order in which they are mentioned. Where paragraph 1 does not apply to any of the joint proprietors, paragraph 2 shall apply.

Article 17 Transfer

1. A Community trade mark may be transferred, separately from any transfer **A3-016** of the undertaking, in respect of some or all of the goods or services for which it is registered.

2. A transfer of the whole of the undertaking shall include the transfer of the Community trade mark except where, in accordance with the law governing the transfer, there is agreement to the contrary or circumstances clearly dictate otherwise. This provision shall apply to the contractual obligation to transfer the undertaking.

3. Without prejudice to paragraph 2, an assignment of the Community trade mark shall be made in writing and shall require the signature of the parties to the contract, except when it is a result of a judgment; otherwise it shall be void.

4. Where it is clear from the transfer documents that because of the transfer the Community trade mark is likely to mislead the public concerning the nature, quality or geographical origin of the goods or services in respect of which it is registered, the Office shall not register the transfer unless the successor agrees to limit registration of the Community trade mark to goods or services in respect of which it is not likely to mislead.

5. On request of one of the parties a transfer shall be entered in the Register and published.

6. As long as the transfer has not been entered in the Register, the successor in title may not invoke the rights arising from the registration of the Community trade mark.

7. Where there are time limits to be observed vis-à-vis the Office, the successor in title may make the corresponding statements to the Office once the request for registration of the transfer has been received by the Office.

8. All documents which require notification to the proprietor of the Community trade mark in accordance with Article 77 shall be addressed to the person registered as proprietor.

Article 18 Transfer of a trade mark registered in the name of an agent

A3-017 Where a Community trade mark is registered in the name of the agent or representative of a person who is the proprietor of that trade mark, without the proprietor's authorization, the latter shall be entitled to demand the assignment in his favour of the said registration, unless such agent or representative justifies his action.

Article 19 Rights in rem

A3-018 1. A Community trade mark may, independently of the undertaking, be given as security or be the subject of rights in rem.

2. On request of one of the parties, rights mentioned in paragraph 1 shall be entered in the Register and published.

Article 22 Licensing

A3-019 1. A Community trade mark may be licensed for some or all of the goods or services for which it is registered and for the whole or part of the Community. A licence may be exclusive or non-exclusive.

2. The proprietor of a Community trade mark may invoke the rights conferred by that trade mark against a licensee who contravenes any provision in his licensing contract with regard to its duration, the form covered by the registration in which the trade mark may be used, the scope of the goods or services for which the licence is granted, the territory in which the trade mark may be affixed, or the quality of the goods manufactured or of the services provided by the licensee.

3. Without prejudice to the provisions of the licensing contract, the licensee may bring proceedings for infringement of a Community trade mark only if its proprietor consents thereto. However, the holder of an exclusive licence may bring such proceedings if the proprietor of the trade mark, after formal notice, does not himself bring infringement proceedings within an appropriate period.

4. A licensee shall, for the purpose of obtaining compensation for damage suffered by him, be entitled to intervene in infringement proceedings brought by the proprietor of the Community trade mark.

5. On request of one of the parties the grant or transfer of a licence in respect of a Community trade mark shall be entered in the Register and published.

Article 23 Effects vis-à-vis third parties

A3-020 1. Legal acts referred to in Article 17, 19 and 22 concerning a Community trade mark shall only have effects vis-à-vis third parties in all the Member States after entry in the Register. Nevertheless, such an act, before it is so entered, shall have effect vis-à-vis third parties who have acquired rights in the trade mark after the date of that act but who knew of the act at the date on which the rights were acquired.

2. Paragraph 1 shall not apply in the case of a person who acquires the Community trade mark or a right concerning the Community trade mark by way of transfer of the whole of the undertaking or by any other universal succession.

3. The effects vis-à-vis third parties of the legal acts referred to in Article 20 shall be governed by the law of the Member State determined in accordance with Article 16.

4. Until such time as common rules for the Member States in the field of bankruptcy enter into force, the effects vis-à-vis third parties of bankruptcy or like proceedings shall be governed by the law of the Member State in which such

proceedings are first brought within the meaning of national law or of conventions applicable in this field.

Article 24 The application for a Community trade mark as an object of property

Articles 16 to 23 shall apply to applications for Community trade marks.   **A3-021**

TITLE III

APPLICATION FOR COMMUNITY TRADE MARKS

FILING OF APPLICATIONS AND THE CONDITIONS WHICH GOVERN THEM

Article 25 Filing of applications

1. An application for a Community trade mark shall be filed, at the choice of **A3-022**
the applicant,
   (a) at the Office; or
   (b) at the central industrial property office of a Member State or at the Benelux Trade Mark Office. An application filed in this way shall have the same effect as if it had been filed on the same date at the Office.

2. Where the application is filed at the central industrial property office of a Member State or at the Benelux Trade Mark Office, that office shall take all steps to forward the application to the Office within two weeks after filing. It may charge the applicant a fee which shall not exceed the administrative costs of receiving and forwarding the application.

3. Applications referred to in paragraph 2 which reach the Office more than one month after filing shall be deemed withdrawn.

4. Ten years after the entry into force of this Regulation, the Commission shall draw up a report on the operation of the system of filing applicationsfor Community trade marks, together with any proposals for modifying this system.

Article 26 Conditions with which applications must comply

1. An application for a Community trade mark shall contain: **A3-023**
   (a) a request for the registration of a Community trade mark;
   (b) information identifying the applicant;
   (c) a list of the goods or services in respect of which the registration is requested;
   (d) a representation of the trade mark.

2. The application for a Community trade mark shall be subject to the payment of the application fee and, when appropriate, of one or more class fees.

3. An application for a Community trade mark must comply with the conditions laid down in the implementing Regulation referred to in Article 140.

Article 27 Date of filing

The date of filing of a Community trade mark application shall be the date **A3-024**
on which documents containing the information specified in Article 26 (1) are filed with the Office by the applicant or, if the application has been filed with the central office of a Member State or with the Benelux Trade Mark Office, with that office, subject to payment of the application fee within a period of one month of filing the abovementioned documents.

Article 28 Classification

A3-025   Goods and services in respect of which Community trade marks are applied for shall be classified in conformity with the system of classification specified in the Implementing Regulation.

PRIORITY

Article 29 Right of priority

A3-026   1. A person who has duly filed an application for a trade mark in or for any State party to the Paris Convention or to the Agreement establishing the World Trade Organization, or his successors in title, shall enjoy, for the purpose of filing a Community trade mark application for the same trade mark in respect of goods or services which are identical with or contained within those for which the application has been filed, a right or priority during a period of six months from the date of filing of the first application.

2. Every filing that is equivalent to a regular national filing under the national law of the State where it was made or under bilateral or multilateral agreements shall be recognized as giving rise to a right of priority.

3. By a regular national filing is meant any filing that is sufficient to establish the date on which the application was filed, whatever may be the outcome of the application.

4. A subsequent application for a trade mark which was the subject of a previous first application in respect of the same goods or services, and which is filed in or in respect of the same State shall be considered as the first application for the purposes of determining priority, provided that, at the date of filing of the subsequent application, the previous application has been withdrawn, abandoned or refused, without being open to public inspection and without leaving any rights outstanding, and has not served as a basis for claiming a right of priority. The previous application may not thereafter serve as a basis for claiming a right of priority.

5. If the first filing has been made in a State which is not a party to the Paris Convention or to the Agreement establishing the World Trade Organization, paragraphs 1 to 4 shall apply only in so far as that State, according to published findings, grants, on the basis of the first filing made at the Office and subject to conditions equivalent to those laid down in this Regulation, a right of priority having equivalent effect.

Article 30 Claiming priority

A3-027   An applicant desiring to take advantage of the priority of a previous application shall file a declaration of priority and a copy of the previous application. If the language of the latter is not one of the languages of the Office, the applicant shall file a translation of the previous application in one of those languages.

Article 31 Effect of priority right

A3-028   The right of priority shall have the effect that the date of priority shall count as the date of filing of the Community trade mark application for the purposes of establishing which rights take precedence.

Article 32 Equivalence of Community filing with national filing

A3-029   A Community trade mark application which has been accorded a date of filing shall, in the Member States, be equivalent to a regular national filing, where appropriate with the priority claimed for the Community trade mark application.

CLAIMING THE SENIORITY OF A NATIONAL TRADE MARK

Article 34 Claiming the seniority of a national trade mark

1. The proprietor of an earlier trade mark registered in a Member State, **A3-030** including a trade mark registered in the Benelux countries, or registered under international arrangements having effect in a Member State, who applies for an identical trade mark for registration as a Community trade mark for goods or services which are identical with or contained within those for which the earlier trade mark has been registered, may claim for the Community trade mark the seniority of the earlier trade mark in respect of the Member State in or for which it is registered.

2. Seniority shall have the sole effect under this Regulation that, where the proprietor of the Community trade mark surrenders the earlier trade mark or allows it to lapse, he shall be deemed to continue to have the same rights as he would have had if the earlier trade mark had continued to be registered.

3. The seniority claimed for the Community trade mark shall lapse if the earlier trade mark the seniority of which is claimed is declared to have been revoked or to be invalid or if it is surrendered prior to the registration of the Community trade mark.

Article 35 Claiming seniority after registration of the Community trade mark

1. The proprietor of a Community trade mark who is the proprietor of an **A3-031** earlier identical trade mark registered in a Member State, including a trade mark registered in the Benelux countries, or of a trade mark registered under international arrangements having effect in a Member State, for identical goods or services, may claim the seniority of the earlier trade mark in respect of the Member State in or for which it is registered.

2. Article 34 (2) and (3) shall apply.

TITLE IV

REGISTRATION PROCEDURE

EXAMINATION OF APPLICATIONS

Article 36 Examination of the conditions of filing

1. The Office shall examine whether: **A3-032**
   (a) the Community trade mark application satisfies the requirements for the accordance of a date of filing in accordance with Article 27;
   (b) the Community trade mark application complies with the conditions laid down in the Implementing Regulation;
   (c) where appropriate, the class fees have been paid within the prescribed period.

2. Where the Community trade mark application does not satisfy the requirements referred to in paragraph 1, the Office shall request the applicant to remedy the deficiencies or the default on payment within the prescribed period.

3. If the deficiencies or the default on payment established pursuant to paragraph 1 (a) are not remedied within this period, the application shall not be dealt with as a Community trade mark application. If the applicant complies with the Office's request, the Office shall accord as the date of filing of the application the date on which the deficiencies or the default on payment established are remedied.

4. If the deficiencies established pursuant to paragraph 1 (b) are not remedied within the prescribed period, the Office shall refuse the application.

5. If the default on payment established pursuant to paragraph 1 (c) is not remedied within the prescribed period, the application shall be deemed to be withdrawn unless it is clear which categories of goods or services the amount paid is intended to cover.

6. Failure to satisfy the requirements concerning the claim to priority shall result in loss of the right of priority for the application.

7. Failure to satisfy the requirements concerning the claiming ofseniority of a national trade mark shall result in loss of that right for the application.

Article 37 Examination of the conditions relating to the entitlement of the proprietor

A3-033   1. Where, pursuant to Article 5, the applicant may not be the proprietor of a Community trade mark, the application shall be refused.

2. The application may not be refused before the applicant has been given the opportunity to withdraw his application or submit his observations.

Article 38 Examination as to absolute grounds for refusal

A3-034   1. Where, under Article 7, a trade mark is ineligible for registration in respect of some or all of the goods or services covered by the Community trade mark application, the application shall be refused as regards those goods or services.

2. Where the trade mark contains an element which is not distinctive, and where the inclusion of said element in the trade mark could give rise to doubts as to the scope of protection of the trade mark, the Office may request, as a condition for registration of said trade mark, that the applicant state that he disclaims any exclusive right to such element. Any disclaimer shall be published together with the application or the registration of the Community trade mark, as the case may be.

3. The application shall not be refused before the applicant has been allowed the opportunity of withdrawing or amending the application or of submitting his observations.

SEARCH

Article 39 Search

A3-035   1. Once the Office has accorded a date of filing to a Community trade mark application and has established that the applicant satisfies the conditions referred to in Article 5, it shall draw up a Community search report citing those earlier Community trade marks or Community trade mark applications discovered which may be invoked under Article 8 against the registration of the Community trade mark applied for.

2. As soon as a Community trade mark application has been accorded a date of filing, the Office shall transmit a copy thereof to the central industrial property office of each Member State which has informed the Office of its decision to

operate a search in its own register of trade marks in respect of Community trade mark applications.

3. Each of the central industrial property offices referred to in paragraph 2 shall communicate to the Office within three months as from the date on which it received the Community trade mark application a search report which shall either cite those earlier national trade marks or trade mark applications discovered which may be invoked under Article 8 against the registration of the Community trade mark applied for, or state that the search has revealed no such rights.

4. An amount shall be paid by the Office to each central industrial property office for each search report provided by that office in accordance with paragraph 3. The amount, which shall be the same for each office, shall be fixed by the Budget Committee by means of a decision adopted by a majority of three-quarters of the representatives of the Member States.

5. The Office shall transmit without delay to the applicant for the Community trade mark the Community search report and the national search reports received within the time limit laid down in paragraph 3.

6. Upon publication of the Community trade mark application, which may not take place before the expiry of a period of one month as from the date on which the Office transmits the search reports to the applicant, the Office shall inform the proprietors of any earlier Community trade marks or Community trade mark applications cited in the Community search report of the publication of the Community trade mark application.

7. The Commission shall, five years after the opening of the Office for the filing of applications, submit to the Council a report on the operation of the system of searching resulting from this Article, including the payments made to Member States under paragraph 4, and, if necessary, appropriate proposals for amending this Regulation with a view to adapting the system of searching on the basis of the experience gained and bearing in mind developments in searching techniques.

PUBLICATION OF THE APPLICATION

Article 40 Publication of the application

1. If the conditions which the application for a Community trade mark must **A3-036** satisfy have been fulfilled and if the period referred to in Article 39 (6) has expired, the application shall be published to the extent that it has not been refused pursuant to Articles 37 and 38.

2. Where, after publication, the application is refused under Articles 37 and 38, the decision that it has been refused shall be published upon becoming final.

OBSERVATIONS BY THIRD PARTIES AND OPPOSITION

Article 41 Observations by third parties

1. Following the publication of the Community trade mark application, any **A3-037** natural or legal person and any group or body representing manufacturers, producers, suppliers of services, traders or consumers may submit to the Office written observations, explaining on which grounds under Article 7, in particular, the trade mark shall not be registered ex officio. They shall not be parties to the proceedings before the Office.

2. The observations referred to in paragraph 1 shall be communicated to the applicant who may comment on them.

Article 42 Opposition

A3-038   1. Within a period of three months following the publication of a Community trade mark application, notice of opposition to registration of the trade mark may be given on the grounds that it may not be registered under Article 8:

    (a) by the proprietors of earlier trade marks referred to in Article 8 (2) as well as licensees authorized by the proprietors of those trade marks, in respect of Article 8 (1) and (5);

    (b) by the proprietors of trade marks referred to in Article 8 (3);

    (c) by the proprietors of earlier marks or signs referred to in Article 8 (4) and by persons authorized under the relevant national law to exercise these rights.

2. Notice of opposition to registration of the trade mark may also be given, subject to the conditions laid down in paragraph 1, in the event of the publication of an amended application in accordance with the second sentence of Article 44 (2).

3. Opposition must be expressed in writing and must specify the grounds on which it is made. It shall not be treated as duly entered until the opposition fee has been paid. Within a period fixed by the Office, the opponent may submit in support of his case facts, evidence and arguments.

Article 43 Examination of opposition

A3-039   1. In the examination of the opposition the Office shall invite the parties, as often as necessary, to file observations, within a period set them by the Office, on communications from the other parties or issued by itself.

2. If the applicant so requests, the proprietor of an earlier Community trade mark who has given notice of opposition shall furnish proof that, during the period of five years preceding the date of publication of the Community trade mark application, the earlier Community trade mark has been put to genuine use in the Community in connection with the goods or services in respect of which it is registered and which he cites as justification for his opposition, or that there are proper reasons for non-use, provided the earlier Community trade mark has at that date been registered for not less than five years. In the absence of proof to this effect, the opposition shall be rejected. If the earlier Community trade mark has been used in relation to part only of the goods or services for which it is registered it shall, for the purposes of the examination of the opposition, be deemed to be registered in respect only of that part of the goods or services.

3. Paragraph 2 shall apply to earlier national trade marks referred to in Article 8 (2) (a), by substituting use in the Member State in which the earlier national trade mark is protected for use in the Community.

4. The Office may, if it thinks fit, invite the parties to make a friendly settlement.

5. If examination of the opposition reveals that the trade mark may not be registered in respect of some or all of the goods or services for which the Community trade mark application has been made, the application shall be refused in respect of those goods or services. Otherwise the opposition shall be rejected.

6. The decision refusing the application shall be published upon becoming final.

WITHDRAWAL, RESTRICTION AND AMENDMENT OF THE APPLICATION

Article 44 Withdrawal, restriction and amendment of the application

1. The applicant may at any time withdraw his Community trade mark application or restrict the list of goods or services contained therein. Where the application has already been published, the withdrawal or restriction shall also be published. **A3-040**

2. In other respects, a Community trade mark application may be amended, upon request of the applicant, only by correcting the name and address of the applicant, errors of wording or of copying, or obvious mistakes, provided that such correction does not substantially change the trade mark or extend the list of goods or services. Where the amendments affect the representation of the trade mark or the list of goods or services and are made after publication of the application, the trade mark application shall be published as amended.

REGISTRATION

Article 45 Registration

Where an application meets the requirements of this Regulation and where no notice of opposition has been given within the period referred to in Article 42 (1) or where opposition has been rejected by a definitive decision, the trade mark shall be registered as a Community trade mark, provided that the registration fee has been paid within the period prescribed. If the fee is not paid within this period the application shall be deemed to be withdrawn. **A3-041**

TITLE V

DURATION, RENEWAL AND ALTERATION OF COMMUNITY TRADE MARKS

Article 46 Duration of registration

Community trade marks shall be registered for a period of ten years from the date of filing of the application. Registration may be renewed in accordance with Article 47 for further periods of ten years. **A3-042**

Article 47 Renewal

1. Registration of the Community trade mark shall be renewed at the request of the proprietor of the trade mark or any person expressly authorized by him, provided that the fees have been paid. **A3-043**

2. The Office shall inform the proprietor of the Community trade mark, and any person having a registered right in respect of the Community trade mark, of the expiry of the registration in good time before the said expiry. Failure to give such information shall not involve the responsibility of the Office.

3. The request for renewal shall be submitted within a period of six months ending on the last day of the month in which protection ends. The fees shall also be paid within this period. Failing this, the request may be submitted and the fees paid within a further period of six months following the day referred to in the first sentence, provided that an additional fee is paid within this further period.

4. Where the request is submitted or the fees paid in respect of only some of the goods or services for which the Community trade mark is registered, registration shall be renewed for those goods or services only.

5. Renewal shall take effect from the day following the date on which the existing registration expires. The renewal shall be registered.

Article 48 Alteration

A3-044   1. The Community trade mark shall not be altered in the register during the period of registration or on renewal thereof.

2. Nevertheless, where the Community trade mark includes the name and address of the proprietor, any alteration thereof not substantially affecting the identity of the trade mark as originally registered may be registered at the request of the proprietor.

3. The publication of the registration of the alteration shall contain a representation of the Community trade mark as altered. Third parties whose rights may be affected by the alteration may challenge the registration thereof within a period of three months following publication.

TITLE VI

SURRENDER, REVOCATION AND INVALIDITY

SURRENDER

Article 49 Surrender

A3-045   1. A Community trade mark may be surrendered in respect of some or all of the goods or services for which it is registered.

2. The surrender shall be declared to the Office in writing by the proprietor of the trade mark. It shall not have effect until it has been entered in the Register.

3. Surrender shall be entered only with the agreement of the proprietor of a right entered in the Register. If a licence has been registered, surrender shall only be entered in the Register if the proprietor of the trade mark proves that he has informed the licensee of his intention to surrender; this entry shall be made on expiry of the period prescribed by the Implementing Regulation.

GROUNDS FOR REVOCATION

Article 50 Grounds for revocation

A3-046   1. The rights of the proprietor of the Community trade mark shall be declared to be revoked on application to the Office or on the basis of a counter-claim in infringement proceedings:

   (a) if, within a continuous period of five years, the trade mark has not been put to genuine use in the Community in connection with the goods or services in respect of which it is registered, and there are no proper reasons for non-use; however, no person may claim that the proprietor's rights in a Community trade mark should be revoked where, during the interval between expiry of the five-year period and filing of the application or counterclaim, genuine use of the trade mark has been started or resumed; the commencement or resumption of use within a period of three months preceding the filing of the application or counterclaim which began at the earliest on expiry of the continuous period of five years of non-use shall, however, be disregarded where preparations for the commencement or resumption occur only after the proprietor becomes aware that the application or counterclaim may be filed;

(b) if, in consequence of acts or inactivity of the proprietor, the trade mark has become the common name in the trade for a product or service in respect of which it is registered;

(c) if, in consequence of the use made of it by the proprietor of the trade mark or with his consent in respect of the goods or services for which it is registered, the trade mark is liable to mislead the public, particularly as to the nature, quality or geographical origin of those goods or services;

(d) if the proprietor of the trade mark no longer satisfies the conditions laid down by Article 5.

2. Where the grounds for revocation of rights exist in respect of only some of the goods or services for which the Community trade mark is registered, the rights of the proprietor shall be declared to be revoked in respect of those goods or services only.

GROUNDS FOR INVALIDITY

Article 51 Absolute grounds for invalidity

1. A Community trade mark shall be declared invalid on application to the **A3-047** Office or on the basis of a counterclaim in infringement proceedings,

(a) where the Community trade mark has been registered in breach of the provisions of Article 5 or of Article 7;

(b) where the applicant was acting in bad faith when he filed the application for the trade mark.

2. Where the Community trade mark has been registered in breach of the provisions of Article 7 (1) (b), (c) or (d), it may nevertheless not be declared invalid if, in consequence of the use which has been made of it, it has after registration acquired a distinctive character in relation to the goods or services for which it is registered.

3. Where the ground for invalidity exists in respect of only some of the goods or services for which the Community trade mark is registered, the trade mark shall be declared invalid as regards those goods or services only.

Article 52 Relative grounds for invalidity

1. A Community trade mark shall be declared invalid on application to the **A3-048** Office or on the basis of a counterclaim in infringement proceedings:

(a) where there is an earlier trade mark as referred to in Article 8 (2) and the conditions set out in paragraph 1 or paragraph 5 of that Article are fulfilled;

(b) where there is a trade mark as referred to in Article 8 (3) and the conditions set out in that paragraph are fulfilled;

(c) where there is an earlier right as referred to in Article 8 (4) and the conditions set out in that paragraph are fulfilled.

2. A Community trade mark shall also be declared invalid on application to the Office or on the basis of a counterclaim in infringement proceedings where the use of such trade mark may be prohibited pursuant to the national law governing the protection of any other earlier right an in particular:

(a) a right to a name;

(b) a right of personal portrayal;

(c) a copyright;

(d) an industrial property right.

3. A Community trade mark may not be declared invalid where the proprietor of a right referred to in paragraphs 1 or 2 consents expressly to the registration of the Community trade mark before submission of the application for a declaration of invalidity or the counterclaim.

4. Where the proprietor of one of the rights referred to in paragraphs 1 or 2 has previously applied for a declaration that a Community trade mark is invalid or made a counterclaim in infringement proceedings, he may not submit a new application for a declaration of invalidity or lodge a counterclaim on the basis of another of the said rights which he could have invoked in support of his first application or counterclaim.

5. Article 51 (3) shall apply.

Article 53 Limitation in consequence of acquiescence

A3-049   1. Where the proprietor of a Community trade mark has acquiesced, for a period of five successive years, in the use of a later Community trade mark in the Community while being aware of such use, he shall no longer be entitled on the basis of the earlier trade mark either to apply for a declaration that the later trade mark is invalid or to oppose the use of the later trade mark in respect of the goods or services for which the later trade mark has been used, unless registration of the later Community trade mark was applied for in bad faith.

2. Where the proprietor of an earlier national trade mark as referred to in Article 8 (2) or of another earlier sign referred to in Article 8 (4) has acquiesced, for a period of five successive years, in the use of a later Community trade mark in the Member State in which the earlier trade mark or the other earlier sign is protected while being aware of such use, he shall no longer be entitled on the basis of the earlier trade mark or of the other earlier sign either to apply for a declaration that the later trade mark is invalid or to oppose the use of the later trade mark in respect of the goods or services for which the later trade mark has been used, unless registration of the later Community trade mark was applied for in bad faith.

3. In the cases referred to in paragraphs 1 and 2, the proprietor of a later Community trade mark shall not be entitled to oppose the use of the earlier right, even though that right may no longer be invoked against the later Community trade mark.

CONSEQUENCES OF REVOCATION AND INVALIDITY

Article 54 Consequences of revocation and invalidity

A3-050   1. The Community trade mark shall be deemed not to have had, as from the date of the application for revocation or of the counterclaim, the effects specified in this Regulation, to the extent that the rights of the proprietor have been revoked. An earlier date, on which one of the grounds for revocation occurred, may be fixed in the decision at the request of one of the parties.

2. The Community trade mark shall be deemed not to have had, as from the outset, the effects specified in this Regulation, to the extent that the trade mark has been declared invalid.

3. Subject to the national provisions relating either to claims for compensation for damage caused by negligence or lack of good faith on the part of the proprietor of the trade mark, or to unjust enrichment, the retroactive effect of revocation or invalidity of the trade mark shall not affect:

    (a) any decision on infringement which has acquired the authority of a final decision and been enforced prior to the revocation or invalidity decision;

    (b) any contract concluded prior to the revocation or invalidity decision, in so far as it has been performed before that decision; however, repayment, to an extent justified by the circumstances, of sums paid under the relevant contract, may be claimed on grounds of equity.

PROCEEDINGS IN THE OFFICE IN RELATION TO REVOCATION OR INVALIDITY

Article 55 Application for revocation or for a declaration of invalidity

1. An application for revocation of the rights of the proprietor of a **A3-051** Community trade mark or for a declaration that the trade mark is invalid may be submitted to the Office:

    (a) where Articles 50 and 51 apply, by any natural or legal person and any group or body set up for the purpose of representing the interests of manufacturers, producers, suppliers of services, traders or consumers, which under the terms of the law governing it has the capacity in its own name to sue and be sued;

    (b) where Article 52 (1) applies, by the persons referred to in Article 42 (1);

    (c) where Article 52 (2) applies, by the owners of the earlier rights referred to in that provision or by the persons who are entitled under the law of the Member State concerned to exercise the rights in question.

2. The application shall be filed in a written reasoned statement. It shall not be deemed to have been filed until the fee has been paid.

3. An application for revocation or for a declaration of invalidity shall be inadmissible if an application relating to the same subject matter and cause of action, and involving the same parties, has been adjudicated on by a court in a Member State and has acquired the authority of a final decision.

Article 56 Examination of the application

1. In the examination of the application for revocation of rights or for a **A3-052** declaration of invalidity, the Office shall invite the parties, as often as necessary, to file observations, within a period to be fixed by the Office, on communications from the other parties or issued by itself.

2. If the proprietor of the Community trade mark so requests, the proprietor of an earlier Community trade mark, being a party to the invalidity proceedings, shall furnish proof that, during the period of five years preceding the date of the application for a declaration of invalidity, the earlier Community trade mark has been put to genuine use in the Community in connection with the goods or services in respect of which it is registered and which he cites as justification for his application, or that there are proper reasons for non-use, provided the earlier Community trade mark has at that date been registered for non-use, provided the earlier Community trade mark has at that date been registered for not less than five years. If, at the date on which the Community trade mark application

was published, the earlier Community trade mark had been registered for not less than five years, the proprietor of the earlier Community trade mark shall furnish proof that, in addition, the conditions contained in Article 43 (2) were satisfied at that date. In the absence of proof to this effect the application for a declaration of invalidity shall be rejected. If the earlier Community trade mark has been used in relation to part only of the goods or services for which it is registered it shall, for the purpose of the examination of the application for a declaration of invalidity, be deemed to be registered in respect only of that part of the goods or services.

3. Paragraph 2 shall apply to earlier national trade marks referred to in Article 8 (2) (a), by substituting use in the Member State in which the earlier national trade mark is protected for use in the Community.

4. The Office may, if it thinks fit, invite the parties to make a friendly settlement.

5. If the examination of the application for revocation of rights or for a declaration of invalidity reveals that the trade mark should not have been registered in respect of some or all of the goods or services for which it is registered, the rights of the proprietor of the Community trade mark shall be revoked or it shall be declared invalid in respect of those goods or services. Otherwise the application for revocation of rights or for a declaration of invalidity shall be rejected.

6. The decision revoking the rights of the proprietor of the Community trade mark or declaring it invalid shall be entered in the Register upon becoming final.

TITLE VII

APPEALS

Article 57 Decisions subject to appeal

A3-053   1. An appeal shall lie from decisions of the examiners, Opposition Divisions, Administration of Trade Marks and Legal Divisions and Cancellation Divisions. It shall have suspensive effect.

2. A decision which does not terminate proceedings as regards one of the parties can only be appealed together with the final decision, unless the decision allows separate appeal.

Article 58 Persons entitled to appeal and to be parties to appeal proceedings

A3-054   Any party to proceedings adversely affected by a decision may appeal. Any other parties to the proceedings shall be parties to the appeal proceedings as of right.

Article 59 Time limit and form of appeal

A3-055   Notice of appeal must be filed in writing at the Office within two months after the date of notification of the decision appealed from. The notice shall be deemed to have been filed only when the fee for appeal has been paid. Within four months after the date of notification of the decision, a written statement setting out the grounds of appeal must be filed.

Article 62 Decisions in respect of appeals

A3-056   1. Following the examination as to the allowability of the appeal, the Board of Appeal shall decide on the appeal. The Board of Appeal may either exercise any power within the competence of the department which was responsible for the decision appealed or remit the case to that department for further prosecution.

2. If the Board of Appeal remits the case for further prosecution to the department whose decision was appealed, that department shall be bound by the ratio decidendi of the Board of Appeal, in so far as the facts are the same.

3. The decisions of the Boards of Appeal shall take effect only as from the date of expiration of the period referred to in Article 63 (5) or, if an action has been brought before the Court of Justice within that period, as from the date of rejection of such action.

Article 63 Actions before the Court of Justice

1. Actions may be brought before the Court of Justice against decisions of **A3-057** the Boards of Appeal on appeals.

2. The action may be brought on grounds of lack of competence, infringement of an essential procedural requirement, infringement of the Treaty, of this Regulation or of any rule of law relating to their application or misuse of power.

3. The Court of Justice has jurisdiction to annul or to alter the contested decision.

4. The action shall be open to any party to proceedings before the Board of Appeal adversely affected by its decision.

5. The action shall be brought before the Court of Justice within two months of the date of notification of the decision of the Board of Appeal.

6. The Office shall be required to take the necessary measures to comply with the judgment of the Court of Justice.

TITLE VIII

COMMUNITY COLLECTIVE MARKS

Article 64 Community collective marks

1. A Community collective mark shall be a Community trade mark which is **A3-058** described as such when the mark is applied for and is capable of distinguishing the goods or services of the members of the association which is the proprietor of the mark from those of other undertakings. Associations of manufacturers, producers, suppliers of services, or traders which, under the terms of the law governing them, have the capacity in their own name to have rights and obligations of all kinds, to make contracts or accomplish other legal acts and to sue and be sued, as well as legal persons governed by public law, may apply for Community collective marks.

2. In derogation from Article 7 (1) (c), signs or indications which may serve, in trade, to designate the geographical origin of the goods or services may constitute Community collective marks within the meaning of paragraph 1. A collective mark shall not entitle the proprietor to prohibit a third party from using in the course of trade such signs or indications, provided he uses them in accordance with honest practices in industrial or commercial matters; in particular, such a mark may not be invoked against a third party who is entitled to use a geographical name.

3. The provisions of this Regulation shall apply to Community collective marks, unless Articles 65 to 72 provide otherwise.

Article 65 Regulations governing use of the mark

A3-059   1. An applicant for a Community collective mark must submit regulations governing its use within the period prescribed.

2. The regulations governing use shall specify the persons authorized to use the mark, the conditions of membership of the association and, where they exist, the conditions of use of the mark including sanctions. The regulations governing use of a mark referred to in Article 64 (2) must authorize any person whose goods or services originate in the geographical area concerned to become a member of the association which is the proprietor of the mark.

Article 66 Refusal of the application

A3-060   1. In addition to the grounds for refusal of a Community trade mark application provided for in Articles 36 and 38, an application for a Community collective mark shall be refused where the provisions of Article 64 or 65 are not satisfied, or where the regulations governing use are contrary to public policy or to accepted principles of morality.

2. An application for a Community collective mark shall also be refused if the public is liable to be misled as regards the character or the significance of the mark, in particular if it is likely to be taken to be something other than a collective mark.

3. An application shall not be refused if the applicant, as a result of amendment of the regulations governing use, meets the requirements of paragraphs 1 and 2.

Article 67 Observations by third parties

A3-061   Apart from the cases mentioned in Article 41, any person, group or body referred to in that Article may submit to the Office written observations based on the particular grounds on which the application for a Community collective mark should be refused under the terms of Article 66.

Article 68 Use of marks

A3-062   Use of a Community collective mark by any person who has authority to use it shall satisfy the requirements of this Regulation, provided that the other conditions which this Regulation imposes with regard to the use of Community trade marks are fulfilled.

Article 70 Persons who are entitled to bring an action for infringement

A3-063   1. The provisions of Article 22 (3) and (4) concerning the rights of licensees shall apply to every person who has authority to use a Community collective mark.

2. The proprietor of a Community collective mark shall be entitled to claim compensation on behalf of persons who have authority to use the mark where they have sustained damage in consequence of unauthorized use of the mark.

Article 71 Grounds for revocation

A3-064   Apart from the grounds for revocation provided for in Article 50, the rights of the proprietor of a Community collective mark shall be revoked on application to the Office or on the basis of a counterclaim in infringement proceedings, if:

(a) the proprietor does not take reasonable steps to prevent the mark being used in a manner incompatible with the conditions of use, where these exist, laid down in the regulations governing use, amendments to which have, where appropriate, been mentioned in the Register;

(b) the manner in which the mark has been used by the proprietor has caused itto become liable to mislead the public in the manner referred to in Article 66 (2);

(c) an amendment to the regulations governing use of the mark has been mentioned in the Register in breach of the provisions of Article 69 (2), unless the proprietor of the mark, by further amending the regulations governing use, complies with the requirements of those provisions.

Article 72 Grounds for invalidity

Apart from the grounds for invalidity provided for in Articles 51 and 52, a **A3-065** Community collective mark which is registered in breach of the provisions of Article 66 shall be declared invalid on application to the Office or on the basis of a counterclaim in infringement proceedings, unless the proprietor of the mark, by amending the regulations governing use, complies with the requirements of those provisions.

TITLE IX

PROCEDURE

GENERAL PROVISIONS

Article 73 Statement of reasons on which decisions are based

Decisions of the Office shall state the reasons on which they are based. They **A3-066** shall be based only on reasons or evidence on which the parties concerned have had on opportunity to present their comments.

Article 74 Examination of the facts by the Office of its own motion

1. In proceedings before it the Office shall examine the facts of its own **A3-067** motion; however, in proceedings relating to relative grounds for refusal of registration, the Office shall be restricted in this examination to the facts, evidence and arguments provided by the parties and the relief sought.

2. The Office may disregard facts or evidence which are not submitted in due time by the parties concerned.

Article 75 Oral proceedings

1. If the Office considers that oral proceedings would be expedient they shall **A3-068** be held either at the instance of the Office or at the request of any party to the proceedings.

2. Oral proceedings before the examiners, the Opposition Division and the Administration of Trade Marks and Legal Division shall not be public.

3. Oral proceedings, including delivery of the decision, shall be public before the Cancellation Division and the Boards of Appeal, in so far as the department before which the proceedings are taking place does not decide otherwise in cases where admission of the public could have serious and unjustified disadvantages, in particular for a party to the proceedings.

Article 79 Reference to general principles

A3-069　　In the absence of procedural provisions in this Regulation, the Implementing Regulation, the fees regulations or the rules of procedure of the Boards of Appeal, the Office shall take into account the principles of procedural law generally recognized in the Member States.

INFORMATION OF THE PUBLIC AND OF THE OFFICIAL AUTHORITIES OF THE MEMBER STATES

Article 83 Register of Community trade marks

A3-070　　The Office shall keep a register to the known as the Register of Community trade marks, which shall contain those particulars the registration or inclusion of which is provided for by this Regulation or by the Implementing Regulation. The Register shall be open to public inspection.

Article 84 Inspection of files

A3-071　　1. The files relating to Community trade mark applications which have not yet been published shall not be made available for inspection without the consent of the applicant.

2. Any person who can prove that the applicant for a Community trade mark has stated that after the trade mark has been registered he will invoke the rights under it against him may obtain inspection of the files prior to the publication of that application and without the consent of the applicant.

3. Subsequent to the publication of the Community trade mark application, the files relating to such application and the resulting trade mark may be inspected on request.

4. However, where the files are inspected pursuant to paragraphs 2 or 3, certain documents in the file may be withheld from inspection in accordance with the provisions of the Implementing Regulation.

Article 85 Periodical publications

A3-072　　The Office shall periodically publish:

(a) a Community Trade Marks Bulletin containing entries made in the Register of Community trade marks as well as other particulars the publication of which is prescribed by this Regulation or by the Implementing Regulation;

(b) an Official Journal containing notices and information of a general character issued by the President of the Office, as well as any other information relevant to this Regulation or its implementation.

TITLE X

JURISDICTION AND PROCEDURE IN LEGAL ACTIONS RELATING TO COMMUNITY TRADE MARKS

APPLICATION OF THE CONVENTION ON JURISDICTION AND ENFORCEMENT

Article 90 Application of the Convention on Jurisdiction and Enforcement

A3-073　　1. Unless otherwise specified in this Regulation, the Convention on Jurisdiction and the Enforcement of Judgments in Civil and Commercial Matters, signed in Brussels on 27 September 1968, as amended by the Conventions on the Accession to that Convention of the States acceding to the European Communities, the whole of which Convention and of which Conventions of Accession are hereinafter referred to as the 'Convention on Jurisdiction and Enforcement', shall apply to proceedings relating to Community trade marks and applications for Community trade marks, as well as to proceedings relating to simultaneous and successive actions on the basis of Community trade marks and national trade marks.

2. In the case of proceedings in respect of the actions and claims referred to in Article 92:

(a) Articles 2, 4, 5 (1), (3), (4) and (5) and Article 24 of the Convention on Jurisdiction and Enforcement shall not apply;

(b) Articles 17 and 18 of that Convention shall apply subject to the limitations in Article 93 (4) of this Regulation;

(c) the provisions of Title II of that Convention which are applicable to persons domiciled in a Member State shall also be applicable to persons who do not have a domicile in any Member State but have an establishment therein.

DISPUTES CONCERNING THE INFRINGEMENT AND VALIDITY OF COMMUNITY TRADE MARKS

Article 91 Community trade mark courts

1. The Member States shall designate in their territories as limited a number **A3-074** as possible of national courts and tribunals of first and second instance, hereinafter referred to as 'Community trade mark courts', which shall perform the functions assigned to them by this Regulation.

2. Each Member State shall communicate to the Commission within three years of the entry into force of this Regulation a list of Community trade mark courts indicating their names and their territorial jurisdiction.

3. Any change made after communication of the list referred to in paragraph 2 in the number, names or territorial jurisdiction of the courts shall be notified without delay by the Member State concerned to the Commission.

4. The information referred to in paragraphs 2 and 3 shall be notified by the Commission to the Member States and published in the Official Journal of the European Communities.

5. As long as a Member State has not communicated the list as stipulated in paragraph 2, jurisdiction for any proceedings resulting from an action or application covered by Article 92, and for which the courts of that State have jurisdiction under Article 93, shall lie with that court of the State in question which would have jurisdiction ratione loci and ratione materiae in the case of proceedings relating to a national trade mark registered in that State.

Article 92 Jurisdiction over infringement and validity

The Community trade mark courts shall have exclusive jurisdiction: **A3-075**

(a) for all infringement actions and – if they are permitted under national law –actions in respect of threatened infringement relating to Community trade marks;

(b) for actions for declaration of non-infringement, if they are permitted under nationallaw;

(c) for all actions brought as a result of acts referred to in Article 9 (3), second sentence;

(d) for counterclaims for revocation or for a declaration of invalidity of the Community trade mark pursuant to Article 96.

Article 93 International jurisdiction

A3-076   1. Subject to the provisions of this Regulation as well as to any provisions of the Convention on Jurisdiction and Enforcement applicable by virtue of Article 90, proceedings in respect of the actions and claims referred to in Article 92 shall be brought in the courts of the Member State in which the defendant is domiciled or, if he is not domiciled in any of the Member States, in which he has an establishment.

2. If the defendant is neither domiciled nor has an establishment in any of the Member States, such proceedings shall be brought in the courts of the Member State in which the plaintiff is domiciled or, if he is not domiciled in any of the Member States, in which he has an establishment.

3. If neither the defendant nor the plaintiff is so domiciled or has such an establishment, such proceedings shall be brought in the courts of the Member State where the Office has its seat.

4. Notwithstanding the provisions of paragraphs 1, 2 and 3:

    (a) Notwithstanding the provisions of paragraphs 1, 2 and 3: (a) Article 17 of the Convention on Jurisdiction and Enforcement shall apply if the parties agree that a different Community trade mark court shall have jurisdiction;

    (b) Article 18 of that Convention shall apply if the defendant enters an appearance before a different Community trade mark court.

5. Proceedings in respect of the actions and claims referred to in Article 92, with the exception of actions for a declaration of non-infringement of a Community trade mark, may also be brought in the courts of the Member State in which the act of infringement has been committed or threatened, or in which an act within the meaning of Article 9 (3), second sentence, has been committed.

Article 94 Extent of jurisdiction

A3-077   1. A Community trade mark court whose jurisdiction is based on Article 93 (1) to (4) shall have jurisdiction in respect of:

2. A Community trade mark court whose jurisdiction is based on Article 93 (5) shall have jurisdiction only in respect of acts committed or threatened within the territory of the Member State in which that court is situated.

    – acts of infringement committed or threatened within the territory of any of the Member States,

    – acts within the meaning of Article 9 (3), second sentence, committed within the territory of any of the Member States.

Article 95 Presumption of validity –Defence as to the merits

A3-078   1. The Community trade mark courts shall treat the Community trade mark as valid unless its validity is put in issue by the defendant with a counterclaim for revocation or for a declaration of invalidity.

2. The validity of a Community trade mark may not be put in issue in an action for a declaration of non-infringement.

3. In the actions referred to in Article 92 (a) and (c) a plea relating to revocation or invalidity of the Community trade mark submitted otherwise than by way of a counterclaim shall be admissible in so far as the defendant claims that

the rights of the proprietor of the Community trade mark could be revoked for lack of use or that Community trade mark could be declared invalid on account of an earlier right of the defendant.

Article 96 Counterclaims

1. A counterclaim for revocation or for a declaration of invalidity may only **A3-079** be based on the grounds for revocation or invalidity mentioned in this Regulation.

2. A Community trade mark court shall reject a counterclaim for revocation or for a declaration of invalidity if a decision taken by the Office relating to the same subject matter and cause of action and involving the same parties has already become final.

3. If the counterclaim is brought in a legal action to which the proprietor of the trade mark is not already a party, he shall be informed thereof and may be joined as a party to the action in accordance with the conditions set out in national law.

4. The Community trade mark court with which a counterclaim for revocation or for a declaration of invalidity of the Community trade mark has been filed shall inform the Office of the date on which the counterclaim was filed. The latter shall record this fact in the Register of Community trade marks.

5. Article 56 (3), (4), (5) and (6) shall apply.

6. Where a Community trade mark court has given a judgment which has become final on a counterclaim for revocation or for invalidity of a Community trade mark, a copy of the judgment shall be sent to the Office. Any party may request information about such transmission. The Office shall mention the judgment in the Register of Community trade marks in accordance with the provisions of the Implementing Regulation.

7. The Community trade mark court hearing a counterclaim for revocation or for a declaration of invalidity may stay the proceedings on application by the proprietor of the Community trade mark and after hearing the other parties and may request the defendant to submit an application for revocation or for a declaration of invalidity to the Office within a time limit which it shall determine. If the application is not made within the time limit, the proceedings shall continue; the counterclaim shall be deemed withdrawn. Article 100 (3) shall apply.

Article 97 Applicable law

1. The Community trade mark courts shall apply the provisions of this **A3-080** Regulation.

2. On all matters not covered by this Regulation a Community trade mark court shall apply its national law, including its private international law.

3. Unless otherwise provided in this Regulation, a Community trade mark court shall apply the rules of procedure governing the same type of action relating to a national trade mark in the Member State where it has its seat.

Article 98 Sanctions

1. Where a Community trade mark court finds that the defendant has **A3-081** infringed or threatened to infringe a Community trade mark, it shall, unless there are special reasons for not doing so, issue an order prohibiting the defendant from proceeding with the acts which infringed or would infringe the Community trade mark. It shall also take such measures in accordance with its national law as are aimed at ensuring that this prohibition is complied with.

2. In all other respects the Community trade mark court shall apply the law of the Member State to which the acts of infringement or threatened infringement were committed, including the private international law.

Article 99 Provisional and protective measures

A3-082   1. Application may be made to the courts of a Member State, including Community trade mark courts, for such provisional, including protective, measures in respect of a Community trade mark or Community trade mark application as may be available under the law of that State in respect of a national trade mark, even if, under this Regulation, a Community trade mark court of another Member State has jurisdiction as to the substance of the matter.

2. A Community trade mark court whose jurisdiction is based on Article 93 (1), (2), (3) or (4) shall have jurisdiction to grant provisional and protective measures which, subject to any necessary procedure for recognition and enforcement pursuant to Title III of the Convention on Jurisdiction and Enforcement, are applicable in the territory of any Member State. No other court shall have such jurisdiction.

Article 101 Jurisdiction of Community trade mark courts of second instance - Further appeal

A3-083   1. An appeal to the Community trade mark courts of second instance shall lie from judgments of the Community trade mark courts of first instance in respect of proceedings arising from the actions and claims referred to in Article 92.

2. The conditions under which an appeal may be lodged with a Community trade mark court of second instance shall be determined by the national law of the Member State in which that court is located.

3. The national rules concerning further appeal shall be applicable in respect of judgments of Community trade mark courts of second instance.

TITLE XI

EFFECTS ON THE LAWS OF THE MEMBER STATES

CIVIL ACTIONS ON THE BASIS OF MORE THAN ONE TRADE MARK

Article 105 Simultaneous and successive civil actions on the basis of Community trade marks and national trade marks

A3-084   1. Where actions for infringement involving the same cause of action and between the same parties are brought in the courts of different Member States, one seized on the basis of a Community trade mark and the other seized on the basis of a national trade mark:

(a) the court other than the court first seized shall of its own motion decline jurisdiction in favour of that court where the trade marks concerned are identical and valid for identical goods or services. The court which would be required to decline jurisdiction may stay its proceedings if the jurisdiction of the other court is contested;

(b) the court other than the court first seized may stay its proceedings where the trade marks concerned are identical and valid for similar goods or services and where the trade marks concerned are similar and valid for identical or similar goods or services.

2. The court hearing an action for infringement on the basis of a Community trade mark shall reject the action if a final judgment on the merits has been given on the same cause of action and between the same parties on the basis of an identical national trade mark valid for identical goods or services.

3. The court hearing an action for infringement on the basis of a national trade mark shall reject the action if a final judgment on the merits has been given on the same cause of action and between the same parties on the basis of an identical Community trade mark valid for identical goods or services.

4. Paragraphs 1, 2 and 3 shall not apply in respect of provisional, including protective, measures.

APPLICATION OF NATIONAL LAWS FOR THE PURPOSE OF PROHIBITING THE USE OF COMMUNITY TRADE MARKS

Article 106 Prohibition of use of Community trade marks

1. This Regulation shall, unless otherwise provided for, not affect the right **A3-085** existing under the laws of the Member States to invoke claims for infringement of earlier rights within the meaning of Article 8 or Article 52 (2) in relation to the use of a later Community trade mark. Claims for infringement of earlier rights within the meaning of Article 8 (2) and (4) may, however, no longer be invoked if the proprietor of the earlier right may no longer apply for a declaration that the Community trade mark is invalid in accordance with Article 53 (2).

2. This Regulation shall, unless otherwise provided for, not affect the right to bring proceedings under the civil, administrative or criminal law of a Member Sate or under provisions of Community law for the purpose of prohibiting the use of a Community trade mark to the extent that the use of a national trade mark may be prohibited under the law of that Member State or under Community law.

Article 107 Prior rights applicable to particular localities

1. The proprietor of an earlier right which only applies to a particular locality may oppose the use of the Community trade mark in the territory where his right is protected in so far as the law of the Member State concerned so permits.

2. Paragraph 1 shall cease to apply if the proprietor of the earlier right has acquiesced in the use of the Community trade mark in the territory where his right is protected for a period of five successive years, being aware of such use, unless the Community trade mark was applied for in bad faith.

3. The proprietor of the Community trade mark shall not be entitled to oppose use of the right referred to in paragraph 1 even though that right may no longer be invoked against the Community trade mark.

CONVERSION INTO A NATIONAL TRADE MARK APPLICATION

Article 108 Request for the application of national procedure

1. The applicant for or proprietor of a Community trade mark may request **A3-086** the conversion of his Community trade mark application or Community trade mark into a national trade mark application

    (a) to the extent that the Community trade mark application is refused, withdrawn, or deemed to be withdrawn;

    (b) to the extent that the Community trade mark ceases to have effect.

2. Conversion shall not take place:

(a) where the rights of the proprietor of the Community trade mark have been revoked on the grounds of non-use, unless in the Member State for which conversion is requested the Community trade mark has been put to use which would be considered to be genuine use under the laws of that Member State;

(b) for the purpose of protection in a Member State in which, in accordance with the decision of the Office or of the national court, grounds for refusal of registration or grounds for revocation or invalidity apply to the Community trade mark application or Community trade mark.

3. The national trade mark application resulting from the conversion of a Community trade mark application or a Community trade mark shall enjoy in respect of the Member State concerned the date of filing or the date of priority of that application or trade mark and, where appropriate, the seniority of a trade mark of that State claimed under Article 34 or 35.

4. Where:

– the Community trade mark application is deemed to be withdrawn or is refused by a decision of the Office which has become final,

– the Community trade mark ceases to have effect as a result of a decision of the Office which has become final or as a result of registration of surrender of the Community trade mark, the Office shall notify to the applicant or proprietor a communication fixing a period of three months from the date of that communication in which a request for conversion may be filed.

5. Where the Community trade mark application is withdrawn or the Community trade mark ceases to have effect as a result of failure to renew the registration, the request for conversion shall be filed within three months after the date on which the Community trade mark application is withdrawn or on which the registration of the Community trade mark expires.

6. Where the Community trade mark ceases to have effect as a result of a decision of a national court, the request for conversion shall be filed within three months after the date on which that decision acquired the authority of a final decision.

7. The effect referred to in Article 32 shall lapse if the request is not filed in due time.

Article 109 Submission, publication and transmission of the request for conversion

A3-087   1. A request for conversion shall be filed with the Office and shall specify the Member States in which application of the procedure for registration of a national trade mark is desired. The request shall not be deemed to be filed until the conversion fee has been paid.

2. If the Community trade mark application has been published, receipt of any such request shall be recorded in the Register of Community trade marks and the request for conversion shall be published.

3. The Office shall check whether conversion may be requested in accordance with Article 108 (1), whether the request has been filed within the period laid down in Article 108 (4), (5) or (6), as the case may be, and whether the conversion fee has been paid. If these conditions are fulfilled, the Office shall transmit the request to the central industrial property offices of the States specified therein. At the request of the central industrial property office of a State concerned, the

Office shall give it any information enabling that office to decide as to the admissibility of the request.

Article 110 Formal requirements for conversion

1. Any central industrial property office to which the request is transmitted **A3-088** shall decide as to its admissibility,

2. A Community trade mark application or a Community trade mark transmitted in accordance with Article 109 shall not be subjected to formal requirements of national law which are different from or additional to those provided for in this Regulation or in the Implementing Regulation.

3. Any central industrial property office to which the request is transmitted may require that the applicant shall, within not less than two months:

    (a) pay the national application fee;

    (b) file a translation in one of the official languages of the State in question of the request and of the documents accompanying it;

    (c) indicate an address for service in the State in question;

    (d) supply a representation of the trade mark in the number of copies specified by the State in question.

Council Regulation (EC) No 6/2002 of 12 December 2001 on Community designs

THE COUNCIL OF THE EUROPEAN UNION,

Having regard to the Treaty establishing the European Community, and in particular Article 308 thereof,

Having regard to the proposal from the Commission,

Having regard to the opinion of the European Parliament,

Having regard to the opinion of the Economic and Social Committee,

Whereas:

(1) A unified system for obtaining a Community design to which uniform protection is given with uniform effect throughout the entire territory of the Community would further the objectives of the Community as laid down in the Treaty.

(2) Only the Benelux countries have introduced a uniform design protection law. In all the other Member States the protection of designs is a matter for the relevant national law and is confined to the territory of the Member State concerned. Identical designs may be therefore protected differently in different Member States and for the benefit of different owners. This inevitably leads to conflicts in the course of trade between Member States.

(3) The substantial differences between Member States' design laws prevent and distort Community-wide competition. In comparison with domestic trade in, and competition between, products incorporating a design, trade and competition within the Community are prevented and distorted by the large number of applications, offices, procedures, laws, nationally circumscribed exclusive rights and the combined administrative expense with correspondingly high costs and fees for the applicant. Directive 98/71/EC of the European Parliament and of the Council of 13 October 1998 on the legal protection of designs contributes to remedying this situation.

(4) The effect of design protection being limited to the territory of the individual Member States whether or not their laws are approximated, leads to a possible division of the internal market with respect to products incorporating a

design which is the subject of national rights held by different individuals, and hence constitutes an obstacle to the free movement of goods.

(5) This calls for the creation of a Community design which is directly applicable in each Member State, because only in this way will it be possible to obtain, through one application made to the Office for Harmonisation in the Internal Market (Trade Marks and Design) in accordance with a single procedure under one law, one design right for one area encompassing all Member States.

(6) Since the objectives of the proposed action, namely, the protection of one design right for one area encompassing all the Member States, cannot be sufficiently achieved by the Member States by reason of the scale and the effects of the creation of a Community design and a Community design authority and can therefore, and can therefore be better achieved at Community level, the Community may adopt measures, in accordance with the principle of subsidiarity as set out in Article 5 of the Treaty. In accordance with the principle of proportionality, as set out in that Article, this Regulation does not go beyond what is necessary in order to achieve those objectives.

(7) Enhanced protection for industrial design not only promotes the contribution of individual designers to the sum of Community excellence in the field, but also encourages innovation and development of new products and investment in their production.

(8) Consequently a more accessible design-protection system adapted to the needs of the internal market is essential for Community industries.

(9) The substantive provisions of this Regulation on design law should be aligned with the respective provisions in Directive 98/71/EC.

(10) Technological innovation should not be hampered by granting design protection to features dictated solely by a technical function. It is understood that this does not entail that a design must have an aesthetic quality. Likewise, the interoperability of products of different makes should not be hindered by extending protection to the design of mechanical fittings. Consequently, those features of a design which are excluded from protection for those reasons should not be taken into consideration for the purpose of assessing whether other features of the design fulfil the requirements for protection.

(11) The mechanical fittings of modular products may nevertheless constitute an important element of the innovative characteristics of modular products and present a major marketing asset, and therefore should be eligible for protection.

(12) Protection should not be extended to those component parts which are not visible during normal use of a product, nor to those features of such part which are not visible when the part is mounted, or which would not, in themselves, fulfil the requirements as to novelty and individual character. Therefore, those features of design which are excluded from protection for these reasons should not be taken into consideration for the purpose of assessing whether other features of the design fulfil the requirements for protection.

(13) Full-scale approximation of the laws of the Member States on the use of protected designs for the purpose of permitting the repair of a complex product so as to restore its original appearance, where the design is applied to or incorporated in a product which constitutes a component part of a complex product upon whose appearance the protected design is dependent, could not be achieved through Directive 98/71/EC. Within the framework of the conciliation procedure on the said Directive, the Commission undertook to review the consequences of the provisions of that Directive three years after the deadline for transposition of the Directive in particular for the industrial sectors which are

most affected. Under these circumstances, it is appropriate not to confer any protection as a Community design for a design which is applied to or incorporated in a product which constitutes a component part of a complex product upon whose appearance the design is dependent and which is used for the purpose of the repair of a complex product so as to restore its original appearance, until the Council has decided its policy on this issue on the basis of a Commission proposal.

(14) The assessment as to whether a design has individual character should be based on whether the overall impression produced on an informed user viewing the design clearly differs from that produced on him by the existing design corpus, taking into consideration the nature of the product to which the design is applied or in which it is incorporated, and in particular the industrial sector to which it belongs and the degree of freedom of the designer in developing the design.

(15) A Community design should, as far as possible, serve the needs of all sectors of industry in the Community.

(16) Some of those sectors produce large numbers of designs for products frequently having a short market life where protection without the burden of registration formalities is an advantage and the duration of protection is of lesser significance. On the other hand, there are sectors of industry which value the advantages of registration for the greater legal certainty it provides and which require the possibility of a longer term of protection corresponding to the foreseeable market life of their products.

(17) This calls for two forms of protection, one being a short-term unregistered design and the other being a longer term registered design.

(18) A registered Community design requires the creation and maintenance of a register in which will be registered all those applications which comply with formal conditions and which have been accorded a date of filing. This registration system should in principle not be based upon substantive examination as to compliance with requirements for protection prior to registration, thereby keeping to a minimum the registration and other procedural burdens on applicants.

(19) A Community design should not be upheld unless the design is new and unless it also possesses an individual character in comparison with other designs.

(20) It is also necessary to allow the designer or his successor in title to test the products embodying the design in the market place before deciding whether the protection resulting from a registered Community design is desirable. To this end it is necessary to provide that disclosures of the design by the designer or his successor in title, or abusive disclosures during a period of 12 months prior to the date of the filing of the application for a registered Community design should not be prejudicial in assessing the novelty or the individual character of the design in question.

(21) The exclusive nature of the right conferred by the registered Community design is consistent with its greater legal certainty. It is appropriate that the unregistered Community design should, however, constitute a right only to prevent copying. Protection could not therefore extend to design products which are the result of a design arrived at independently by a second designer. This right should also extend to trade in products embodying infringing designs.

(22) The enforcement of these rights is to be left to national laws. It is necessary therefore to provide for some basic uniform sanctions in all Member

States. These should make it possible, irrespective of the jurisdiction under which enforcement is sought, to stop the infringing acts.

(23) Any third person who can establish that he has in good faith commenced use even for commercial purposes within the Community, or has made serious and effective preparations to that end, of a design included within the scope of protection of a registered Community design, which has not been copied from the latter, may be entitled to a limited exploitation of that design.

(24) It is a fundamental objective of this Regulation that the procedure for obtaining a registered Community design should present the minimum cost and difficulty to applicants, so as to make it readily available to small and medium-sized enterprises as well as to individual designers.

(25) Those sectors of industry producing large numbers of possibly short-lived designs over short periods of time of which only some may be eventually commercialised will find advantage in the unregistered Community design. Furthermore, there is also a need for these sectors to have easier recourse to the registered Community design. Therefore, the option of combining a number of designs in one multiple application would satisfy that need. However, the designs contained in a multiple application may be dealt with independently of each other for the purposes of enforcement of rights, licensing, rights in rem, levy of execution, insolvency proceedings, surrender, renewal, assignment, deferred publication or declaration of invalidity.

(26) The normal publication following registration of a Community design could in some cases destroy or jeopardise the success of a commercial operation involving the design. The facility of a deferment of publication for a reasonable period affords a solution in such cases.

(27) A procedure for hearing actions concerning validity of a registered Community design in a single place would bring savings in costs and time compared with procedures involving different national courts.

(28) It is therefore necessary to provide safeguards including a right of appeal to a Board of Appeal, and ultimately to the Court of Justice. Such a procedure would assist the development of uniform interpretation of the requirements governing the validity of Community designs.

(29) It is essential that the rights conferred by a Community design can be enforced in an efficient manner throughout the territory of the Community.

(30) The litigation system should avoid as far as possible "forum shopping". It is therefore necessary to establish clear rules of international jurisdiction.

(31) This Regulation does not preclude the application to designs protected by Community designs of the industrial property laws or other relevant laws of the Member States, such as those relating to design protection acquired by registration or those relating to unregistered designs, trade marks, patents and utility models, unfair competition or civil liability.

(32) In the absence of the complete harmonisation of copyright law, it is important to establish the principle of cumulation of protection under the Community design and under copyright law, whilst leaving Member States free to establish the extent of copyright protection and the conditions under which such protection is conferred.

(33) The measures necessary for the implementation of this Regulation should be adopted in accordance with Council Decision 1999/468/EC of 28 June 1999 laying down the procedures for the exercise of implementing powers conferred on the Commission,

HAS ADOPTED THIS REGULATION:

TITLE I

GENERAL PROVISIONS

Article 1 Community design

1. A design which complies with the conditions contained in this Regulation **A4-001** is hereinafter referred to as a "Community design".
2. A design shall be protected:
   (a) by an "unregistered Community design", if made available to the public in the manner provided for in this Regulation;
   (b) by a "registered Community design", if registered in the manner provided for in this Regulation.
3. A Community design shall have a unitary character. It shall have equal effect throughout the Community. It shall not be registered, transferred or surrendered or be the subject of a decision declaring it invalid, nor shall its use be prohibited, save in respect of the whole Community. This principle and its implications shall apply unless otherwise provided in this Regulation.

Article 2 Office

The Office for Harmonisation in the Internal Market (Trade Marks and **A4-002** Designs), hereinafter referred to as "the Office", instituted by Council Regulation (EC) No 40/94 of 20 December 1993 on the Community trade mark(6), hereinafter referred to as the "Regulation on the Community trade mark", shall carry out the tasks entrusted to it by this Regulation.

TITLE II

THE LAW RELATING TO DESIGNS

Requirements for protection

Article 3 Definitions

For the purposes of this Regulation: **A4-003**
   (a) "design" means the appearance of the whole or a part of a product resulting from the features of, in particular, the lines, contours, colours, shape, texture and/or materials of the product itself and/or its ornamentation;
   (b) "product" means any industrial or handicraft item, including inter alia parts intended to be assembled into a complex product, packaging, get-up, graphic symbols and typographic typefaces, but excluding computer programs;
   (c) "complex product" means a product which is composed of multiple components which can be replaced permitting disassembly and re-assembly of the product.

Article 4 Requirements for protection

1. A design shall be protected by a Community design to the extent that it is **A4-004** new and has individual character.
2. A design applied to or incorporated in a product which constitutes a component part of a complex product shall only be considered to be new and to have individual character:

(a) if the component part, once it has been incorporated into the complex product, remains visible during normal use of the latter; and

(b) to the extent that those visible features of the component part fulfil in themselves the requirements as to novelty and individual character.

3. "Normal use" within the meaning of paragraph (2)(a) shall mean use by the end user, excluding maintenance, servicing or repair work.

Article 5 Novelty

A4-005   1. A design shall be considered to be new if no identical design has been made available to the public:

(a) in the case of an unregistered Community design, before the date on which the design for which protection is claimed has first been made available to the public;

(b) in the case of a registered Community design, before the date of filing of the application for registration of the design for which protection is claimed, or, if priority is claimed, the date of priority.

2. Designs shall be deemed to be identical if their features differ only in immaterial details.

Article 6 Individual character

A4-006   1. A design shall be considered to have individual character if the overall impression it produces on the informed userdiffers from the overall impression produced on such a user by any design which has been made available to the public:

(a) in the case of an unregistered Community design, before the date on which the design for which protection is claimed has first been made available to the public;

(b) in the case of a registered Community design, before the date of filing the application for registration or, if a priority is claimed, the date of priority.

2. In assessing individual character, the degree of freedom of the designer in developing the design shall be taken into consideration.

Article 7 Disclosure

A4-007   1. For the purpose of applying Articles 5 and 6, a design shall be deemed to have been made available to the public if it has been published following registration or otherwise, or exhibited, used in trade or otherwise disclosed, before the date referred to in Articles 5(1)(a) and 6(1)(a) or in Articles 5(1)(b) and 6(1)(b), as the case may be, except where these events could not reasonably have become known in the normal course of business to the circles specialised in the sector concerned, operating within the Community. The design shall not, however, be deemed to have been made available to the public for the sole reason that it has been disclosed to a third person under explicit or implicit conditions of confidentiality.

2. A disclosure shall not be taken into consideration for the purpose of applying Articles 5 and 6 and if a design for which protection is claimed under a registered Community design has been made available to the public:

(a) by the designer, his successor in title, or a third person as a result of information provided or action taken by the designer or his successor in title; and

(i) Community trade marks;

(b) during the 12-month period preceding the date of filing of the application or, if a priority is claimed, the date of priority.

3. Paragraph 2 shall also apply if the design has been made available to the public as a consequence of an abuse in relation to the designer or his successor in title.

Article 8 Designs dictated by their technical function and designs of interconnections

1. A Community design shall not subsist in features of appearance of a **A4-008** product which are solely dictated by its technical function.

2. A Community design shall not subsist in features of appearance of a product which must necessarily be reproduced in their exact form and dimensions in order to permit the product in which the design is incorporated or to which it is applied to be mechanically connected to or placed in, around or against another product so that either product may perform its function.

3. Notwithstanding paragraph 2, a Community design shall under the conditions set out in Articles 5 and 6 subsist in a design serving the purpose of allowing the multiple assembly or connection of mutually interchangeable products within a modular system.

Article 9 Designs contrary to public policy or morality

A Community design shall not subsist in a design which is contrary to public **A4-009** policy or to accepted principles of morality.

Scope and term of protection

Article 10 Scope of protection

1. The scope of the protection conferred by a Community design shall **A4-010** include any design which does not produce on the informed user a different overall impression.

2. In assessing the scope of protection, the degree of freedom of the designer in developing his design shall be taken into consideration.

Article 11 Commencement and term of protection of the unregistered Community design

1. A design which meets the requirements under Section 1 shall be protected **A4-011** by an unregistered Community design for a period of three years as from the date on which the design was first made available to the public within the Community.

2. For the purpose of paragraph 1, a design shall be deemed to have been made available to the public within the Community if it has been published, exhibited, used in trade or otherwise disclosed in such a way that, in the normal course of business, these events could reasonably have become known to the circles specialised in the sector concerned, operating within the Community. The design shall not, however, be deemed to have been made available to the public for the sole reason that it has been disclosed to a third person under explicit or implicit conditions of confidentiality.

Article 12 Commencement and term of protection of the registered Community design

A4-012   Upon registration by the Office, a design which meets the requirements under Section 1 shall be protected by a registered Community design for a period of five years as from the date of the filing of the application. The right holder may have the term of protection renewed for one or more periods of five years each, up to a total term of 25 years from the date of filing.

Article 13 Renewal

A4-013   1. Registration of the registered Community design shall be renewed at the request of the right holder or of any person expressly authorised by him, provided that the renewal fee has been paid.

2. The Office shall inform the right holder of the registered Community design and any person having a right entered in the register of Community designs, referred to in Article 72, hereafter referred to as the "register" in respect of the registered Community design, of the expiry of the registration in good time before the said expiry. Failure to give such information shall not involve the responsibility of the Office.

3. The request for renewal shall be submitted and the renewal fee paid within a period of six months ending on the last day of the month in which protection ends. Failing this, the request may be submitted and the fee paid within a further period of six months from the day referred to in the first sentence, provided that an additional fee is paid within this further period.

4. Renewal shall take effect from the day following the date on which the existing registration expires. The renewal shall be entered in the register.

Right to the Community design

Article 14 Right to the Community design

A4-014   1. The right to the Community design shall vest in the designer or his successor in title.

2. If two or more persons have jointly developed a design, the right to the Community design shall vest in them jointly.

3. However, where a design is developed by an employee in the execution of his duties or following the instructions given by his employer, the right to the Community design shall vest in the employer, unless otherwise agreed or specified under national law.

Article 15 Claims relating to the entitlement to a Community design

A4-015   1. If an unregistered Community design is disclosed or claimed by, or a registered Community design has been applied for or registered in the name of, a person who is not entitled to it under Article 14, the person entitled to it under that provision may, without prejudice to any other remedy which may be open to him, claim to become recognised as the legitimate holder of the Community design.

2. Where a person is jointly entitled to a Community design, that person may, in accordance with paragraph 1, claim to become recognised as joint holder.

3. Legal proceedings under paragraphs 1 or 2 shall be barred three years after the date of publication of a registered Community design or the date of disclosure of an unregistered Community design. This provision shall not apply if the person who is not entitled to the Community design was acting in bad faith

at the time when such design was applied for or disclosed or was assigned to him.

4. In the case of a registered Community design, the following shall be entered in the register:

(a) the mention that legal proceedings under paragraph 1 have been instituted;

(b) the final decision or any other termination of the proceedings;

(c) any change in the ownership of the registered Community design resulting fromthe final decision.

Article 16 Effects of a judgement on entitlement to a registered Community design

1. Where there is a complete change of ownership of a registered Community **A4-016** design as a result of legal proceedings under Article 15(1), licences and other rights shall lapse upon the entering in the register of the person entitled.

2. If, before the institution of the legal proceedings under Article 15(1) has been registered, the holder of the registered Community design or a licensee has exploited the design within the Community or made serious and effective preparations to do so, he may continue such exploitation provided that he requests within the period prescribed by the implementing regulation a non-exclusive licence from the new holder whose name is entered in the register. The licence shall be granted for a reasonable period and upon reasonable terms.

3. Paragraph 2 shall not apply if the holder of the registered Community design or the licensee was acting in bad faith at the time when he began to exploit the design or to make preparations to do so.

Article 17 Presumption in favour of the registered holder of the design

The person in whose name the registered Community design is registered or, **A4-017** prior to registration, the person in whose name the application is filed, shall be deemed to be the person entitled in any proceedings before the Office as well as in any other proceedings.

Article 18 Right of the designer to be cited

The designer shall have the right, in the same way as the applicant for or the **A4-018** holder of a registered Community design, to be cited as such before the Office and in the register. If the design is the result of teamwork, the citation of the team may replace the citation of the individual designers.

Effects of the Community design

Article 19 Rights conferred by the Community design

1. A registered Community design shall confer on its holder the exclusive **A4-019** right to use it and to prevent any third party not having his consent from using it. The aforementioned use shall cover, in particular, the making, offering, putting on the market, importing, exporting or using of a product in which the design is incorporated or to which it is applied, or stocking such a product for those purposes.

2. An unregistered Community design shall, however, confer on its holder the right to prevent the acts referred to in paragraph 1 only if the contested use results from copying the protected design. The contested use shall not be deemed to result from copying the protected design if it results from an independent

work of creation by a designer who may be reasonably thought not to be familiar with the design made available to the public by the holder.

3. Paragraph 2 shall also apply to a registered Community design subject to deferment of publication as long as the relevant entries in the register and the file have not been made available to the public in accordance with Article 50(4).

Article 20 Limitation of the rights conferred by a Community design

A4-020   1. The rights conferred by a Community design shall not be exercised in respect of:

    (a) acts done privately and for non-commercial purposes;

    (b) acts done for experimental purposes;

    (c) acts of reproduction for the purpose of making citations or of teaching, provided that such acts are compatible with fair trade practice and do not unduly prejudice the normal exploitation of the design, and that mention is made of the source.

2. In addition, the rights conferred by a Community design shall not be exercised in respect of:

    (a) the equipment on ships and aircraft registered in a third country when these temporarily enter the territory of the Community;

    (b) the importation in the Community of spare parts and accessories for the purpose of repairing such craft;

    (c) the execution of repairs on such craft.

Article 21 Exhaustion of rights

A4-021   The rights conferred by a Community design shall not extend to acts relating to a product in which a design included within the scope of protection of the Community design is incorporated or to which it is applied, when the product has been put on the market in the Community by the holder of the Community design or with his consent.

Article 22 Rights of prior use in respect of a registered Community design

A4-022   1. A right of prior use shall exist for any third person who can establish that before the date of filing of the application, or, if a priority is claimed, before the date of priority, he has in good faith commenced use within the Community, or has made serious and effective preparations to that end, of a design included within the scope of protection of a registered Community design, which has not been copied from the latter.

2. The right of prior use shall entitle the third person to exploit the design for the purposes for which its use had been effected, or for which serious and effective preparations had been made, before the filing or priority date of the registered Community design.

3. The right of prior use shall not extend to granting a licence to another person to exploit the design.

4. The right of prior use cannot be transferred except, where the third person is a business, along with that part of the business in the course of which the act was done or the preparations were made.

Article 23 Government use

A4-023   Any provision in the law of a Member State allowing use of national designs by or for the government may be applied to Community designs, but only to the extent that the use is necessary for essential defence or security needs.

Invalidity

Article 24 Declaration of invalidity

1. A registered Community design shall be declared invalid on application to **A4-024** the Office in accordance with the procedure in Titles VI and VII or by a Community design court on the basis of a counterclaim in infringement proceedings.

2. A Community design may be declared invalid even after the Community design has lapsed or has been surrendered.

3. An unregistered Community design shall be declared invalid by a Community design court on application to such a court or on the basis of a counterclaim in infringement proceedings.

Article 25 Grounds for invalidity

1. A Community design may be declared invalid only in the following cases: **A4-025**
   (a) if the design does not correspond to the definition under Article 3(a);
   (b) if it does not fulfil the requirements of Articles 4 to 9;
   (c) if, by virtue of a court decision, the right holder is not entitled to the Community design under Article 14;
   (d) if the Community design is in conflict with a prior design which has been made available to the public after the date of filing of the application or, if a priority is claimed, the date of priority of the Community design, and which is protected from a date prior to the said date by a registered Community design or an application for such a design, or by a registered design right of a Member State, or by an application for such a right;
   (e) if a distinctive sign is used in a subsequent design, and Community law or the law of the Member State governing that sign confers on the right holder of the sign the right to prohibit such use;
   (f) if the design constitutes an unauthorised use of a work protected under the copyright law of a Member State;
   (g) if the design constitutes an improper use of any of the items listed in Article 6ter of the "Paris Convention" for the Protection of Industrial Property hereafter referred to as the "Paris Convention", or of badges, emblems and escutcheons other than those covered by the said Article 6ter and which are of particular public interest in a Member State.

2. The ground provided for in paragraph (1)(c) may be invoked solely by the person who is entitled to the Community design under Article 14.

3. The grounds provided for in paragraph (1)(d), (e) and (f) may be invoked solely by the applicant for or holder of the earlier right.

4. The ground provided for in paragraph (1)(g) may be invoked solely by the person or entity concerned by the use.

5. Paragraphs 3 and 4 shall be without prejudice to the freedom of Member States to provide that the grounds provided for in paragraphs 1(d) and (g) may also be invoked by the appropriate authority of the Member State in question on its own initiative.

6. A registered Community design which has been declared invalid pursuant to paragraph (1)(b), (e), (f) or (g) may be maintained in an amended form, if in that form it complies with the requirements for protection and the identity of the design is retained. ιMaintenanceι in an amended form may include registration accompanied by a partial disclaimer by the holder of the registered Community

design or entry in the register of a court decision or a decision by the Office declaring the partial invalidity of the registered Community design.

Article 26 Consequences of invalidity

A4-026   1. A Community design shall be deemed not to have had, as from the outset, the effects specified in this Regulation, to the extent that it has been declared invalid.

2. Subject to the national provisions relating either to claims for compensation for damage caused by negligence or lack of good faith on the part of the holder of the Community design, or to unjust enrichment, the retroactive effect of invalidity of the Community design shall not affect:

    (a) any decision on infringement which has acquired the authority of a final decision and been enforced prior to the invalidity decision;

    (b) any contract concluded prior to the invalidity decision, in so far as it has been performed before the decision; however, repayment, to an extent justified by the circumstances, of sums paid under the relevant contract may be claimed on grounds of equity.

TITLE III

COMMUNITY DESIGNS AS OBJECTS OF PROPERTY

Article 27 Dealing with Community designs as national design rights

A4-027   1. Unless Articles 28, 29, 30, 31 and 32 provide otherwise, a Community design as an object of property shall be dealt with in its entirety, and for the whole area of the Community, as a national design right of the Member State in which:

    (a) the holder has his seat or his domicile on the relevant date; or

    (b) where point (a) does not apply, the holder has an establishment on the relevant date.

2. In the case of a registered Community design, paragraph 1 shall apply according to the entries in the register.

3. In the case of joint holders, if two or more of them fulfil the condition under paragraph 1, the Member State referred to in that paragraph shall be determined:

    (a) in the case of an unregistered Community design, by reference to the relevant joint holder designated by them by common agreement;

    (b) in the case of a registered Community design, by reference to the first of the relevant joint holders in the order in which they are mentioned in the register.

4. Where paragraphs 1, 2 and 3 do not apply, the Member State referred to in paragraph 1 shall be the Member State in which the seat of the Office is situated.

Article 28 Transfer of the registered Community design

A4-028   The transfer of a registered Community design shall be subject to the following provisions:

    (a) at the request of one of the parties, a transfer shall be entered in the register and published;

    (b) until such time as the transfer has been entered in the register, the successor in title may not invoke the rights arising from the registration of the Community design;

(c) where there are time limits to be observed in dealings with the Office, the successor in title may make the corresponding statements to the Office once the request for registration of the transfer has been received by the Office;

(d) all documents which by virtue of Article 66 require notification to the holder of the registered Community design shall be addressed by the Office to the person registered as holder or his representative, if one has been appointed.

Article 29 Rights in rem on a registered Community design

1. A registered Community design may be given as security or be the subject **A4-029** of rights in rem.

2. On request of one of the parties, the rights mentioned in paragraph 1 shall be entered in the register and published.

Article 32 Licensing

1. A Community design may be licensed for the whole or part of the **A4-030** Community. A licence may be exclusive or non-exclusive.

2. Without prejudice to any legal proceedings based on the law of contract, the holder may invoke the rights conferred by the Community design against a licensee who contravenes any provision in his licensing contract with regard to its duration, the form in which the design may be used, the range of products for which the licence is granted and the quality of products manufactured by the licensee.

3. Without prejudice to the provisions of the licensing contract, the licensee may bring proceedings for infringement of a Community design only if the right holder consents thereto. However, the holder of an exclusive licence may bring such proceedings if the right holder in the Community design, having been given notice to do so, does not himself bring infringement proceedings within an appropriate period.

4. A licensee shall, for the purpose of obtaining compensation for damage suffered by him, be entitled to intervene in an infringement action brought by the right holder in a Community design.

5. In the case of a registered Community design, the grant or transfer of a licence in respect of such right shall, at the request of one of the parties, be entered in the register and published.

Article 33 Effects vis-à-vis third parties

1. The effects vis-à-vis third parties of the legal acts referred to in Articles 28, **A4-031** 29, 30 and 32 shall be governed by the law of the Member State determined in accordance with Article 27.

2. However, as regards registered Community designs, legal acts referred to in Articles 28, 29 and 32 shall only have effect vis-à-vis third parties in all the Member States after entry in the register. Nevertheless, such an act, before it is so entered, shall have effect vis-à-vis third parties who have acquired rights in the registered Community design after the date of that act but who knew of the act at the date on which the rights were acquired.

3. Paragraph 2 shall not apply to a person who acquires the registered Community design or a right concerning the registered Community design by way of transfer of the whole of the undertaking or by any other universal succession.

4. Until such time as common rules for the Member States in the field of insolvency enter into force, the effects vis-à-vis third parties of insolvency proceedings shall be governed by the law of the Member State in which such

proceedings are first brought under the national law or the regulations applicable in this field.

Article 34 The application for a registered Community design as an object of property

A4-032   1. An application for a registered Community design as an object of property shall be dealt with in its entirety, and for the whole area of the Community, as a national design right of the Member State determined in accordance with Article 27.

2. Articles 28, 29, 30, 31, 32 and 33 shall apply mutatis mutandis to applications for registered Community designs. Where the effect of one of these provisions is conditional upon an entry in the register, that formality shall be performed upon registration of the resulting registered Community design.

TITLE IV

APPLICATION FOR A REGISTERED COMMUNITY DESIGN

Filing of applications and the conditions which govern them

Article 35 Filing and forwardingof applications

A4-033   1. An application for a registered Community design shall be filed, at the option of the applicant:

(a) at the Office; or

(b) at the central industrial property office of a Member State; or

(c) in the Benelux countries, at the Benelux Design Office.

2. Where the application is filed at the central industrial property office of a Member State or at the Benelux Design Office, that office shall take all steps to forward the application to the Office within two weeks after filing. It may charge the applicant a fee which shall not exceed the administrative costs of receiving and forwarding the application.

3. As soon as the Office has received an application which has been forwarded by a central industrial property office of a Member State or by the Benelux Design Office, it shall inform the applicant accordingly, indicating the date of its receipt at the Office.

4. No less than 10 years after the entry into force of this Regulation, the Commission shall draw up a report on the operation of the system of filing applications for registered Community designs, accompanied by any proposals for revision that it may deem appropriate.

Article 36 Conditions with which applications must comply

A4-034   1. An application for a registered Community design shall contain:

(a) a request for registration;

(b) information identifying the applicant;

(c) a representation of the design suitable for reproduction. However, if the object of the application is a two-dimensional design and the application contains a request for deferment of publication in accordance with Article 50, the representation of the design may be replaced by a specimen.

2. The application shall further contain an indication of the products in which the design is intended to be incorporated or to which it is intended to be applied.

3. In addition, the application may contain:

(a) a description explaining the representation or the specimen;

(b) a request for deferment of publication of the registration in accordance with Article 50;

(c) information identifying the representative if the applicant has appointed one;

(d) the classification of the products in which the design is intended to be incorporated or to which it is intended to be applied according to class;

(e) the citation of the designer or of the team of designers or a statement under the applicant's responsibility that the designer or the team of designers has waived the right to be cited.

4. The application shall be subject to the payment of the registration fee and the publication fee. Where a request for deferment under paragraph 3(b) is filed, the publication fee shall be replaced by the fee for deferment of publication.

5. The application shall comply with the conditions laid down in the implementing regulation.

6. The information contained in the elements mentioned in paragraph 2 and in paragraph 3(a) and (d) shall not affect the scope of protection of the design as such.

Article 38 Date of filing

1. The date of filing of an application for a registered Community design **A4-035** shall be the date on which documents containing the information specified in Article 36(1) are filed with the Office by the applicant, or, if the application has been filed with the central industrial property office of a Member State or with the Benelux Design Office, with that office.

2. By derogation from paragraph 1, the date of filing of an application filed with the central industrial property office of a Member State or with the Benelux Design Office and reaching the Office more than two months after the date on which documents containing the information specified in Article 36(1) have been filed shall be the date of receipt of such documents by the Office.

Article 39 Equivalence of Community filing with national filing

An application for a registered Community design which has been accorded **A4-036** a date of filing shall, in the Member States, be equivalent to a regular national filing, including where appropriate the priority claimed for the said application.

Article 40 Classification

For the purpose of this Regulation, use shall be made of the Annex to the **A4-037** Agreement establishing an International Classification for Industrial Designs, signed at Locarno on 8 October 1968.

Priority

Article 41 Right of priority

1. A person who has duly filed an application for a design right or for a **A4-038** utility model in or for any State party to the Paris Convention for the Protection

of Industrial Property, or to the Agreement establishing the World Trade Organisation, or his successors in title, shall enjoy, for the purpose of filing an application for a registered Community design in respect of the same design or utility model, a right of priority of six months from the date of filing of the first application.

2. Every filing that is equivalent to a regular national filing under the national law of the State where it was made or under bilateral or multilateral agreements shall be recognised as giving rise to a right of priority.

3. "Regular national filing" means any filing that is sufficient to establish the date on which the application was filed, whatever may be the outcome of the application.

4. A subsequent application for a design which was the subject of a previous first application, and which is filed in or in respect of the same State, shall be considered as the first application for the purpose of determining priority, provided that, at the date of the filing of the subsequent application, the previous application has been withdrawn, abandoned or refused without being open to public inspection and without leaving any rights outstanding, and has not served as a basis for claiming priority. The previous application may not thereafter serve as a basis for claiming a right of priority.

5. If the first filing has been made in a State which is not a party to the Paris Convention, or to the Agreement establishing the World Trade Organisation, paragraphs 1 to 4 shall apply only in so far as that State, according to published findings, grants, on the basis of a filing made at the Office and subject to conditions equivalent to those laid down in this Regulation, a right of priority having equivalent effect.

Article 42 Claiming priority

A4-039   An applicant for a registered Community design desiring to take advantage of the priority of a previous application shall file a declaration of priority and a copy of the previous application. If the language of the latter is not one of the languages of the Office, the Office may require a translation of the previous application in one of those languages.

Article 43 Effect of priority right

A4-040   The effect of the right of priority shall be that the date of priority shall count as the date of the filing of the application for a registered Community design for the purpose of Articles 5, 6, 7, 22, 25(1)(d) and 50(1).

Article 44 Exhibition priority

A4-041   1. If an applicant for a registered Community design has disclosed products in which the design is incorporated, or to which it is applied, at an official or officially recognised international exhibition falling within the terms of the Convention on International Exhibitions signed in Paris on 22 November 1928 and last revised on 30 November 1972, he may, if he files the application within a period of six months from the date of the first disclosure of such products, claim a right of priority from that date within the meaning of Article 43.

2. An applicant who wishes to claim priority pursuant to paragraph 1, under the conditions laid down in the implementing regulation, must file evidence that he has disclosed at an exhibition the products in or to which the design is incorporated or applied.

3. An exhibition priority granted in a Member State or in a third country does not extend the period of priority laid down in Article 41.

TITLE V

REGISTRATION PROCEDURE

Article 45 Examination as to formal requirements for filing

1. The Office shall examine whether the application complies with the require- **A4-042** ments laid down in Article 36(1) for the accordance of a date of filing.

2. The Office shall examine whether:
   (a) the application complies with the other requirements laid down in Article 36(2), (3), (4) and (5) and, in the case of a multiple application, Article 37(1) and (2);
   (b) the application meets the formal requirements laid down in the implementing regulation for the implementation of Articles 36 and 37;
   (c) the requirements of Article 77(2) are satisfied;
   (d) the requirements concerning the claim to priority are satisfied, if a priority is claimed.

3. The conditions for the examination as to the formal requirements for filing shall be laid down in the implementing regulation.

Article 47 Grounds for non-registrability

1. If the Office, in carrying out the examination pursuant to Article 45, **A4-043** notices that the design for which protection is sought:
   (a) does not correspond to the definition under Article 3(a); or
   (b) is contrary to public policy or to accepted principles of morality, it shall refuse the application.

2. The application shall not be refused before the applicant has been allowed the opportunity of withdrawing or amending the application or of submitting his observations.

Article 48 Registration

If the requirements that an application for a registered Community design **A4-044** must satisfy have been fulfilled and to the extent that the application has not been refused by virtue of Article 47, the Office shall register the application in the Community design Register as a registered Community design. The registration shall bear the date of filing of the application referred to in Article 38.

Article 49 Publication

Upon registration, the Office shall publish the registered Community design **A4-045** in the Community Designs Bulletin as mentioned in Article 73(1). The contents of the publication shall be set out in the implementing regulation.

TITLE VI

SURRENDER AND INVALIDITY OF THE REGISTERED COMMUNITY DESIGN

Article 51 Surrender

1. The surrender of a registered Community design shall be declared to the **A4-046** Office in writing by the right holder. It shall not have effect until it has been entered in the register.

2. If a Community design which is subject to deferment of publication is surrendered it shall be deemed from the outset not to have had the effects specified in this Regulation.

3. A registered Community design may be partially surrendered provided that its amended form complies with the requirements for protection and the identity of the design is retained.

4. Surrender shall be registered only with the agreement of the proprietor of a right entered in the register. If a licence has been registered, surrender shall be entered in the register only if the right holder in the registered Community design proves that he has informed the licensee of his intention to surrender. This entry shall be made on expiry of the period prescribed by the implementing regulation.

5. If an action pursuant to Article 14 relating to the entitlement to a registered Community design has been brought before a Community design court, the Office shall not enter the surrender in the register without the agreement of the claimant.

Article 52 Application for a declaration of invalidity

A4-047   1. Subject to Article 25(2), (3), (4) and (5), any natural or legal person, as well as a public authority empowered to do so, may submit to the Office an application for a declaration of invalidity of a registered Community design.

2. The application shall be filed in a written reasoned statement. It shall not be deemed to have been filed until the fee for an application for a declaration of invalidity has been paid.

3. An application for a declaration of invalidity shall not be admissible if an application relating to the same subject matter and cause of action, and involving the same parties, has been adjudicated on by a Community design court and has acquired the authority of a final decision.

Article 53 Examination of the application

A4-048   1. If the Office finds that the application for a declaration of invalidity is admissible, the Office shall examine whether the grounds for invalidity referred to in Article 25 prejudice the maintenance of the registered Community design.

2. In the examination of the application, which shall be conducted in accordance with the implementing regulation, the Office shall invite the parties, as often as necessary, to file observations, within a period to be fixed by the Office, on communications from the other parties or issued by itself.

3. The decision declaring the registered Community design invalid shall be entered in the register upon becoming final.

TITLE VII

APPEALS

Article 55 Decisions subject to appeal

A4-049   1. An appeal shall lie from decisions of the examiners, the Administration of Trade Marks and Designs and Legal Division and Invalidity Divisions. It shall have suspensive effect.

2. A decision which does not terminate proceedings as regards one of the parties can only be appealed together with the final decision, unless the decision allows separate appeal.

Article 56 Persons entitled to appeal and to be parties to appeal proceedings

Any party to proceedings adversely affected by a decision may appeal. Any **A4-050** other parties to the proceedings shall be parties to the appeal proceedings as of right.

Article 57 Time limit and form of appeal

Notice of appeal must be filed in writing at the Office within two months **A4-051** after the date of notification of the decision appealed from. The notice shall be deemed to have been filed only when the fee for appeal has been paid. Within four months after the date of notification of the decision, a written statement setting out the grounds of appeal must be filed.

Article 60 Decisions in respect of appeals

1. Following the examination as to the merits of the appeal, the Board of **A4-052** Appeal shall decide on the appeal. The Board of Appeal may either exercise any power within the competence of the department which was responsible for the decision appealed against or remit the case to that department for further prosecution.

2. If the Board of Appeal remits the case for further prosecution to the department whose decision was appealed, that department shall be bound by the ratio decidendi of the Board of Appeal, in so far as the facts are the same.

3. The decisions of the Boards of Appeal shall take effect only from the date of expiry of the period referred to in Article 61(5) or, if an action has been brought before the Court of Justice within that period, from the date of rejection of such action.

Article 61 Actions before the Court of Justice

1. Actions may be brought before the Court of Justice against decisions of **A4-053** the Boards of Appeal on appeals.

2. The action may be brought on grounds of lack of competence, infringement of an essential procedural requirement, infringement of the Treaty, of this Regulation or of any rule of law relating to their application or misuse of power.

3. The Court of Justice has jurisdiction to annul or to alter the contested decision.

4. The action shall be open to any party to proceedings before the Board of Appeal adversely affected by its decision.

5. The action shall be brought before the Court of Justice within two months of the date of notification of the decision of the Board of Appeal.

6. The Office shall be required to take the necessary measures to comply with the judgment of the Court of Justice.

TITLE VIII

PROCEDURE BEFORE THE OFFICE

General provisions

Article 62 Statement of reasons on which decisions are based

A4-054　Decisions of the Office shall state the reasons on which they are based. They shall be based only on reasons or evidence on which the parties concerned have had an opportunity to present their comments.

Article 63 Examination of the facts by the Office of its own motion

A4-055　1. In proceedings before it the Office shall examine the facts of its own motion. However, in proceedings relating to a declaration of invalidity, the Office shall be restricted in this examination to the facts, evidence and arguments provided by the parties and the relief sought.

2. The Office may disregard facts or evidence which are not submitted in due time by the parties concerned.

Article 64 Oral proceedings

A4-056　1. If the Office considers that oral proceedings would be expedient, they shall be held either at the instance of the Office or at the request of any party to the proceedings.

2. Oral proceedings, including delivery of the decision, shall be public, unless the department before which the proceedings are taking place decides otherwise in cases where admission of the public could have serious and unjustified disadvantages, in particular for a party to the proceedings.

Article 68 Reference to general principles

A4-057　In the absence of procedural provisions in this Regulation, the implementing regulation, the fees regulation or the rules of procedure of the Boards of Appeal, the Office shall take into account the principles of procedural law generally recognised in the Member States.

Costs

Article 70 Apportionment of costs

A4-058　1. The losing party in proceedings for a declaration of invalidity of a registered Community design or appeal proceedings shall bear the fees incurred by the other party as well as all costs incurred by him essential to the proceedings, including travel and subsistence and the remuneration of an agent, adviser or advocate, within the limits of scales set for each category of costs under the conditions laid down in the implementing regulation.

2. However, where each party succeeds on some and fails on other heads, or if reasons of equity so dictate, the Invalidity Division or Board of Appeal shall decide a different apportionment of costs.

3. A party who terminates the proceedings by surrendering the registered Community design or by not renewing its registration or by withdrawing the application for a declaration of invalidity or the appeal, shall bear the fees and the costs incurred by the other party as stipulated in paragraphs 1 and 2.

4. Where a case does not proceed to judgment, the costs shall be at the discretion of the Invalidity Division or Board of Appeal.

5. Where the parties conclude before the Invalidity Division or Board of Appeal a settlement of costs differing from that provided for in paragraphs 1, 2, 3 and 4, the body concerned shall take note of that agreement.

6. On request, the registry of the Invalidity Division or Board of Appeal shall fix the amount of the costs to be paid pursuant to the preceding paragraphs. The amount so determined may be reviewed by a decision of the Invalidity Division or Board of Appeal on a request filed within the period prescribed by the implementing regulation.

Article 71 Enforcement of decisions fixing the amount of costs

1. Any final decision of the Office fixing the amount of costs shall be enforce- **A4-059** able.

2. Enforcement shall be governed by the rules of civil procedure in force in the State in the territory of which it is carried out. The order for its enforcement shall be appended to the decision, without any other formality than verification of the authenticity of the decision, by the national authority which the government of each Member State shall designate for this purpose and shall make known to the Office and to the Court of Justice.

3. When these formalities have been completed on application by the party concerned, the latter may proceed to enforcement in accordance with the national law, by bringing the matter directly before the competent authority.

4. Enforcement may be suspended only by a decision of the Court of Justice. However, the courts of the Member State concerned shall have jurisdiction over complaints that enforcement is being carried out in an irregular manner.

Informing the public and the official authorities of the Member States

Article 72 Register of Community designs

The Office shall keep a register to be known as the register of Community **A4-060** designs, which shall contain those particulars of which the registration is provided for by this Regulation or by the implementing regulation. The register shall be open to public inspection, except to the extent that Article 50(2) provides otherwise.

Article 73 Periodical publications

1. This Office shall periodically publish a Community Designs Bulletin **A4-061** containing entries open to public inspection in the register as well as other particulars the publication of which is prescribed by this Regulation or by the implementing regulation.

2. Notices and information of a general character issued by the President of the Office, as well as any other information relevant to this Regulation or its implementation, shall be published in the Official Journal of the Office.

Article 74 Inspection of files

1. The files relating to applications for registered Community designs which **A4-062** have not yet been published or the files relating to registered Community designs which are subject to deferment of publication in accordance with Article 50 or which, being subject to such deferment, have been surrendered before or on the expiry of that period, shall not be made available for inspection without the

consent of the applicant for or the right holder in the registered Community design.

2. Any person who can establish a legitimate interest may inspect a file without the consent of the applicant for or holder of the registered Community design prior to the publication or after the surrender of the latter in the case provided for in paragraph 1. This shall in particular apply if the interested person proves that the applicant for or the holder of the registered Community design has taken steps with a view to invoking against him the right under the registered Community design.

3. Subsequent to the publication of the registered Community design, the file may be inspected on request.

4. However, where a file is inspected pursuant to paragraph 2 or 3, certain documents in the file may be withheld from inspection in accordance with the provisions of the implementing regulation.

Article 75 Administrative cooperation

A4-063   Unless otherwise provided in this Regulation or in national laws, the Office and the courts or authorities of the Member States shall on request give assistance to each other by communicating information or opening files for inspection.

Where the Office opens files to inspection by courts, public prosecutors' offices or central industrial property offices, the inspection shall not be subject to the restrictions laid down in Article 74

TITLE IX

JURISDICTION AND PROCEDURE IN LEGAL ACTIONS RELATING
TO COMMUNITY DESIGNS

Jurisdiction and enforcement

Article 79 Application of the Convention on Jurisdiction and Enforcement

A4-064   1. Unless otherwise specified in this Regulation, the Convention on Jurisdiction and the Enforcement of Judgements in Civil and Commercial Matters, signed in Brussels on 27 September 1968(7), hereinafter referred to as the "Convention on Jurisdiction and Enforcement", shall apply to proceedings relating to Community designs and applications for registered Community designs, as well as to proceedings relating to actions on the basis of Community designs and national designs enjoying simultaneous protection.

2. The provisions of the Convention on Jurisdiction and Enforcement which are rendered applicable by the paragraph 1 shall have effect in respect of any Member Statesolely in the text which is in force in respect of that State at any given time.

3. 3. In the event of proceedings in respect of the actions and claims referred to in Article 85:

(a) Articles 2, 4, 5(1), (3), (4) and (5), 16(4) and 24 of the Convention on Jurisdiction and Enforcement shall not apply;

(b) Articles 17 and 18 of that Convention shall apply subject to the limitations in Article 82(4) of this Regulation;

(c) the provisions of Title II of that Convention which are applicable to persons domiciled in a Member State shall also be applicable to persons who do not have a domicile in any Member State but have an establishment therein.

4. The provisions of the Convention on Jurisdiction and Enforcement shall not have effect in respect of any Member State for which that Convention has not yet entered into force. Until such entry into force, proceedings referred to in paragraph 1 shall be governed in such a Member State by any bilateral or multilateral convention governing its relationship with another Member State concerned, or, if no such convention exists, by its domestic law on jurisdiction, recognition and enforcement of decisions.

Disputes concerning the infringement and validity of Community designs

Article 80 Community design courts

1. The Member States shall designate in their territories as limited a number **A4-065** as possible of national courts and tribunals of first and second instance (Community design courts) which shall perform the functions assigned to them by this Regulation.

2. Each Member State shall communicate to the Commission not later than 6 March 2005 a list of Community design courts, indicating their names and their territorial jurisdiction.

3. Any change made after communication of the list referred to in paragraph 2 in the number, names or territorial jurisdiction of the Community design courts shall be notified without delay by the Member State concerned to the Commission.

4. The information referred to in paragraphs 2 and 3 shall be notified by the Commission to the Member States and published in the Official Journal of the European Communities.

5. As long as a Member State has not communicated the list as stipulated in paragraph 2, jurisdiction for any proceedings resulting from an action covered by Article 81 for which the courts of that State have jurisdiction pursuant to Article 82 shall lie with that court of the State in question which would have jurisdiction ratione loci and ratione materiae in the case of proceedings relating to a national design right of that State.

Article 81 Jurisdiction over infringement and validity

The Community design courts shall have exclusive jurisdiction: **A4-066**

(a) for infringement actions and - if they are permitted under national law - actions in respect of threatened infringement of Community designs;

(b) for actions for declaration of non-infringement of Community designs, if they are permitted under national law;

(c) for actions for a declaration of invalidity of an unregistered Community design;

(d) for counterclaims for a declaration of invalidity of a Community design raised in connection with actions under (a).

Article 82 International jurisdiction

1. Subject to the provisions of this Regulation and to any provisions of the **A4-067** Convention on Jurisdiction and Enforcement applicable by virtue of Article 79, proceedings in respect of the actions and claims referred to in Article 81 shall be brought in the courts of the Member State in which the defendant is domiciled or,

if he is not domiciled in any of the Member States, in any Member State in which he has an establishment.

2. If the defendant is neither domiciled nor has an establishment in any of the Member States, such proceedings shall be brought in the courts of the Member State in which the plaintiff is domiciled or, if he is not domiciled in any of the Member States, in any Member State in which he has an establishment.

3. If neither the defendant nor the plaintiff is so domiciled or has such an establishment, such proceedings shall be brought in the courts of the Member State where the Office has its seat.

4. Notwithstanding paragraphs 1, 2 and 3:
   (a) Article 17 of the Convention on Jurisdiction and Enforcement shall apply if the parties agree that a different Community design court shall have jurisdiction;
   (b) Article 18 of that Convention shall apply if the defendant enters an appearance before a different Community design court.

5. Proceedings in respect of the actions and claims referred to in Article 81(a) and (d) may also be brought in the courts of the Member State in which the act of infringement has been committed or threatened.

Article 83 Extent of jurisdiction on infringement

A4-068   1. A Community design court whose jurisdiction is based on Article 82(1), (2) (3) or (4) shall have jurisdiction in respect of acts of infringement committed or threatened within the territory of any of the Member States.

2. A Community design court whose jurisdiction is based on Article 82(5) shall have jurisdiction only in respect of acts of infringement committed or threatened within the territory of the Member State in which that court is situated.

Article 84 Action or counterclaim for a declaration of invalidity of a Community design

A4-069   1. An action or a counterclaim for a declaration of invalidity of a Community design may only be based on the grounds for invalidity mentioned in Article 25.

2. In the cases referred to in Article 25(2), (3), (4) and (5) the action or the counterclaim may be brought solely by the person entitled under those provisions.

3. If the counterclaim is brought in a legal action to which the right holder of the Community design is not already a party, he shall be informed thereof and may be joined as a party to the action in accordance with the conditions set out in the law of the Member State where the court is situated.

4. The validity of a Community design may not be put in issue in an action for a declaration of non-infringement.

Article 85 Presumption of validity - defence as to the merits

A4-070   1. In proceedings in respect of an infringement action or an action for threatened infringement of a registered Community design, the Community design court shall treat the Community design as valid. Validity may be challenged only with a counterclaim for a declaration of invalidity. However, a plea relating to the invalidity of a Community design, submitted otherwise than by way of counterclaim, shall be admissible in so far as the defendant claims that the Community design could be declared invalid on account of an earlier national design right, within the meaning of Article 25(1)(d), belonging to him.

2. In proceedings in respect of an infringement action or an action for threatened infringement of an unregistered Community design, the Community design court shall treat the Community design as valid if the right holder produces proof that the conditions laid down in Article 11 have been met and indicates what constitutes the individual character of his Community design. However, the defendant may contest its validity by way of a plea or with a counterclaim for a declaration of invalidity.

Article 86 Judgements of invalidity

1. Where in a proceeding before a Community design court the Community **A4-071** design has been put in issue by way of a counterclaim for a declaration of invalidity:
> (a) if any of the grounds mentioned in Article 25 are found to prejudice the maintenance of the Community design, the court shall declare the Community design invalid;
> (b) if none of the grounds mentioned in Article 25 is found to prejudice the maintenance of the Community design, the court shall reject the counterclaim.

2. The Community design court with which a counterclaim for a declaration of invalidity of a registered Community design has been filed shall inform the Office of the date on which the counterclaim was filed. The lattershall record this fact in the register.

3. The Community design court hearing a counterclaim for a declaration of invalidity of a registered Community design may, on application by the right holder of the registered Community design and after hearing the other parties, stay the proceedings and request the defendant to submit an application for a declaration of invalidity to the Office within a time limit which the court shall determine. If the application is not made within the time limit, the proceedings shall continue; the counterclaim shall be deemed withdrawn. Article 91(3) shall apply.

4. Where a Community design court has given a judgment which has become final on a counterclaim for a declaration of invalidity of a registered Community design, a copy of the judgment shall be sent to the Office. Any party may request information about such transmission. The Office shall mention the judgment in the register in accordance with the provisions of the implementing regulation.

5. No counterclaim for a declaration of invalidity of a registered Community design may be made if an application relating to the same subject matter and cause of action, and involving the same parties, has already been determined by the Office in a decision which has become final.

Article 87 Effects of the judgement on invalidity

When it has become final, a judgment of a Community design court **A4-072** declaring a Community design invalid shall have in all the Member States the effects specified in Article 26.

Article 88 Applicable law

1. The Community design courts shall apply the provisions of this **A4-073** Regulation.

2. On all matters not covered by this Regulation, a Community design court shall apply its national law, including its private international law.

3. Unless otherwise provided in this Regulation, a Community design court shall apply the rules of procedure governing the same type of action relating to a national design right in the Member State where it is situated.

Article 89 Sanctions in actions for infringement

A4-074   1. Where in an action for infringement or for threatened infringement a Community design court finds that the defendant has infringed or threatened to infringe a Community design, it shall, unless there are special reasons for not doing so, order the following measures:

(a) an order prohibiting the defendant from proceeding with the acts which have infringed or would infringe the Community design;

(b) an order to seize the infringing products;

(c) an order to seize materials and implements predominantly used in order to manufacture the infringing goods, if their owner knew the effect for which such use was intended or if such effect would have been obvious in the circumstances;

(d) any order imposing other sanctions appropriate under the circumstances which are provided by the law of the Member State in which the acts of infringement or threatened infringement are committed, including its private international law.

2. The Community design court shall take such measures in accordance with its national law as are aimed at ensuring that the orders referred to in paragraph 1 are complied with.

Article 90 Provisional measures, including protective measures

A4-075   1. Application may be made to the courts of a Member State, including Community design courts, for such provisional measures, including protective measures, in respect of a Community design as may be available under the law of that State in respect of national design rights even if, under this Regulation, a Community design court of another Member State has jurisdiction as to the substance of the matter.

2. In proceedings relating to provisional measures, including protective measures, a plea otherwise than by way of counterclaim relating to the invalidity of a Community design submitted by the defendant shall be admissible. Article 85(2) shall, however, apply mutatis mutandis.

3. A Community design court whose jurisdiction is based on Article 82(1), (2), (3) or (4) shall have jurisdiction to grant provisional measures, including protective measures, which, subject to any necessary procedure for recognition and enforcement pursuant to Title III of the Convention on Jurisdiction and Enforcement, are applicable in the territory of any Member State. No other court shall have such jurisdiction.

TITLE X

EFFECTS ON THE LAWS OF THE MEMBER STATES

Article 96 Relationship to other forms of protection under national law

A4-076   1. The provisions of this Regulation shall be without prejudice to any provisions of Community law or of the law of the Member States concerned relating to unregistered designs, trade marks or other distinctive signs, patents and utility models, typefaces, civil liability and unfair competition.

2. A design protected by a Community design shall also be eligible for protection under the law of copyright of Member States as from the date on which the design was created or fixed in any form. The extent to which, and the conditions under which, such a protection is conferred, including the level of originality required, shall be determined by each Member State.

TITLE XII

FINAL PROVISIONS

Article 110 Transitional provision

1. Until such time as amendments to this Regulation enter into force on a **A4-077** proposal from the Commission on this subject, protection as a Community design shall not exist for a design which constitutes a component part of a complex product used within the meaning of Article 19(1) for the purpose of the repair of that complex product so as to restore its original appearance.

2. The proposal from the Commission referred to in paragraph 1 shall be submitted together with, and take into consideration, any changes which the Commission shall propose on the same subject pursuant to Article 18 of Directive 98/71/EC.

COUNCIL DIRECTIVE of 10 September 1984 concerning misleading and comparative advertising. Amended by: Directive 97/55/EC of European Parliament and of the Council of 6 October 1997

THE COUNCIL OF THE EUROPEAN COMMUNITIES,

Having regard to the Treaty establishing the European Economic Community, and in particular Article 100 thereof,

Having regard to the proposal from the Commission,

Having regard to the opinion of the European Parliament,

Having regard to the opinion of the Economic and Social Committee,

Whereas the laws against misleading advertising now in force in the Member States differ widely; whereas, since advertising reaches beyond the frontiers of individual Member States, it has a direct effect on the establishment and the functioning of the common market;

Whereas misleading advertising can lead to distortion of competition within the common market;

Whereas advertising, whether or not it induces a contract, affects the economic welfare of consumers;

Whereas misleading advertising may cause a consumer to take decisions prejudicial to him when acquiring goods or other property, or using services, and the differences between the laws of the Member States not only lead, in many cases, to inadequate levels of consumer protection, but also hinder the execution of advertising campaigns beyond national boundaries and thus affect the free circulation of goods and provision of services;

Whereas the second programme of the European Economic Community for a consumer protection and information policy provides for appropriate action for the protection of consumers against misleading and unfair advertising;

Whereas it is in the interest of the public in general, as well as that of consumers and all those who, in competition with one another, carry on a trade, business, craft or profession, in the common market, to harmonize in the first instance national provisions against misleading advertising and that, at a second stage, unfair advertising and, as far as necessary, comparative advertising should be dealt with, on the basis of appropriate Commission proposals;

Whereas minimum and objective criteria for determining whether advertising is misleading should be established for this purpose;

Whereas the laws to be adopted by Member States against misleading advertising must be adequate and effective; Whereas persons or organizations regarded under national law as having a legitimate interest in the matter must have facilities for initiating proceedings against misleading advertising, either before a court or before an administrative authority which is competent to decide upon complaints or to initiate appropriate legal proceedings;

Whereas it should be for each Member State to decide whether to enable the courts or administrative authorities to require prior recourse to other established means of dealing with the complaint;

Whereas the courts or administrative authorities must have powers enabling them to order or obtain the cessation of misleading advertising;

Whereas in certain cases it may be desirable to prohibit misleading advertising even before it is published; whereas, however, this in no way implies that Member States are under an obligation to introduce rules requiring the systematic prior vetting of advertising;

Whereas provision should be made for accelerated procedures under which measures with interim or definitive effect can be taken;

Whereas it may be desirable to order the publication of decisions made by courts or administrative authorities or of corrective statements in order to eliminate any continuing effects of misleading advertising;

Whereas administrative authorities must be impartial and the exercise of their powers must be subject to judicial review;

Whereas the voluntary control exercised by self-regulatory bodies to eliminate misleading advertising may avoid recourse to administrative or judicial action and ought therefore to be encouraged;

Whereas the advertiser should be able to prove, by appropriate means, the material accuracy of the factual claims he makes in his advertising, and may in appropriate cases be required to do so by the court or administrative authority;

Whereas this Directive must not preclude Member States from retaining or adopting provisions with a view to ensuring more extensive protection of consumers, persons carrying on a trade, business, craft or profession, and the general public,

HAS ADOPTED THIS DIRECTIVE:

Article 1

A5-001   The purpose of this Directive is to protect consumers, persons carrying on a trade or business or practising a craft or profession and the interests of the public in general against misleading advertising and the unfair consequences thereof.

Article 2

A5-002   For the purposes of this Directive:

1. 'advertising' means the making of a representation in any form in connection with a trade, business, craft or profession in order to promote the supply of goods or services, including immovable property, rights and obligations;

2. 'misleading advertising' means any advertising which in any way, including its presentation, deceives or is likely to deceive the persons to whom it is addressed or whom it reaches and which, by reason of its deceptive nature, is likely to affect their economic behaviour or which, for those reasons, injures or is likely to injure a competitor;

2a. 'comparative advertising' means any advertising which explicitly or by implication identifies a competitororgoods orser vices offered by a competitor;

3. 'person' means any natural or legal person.

Article 3

In determining whether advertising is misleading, account shall be taken of **A5-003** all its features, and in particular of any information it contains concerning:

(a) the characteristics of goods or services, such as their availability, nature, execution, composition, method and date of manufacture or provision, fitness for purpose, uses, quantity, specification, geographical or commercial origin or the results to be expected from their use, or the results and material features of tests or checks carried out on the goods or services;

(b) the price or the manner in which the price is calculated, and the conditions on which the goods are supplied or the services provided;

(c) the nature, attributes and rights of the advertiser, such as his identity and assets, his qualifications and ownership of industrial, commercial or intellectual property rights or his awards and distinctions.

Article 3a

1. Comparative advertising shall, as far as the comparison is concerned, be **A5-004** permitted when the following conditions are met:
   (a) it is not misleading according to Articles 2 (2), 3 and 7 (1);
   (b) it compares goods or services meeting the same needs or intended for the same purpose;
   (c) it objectively compares one or more material, relevant, verifiable and representative features of those goods and services, which may include price;
   (d) it does not create confusion in the market place beween the advertiser and a competitor or between the advertiser's trade marks, trade names, other distinguishing marks, goods orser vices and those of a competitor;
   (e) it does not discredit or denigrate the trade marks, trade names, other distinguishing marks, goods, services, activities, or circumstances of a competitor;
   (f) for products with designation of origin, it relates in each case to products with the same designation;
   (g) it does not take unfair advantage of the reputation of a trade mark, trade name or other distinguishing marks of a competitor or of the designation of origin of competing products;
   (h) it does not present goods or services as imitations or replicas of goods or services bearing a protected trade mark or trade name.

2. Any comparison referring to a special offer shall indicate in a clear and unequivocal way the date on which the offerends or, where appropriate, that the special offer is subject to the availability of the goods and services, and, where the special offer has not yet begun, the date of the start of the period during which the special price or other specific conditions shall apply.

Article 4

A5-005   1. Member States shall ensure that adequate and effective means exist to combat misleading advertising and for the compliance with the provisions on comparative advertising in the interests of consumers as well as competitors and the general public

Such means shall include legal provisions under which persons or organizations regarded under national law as having a legitimate interest in prohibiting misleading advertising or regulating comparative advertising may:

(a) take legal action against such advertising; and/or

(b) bring such advertising before an administrative authority competent either to decide on complaints or to initiate appropriate legal proceedings.

It shall be for each Member State to decide which of these facilities shall be available and whether to enable the courts or administrative authorities to require prior recourse to other established means of dealing with complaints, including those referred to in Article 5.

2. Under the legal provisions referred to in paragraph 1, Member States shall confer upon the courts or administrative authorities powers enabling them, in cases where they deem such measures to be necessary taking into account all the interests involved and in particular the public interest:

– to order the cessation of, or to institute appropriate legal proceedings for an order for the cessation of, misleading advertising or unpermitted comparative advertising, or

–if the misleading advertising or unpermitted comparative advertising has not yet been published but publication is imminent, to order the prohibition of, or to institute appropriate legal proceedings for an order for the prohibition of, such publication,

even without proof of actual loss or damage or of intention or negligence on the part of the advertiser.

–either with interim effect, or

–with definitive effect,

on the understanding that it is for each Member State to decide which of the two options to select.

Furthermore, Member States may confer upon the courts or administrative authorities powers enabling them, with a view to eliminating the continuing effects of misleading advertising or unpermitted comparative advertising, the cessation of which has been ordered by a final decision:

– to require publication of that decision in full or in part and in such form as they deem adequate,

– to require in addition the publication of a corrective statement.

3. The administrative authorities referred to in paragraph 1 must:

(a) be composed so as not to cast doubt on their impartiality;

(b) have adequate powers, where they decide on complaints, to monitor and enforce the observance of their decisions effectively;

(c) normally give reasons for their decisions.

Where the powers referred to in paragraph 2 are exercised exclusively by an administrative authority, reasons for its decisions shall always be given. Furthermore in this case, provision must be made for procedures whereby improper or unreasonable exercise of its powers by the administrative authority or improper or unreasonable failure to exercise the said powers can be the subject of judicial review.

Article 5

This Directive does not exclude the voluntary control, which Member States **A5-006** may encourage, of misleading or comparative advertising by self-regulatory bodies and recourse to such bodies by the persons or organisations referred to in Article 4 if proceedings before such bodies are in addition to the court or administrative proceedings referred to in that Article.

Article 6

Member States shall confer upon the courts or administrative authorities **A5-007** powers enabling them in the civil or administrative proceedings provided for in Article 4:

(a) to require the advertiser to furnish evidence as to the accuracy of factual claims in advertising if, taking into account the legitimate interest of the advertiser and any other party to the proceedings, such a requirement appears appropriate on the basis of the circumstances of the particular case and in the case of comparative advertising to require the advertiser to furnish such evidence in a short period of time; and

(b) to consider factual claims as inaccurate if the evidence demanded in accordance with (a) is not furnished or is deemed insufficient by the court or administrative authority.

Article 7

1. This Directive shall not preclude Member States from retaining or **A5-008** adopting provisions with a view to ensuring more extensive protection, with regard to misleading advertising, for consumers, persons carrying on a trade, business, craft or profession, and the general public.

2. Paragraph 1 shall not apply to comparative advertising as far as the comparison is concerned.

3. The provisions of this Directive shall apply without prejudice to Community provisions on advertising for specific products and/or services or to restrictions or prohibitions on advertising in particular media.

4. The provisions of this Directive concerning comparative advertising shall not oblige Member States which, in compliance with the provisions of the Treaty, maintain or introduce advertising bans regarding certain goods or services, whether imposed directly or by a body or organization responsible, under the law of the Member States, for regulating the exercise of a commercial, industrial, craft or professional activity, to permit comparative advertising regarding those goods or services. Where these bans are limited to particular media, the Directive shall apply to the media not covered by these bans.

5. Nothing in this Directive shall prevent Member States from, in compliance with the provisions of the Treaty, maintaining or introducing bans or limitations on the use of comparisons in the advertising of professional services, whether imposed directly or by a body or organization responsible, under the law of the Member States, for regulating the exercise of a professional activity.

Article 8

Member States shall bring into force the measures necessary to comply with **A5-009** this Directive by 1 October 1986 at the latest. They shall forthwith inform the Commission thereof.

Member States shall communicate to the Commission the text of all provisions of national law which they adopt in the field covered by this Directive.

Article 9

A5-010   This Directive is addressed to the Member States.

COUNCIL DIRECTIVE of 16 December 1986 on the legal protection of topographies of semiconductor products (87/54/ EEC)

THE COUNCIL OF THE EUROPEAN COMMUNITIES,

Having regard to the Treaty establishing the European Economic Community and in particular Article 100 thereof,

Having regard to the proposal from the Commission,

Having regard to the opinion of the European Parliament,

Having regard to the opinion of the Economic and Social Committee,

Whereas semiconductor products are playing an increasingly important role in a broad range of industries and semiconductor technology can accordingly be considered as being of fundamental importance for the Community's industrial development;

Whereas the functions of semiconductor products depend in large part on the topographies of such products and whereas the development of such topographies requires the investment of considerable resources, human, technical and financial, while topographies of such products can be copied at a fraction of the cost needed to develop them independently;

Whereas topographies of semiconductor products are at present not clearly protected in all Member States by existing legislation and such protection, where it exists, has different attributes;

Whereas certain existing differences in the legal protection of semiconductor products offered by the laws of the Member States have direct and negative effects on the functioning of the common market as regards semiconductor products and such differences could well become greater as Member States introduce new legislation on this subject;

Whereas existing differences having such effects need to be removed and new ones having a negative effect on the common market prevented from arising;

Whereas, in relation to extension of protection to persons outside the Community, Member States should be free to act on their own behalf in so far as Community decisions have not been taken within a limited period of time;

Whereas the Community's legal framework on the protection of topographies of semiconductor products can, in the first instance, be limited to certain basic principles by provisions specifying whom and what should be protected, the exclusive rights on which protected persons should be able to rely to authorize or prohibit certain acts, exceptions to these rights and for how long the protection should last;

Whereas other matters can for the time being be decided in accordance with national law, in particular, whether registration or deposit is required as a condition for protection and, subject to an exclusion of licences granted for the sole reason that a certain period of time has elapsed, whether and on what conditions non-voluntary licences may be granted in respect of protected topographies;

Whereas protection of topographies of semiconductor products in accordance with this Directive should be without prejudice to the application of some other forms of protection;

Whereas further measures concerning the legal protection of topographies of semiconductor products in the Community can be considered at a later stage, if necessary, while the application of common basic principles by all Member States in accordance with the provisions of this Directive is an urgent necessity,

HAS ADOPTED THIS DIRECTIVE:

CHAPTER I

DEFINITIONS

Article 1

1. For the purposes of this Directive: A6-001
   (a) a 'semiconductor product' shall mean the final or an intermediate form of any product:
      (i) consisting of a body of material which includes a layer of semiconducting material; and
      (ii) having one or more other layers composed of conducting, insulating or semiconducting material, the layers being arranged in accordance with a predetermined three-dimensional pattern; and
      (iii) intended to perform, exclusively or together with other functions, an electronic function;
   (b) the 'topography' of a semiconductor product shall mean a series of related images, however fixed or encoded;
      (i) representing the three-dimensional pattern of the layers of which a semiconductor product is composed; and
      (ii) in which series, each image has the pattern or part of the pattern of a surface of the semiconductor product at any stage of its manufacture;
   (c) 'commercial exploitation' means the sale, rental, leasing or any other method of commercial distribution, or an offer for these purposes. However, for the purposes of Articles 3 (4), 4 (1), 7 (1), (3) and (4) 'commercial exploitation' shall not include exploitation under conditions of confidentiality to the extent that no further distribution to third parties occurs, except where exploitation of a topography takes place under conditions of confidentiality required by a measure taken in conformity with Article 223 (1) (b) of the Treaty.

2. The Council acting by qualified majority on a proposal from the Commission, may amend paragraph 1 (a) (i) and (ii) in order to adapt these provisions in the light of technical progress.

CHAPTER 2

PROTECTION OF TOPOGRAPHIES OF SEMICONDUCTOR PRODUCTS

Article 2

A6-002   1. Member States shall protect the topographies of semiconductor products by adopting legislative provisions conferring exclusive rights in accordance with the provisions of the Directive.

1. The topography of a semiconductor product shall be protected in so far as it satisfies the conditions that it is the result of its creator's own intellectual effort and is not commonplace in the semiconductor industry. Where the topography of a semiconductor product consists of elements that are commonplace in the semiconductor industry, it shall be protected only to the extent that the combination of such elements, taken as a whole, fulfils the abovementioned conditions.

Article 3

A6-003   1. Subject to paragraphs 2 to 5, the right to protection shall apply in favour of persons who are the creators of the topographies of semiconductor products.

2. Member States may provide that,
  - (a) where a topography is created in the course of the creator's employment, the right to protection shall apply in favour of the creator's employer unless the terms of employment provide to the contrary;
  - (b) where a topography is created under a contract other than a contract of employment, the right to protection shall apply in favour of a party to the contract by whom the topography has been commissioned, unless the contract provides to the contrary.

3. (a) As regards the persons referred to in paragraph 1, the right to protection shall apply in favour of natural persons who are nationals of a Member State or who have their habitual residence on the territory of a Member State.
  - (b) Where Member States make provision in accordance with paragraph 2, the right to protection shall apply in favour of:
    - (i) natural persons who are nationals of a Member State or who have their habitual residence on the territory of a Member State;
    - (ii) companies or other legal persons which have a real and effective industrial or commercial establishment on the territory of a Member State.

4. Where no right to protection exists in accordance with other provisions of this Article, the right to protection shall also apply in favour of the persons referred to in paragraph 3 (b) (i) and (ii) who:
  - (a) first commercially exploit within a Member State a topography which has not yet been exploited commercially anywhere in the world; and
  - (b) have been exclusively authorized to exploit commercially the topography throughout the Community by the person entitled to dispose of it.

5. The right to protection shall also apply in favour of the successors in title of the persons mentioned in paragraphs 1 to 4.

6. Subject to paragraph 7, Member States may negotiate and conclude agreements or understandings with third States and multilateral Conventions concerning the legal protection of topographies of semiconductor products

whilst respecting Community lawand in particular the rules laid down in this Directive.

7. Member States may enter into negotiations which third States with a view to extending the right to protection to persons who do not benefit from the right to protection according to the provisions of this Directive. Member States who enter into such negotiations shall inform the Commission thereof.

When a Member State wishes to extend protection to persons who otherwise do not benefit from the right to protection according to the provisions of this Directive or to conclude an agreement or understanding on the extension of protection with a non-Member State it shall notify the Commission. The Commission shall inform the other Member States thereof. The Member State shall hold the extension of protection or the conclusion of the agreement or understanding in abeyance for one month from the date on which it notifies the Commission. However, if within that period the Commission notifies the Member State concerned of its intention to submit a proposal to the Council for all Member States to extend protection in respect of the persons or non-Member State concerned, the Member State shall hold the extension of protection or the conclusion of the agreement or undestanding in abeyance for a period of two months from the date of the notification by the Member State.

Where, before the end of this two-month period, the Commission submits such a proposal to the Council, the Member State shall hold the extension of protection or the conclusion of the agreement or understanding in abeyance for a further period of four months from the date on which the proposal was submitted. In the absence of a Commission notification or proposal or a Council decision within the time limits prescribed above, the Member State may extend protection or conclude the agreement or understanding. A proposal by the Commission to extend protection, whether or not it is made following a notification by a Member State in accordance with the preceding paragraphs shall be adopted by the Council acting by qualified majority.

A Decision of the Council on the basis of a Commission proposal shall not prevent a Member State from extending protection to persons, in addition to those to benefit from protection in all Member States, who were included in the envisaged extension, agreement or understanding as notified, unless the Council acting by qualified majority has decided otherwise.

8. Commission proposals and Council decisions pursuant to paragraph 7 shall be published for information in the Official Journal of the European Communities.

Article 4

1. Member States may provide that the exclusive rights conferred in **A6-004** conformity with Article 2 shall not come into existence or shall no longer apply to the topography of a semiconductor product unless an application for registration in due form has been filed with a public authority within two years of its first commercial exploitation. Member States may require in addition to such registration that material identifying or exemplifying the topography or any combination thereof has been deposited with a public authority, as well as a statement as to the date of first commercial exploitation of the topography where it precedes the date of the applciation for registration.

2. Member States shall ensure that material deposited in conformity with paragraph 1 is not made available to the public where it is a trade secret. This provision shall be without prejudice to the disclosure of such material pursuant to an order of a court or other competent authority to persons involved in litigation

concerning the validity or infringement of the excusive rights referred to in Article 2.

3. Member States may require that transfers of rights in protected topographies be registered.

4. Member States may subject registration and deposit in accordance with paragraphs 1 and 3 to the payment of fees not exceeding their administrative costs.

5. Conditions prescribing the fulfilment of additional formalities for obtaining or maintaining protection shall not be admitted.

6. Member States which require registration shall provide for legal remedies in favour of a person having the right to protection in accordance with the provisions of this Directive who can prove that another person has applied for or obtained the registration of a topography without his authorization.

Article 5

A6-005   1. The exclusive rights referred to in Article 2 shall include the rights to authorize or prohibit any of the following acts:

(a) reproduction of a topography in so far as it is protected under Article 2 (2);

(b) commercial exploitation or the importation for that purpose of a topography or of a semiconductor product manufactured by using the topography.

2. Notwithstanding paragraph 1, a Member State pay permit the reproduction of a topography privately for non commercial aims.

3. The exclusive rights referred to in paragraph 1 (a) shall not apply to reproduction for the purpose of analyzing, evaluating or teaching the concepts, processes, systems or techniques embodied in the topography or the topography itself.

4. The exclusive rights referred to in paragraph 1 shall not extend to any such act in relation to a topography meeting the requirements of Article 2 (2) and created on the basis of an analysis and evaluation of another topography, carried out in conformity with paragraph 3.

5. The exclusive rights to authorize or prohibit the acts specified in paragraph 1 (b) shall not apply to any such act committed after the topography or the semiconductor product has been put on the market in a Member State by the person entitled to authorize its marketing or with his consent.

6. A person who, when he acquires a semiconductor product, does not know, or has no reasonable grounds to believe, that the product is protected by an exclusive right conferred by a Member State in conformity with this Directive shall not be prevented from commercially exploiting that product. However, for acts committed after that person knows, or has reasonable grounds to believe, that the semiconductor product is so protected, Member States shall ensure that on the demand of the rightholder a tribunal may require, in accordance with the provisions of the national law applicable, the payment of adequate remuneration.

7. The provisions of paragraph 6 shall apply to the successors in title of the person referred to in the first sentence of that paragraph.

Article 6

A6-006   Member States shall not subject the exclusive rights referred to in Article 2 to licences granted, for the sole reason that a certain period of time has elapsed, automatically, and by operation of law.

Article 7

1. Member States shall provide that the exclusive rights referred to in Article **A6-007** 2 shall come into existence:

 (a) where registration is the condition for the coming into existence of the exclusive rights in accordance with Article 4, on the earlier of the following dates:

  (i) the date when the topography is first commercially exploited anywhere in the world;

  (ii) the date when an application or registration has been filed in due form; or

 (b) when the topography is first commercially exploited anywhere in the world; or

 (c) when the topography is first fixed or encoded.

2. Where the exclusive rights come into existence in accordance with paragraph 1 (a) or (b), the Member States shall provide, for the period prior to those rights coming into existence, legal remedies in favour of a person having the right to protection in accordance with the provisions of this Directive who can prove that another person has fraudulently reproduced or commercially exploited or imported for that purpose a topography. This paragraph shall be without prejudice to legal remedies made available to enforce the exclusive rights conferred in conformity with Article 2.

3. The exclusive rights shall come to an end 10 years from the end of the calendar year in which the topography is first commercially exploited anywhere in the world or, where registration is a condition for the coming into existence or continuing application of the exclusive rights, 10 years from the earlier of the following dates:

 (a) the end of the calendar year in which the topography is first commercially exploited anywhere in the world;

 (b) the end of the calendar year in which the application for registration has been filed in due form.

4. Where a topography has not been commercially exploited anywhere in the world within a period of 15 years from its first fixation or encoding, any exclusive rights in existence pursuant to paragraph 1 shall come to an end and no new exclusive rights shall come into existence unless an application for registration in due form has been filed within that period in those Member States where registration is a condition for the coming into existence or continuing application of the exclusive rights.

Article 8

The protection granted to the topographies of semiconductor products in **A6-008** accordance with Article 2 shall not extend to any concept, process, system, technique or encoded information embodied in the topography other than the topography itself.

Article 9

Where the legislation of Member States provides that semiconductor **A6-009** products manufactured using protected topographies may carry an indication, the indication to be used shall be a capital T as follows: T, 'T', [T], T, T * or T.

CHAPTER 3

CONTINUED APPLICATION OF OTHER LEGAL PROVISIONS

Article 10

A6-010   1. The provisions of this Directive shall be without prejudice to legal provisions concerning patent and utility model rights.
2. The provisions of this Directive shall be without prejudice:
   (a) to rights conferred by the Member States in fulfilment of their obligations under international agreements, including provisions extending such rights to nationals of, or residents in, the territory of the Member State concerned;
   (b) to the law of copyright in Member States, restricting the reproduction of drawing or other artistic representations of topographies by copying them in two dimensions.
3. Protection granted by national law to topographies of semiconductor products fixed or encoded before the entry into force of the national provisions enacting the Directive, but no later than the date set out in Article 11 (1), shall not be affected by the provisions of this Directive.

CHAPTER 4

FINAL PROVISIONS

Article 11

A6-011   1. Member States shall bring into force the laws, regulations or administrative provisions necessary to comply with this Directive by 7 November 1987.
2. Member States shall ensure that they communicate to the Commission the texts of the main provisions of national law which they adopt in the field covered by this Directive.

Article 12

A6-012   This Directive is addressed to the Member States.

FIRST COUNCIL DIRECTIVE of 21 December 1988 to approximate the laws of the Member States relating to trade marks (89/104/EEC)

THE COUNCIL Of THE EUROPEAN COMMUNITIES,
Having regard to the Treaty establishing the European Economic Community, and in particular Article 100a thereof,
Having regard to the proposal from the Commission,
In cooperation with the European Parliament,
Having regard to the opinion of the Economic and Social Committee,
Whereas the trade mark laws at present applicable in the Member States contain disparities which may impede the free movement of goods and freedom to provide services and may distort competition within the common market; whereas it is therefore necessary, in view of the establishment and functioning of the internmal market, to approximate the laws of Member States;

Whereas it is important not to disregard the solutions and advantages which the Community trade mark system may afford to undertakings wishing to acquire trade marks;

Whereas it does not appear to be necessary at present to undertake full-scale approximation of the trade mark laws of the Member States and it will be sufficient if approximation is limited to those national provisions of law which most directly affect the functioning of the internal market;

Whereas the Directive does not deprive the Member States of the right to continue to protect trademarks acquired through use but takes them into account only in regard to the relationship between them and trade marks acquired by registration;

Whereas Member States also remain free to fix the provisions of procedure concerning the registration, the revocation and the invalidity of trade marks acquired by registration; whereas they can, for example, determine the form of trade mark registration and invalidity procedures, decide whether earlier rights should be invoked either in the registration procedure or in the invalidity procedure or in both and, if they allow earlier rights to be invoked in the registration procedure, have an opposition procedure or an ex officio examination procedure or both; whereas Member States remain free to determine the effects of revocation or invalidity of trade marks;

Whereas this Directive does not exclude the application to trade marks of provisions of law of the Member States other than trade mark law, such as the provisions relating to unfair competition, civil liability or consumer protection;

Whereas attainment of the objectives at which this approximation of laws is aiming requires that the conditions for obtaining and continuing to hold a registered trade mark are, in general, identical in all Member States; whereas, to this end, it is necessary to list examples of signs which may constitute a trade mark, provided that such signs are capable of distinguishing the goods or services of one undertaking from those of othrefusal or invalidity concemning the trade mark itself, for example, the absence of any distinctive character, or concerning conflicts between the trade mark and earlier rights, are to be listed in an exhaustive manner, even if some of these grounds are listed as an option for the Member States which will therefore be able to maintain or introduce those grounds in their legislation; whereas Member States will be able to maintain or introduce into their legislation grounds of refusal or invalidity linked to conditions for obtaining and continning to hold a trade mark for which there is no provision of approximation, concerning, for example, the eligibility for the grant of a trade mark, the renewal of the trade mark or rules on fees, or related to the non-compliance with procedural rules;

Whereas in order to reduce the total number of trade marks registered and protected in the Community and, consequently, the number of conflicts which arise between them, it is essential to require that registered trade marks must actually be used or, if not used, be subject to revocation; whereas it is necessary to provide that a trade mark cannot be invalidated on the basis of the existence of a non-used earlier trade mark, while the Member States remain free to apply the same principle in respect of the registration of a trade mark or to provide that a trade mark may not be successfully invoked in infringement proceedings if it is established as a result of a plea that the trade mark could be revoked; whereas in all these cases it is up to the Member States to establish the applicable rules of procedure;

Whereas it is fundamental, in order to facilitate the free circulation of goods and services, to ensure that henceforth registered trade marks enjoy the same protection under the legal systems of all the Member States; whereas this should however not prevent the Member States from granting at their option extensive protection to those trade marks which have a reputation;

Whereas the protection afforded by the registered trade mark, the function of which is in particular to guarantee the trade mark as an indication of origin, is absolute in the case of identity between the mark and the sign and goods or services; whereas the protection applies also in case of similarity between the mark and the sign and the goods or services; whereas it is indispensable to give an interpretation of the concept of similarity in relation to the likelihood of confusion; whereas the likelihood of confusion, the appreciation of which depends on numerous elements and, in particular, on the recognition of the trade mark on the market, of the association which can be made with the used or registered sign, of the degree of similarity between the trade mark and the sign and between the goods or services identified, constitutes the specific condition for such protection; whereas the ways in which likelihood of confusion may be established, and in particular the onus of proof, are a matter for national procedural rules which are not prejudiced by the Directive;

Whereas it is important, for reasons of legal certainty and without inequitably prejudicing the interests of a proprietor of an earlier trade mark, to provide that the latter may no longer request a declaration of invalidity nor may he oppose the use of a trade mark subsequent to his own of which he has knowingly tolerated the use for a substantial length of time, unless the application for the subsequent trade mark was made in bad faith:

Whereas all Member States of the Community are bound by the Paris Convention for the Protection of Industrial Property; whereas it is necessary that the provisions of this Directive are entirely consistent with those of the Paris Convention; whereas the obligations of the Member States resulting from this Convention are not affected by this Directive; whereas, where appropriate, the second subparagraph of Article 234 of the Treaty is applicable,

HAS ADOPTED THIS DIRECTIVE:

Article 1 Scope

A7-001   This Directive shall apply to every trade mark in respect of goods or services which is the subject of registration or of an application in a Member State for registration as an individual trade mark, a collective mark or a guarantee or certification mark, or which is the subject of a registration or an application for registration in the Benelux Trade Mark Office or of an international registration having effect in a Member State.

Article 2 Signs of which a trade mark may consist

A7-002   A trade mark may consist of any sign capable of being represented graphically, particularly words, including personal names, designs, letters, numerals, the shape of goods or of their packaging, provided that such signs are capable of distinguishing the goods or services of one undertaking from those of other undertakings.

Article 3 Grounds for refusal or invalidity

A7-003   1. he following shall not be registered or if registered shall be liable to be declared invalid:
(a) signs which cannot constitute a trade mark;
(b) trade marks which are devoid of any distinctive character;

    (c) trade marks which consist exclusively of signs or indications which may serve, in trade, to designate the kind, quality, quantity, intended purpose, value, geographical origin, or the time of production of the goods or of rendering of the service, or other characteristics of the goods

    (d) trade marks which consist exclusively of signs or indications which have become customary in the current language or in the bona fide and established practices of the trade;

    (e) signs which consist exclusively of:
        – the shape which results from the nature of the goods themselves, or
        – the shape of goods which is necessary to obtain a technical result, or
        – the shape which gives substantial value to the goods;

    (f) trademarks which are contrary to public policy or to accepted principles of morality;

    (g) trade marks which are of such a nature as to deceive the public, for instance as to the nature, quality or geographical origin of the goods or service;

    (h) trade marks which have not been authorized by the competent authorities and are to be refused or invalidated pursuant to Article 6 ter of the Paris Convention for the Protection of Industrial Property, hereinafter referred to as the 'Paris Convention'.

2. Any Member State may provide that a trade mark shall not be registered or, if registered, shall be liable to be declared invalid where and to the extent that:

    (a) the use of that trade mark may be prohibited pursuant to provisions of law other than trade mark law of the Member State concerned or of the Community;

    (b) the trade mark covers a sign of high symbolic value, in particular a religious symbol;

    (c) the trade mark includes badges, emblems and escutcheons other than those coved by Article 6 ter of the Paris Convention and which are of public interest, unless the consent of the appropriate authorities to its registration has been given in conformity with the legislation of the Member State;

    (d) the application for registration of the trade mark was made in bad faith by the applicant.

3. A trade mark shall not be refused registration or be declared invalid in accordance with paragraph 1 (b), (c) or (d) if, before the date of application for registration and following the use which has been made of it, it has acquired a distinctive character. Any Member State may in addition provide that this provision shall also apply where the distinctive character was acquired after the date of application for registration or after the date of registration.

4. Any Member State may provide that, by derogation from the preceding paragraphs, the grounds of refusal of registration or invalidity in force in that State prior to the date on which the provisions necessary to comply with this Directive enter into force, shall apply to trade marks for which application has been made prior to that date.

Article 4 Further grounds for refusal or invalidity concerning conflicts with earlier rights

A7-004   1. A trade mark shall not be registered or, if registered, shall be liable to be declared invalid:

    (a) if it is identical with an earlier trade mark, and the goods or services for which the trade mark is applied for or is registered are identical with the goods or services for which the earlier trade mark is protected;

    (b) if because of its identity with, or similarity to,the earlier trade mark and the identity or similarity of the goods or services covered by the trade marks, there exists a likelihood of confusion on the part of the public, which includes the likelihood of association with the earlier trade mark.

  2. "Earlier trade marks" within the meaning of paragraph 1 means:

    (a) trade marks of the following kinds with a date of application for registration which is earlier than the date of application for registration of the trade mark, taking account, where appropriate, of the priorities claimed in respect of those trade marks;

      (i) Community trade marks;

      (ii) trade marks registered in the Member State or, in the case of Belgium, Luxembourg or the Netherlands, at the Benelux Trade Mark Office;

      (iii) trade marks registered under international arrangements which have effect in the Member State;

    (b) Community trade marks which validly claim seniority, in accordance with the Regulation on the Community trade mark, from a trade mark referred to in (a) (ii) and (iii), even when the latter trade mark has been surrendered or allowed to lapse;

    (c) applications for the trade marks referred to in (a) and (b), subject to their registration;

    (d) trade marks which, on the date of application for registration of the trade mark, or, where appropriate, of the priority claimed in respect of the application for registration of the trade mark, are well known in a Member State, in the sense in which the words 'well known' are used in Article 6 bis of the Paris Convention.

  3. A trade mark shall furthermore not be registered or, if registered, shall be liable to be declared invalid if it is identical with, or similar to, an earlier Community trade mark within the meaning of paragraph 2 and is to be, or has been, registered for goods or services which are not similar to those for which the earlier Community trade mark is registered, where the earlier Community trade mark has a reputation in the Community and where the use of the later trade mark without due cause would take unfair advantage of, or be detrimental to, the distinctive character or the repute of the earlier Community trade mark.

  4. Any Member State may furthermore provide that a trade mark shall not be registered or, if registered, shall be liable to be declared invalid where, and to the extent that:

    (a) the trade mark is identical with, or similar to, an earlier national trade mark within the meaning of paragraph 2 and is to he, or has been, registered for goods or services which are not similar to those for which the earlier trade mark is registered, where the earlier trade mark has a reputation in the Member State concerned and where the use of the later trade mark without due cause would take unfair advantage of, or be detrimental to, the distinctive character or che repute of the earlier trade mark;

(b) rights to a non-registered trade mark or to another sign used in the course oftrade were acquired prior to the date of application for registration of the subsequent trade mark, or the date of the priority claimed for the application for registration of the subsequent trade mark and that non-registered trade mark or other sign confers on its proprietor the right to prohibit the use of a subsequent trade mark;

(c) the use of the trade mark may be prohibited by virtue of an earlier right other than the rights referred to in paragraphs 2 and 4 (b) and in particular:
   (i) a right to a name;
   (ii) a right of personal portrayal;
   (iii) a copyright;
   (iv) an industrial property right;

(d) the trade mark is identical with, or similar to, an earlier collective trade mark conferring a right which expired within a period of a maximum of three years preceding application;

(e) the trade mark is identical with, or similar to, an earlier guarantee or certification mark conferring a right which expired within a period preceding application the length of which is fixed by the Member State;

(f) the trade mark is identical with, or similar to, an earlier trade mark which was registered for identical or similar goods or services and conferred on them a right which has expired for failure to renew within a period of a maximum of two years preceding application, unless the proprietor of the earlier trade mark gave his agreement for the registration of the later mark or did not use his trade mark;

(g) the trade mark is liable to be confused with a mark which was in use abroad on the filing date of the application and which is still in use there, provided that at the date of the application the applicant was acting in bad faith.

5. The Member States may permit that in appropriate circumstances registration need not be refused or the trade mark need not be declared invalid where the proprietor of the earlier trade mark or other earlier right consents to the registration of the later trade mark.

6. Any Member State may provide that, by derogation from paragraphs 1 to 5, the grounds for refusal of registration or invalidity in force in that State prior to the date on which the provisions necessary to comply with this Directive enter into force, shall apply to trade marks for which application has been made prior to that date.

Article 5 Rights conferred by a trade mark

1. The registered trade mark shall confer on the proprietor exclusive rights **A7-005** therein. The proprietor shall be entitled to prevent all third parties not having his consent from using in the course of trade:

(a) any signwhich is identical with the trade mark in relation to goods or services which are identical with those for which the trade mark is registered;

(b) any sign where, because of its identity with, or similarity to, the trade mark and the identity or similarity of the goods or services covered by the trade mark and the sign, there exists a likelihood of confusion on the part of the public, which includes the likelihood of association between the sign and the trade mark.

2. Any Member State may also provide that the proprietor shall be entitled to prevent all third parties not having his consent from using in the course of trade any sign which is identical with, or similar to, the trade mark in relation to goods or services which are not similar to those for which the trade mark is registered, where the latter has a reputation in the Member State and where use of that sign without due cause takes unfair advantage of, or is detrimental to, the distinctive character or the repute of the trade mark.

3. The following, inter alia, may be prohibited under paragraphs 1 and 2:

    (a) affixing the sign to the goods or to the packaging thereof;

    (b) offering the goods, or putting them on the market or stocking them for these purposes under that sign, or offering or supplying services thereunder;

    (c) importing or exporting the goods under the sign;

    (d) using the sign on business papers and in advertising.

4. Where, under the law of the Member State, the use of a sign under the conditions referred to in 1 (b) or 2 could not be prohibited before the date on which the provisions necessary to comply with this Directive entered into force in the Member State concerned, the rights conferred by the trade mark may not be relied on to prevent the continued use of the sign.

5. Paragraphs 1 to 4 shall not affect provisions in any Member State relating to the protection against the use of a sign other than for the purposes of distinguishing goods or services, where use of that sign without due cause takes unfair advantage of, or is detrimental to, the distinctive character or the repute of the trade mark

Article 6 Limitation of the effects of a trade mark

A7-006   1. The trade mark shall not entitle the proprietor to prohibit a third party from using, in the course of trade,

    (a) his own name or address;

    (b) indications concerning the kind, quality, quantity, intended purpose, value, geographical origin, the time of production of goods or of rendering of the service, or other characteristics of goods or services;

    (c) the trade mark where it is necessary to indicate the intended purpose of a product or service, in particular as accessories or spare parts; provided he uses them in accordance with honest practices in industrial or commercial matters

2. The trade mark shall not entitle the proprietor to prohibit a third party from using, in the course of trade, an earlier right which only applies in a particular locality if that right is recognized by the laws of the Member State in question and within the limits of the territory in which it is recognized.

Article 7 Exhaustion of the rights conferred by a trade mark

A7-007   1. The trade mark shall not entitle the proprietor to prohibit its use in relation to goods which have been put on the market in the Community under that trade mark by the proprietor or with his consent.

2. Paragraph 1 shall not apply where there exist legitimate reasons for the proprietor to oppose further commercialization of the goods, especially where the condition of the goods is changed or impaired after they have been put on the market.

Article 8 Licensing

1. A trade mark may be licensed for some or all of the goods or services for **A7-008** which it is registered and for the whole or part of the Member State concerned. A license may be exclusive or non-exclusive.

2. The proprietor of a trade mark may invoke the rights conferred by that trade mark against a licensee who contravenes any provision in his licensing contract with regard to its duration, the form covered by the registration in which the trade mark may be used, the scope of the goods or services for which the licence is granted, the territory in which the trade mark may be affixed, or the quality of the goods manufactured or of the services provided by the licensee.

Article 9 Limitation in consequence of acquiescence

1. Where, in a Member State, the proprietor of an earlier trade mark as **A7-009** referred to in Article 4 (2) has acquiesced, for a period of five successive years, in the use of a later trade mark registered in that Member State while being aware of such use, he shall no longer be entitled on the basis of the earlier trade mark either to apply for a declaration that the later trade mark is invalid or to oppose the use of the later trade mark in respect of the goods or services for which the later trade mark has been used, unless registration of the later trade mark was applied for in bad faith.

2. Any Member State may provide that paragraph 1 shall apply mutatis mutandis to the proprietor of an earlier trade mark referred to in Article 4 (4) (a) or an other earlier right referred to in Article 4 (4) (b) or (c).

3. In the cases referred to in paragraphs 1 and 2, the proprietor of a later registered trade mark shall not be entitled to oppose the use of the earlier right, even though that right may no longer be invoked against the later trade mark.

Article 10 Use of trade marks

1. If, within a period of five years following the date of the completion of the **A7-010** registration procedure, the proprietor has not put the trade mark to genuine use in the Member State in connection with the goods or services in respect of which it is registered, or if such use has been suspended during an uninterrupted period of five years, the trade mark shall be subject to the sanctions provided for in this Directive, unless there are proper reasons for non-use.

2. The following shall also constitute use within the meaning of paragraph 1:
   (a) use of the trade mark in a form differing in elements which do not alter the distinctive character of the mark in the form in which it was registered;
   (b) affixing of the trade mark to goods or to the packaging thereof in the Member State concerned solely for export purposes.

3. Use of the trade mark with the consent of the proprietor or by any person who has authority to use a collective mark or a guarantee or certification mark shall be deemed to constitute use by the proprietor.

4. In relation to trade marks registered before the date on which the provisions necessary to comply with this Directive enter into force in the Member State concerned:
   (a) where a provision in force prior to that date attaches sanctions to non-use of a trade mark during an uninterrupted period, the relevant period of five years mentioned in paragraph 1 shall be deemed to have begun to run at the same time as any period of non-use which is already running at that date;

(b) where there is no use provision in force prior to that date, the periods of five years mentioned in paragraph 1 shall be deemed to run from that date at the earliest.

Article 11 Sanctions for non use of a trade mark in legal or administrative proceedings

A7-011   1. A trade mark may not be declared invalid on the ground that there is an earlier conflicting trade mark if the latter does not fulfil the requirements of use set out in Article 10 (1), (2) and (3) or in Article 10 (4), as the case may be.

2. Any Member State may provide that registration of a trade mark may not be refused on the ground that there is an earlier conflicting trade mark if the latter does not fulfil the requirements of use set out in Article 10 (1), (2) and (3) or in Article 10 (4), as the case may be.

3. Without prejudice to the application of Article 12, where a counter-claim for revocation is made, any Member State may provide that a trade mark may not be successfully invoked in infringement proceedings if it is established as a result of a plea that the trade mark could be revoked pursuant to Article 12 (1).

4. If the earlier trade mark has been used in relation to part only of the goods or services for which it is registered, it shall, for purposes of applying paragraphs 1, 2 and 3, be deemed to be registered in respect only of that part of the goods or services.

Article 12 Grounds for revocation

A7-012   1. A trade mark shall be liable to revocation if, within a continous period of five years, it has not been put to genuine use in the Member State in connection with the goods or. services in respect of which it is registered, and there are no proper reasons for non-use; however, no person may claim that the proprietor's rights in a trade mark should be revoked where, during the interval between expiry of the five-year period and filing of the application for revocation, genuine use of the trade mark has been started or resumed; the commencement or resumption of use within a period of three months preceding the filing of the application for revocation which began at the earliest on expiry of the continuous period of five years of non-use, shall, however, be disregarded where preparations for the commencement or resumption occur only after the proprietor becomes aware that the application for revocation may be filed.

2. A trade mark shall also be liable to revocation if, after the date on which it was registered,
- (a) in consequence of acts or inactivity of the proprietor, it has become the common name in the trade for a product or service in respect of which it is registered;
- (b) in consequence of the use made of it by the proprietor of the trade mark or with his consent in respect of the goods or services for which it is registered, it is liable to mislead the public, particularly as to the nature, quality or geographical origin of those goods or services.

Article 13 Grounds for refusal or revocation or invalidity relating to only some of the goods or services

A7-013   Where grounds for refusal of registration or for revocation or invalidity of a trade mark exist in respect of only some of the goods or services for which that trade mark has been applied for or registered, refusal of registration or revocation or invalidity shall cover those goods or services only.

Article 14 Establishment a posteriori of invalidity or revocation of a trade mark

Where the seniority of an earlier trade mark which has been surrendered or **A7-014** allowed to lapse, is claimed for a Community trade mark, the invalidity or revocation of the earlier trade mark may be established a posteriori

Article 15 Special provisions in respect of collective marks, guarantee marks and certification marks

1. Without prejudice to Article 4, Member States whose laws authorize the **A7-015** registration of collective marks or of guarantee or certification marks may provide that such marks shall not be registered, or shall be revoked or declared invalid, on grounds additional to those specified in Articles 3 and 12 where the function of those marks so requires.

2. By way of derogation from Article 3 (1) (c), Member States may provide that signs or indications which may serve, in trade, to designate the geographical origin of the goods or services may constitute collective, guarantee or certification marks. Such a mark does not entitle the proprietor to prohibit a third party from using in the course of trade such signs or indications, provided he uses them in accordance with honest practices in industrial or commercial matters; in particular, such a mark may not be invoked against a third party who is entitled to use a geographical name

Article 16 National provisions to be adopted pursuant to this Directive

1. The Member States shall bring into force the laws, regulations and adminis- **A7-016** trative provisions necessary to comply with this Directive not later than 28 December 1991. They shall immediately inform the Commission thereof.

2. Acting on a proposal from the Commission, the Council, acting by qualified majority, may defer the date referred to in paragraph 1 until 31 December 1992 at the latest.

3. Member States shall communicate to the Commission the text of the main.- provisions of national law which they adopt in the field governed by this Directive.

Article 17 Addressees

This Directive is addressed to the Member States. **A7-017**

COUNCIL DIRECTIVE of 14 May 1991 on the legal protection of computer programs (91/250/EEC)

THE COUNCIL OF THE EUROPEAN COMMUNITIES,
Having regard to the Treaty establishing the European Economic Community and in particular Article 100a thereof,
Having regard to the proposal from the Commission,
In cooperation with the European Parliament,
Having regard to the opinion of the Economic and Social Committee,
Whereas computer programs are at present not clearly protected in all Member States by existing legislation and such protection, where it exists, has different attributes;
Whereas the development of computer programs requires the investment of considerable human, technical and financial resources while computer programs can be copied at a fraction of the cost needed to develop them independently;

Whereas computer programs are playing an increasingly important role in a broad range of industries and computer program technology can accordingly be considered as being of fundamental importance for the Community's industrial development;

Whereas certain differences in the legal protection of computer programs offered by the laws of the Member States have direct and negative effects on the functioning of the common market as regards computer programs and such differences could well become greater as Member States introduce new legislation on this subject;

Whereas existing differences having such effects need to be removed and new ones prevented from arising, while differences not adversely affecting the functioning of the common market to a substantial degree need not be removed or prevented from arising;

Whereas the Community's legal framework on the protection of computer programs can accordingly in the first instance be limited to establishing that Member States should accord protection to computer programs under copyright law as literary works and, further, to establishing who and what should be protected, the exclusive rights on which protected persons should be able to rely in order to authorize or prohibit certain acts and for how long the protection should apply;

Whereas, for the purpose of this Directive, the term 'computer program' shall include programs in any form, including those which are incorporated into hardware;

Whereas this term also includes preparatory design work leading to the development of a computer program provided that the nature of the preparatory work is such that a computer program can result from it at a later stage;

Whereas, in respect of the criteria to be applied in determining whether or not a computer program is an original work, no tests as to the qualitative or aesthetic merits of the program should be applied;

Whereas the Community is fully committed to the promotion of international standardization;

Whereas the function of a computer program is to communicate and work together with other components of a computer system and with users and, for this purpose, a logical and, where appropriate, physical interconnection and interaction is required to permit all elements of software and hardware to work with other software and hardware and with users in all the ways in which they are intended to function;

Whereas the parts of the program which provide for such interconnection and interaction between elements of software and hardware are generally known as 'interfaces';

Whereas this functional interconnection and interaction is generally known as 'interoperability'; whereas such interoperability can be defined as the ability to exchange information and mutually to use the information which has been exchanged;

Whereas, for the avoidance of doubt, it has to be made clear that only the expression of a computer program is protected and that ideas and principles which underlie any element of a program, including those which underlie its interfaces, are not protected by copyright under this Directive;

Whereas, in accordance with this principle of copyright, to the extent that logic, algorithms and programming languages comprise ideas and principles, those ideas and principles are not protected under this Directive;

Whereas, in accordance with the legislation and jurisprudence of the Member States and the international copyright conventions, the expression of those ideas and principles is to be protected by copyright;

Whereas, for the purposes of this Directive, the term 'rental' means the making available for use, for a limited period of time and for profit-making purposes, of a computer program or a copy thereof; whereas this term does not include public lending, which, accordingly, remains outside the scope of this Directive;

Whereas the exclusive rights of the author to prevent the unauthorized reproduction of his work have to be subject to a limited exception in the case of a computer program to allow the reproduction technically necessary for the use of that program by the lawful acquirer;

Whereas this means that the acts of loading and running necessary for the use of a copy of a program which has been lawfully acquired, and the act of correction of its errors, may not be prohibited by contract; whereas, in the absence of specific contractual provisions, including when a copy of the program has been sold, any other act necessary for the use of the copy of a program may be performed in accordance with its intended purpose by a lawful acquirer of that copy;

Whereas a person having a right to use a computer program should not be prevented from performing acts necessary to observe, study or test the functioning of the program, provided that these acts do not infringe the copyright in the program;

Whereas the unauthorized reproduction, translation, adaptation or transformation of the form of the code in which a copy of a computer program has been made available constitutes an infringement of the exclusive rights of the author;

Whereas, nevertheless, circumstances may exist when such a reproduction of the code and translation of its form within the meaning of Article 4 (a) and (b) are indispensable to obtain the necessary information to achieve the interoperability of an independently created program with other programs;

Whereas it has therefore to be considered that in these limited circumstances only, performance of the acts of reproduction and translation by or on behalf of a person having a right to use a copy of the program is legitimate and compatible with fair practice and must therefore be deemed not to require the authorization of the rightholder;

Whereas an objective of this exception is to make it possible to connect all components of a computer system, including those of different manufacturers, so that they can work together;

Whereas such an exception to the author's exclusive rights may not be used in a way which prejudices the legitimate interests of the rightholder or which conflicts with a normal exploitation of the program;

Whereas, in order to remain in accordance with the provisions of the Berne Convention for the Protection of Literary and Artistic Works, the term of protection should be the life of the author and fifty years from the first of January of the year following the year of his death or, in the case of an anonymous or pseudonymous work, 50 years from the first of January of the year following the year in which the work is first published; Whereas protection of computer programs under copyright laws should be without prejudice to the application, in appropriate cases, of other forms of protection; whereas, however, any contractual provisions contrary to Article 6 or to the exceptions provided for in Article 5 (2) and (3) should be null and void;

Whereas the provisions of this Directive are without prejudice to the application of the competition rules under Articles 85 and 86 of the Treaty if a dominant supplier refuses to make information available which is necessary for interoperability as defined in this Directive;

Whereas the provisions of this Directive should be without prejudice to specific requirements of Community law already enacted in respect of the publication of interfaces in the telecommunications sector or Council Decisions relating to standardization in the field of information technology and telecommunication;

Whereas this Directive does not affect derogations provided for under national legislation in accordance with the Berne Convention on points not covered by this Directive,

HAS ADOPTED THIS DIRECTIVE:

Article 1 Object of protection

A8-001   1. In accordance with the provisions of this Directive, Member States shall protect computer programs, by copyright, as literary works within the meaning of the Berne Convention for the Protection of Literary and Artistic Works. For the purposes of this Directive, the term 'computer programs' shall include their preparatory design material.

2. Protection in accordancewith this Directive shall apply to the expression in any form of a computer program. Ideas and principles which underlie any element of a computer program, including those which underlie its interfaces, are not protected by copyright under this Directive.

3. A computer program shall be protected if it is original in the sense that it is the author's own intellectual creation. No other criteria shall be applied to determine its eligibility for protection.

Article 2 Authorship of computer programs

A8-002   1. The author of a computer program shall be the natural person or group of natural persons who has created the program or, where the legislation of the Member State permits, the legal person designated as the rightholder by that legislation. Where collective works are recognized by the legislation of a Member State, the person considered by the legislation of the Member State to have created the work shall be deemed to be its author.

2. In respect of a computer program created by a group of natural persons jointly, the exclusive rights shall be owned jointly.

3. Where a computer program is created by an employee in the execution of his duties or following the instructions given by his employer, the employer exclusively shall be entitled to exercise all economic rights in the program so created, unless otherwise provided by contract.

Article 3 Beneficiaries of protection

A8-003   Protection shall be granted to all natural or legal persons eligible under national copyright legislation as applied to literary works.

Article 4 Restricted Acts

A8-004   Subject to the provisions of Articles 5 and 6, the exclusive rights of the rightholder within the meaning of Article 2, shall include the right to do or to authorize:

(a) the permanent or temporary reproduction of a computer program by any means and in any form, in part or in whole. Insofar as loading, displaying, running, transmision or storage of the computer program necessitate such reproduction, such acts shall be subject to authorization by the rightholder;

(b) the translation, adaptation, arrangement and any other alteration of a computer program and the reproduction of the results thereof, without prejudice to the rights of the person who alters the program;

(c) any form of distribution to the public, including the rental, of the original computer program or of copies thereof. The first sale in the Community of a copy of a program by the rightholder or with his consent shall exhaust the distribution right within the Community of that copy, with the exception of the right to control further rental of the program or a copy thereof.

Article 5 Exceptions to the restricted acts

1. In the absence of specific contractual provisions, the acts referred to in **A8-005** Article 4 (a) and (b) shall not require authorization by the rightholder where they are necessary for the use of the computer program by the lawful acquirer in accordance with its intended purpose, including for error correction.

2. The making of a back-up copy by a person having a right to use the computer program may not be prevented by contract insofar as it is necessary for that use.

3. The person having a right to use a copy of a computer program shall be entitled, without the authorization of the rightholder, to observe, study or test the functioning of the program in order to determine the ideas and principles which underlie any element of the program if he does so while performing any of the acts of loading, displaying, running, transmitting or storing the program which he is entitled to do.

Article 6 Decompilation

1. The authorization of the rightholder shall not be required where reproduc- **A8-006** tion of the code and translation of its form within the meaning of Article 4 (a) and (b) are indispensable to obtain the information necessary to achieve the interoperability of an independently created computer program with other programs, provided that the following conditions are met:

(a) these acts are performed by the licensee or by another person having a right to use a copy of a program, or on their behalf by a person authorized to to so;

(b) the information necessary to achieve interoperability has not previously been readily available to the persons referred to in subparagraph (a); and (c) these acts are confined to the parts of the original program which are necessary to achieve interoperability.

2. The provisions of paragraph 1 shall not permit the information obtained through its application:

(a) to be used for goals other than to achieve the interoperability of the independently created computer program;

(b) to be given to others, except when necessary for the interoperability of the independently created computer program; or (c) to be used for the development, production or marketing of a computer program substantially similar in its expression, or for any other act which infringes copyright.

3. In accordance with the provisions of the Berne Convention for the protection of Literary and Artistic Works, the provisions of this Article may not be interpreted in such a way as to allow its application to be used in a manner which unreasonably prejudices the right holder's legitimate interests or conflicts with a normal exploitation of the computer program.

Article 7 Special measures of protection

A8-007   1. Without prejudice to the provisions of Articles 4, 5 and 6, Member States shall provide, in accordance with their national legislation, appropriate remedies against a person committing any of the acts listed in subparagraphs (a), (b) and (c) below:

> (a) any act of putting into circulation a copy of a computer program knowing, or having reason to believe, that it is an infringing copy;
>
> (b) the possession, for commercial purposes, of a copy of a computer program knowing, or having reason to believe, that it is an infringing copy;
>
> (c) any act of putting into circulation, or the possession for commercial purposes of, any means the sole intended purpose of which is to facilitate the unauthorized removal or circumvention of any technical device which may have been applied to protect a computer program.

2. Any infringing copy of a computer program shall be liable to seizure in accordance with the legislation of the Member State concerned.

3. Member States may provide for the seizure of any means referred to in paragraph 1 (c).

Article 9 Continued application of other legal provisions

A8-008   1. The provisions of this Directive shall be without prejudice to any other legal provisions such as those concerning patent rights, trade-marks, unfair competition, trade secrets, protection of semi-conductor products or the law of contract. Any contractual provisions contrary to Article 6 or to the exceptions provided for in Article 5 (2) and (3) shall be null and void.

2. The provisions of this Directive shall apply also to programs created before 1 January 1993 without prejudice to any acts concluded and rights acquired before that date.

Article 10 Final provisions

A8-009   1. Member States shall bring into force the laws, regulations and administrative provisions necessary to comply with this Directive before 1 January 1993. When Member States adopt these measures, the latter shall contain a reference to this Directive or shall be accompanied by such reference on the occasion of their official publication. The methods of making such a reference shall be laid down by the Member States.

2. Member States shall communicate to the Commission the provisions of national law which they adopt in the field governed by this Directive.

Article 11

This Directive is addressed to the Member States.

Council Directive 92/100/EEC of 19 November 1992 on rental
right and lending right and on certain rights related to copyright
in the field of intellectual property. Amended by: Council
Directive 93/98/EEC of 29 October 1993 and Directive 2001/
29/EC of the European Parliament and the Council of 22 May
2001

THE COUNCIL OF THE EUROPEAN COMMUNITIES,
Having regard to the Treaty establishing the European Economic Community,
and in particular Articles 57 (2), 66 and 100a thereof,
Having regard to the proposal from the Commission,
In cooperation with the European Parliament,
Having regard to the opinion of the Economic and Social Committee,
Whereas differences exist in the legal protection provided by the laws and
practices of the Member States for copyright works and subject matter of related
rights protection as regards rental and lending; whereas such differences are
sources of barriers to trade and distortions of competition which impede the
achievement and proper functioning of the internal market;
Whereas such differences in legal protection could well become greater as
Member States adopt new and different legislation or as national case-law interpreting such legislation develops differently;
Whereas such differences should therefore be eliminated in accordance with the
objective of introducing an area without internal frontiers as set out in Article 8a
of the Treaty so as to institute, pursuant to Article 3 (f) of the Treaty, a system
ensuring that competition in the common market is not distorted;
Whereas rental and lending of copyright works and the subject matter of related
rights protection is playing an increasingly important role in particular for
authors, performers and producers of phonograms and films; whereas piracy is
becoming an increasing threat;
Whereas the adequate protection of copyright works and subject matter of
related rights protection by rental and lending rights as well as the protection of
the subject matter of related rights protection by the fixation right, reproduction
right, distribution right, right to broadcast and communication to the public can
accordingly be considered as being of fundamental importance for the Community's economic and cultural development;
Whereas copyright and related rights protection must adapt to new economic
developments such as new forms of exploitation;
Whereas the creative and artistic work of authors and performers necessitates
an adequate income as a basis for further creative and artistic work, and the
investments required particularly for the production of phonograms and films
are especially high and risky; whereas the possibility for securing that income
and recouping that investment can only effectively be guaranteed through
adequate legal protection of the rightholders concerned;
Whereas these creative, artistic and entrepreneurial activities are, to a large
extent, activities of self-employed persons; whereas the pursuit of such activities
must be made easier by providing a harmonized legal protection within the
Community;
Whereas, to the extent that these activities principally constitute services, their
provision must equally be facilitated by the establishment in the Community of a
harmonized legal framework;

Whereas the legislation of the Member States should be approximated in such a way so as not to conflict with the international conventions on which many Member States' copyright and related rights laws are based;

Whereas the Community's legal framework on the rental right and lending right and on certain rights related to copyright can be limited to establishing that Member States provide rights with respect to rental and lending for certain groups of rightholders and further to establishing the rights of fixation, reproduction, distribution, broadcasting and communication to the public for certain groups of rightholders in the field of related rights protection;

Whereas it is necessary to define the concepts of rental and lending for the purposes of this Directive;

Whereas it is desirable, with a view to clarity, to exclude from rental and lending within the meaning of this Directive certain forms of making available, as for instance making available phonograms or films (cinematographic or audiovisual works or moving images, whether or not accompanied by sound) for the purpose of public performance or broadcasting, making available for the purpose of exhibition, or making available for on-the-spot reference use; whereas lending within the meaning of this Directive does not include making available between establishments which are accessible to the public;

Whereas, where lending by an establishment accessible to the public gives rise to a payment the amount of which does not go beyond what is necessary to cover the operating costs of the establishment, there is no direct or indirect economic or commercial advantage within the meaning of this Directive;

Whereas it is necessary to introduce arrangements ensuring that an unwaivable equitable remuneration is obtained by authors and performers who must retain the possibility to entrust the administration of this right to collecting societies representing them;

Whereas the equitable remuneration may be paid on the basis of one or several payments an any time on or after the conclusion of the contract;

Whereas the equitable remuneration must take account of the importance of the contribution of the authors and performers concerned to the phonogram or film;

Whereas it is also necessary to protect the rights at least of authors as regards public lending by providing for specific arrangements; whereas, however, any measures based on Article 5 of this Directive have to comply with Community law, in particular with Article 7 of the Treaty;

Whereas the provisions of Chapter II do not prevent Member States from extending the presumption set out in Article 2 (5) to the exclusive rights included in that chapter; whereas furthermore the provisions of Chapter II do not prevent Member States from providing for a rebuttable presumption of the authorization of exploitation in respect of the exclusive rights of performers provided for in those articles, in so far as such presumption is compatible with the International Convention for the Protection of Performers, Producers of Phonograms and Broadcasting Organizations (hereinafter referred to as the Rome Convention);

Whereas Member States may provide for more far-reaching protection for owners of rights related to copyright than that required by Article 8 of this Directive;

Whereas the harmonized rental and lending rights and the harmonized protection in the field of rights related to copyright should not be exercised in a way which constitutes a disguised restriction on trade between Member States or

in a way which is contrary to the rule of media exploitation chronology, as recognized in the Judgment handed down in Société Cinéthèque v. FNCF,
HAS ADOPTED THIS DIRECTIVE:

Chapter I

Rental and Lending Right

Article 1 Object of harmonization

1. In accordance with the provisions of this Chapter, Member States shall **A9-001** provide, subject to Article 5, a right to authorize or prohibit the rental and lending of originals and copies of copyright works, and other subject matter as set out in Article 2 (1).

2. For the purposes of this Directive, 'rental' means making available for use, for a limited period of time and for direct or indirect economic or commercial advantage.

3. For the purposes of this Directive, 'lending' means making available for use, for a limited period of time and not for direct or indirect economic or commercial advantage, when it is made through establishments which are accessible to the public.

4. The rights referred to in paragraph 1 shall not be exhausted by any sale or other act of distribution of originals and copies of copyright works and other subject matter as set out in Article 2 (1).

Article 2 Rightholders and subject matter of rental and lending right

1. The exclusive right to authorize or prohibit rental and lending shall **A9-002** belong:
   – to the author in respect of the original and copies of his work,
   – to the performer in respect of fixations of his performance,
   – to the phonogram producer in respect of his phonograms, and
   – to the producer of the first fixation of a film in respect of the original and copies of his film. For the purposes of this Directive, the term 'film' shall designate a cinematographic or audiovisualwork or moving images, whether or not accompanied by sound.

2. For the purposes of this Directive the principal director of a cinematographic or audiovisual work shall be considered as its author or one of its authors. Member States may provide for others to be considered as its co-authors.

3. This Directive does not cover rental and lending rights in relation to buildings and to works of applied art.

4. The rights referred to in paragraph 1 may be transferred, assigned or subjet to the granting of contractual licences.

5. Without prejudice to paragraph 7, when a contract concerning film production is concluded, individually or collectively, by performers with a film producer, the performer covered by this contract shall be presumed, subject to contractual clauses to the contrary, to have transferred his rental right, subject to Article 4.

6. Member States may provide for a similar presumption as set out in paragraph 5 with respect to authors.

7. Member States may provide that the signing of a contract concluded between a performer and a film producer concerning the production of a film

has the effect of authorizing rental, provided that such contract provides for an equitable remuneration within the meaning of Article 4. Member States may also provide that this paragraph shall apply mutatis mutandis to the rights included in Chapter II.

Article 3 Rental of computer programs

A9-003   This Directive shall be without prejudice to Article 4 (c) of Council Directive 91/250/EEC of 14 May 1991 on the legal protection of computer programs (5).

Article 4 Unwaivable right to equitable remuneration

A9-004   1. Where an author or performer has transferred or assigned his rental right concerning a phonogram or an original or copy of a film to a phonogram or film producer, that author or performer shall retain the right to obtain an equitable remuneration for the rental.

2. The right to obtain an equitable remuneration for rental cannot be waived by authors or performers.

3. The administration of this right to obtain an equitable remuneration may be entrusted to collecting societies representing authors or performers.

4. Member States may regulate whether and to what extent administration by collecting societies of the right to obtain an equitable remuneration may be imposed, as well as the question from whom this remuneration may be claimed or collected.

Article 5 Derogation from the exclusive public lending right

A9-005   1. Member States may derogate from the exclusive right provided for in Article 1 in respect of public lending, provided that at least authors obtain a remuneration for such lending. Member States shall be free to determine this remuneration taking account of their cultural promotion objectives.

2. When Member States do not apply the exclusive lending right provided for in Article 1 as regards phonograms, films and computer programs, they shall introduce, at least for authors, a remuneration.

3. Member States may exempt certain categories of establishments from the payment of the remuneration referred to in paragraphs 1 and 2.

4. The Commission, in cooperation with the Member States, shall draw up before 1 July 1997 a report on public lending in the Community. It shall forward this report to the European Parliament and to the Council.

CHAPTER II

RIGHTS RELATED TO COPYRIGHT

Article 6 Fixation right

A9-006   1. Member States shall provide for performers the exclusive right to authorize or prohibit the fixation of their performances.

2. Member States shall provide for broadcasting organizations the exclusive right to authorize or prohibit the fixation of their broadcasts, whether these broadcasts are transmitted by wire or over the air, including by cable or satellite.

3. A cable distributor shall not have the right provided for in paragraph 2 where it merely retransmits by cable the broadcasts of broadcasting organizations.

Article 8 Broadcasting and communication to the public

1. Member States shall provide for performers the exclusive right to **A9-007** authorize or prohibit the broadcasting by wireless means and the communication to the public of their performances, except where the performance is itself already a broadcast performance or is made from a fixation.

2. Member States shall provide a right in order to ensure that a single equitable remuneration is paid by the user, if a phonogram published for commercial purposes, or a reproduction of such phonogram, is used for broadcasting by wireless means or for any communication to the public, and to ensure that this remuneration is shared between the relevant performers and phonogram producers. Member States may, in the absence of agreement between the performers and phonogram producers, lay down the conditions as to the sharing of this remuneration between them.

3. Member States shall provide for broadcasting organizations the exclusive right to authorize or prohibit the rebroadcasting of their broadcasts by wireless means, as well as the communication to the public of their broadcasts if such communication is made in places accessible to the public against payment of an entrance fee.

Article 9 Distribution right

1. Member States shall provide **A9-008**
   – for performers, in respect of fixations of their performances,
   – for phonogram producers, in respect of their phonograms,
   – for producers of the first fixations of films, in respect of the original and copies of their films,
   – for broadcasting organizations, in respect of fixations of their broadcast as set out in Article 6 (2),

the exclusive right to make available these objects, including copies thereof, to the public by sale or otherwise, hereafter referred to as the 'distribution right'.

2. The distribution right shall not be exhausted within the Community in respect of an object as referred to in paragraph 1, except where the first sale in the Community of that object is made by the rightholder or with his consent.

3. The distribution right shall be without prejudice to the specific provisions of Chapter I, in particular Article 1 (4).

4. The distribution right may be transferred, assigned or subject to the granting of contractual licences.

Article 10 Limitations to rights

1. Member States may provide for limitations to the rights referred to in **A9-009** Chapter II in respect of:
   (a) private use;
   (b) use of short excerpts in connection with the reporting of current events;
   (c) ephemeral fixation by a broadcasting organization by means of its own facilities and for its own broadcasts;
   (d) use solely for the purposes of teaching or scientific research.

2. Irrespective of paragraph 1, any Member State may provide for the same kinds of limitations with regard to the protection of performers, producers of phonograms, broadcasting organizations and of producers of the first fixations of films, as it provides for in connection with the protection of copyright in

literary and artistic works. However, compulsory licences may be provided for only to the extent to which they are compatible with the Rome Convention.

3. Paragraph 1 (a) shall be without prejudice to any existing or future legislation on remuneration for reproduction for private use.

CHAPTER IV

COMMON PROVISIONS

Article 13 Application in time

A9-010 1. This Directive shall apply in respect of all copyright works, performances, phonograms, broadcasts and first fixations of films referred to in this Directive which are, on 1 July 1994, still protected by the legislation of the Member States in the field of copyright and related rights or meet the criteria for protection under the provisions of this Directive on that date.

2. This Directive shall apply without prejudice to any acts of exploitation performed before 1 July 1994.

3. Member States may provide that the rightholders are deemed to have given their authorization to the rental or lending of an object referred to in Article 2 (1) which is proven to have been made available to third parties for this purpose or to have been acquired before 1 July 1994. However, in particular where such an object is a digital recording, Member States may provide that rightholders shall have a right to obtain an adequate remuneration for the rental or lending of that object.

4. Member States need not apply the provisions of Article 2 (2) to cinematographic or audiovisual works created before 1 July 1994.

5. Member States may determine the date as from which the Article 2 (2) shall apply, provided that that date is no later than 1 July 1997.

6. This Directive shall, without prejudice to paragraph 3 and subject to paragraphs 8 and 9, not affect any contracts concluded before the date of its adoption.

7. Member States may provide, subject to the provisions of paragraphs 8 and 9, that when rightholders who acquire new rights under the national provisions adopted in implementation of this Directive have, before 1 July 1994, given their consent for exploitation, they shall be presumed to have transferred the new exclusive rights.

8. Member States may determine the date as from which the unwaivable right to an equitable remuneration referred to in Article 4 exists, provided that that date is no later than 1 July 1997.

9. For contracts concluded before 1 July 1994, the unwaivable right to an equitable remuneration provided for in Article 4 shall apply only where authors or performers or those representing them have submitted a request to that effect before 1 January 1997. In the absence of agreement between rightholders concerning the level of remuneration, Member States may fix the level of equitable remuneration

Article 14 Relation between copyright and related rights

A9-011 Protection of copyright-related rights under this Directive shall leave intact and shall in no way affect the protection of copyright.

Article 15 Final provisions

1. Member States shall bring into force the laws, regulations and administra- **A9-012** tive provisions necessary to comply with this Directive not later than 1 July 1994. They shall forthwith inform the Commission thereof.

When Member States adopt these measures, they shall contain a reference to this Directive or shall be accompanied by such reference at the time of their official publication. The methods of making such a reference shall be laid down by the Member States.

2. Member States shall communicate to the Commission the main provisions of domestic law which they adopt in the field covered by this Directive.

Article 16

This Directive is addressed to the Member States.

COUNCIL DIRECTIVE 93/83/EEC of 27 September 1993 on the coordination of certain rules concerning copyright and rights related to copyright applicable to satellite broadcasting and cable retransmission

THE COUNCIL OF THE EUROPEAN COMMUNITIES,
Having regard to the Treaty establishing the European Economic Community, and in particular Articles 57 (2) and 66 thereof,
Having regard to the proposal from the Commission,
In cooperation with the European Parliament,
Having regard to the opinion of the Economic and Social Committee,
(1) Whereas the objectives of the Community as laid down in the Treaty include establishing an ever closer union among the peoples of Europe, fostering closer relations between the States belonging to the Community and ensuring the economic and social progress of the Community countries by common action to eliminate the barriers which divide Europe;
(2) Whereas, to that end, the Treaty provides for the establishment of a common market and an area without internal frontiers; whereas measures to achieve this include the abolition of obstacles to the free movement of services and the institution of a system ensuring that competition in the common market is not distorted; whereas, to that end, the Council may adopt directives for the coordination of the provisions laid down by law, regulation or administrative action in Member States concerning the taking up and pursuit of activities as self-employed persons;
(3) Whereas broadcasts transmitted across frontiers within the Community, in particular by satellite and cable, are one of the most important ways of pursuing these Community objectives, which are at the same time political, economic, social, cultural and legal;
(4) Whereas the Council has already adopted Directive 89/552/EEC of 3 October 1989 on the coordination of certain provisions laid down by law, regulation or administrative action in Member States concerning the pursuit of television broadcasting activities, which makes provision for the promotion of the distribution and production of European television programmes and for advertising and sponsorship, the protection of minors and the right of reply;
(5) Whereas, however, the achievement of these objectives in respect of cross-border satellite broadcasting and the cable retransmission of programmes from

other Member States is currently still obstructed by a series of differences between national rules of copyright and some degree of legal uncertainty; whereas this means that holders of rights are exposed to the threat of seeing their works exploited without payment of remuneration or that the individual holders of exclusive rights in various Member States block the exploitation of their rights; whereas the legal uncertainty in particular constitutes a direct obstacle in the free circulation of programmes within the Community;

(6) Whereas a distinction is currently drawn for copyright purposes between communication to the public by direct satellite and communication to the public by communications satellite; whereas, since individual reception is possible and affordable nowadays with both types of satellite, there is no longer any justification for this differing legal treatment;

(7) Whereas the free broadcasting of programmes is further impeded by the current legal uncertainty over whether broadcastsing by a satellite whose signals can be received directly affects the rights in the country of transmission only or in all countries of reception together; whereas, since communications satellites and direct satellites are treated alike for copyright purposes, this legal uncertainty now affects almost all programmes broadcast in the Community by satellite;

(8) Whereas, furthermore, legal certainty, which is a prerequisite for the free movement of broadcasts within the Community, is missing where programmes transmitted across frontiers are fed into and retransmitted through cable networks;

(9) Whereas the development of the acquisition of rights on a contractual basis by authorization is already making a vigorous contribution to the creation of the desired European audiovisual area; whereas the continuation of such contractual agreements should be ensured and their smooth application in practice should be promoted wherever possible;

(10) Whereas at present cable operators in particular cannot be sure that they have actually acquired all the programme rights covered by such an agreement;

(11) Whereas, lastly, parties in different Member States are not all similarly bound by obligations which prevent them from refusing without valid reason to negotiate on the acquisition of the rights necessary for cable distribution or allowing such negotiations to fail;

(12) Whereas the legal framework for the creation of a single audiovisual area laid down in Directive 89/552/EEC must, therefore, be supplemented with reference to copyright;

(13) Whereas, therefore, an end should be put to the differences of treatment of the transmission of programmes by communications satellite which exist in the Member States, so that the vital distinction throughout the Community becomes whether works and other protected subject matter are communicated to the public; whereas this will also ensure equal treatment of the suppliers of cross–border broadcasts, regardless of whether they use a direct broadcasting satellite or a communications satellite;

(14) Whereas the legal uncertainty regarding the rights to be acquired which impedes cross–border satellite broadcasting should be overcome by defining the notion of communication to the public by satellite at a Community level; whereas this definition should at the same time specify where the act of communication takes place; whereas such a definition is necessary to avoid the cumulative application of several national laws to one single act of broadcasting; whereas communication to the public by satellite occurs only when, and in the Member State where, the programme-carrying signals are introduced under the control and responsibility of the broadcasting organization into an uninterrupted chain

of communication leading to the satellite and down towards the earth; whereas normal technical procedures relating to the programme-carrying signals should not be considered as interruptions to the chain of broadcasting;

(15) Whereas the acquisition on a contractual basis of exclusive broadcasting rights should comply with any legislation on copyright and rights related to copyright in the Member State in which communication to the public by satellite occurs;

(16) Whereas the principle of contractual freedom on which this Directive is based will make it possible to continue limiting the exploitation of these rights, especially as far as certain technical means of transmission or certain language versions are concerned;

(17) Whereas, in ariving at the amount of the payment to be made for the rights acquired, the parties should take account of all aspects of the broadcast, such as the actual audience, the potential audience and the language version;

(18) Whereas the application of the country-of-origin principle contained in this Directive could pose a problem with regard to existing contracts; whereas this Directive should provide for a period of five years for existing contracts to be adapted, where necessary, in the light of the Directive; whereas the said country-of-origin principle should not, therefore, apply to existing contracts which expire before 1 January 2000; whereas if by that date parties still have an interest in the contract, the same parties should be entitled to renegotiate the conditions of the contract;

(19) Whereas existing international co-production agreements must be interpreted in the light of the economic purpose and scope envisaged by the parties upon signature; whereas in the past international co-production agreements have often not expressly and specifically addressed communication to the public by satellite within the meaning of this Directive a particular form of exploitation; whereas the underlying philosophy of many existing international co-production agreements is that the rights in the co-production are exercised separately and independently by each co-producer, by dividing the exploitation rights between them along territorial lines; whereas, as a general rule, in the situation where a communication to the public by satellite authorized by one co-producer would prejudice the value of the exploitation rights of another co-producer, the interpretation of such an existing agreement would normally suggest that the latter co-producer would have to give his consent to the authorization, by the former co-producer, of the communication to the public by satellite; whereas the language exclusivity of the latter co-producer will be prejudiced where the language version or versions of the communication to the public, including where the version is dubbed or subtitled, coincide(s) with the language or the languages widely understood in the territory allotted by the agreement to the latter co-producer; whereas the notion of exclusivity should be understood in a wider sense where the communication to the public by satellite concerns a work which consists merely of images and contains no dialogue or subtitles; whereas a clear rule is necessary in cases where the international co-production agreement does not expressly regulate the division of rights in the specific case of communication to the public by satellite within the meaning of this Directive;

(20) Whereas communications to the public by satellite from non-member countries will under certain conditions be deemed to occur within a Member State of the Community;

(21) Whereas it is necessary to ensure that protection for authors, performers, producers of phonograms and broadcasting organizations is accorded in all

Member States and that this protection is not subject to a statutory licence system; whereas only in this way is it possible to ensure that any difference in the level of protection within the common market will not create distortions of competition;

(22) Whereas the advent of new technologies is likely to have an impact on both the quality and the quantity of the exploitation of works and other subject matter;

(23) Whereas in the light of these developments the level of protection granted pursuant to this Directive to all rightholders in the areas covered by this Directive should remain under consideration;

(24) Whereas the harmonization of legislation envisaged in this Directive entails the harmonization of the provisions ensuring a high level of protection of authors, performers, phonogram producers and broadcasting organizations; whereas this harmonization should not allow a broadcasting organization to take advantage of differences in levels of protection by relocating activities, to the detriment of audiovisual productions;

(25) Wheres the protection provided for rights related to copyright should be aligned on that contained in Council Directive 92/100/EEC of 19 November 1992 on rental right and lending right and on certain rights related to copyright in the field of intellectual property (5) for the purposes of communication to the public by satellite; whereas, in particular, this will ensure that peformers and phonogram producers are guaranteed an appropriate remuneration for the communication to the public by satellite of their performances or phonograms;

(26) Whereas the provisions of Article 4 do not prevent Member States from extending the presumption set out in Article 2 (5) of Directive 92/100/EEC to the exclusive rights referred to in Article 4; whereas, furthermore, the provisions of Article 4 do not prevent Member States from providing for a rebuttable presumption of the authoriztion of exploitation in respect of the exclusive rights of performers referred to in that Article, in so far as such presumption is compatible with the International Convention for the Protection of Performers, Producers of Phonograms and Broadcasting Organizations;

(27) Whereas the cable retransmission of programmes from other Member States is an act subject to copyright and, as the case may be, rights related to copyright; whereas the cable operator must, therefore, obtain the authorization from every holder of rights in each part of the programme retransmitted; whereas, pursuant to this Directive, the authorizations should be granted contractually unless a temporary exception is provided for in the case of existing legal licence schemes;

(28) Whereas, in order to ensure that the smooth operation of contractual arrangements is not called into question by the intervention of outsiders holding rights in individual parts of the programme, provision should be made, through the obligation to have recourse to a collecting society, for the exclusive collective exercise of the authorization right to the extent that this is required by the special features of cable retransmission; whereas the authorization right as such remains intact and only the exercise of this right is regulated to some extent, so that the right to authorize a cable retransmission can still be assigned; whereas this Directive does not affect the exercise of moral rights;

(29) Whereas the exemption provided for in Article 10 should not limit the choice of holders of rights to transfer their rights to a collecting society and thereby have a direct share in the remuneration paid by the cable distributor for cable retransmission;

(30) Whereas contractual arrangements regarding the authorization of cable retransmission should be promoted by additional measures; whereas a party seeking the conclusion of a general contract should, for its part, be obliged to submit collective proposals for an agreement; whereas, furthermore, any party shall be entitled, at any moment, to call upon the assistance of impartial mediators whose task is to assist negotiations and who may submit proposals; whereas any such proposals and any opposition thereto should be served on the parties concerned in accordance with the applicable rules concerning the service of legal documents, in particular as set out in existing international conventions; whereas, finally, it is necessary to ensure that the negotiations are not blocked without valid justification or that individual holders are not prevented without valid justification from taking part in the negotiations; whereas none of these measures for the promotion of the acquisition of rights calls into question the contractual nature of the acquisition of cable retransmission rights;

(31) Whereas for a transitional period Member States should be allowed to retain existing bodies with jurisdiction in their territory over cases where the right to retransmit a programme by cable to the public has been unreasonably refused or offered on unreasonable terms by a broadcasting organization; whereas it is understood that the right of parties concerned to be heard by the body should be guaranteed and that the existence of the body should not prevent the parties concerned from having normal access to the courts;

(32) Whereas, however, Community rules are not needed to deal with all of those matters, the effects of which perhaps with some commercially insignificant exceptions, are felt only inside the borders of a single Member State;

(33) Whereas minimum rules should be laid down in order to establish and guarantee free and uninterrupted cross-border broadcasting by satellite and simultaneous, unaltered cable retransmission of programmes broadcast from other Member States, on an essentially contractual basis;

(34) Whereas this Directive should not prejudice further harmonization in the field of copyright and rights related to copyright and the collective administration of such rights; whereas the possibility for Member States to regulate the activities of collecting societies should not prejudice the freedom of contractual negotiation of the rights provided for in this Directive, on the understanding that such negotiation takes place within the framework of general or specific national rules with regard to competition law or the prevention of abuse of monopolies;

(35) Whereas it should, therefore, be for the Member States to supplement the general provisions needed to achieve the objectives of this Directive by taking legislative and administrative measures in their domestic law, provided that these do not run counter to the objectives of this Directive and are compatible with Community law;

(36) Whereas this Directive does not affect the applicability of the competition rules in Articles 85 and 86 of the Treaty,

HAS ADOPTED THIS DIRECTIVE:

Chapter I

Definitions

Article 1 Definitions

A10-001   1. For the purpose of this Directive, 'satellite' means any satellite operating on frequency bands which, under telecommunications law, are reserved for the broadcast of signals for reception by the public or which are reserved for closed, point-to-point communication. In the latter case, however, the circumstances in which individual reception of the signals takes place must be comparable to those which apply in the first case.

   2.

   (a) For the purpose of this Directive, 'communication to the public by satellite' means the act of introducing, under the control and responsibility of the broadcasting organization, the programme–carrying signals intended for reception by the public into an uninterrupted chain of communication leading to the satellite and down towards the earth.

   (b) The act of communication to the public by satellite occurs solely in the Member State where, under the control and responsibility of the broadcasting organization, the programme–carrying signals are introduced into an uninterrupted chain of communication leading to the satellite and down towards the earth.

   (c) If the programme-carrying signals are encrypted, then there is communication to the public by satellite on condition that the means for decrypting the broadcast are provided to the public by the broadcasting organization or with its consent.

   (d) Where an act of communication to the public by satellite occurs in a non–Community State which does not provide the level of protection provided for under Chapter II,

   (i) if the programme-carrying signals are transmitted to the satellite from an uplink situation situated in a Member State, that act of communication to the public by satellite shall be deemed to have occurred in that Member State and the rights provided for under Chapter II shall be exercisable against the person operating the uplink station; or

   (ii) if there is no use of an uplink station situated in a Member State but a broadcasting organization established in a Member State has commissioned the act of communication to the public by satellite, that act shall be deemed to have occured in the Member State in which the broadcasting organization has its principal establishment in the Community and the rights provided for under Chapter II shall be exercisable against the broadcasting organization.

   3. For the purposes of this Directive, 'cable retransmission' means the simultaneous, unaltered and unabridged retransmission by a cable or microwave system for reception by the public of an initial transmission from another Member State, by wire or over the air, including that by satellite, of television or radio programmes intended for reception by the public.

   4. For the purposes of this Directive 'collecting society' means any organization which manages or administers copyright or rights related to copyright as its sole purpose or as one of its main purposes.

5. For the purposes of this Directive, the principal director of a cinematographic or audiovisual work shall be considered as its author or one of its authors. Member States may provide for others to be considered as its co-authors.

CHAPTER II

BROADCASTING OF PROGRAMMES BY SATELLITE

Article 2

Broadcasting right Member States shall provide an exclusive right for the **A10-002** author to authorize the communication to the public by satellite of copyright works, subject to the provisions set out in this chapter.

Article 3 Acquisition of broadcasting rights

1. Member States shall ensure that the authorization referred to in Article 2 **A10-003** may be acquired only be agreement.

2. A Member State may provide that a collective agreement between a collecting society and a broadcasting organization concerning a given category of works may be extended to rightholders of the same category who are not represented by the collecting society, provided that:
  – the communication to the public by satellite simulcasts a terrestrial broadcast by the same broadcaster, and
  –the unrepresented rightholder shall, at any time, have the possibility of excluding the extension of the collective agreement to his works and of exercising his rights either individually or collectively.

3. Paragraph 2 shall not apply to cinematographic works, including works created by a process analogous to cinematography.

4. Where the law of a Member State provides for the extension of a collective agreement in accordance with the provisions of paragraph 2, that Member States shall inform the Commission which broadcasting organizations are entitled to avail themselves of that law. The Commission shall publish this information in the Official Journal of the European Communities (C series).

Article 4 Rights of performers, phonogram producers and broadcasting organizations

1. For the purposes of communication to the public by satellite, the rights of **A10-004** performers, phonogram producers and broadcasting organizations shall be protected in accordance with the provisions of Articles 6, 7, 8 and 10 of Directive 92/100/EEC.

2. For the purposes of paragraph 1, 'broadcasting by wireless means' in Directive 92/100/EEC shall be understood as including communication to the public by satellite.

3. With regard to the exercise of the rights referred to in paragraph 1, Articles 2 (7) and 12 of Directive 92/100/EEC shall apply.

Article 5 Relation between copyright and related rights

Protection of copyright-related rights under this Directive shall leave intact **A10-005** and shall in no way affect the protection of copyright.

Article 6 Minimum protection

A10-006   1. Member States may provide for more far-reaching protection for holders of rights related to copyright than that required by Article 8 of Directive 92/100/EEC.

2. In applying paragraph 1 Member States shall observe the definitions contained in Article 1 (1) and (2).

Article 7 Transitional provisions

A10-007   1. With regard to the application in time of the rights referred to in Article 4 (1) of this Directive, Article 13 (1), (2), (6) and (7) of Directive 92/100/EEC shall apply. Article 13 (4) and (5) of Directive 92/100/EEC shall apply mutatis mutandis.

2. Agreements concerning the exploitation of works and other protected subject matter which are in force on the date mentioned in Article 14 (1) shall be subject to the provisions of Articles 1 (2), 2 and 3 as from 1 January 2000 if they expire after that date.

3. When an international co-production agreement concluded before the date mentioned in Article 14 (1) between a co-producer from a Member State and one or more co-producers from other Member States or third countries expressly provides for a system of division of exploitation rights between the co-producers by geographical areas for all means of communication to the public, without distinguishing the arrangement applicable to communication to the public by satellite from the provisions applicable to the other means of communication, and where communication to the public by satellite of the co-production would prejudice the exclusivity, in particular the language exclusivity, of one of the co-producers or his assignees in a given territory, the authorization by one of the co-producers or his assignees for a communication to the public by satellite shall require the prior consent of the holder of that exclusivity, whether co-producer or assignee.

CHAPTER III

CABLE RETRANSMISSION

Article 8 Cable retransmission right

A10-008   1. Member States shall ensure that when programmes from other Member States are retransmitted by cable in their territory the applicable copyright and related rights are observed and that such retransmission takes place on the basis of individual or collective contractual agreements between copyright owners, holders of related rights and cable operators.

2. Notwithstanding paragraph 1, Member States may retain until 31 December 1997 such statutory licence systems which are in operation or expressly provided for by national law on 31 July 1991.

Article 9 Exercise of the cable retransmission right

A10-009   1. Member States shall ensure that the right of copyright owners and holders or related rights to grant or refuse authorization to a cable operator for a cable retransmission may be exercised only through a collecting society.

2. Where a rightholder has not transferred the management of his rights to a collecting society, the collecting society which manages rights of the same category shall be deemed to be mandated to manage his rights. Where more than

one collecting society manages rights of that category, the rightholder shall be free to choose which of those collecting societies is deemed to be mandated to manage his rights. A rightholder referred to in this paragraph shall have the same rights and obligations resulting from the agreement between the cable operator and the collecting society which is deemed to be mandated to manage his rights as the rightholders who have mandated that collecting society and he shall be able to claim those rights within a period, to be fixed by the Member State concerned, which shallnot be shorter than three years from the date of the cable retransmission which includes his work or other protected subject matter.

3. A Member State may provide that, when a rightholder authorizes the initial transmission within its territory of a work or other protected subject matter, he shall be deemed to have agreed not to exercise his cable retransmission rights on an individual basis but to exercise them in accordance with the provisions of this Directive.

Article 10 Exercise of the cable retransmission right by broadcasting organizations

Member States shall ensure that Article 9 does not apply to the rights **A10-010** exercised by a broadcasting organization in respect of its own transmission, irrespective of whether the rights concerned are its own or have been transferred to it by other copyright owners and/or holders of related rights.

Article 11 Mediators

1. Where no agreement is concluded regarding authorization of the cable **A10-011** retransmission of a broadcast. Member States shall ensure that either party may call upon the assistance of one or more mediators.

2. The task of the mediators shall be to provide assistance with negotiation. They may also submit proposals to the parties.

3. It shall be assumed that all the parties accept a proposal as referred to in paragraph 2 if none of them expresses its opposition within a period of three months. Notice of the proposal and of any opposition thereto shall be served on the parties concerned in accordance with the applicable rules concerning the service of legal documents.

4. The mediators shall be so selected that their independence and impartiality are beyond reasonable doubt.

Article 12 Prevention of the abuse of negotiating positions

1. Member States shall ensure by means of civil or administrative law, as **A10-012** appropriate, that the parties enter and conduct negotiations regarding authorization for cable retransmission in good faith and do not prevent or hinder negotiation without valid justification.

2. A Member State which, on the date mentioned in Article 14 (1), has a body with jurisdiction in its territory over cases where the right to retransmit a programme by cable to the public in that Member State has been unreasonably refused or offered on unreasonable terms by a broadcasting organization may retain that body.

3. Paragraph 2 shall apply for a transitional period of eight years from the date mentioned in Article 14 (1).

CHAPTER IV

GENERAL PROVISIONS

Article 13 Collective administration of rights

A10-013　This Directive shall be without prejudice to the regulation of the activities of collecting societies by the Member States.

Article 14 Final Provisions

A10-014　1. Member States shall bring into force the laws, regulations and administrative provisions necessary to comply with this Directive before 1 January 1995. They shall immediately inform the Commission thereof.

When Member States adopt these measures, the latter shall contain a reference to this Directive or shall be accompanied by such reference at the time of their offical publication. The methods of making such a reference shall be laid down by the Member States.

2. Member States shall communicate to the Commission the provisions of national law which they adopt in the field covered by this Directive.

3. Not later than 1 January 2000, the Commission shall submit to the European Parliament, the Council and the Economic and Social Committee a report on the application of this Directive and, if necessary, make further proposals to adapt it to developments in the audio and audiovisual sector.

Article 15

A10-015　This Directive is addressed to the Member States.

**COUNCIL DIRECTIVE 93/98/EEC of 29 October 1993
harmonizing the term of protection of copyright and certain
related rights. Amended by: Directive 2001/29/EC of the
European Parliment and of the Council of 22 May 2001**

THE COUNCIL OF THE EUROPEAN COMMUNITIES,

Having regard to the Treaty establishing the European Economic Community, and in particular Articles 57 (2), 66 and 100a thereof,

Having regard to the proposal from the Commission,

In cooperation with the European Parliament

Having regard to the opinion of the Economic and Social Committee,

(1) Whereas the Berne Convention for the protection of literary and artistic works and the International Convention for the protection of performers, producers of phonograms and broadcasting organizations (Rome Convention) lay down only minimum terms of protection of the rights they refer to, leaving the Contracting States free to grant longer terms; whereas certain Member States have exercised this entitlement; whereas in addition certain Member States have not become party to the Rome Convention;

(2) Whereas there are consequently differences between the national laws governing the terms of protection of copyright and related rights, which are liable to impede the free movement of goods and freedom to provide services, and to distort competition in the common market; whereas therefore with a view to the smooth operation of the internal market, the laws of the Member States should be harmonized so as to make terms of protection identical throughout the Community;

(3) Whereas harmonization must cover not only the terms of protection as such, but also certain implementing arrangements such as the date from which each term of protection is calculated;

(4) Whereas the provisions of this Directive do not affect the application by the Member States of the provisions of Article 14a (2) (b), (c) and (d) and (3) of the Berne Convention;

(5) Whereas the minimum term of protection laid down by the Berne Convention, namely the life of the author and 50 years after his death, was intended to provide protection for the author and the first two generations of his descendants; whereas the average lifespan in the Community has grown longer, to the point where this term is no longer sufficient to cover two generations;

(6) Whereas certain Member States have granted a term longer than 50 years after the death of the author in order to offset the effects of the world wars on the exploitation of authors' works;

(7) Whereas for the protection of related rights certain Member States have introduced a term of 50 years after lawful publication or lawful communication to the public;

(8) Whereas under the Community position adopted for the Uruguay Round negotiations under the General Agreement on Tariffs and Trade (GATT) the term of protection for producers of phonograms should be 50 years after first publication;

(9) Whereas due regard for established rights is one of the general principles of law protected by the Community legal order; whereas, therefore, a harmonization of the terms of protection of copyright and related rights cannot have the effect of reducing the protection currently enjoyed by rightholders in the Community; whereas in order to keep the effects of transitional measures to a minimum and to allow the internal market to operate in practice, the harmonization of the term of protection should take place on a long term basis;

(10) Whereas in its communication of 17 January 1991 'Follow-up to the Green Paper - Working programme of the Commission in the field of copyright and neighbouring rights' the Commission stresses the need to harmonize copyright and neighbouring rights at a high level of protection since these rights are fundamental to intellectual creation and stresses that their protection ensures the maintenance and development of creativity in the interest of authors, cultural industries, consumers and society as a whole;

(11) Whereas in order to establish a high level of protection which at the same time meets the requirements of the internal market and the need to establish a legal environment conducive to the harmonious development of literary and artistic creation in the Community, the term of protection for copyright should be harmonized at 70 years after the death of the author or 70 years after the work is lawfully made available to the public, and for related rights at 50 years after the event which sets the term running;

(12) Whereas collections are protected according to Article 2 (5) of the Berne Convention when, by reason of the selection and arrangement of their content, they constitute intellectual creations; whereas those works are protected as such, without prejudice to the copyright in each of the works forming part of such collections, whereas in consequence specific terms of protection may apply to works included in collections;

(13) Whereas in all cases where one or more physical persons are identified as authors the term of protection should be calculated after their death; whereas the question of authorship in the whole or a part of a work is a question of fact which the national courts may have to decide;

(14) Whereas terms of protection should be calculated from the first day of January of the year following the relevant event, as they are in the Berne and Rome Conventions;

(15) Whereas Article 1 of Council Directive 91/250/EEC of 14 May 1991 on the legal protection of computer programs (4) provides that Member States are to protect computer programs, by copyright, as literary works within the meaning of the Berne Convention; whereas this Directive harmonizes the term of protection of literary works in the Community; whereas Article 8 of Directive 91/250/EEC, which merely makes provisional arrangements governing the term of protection of computer programs, should accordingly be repealed;

(16) Whereas Articles 11 and 12 of Council Directive 92/100/EEC of 19 November 1992 on rental right and lending right and on certain rights related to copyright in the field of intellectual property (5) make provision for minimum terms of protection only, subject to any further harmonization; whereas this Directive provides such further harmonization; whereas these Articles should accordingly be repealed;

(17) Whereas the protection of photographs in the Member States is the subject of varying regimes; whereas in order to achieve a sufficient harmonization of the term of protection of photographic works, in particular of those which, due to their artistic or professional character, are of importance within the internal market, it is necessary to define the level of originality required in this Directive; whereas a photographic work within the meaning of the Berne Convention is to be considered original if it is the author's own intellectual creation reflecting his personality, no other criteria such as merit or purpose being taken into account; whereas the protection of other photographs should be left to national law;

(18) Whereas, in order to avoid differences in the term of protection as regards related rights it is necessary to provide the same starting point for the calculation of the term throughout the Community; whereas the performance, fixation, transmission, lawful publication, and lawful communication to the public, that is to say the means of making a subject of a related right perceptible in all appropriate ways to persons in general, should be taken into account for the calculation of the term of protection regardless of the country where this performance, fixation, transmission, lawful publication, or lawful communication to the public takes place;

(19) Whereas the rights of broadcasting organizations in their broadcasts, whether these broadcasts are transmitted by wire or over the air, including by cable or satellite, should not be perpetual; whereas it is therefore necessary to have the term of protection running from the first transmission of a particular broadcast only; whereas this provision is understood to avoid a new term running in cases where a broadcast is identical to a previous one;

(20) Whereas the Member States should remain free to maintain or introduce other rights related to copyright in particular in relation to the protection of critical and scientific publications; whereas, in order to ensure transparency at Community level, it is however necessary for Member States which introduce new related rights to notify the Commission;

(21) Whereas it is useful to make clear that the harmonization brought about by this Directive does not apply to moral rights;

(22) Whereas, for works whose country of origin within the meaning of the Berne Convention is a third country and whose author is not a Community national, comparison of terms of protection should be applied, provided that the term accorded in the Community does not exceed the term laid down in this Directive

(23) Whereas where a rightholder who is not a Community national qualifies for protection under an international agreement the term of protection of related rights should be the same as that laid down in this Directive, except that it should not exceed that fixed in the country of which the rightholder is a national;

(24) Whereas comparison of terms should not result in Member States being brought into conflict with their international obligations;

(25) Whereas, for the smooth functioning of the internal market this Directive should be applied as from 1 July 1995;

(26) Whereas Member States should remain free to adopt provisions on the interpretation, adaptation and further execution of contracts on the exploitation of protected works and other subject matter which were concluded before the extension of the term of protection resulting from this Directive;

(27) Whereas respect of acquired rights and legitimate expectations is part of the Community legal order; whereas Member States may provide in particular that in certain circumstances the copyright and related rights which are revived pursuant to this Directive may not give rise to payments by persons who undertook in good faith the exploitation of the works at the time when such works lay within the public domain,

HAS ADOPTED THIS DIRECTIVE:

Article 1 Duration of authors' rights

1. The rights of an author of a literary or artistic work within the meaning of **A11-001** Article 2 of the Berne Convention shall run for the life of the author and for 70 years after his death, irrespective of the date when the work is lawfully made available to the public.

2. In the case of a work of joint authorship the term referred to in paragraph 1 shall be calculated from the death of the last surviving author.

3. In the case of anonymous or pseudonymous works, the term of protection shall run for seventy years after the work is lawfully made available to the public. However, when the pseudonym adopted by the author leaves no doubt as to his identity, or if the author discloses his identity during the period referred to in the first sentence, the term of protection applicable shall be that laid down in paragraph 1

4. Where a Member State provides for particular provisions on copyright in respect of collective works or for a legal person to be designated as the rightholder, the term of protection shall be calculated according to the provisions of paragraph 3, except if the natural persons who have created the work as such are identified as such in the versions of the work which are made available to the public. This paragraph is without prejudice to the rights of identified authors whose identifiable contributions are included in such works, to which contributions paragraph 1 or 2 shall apply.

5. Where a work is published in volumes, parts, instalments, issues or episodes and the term of protection runs from the time when the work was lawfully made available to the public, the term of protection shall run for each such item separately.

6. In the case of works for which the term of protection is not calculated from the death of the author or authors and which have not been lawfully made available to the public within seventy years from their creation, the protection shall terminate.

Article 2 Cinematographic or audiovisual works

A11-002   1. The principal director of a cinematographic or audiovisual work shall be considered as its author or one of its authors. Member States shall be free to designate other co-authors.

2. The term of protection of cinematographic or audiovisual works shall expire 70 years after the death of the last of the following persons to survive, whether or not these persons are designated as co-authors: the principal director, the author of the screenplay, the author of the dialogue and the composer of music specifically created for use in the cinematographic or audiovisual work.

Article 3 Duration of related rights

A11-003   1. The rights of performers shall expire 50 years after the date of the performance. However, if a fixation of the performance is lawfully published or lawfully communicated to the public within this period, the rights shall expire 50 years from the date of the first such publication or the first such communication to the public, whichever is the earlier.

2. The rights of producers of phonograms shall expire 50 years after the fixation is made. However, if the phonogram is lawfully published or lawfully communicated to the public during this period, the rights shall expire 50 years from the date of the first such publication or the first such communication to the public, whichever is the earlier.

3. The rights of producers of the first fixation of a film shall expire 50 years after the fixation is made. However, if the film is lawfully published or lawfully communicated to the public during this period, the rights shall expire 50 years from the date of the first such publication or the first such communication to the public, whichever is the earlier. The term 'film' shall designate a cinematographic or audiovisual work or moving images, whether or not accompanied by sound.

4. The rights of broadcasting organizations shall expire 50 years after the first transmission of a broadcast, whether this broadcast is transmitted by wire or over the air, including by cable or satellite.

Article 4 Protection of previously unpublished works

A11-004   Any person who, after the expiry of copyright protection, for the first time lawfully publishes or lawfully communicates to the public a previously unpublished work, shall benefit from a protection equivalent to the economic rights of the author. The term of protection of such rights shall be 25 years from the time when the work was first lawfully published or lawfully communicated to the public.

Article 5 Critical and scientific publications

A11-005   Member States may protect critical and scientific publications of works which have come into the public domain. The maximum term of protection of such rights shall be 30 years from the time when the publication was first lawfully published.

Article 6 Protection of photographs

A11-006   Photographs which are original in the sense that they are the author's own intellectual creation shall be protected in accordance with Article 1. No other criteria shall be applied to determine their eligibility for protection. Member States may provide for the protection of other photographs.

Article 7 Protection vis-à-vis third countries

1. Where the country of origin of a work, within the meaning of the Berne **A11-007** Convention, is a third country, and the author of the work is not a Community national, the term of protection granted by the Member States shall expire on the date of expiry of the protection granted in the country of origin of the work, but may not exceed the term laid down in Article 1.

2. The terms of protection laid down in Article 3 shall also apply in the case of rightholders who are not Community nationals, provided Member States grant them protection. However, without prejudice to the international obligations of the Member States, the term of protection granted by Member States shall expire no later than the date of expiry of the protection granted in the country of which the rightholder is a national and may not exceed the term laid down in Article 3.

3. Member States which, at the date of adoption of this Directive, in particular pursuant to their international obligations, granted a longer term of protection than that which would result from the provisions, referred to in paragraphs 1 and 2 may maintain this protection until the conclusion of international agreements on the term of protection by copyright or related rights.

Article 8 Calculation of terms

The terms laid down in this Directive are calculated from the first day of **A11-008** January of the year following the event which gives rise to them.

Article 9 Moral rights

This Directive shall be without prejudice to the provisions of the Member **A11-009** States regulating moral rights

Article 10 Application in time

1. Where a term of protection, which is longer than the corresponding term **A11-010** provided for by this Directive, is already running in a Member State on the date referred to in Article 13 (1), this Directive shall not have the effect of shortening that term of protection in that Member State.

2. The terms of protection provided for in this Directive shall apply to all works and subject matter which are protected in at least one Member State, on the date referred to in Article 13 (1), pursuant to national provisions on copyright or related rights or which meet the criteria for protection under Directive 92/100/EEC.

3. This Directive shall be without prejudice to any acts of exploitation performed before the date referred to in Article 13 (1). Member States shall adopt the necessary provisions to protect in particular acquired rights of third parties.

4. Member States need not apply the provisions of Article 2 (1) to cinematographic or audiovisual works created before 1 July 1994.

5. Member States may determine the date as from which Article 2 (1) shall apply, provided that date is no later than 1 July 1997.

Article 12 Notification procedure

Member States shall immediately notify the Commission of any governmental **A11-011** plan to grant new related rights, including the basic reasons for their introduction and the term of protection envisaged.

Article 13 General provisions

A11-012   1. Member States shall bring into force the laws, regulations and administrative provisions necessary to comply with Articles 1 to 11 of this Directive before 1 July 1995.

When Member States adopt these provisions, they shall contain a reference to this Directive or shall be accompanied by such reference at the time of their official publication. The methods of making such a reference shall be laid down by the Member States.

Member States shall communicate to the Commission the texts of the provisions of national law which they adopt in the field governed by this Directive.

2. Member States shall apply Article 12 from the date of notification of this Directive.

Article 14

A11-013   This Directive is addressed to the Member States.

DIRECTIVE 96/9/EC OF THE EUROPEAN PARLIAMENT AND OF THE COUNCIL of 11 March 1996 on the legal protection of databases

THE EUROPEAN PARLIAMENT AND THE COUNCIL OF THE EUROPEAN UNION,

Having regard to the Treaty establishing the European Community, and in particular Article 57 (2), 66 and 100a thereof,

Having regard to the proposal from the Commission,

Having regard to the opinion of the Economic and Social Committee,

Acting in accordance with the procedure laid down in Article 189b of the Treaty,

(1) Whereas databases are at present not sufficiently protected in all Member States by existing legislation; whereas such protection, where it exists, has different attributes;

(2) Whereas such differences in the legal protection of databases offered by the legislation of the Member States have direct negative effects on the functioning of the internal market as regards databases and in particular on the freedom of natural and legal persons to provide on-line database goods and services on the basis of harmonized legal arrangements throughout the Community; whereas such differences could well become more pronounced as Member States introduce new legislation in this field, which is now taking on an increasingly international dimension;

(3) Whereas existing differences distorting the functioning of the internal market need to be removed and new ones prevented from arising, while differences not adversely affecting the functioning of the internal market or the development of an information market within the Community need not be removed or prevented from arising;

(4) Whereas copyright protection for databases exists in varying forms in the Member States according to legislation or case-law, and whereas, if differences in legislation in the scope and conditions of protection remain between the Member States, such unharmonized intellectual property rights can have the effect of preventing the free movement of goods or services within the Community;

(5) Whereas copyright remains an appropriate form of exclusive right for authors who have created databases;

(6) Whereas, nevertheless, in the absence of a harmonized system of unfair-competition legislation or of case-law, other measures are required in addition to prevent the unauthorized extraction and/or re-utilization of the contents of a database;

(7) Whereas the making of databases requires the investment of considerable human, technical and financial resources while such databases can be copied or accessed at a fraction of the cost needed to design them independently;

(8) Whereas the unauthorized extraction and/or re-utilization of the contents of a database constitute acts which can have serious economic and technical consequences;

(9) Whereas databases are a vital tool in the development of an information market within the Community; whereas this tool will also be of use in many other fields;

(10) Whereas the exponential growth, in the Community and worldwide, in the amount of information generated and processed annually in all sectors of commerce and industry calls for investment in all the Member States in advanced information processing systems;

(11) Whereas there is at present a very great imbalance in the level of investment in the database sector both as between the Member States and between the Community and the world's largest database–producing third countries;

(12) Whereas such an investment in modern information storage and processing systems will not take place within the Community unless a stable and uniform legal protection regime is introduced for the protection of the rights of makers of databases;

(13) Whereas this Directive protects collections, sometimes called 'compilations', of works, data or other materials which are arranged, stored and accessed by means which include electronic, electromagnetic or electro-optical processes or analogous processes;

(14) Whereas protection under this Directive should be extended to cover non-electronic databases;

(15) Whereas the criteria used to determine whether a database should be protected by copyright should be defined to the fact that the selection or the arrangement of the contents of the database is the author's own intellectual creation; whereas such protection should cover the structure of the database;

(16) Whereas no criterion other than originality in the sense of the author's intellectual creation should be applied to determine the eligibility of the database for copyright protection, and in particular no aesthetic or qualitative criteria should be applied;

(17) Whereas the term 'database' should be understood to include literary, artistic, musical or other collections of works or collections of other material such as texts, sound, images, numbers, facts, and data; whereas it should cover collections of independent works, data or other materials which are systematically or methodically arranged and can be individually accessed; whereas this means that a recording or an audiovisual, cinematographic, literary or musical work as such does not fall within the scope of this Directive;

(18) Whereas this Directive is without prejudice to the freedom of authors to decide whether, or in what manner, they will allow their works to be included in a database, in particular whether or not the authorization given is exclusive; whereas the protection of databases by the sui generis right is without prejudice to existing rights over their contents, and whereas in particular where an author or the holder of a related right permits some of his works or subject matter to be included in a database pursuant to a non-exclusive agreement, a third party may make use of those works or subject matter subject to the required consent of the author or of the holder of the related right without the sui generis right of the maker of the database being invoked to prevent him doing so, on condition that those works or subject matter are neither extracted from the database nor re–utilized on the basis thereof;

(19) Whereas, as a rule, the compilation of several recordings of musical performances on a CD does not come within the scope of this Directive, both because, as a compilation, it does not meet the conditions for copyright protection and because it does not represent a substantial enough investment to be eligible under the sui generis right;

(20) Whereas protection under this Directive may also apply to the materials necessary for the operation or consultation of certain databases such as thesaurus and indexation systems;

(21) Whereas the protection provided for in this Directive relates to databases in which works, data or other materials have been arranged systematically or methodically; whereas it is not necessary for those materials to have been physically stored in an organized manner;

(22) Whereas electronic databases within the meaning of this Directive may also include devices such as CD-ROM and CD-i;

(23) Whereas the term 'database' should not be taken to extend to computer programs used in the making or operation of a database, which are protected by Council Directive 91/250/EEC of 14 May 1991 on the legal protection of computer programs (4);

(24) Whereas the rental and lending of databases in the field of copyright and related rights are governed exclusively by Council Directive 92/100/EEC of 19 November 1992 on rental right and lending right and on certain rights related to copyright in the field of intellectual property (5);

(25) Whereas the term of copyright is already governed by Council Directive 93/98/EEC of 29 October 1993 harmonizing the term of protection of copyright and certain related rights (6);

(26) Whereas works protected by copyright and subject matter protected by related rights, which are incorporated into a database, remain nevertheless protected by the respective exclusive rights and may not be incorporated into, or extracted from, the database without the permission of the rightholder or his successors in title;

(27) Whereas copyright in such works and related rights in subject matter thus incorporated into a database are in no way affected by the existence of a separate right in the selection or arrangement of these works and subject matter in a database;

(28) Whereas the moral rights of the natural person who created the database belong to the author and should be exercised according to the legislation of the Member States and the provisions of the Berne Convention for the Protection of Literary and Artistic Works; whereas such moral rights remain outside the scope of this Directive;

(29) Whereas the arrangements applicable to databases created by employees are left to the discretion of the Member States; whereas, therefore nothing in this Directive prevents Member States from stipulating in their legislation that where a database is created by an employee in the execution of his duties or following the instructions given by his employer, the employer exclusively shall be entitled to

exercise all economic rights in the database so created, unless otherwise provided by contract;

(30) Whereas the author's exclusive rights should include the right to determine the way in which his work is exploited and by whom, and in particular to control the distribution of his work to unauthorized persons;

(31) Whereas the copyright protection of databases includes making databases available by means other than the distribution of copies;

(32) Whereas Member States are required to ensure that their national provisions are at least materially equivalent in the case of such acts subject to restrictions as are provided for by this Directive;

(33) Whereas the question of exhaustion of the right of distribution does not arise in the case of on-line databases, which come within the field of provision of services; whereas this also applies with regard to a material copy of such a database made by the user of such a service with the consent of the rightholder; whereas, unlike CD–ROM or CD–i, where the intellectual property is incorporated in a material medium, namely an item of goods, every on–line service is in fact an act which will have to be subject to authorization where the copyright so provides;

(34) Whereas, nevertheless, once the rightholder has chosen to make available a copy of the database to a user, whether by an on-line service or by other means of distribution, that lawful user must be able to access and use the database for the purposes and in the way set out in the agreement with the rightholder, even if such access and use necessitate performance of otherwise restricted acts;

(35) Whereas a list should be drawn up of exceptions to restricted acts, taking into account the fact that copyright as covered by this Directive applies only to the selection or arrangements of the contents of a database; whereas Member States should be given the option of providing for such exceptions in certain cases; whereas, however, this option should be exercised in accordance with the Berne Convention and to the extent that the exceptions relate to the structure of the database; whereas a distinction should be drawn between exceptions for private use and exceptions for reproduction for private purposes, which concerns provisions under national legislation of some Member States on levies on blank media or recording equipment;

(36) Whereas the term 'scientific research' within the meaning of this Directive covers both the natural sciences and the human sciences;

(37) Whereas Article 10 (1) of the Berne Convention is not affected by this Directive;

(38) Whereas the increasing use of digital recording technology exposes the database maker to the risk that the contents of his database may be copied and rearranged electronically, without his authorization, to produce a database of identical content which, however, does not infringe any copyright in the arrangement of his database;

(39) Whereas, in addition to aiming to protect the copyright in the original selection or arrangement of the contents of a database, this Directive seeks to safeguard the position of makers of databases against misappropriation of the results of the financial and professional investment made in obtaining and collection the contents by protecting the whole or substantial parts of a database against certain acts by a user or competitor;

(40) Whereas the object of this sui generis right is to ensure protection of any investment in obtaining, verifying or presenting the contents of a database for the limited duration of the right; whereas such investment may consist in the deployment of financial resources and/or the expending of time, effort and energy;

(41) Whereas the objective of the sui generis right is to give the maker of a database the option of preventing the unauthorized extraction and/or re-utilization of all or a substantial part of the contents of that database; whereas the maker of a database is the person who takes the initiative and the risk of investing; whereas this excludes subcontractors in particular from the definition of maker;

(42) Whereas the special right to prevent unauthorized extraction and/or re-utilization relates to acts by the user which go beyond his legitimate rights and thereby harm the investment; whereas the right to prohibit extraction and/or re–utilization of all or a substantial part of the contents relates not only to the manufacture of a parasitical competing product but also to any user who, through his acts, causes significant detriment, evaluated qualitatively or quantitatively, to the investment;

(43) Whereas, in the case of on-line transmission, the right to prohibit re–utilization is not exhausted either as regards the database or as regards a material copy of the database or of part thereof made by the addressee of the transmission with the consent of the rightholder;

(44) Whereas, when on-screen display of the contents of a database necessitates the permanent or temporary transfer of all or a substantial part of such contents to another medium, that act should be subject to authorization by the rightholder;

(45) Whereas the right to prevent unauthorized extraction and/or re-utilization does not in any way constitute an extension of copyright protection to mere facts or data;

(46) Whereas the existence of a right to prevent the unauthorized extraction and/or re–utilization of the whole or a substantial part of works, data or materials from a database should not give rise to the creation of a new right in the works, data or materials themselves;

(47) Whereas, in the interests of competition between suppliers of information products and services, protection by the sui generis right must not be afforded in such a way as to facilitate abuses of a dominant position, in particular as regards the creation and distribution of new products and services which have an intellectual, documentary, technical, economic or commercial added value; whereas, therefore, the provisions of this Directive are without prejudice to the application of Community or national competition rules;

(48) Whereas the objective of this Directive, which is to afford an appropriate and uniform level of protection of databases as a means to secure the remuneration of the maker of the database, is different from the aim of Directive 95/46/EC of the European Parliament and of the Council of 24 October 1995 on the protection of individuals with regard to the processing of personal data and on the free movement of such data (7), which is to guarantee free circulation of personal data on the basis of harmonized rules designed to protect fundamental rights, notably the right to privacy which is recognized in Article 8 of the European Convention for the Protection of Human Rights and Fundamental Freedoms; whereas the provisions of this Directive are without prejudice to data protection legislation;

(49) Whereas, notwithstanding the right to prevent extraction and/or re–utilization of all or a substantial part of a database, it should be laid down that the maker of a database or rightholder may not prevent a lawful user of the database from extracting and re-utilizing insubstantial parts; whereas, however, that user may not unreasonably prejudice either the legitimate interests of the holder of the sui generis right or the holder of copyright or a related right in respect of the works or subject matter contained in the database;

(50) Whereas the Member States should be given the option of providing for exceptions to the right to prevent the unauthorized extraction and/or re-utilization of a substantial part of the contents of a database in the case of extraction for private purposes, for the purposes of illustration for teaching or scientific research, or where extraction and/or re-utilization are/is carried out in the interests of public security or for the purposes of an administrative or judicial procedure; whereas such operations must not prejudice the exclusive rights of the maker to exploit the database and their purpose must not be commercial;

(51) Whereas the Member States, where they avail themselves of the option to permit a lawful user of a database to extract a substantial part of the contents for the purposes of illustration for teaching or scientific research, may limit that permission to certain categories of teaching or scientific research institution;

(52) Whereas those Member States which have specific rules providing for a right comparable to the sui generis right provided for in this Directive should be permitted to retain, as far as the new right is concerned, the exceptions traditionally specified by such rules;

(53) Whereas the burden of proof regarding the date of completion of the making of a database lies with the maker of the database;

(54) Whereas the burden of proof that the criteria exist for concluding that a substantial modification of the contents of a database is to be regarded as a substantial new investment lies with the maker of the database resulting from such investment;

(55) Whereas a substantial new investment involving a new term of protection may include a substantial verification of the contents of the database;

(56) Whereas the right to prevent unauthorized extraction and/or re-utilization in respect of a database should apply to databases whose makers are nationals or habitual residents of third countries or to those produced by legal persons not established in a Member State, within the meaning of the Treaty, only if such third countries offer comparable protection to databases produced by nationals of a Member State or persons who have their habitual residence in the territory of the Community;

(57) Whereas, in addition to remedies provided under the legislation of the Member States for infringements of copyright or other rights, Member States should provide for appropriate remedies against unauthorized extraction and/or re-utilization of the contents of a database;

(58) Whereas, in addition to the protection given under this Directive to the structure of the database by copyright, and to its contents against unauthorized extraction and/or re-utilization under the sui generis right, other legal provisions in the Member States relevant to the supply of database goods and services continue to apply;

(59) Whereas this Directive is without prejudice to the application to databases composed of audiovisual works of any rules recognized by a Member State's legislation concerning the broadcasting of audiovisual programmes;

(60) Whereas some Member States currently protect under copyright arrangements databases which do not meet the criteria for eligibility for copyright protection laid down in this Directive; whereas, even if the databases concerned are eligible for protection under the right laid down in this Directive to prevent unauthorized extraction and/or re-utilization of their contents, the term of protection under that right is considerably shorter than that which they enjoy under the national arrangements currently in force; whereas harmonization of

the criteria for determining whether a database is to be protected by copyright may not have the effect of reducing the term of protection currently enjoyed by the rightholders concerned; whereas a derogation should be laid down to that effect; whereas the effects of such derogation must be confined to the territories of the Member States concerned,
HAS ADOPTED THIS DIRECTIVE:

CHAPTER I

SCOPE

Article 1 Scope

A12-001   1 This Directive concerns the legal protection of databases in any form.
2. For the purposes of this Directive, 'database' shall mean a collection of independent works, data or other materials arranged in a systematic or methodical way and individually accessible by electronic or other means.
3. Protection under this Directive shall not apply to computer programs used in the making or operation of databases accessible by electronic means.

Article 2 Limitations on the scope

A12-002   This Directive shall apply without prejudice to Community provisions relating to:
(a) the legal protection of computer programs;
(b) rental right, lending right and certain rights related to copyright in the field of intellectual property;
(c) the term of protection of copyright and certain related rights.

CHAPTER II

COPYRIGHT

Article 3 Object of protection

A12-003   1. In accordance with this Directive, databases which, by reason of the selection or arrangement of their contents, constitute the author's own intellectual creation shall be protected as such by copyright. No other criteria shall be applied to determine their eligibility for that protection.
2. The copyright protection of databases provided for by this Directive shall not extend to their contents and shall be without prejudice to any rights subsisting in those contents themselves.

Article 4 Database authorship

A12-004   1. The author of a database shall be the natural person or group of natural persons who created the base or, where the legislation of the Member States so permits, the legal person designated as the rightholder by that legislation.
2. Where collective works are recognized by the legislation of a Member State, the economic rights shall be owned by the person holding the copyright.
3. In respect of a database created by a group of natural persons jointly, the exclusive rights shall be owned jointly.

Article 5 Restricted acts

In respect of the expression of the database which is protectable by copyright, **A12-005** the author of a database shall have the exclusive right to carry out or to authorize:

(a) temporary or permanent reproduction by any means and in any form, in whole or in part;

(b) translation, adaptation, arrangement and any other alteration;

(c) any form of distribution to the public of the database or of copies thereof. The first sale in the Community of a copy of the database by the rightholder or with his consent shall exhaust the right to control resale of that copy within the Community;

(d) any form of distribution to the public of the database or of copies thereof. The first sale in the Community of a copy of the database by the rightholder or with his consent shall exhaust the right to control resale of that copy within the Community;

(e) any reproduction, distribution, communication, display or performance to the public of the results of the acts referred to in (b).

Article 6 Exceptions to restricted acts

1. The performance by the lawful user of a database or of a copy thereof of **A12-006** any of the acts listed in Article 5 which is necessary for the purposes of access to the contents of the databases and normal use of the contents by the lawful user shall not require the authorization of the author of the database. Where the lawful user is authorized to use only part of the database, this provision shall apply only to that part.

2. Member States shall have the option of providing for limitations on the rights set out in Article 5 in the following cases:

(a) in the case of reproduction for private purposes of a non-electronic database;

(b) where there is use for the sole purpose of illustration for teaching or scientific research, as long as the source is indicated and to the extent justified by the non-commercial purpose to be achieved;

(c) where there is use for the purposes of public security of for the purposes of an administrative or judicial procedure;

(d) where other exceptions to copyright which are traditionally authorized under national law are involved, without prejudice to points (a), (b) and (c).

3. In accordance with the Berne Convention for the protection of Literary and Artistic Works, this Article may not be interpreted in such a way as to allow its application to be used in a manner which unreasonably prejudices the rightholder's legitimate interests or conflicts with normal exploitation of the database.

CHAPTER III

SUI GENERISRIGHT

Article 7 Object of protection

1. Member States shall provide for a right for the maker of a database which **A12-007** shows that there has been qualitatively and/or quantitatively a substantial investment in either the obtaining, verification or presentation of the contents to

prevent extraction and/or re-utilization of the whole or of a substantial part, evaluated qualitatively and/or quantitatively, of the contents of that database.

2. For the purposes of this Chapter:

(a) 'extraction' shall mean the permanent or temporary transfer of all or a substantial part of the contents of a database to another medium by any means or in any form;

(b) 're-utilization' shall mean any form of making available to the public all or a substantial part of the contents of a database by the distribution of copies, by renting, by on-line or other forms of transmission. The first sale of a copy of a database within the Community by the righthold-er or with his consent shall exhaust the right to control resale of that copy within the Community;

Public lending is not an act of extraction or re-utilization.

3. The right referred to in paragraph 1 may be transferred, assigned or granted under contractual licence.

4. The right provided for in paragraph 1 shall apply irrespective of the eligibil-ity of that database for protection by copyright or by other rights. Moreover, it shall apply irrespective of eligibility of the contents of that database for protection by copyright or by other rights. Protection of databases under the right provided for in paragraph 1 shall be without prejudice to rights existing in respect of their contents.

5. The repeated and systematic extraction and/or re-utilization of insubstan-tial parts of the contents of the database implying acts which conflict with a normal exploitation of that database or which unreasonably prejudice the legitimate interests of the maker of the database shall not be permitted.

Article 8 Rights and obligations of lawful users

A12-008   1. The maker of a database which is made available to the public in whatever manner may not prevent a lawful user of the database from extracting and/or re-utilizing insubstantial parts of its contents, evaluated qualitatively and/or quanti-tatively, for any purposes whatsoever. Where the lawful user is authorized to extract and/or re-utilize only part of the database, this paragraph shall apply only to that part.

2. A lawful user of a database which is made available to the public in whatever manner may not perform acts which conflict with normal exploitation of the database or unreasonably prejudice the legitimate interests of the maker of the database

3. A lawful user of a database which is made available to the public in any manner may not cause prejudice to the holder of a copyright or related right in respect of the works or subject matter contained in the database.

Article 9 Exceptions to the sui generis right

A12-009   Member States may stipulate that lawful users of a database which is made available to the public in whatever manner may, without the authorization of its maker, extract or re-utilize a substantial part of its contents:

(b) in the case of extraction for the purposes of illustration for teaching or scientific research, as long as the source is indicated and to the extent justified by the non-commercial purpose to be achieved;

(a) in the case of extraction for private purposes of the contents of a non-electronic database;

(c) in the case of extraction and/or re-utilization for the purposes of public security or an administrative or judicial procedure.

Article 10 Term of protection

1. The right provided for in Article 7 shall run from the date of completion **A12-010** of the making of the database. It shall expire fifteen years from the first of January of the year following the date of completion.

2. In the case of a database which is made available to the public in whatever manner before expiry of the period provided for in paragraph 1, the term of protection by that right shall expire fifteen years from the first of January of the year following the date when the database was first made available to the public.

3. Any substantial change, evaluated qualitatively or quantitatively, to the contents of a database, including any substantial change resulting from the accumulation of successive additions, deletions or alterations, which would result in the database being considered to be a substantial new investment, evaluated qualitatively or quantitatively, shall qualify the database resulting from that investment for its own term of protection.

Article 11 Beneficiaries of protection under the sui generis right

1. The right provided for in Article 7 shall apply to database whose makers **A12-011** or rightholders are nationals of a Member State or who have their habitual residence in the territory of the Community.

2. Paragraph 1 shall also apply to companies and firms formed in accordance with the law of a Member State and having their registered office, central administration or principal place of business within the Community; however, where such a company or firm has only its registered office in the territory of the Community, its operations must be genuinely linked on an ongoing basis with the economy of a Member State.

3. Agreements extending the right provided for in Article 7 to databases made in third countries and falling outside the provisions of paragraphs 1 and 2 shall be concluded by the Council acting on a proposal from the Commission. The term of any protection extended to databases by virtue of that procedure shall not exceed that available pursuant to Article 10.

CHAPTER IV

COMMON PROVISIONS

Article 12 Remedies

Member States shall provide appropriate remedies in respect of infringements **A12-012** of the rights provided for in this Directive.

Article 13 Continued application of other legal provisions

This Directive shall be without prejudice to provisions concerning in **A12-013** particular copyright, rights related to copyright or any other rights or obligations subsisting in the data, works or other materials incorporated into a database, patent rights, trade marks, design rights, the protection of national treasures, laws on restrictive practices and unfair competition, trade secrets, security, confidentiality, data protection and privacy, access to public documents, and the law of contract.

Article 14 Application over time

1. Protection pursuant to this Directive as regards copyright shall also be **A12-014** available in respect of databases created prior to the date referred to Article 16 (1)

which on that date fulfil the requirements laid down in this Directive as regards copyright protection of databases.

2. Notwithstanding paragraph 1, where a database protected under copyright arrangements in a Member State on the date of publication of this Directive does not fulfil the eligibility criteria for copyright protection laid down in Article 3 (1), this Directive shall not result in any curtailing in that Member State of the remaining term of protection afforded under those arrangements.

3. Protection pursuant to the provisions of this Directive as regards the right provided for in Article 7 shall also be available in respect of databases the making of which was completed not more than fifteen years prior to the date referred to in Article 16 (1) and which on that date fulfil the requirements laid down in Article 7.

4. The protection provided for in paragraphs 1 and 3 shall be without prejudice to any acts concluded and rights acquired before the date referred to in those paragraphs.

5. In the case of a database the making of which was completed not more than fifteen years prior to the date referred to in Article 16 (1), the term of protection by the right provided for in Article 7 shall expire fifteen years from the first of January following that date.

Article 15 Binding nature of certain provisions

A12-015   Any contractual provision contrary to Articles 6 (1) and 8 shall be null and void.

Article 16 Final provisions

A12-016   1. Member States shall bring into force the laws, regulations and administrative provisions necessary to complywith this Directive before 1 January 1998. When Member States adopt these provisions, they shall contain a reference to this Directive or shall be accompanied by such reference on the occasion of their official publication. The methods of making such reference shall be laid down by Member States.

2. Member States shall communicate to the Commission the text of the provisions of domestic law which they adopt in the field governed by this Directive.

3. Not later than at the end of the third year after the date referred to in paragraph 1, and every three years thereafter, the Commission shall submit to the European Parliament, the Council and the Economic and Social Committee a report on the application of this Directive, in which, inter alia, on the basis of specific information supplied by the Member States, it shall examine in particular the application of the sui generis right, including Articles 8 and 9, and shall verify especially whether the application of this right has led to abuse of a dominant position or other interference with free competition which would justify appropriate measures being taken, including the establishment of non-voluntary licensing arrangements. Where necessary, it shall submit proposals for adjustment of this Directive in line with developments in the area of databases.

Article 17

A12-017   This Directive is addressed to the Member States.

DIRECTIVE 98/44/ EC OF THE EUROPEAN PARLIAMENT AND OF THE COUNCIL of 6 July 1998 on the legal protection of biotechnological inventions

THE EUROPEAN PARLIAMENT AND THE COUNCIL OF THE EUROPEAN UNION,

Having regard to the Treaty establishing the European Community, and in particular Article 57 (2), 66 and 100a thereof,

Having regard to the proposal from the Commission,

Having regard to the opinion of the Economic and Social Committee,

Acting in accordance with the procedure laid down in Article 189b of the Treaty,

(1) Whereas biotechnology and genetic engineering are playing an increasingly important role in a broad range of industries and the protection of biotechnological inventions will certainly be of fundamental importance for the Community's industrial development;

(2) Whereas, in particular in the field of genetic engineering, research and development require a considerable amount of high-risk investment and therefore only adequate legal protection can make them profitable;

(3) Whereas effective and harmonised protection throughout the Member States is essential in order to maintain and encourage investment in the field of biotechnology;

(4) Whereas following the European Parliament's rejection of the joint text, approved by the Conciliation Committee, for a European Parliament and Council Directive on the legal protection of biotechnological inventions (4), the European Parliament and the Council have determined that the legal protection of biotechnological inventions requires clarification;

(5) Whereas differences exist in the legal protection of biotechnological inventions offered by the laws and practices of the different Member States; whereas such differences could create barriers to trade and hence impede the proper functioning of the internal market;

(6) Whereas such differences could well become greater as Member States adopt new and different legislation and administrative practices, or whereas national case-law interpreting such legislation develops differently;

(7) Whereas uncoordinated development of national laws on the legal protection of biotechnological inventions in the Community could lead to further disincentives to trade, to the detriment of the industrial development of such inventions and of the smooth operation of the internal market;

(8) Whereas legal protection of biotechnological inventions does not necessitate the creation of a separate body of law in place of the rules of national patent law; whereas the rules of national patent law remain the essential basis for the legal protection of biotechnological inventions given that they must be adapted or added to in certain specific respects in order to take adequate account of technological developments involving biological material which also fulfil the requirements for patentability;

(9) Whereas in certain cases, such as the exclusion from patentability of plant and animal varieties and of essentially biological processes for the production of plants and animals, certain concepts in national laws based upon international patent and plant variety conventions have created uncertainty regarding the protection of biotechnological and certain microbiological inventions; whereas harmonisation is necessary to clarify the said uncertainty;

(10) Whereas regard should be had to the potential of the development of biotechnology for the environment and in particular the utility of this technology for

the development of methods of cultivation which are less polluting and more economical in their use of ground; whereas the patent system should be used to encourage research into, and the application of, such processes;

(11) Whereas the development of biotechnology is important to developing countries, both in the field of health and combating major epidemics and endemic diseases and in that of combating hunger in the world; whereas the patent system should likewise be used to encourage research in these fields; whereas international procedures for the dissemination of such technology in the Third World and to the benefit of the population groups concerned should be promoted;

(12) Whereas the Agreement on Trade-Related Aspects of Intellectual Property Rights (TRIPs) signed by the European Community and the Member States, has entered into force and provides that patent protection must be guaranteed for products and processes in all areas of technology;

(13) Whereas the Community's legal framework for the protection of biotechnological inventions can be limited to laying down certain principles as they apply to the patentability of biological material as such, such principles being intended in particular to determine the difference between inventions and discoveries with regard to the patentability of certain elements of human origin, to the scope of protection conferred by a patent on a biotechnological invention, to the right to use a deposit mechanism in addition to written descriptions and lastly to the option of obtaining non-exclusive compulsory licences in respect of interdependence between plant varieties and inventions, and conversely;

(14) Whereas a patent for invention does not authorise the holder to implement that invention, but merely entitles him to prohibit third parties from exploiting it for industrial and commercial purposes; whereas, consequently, substantive patent law cannot serve to replace or render superfluous national, European or international law which may impose restrictions or prohibitions or which concerns the monitoring of research and of the use or commercialisation of its results, notably from the point of view of the requirements of public health, safety, environmental protection, animal welfare, the preservation of genetic diversity and compliance with certain ethical standards;

(15) Whereas no prohibition or exclusion exists in national or European patent law (Munich Convention) which precludes a priori the patentability of biological matter;

(16) Whereas patent law must be applied so as to respect the fundamental principles safeguarding the dignity and integrity of the person; whereas it is important to assert the principle that the human body, at any stage in its formation or development, including germ cells, and the simple discovery of one of its elements or one of its products, including the sequence or partial sequence of a human gene, cannot be patented; whereas these principles are in line with the criteria of patentability proper to patent law, whereby a mere discovery cannot be patented;

(17) Whereas significant progress in the treatment of diseases has already been made thanks to the existence of medicinal products derived from elements isolated from the human body and/or otherwise produced, such medicinal products resulting from technical processes aimed at obtaining elements similar in structure to those existing naturally in the human body and whereas, consequently, research aimed at obtaining and isolating such elements valuable to medicinal production should be encouraged by means of the patent system;

(18) Whereas, since the patent system provides insufficient incentive for encouraging research into and production of biotechnological medicines which are needed to combat rare or 'orphan' diseases, the Community and the Member States have a duty to respond adequately to this problem;

(19) Whereas account has been taken of Opinion No 8 of the Group of Advisers on the Ethical Implications of Biotechnology to the European Commission;

(20) Whereas, therefore, it should be made clear that an invention based on an element isolated from the human body or otherwise produced by means of a technical process, which is susceptible of industrial application, is not excluded from patentability, even where the structure of that element is identical to that of a natural element, given that the rights conferred by the patent do not extend to the human body and its elements in their natural environment;

(21) Whereas such an element isolated from the human body or otherwise produced is not excluded from patentability since it is, for example, the result of technical processes used to identify, purify and classify it and to reproduce it outside the human body, techniques which human beings alone are capable of putting into practice and which nature is incapable of accomplishing by itself;

(22) Whereas the discussion on the patentability of sequences or partial sequences of genes is controversial; whereas, according to this Directive, the granting of a patent for inventions which concern such sequences or partial sequences should be subject to the same criteria of patentability as in all other areas of technology: novelty, inventive step and industrial application; whereas the industrial application of a sequence or partial sequence must be disclosed in the patent application as filed;

(23) Whereas a mere DNA sequence without indication of a function does not contain any technical information and is therefore not a patentable invention;

(24) Whereas, in order to comply with the industrial application criterion it is necessary in cases where a sequence or partial sequence of a gene is used to produce a protein or part of a protein, to specify which protein or part of a protein is produced or what function it performs;

(25) Whereas, for the purposes of interpreting rights conferred by a patent, when sequences overlap only in parts which are not essential to the invention, each sequence will be considered as an independent sequence in patent law terms;

(26) Whereas if an invention is based on biological material of human origin or if it uses such material, where a patent application is filed, the person from whose body the material is taken must have had an opportunity of expressing free and informed consent thereto, in accordance with national law;

(27) Whereas if an invention is based on biological material of plant or animal origin or if it uses such material, the patent application should, where appropriate, include information on the geographical origin of such material, if known; whereas this is without prejudice to the processing of patent applications or the validity of rights arising from granted patents;

(28) Whereas this Directive does not in any way affect the basis of current patent law, according to which a patent may be granted for any new application of a patented product;

(29) Whereas this Directive is without prejudice to the exclusion of plant and animal varieties from patentability; whereas on the other hand inventions which concern plants or animals are patentable provided that the application of the invention is not technically confined to a single plant or animal variety;

(30) Whereas the concept 'plant variety' is defined by the legislation protecting new varieties, pursuant to which a variety is defined by its whole genome and

therefore possesses individuality and is clearly distinguishable from other varieties;

(31) Whereas a plant grouping which is characterised by a particular gene (and not its whole genome) is not covered by the protection of new varieties and is therefore not excluded from patentability even if it comprises new varieties of plants;

(32) Whereas, however, if an invention consists only in genetically modifying a particular plant variety, and if a new plant variety is bred, it will still be excluded from patentability even if the genetic modification is the result not of an essentially biological process but of a biotechnological process;

(33) Whereas it is necessary to define for the purposes of this Directive when a process for the breeding of plants and animals is essentially biological;

(34) Whereas this Directive shall be without prejudice to concepts of invention and discovery, as developed by national, European or international patent law;

(35) Whereas this Directive shall be without prejudice to the provisions of national patent law whereby processes for treatment of the human or animal body by surgery or therapy and diagnostic methods practised on the human or animal body are excluded from patentability;

(36) Whereas the TRIPs Agreement provides for the possibility that members of the World Trade Organisation may exclude from patentability inventions, the prevention within their territory of the commercial exploitation of which is necessary to protect ordre public or morality, including to protect human, animal or plant life or health or to avoid serious prejudice to the environment, provided that such exclusion is not made merely because the exploitation is prohibited by their law;

(37) Whereas the principle whereby inventions must be excluded from patentability where their commercial exploitation offends against ordre public or morality must also be stressed in this Directive;

(38) Whereas the operative part of this Directive should also include an illustrative list of inventions excluded from patentability so as to provide national courts and patent offices with a general guide to interpreting the reference to ordre public and morality; whereas this list obviously cannot presume to be exhaustive; whereas processes, the use of which offend against human dignity, such as processes to produce chimeras from germ cells or totipotent cells of humans and animals, are obviously also excluded from patentability;

(39) Whereas ordre public and morality correspond in particular to ethical or moral principles recognised in a Member State, respect for which is particularly important in the field of biotechnology in view of the potential scope of inventions in this field and their inherent relationship to living matter; whereas such ethical or moral principles supplement the standard legal examinations under patent law regardless of the technical field of the invention;

(40) Whereas there is a consensus within the Community that interventions in the human germ line and the cloning of human beings offends against ordre public and morality; whereas it is therefore important to exclude unequivocally from patentability processes for modifying the germ line genetic identity of human beings and processes for cloning human beings;

(41) Whereas a process for cloning human beings may be defined as any process, including techniques of embryo splitting, designed to create a human being with the same nuclear genetic information as another living or deceased human being;

(42) Whereas, moreover, uses of human embryos for industrial or commercial purposes must also be excluded from patentability; whereas in any case such exclusion does not affect inventions for therapeutic or diagnostic purposes which are applied to the human embryo and are useful to it;

(43) Whereas pursuant to Article F(2) of the Treaty on European Union, the Union is to respect fundamental rights, as guaranteed by the European Convention for the Protection of Human Rights and Fundamental Freedoms signed in Rome on 4 November 1950 and as they result from the constitutional traditions common to the Member States, as general principles of Community law;

(44) Whereas the Commission's European Group on Ethics in Science and New Technologies evaluates all ethical aspects of biotechnology; whereas it should be pointed out in this connection that that Group may be consulted only where biotechnology is to be evaluated at the level of basic ethical principles, including where it is consulted on patent law;

(45) Whereas processes for modifying the genetic identity of animals which are likely to cause them suffering without any substantial medical benefit in terms of research, prevention, diagnosis or therapy to man or animal, and also animals resulting from such processes, must be excluded from patentability;

(46) Whereas, in view of the fact that the function of a patent is to reward the inventor for his creative efforts by granting an exclusive but time-bound right, and thereby encourage inventive activities, the holder of the patent should be entitled to prohibit the use of patented self-reproducing material in situations analogous to those where it would be permitted to prohibit the use of patented, non-self-reproducing products, that is to say the production of the patented product itself;

(47) Whereas it is necessary to provide for a first derogation from the rights of the holder of the patent when the propagating material incorporating the protected invention is sold to a farmer for farming purposes by the holder of the patent or with his consent; whereas that initial derogation must authorise the farmer to use the product of his harvest for further multiplication or propagation on his own farm; whereas the extent and the conditions of that derogation must be limited in accordance with the extent and conditions set out in Council Regulation (EC) No 2100/94 of 27 July 1994 on Community plant variety rights;

(48) Whereas only the fee envisaged under Community law relating to plant variety rights as a condition for applying the derogation from Community plant variety rights can be required of the farmer;

(49) Whereas, however, the holder of the patent may defend his rights against a farmer abusing the derogation or against a breeder who has developed a plant variety incorporating the protected invention if the latter fails to adhere to his commitments;

(50) Whereas a second derogation from the rights of the holder of the patent must authorise the farmer to use protected livestock for agricultural purposes;

(51) Whereas the extent and the conditions of that second derogation must be determined by national laws, regulations and practices, since there is no Community legislation on animal variety rights;

(52) Whereas, in the field of exploitation of new plant characteristics resulting from genetic engineering, guaranteed access must, on payment of a fee, be granted in the form of a compulsory licence where, in relation to the genus or species concerned, the plant variety represents significant technical progress of considerable economic interest compared to the invention claimed in the patent;

(53) Whereas, in the field of the use of new plant characteristics resulting from new plant varieties in genetic engineering, guaranteed access must, on payment of a fee, be granted in the form of a compulsory licence where the invention represents significant technical progress of considerable economic interest;

(54) Whereas Article 34 of the TRIPs Agreement contains detailed provisions on the burden of proof which is binding on all Member States; whereas, therefore, a provision in this Directive is not necessary;

(55) Whereas following Decision 93/626/EEC (7) the Community is party to the Convention on Biological Diversity of 5 June 1992; whereas, in this regard, Member States must give particular weight to Article 3 and Article 8(j), the second sentence of Article 16(2) and Article 16(5) of the Convention when bringing into force the laws, regulations and administrative provisions necessary to comply with this Directive;

(56) Whereas the Third Conference of the Parties to the Biodiversity Convention, which took place in November 1996, noted in Decision III/17 that 'further work is required to help develop a common appreciation of the relationship between intellectual property rights and the relevant provisions of the TRIPs Agreement and the Convention on Biological Diversity, in particular on issues relating to technology transfer and conservation and sustainable use of biological diversity and the fair and equitable sharing of benefits arising out of the use of genetic resources, including the protection of knowledge, innovations and practices of indigenous and local communities embodying traditional lifestyles relevant for the conservation and sustainable use of biological diversity',

HAS ADOPTED THIS DIRECTIVE:

Chapter I

Patentability

Article 1

A13-001   1. Member States shall protect biotechnological inventions under national patent law. They shall, if necessary, adjust their national patent law to take account of the provisions of this Directive.

2. This Directive shall be without prejudice to the obligations of the Member States pursuant to international agreements, and in particular the TRIPs Agreement and the Convention on Biological Diversity.

Article 2

A13-002   1 For the purposes of this Directive,

  (a) 'biological material' means any material containing genetic information and capable of reproducing itself or being reproduced in a biological system;

  (b) 'microbiological process' means any process involving or performed upon or resulting in microbiological material.

2. A process for the production of plants or animals is essentially biological if it consists entirely of natural phenomena such as crossing or selection.

3. The concept of 'plant variety' is defined by Article 5 of Regulation (EC) No 2100/94.

Article 3

1. For the purposes of this Directive, inventions which are new, which involve   **A13-003**
an inventive step and which are susceptible of industrial application shall be
patentable even if they concern a product consisting of or containing biological
material or a process by means of which biological material is produced,
processed or used.

2. Biological material which is isolated from its natural environment or
produced by means of a technical process may be the subject of an invention even
if it previously occurred in nature.

Article 4

1 The following shall not be patentable: **A13-004**
   (a) plant and animal varieties;
   (b) essentially biological processes for the production of plants or animals.

2. Inventions which concern plants or animals shall be patentable if the
technical feasibility of the invention is not confined to a particular plant or
animal variety.

3. Paragraph 1(b) shall be without prejudice to the patentability of inventions
which concern a microbiological or other technical process or a product
obtained by means of such a process.

Article 5

1. The human body, at the various stages of its formation and development,   **A13-005**
and the simple discovery of one of its elements, including the sequence or partial
sequence of a gene, cannot constitute patentable inventions.

2. An element isolated from the human body or otherwise produced by
means of a technical process, including the sequence or partial sequence of a
gene, may constitute a patentable invention, even if the structure of that element is
identical to that of a natural element.

3. The industrial application of a sequence or a partial sequence of a gene
must be disclosed in the patent application.

Article 6

1. Inventions shall be considered unpatentable where their commercial exploi-   **A13-006**
tation would be contrary to ordre public or morality; however, exploitation shall
not be deemed to be so contrary merely because it is prohibited by law or
regulation.

2. On the basis of paragraph 1, the following, in particular, shall be
considered unpatentable:
   (a) processes for cloning human beings;
   (b) processes for modifying the germ line genetic identity of human
       beings;
   (c) uses of human embryos for industrial or commercial purposes;
   (d) processes for modifying the genetic identity of animals which are likely
       to cause them suffering without any substantial medical benefit to man
       or animal, and also animals resulting from such processes.

Article 7

The Commission's European Group on Ethics in Science and New Technolo-   **A13-007**
gies evaluates all ethical aspects of biotechnology.

Chapter II

Scope of protection

Article 8

A13-008   1. The protection conferred by a patent on a biological material possessing specific characteristics as a result of the invention shall extend to any biological material derived from that biological material through propagation or multiplication in an identical or divergent form and possessing those same characteristics.

2. The protection conferred by a patent on a process that enables a biological material to be produced possessing specific characteristics as a result of the invention shall extend to biological material directly obtained through that process and to any other biological material derived from the directly obtained biological material through propagation or multiplication in an identical or divergent form and possessing those same characteristics.

Article 9

A13-009   The protection conferred by a patent on a product containing or consisting of genetic information shall extend to all material, save as provided in Article 5(1), in which the product in incorporated and in which the genetic information is contained and performs its function.

Article 10

A13-010   The protection referred to in Articles 8 and 9 shall not extend to biological material obtained from the propagation or multiplication of biological material placed on the market in the territory of a Member State by the holder of the patent or with his consent, where the multiplication or propagation necessarily results from the application for which the biological material was marketed, provided that the material obtained is not subsequently used for other propagationor multiplication.

Article 11

A13-011   1. By way of derogation from Articles 8 and 9, the sale or other form of commercialisation of plant propagating material to a farmer by the holder of the patent or with his consent for agricultural use implies authorisation for the farmer to use the product of his harvest for propagation or multiplication by him on his own farm, the extent and conditions of this derogation corresponding to those under Article 14 of Regulation (EC) No 2100/94.

2. By way of derogation from Articles 8 and 9, the sale or any other form of commercialisation of breeding stock or other animal reproductive material to a farmer by the holder of the patent or with his consent implies authorisation for the farmer to use the protected livestock for an agricultural purpose. This includes making the animal or other animal reproductive material available for the purposes of pursuing his agricultural activity but not sale within the framework or for the purpose of a commercial reproduction activity.

3. The extent and the conditions of the derogation provided for in paragraph 2 shall be determined by national laws, regulations and practices.

Chapter III

Compulsory cross-licensing

Article 12

1. Where a breeder cannot acquire or exploit a plant variety right without **A13-012** infringing a prior patent, he may apply for a compulsory licence for non-exclusive use of the invention protected by the patent inasmuch as the licence is necessary for the exploitation of the plant variety to be protected, subject to payment of an appropriate royalty. Member States shall provide that, where such a licence is granted, the holder of the patent will be entitled to a cross-licence on reasonable terms to use the protected variety.

2. Where the holder of a patent concerning a biotechnological invention cannot exploit it without infringing a prior plant variety right, he may apply for a compulsory licence for non-exclusive use of the plant variety protected by that right, subject to payment of an appropriate royalty. Member States shall provide that, where such a licence is granted, the holder of the variety right will be entitled to a cross-licence on reasonable terms to use the protected invention.

3. Applicants for the licences referred to in paragraphs 1 and 2 must demonstrate that:

(a) they have applied unsuccessfully to the holder of the patent or of the plant variety right to obtain a contractual licence;

(b) the plant variety or the invention constitutes significant technical progress of considerable economic interest compared with the invention claimed in the patent or the protected plant variety.

4. Each Member State shall designate the authority or authorities responsible for granting the licence. Where a licence for a plant variety can be granted only by the Community Plant Variety Office, Article 29 of Regulation (EC) No 2100/94 shall apply.

Chapter IV

Deposit, access and re-deposit of a biological material

Article 13

1. Where an invention involves the use of or concerns biological material **A13-013** which is not available to the public and which cannot be described in a patent application in such a manner as to enable the invention to be reproduced by a person skilled in the art, the description shall be considered inadequate for the purposes of patent law unless:

(a) the biological material has been deposited no later than the date on which the patent application was filed with a recognised depositary institution. At least the international depositary authorities which acquired this status by virtue of Article 7 of the Budapest Treaty of 28 April 1977 on the international recognition of the deposit of micro-organisms for the purposes of patent procedure, hereinafter referred to as the 'Budapest Treaty', shall be recognised;

(b) the application as filed contains such relevant information as is available to the applicant on the characteristics of the biological material deposited;

(c) the patent application states the name of the depository institution and the accession number.

2. Access to the deposited biological material shall be provided through the supply of a sample:

(a) up to the first publication of the patent application, only to those persons who are authorised under national patent law;

(b) between the first publication of the application and the granting of the patent, to anyone requesting it or, if the applicant so requests, only to an independent expert;

(c) after the patent has been granted, and notwithstanding revocation or cancellation of the patent, to anyone requesting it.

3. The sample shall be supplied only if the person requesting it undertakes, for the term during which the patent is in force:

(a) not to make it or any material derived from it available to third parties; and

(b) not to use it or any material derived from it except for experimental purposes, unless the applicant for or proprietor of the patent, as applicable, expressly waives such an undertaking.

4. At the applicant's request, where an application is refused or withdrawn, access to the deposited material shall be limited to an independent expert for 20 years from the date on which the patent application was filed. In that case, paragraph 3 shall apply.

5. The applicant's requests referred to in point (b) of paragraph 2 and in paragraph 4 may only be made up to the date on which the technical preparations for publishing the patent application are deemed to have been completed.

Article 14

A13-014   1. If the biological material deposited in accordance with Article 13 ceases to be available from the recognised depositary institution, a new deposit of the material shall be permitted on the same terms as those laid down in the Budapest Treaty.

2. Any new deposit shall be accompanied by a statement signed by the depositor certifying that the newly deposited biological material is the same as that originally deposited.

CHAPTER V

FINAL PROVISIONS

Article 15

A13-015   1. Member States shall bring into force the laws, regulations and administrative provisions necessary to comply with this Directive not later than 30 July 2000. They shall forthwith inform the Commission thereof.

When Member States adopt these measures, they shall contain a reference to this Directive or shall be accompanied by such reference on the occasion of their official publication. The methods of making such reference shall be laid down by Member States.

2. Member States shall communicate to the Commission the text of the provisions of national law which they adopt in the field covered by this Directive.

Article 16

The Commission shall send the European Parliament and the Council:

(a) every five years as from the date specified in Article 15(1) a report on any problems encountered with regard to the relationship between this Directive and international agreements on the protection of human rights to which the Member States have acceded; **A13-016**

(b) within two years of entry into force of this Directive, a report assessing the implications for basic genetic engineering research of failure to publish, or late publication of, papers on subjects which could be patentable;

(c) annually as from the date specified in Article 15(1), a report on the development and implications of patent law in the field of biotechnology and genetic engineering.

Article 17

This Directive shall enter into force on the day of its publication in the **A13-017** Official Journal of the European Communities.

Article 18

This Directive is addressed to the Member States. **A13-018**

DIRECTIVE 98/71/EC OF THE EUROPEAN PARLIAMENT AND OF THE COUNCIL of 13 October 1998 on the legal protection of designs

THE EUROPEAN PARLIAMENT AND THE COUNCIL OF THE EUROPEAN UNION,

Having regard to the Treaty establishing the European Community and in particular Article 100a thereof,

Having regard to the proposal from the Commission,

Having regard to the opinion of the Economic and Social Committee,

Acting in accordance with the procedure laid down in Article 189b of the Treaty, in the light of the joint text approved by the Conciliation Committee on 29 July 1998,

(1) Whereas the objectives of the Community, as laid down in the Treaty, include laying the foundations of an ever closer union among the peoples of Europe, fostering closer relations between Member States of the Community, and ensuring the economic and social progress of the Community countries by common action to eliminate the barriers which divide Europe; whereas to that end the Treaty provides for the establishment of an internal market characterised by the abolition of obstacles to the free movement of goods and also for the institution of a system ensuring that competition in the internal market is not distorted; whereas an approximation of the laws of the Member States on the legal protection of designs would further those objectives;

(2) Whereas the differences in the legal protection of designs offered by the legislation of the Member States directly affect the establishment and functioning of the internal market as regards goods embodying designs; whereas such differences can distort competition within the internal market;

(3) Whereas it is therefore necessary for the smooth functioning of the internal market to approximate the design protection laws of the Member States;

(4) Whereas, in doing so, it is important to take into consideration the solutions and the advantages with which the Community design system will provide undertakings wishing to acquire design rights;

(5) Whereas it is unnecessary to undertake a full-scale approximation of the design laws of the Member States, and it will be sufficient if approximation is limited to those national provisions of law which most directly affect the functioning of the internal market; whereas provisions on sanctions, remedies and enforcement should be left to national law; whereas the objectives of this limited approximation cannot be sufficiently achieved by the Member States acting alone;

(6) Whereas Member States should accordingly remain free to fix the procedural provisions concerning registration, renewal and invalidation of design rights and provisions concerning the effects of such invalidity;

(7) Whereas this Directive does not exclude the application to designs of national or Community legislation providing for protection other than that conferred by registration or publication as design, such as legislation relating to unregistered design rights, trade marks, patents and utility models, unfair competition or civil liability;

(8) Whereas, in the absence of harmonisation of copyright law, it is important to establish the principle of cumulation of protection under specific registered design protection law and under copyright law, whilst leaving Member States free to establish the extent of copyright protection and the conditions under which such protection is conferred;

(9) Whereas the attainment of the objectives of the internal market requires that the conditions for obtaining a registered design right be identical in all the Member States; whereas to that end it is necessary to give a unitary definition of the notion of design and of the requirements as to novelty and individual character with which registered design rights must comply;

(10) Whereas it is essential, in order to facilitate the free movement of goods, to ensure in principle that registered design rights confer upon the right holder equivalent protection in all Member States;

(11) Whereas protection is conferred by way of registration upon the right holder for those design features of a product, in whole or in part, which are shown visibly in an application and made available to the public by way of publication or consultation of the relevant file;

(12) Whereas protection should not be extended to those component parts which are not visible during normal use of a product, or to those features of such part which are not visible when the part is mounted, or which would not, in themselves, fulfil the requirements as to novelty and individual character; whereas features of design which are excluded from protection for these reasons should not be taken into consideration for the purpose of assessing whether other features of the design fulfil the requirements for protection;

(13) Whereas the assessment as to whether a design has individual character should be based on whether the overall impression produced on an informed user viewing the design clearly differs from that produced on him by the existing design corpus, taking into consideration the nature of the product to which the design is applied or in which it is incorporated, and in particular the industrial sector to which it belongs and the degree of freedom of the designer in developing the design;

(14) Whereas technological innovation should not be hampered by granting design protection to features dictated solely by a technical function; whereas

it is understood that this does not entail that a design must have an aesthetic quality; whereas, likewise, the interoperability of products of different makes should not be hindered by extending protection to the design of mechanical fittings; whereas features of a design which are excluded from protection for these reasons should not be taken into consideration for the purpose of assessing whether other features of the design fulfil the requirements for protection;

(15) Whereas the mechanical fittings of modular products may nevertheless constitute an important element of the innovative characteristics of modular products and present a major marketing asset and therefore should be eligible for protection;

(16) Whereas a design right shall not subsist in a design which is contrary to public policy or to accepted principles of morality; whereas this Directive does not constitute a harmonisation of national concepts of public policy or accepted principles of morality;

(17) Whereas it is fundamental for the smooth functioning of the internal market to unify the term of protection afforded by registered design rights;

(18) Whereas the provisions of this Directive are without prejudice to the application of the competition rules under Articles 85 and 86 of the Treaty;

(19) Whereas the rapid adoption of this Directive has become a matter of urgency for a number of industrial sectors; whereas full-scale approximation of the laws of the Member States on the use of protected designs for the purpose of permitting the repair of a complex product so as to restore its original appearance, where the product incorporating the design or to which the design is applied constitutes a component part of a complex product upon whose appearance the protected design is dependent, cannot be introduced at the present stage; whereas the lack of full-scale approximation of the laws of the Member States on the use of protected designs for such repair of a complex product should not constitute an obstacle to the approximation of those other national provisions of design law which most directly affect the functioning of the internal market; whereas for this reason Member States should in the meantime maintain in force any provisions in conformity with the Treaty relating to the use of the design of a component part used for the purpose of the repair of a complex product so as to restore its original appearance, or, if they introduce any new provisions relating to such use, the purpose of these provisions should be only to liberalise the market in such parts; whereas those Member States which, on the date of entry into force of this Directive, do not provide for protection for designs of component parts are not required to introduce registration of designs for such parts; whereas three years after the implementation date the Commission should submit an analysis of the consequences of the provisions of this Directive for Community industry, for consumers, for competition and for the functioning of the internal market; whereas, in respect of component parts of complex products, the analysis should, in particular, consider harmonisation on the basis of possible options, including a remuneration system and a limited term of exclusivity; whereas, at the latest one year after the submission of its analysis, the Commission should, after consultation with the parties most affected, propose to the European Parliament and the Council any changes to this Directive needed to complete the internal market in respect of component parts of complex products, and any other changes which it considers necessary;

(20) Whereas the transitional provision in Article 14 concerning the design of a component part used for the purpose of the repair of a complex product so as to restore its original appearance is in no case to be construed as constituting an obstacle to the free movement of a product which constitutes such a component part;

(21) Whereas the substantive grounds for refusal of registration in those Member States which provide for substantive examination of applications prior to registration, and the substantive grounds for the invalidation of registered design rights in all the Member States, must be exhaustively enumerated,

HAS ADOPTED THIS DIRECTIVE:

Article 1 Definitions

A15-001   For the purpose of this Directive:

(a) 'design' means the appearance of the whole or a part of a product resulting from the features of, in particular, the lines, contours, colours, shape, texture and/or materials of the product itself and/or its ornamentation;

(b) 'product' means any industrial or handicraft item, including inter alia parts intended to be assembled into a complex product, packaging, get–up, graphic symbols and typographic typefaces, but excluding computer programs;

(c) 'complex product' means a product which is composed of multiple components which can be replaced permitting disassembly and reassembly of the product.

Article 2 Scope of application

A15-002   1. This Directive shall apply to:

(a) design rights registered with the central industrial property offices of the Member States;

(b) design rights registered at the Benelux Design Office;

(c) design rights registered under international arrangements which have effect in a Member State;

(d) applications for design rights referred to under (a), (b) and (c).

2. For the purpose of this Directive, design registration shall also comprise the publication following filing of the design with the industrial property office of a Member State in which such publication has the effect of bringing a design right into existence.

Article 3 Protection requirements

A15-003   1. Member States shall protect designs by registration, and shall confer exclusive rights upon their holders in accordance with the provisions of this Directive.

2. A design shall be protected by a design right to the extent that it is new and has individual character.

3. A design applied to or incorporated in a product which constitutes a component part of a complex product shall only be considered to be new and to have individual character:

(a) if the component part, once it has been incorporated into the complex product, remains visible during normal use of the latter, and

(b) to the extent that those visible features of the component part fulfil in themselves the requirements as to novelty and individual character.

4. 'Normal use' within the meaning of paragraph (3)(a) shall mean use by the end user, excluding maintenance, servicing or repair work.

Article 4 Novelty

A design shall be considered new if no identical design has been made A15-004 available to the public before the date of filing of the application for registration or, if priority is claimed, the date of priority. Designs shall be deemed to be identical if their features differ only in immaterial details.

Article 5 Individual character

1. A design shall be considered to have individual character if the overall A15-005 impression it produces on the informed user differs from the overall impression produced on such a user by any design which has been made available to the public before the date of filing of the application for registration or, if priority is claimed, the date of priority.

2. In assessing individual character, the degree of freedom of the designer in developing the design shall be taken into consideration.

Article 6 Disclosure

1. For the purpose of applying Articles 4 and 5, a design shall be deemed to A15-006 have been made available to the public if it has been published following registration or otherwise, or exhibited, used in trade or otherwise disclosed, except where these events could not reasonably have become known in the normal course of business to the circles specialised in the sector concerned, operating within the Community, before the date of filing of the application for registration or, if priority is claimed, the date of priority. The design shall not, however, be deemed to have been made available to the public for the sole reason that it has been disclosed to a third person under explicit or implicit conditions of confidentiality.

2. A disclosure shall not be taken into consideration for the purpose of applying Articles 4 and 5 if a design for which protection is claimed under a registered design right of a Member State has been made available to the public:
   (a) by the designer, his successor in title, or a third person as a result of information provided or action taken by the designer, or his successor in title; and
   (b) during the 12-month period preceding the date of filing of the application or, if priority is claimed, the date of priority.

3. Paragraph 2 shall also apply if the design has been made available to the public as a consequence of an abuse in relation to the designer or his successor in title.

Article 7 Designs dictated by their technical function and designs of interconnections

1. A design right shall not subsist in features of appearance of a product A15-007 which are solely dictated by its technical function.

2. A design right shall not subsist in features of appearance of a product which must necessarily be reproduced in their exact form and dimensions in order to permit the product in which the design is incorporated or to which it is applied to be mechanically connected to or placed in, around or against another product so that either product may perform its function.

3. Notwithstanding paragraph 2, a design right shall, under the conditions set out in Articles 4 and 5, subsist in a design serving the purpose of allowing

multiple assembly or connection of mutually interchangeable products within a modular system.

Article 8 Designs contrary to public policy or moralit

A15-008   A design right shall not subsist in a design which is contrary to public policy or to accepted principles of morality.

Article 9 Scope of protection

A15-009   1. The scope of the protection conferred by a design right shall include any design which does not produce on the informed user a different overall impression.

2. In assessing the scope of protection, the degree of freedom of the designer in developing his design shall be taken into consideration.

Article 10 Term of protection

A15-010   Upon registration, a design which meets the requirements of Article 3(2) shall be protected by a design right for one or more periods of five years from the date of filing of the application. The right holder may have the term of protection renewed for one or more periods of five years each, up to a total term of 25 years from the date of filing.

Article 11 Invalidity or refusal of registration

A15-011   1. A design shall be refused registration, or, if the design has been registered, the design right shall be declared invalid:

(a) if the design is not a design within the meaning of Article 1(a); or

(b) if it does not fulfil the requirements of Articles 3 to 8; or

(c) if the applicant for or theholder of the design right is not entitled to it under the law of the Member State concerned; or

(d) if the design is in conflict with a prior design which has been made available to the public after the date of filing of the application or, if priority is claimed, the date of priority, and which is protected from a date prior to the said date by a registered Community design or an application for a registered Community design or by a design right of the Member State concerned, or by an application for such a right.

2. Any Member State may provide that a design shall be refused registration, or, if the design has been registered, that the design right shall be declared invalid:

(a)   if a distinctive sign is used in a subsequent design, and Community law or the law of the Member State concerned governing that sign confers on the right holder of the sign the right to prohibit such use; or

(b) if the design constitutes an unauthorised use of a work protected under the copyright law of the Member State concerned; or

(c) if the design constitutes an improper use of any of the items listed in Article 6b of the Paris Convention for the Protection of Industrial Property, or of badges, emblems and escutcheons other than those covered by Article 6b of the said Convention which are of particular public interest in the Member State concerned.

3. The ground provided for in paragraph 1(c) may be invoked solely by the person who is entitled to the design right under the law of the Member State concerned.

4. The grounds provided for in paragraph 1(d) and in paragraph 2(a) and (b) may be invoked solely by the applicant for or the holder of the conflicting right.

5. The ground provided for in paragraph 2(c) may be invoked solely by the person or entity concerned by the use.

6. Paragraphs 4 and 5 shall be without prejudice to the freedom of Member States to provide that the grounds provided for in paragraphs 1(d) and 2(c) may also be invoked by the appropriate authority of the Member State in question on its own initiative.

7. When a design has been refused registration or a design right has been declared invalid pursuant to paragraph 1(b) or to paragraph 2, the design may be registered or the design right maintained in an amended form, if in that form it complies with the requirements for protection and the identity of the design is retained. Registration or maintenance in an amended form may include registration accompanied by a partial disclaimer by the holder of the design right or entry in the design Register of a court decision declaring the partial invalidity of the design right.

8. Any Member State may provide that, by way of derogation from paragraphs 1 to 7, the grounds for refusal of registration or for invalidation in force in that State prior to the date on which the provisions necessary to comply with this Directive enter into force shall apply to design applications which have been made prior to that date and to resulting registrations.

9. A design right may be declared invalid even after it has lapsed or has been surrendered.

Article 12 Rights conferred by the design right

1. The registration of a design shall confer on its holder the exclusive right to **A15-012** use it and to prevent any third party not having his consent from using it. The aforementioned use shall cover, in particular, the making, offering, putting on the market, importing, exporting or using of a product in which the design is incorporated or to which it is applied, or stocking such a product for those purposes.

2. Where, under the law of a Member State, acts referred to in paragraph 1 could not be prevented before the date on which the provisions necessary to comply with this Directive entered into force, the rights conferred by the design right may not be invoked to prevent continuation of such acts by any person who had begun such acts prior to that date.

Article 13 Limitation of the rights conferred by the design right

1. The rights conferred by a design right upon registration shall not be **A15-013** exercised in respect of:
   (a) acts done privately and for non-commercial purposes;
   (b) acts done for experimental purposes;
   (c) acts of reproduction for the purposes of making citations or of teaching, provided that such acts are compatible with fair trade practice and do not unduly prejudice the normal exploitation of the design, and that mention is made of the source.

2. In addition, the rights conferred by a design right upon registration shall not be exercised in respect of:
   (a) the equipment on ships and aircraft registered in another country when these temporarily enter the territory of the Member State concerned;
   (b) the importation in the Member State concerned of spare parts and accessories for the purpose of repairing such craft;
   (c) the execution of repairs on such craft.

Article 14 Transitional provision

A15-014   Until such time as amendments to this Directive are adopted on a proposal from the Commission in accordance with the provisions of Article 18, Member States shall maintain in force their existing legal provisions relating to the use of the design of a component part used for the purpose of the repair of a complex product so as to restore its original appearance and shall introduce changes to those provisions only if the purpose is to liberalise the market for such parts.

Article 15 Exhaustion of rights

A15-015   The rights conferred by a design right upon registration shall not extend to acts relating to a product in which a design included within the scope of protection of the design right is incorporated or to which it is applied, when the product has been put on the market in the Community by the holder of the design right or with his consent.

Article 16 Relationship to other forms of protection

A15-016   The provisions of this Directive shall be without prejudice to any provisions of Community law or of the law of the Member State concerned relating to unregistered design rights, trade marks or other distinctive signs, patents and utility models, typefaces, civil liability or unfair competition.

Article 17 Relationship to copyright

A15-017   A design protected by a design right registered in or in respect of a Member State in accordance with this Directive shall also be eligible for protection under the law of copyright of that State as from the date on which the design was created or fixed in any form. The extent to which, and the conditions under which, such a protection is conferred, including the level of originality required, shall be determined by each Member State.

Article 18 Revision

A15-018   Three years after the implementation date specified in Article 19, the Commission shall submit an analysis of the consequences of the provisions of this Directive for Community industry, in particular the industrial sectors which are most affected, particularly manufacturers of complex products and component parts, for consumers, for competition and for the functioning of the internal market. At the latest one year later the Commission shall propose to the European Parliament and the Council any changes to this Directive needed to complete the internal market in respect of component parts of complex products and any other changes which it considers necessary in light of its consultations with the parties most affected.

Article 19 Implementation

A15-019   1. Member States shall bring into force the laws, regulations or administrative provisions necessary to comply with this Directive not later than 28 October 2001.

When Member States adopt these provisions, they shall contain a reference to this Directive or shall be accompanied by such reference on the occasion of their official publication. The methods of making such reference shall be laid down by Member States.

2. Member States shall communicate to the Commission the provisions of national law which they adopt in the field governed by this Directive.

Article 20 Entry into force

This Directive shall enter into force on the 20th day following its publication **A15-020** in the Official Journal of the European Communities.

Article 21 Addressees

his Directive is addressed to the Member States.   **A15-021**

Directive 2001/29/EC of the European Parliament and of the Council of 22 May 2001 on the harmonisation of certain aspects of copyright and related rights in the information society

THE EUROPEAN PARLIAMENT AND THE COUNCIL OF THE EUROPEAN UNION,

Having regard to the Treaty establishing the European Community, and in particular Articles 47(2), 55 and 95 thereof,

Having regard to the proposal from the Commission,

Having regard to the opinion of the Economic and Social Committee,

Acting in accordance with the procedure laid down in Article 251 of the Treaty,

Whereas:

(1) The Treaty provides for the establishment of an internal market and the institution of a system ensuring that competition in the internal market is not distorted. Harmonisation of the laws of the Member States on copyright and related rights contributes to the achievement of these objectives.

(2) The European Council, meeting at Corfu on 24 and 25 June 1994, stressed the need to create a general and flexible legal framework at Community level in order to foster the development of the information society in Europe. This requires, inter alia, the existence of an internal market for new products and services. Important Community legislation to ensure such a regulatory framework is already in place or its adoption is well under way. Copyright and related rights play an important role in this context as they protect and stimulate the development and marketing of new products and services and the creation and exploitation of their creative content.

(3) The proposed harmonisation will help to implement the four freedoms of the internal market and relates to compliance with the fundamental principles of law and especially of property, including intellectual property, and freedom of expression and the public interest.

(4) A harmonised legal framework on copyright and related rights, through increased legal certainty and while providing for a high level of protection of intellectual property, will foster substantial investment in creativity and innovation, including network infrastructure, and lead in turn to growth and increased competitiveness of European industry, both in the area of content provision and information technology and more generally across a wide range of industrial and cultural sectors. This will safeguard employment and encourage new job creation.

(5) Technological development has multiplied and diversified the vectors for creation, production and exploitation. While no new concepts for the protection of intellectual property are needed, the current law on copyright and related rights should be adapted and supplemented to respond adequately to economic realities such as new forms of exploitation.

(6) Without harmonisation at Community level, legislative activities at national level which have already been initiated in a number of Member States in

order to respond to the technological challenges might result in significant differences in protection and thereby in restrictions on the free movement of services and products incorporating, or based on, intellectual property, leading to a refragmentation of the internal market and legislative inconsistency. The impact of such legislative differences and uncertainties will become more significant with the further development of the information society, which has already greatly increased transborder exploitation of intellectual property. This development will and should further increase. Significant legal differences and uncertainties in protection may hinder economies of scale for new products and services containing copyright and related rights.

(7) The Community legal framework for the protection of copyright and related rights must, therefore, also be adapted and supplemented as far as is necessary for the smooth functioning of the internal market. To that end, those national provisions on copyright and related rights which vary considerably from one Member State to another or which cause legal uncertainties hindering the smooth functioning of the internal market and the proper development of the information society in Europe should be adjusted, and inconsistent national responses to the technological developments should be avoided, whilst differences not adversely affecting the functioning of the internal market need not be removed or prevented.

(8) The various social, societal and cultural implications of the information society require that account be taken of the specific features of the content of products and services.

(9) Any harmonisation of copyright and related rights must take as a basis a high level of protection, since such rights are crucial to intellectual creation. Their protection helps to ensure the maintenance and development of creativity in the interests of authors, performers, producers, consumers, culture, industry and the public at large. Intellectual property has therefore been recognised as an integral part of property.

(10) If authors or performers are to continue their creative and artistic work, they have to receive an appropriate reward for the use of their work, as must producers in order to be able to finance this work. The investment required to produce products such as phonograms, films or multimedia products, and services such as "on-demand" services, is considerable. Adequate legal protection of intellectual property rights is necessary in order to guarantee the availability of such a reward and provide the opportunity for satisfactory returns on this investment.

(11) A rigorous, effective system for the protection of copyright and related rights is one of the main ways of ensuring that European cultural creativity and production receive the necessary resources and of safeguarding the independence and dignity of artistic creators and performers.

(12) Adequate protection of copyright works and subject-matter of related rights is also of great importance from a cultural standpoint. Article 151 of the Treaty requires the Community to take cultural aspects into account in its action.

(13) A common search for, and consistent application at European level of, technical measures to protect works and other subject-matter and to provide the necessary information on rights are essential insofar as the ultimate aim of these measures is to give effect to the principles and guarantees laid down in law.

(14) This Directive should seek to promote learning and culture by protecting works and other subject-matter while permitting exceptions or limitations in the public interest for the purpose of education and teaching.

(15) The Diplomatic Conference held under the auspices of the World Intellectual Property Organisation (WIPO) in December 1996 led to the adoption of two new Treaties, the "WIPO Copyright Treaty" and the "WIPO Performances and Phonograms Treaty", dealing respectively with the protection of authors and the protection of performers and phonogram producers. Those Treaties update the international protection for copyright and related rights significantly, not least with regard to the so-called "digital agenda", and improve the means to fight piracy world-wide. The Community and a majority of Member States have already signed the Treaties and the process of making arrangements for the ratification of the Treaties by the Community and the Member States is under way. This Directive also serves to implement a number of the new international obligations.

(16) Liability for activities in the network environment concerns not only copyright and related rights but also other areas, such as defamation, misleading advertising, or infringement of trademarks, and is addressed horizontally in Directive 2000/31/EC of the European Parliament and of the Council of 8 June 2000 on certain legal aspects of information society services, in particular electronic commerce, in the internal market ("Directive on electronic commerce"), which clarifies and harmonises various legal issues relating to information society services including electronic commerce. This Directive should be implemented within a timescale similar to that for the implementation of the Directive on electronic commerce, since that Directive provides a harmonised framework of principles and provisions relevant inter alia to important parts of this Directive. This Directive is without prejudice to provisions relating to liability in that Directive.

(17) It is necessary, especially in the light of the requirements arising out of the digital environment, to ensure that collecting societies achieve a higher level of rationalisation and transparency with regard to compliance with competition rules.

(18) This Directive is without prejudice to the arrangements in the Member States concerning the management of rights such as extended collective licences.

(19) The moral rights of rightholders should be exercised according to the legislation of the Member States and the provisions of the Berne Convention for the Protection of Literary and Artistic Works, of the WIPO Copyright Treaty and of the WIPO Performances and Phonograms Treaty. Such moral rights remain outside the scope of this Directive.

(20) This Directive is based on principles and rules already laid down in the Directives currently in force in this area, in particular Directives 91/250/EEC, 92/100/EEC, 93/83/EEC, 93/98/EEC and 96/9/EC, and it develops those principles and rules and places them in the context of the information society. The provisions of this Directive should be without prejudice to the provisions of those Directives, unless otherwise provided in this Directive.

(21) This Directive should define the scope of the acts covered by the reproduction right with regard to the different beneficiaries. This should be done in conformity with the acquis communautaire. A broad definition of these acts is needed to ensure legal certainty within the internal market.

(22) The objective of proper support for the dissemination of culture must not be achieved by sacrificing strict protection of rights or by tolerating illegal forms of distribution of counterfeited or pirated works.

(23) This Directive should harmonise further the author's right of communication to the public. This right should be understood in a broad sense covering all communication to the public not present at the place where the communication originates. This right should cover any such transmission or retransmission of a work to the public by wire or wireless means, including broadcasting. This right should not cover any other acts.

(24) The right to make available to the public subject-matter referred to in Article 3(2) should be understood as covering all acts of making available such subject-matter to members of the public not present at the place where the act of making available originates, and as not covering any other acts.

(25) The legal uncertainty regarding the nature and the level of protection of acts of on-demand transmission of copyright works and subject-matter protected by related rights over networks should be overcome by providing for harmonised protection at Community level. It should be made clear that all rightholders recognised by this Directive should have an exclusive right to make available to the public copyright works or any other subject-matter by way of interactive on-demand transmissions. Such interactive on-demand transmissions are characterised by the fact that members of the public may access them from a place and at a time individually chosen by them.

(26) With regard to the making available in on-demand services by broadcasters of their radio or television productions incorporating music from commercial phonograms as an integral part thereof, collective licensing arrangements are to be encouraged in order to facilitate the clearance of the rights concerned.

(27) The mere provision of physical facilities for enabling or making a communication does not in itself amount to communication within the meaning of this Directive.

(28) Copyright protection under this Directive includes the exclusive right to control distribution of the work incorporated in a tangible article. The first sale in the Community of the original of a work or copies thereof by the rightholder or with his consent exhausts the right to control resale of that object in the Community. This right should not be exhausted in respect of the original or of copies thereof sold by the rightholder or with his consent outside the Community. Rental and lending rights for authors have been established in Directive 92/100/EEC. The distribution right provided for in this Directive is without prejudice to the provisions relating to the rental and lending rights contained in Chapter I of that Directive.

(29) The question of exhaustion does not arise in the case of services and on-line services in particular. This also applies with regard to a material copy of a work or other subject-matter made by a user of such a service with the consent of the rightholder. Therefore, the same applies to rental and lending of the original and copies of works or other subject-matter which are services by nature. Unlike CD-ROM or CD-I, where the intellectual property is incorporated in a material medium, namely an item of goods, every on-line service is in fact an act which should be subject to authorisation where the copyright or related right so provides.

(30) The rights referred to in this Directive may be transferred, assigned or subject to the granting of contractual licences, without prejudice to the relevant national legislation on copyright and related rights.

(31) A fair balance of rights and interests between the different categories of rightholders, as well as between the different categories of rightholders and users of protected subject-matter must be safeguarded. The existing exceptions and limitations to the rights as set out by the Member States have to be reassessed in the light of the new electronic environment. Existing differences in the exceptions and limitations to certain restricted acts have direct negative effects on the functioning of the internal market of copyright and related rights. Such differences could well become more pronounced in view of the further development of transborder exploitation of works and cross-border activities. In order to ensure the proper functioning of the internal market, such exceptions and limitations should be defined more harmoniously. The degree of their harmonisation should be based on their impact on the smooth functioning of the internal market.

(32) This Directive provides for an exhaustive enumeration of exceptions and limitations to the reproduction right and the right of communication to the public. Some exceptions or limitations only apply to the reproduction right, where appropriate. This list takes due account of the different legal traditions in Member States, while, at the same time, aiming to ensure a functioning internal market. Member States should arrive at a coherent application of these exceptions and limitations, which will be assessed when reviewing implementing legislation in the future.

(33) The exclusive right of reproduction should be subject to an exception to allow certain acts of temporary reproduction, which are transient or incidental reproductions, forming an integral and essential part of a technological process and carried out for the sole purpose of enabling either efficient transmission in a network between third parties by an intermediary, or a lawful use of a work or other subject-matter to be made. The acts of reproduction concerned should have no separate economic value on their own. To the extent that they meet these conditions, this exception should include acts which enable browsing as well as acts of caching to take place, including those which enable transmission systems to function efficiently, provided that the intermediary does not modify the information and does not interfere with the lawful use of technology, widely recognised and used by industry, to obtain data on the use of the information. A use should be considered lawful where it is authorised by the rightholder or not restricted by law.

(34) Member States should be given the option of providing for certain exceptions or limitations for cases such as educational and scientific purposes, for the benefit of public institutions such as libraries and archives, for purposes of news reporting, for quotations, for use by people with disabilities, for public security uses and for uses in administrative and judicial proceedings.

(35) In certain cases of exceptions or limitations, rightholders should receive fair compensation to compensate them adequately for the use made of their protected works or other subject-matter. When determining the form, detailed arrangements and possible level of such fair compensation, account should be taken of the particular circumstances of each case. When evaluating these circumstances, a valuable criterion would be the possible harm to the rightholders resulting from the act in question. In cases where

rightholders have already received payment in some other form, for instance as part of a licence fee, no specific or separate payment may be due. The level of fair compensation should take full account of the degree of use of technological protection measures referred to in this Directive. In certain situations where the prejudice to the rightholder would be minimal, no obligation for payment may arise.

(36) The Member States may provide for fair compensation for rightholders also when applying the optional provisions on exceptions or limitations which do not require such compensation.

(37) Existing national schemes on reprography, where they exist, do not create major barriers to the internal market. Member States should be allowed to provide for an exception or limitation in respect of reprography.

(38) Member States should be allowed to provide for an exception or limitation to the reproduction right for certain types of reproduction of audio, visual and audio-visual material for private use, accompanied by fair compensation. This may include the introduction or continuation of remuneration schemes to compensate for the prejudice to rightholders. Although differences between those remuneration schemes affect the functioning of the internal market, those differences, with respect to analogue private reproduction, should not have a significant impact on the development of the information society. Digital private copying is likely to be more widespread and have a greater economic impact. Due account should therefore be taken of the differences between digital and analogue private copying and a distinction should be made in certain respects between them.

(39) When applying the exception or limitation on private copying, Member States should take due account of technological and economic developments, in particular with respect to digital private copying and remuneration schemes, when effective technological protection measures are available. Such exceptions or limitations should not inhibit the use of technological measures or their enforcement against circumvention.

(40) Member States may provide for an exception or limitation for the benefit of certain non-profit making establishments, such as publicly accessible libraries and equivalent institutions, as well as archives. However, this should be limited to certain special cases covered by the reproduction right. Such an exception or limitation should not cover uses made in the context of on-line delivery of protected works or other subject-matter. This Directive should be without prejudice to the Member States' option to derogate from the exclusive public lending right in accordance with Article 5 of Directive 92/100/EEC. Therefore, specific contracts or licences should be promoted which, without creating imbalances, favour such establishments and the disseminative purposes they serve.

(41) When applying the exception or limitation in respect of ephemeral recordings made by broadcasting organisations it is understood that a broadcaster's own facilities include those of a person acting on behalf of and under the responsibility of the broadcasting organisation.

(42) When applying the exception or limitation for non-commercial educational and scientific research purposes, including distance learning, the non-commercial nature of the activity in question should be determined by that activity as such. The organisational structure and the means of funding of the establishment concerned are not the decisive factors in this respect.

(43) It is in any case important for the Member States to adopt all necessary measures to facilitate access to works by persons suffering from a disability

which constitutes an obstacle to the use of the works themselves, and to pay particular attention to accessible formats.

(44) When applying the exceptions and limitations provided for in this Directive, they should be exercised in accordance with international obligations. Such exceptions and limitations may not be applied in a way which prejudices the legitimate interests of the rightholder or which conflicts with the normal exploitation of his work or other subject-matter. The provision of such exceptions or limitations by Member States should, in particular, duly reflect the increased economic impact that such exceptions or limitations may have in the context of the new electronic environment. Therefore, the scope of certain exceptions or limitations may have to be even more limited when it comes to certain new uses of copyright works and other subject-matter.

(45) The exceptions and limitations referred to in Article 5(2), (3) and (4) should not, however, prevent the definition of contractual relations designed to ensure fair compensation for the rightholders insofar as permitted by national law.

(46) Recourse to mediation could help users and rightholders to settle disputes. The Commission, in cooperation with the Member States within the Contact Committee, should undertake a study to consider new legal ways of settling disputes concerning copyright and related rights.

(47) Technological development will allow rightholders to make use of technological measures designed to prevent or restrict acts not authorised by the rightholders of any copyright, rights related to copyright or the sui generis right in databases. The danger, however, exists that illegal activities might be carried out in order to enable or facilitate the circumvention of the technical protection provided by these measures. In order to avoid fragmented legal approaches that could potentially hinder the functioning of the internal market, there is a need to provide for harmonised legal protection against circumvention of effective technological measures and against provision of devices and products or services to this effect.

(48) Such legal protection should be provided in respect of technological measures that effectively restrict acts not authorised by the rightholders of any copyright, rights related to copyright or the sui generis right in databases without, however, preventing the normal operation of electronic equipment and its technological development. Such legal protection implies no obligation to design devices, products, components or services to correspond to technological measures, so long as such device, product, component or service does not otherwise fall under the prohibition of Article 6. Such legal protection should respect proportionality and should not prohibit those devices or activities which have a commercially significant purpose or use other than to circumvent the technical protection. In particular, this protection should not hinder research into cryptography.

(49) The legal protection of technological measures is without prejudice to the application of any national provisions which may prohibit the private possession of devices, products or components for the circumvention of technological measures.

(50) Such a harmonised legal protection does not affect the specific provisions on protection provided for by Directive 91/250/EEC. In particular, it should not apply to the protection of technological measures used in connection with computer programs, which is exclusively addressed in that Directive. It should neither inhibit nor prevent the development or use of any means of

circumventing a technological measure that is necessary to enable acts to be undertaken in accordance with the terms of Article 5(3) or Article 6 of Directive 91/250/EEC. Articles 5 and 6 of that Directive exclusively determine exceptions to the exclusive rights applicable to computer programs.

(51) The legal protection of technological measures applies without prejudice to public policy, as reflected in Article 5, or public security. Member States should promote voluntary measures taken by rightholders, including the conclusion and implementation of agreements between rightholders and other parties concerned, to accommodate achieving the objectives of certain exceptions or limitations provided for in national law in accordance with this Directive. In the absence of such voluntary measures or agreements within a reasonable period of time, Member States should take appropriate measures to ensure that rightholders provide beneficiaries of such exceptions or limitations with appropriate means of benefiting from them, by modifying an implemented technological measure or by other means. However, in order to prevent abuse of such measures taken by rightholders, including within the framework of agreements, or taken by a Member State, any technological measures applied in implementation of such measures should enjoy legal protection.

(52) When implementing an exception or limitation for private copying in accordance with Article 5(2)(b), Member States should likewise promote the use of voluntary measures to accommodate achieving the objectives of such exception or limitation. If, within a reasonable period of time, no such voluntary measures to make reproduction for private use possible have been taken, Member States may take measures to enable beneficiaries of the exception or limitation concerned to benefit from it. Voluntary measures taken by rightholders, including agreements between rightholders and other parties concerned, as well as measures taken by Member States, do not prevent rightholders from using technological measures which are consistent with the exceptions or limitations on private copying in national law in accordance with Article 5(2)(b), taking account of the condition of fair compensation under that provision and the possible differentiation between various conditions of use in accordance with Article 5(5), such as controlling the number of reproductions. In order to prevent abuse of such measures, any technological measures applied in their implementation should enjoy legal protection.

(53) The protection of technological measures should ensure a secure environment for the provision of interactive on-demand services, in such a way that members of the public may access works or other subject-matter from a place and at a time individually chosen by them. Where such services are governed by contractual arrangements, the first and second subparagraphs of Article 6(4) should not apply. Non-interactive forms of online use should remain subject to those provisions.

(54) Important progress has been made in the international standardisation of technical systems of identification of works and protected subject-matter in digital format. In an increasingly networked environment, differences between technological measures could lead to an incompatibility of systems within the Community. Compatibility and interoperability of the different systems should be encouraged. It would be highly desirable to encourage the development of global systems.

(55) Technological development will facilitate the distribution of works, notably on networks, and this will entail the need for rightholders to identify better the work or other subject-matter, the author or any other rightholder, and to provide information about the terms and conditions of use of the work or other subject-matter in order to render easier the management of rights attached to them. Rightholders should be encouraged to use markings indicating, in addition to the information referred to above, inter alia their authorisation when putting works or other subject-matter on networks.

(56) There is, however, the danger that illegal activities might be carried out in order to remove or alter the electronic copyright-management information attached to it, or otherwise to distribute, import for distribution, broadcast, communicate to the public or make available to the public works or other protected subject-matter from which such information has been removed without authority. In order to avoid fragmented legal approaches that could potentially hinder the functioning of the internal market, there is a need to provide for harmonised legal protection against any of these activities.

(57) Any such rights-management information systems referred to above may, depending on their design, at the same time process personal data about the consumption patterns of protected subject-matter by individuals and allow for tracing of on-line behaviour. These technical means, in their technical functions, should incorporate privacy safeguards in accordance with Directive 95/46/EC of the European Parliament and of the Council of 24 October 1995 on the protection of individuals with regard to the processing of personal data and the free movement of such data(10).

(58) Member States should provide for effective sanctions and remedies for infringements of rights and obligations as set out in this Directive. They should take all the measures necessary to ensure that those sanctions and remedies are applied. The sanctions thus provided for should be effective, proportionate and dissuasive and should include the possibility of seeking damages and/or injunctive relief and, where appropriate, of applying for seizure of infringing material.

(59) In the digital environment, in particular, the services of intermediaries may increasingly be used by third parties for infringing activities. In many cases such intermediaries are best placed to bring such infringing activities to an end. Therefore, without prejudice to any other sanctions and remedies available, rightholders should have the possibility of applying for an injunction against an intermediary who carries a third party's infringement of a protected work or other subject-matter in a network. This possibility should be available even where the acts carried out by the intermediary are exempted under Article 5. The conditions and modalities relating to such injunctions should be left to the national law of the Member States.

(60) The protection provided under this Directive should be without prejudice to national or Community legal provisions in other areas, such as industrial property, data protection, conditional access, access to public documents, and the rule of media exploitation chronology, which may affect the protection of copyright or related rights.

(61) In order to comply with the WIPO Performances and Phonograms Treaty, Directives 92/100/EEC and 93/98/EEC should be amended,

HAS ADOPTED THIS DIRECTIVE:

CHAPTER I

SCOPE

Article 1 Scope

A16-001   1 This Directive concerns the legal protection of copyright and related rights in the framework of the internal market, with particular emphasis on the information society.

2. Except in the cases referred to in Article 11, this Directive shall leave intact and shall in no way affect existing Community provisions relating to:

(a) the legal protection of computer programs;

(b) rental right, lending right and certain rights related to copyright in the field of intellectual property;

(c) copyright and related rights applicable to broadcasting of programmes by satellite and cable retransmission;

(d) the term of protection of copyright and certain related rights;

(e) the legal protection of databases.

CHAPTER II

RIGHTS AND EXCEPTIONS

Article 2 Reproduction right

A16-002   Member States shall provide for the exclusive right to authorise or prohibit direct or indirect, temporary or permanent reproduction by any means and in any form, in whole or in part:

(a) for authors, of their works;

(b) for performers, of fixations of their performances;

(c) for phonogram producers, of their phonograms;

(d) for the producers of the first fixations of films, in respect of the original and copies of their films;

(e) for broadcasting organisations, of fixations of their broadcasts, whether those broadcasts are transmitted by wire or over the air, including by cable or satellite.

Article 3 Right of communication to the public of works and right of making available to the public other subject-matter

A16-003   1. Member States shall provide authors with the exclusive right to authorise or prohibit any communication to the public of their works, by wire or wireless means, including the making available to the public of their works in such a way that members of the public may access them from a place and at a time individually chosen by them.

2. Member States shall provide for the exclusive right to authorise or prohibit the making available to the public, by wire or wireless means, in such a way that members of the public may access them from a place and at a time individually chosen by them:

(a) for performers, of fixations of their performances;

(b) for phonogram producers, of their phonograms;

(c) for the producers of the first fixations of films, of the original and copies of their films;

(d) for broadcasting organisations, of fixations of their broadcasts, whether these broadcasts are transmitted by wire or over the air, including by cable or satellite.

3. The rights referred to in paragraphs 1 and 2 shall not be exhausted by any act of communication to the public or making available to the public as set out in this Article.

Article 4 Distribution right

1. Member States shall provide for authors, in respect of the original of their **A16-004** works or of copies thereof, the exclusive right to authorise or prohibit any form of distribution to the public by sale or otherwise.

2. The distribution right shall not be exhausted within the Community in respect of the original or copies of the work, except where the first sale or other transfer of ownership in the Community of that object is made by the rightholder or with his consent.

Article 5 Exceptions and limitations

1. Temporary acts of reproduction referred to in Article 2, which are transient **A16-005** or incidental, which are an integral and essential part of a technological process and the sole purpose is to enable:
  (a) a transmission in a network between third parties by an intermediary, or
  (b) alawful use of a work or other subject-matter to be made, and which have no independent economic significance, shall be exempted from the reproduction right provided for in Article 2.

2. Member States may provide for exceptions or limitations to the reproduction right provided for in Article 2 in the following cases:
  (a) in respect of reproductions on paper or any similar medium, effected by the use of any kind of photographic technique or by some other process having similar effects, with the exception of sheet music, provided that the rightholders receive fair compensation;
  (b) in respect of reproductions on any medium made by a natural person for private use and for ends that are neither directly nor indirectly commercial, on condition that the rightholders receive fair compensation which takes account of the application or non-application of technological measures referred to in Article 6 to the work or subject-matter concerned;
  (c) in respect of specific acts of reproduction made by publicly accessible libraries, educational establishments or museums, or by archives, which are not for direct or indirect economic or commercial advantage;
  (d) in respect of ephemeral recordings of works made by broadcasting organisations by means of their own facilities and for their own broadcasts; the preservation of these recordings in official archives may, on the grounds of their exceptional documentary character, be permitted;
  (e) in respect of reproductions of broadcasts made by social institutions pursuing non-commercial purposes, such as hospitals or prisons, on condition that the rightholders receive fair compensation.

3. Member States may provide for exceptions or limitations to the rights provided for in Articles 2 and 3 in the following cases:
  (a) use for the sole purpose of illustration for teaching or scientific research, as long as the source, including the author's name, is

indicated, unless this turns out to be impossible and to the extent justified by the non-commercial purpose to be achieved;

(b) uses, for the benefit of people with a disability, which are directly related to the disability and of a non-commercial nature, to the extent required by the specific disability;

(c) reproduction by the press, communication to the public or making available of published articles on current economic, political or religious topics or of broadcast works or other subject-matter of the same character, in cases where such use is not expressly reserved, and as long as the source, including the author's name, is indicated, or use of works or other subject-matter in connection with the reporting of current events, to the extent justified by the informatory purpose and as long as the source, including the author's name, is indicated, unless this turns out to be impossible;

(d) quotations for purposes such as criticism or review, provided that they relate to a work or other subject-matter which has already been lawfully made available to the public, that, unless this turns out to be impossible, the source, including the author's name, is indicated, and that their use is in accordance with fair practice, and to the extent required by the specific purpose;

(e) use for the purposes of public security or to ensure the proper performance or reporting of administrative, parliamentary or judicial proceedings;

(f) use of political speeches as well as extracts of public lectures or similar works or subject-matter to the extent justified by the informatory purpose and provided that the source, including the author's name, is indicated, except where this turns out to be impossible;

(g) use during religious celebrations or official celebrations organised by a public authority;

(h) use of works, such as works of architecture or sculpture, made to be located permanently in public places;

(i) incidental inclusion of a work or other subject-matter in other material;

(j) use for the purpose of advertising the public exhibition or sale of artistic works, to the extent necessary to promote the event, excluding any other commercial use;

(k) use for the purpose of caricature, parody or pastiche;

(l) use in connection with the demonstration or repair of equipment;

(m) use of an artistic work in the form of a building or a drawing or plan of a building for the purposes of reconstructing the building;

(n) use by communication or making available, for the purpose of research or private study, to individual members of the public by dedicated terminals on the premises of establishments referred to in paragraph 2(c) of works and other subject-matter not subject to purchase or licensing terms which are contained in their collections;

(o) use in certain other cases of minor importance where exceptions or limitations already exist under national law, provided that they only concern analogue uses and do not affect the free circulation of goods and services within the Community, without prejudice to the other exceptions and limitations contained in this Article.

4. Where the Member States may provide for an exception or limitation to the right of reproduction pursuant to paragraphs 2 and 3, they may provide similarly for an exception or limitation to the right of distribution as referred to in

Article 4 to the extent justified by the purpose of the authorised act of reproduction.

5. The exceptions and limitations provided for in paragraphs 1, 2, 3 and 4 shall only be applied in certain special cases which do not conflict with a normal exploitation of the work or other subject-matter and do not unreasonably prejudice the legitimate interests of the rightholder.

CHAPTER III

PROTECTION OF TECHNOLOGICAL MEASURES AND RIGHTS-MANAGEMENT INFORMATION

Article 6 Obligations as to technological measures

1. Member States shall provide adequate legal protection against the circum- **A16-006** vention of any effective technological measures, which the person concerned carries out in the knowledge, or with reasonable grounds to know, that he or she is pursuing that objective.

2. Member States shall provide adequate legal protection against the manufacture, import, distribution, sale, rental, advertisement for sale or rental, or possession for commercial purposes of devices, products or components or the provision of services which:

(a) are promoted, advertised or marketed for the purpose of circumvention of, or

(b) have only a limited commercially significant purpose or use other than to circumvent, or

(c) are primarily designed, produced, adapted or performed for the purpose of enabling or facilitating the circumvention of, any effective technological measures.

3. For the purposes of this Directive, the expression "technological measures" means any technology, device or component that, in the normal course of its operation, is designed to prevent or restrict acts, in respect of works or other subject-matter, which are not authorised by the rightholder of any copyright or any right related to copyright as provided for by law or the sui generis right provided for in Chapter III of Directive 96/9/EC. Technological measures shall be deemed "effective" where the use of a protected work or other subject-matter is controlled by the rightholders through application of an access control or protection process, such as encryption, scrambling or other transformation of the work or other subject-matter or a copy control mechanism, which achieves the protection objective.

4. Notwithstanding the legal protection provided for in paragraph 1, in the absence of voluntary measures taken by rightholders, including agreements between rightholders and other parties concerned, Member States shall take appropriate measures to ensure that rightholders make available to the beneficiary of an exception or limitation provided for in national law in accordance with Article 5(2)(a), (2)(c), (2)(d), (2)(e), (3)(a), (3)(b) or (3)(e) the means of benefiting from that exception or limitation, to the extent necessary to benefit from that exception or limitation and where that beneficiary has legal access to the protected work or subject-matter concerned. A Member State may also take such measures in respect of a beneficiary of an exception or limitation provided for in accordance with Article 5(2)(b), unless reproduction for private use has already beenmade possible by rightholders to the extent necessary to benefit from the exception or limitation concerned and in accordance with the provisions of

Article 5(2)(b) and (5), without preventing rightholders from adopting adequate measures regarding the number of reproductions in accordance with these provisions. The technological measures applied voluntarily by rightholders, including those applied in implementation of voluntary agreements, and technological measures applied in implementation of the measures taken by Member States, shall enjoy the legal protection provided for in paragraph 1. The provisions of the first and second subparagraphs shall not apply to works or other subject-matter made available to the public on agreed contractual terms in such a way that members of the public may access them from a place and at a time individually chosen by them. When this Article is applied in the context of Directives 92/100/EEC and 96/9/EC, this paragraph shall apply mutatis mutandis.

Article 7 Obligations concerning rights-management information

A16-007   1. Member States shall provide for adequate legal protection against any person knowingly performing without authority any of the following acts:

    (a) the removal or alteration of any electronic rights-management information;

    (b) the distribution, importation for distribution, broadcasting, communication or making available to the public of works or other subject-matter protected under this Directive or under Chapter III of Directive 96/9/EC from which electronic rights-management information has been removed or altered without authority, if such person knows, or has reasonable grounds to know, that by so doing he is inducing, enabling, facilitating or concealing an infringement of any copyright or any rights related to copyright as provided by law, or of the sui generis right provided for in Chapter III of Directive 96/9/EC.

2. For the purposes of this Directive, the expression ɪrights-management informationɪ means any information provided by rightholders which identifies the work or other subject-matter referred to in this Directive or covered by the sui generis right provided for in Chapter III of Directive 96/9/EC, the author or any other rightholder, or information about the terms and conditions of use of the work or other subject-matter, and any numbers or codes that represent such information. The first subparagraph shall apply when any of these items of information is associated with a copy of, or appears in connection with the communication to the public of, a work or other subjectmatter referred to in this Directive or covered by the sui generis right provided for in Chapter III of Directive 96/9/EC

CHAPTER IV

COMMON PROVISIONS

Article 8 Sanctions and remedies

A16-008   1. Member States shall provide appropriate sanctions and remedies in respect of infringements of the rights and obligations set out in this Directive and shall take all the measures necessary to ensure that those sanctions and remedies are applied. The sanctions thus provided for shall be effective, proportionate and dissuasive.

2. Each Member State shall take the measures necessary to ensure that rightholders whose interests are affected by an infringing activity carried out on its territory can bring an action for damages and/or apply for an injunction and,

where appropriate, for the seizure of infringing material as well as of devices, products or components referred to in Article 6(2).

3. Member States shall ensure that rightholders are in a position to apply for an injunction against intermediaries whose services are used by a third party to infringe a copyright or related right.

Article 9 Continued application of other legal provisions

This Directive shall be without prejudice to provisions concerning in **A16-009** particular patent rights, trade marks, design rights, utility models, topographies of semi-conductor products, type faces, conditional access, access to cable of broadcasting services, protection of national treasures, legal deposit require-ments, laws on restrictive practices and unfair competition, trade secrets, security, confidentiality, data protection and privacy, access to public documents, the law of contract.

Article 10 Application over time

1. The provisions of this Directive shall apply in respect of all works and **A16-010** other subject-matter referred to in this Directive which are, on 22 December 2002, protected by the Member States' legislation in the field of copyright and related rights, or which meet the criteria for protection under the provisions of this Directive or the provisions referred to in Article 1(2).

2. This Directive shall apply without prejudice to any acts concluded and rights acquired before 22 December 2002.

Article 12 Final provisions

1. Not later than 22 December 2004 and every three years thereafter, the **A16-011** Commission shall submit to the European Parliament, the Council and the Economic and Social Committee a report on the application of this Directive, in which, inter alia, on the basis of specific information supplied by the Member States, it shall examine in particular the application of Articles 5, 6 and 8 in the light of the development of the digital market. In the case of Article 6, it shall examine in particular whether that Article confers a sufficient level of protection and whether acts which are permitted by law are being adversely affected by the use of effective technological measures. Where necessary, in particular to ensure the functioning of the internal market pursuant to Article 14 of the Treaty, it shall submit proposals for amendments to this Directive.

2. Protection of rights related to copyright under this Directive shall leave intact and shall in no way affect the protection of copyright.

3. A contact committee is hereby established. It shall be composed of repre-sentatives of the competent authorities of the Member States. It shall be chaired by a representative of the Commission and shall meet either on the initiative of the chairman or at the request of the delegation of a Member State.

4. The tasks of the committee shall be as follows:

    (a) to examine the impact of this Directive on the functioning of the internal market, and to highlight any difficulties;

    (b) to organise consultations on all questions deriving from the application of this Directive;

    (c) to facilitate the exchange of information on relevant developments in legislation and case-law, as well as relevant economic, social, cultural and technological developments;

(d) to act as a forum for the assessment of the digital market in works and other items, including private copying and the use of technological measures.

Article 13 Implementation

A16-012   1. Member States shall bring into force the laws, regulations and administrative provisions necessary to comply with this Directive before 22 December 2002. They shall forthwith inform the Commission thereof. When Member States adopt these measures, they shall contain a reference to this Directive or shall be accompanied by such reference on the occasion of their official publication. The methods of making such reference shall be laid down by Member States.

2. Member States shall communicate to the Commission the text of the provisions of domestic law which they adopt in the field governed by this Directive.

Article 14 Entry into force

A16-013   This Directive shall enter into force on the day of its publication in the Official Journal of the European Communities.

Article 15 Addressees

A16-014   This Directive is addressed to the Member States.

Directive 2001/84/EC of the European Parliament and of the Council of 27 September 2001 on the resale right for the benefit of the author of an original work of art

THE EUROPEAN PARLIAMENT AND THE COUNCIL OF THE EUROPEAN UNION,

Having regard to the Treaty establishing the European Community, and in particular Articles 47(2), 55 and 95 thereof,

Having regard to the proposal from the Commission,

Having regard to the opinion of the Economic and Social Committee,

Acting in accordance with the procedure laid down in Article 251 of the Treaty, and in the light of the joint text approved by the Conciliation Committee on 6 June 2001,

Whereas:

(1) In the field of copyright, the resale right is an unassignable and inalienable right, enjoyed by the author of an original work of graphic or plastic art, to an economic interest in successive sales of the work concerned.

(2) The resale right is a right of a productive character which enables the author/artist to receive consideration for successive transfers of the work. The subject-matter of the resale right is the physical work, namely the medium in which the protected work is incorporated.

(3) The resale right is intended to ensure that authors of graphic and plastic works of art share in the economic success of their original works of art. It helps to redress the balance between the economic situation of authors of graphic and plastic works of art and that of other creators who benefit from successive exploitations of their works.

(4) The resale right forms an integral part of copyright and is an essential prerogative for authors. The imposition of such a right in all Member States meets the need for providing creators with an adequate and standard level of protection.

(5) Under Article 151(4) of the Treaty the Community is to take cultural aspects into account in its action under other provisions of the Treaty.

(6) The Berne Convention for the Protection of Literary and Artistic Works provides that the resale right is available only if legislation in the country to which the author belongs so permits. The right is therefore optional and subject to the rule of reciprocity. It follows from the case-law of the Court of Justice of the European Communities on the application of the principle of non-discrimination laid down in Article 12 of the Treaty, as shown in the judgment of 20 October 1993 in Joined Cases C-92/92 and C-326/92 Phil Collins and Others, that domestic provisions containing reciprocity clauses cannot be relied upon in order to deny nationals of other Member States rights conferred on national authors. The application of such clauses in the Community context runs counter to the principle of equal treatment resulting from the prohibition of any discrimination on grounds of nationality.

(7) The process of internationalisation of the Community market in modern and contemporary art, which is now being speeded up by the effects of the new economy, in a regulatory context in which few States outside the EU recognise the resale right, makes it essential for the European Community, in the external sphere, to open negotiations with a view to making Article 14b of the Berne Convention compulsory.

(8) The fact that this international market exists, combined with the lack of a resale right in several Member States and the current disparity as regards national systems which recognise that right, make it essential to lay down transitional provisions as regards both entry into force and the substantive regulation of the right, which will preserve the competitiveness of the European market.

(9) The resale right is currently provided for by the domestic legislation of a majority of Member States. Such laws, where they exist, display certain differences, notably as regards the works covered, those entitled to receive royalties, the rate applied, the transactions subject to payment of a royalty, and the basis on which these are calculated. The application or non-application of such a right has a significant impact on the competitive environment within the internal market, since the existence or absence of an obligation to pay on the basis of the resale right is an element which must be taken into account by each individual wishing to sell a work of art. This right is therefore a factor which contributes to the creation of distortions of competition as well as displacement of sales within the Community.

(10) Such disparities with regard to the existence of the resale right and its application by the Member States have a direct negative impact on the proper functioning of the internal market in works of art as provided for by Article 14 of the Treaty. In such a situation Article 95 of the Treaty constitutes the appropriate legal basis.

(11) The objectives of the Community as set out in the Treaty include laying the foundations of an ever closer union among the peoples of Europe, promoting closer relations between the Member States belonging to the Community, and ensuring their economic and social progress by common action to eliminate the barriers which divide Europe. To that end the Treaty provides for the establishment of an internal market which presupposes the abolition of obstacles to the free movement of goods, freedom to provide services and freedom of establishment, and for the introduction of a system ensuring that competition in the

common market is not distorted. Harmonisation of Member States' laws on the resale right contributes to the attainment of these objectives.

(12) The Sixth Council Directive (77/388/EEC) of 17 May 1977 on the harmonisation of the laws of the Member States relating to turnover taxes - common system of value added tax: uniform basis of assessment, progressively introduces a Community system of taxation applicable inter alia to works of art. Measures confined to the tax field are not sufficient to guarantee the harmonious functioning of the art market. This objective cannot be attained without harmonisation in the field of the resale right.

(13) Existing differences between laws should be eliminated where they have a distorting effect on the functioning of the internal market, and the emergence of any new differences of that kind should be prevented. There is no need to eliminate, or prevent the emergence of, differences which cannot be expected to affect the functioning of the internal market.

(14) A precondition of the proper functioning of the internal market is the existence of conditions of competition which are not distorted. The existence of differences between national provisions on the resale right creates distortions of competition and displacement of sales within the Community and leads to unequal treatment between artists depending on where their works are sold. The issue under consideration has therefore transnational aspects which cannot be satisfactorily regulated by action by Member States. A lack of Community action would conflict with the requirement of the Treaty to correct distortions of competition and unequal treatment.

(15) In view of the scale of divergences between national provisions it is therefore necessary to adopt harmonising measures to deal with disparities between the laws of the Member States in areas where such disparities are liable to create or maintain distorted conditions of competition. It is not however necessary to harmonise every provision of the Member States' laws on the resale right and, in order to leave as much scope for national decision as possible, it is sufficient to limit the harmonisation exercise to those domestic provisions that have the most direct impact on the functioning of the internal market.

(16) This Directive complies therefore, in its entirety, with the principles of subsidiarity and proportionality as laid down in Article 5 of the Treaty.

(17) Pursuant to Council Directive 93/98/EEC of 29 October 1993 harmonising the term of protection of copyright and certain related rights(6), the term of copyright runs for 70 years after the author's death. The same period should be laid down for the resale right. Consequently, only the originals of works of modern and contemporary art may fall within the scope of the resale right. However, in order to allow the legal systems of Member States which do not, at the time of the adoption of this Directive, apply a resale right for the benefit of artists to incorporate this right into their respective legal systems and, moreover, to enable the economic operators in those Member States to adapt gradually to the aforementioned right whilst maintaining their economic viability, the Member States concerned should be allowed a limited transitional period during which they may choose not to apply the resale right for the benefit of those entitled under the artist after his death.

(18) The scope of the resale right should be extended to all acts of resale, with the exception of those effected directly between persons acting in their private capacity without the participation of an art market professional. This right should not extend to acts of resale by persons acting in their private capacity to museums which are not for profit and which are open to the public. With regard to the particular situation of art galleries which acquire works directly from the

author, Member States should be allowed the option of exempting from the resale right acts of resale of those works which take place within three years of that acquisition. The interests of the artist should also be taken into account by limiting this exemption to such acts of resale where the resale price does not exceed EUR 10000.

(19) It should be made clear that the harmonisation brought about by this Directive does not apply to original manuscripts of writers and composers.

(20) Effective rules should be laid down based on experience already gained at national level with the resale right. It is appropriate to calculate the royalty as a percentage of the sale price and not of the increase in value of works whose original value has increased.

(21) The categories of works of art subject to the resale right should be harmonised.

(22) The non-application of royalties below the minimum threshold may help to avoid disproportionately high collection and administration costs compared with the profit for the artist. However, in accordance with the principle of subsidiarity, the Member States should be allowed to establish national thresholds lower than the Community threshold, so as to promote the interests of new artists. Given the small amounts involved, this derogation is not likely to have a significant effect on the proper functioning of the internal market.

(23) The rates set by the different Member States for the application of the resale right vary considerably at present. The effective functioning of the internal market in works of modern and contemporary art requires the fixing of uniform rates to the widest possible extent.

(24) It is desirable to establish, with the intention of reconciling the various interests involved in the market for original works of art, a system consisting of a tapering scale of rates for several price bands. It is important to reduce the risk of sales relocating and of the circumvention of the Community rules on the resale right.

(25) The person by whom the royalty is payable should, in principle, be the seller. Member States should be given the option to provide for derogations from this principle in respect of liability for payment. The seller is the person or undertaking on whose behalf the sale is concluded.

(26) Provision should be made for the possibility of periodic adjustment of the threshold and rates. To this end, it is appropriate to entrust to the Commission the task of drawing up periodic reports on the actual application of the resale right in the Member States and on the impact on the art market in the Community and, where appropriate, of making proposals relating to the amendment of this Directive.

(27) The persons entitled to receive royalties must be specified, due regard being had to the principle of subsidiarity. It is not appropriate to take action through this Directive in relation to Member States' laws of succession. However, those entitled under the author must be able to benefit fully from the resale right after his death, at least following the expiry of the transitional period referred to above.

(28) The Member States are responsible for regulating the exercise of the resale right, particularly with regard to the way this is managed. In this respect management by a collecting society is one possibility. Member States should ensure that collecting societies operate in a transparent and efficient manner. Member States must also ensure that amounts intended for authors who are nationals of other Member States are in fact collected and distributed. This

Directive is without prejudice to arrangements in Member States for collection and distribution.

(29) Enjoyment of the resale right should be restricted to Community nationals as well as to foreign authors whose countries afford such protection to authors who are nationals of Member States. A Member State should have the option of extending enjoyment of this right to foreign authors who have their habitual residence in that Member State.

(30) Appropriate procedures for monitoring transactions should be introduced so as to ensure by practical means that the resale right is effectively applied by Member States. This implies also a right on the part of the author or his authorised representative to obtain any necessary information from the natural or legal person liable for payment of royalties. Member States which provide for collective management of the resale right may also provide that the bodies responsible for that collective management should alone be entitled to obtain information,

HAS ADOPTED THIS DIRECTIVE:

CHAPTER I

SCOPE

Article 1 Subject matter of the resale right

A17-001   1 Member States shall provide, for the benefit of the author of an original work of art, a resale right, to be defined as an inalienable right, which cannot be waived, even in advance, to receive a royalty based on the sale price obtained for any resale of the work, subsequent to the first transfer of the work by the author.

2. The right referred to in paragraph 1 shall apply to all acts of resale involving as sellers, buyers or intermediaries art market professionals, such as salesrooms, art galleries and, in general, any dealers in works of art.

3. Member States may provide that the right referred to in paragraph 1 shall not apply to acts of resale where the seller has acquired the work directly from the author less than three years before that resale and where the resale price does not exceed EUR 10000.

4. The royalty shall be payable by the seller. Member States may provide that one of the natural or legal persons referred to in paragraph 2 other than the seller shall alone be liable or shall share liability with the seller for payment of the royalty.

Article 2 Works of art to which the resale right relates

A17-002   1. For the purposes of this Directive, "original work of art" means works of graphic or plastic art such as pictures, collages, paintings, drawings, engravings, prints, lithographs, sculptures, tapestries, ceramics, glassware and photographs, provided they are made by the artist himself or are copies considered to be original works of art.

2. Copies of works of art covered by this Directive, which have been made in limited numbers by the artist himself or under his authority, shall be considered to be original works of art for the purposes of this Directive. Such copies will normally have been numbered, signed or otherwise duly authorised by the artist.

CHAPTER II

PARTICULAR PROVISIONS

Article 3 Threshold

1. It shall be for the Member States to set a minimum sale price from which **A17-003** the sales referred to in Article 1 shall be subject to resale right.

2. This minimum sale price may not under any circumstances exceed EUR 3000.

Article 4 Rates

1. The royalty provided for in Article 1 shall be set at the following rates: **A17-004**
   (a) 4 % for the portion of the sale price up to EUR 50000;
   (b) 3 % for the portion of the sale price from EUR 50000,01 to EUR 200000;
   (c) 1 % for the portion of the sale price from EUR 200000,01 to EUR 350000;
   (d) 0,5 % for the portion of the sale price from EUR 350000,01 to EUR 500000;
   (e) 0,25 % for the portion of the sale price exceeding EUR 500000.
However, the total amount of the royalty may not exceed EUR 12500.

2. By way of derogation from paragraph 1, Member States may apply a rate of 5 % for the portion of the sale price referred to in paragraph 1(a).

3. If the minimum sale price set should be lower than EUR 3000, the Member State shall also determine the rate applicable to the portion of the sale price up to EUR 3000; this rate may not be lower than 4 %

Article 5 Calculation basis

The sale prices referred to in Articles 3 and 4 are net of tax. **A17-005**

Article 6 Persons entitled to receive royalties

1. The royalty provided for under Article 1 shall be payable to the author of **A17-006** the work and, subject to Article 8(2), after his death to those entitled under him/ her.

2. Member States may provide for compulsory or optional collective management of the royalty provided for under Article 1.

Article 7 Third-country nationals entitled to receive royalties

1. Member States shall provide that authors who are nationals of third **A17-007** countries and, subject to Article 8(2), their successors in title shall enjoy the resale right in accordance with this Directive and the legislation of the Member State concerned only if legislation in the country of which the author or his/her successor in title is a national permits resale right protection in that country for authors from the Member States and their successors in title.

2. On the basis of information provided by the Member States, the Commission shall publish as soon as possible an indicative list of those third countries which fulfil the condition set out in paragraph 1. This list shall be kept up to date.

3. Any Member State may treat authors who are not nationals of a Member State but who have their habitual residence in that Member State in the same way as its own nationals for the purpose of resale right protection.

Article 8 Term of protection of the resale right

A17-008 1. The term of protection of the resale right shall correspond to that laid down in Article 1 of Directive 93/98/EEC.

2. By way of derogation from paragraph 1, those Member States which do not apply the resale right on (the entry into force date referred to in Article 13), shall not be required, for a period expiring not later than 1 January 2010, to apply the resale right for the benefit of those entitled under the artist after his/her death.

3. A Member State to which paragraph 2 applies may have up to two more years, if necessary to enable the economic operators in that Member State to adapt gradually to the resale right system while maintaining their economic viability, before it is required to apply the resale right for the benefit of those entitled under the artist after his/her death. At least 12 months before the end of the period referred to in paragraph 2, the Member State concerned shall inform the Commission giving its reasons, so that the Commission can give an opinion, after appropriate consultations, within three months following the receipt of such information. If the Member State does not follow the opinion of the Commission, it shall within one month inform the Commission and justify its decision. The notification and justification of the Member State and the opinion of the Commission shall be published in the Official Journal of the European Communities and forwarded to the European Parliament.

4. In the event of the successful conclusion, within the periods referred to in Article 8(2) and (3), of international negotiations aimed at extending the resale right at international level, the Commission shall submit appropriate proposals.

Article 9 Right to obtain information

A17-009 The Member States shall provide that for a period of three years after the resale, the persons entitled under Article 6 may require from any art market professional mentioned in Article 1(2) to furnish any information that may be necessary in order to secure payment of royalties in respect of the resale.

CHAPTER III

FINAL PROVISIONS

Article 10 Application in time

A17-010 This Directive shall apply in respect of all original works of art as defined in Article 2 which, on 1 January 2006, are still protected by the legislation of the Member States in the field of copyright or meet the criteria for protection under the provisions of this Directive at that date.

Article 11 Revision clause

A17-011 1. The Commission shall submit to the European Parliament, the Council and the Economic and Social Committee not later than 1 January 2009 and every four years thereafter a report on the implementation and the effect of this Directive, paying particular attention to the competitiveness of the market in modern and contemporary art in the Community, especially as regards the position of the Community in relation to relevant markets that do not apply the resale right and the fostering of artistic creativity and the management procedures in the Member States. It shall examine in particular its impact on the internal market and the effect of the introduction of the resale right in those

Member States that did not apply the right in national law prior to the entry into force of this Directive. Where appropriate, the Commission shall submit proposals for adapting the minimum threshold and the rates of royalty to take account of changes in the sector, proposals relating to the maximum amount laid down in Article 4(1) and any other proposal it may deem necessary in order to enhance the effectiveness of this Directive.

2. A Contact Committee is hereby established. It shall be composed of representatives of the competent authorities of the Member States. It shall be chaired by a representative of the Commission and shall meet either on the initiative of the Chairman or at the request of the delegation of a Member State.

3. The task of the Committee shall be as follows:
- to organise consultations on all questions deriving from application of this Directive,
- to facilitate the exchange of information between the Commission and the Member States on relevant developments in the art market in the Community.

Article 12 Implementation

1. Member States shall bring into force the laws, regulations and administra- **A17-012** tive provisions necessary to comply with this Directive before 1 January 2006. They shall forthwith inform the Commission thereof. When Member States adopt these measures, they shall contain a reference to this Directive or shall be accompanied by such reference on the occasion of their official publication. The methods of making such a reference shall be laid down by the Member States.

2. Member States shall communicate to the Commission the provisions of national law which they adopt in the field covered by this Directive.

Article 13 Entry into force

This Directive shall enter into force on the day of its publication in the **A17-013** Official Journal of the European Communities.

Article 14 Addressees

This Directive is addressed to the Member States. **A17-014**

DIRECTIVE 2004/48/EC OF THE EUROPEAN PARLIAMENT AND OF THE COUNCIL of 29 April 2004 on the enforcement of intellectual property rights (Text with EEA relevance)

THE EUROPEAN PARLIAMENT AND THE COUNCIL OF THE EUROPEAN UNION,

Having regard to the Treaty establishing the European Community, and in particular Article 95 thereof,

Having regard to the proposal from the Commission,

Having regard to the Opinion of the European Economic and Social Committee,

After consulting the Committee of the Regions,

Acting in accordance with the procedure laid down in Article 251 of the Treaty,

Whereas:

(1) The achievement of the Internal Market entails eliminating restrictions on freedom of movement and distortions of competition, while creating an envir-

onment conducive to innovation and investment. In this context, the protection of intellectual property is an essential element for the success of the Internal Market. The protection of intellectual property is important not only for promoting innovation and creativity, but also for developing employment and improving competitiveness.

(2) The protection of intellectual property should allow the inventor or creator to derive a legitimate profit from his invention or creation. It should also allow the widest possible dissemination of works, ideas and new know-how. At the same time, it should not hamper freedom of expression, the free movement of information, or the protection of personal data, including on the Internet.

(3) However, without effective means of enforcing intellectual property rights, innovation and creativity are discouraged and investment diminished. It is therefore necessary to ensure that the substantive law on intellectual property, which is nowadays largely part of the acquis communautaire, is applied effectively in the Community. In this respect, the means of enforcing intellectual property rights are of paramount importance for the success of the Internal Market.

(4) At international level, all Member States, as well as the Community itself as regards matters within its competence, are bound by the Agreement on Trade-Related Aspects of Intellectual Property (the "TRIPS Agreement"), approved, as part of the multilateral negotiations of the Uruguay Round, by Council Decision 94/800/EC and concluded in the framework of the World Trade Organisation.

(5) The TRIPS Agreement contains, in particular, provisions on the means of enforcing intellectual property rights, which are common standards applicable at international level and implemented in all Member States. This Directive should not affect Member States' international obligations, including those under the TRIPS Agreement.

(6) There are also international conventions to which all Member States are parties and which also contain provisions on the means of enforcing intellectual property rights. These include, in particular, the Paris Convention for the Protection of Industrial Property, the Berne Convention for the Protection of Literary and Artistic Works, and the Rome Convention for the Protection of Performers, Producers of Phonograms and Broadcasting Organisations.

(7) It emerges from the consultations held by the Commission on this question that, in the Member States, and despite the TRIPS Agreement, there are still major disparities as regards the means of enforcing intellectual property rights. For instance, the arrangements for applying provisional measures, which are used in particular to preserve evidence, the calculation of damages, or the arrangements for applying injunctions, vary widely from one Member State to another. In some Member States, there are no measures, procedures and remedies such as the right of information and the recall, at the infringer's expense, of the infringing goods placed on the market.

(8) The disparities between the systems of the Member States as regards the means of enforcing intellectual property rights are prejudicial to the proper functioning of the Internal Market and make it impossible to ensure that intellectual property rights enjoy an equivalent level of protection throughout the Community. This situation does not promote free movement within the Internal Market or create an environment conducive to healthy competition.

(9) The current disparities also lead to a weakening of the substantive law on intellectual property and to a fragmentation of the Internal Market in this field. This causes a loss of confidence in the Internal Market in business circles, with a consequent reduction in investment in innovation and creation. Infringements of intellectual property rights appear to be increasingly linked to organised crime. Increasing use of the Internet enables pirated products to be distributed instantly around the globe. Effective enforcement of the substantive law on intellectual property should be ensured by specific action at Community level. Approximation of the legislation of the Member States in this field is therefore an essential prerequisite for the proper functioning of the Internal Market.

(10) The objective of this Directive is to approximate legislative systems so as to ensure a high, equivalent and homogeneous level of protection in the Internal Market.

(11) This Directive does not aim to establish harmonised rules for judicial cooperation, jurisdiction, the recognition and enforcement of decisions in civil and commercial matters, or deal with applicable law. There are Community instruments which govern such matters in general terms and are, in principle, equally applicable to intellectual property.

(12) This Directive should not affect the application of the rules of competition, and in particular Articles 81 and 82 of the Treaty. The measures provided for in this Directive should not be used to restrict unduly competition in a manner contrary to the Treaty.

(13) It is necessary to define the scope of this Directive as widely as possible in order to encompass all the intellectual property rights covered by Community provisions in this field and/or by the national law of the Member State concerned. Nevertheless, that requirement does not affect the possibility, on the part of those Member States which so wish, to extend, for internal purposes, the provisions of this Directive to include acts involving unfair competition, including parasitic copies, or similar activities.

(14) The measures provided for in Articles 6(2), 8(1) and 9(2) need to be applied only in respect of acts carried out on a commercial scale. This is without prejudice to the possibility for Member States to apply those measures also in respect of other acts. Acts carried out on a commercial scale are those carried out for direct or indirect economic or commercial advantage; this would normally exclude acts carried out by end-consumers acting in good faith.

(15) This Directive should not affect substantive law on intellectual property, Directive 95/46/EC of 24 October 1995 of the European Parliament and of the Council on the protection of individuals with regard to the processing of personal data and on the free movement of such data, Directive 1999/93/EC of the European Parliament and of the Council of 13 December 1999 on a Community framework for electronic signatures and Directive 2000/31/EC of the European Parliament and of the Council of 8 June 2000 on certain legal aspects of information society services, in particular electronic commerce, in the Internal Market.

(16) The provisions of this Directive should be without prejudice to the particular provisions for the enforcement of rights and on exceptions in the domain of copyright and related rights set out in Community instruments and notably those found in Council Directive 91/250/EEC of 14 May 1991 on the legal protection of computer programs or in Directive 2001/29/EC of the European Parliament and of the Council of 22 May 2001 on the harmo-

nisation of certain aspects of copyright and related rights in the information society.

(17) The measures, procedures and remedies provided for in this Directive should be determined in each case in such a manner as to take due account of the specific characteristics of that case, including the specific features of each intellectual property right and, where appropriate, the intentional or unintentional character of the infringement.

(18) The persons entitled to request application of those measures, procedures and remedies should be not only the rightholders but also persons who have a direct interest and legal standing in so far as permitted by and in accordance with the applicable law, which may include professional organisations in charge of the management of those rights or for the defence of the collective and individual interests for which they are responsible.

(19) Since copyright exists from the creation of a work and does not require formal registration, it is appropriate to adopt the rule laid down in Article 15 of the Berne Convention, which establishes the presumption whereby the author of a literary or artistic work is regarded as such if his name appears on the work. A similar presumption should be applied to the owners of related rights since it is often the holder of a related right, such as a phonogram producer, who will seek to defend rights and engage in fighting acts of piracy.

(20) Given that evidence is an element of paramount importance for establishing the infringement of intellectual property rights, it is appropriate to ensure that effective means of presenting, obtaining and preserving evidence are available. The procedures should have regard to the rights of the defence and provide the necessary guarantees, including the protection of confidential information. For infringements committed on a commercial scale it is also important that the courts may order access, where appropriate, to banking, financial or commercial documents under the control of the alleged infringer.

(21) Other measures designed to ensure a high level of protection exist in certain Member States and should be made available in all the Member States. This is the case with the right of information, which allows precise information to be obtained on the origin of the infringing goods or services, the distribution channels and the identity of any third parties involved in the infringement.

(22) It is also essential to provide for provisional measures for the immediate termination of infringements, without awaiting a decision on the substance of the case, while observing the rights of the defence, ensuring the proportionality of the provisional measures as appropriate to the characteristics of the case in question and providing the guarantees needed to cover the costs and the injury caused to the defendant by an unjustified request. Such measures are particularly justified where any delay would cause irreparable harm to the holder of an intellectual property right.

(23) Without prejudice to any other measures, procedures and remedies available, rightholders should have the possibility of applying for an injunction against an intermediary whose services are being used by a third party to infringe the rightholder's industrial property right. The conditions and procedures relating to such injunctions should be left to the national law of the Member States. As far as infringements of copyright and related rights are concerned, a comprehensive level of harmonisation is already

provided for in Directive 2001/29/EC. Article 8(3) of Directive 2001/29/EC should therefore not be affected by this Directive.

(24) Depending on the particular case, and if justified by the circumstances, the measures, procedures and remedies to be provided for should include prohibitory measures aimed at preventing further infringements of intellectual property rights. Moreover there should be corrective measures, where appropriate at the expense of the infringer, such as the recall and definitive removal from the channels of commerce, or destruction, of the infringing goods and, in appropriate cases, of the materials and implements principally used in the creation or manufacture of these goods. These corrective measures should take account of the interests of third parties including, in particular, consumers and private parties acting in good faith.

(25) Where an infringement is committed unintentionally and without negligence and where the corrective measures or injunctions provided for by this Directive would be disproportionate, Member States should have the option of providing for the possibility, in appropriate cases, of pecuniary compensation being awarded to the injured party as an alternative measure. However, where the commercial use of counterfeit goods or the supply of services would constitute an infringement of law other than intellectual property law or would be likely to harm consumers, such use or supply should remain prohibited.

(26) With a view to compensating for the prejudice suffered as a result of an infringement committed by an infringer who engaged in an activity in the knowledge, or with reasonable grounds for knowing, that it would give rise to such an infringement, the amount of damages awarded to the rightholder should take account of all appropriate aspects, such as loss of earnings incurred by the rightholder, or unfair profits made by the infringer and, where appropriate, any moral prejudice caused to the rightholder. As an alternative, for example where it would be difficult to determine the amount of the actual prejudice suffered, the amount of the damages might be derived from elements such as the royalties or fees which would have been due if the infringer had requested authorisation to use the intellectual property right in question. The aim is not to introduce an obligation to provide for punitive damages but to allow for compensation based on an objective criterion while taking account of the expenses incurred by the rightholder, such as the costs of identification and research.

(27) To act as a supplementary deterrent to future infringers and to contribute to the awareness of the public at large, it is useful to publicise decisions in intellectual property infringement cases.

(28) In addition to the civil and administrative measures, procedures and remedies provided for under this Directive, criminal sanctions also constitute, in appropriate cases, a means of ensuring the enforcement of intellectual property rights.

(29) Industry should take an active part in the fight against piracy and counterfeiting. The development of codes of conduct in the circles directly affected is a supplementary means of bolstering the regulatory framework. The Member States, in collaboration with the Commission, should encourage the development of codes of conduct in general. Monitoring of the manufacture of optical discs, particularly by means of an identification code embedded in discs produced in the Community, helps to limit infringements of intellectual property rights in this sector, which suffers from piracy on a

large scale. However, these technical protection measures should not be misused to protect markets and prevent parallel imports.

(30) In order to facilitate the uniform application of this Directive, it is appropriate to provide for systems of cooperation and the exchange of information between Member States, on the one hand, and between the Member States and the Commission on the other, in particular by creating a network of correspondents designated by the Member States and by providing regular reports assessing the application of this Directive and the effectiveness of the measures taken by the various national bodies.

(31) Since, for the reasons already described, the objective of this Directive can best be achieved at Community level, the Community may adopt measures, in accordance with the principle of subsidiarity as set out in Article 5 of the Treaty. In accordance with the principle of proportionality as set out in that Article, this Directive does not go beyond what is necessary in order to achieve that objective.

(32) This Directive respects the fundamental rights and observes the principles recognised in particular by the Charter of Fundamental Rights of the European Union. In particular, this Directive seeks to ensure full respect for intellectual property, in accordance with Article 17(2) of that Charter,

HAVE ADOPTED THIS DIRECTIVE:

CHAPTER I

OBJECTIVE AND SCOPE

Article 1 Subject matter

A18-001   This Directive concerns the measures, procedures and remedies necessary to ensure the enforcement of intellectual property rights. For the purposes of this Directive, the term "intellectual property rights" includes industrial property rights.

Article 2 Scope

A18-002   1. Without prejudice to the means which are or may be provided for in Community or national legislation, in so far as those means may be more favourable for rightholders, the measures, procedures and remedies provided for by this Directive shall apply, in accordance with Article 3, to any infringement of intellectual property rights as provided for by Community law and/or by the national law of the Member State concerned.

2. This Directive shall be without prejudice to the specific provisions on the enforcement of rights and on exceptions contained in Community legislation concerning copyright and rights related to copyright, notably those found in Directive 91/250/EEC and, in particular, Article 7 thereof or in Directive 2001/29/EC and, in particular, Articles 2 to 6 and Article 8 thereof.

3. This Directive shall not affect:

(a) the Community provisions governing the substantive law on intellectual property, Directive 95/46/EC, Directive 1999/93/EC or Directive 2000/31/EC, in general, and Articles 12 to 15 of Directive 2000/31/EC in particular;

(b) Member States' international obligations and notably the TRIPS Agreement, including those relating to criminal procedures and penalties;

(c) any national provisions in Member States relating to criminal procedures or penalties in respect of infringement of intellectual property rights.

CHAPTER II

MEASURES, PROCEDURES AND REMEDIES

Section 1 General provisions

Article 3 General obligation

1. Member States shall provide for the measures, procedures and remedies **A18-003** necessary to ensure the enforcement of the intellectual property rights covered by this Directive. Those measures, procedures and remedies shall be fair and equitable and shall not be unnecessarily complicated or costly, or entail unreasonable time-limits or unwarranted delays.

2. Those measures, procedures and remedies shall also be effective, proportionate and dissuasive and shall be applied in such a manner as to avoid the creation of barriers to legitimate trade and to provide for safeguards against their abuse.

Article 4 Persons entitled to apply for the application of the measures, procedures and remedies

1. Member States shall recognise as persons entitled to seek application of **A18-004** the measures, procedures and remedies referred to in this Chapter:
  (a) the holders of intellectual property rights, in accordance with the provisions of the applicable law,
  (b) all other persons authorised to use those rights, in particular licensees, in so far as permitted by and in accordance with the provisions of the applicable law,
  (c) intellectual property collective rights management bodies which are regularly recognised as having a right to represent holders of intellectual property rights, in so far as permitted by and in accordance with the provisions of the applicable law,
  (d) professional defence bodies which are regularly recognised as having a right to represent holders of intellectual property rights, in so far as permitted by and in accordance with the provisions of the applicable law.

Article 5 Presumption of authorship or ownership

For the purposes of applying the measures, procedures and remedies **A18-005** provided for in this Directive,
  (a) for the author of a literary or artistic work, in the absence of proof to the contrary, to be regarded as such, and consequently to be entitled to institute infringement proceedings, it shall be sufficient for his name to appear on the work in the usual manner;
  (b) the provision under (a) shall apply mutatis mutandis to the holders of rights related to copyright with regard to their protected subject matter.

Section 2 Evidence

Article 6 Evidence

A18-006   1. Member States shall ensure that, on application by a party which has presented reasonably available evidence sufficient to support its claims, and has, in substantiating those claims, specified evidence which lies in the control of the opposing party, the competent judicial authorities may order that such evidence be presented by the opposing party, subject to the protection of confidential information. For the purposes of this paragraph, Member States may provide that a reasonable sample of a substantial number of copies of a work or any other protected object be considered by the competent judicial authorities to constitute reasonable evidence.

2. Under the same conditions, in the case of an infringement committed on a commercial scale Member States shall take such measures as are necessary to enable the competent judicial authorities to order, where appropriate, on application by a party, the communication of banking, financial or commercial documents under the control of the opposing party, subject to the protection of confidential information.

Article 7 Measures for preserving evidence

A18-007   1. Member States shall ensure that, even before the commencement of proceedings on the merits of the case, the competent judicial authorities may, on application by a party who has presented reasonably available evidence to support his claims that his intellectual property right has been infringed or is about to be infringed, order prompt and effective provisional measures to preserve relevant evidence in respect of the alleged infringement, subject to the protection of confidential information. Such measures may include the detailed description, with or without the taking of samples, or the physical seizure of the infringing goods, and, in appropriate cases, the materials and implements used in the production and/or distribution of these goods and the documents relating thereto. Those measures shall be taken, if necessary without the other party having been heard, in particular where any delay is likely to cause irreparable harm to the rightholder or where there is a demonstrable risk of evidence being destroyed.

Where measures to preserve evidence are adopted without the other party having been heard, the parties affected shall be given notice, without delay after the execution of the measures at the latest. A review, including a right to be heard, shall take place upon request of the parties affected with a view to deciding, within a reasonable period after the notification of the measures, whether the measures shall be modified, revoked or confirmed.

2. Member States shall ensure that the measures to preserve evidence may be subject to the lodging by the applicant of adequate security or an equivalent assurance intended to ensure compensation for any prejudice suffered by the defendant as provided for in paragraph 4.

3. Member States shall ensure that the measures to preserve evidence are revoked or otherwise cease to have effect, upon request of the defendant, without prejudice to the damages which may be claimed, if the applicant does not institute, within a reasonable period, proceedings leading to a decision on the merits of the case before the competent judicial authority, the period to be determined by the judicial authority ordering the measures where the law of a Member State so permits or, in the absence of such determination, within a

period not exceeding 20 working days or 31 calendar days, whichever is the longer.

4. Where the measures to preserve evidence are revoked, or where they lapse due to any act or omission by the applicant, or where it is subsequently found that there has been no infringement or threat of infringement of an intellectual property right, the judicial authorities shall have the authority to order the applicant, upon request of the defendant, to provide the defendant appropriate compensation for any injury caused by those measures.

5. Member States may take measures to protect witnesses' identity.

Section 3 Right of information

Article 8 Right of information

1. Member States shall ensure that, in the context of proceedings concerning **A18-008** an infringement of an intellectual property right and in response to a justified and proportionate request of the claimant, the competent judicial authorities may order that information on the origin and distribution networks of the goods or services which infringe an intellectual property right be provided by the infringer and/or any other person who:

   (a) was found in possession of the infringing goods on a commercial scale;

   (b) was found to be using the infringing services on a commercial scale;

   (c) was found to be providing on a commercial scale services used in infringing activities; or

   (d) was indicated by the person referred to in point (a), (b) or (c) as being involved in the production, manufacture or distribution of the goods or the provision of the services.

2. The information referred to in paragraph 1 shall, as appropriate, comprise:

   (a) the names and addresses of the producers, manufacturers, distributors, suppliers and other previous holders of the goods or services, as well as the intended wholesalers and retailers;

   (b) information on the quantities produced, manufactured, delivered, received or ordered, as well as the price obtained for the goods or services in question.

3. Paragraphs 1 and 2 shall apply without prejudice to other statutory provisions which:

   (a) grant the rightholder rights to receive fuller information;

   (b) govern the use in civil or criminal proceedings of the information communicated pursuant to this Article;

   (c) govern responsibility for misuse of the right of information; or

   (d) afford an opportunity for refusing to provide information which would force the person referred to in paragraph 1 to admit to his own participation or that of his close relatives in an infringement of an intellectual property right; or

   (e) govern the protection of confidentiality of information sources or the processing of personal data.

Section 4 Provisional and precautionary measures

Article 9 Provisional and precautionary measures

A18-009 1. Member States shall ensure that the judicial authorities may, at the request of the applicant:

(a) issue against the alleged infringer an interlocutory injunction intended to prevent any imminent infringement of an intellectual property right, or to forbid, on a provisional basis and subject, where appropriate, to a recurring penalty payment where provided for by national law, the continuation of the alleged infringements of that right, or to make such continuation subject to the lodging of guarantees intended to ensure the compensation of the rightholder; an interlocutory injunction may also be issued, under the same conditions, against an intermediary whose services are being used by a third party to infringe an intellectual property right; injunctions against intermediaries whose services are used by a third party to infringe a copyright or a related right are covered by Directive 2001/29/EC;

(b) order the seizure or delivery up of the goods suspected of infringing an intellectual property right so as to prevent their entry into or movement within the channels of commerce.

2. In the case of an infringement committed on a commercial scale, the Member States shall ensure that, if the injured party demonstrates circumstances likely to endanger the recovery of damages, the judicial authorities may order the precautionary seizure of the movable and immovable property of the alleged infringer, including the blocking of his bank accounts and other assets. To that end, the competent authorities may order the communication of bank, financial or commercial documents, or appropriate access to the relevant information.

3. The judicial authorities shall, in respect of the measures referred to in paragraphs 1 and 2, have the authority to require the applicant to provide any reasonably available evidence in order to satisfy themselves with a sufficient degree of certainty that the applicant is the rightholder and that the applicant's right is being infringed, or that such infringement is imminent.

4. Member States shall ensure that the provisional measures referred to in paragraphs 1 and 2 may, in appropriate cases, be taken without the defendant having been heard, in particular where any delay would cause irreparable harm to the rightholder. In that event, the parties shall be so informed without delay after the execution of the measures at the latest.

A review, including a right to be heard, shall take place upon request of the defendant with a view to deciding, within a reasonable time after notification of the measures, whether those measures shall be modified, revoked or confirmed.

5. Member States shall ensure that the provisional measures referred to in paragraphs 1 and 2 are revoked or otherwise cease to have effect, upon request of the defendant, if the applicant does not institute, within a reasonable period, proceedings leading to a decision on the merits of the case before the competent judicial authority, the period to be determined by the judicial authority ordering the measures where the law of a Member State so permits or, in the absence of such determination, within a period not exceeding 20 working days or 31 calendar days, whichever is the longer.

6. The competent judicial authorities may make the provisional measures referred to in paragraphs 1 and 2 subject to the lodging by the applicant of adequate security or an equivalent assurance intended to ensure compensation for any prejudice suffered by the defendant as provided for in paragraph 7.

7. Where the provisional measures are revoked or where they lapse due to any act or omission by the applicant, or where it is subsequently found that there has been no infringement or threat of infringement of an intellectual property right, the judicial authorities shall have the authority to order the applicant, upon request of the defendant, to provide the defendant appropriate compensation for any injury caused by those measures.

Section 5 Measures resulting from a decision on the merits of the case

Article 10 Corrective measures

1. Without prejudice to any damages due to the rightholder by reason of the **A18-010** infringement, and without compensation of any sort, Member States shall ensure that the competent judicial authorities may order, at the request of the applicant, that appropriate measures be taken with regard to goods that they have found to be infringing an intellectual property right and, in appropriate cases, with regard to materials and implements principally used in the creation or manufacture of those goods. Such measures shall include:
   (a) recall from the channels of commerce,
   (b) definitive removal from the channels of commerce, or
   (c) destruction.

2. The judicial authorities shall order that those measures be carried out at the expense of the infringer, unless particular reasons are invoked for not doing so.

3. In considering a request for corrective measures, the need for proportionality between the seriousness of the infringement and the remedies ordered as well as the interests of third parties shall be taken into account.

Article 11 Injunctions

Member States shall ensure that, where a judicial decision is taken finding an **A18-011** infringement of an intellectual property right, the judicial authorities may issue against the infringer an injunction aimed at prohibiting the continuation of the infringement. Where provided for by national law, non-compliance with an injunction shall, where appropriate, be subject to a recurring penalty payment, with a view to ensuring compliance. Member States shall also ensure that rightholders are in a position to apply for an injunction against intermediaries whose services are used by a third party to infringe an intellectual property right, without prejudice to Article 8(3) of Directive 2001/29/EC.

Article 12 Alternative measures

Member States may provide that, in appropriate cases and at the request of **A18-012** the person liable to be subject to the measures provided for in this Section, the competent judicial authorities may order pecuniary compensation to be paid to the injured party instead of applying the measures provided for in this Section if that person acted unintentionally and without negligence, if execution of the measures in question would cause him disproportionate harm and if pecuniary compensation to the injured party appears reasonably satisfactory.

Section 6 Damages and legal costs

Article 13 Damages

A18-013   1. Member States shall ensure that the competent judicial authorities, on application of the injured party, order the infringer who knowingly, or with reasonable grounds to know, engaged in an infringing activity, to pay the right-holder damages appropriate to the actual prejudice suffered by him as a result of the infringement.

When the judicial authorities set the damages:
  (a) they shall take into account all appropriate aspects, such as the negative economic consequences, including lost profits, which the injured party has suffered, any unfair profits made by the infringer and, in appropriate cases, elements other than economic factors, such as the moral prejudice caused to the rightholder by the infringement; or
  (b) as an alternative to (a), they may, in appropriate cases, set the damages as a lump sum on the basis of elements such as at least the amount of royalties or fees which would have been due if the infringer had requested authorisation to use the intellectual property right in question.

2. Where the infringer did not knowingly, or with reasonable grounds to know, engage in infringing activity, Member States may lay down that the judicial authorities may order the recovery of profits or the payment of damages, which may be pre-established.

Article 14 Legal costs

A18-014   Member States shall ensure that reasonable and proportionate legal costs and other expenses incurred by the successful party shall, as a general rule, be borne by the unsuccessful party, unless equity does not allow this.

Section 7 Publicity measures

Article 15 Publication of judicial decisions

A18-015   Member States shall ensure that, in legal proceedings instituted for infringement of an intellectual property right, the judicial authorities may order, at the request of the applicant and at the expense of the infringer, appropriate measures for the dissemination of the information concerning the decision, including displaying the decision and publishing it in full or in part. Member States may provide for other additional publicity measures which are appropriate to the particular circumstances, including prominent advertising.

CHAPTER III

SANCTIONS BY MEMBER STATES

Article 16 Sanctions by Member States

A18-016   Without prejudice to the civil and administrative measures, procedures and remedies laid down by this Directive, Member States may apply other appropriate sanctions in cases where intellectual property rights have been infringed.

CHAPTER IV

CODES OF CONDUCT AND ADMINISTRATIVE COOPERATION

Article 17 Codes of conduct

Member States shall encourage:
    (a) the development by trade or professional associations or organisations of codes of conduct at Community level aimed at contributing towards the enforcement of the intellectual property rights, particularly by recommending the use on optical discs of a code enabling the identification of the origin of their manufacture;
    (b) the submission to the Commission of draft codes of conduct at national and Community level and of any evaluations of the application of these codes of conduct.

A18-017

Article 18 Assessment

1. Three years after the date laid down in Article 20(1), each Member State shall submit to the Commission a report on the implementation of this Directive.

A18-018

On the basis of those reports, the Commission shall draw up a report on the application of this Directive, including an assessment of the effectiveness of the measures taken, as well as an evaluation of its impact on innovation and the development of the information society. That report shall then be transmitted to the European Parliament, the Council and the European Economic and Social Committee. It shall be accompanied, if necessary and in the light of developments in the Community legal order, by proposals for amendments to this Directive.

2. Member States shall provide the Commission with all the aid and assistance it may need when drawing up the report referred to in the second subparagraph of paragraph 1.

Article 19 Exchange of information and correspondents

For the purpose of promoting cooperation, including the exchange of information, among Member States and between Member States and the Commission, each Member State shall designate one or more national correspondents for any question relating to the implementation of the measures provided for by this Directive. It shall communicate the details of the national correspondent(s) to the other Member States and to the Commission.

A18-019

CHAPTER V

FINAL PROVISIONS

Article 20 Implementation

1. Member States shall bring into force the laws, regulations and administrative provisions necessary to comply with this Directive by ... [1]. They shall forthwith inform the Commission thereof.
    When Member States adopt these measures, they shall contain a reference to this Directive or shall be accompanied by such reference on the occasion of their

A18-020

---

[1] Twenty-four months after the date of adoption of this Directive.

official publication. The methods of making such reference shall be laid down by Member States.

2. Member States shall communicate to the Commission the texts of the provisions of national law which they adopt in the field governed by this Directive.

Article 21 Entry into force

A18-021   This Directive shall enter into force on the twentieth day following that of its publication in the Official Journal of the European Union.

Article 22 Addressees

A18-022   This Directive is addressed to the Member States.

Paris Convention for the Protection of Industrial Property

(of March 20, 1883, as revised at Brussels on December 14, 1900, at Washington on June 2, 1911, at The Hague on November 6, 1925, at London on June 2, 1934, at Lisbon on October 31, 1958, and at Stockholm on July 14, 1967, and as amended on September 28, 1979)

Article 1 Establishment of the Union; Scope of Industrial Property

A19-001   (1) The countries to which this Convention applies constitute a Union for the protection of industrial property.

(2) The protection of industrial property has as its object patents, utility models, industrial designs, trademarks, service marks, trade names, indications of source or appellations of origin, and the repression of unfair competition.

(3) Industrial property shall be understood in the broadest sense and shall apply not only to industry and commerce proper, but likewise to agricultural and extractive industries and to all manufactured or natural products, for example, wines, grain, tobacco leaf, fruit, cattle, minerals, mineral waters, beer, flowers, and flour.

(4) Patents shall include the various kinds of industrial patents recognized by the laws of the countries of the Union, such as patents of importation, patents of improvement, patents and certificates of addition, etc.

Article 2 National Treatment for Nationals of Countries of the Union

A19-002   (1) Nationals of any country of the Union shall, as regards the protection of industrial property, enjoy in all the other countries of the Union the advantages that their respective laws now grant, or may hereafter grant, to nationals; all without prejudice to the rights specially provided for by this Convention. Consequently, they shall have the same protection as the latter, and the same legal remedy against any infringement of their rights, provided that the conditions and formalities imposed upon nationals are complied with.

(2) However, no requirement as to domicile or establishment in the country where protection is claimed may be imposed upon nationals of countries of the Union for the enjoyment of any industrial property rights.

(3) The provisions of the laws of each of the countries of the Union relating to judicial and administrative procedure and to jurisdiction, and to the designa-

tion of an address for service or the appointment of an agent, which may be required by the laws on industrial property are expressly reserved.

Article 3 Same Treatment for Certain Categories of Persons as for Nationals of Countries of the Union

Nationals of countries outside the Union who are domiciled or who have real **A19-003** and effective industrial or commercial establishments in the territory of one of the countries of the Union shall be treated in the same manner as nationals of the countries of the Union.

Article 4 A to I. Patents, Utility Models, Industrial Designs, Marks, Inventors' Certificates: Right of Priority. - G. Patents: Division of the Application

A.- **A19-004**
  (1) Any person who has duly filed an application for a patent, or for the registration of a utility model, or of an industrial design, or of a trademark, in one of the countries of the Union, or his successor in title, shall enjoy, for the purpose of filing in the other countries, a right of priority during the periods hereinafter fixed.
  (2) Any filing that is equivalent to a regular national filing under the domestic legislation of any country of the Union or under bilateral or multilateral treaties concluded between countries of the Union shall be recognized as giving rise to the right of priority.
  (3) By a regular national filing is meant any filing that is adequate to establish the date on which the application was filed in the country concerned, whatever may be the subsequent fate of the application.

B.- Consequently, any subsequent filing in any of the other countries of the Union before the expiration of the periods referred to above shall not be invalidated by reason of any acts accomplished in the interval, in particular, another filing, the publication or exploitation of the invention, the putting on sale of copies of the design, or the use of the mark, and such acts cannot give rise to any third-party right or any right of personal possession. Rights acquired by third parties before the date of the first application that serves as the basis for the right of priority are reserved in accordance with the domestic legislation of each country of the Union

C.-
  (1) The periods of priority referred to above shall be twelve months for patents and utility models, and six months for industrial designs and trademarks.
  (2) These periods shall start from the date of filing of the first application; the day of filing shall not be included in the period.
  (3) If the last day of the period is an official holiday, or a day when the Office is not open for the filing of applications in the country where protection is claimed, the period shall be extended until the first following working day.
  (4) A subsequent application concerning the same subject as a previous first application within the meaning of paragraph (2), above, filed in the same country of the Union shall be considered as the first application, of which the filing date shall be the starting point of the period of priority, if, at the time of filing the subsequent application, the said previous application has been withdrawn, abandoned, or refused, without having been laid open to public inspection and without leaving

any rights outstanding, and if it has not yet served as a basis for claiming a right of priority. The previous application may not thereafter serve as a basis for claiming a right of priority.

D.-

(1) Any person desiring to take advantage of the priority of a previous filing shall be required to make a declaration indicating the date of such filing and the country in which it was made. Each country shall determine the latest date on which such declaration must be made.

(2) These particulars shall be mentioned in the publications issued by the competent authority, and in particular in the patents and the specifications relating thereto.

(3) The countries of the Union may require any person making a declaration of priority to produce a copy of the application (description, drawings, etc.) previously filed. The copy, certified as correct by the authority which received such application, shall not require any authentication, and may in any case be filed, without fee, at any time within three months of the filing of the subsequent application. They may require it to be accompanied by a certificate from the same authority showing the date of filing, and by a translation.

(4) No other formalities may be required for the declaration of priority at the time of filing the application. Each country of the Union shall determine the consequences of failure to comply with the formalities prescribed by this Article, but such consequences shall in no case go beyond the loss of the right of priority.

(5) Subsequently, further proof may be required.

Any person who avails himself of the priority of a previous application shall be required to specify the number of that application; this number shall be published as provided for by paragraph (2), above.

E. -

(1) Where an industrial design is filed in a country by virtue of a right of priority based on the filing of a utility model, the period of priority shall be the same as that fixed for industrial designs.

(2) Furthermore, it is permissible to file a utility model in a country by virtue of a right of priority based on the filing of a patent application, and vice versa.

F. - No country of the Union may refuse a priority or a patent application on the ground that the applicant claims multiple priorities, even if they originate in different countries, or on the ground that an application claiming one or more priorities contains one or more elements that were not included in the application or applications whose priority is claimed, provided that, in both cases, there is unity of invention within the meaning of the law of the country.

With respect to the elements not included in the application or applications whose priority is claimed, the filing of the subsequent application shall give rise to a right of priority under ordinary conditions.

G. -

(1) If the examination reveals that an application for a patent contains more than one invention, the applicant may divide the application into a certain number of divisional applications and preserve as the date of each the date of the initial application and the benefit of the right of priority, if any.

(2) The applicant may also, on his own initiative, divide a patent application and preserve as the date of each divisional application the date of the initial application and the benefit of the right of priority, if any. Each country of the Union shall have the right to determine the conditions under which such division shall be authorized.

H. - Priority may not be refused on the ground that certain elements of the invention for which priority is claimed do not appear among the claims formulated in the application in the country of origin, provided that the application documents as a whole specifically disclose such elements.

I. -

(1) Applications for inventors' certificates filed in a country in which applicants have the right to apply at their own option eitherfor a patent or for an inventor's certificate shall give rise to the right of priority provided for by this Article, under the same conditions and with the same effects as applications for patents.

(2) In a country in which applicants have the right to apply at their own option either for a patent or for an inventor's certificate, an applicant for an inventor's certificate shall, in accordance with the provisions of this Article relating to patent applications, enjoy a right of priority based on an application for a patent, a utility model, or an inventor's certificate.

Article 4bis Patents: Independence of Patents Obtained for the Same Invention in Different Countries

(1) Patents applied for in the various countries of the Union by nationals of **A19-005** countries of the Union shall be independent of patents obtained for the same invention in other countries, whether members of the Union or not.

(2) The foregoing provision is to be understood in an unrestricted sense, in particular, in the sense that patents applied for during the period of priority are independent, both as regards the grounds for nullity and forfeiture, and as regards their normal duration.

(3) The provision shall apply to all patents existing at the time when it comes into effect.

(4) Similarly, it shall apply, in the case of the accession of new countries, to patents in existence

(5) Patents obtained with the benefit of priority shall, in the various countries of the Union, have a duration equal to that which they would have, had they been applied for or granted without the benefit of priority.

Article 4ter Patents: Mention of the Inventor in the Patent

The inventor shall have the right to be mentioned as such in the patent. **A19-006**

Article 4quater Patents: Patentability in Case of Restrictions of Sale by Law

The grant of a patent shall not be refused and a patent shall not be invalidated **A19-007** on the ground that the sale of the patented product or of a product obtained by means of a patented process is subject to restrictions or limitations resulting from the domestic law.

Article 5 A. Patents: Importation of Articles; Failure to Work or Insufficient Working; Compulsory Licenses. - B. Industrial Designs: Failure to Work; Importation of Articles. - C. Marks: Failure to Use; Different Forms; Use by Co-proprietors. - D. Patents, Utility Models, Marks, Industrial Designs: Marking

A19-008   A.-

(1) Importation by the patentee into the country where the patent has been granted of articles manufactured in any of the countries of the Union shall not entail forfeiture of the patent.

(2) Each country of the Union shall have the right to take legislative measures providing for the grant of compulsory licenses to prevent the abuses which might result from the exercise of the exclusive rights conferred by the patent, for example, failure to work.

(3) Forfeiture of the patent shall not be provided for except in cases where the grant of compulsory licenses would not have been sufficient to prevent the said abuses. No proceedings for the forfeiture or revocation of a patent may be instituted before the expiration of two years from the grant of the first compulsory license.

(4) A compulsory license may not be applied for on the ground of failure to work or insufficient working before the expiration of a period of four years from the date of filing of the patent application or three years from the date of the grant of the patent, whichever period expires last; it shall be refused if the patentee justifies his inaction by legitimate reasons. Such a compulsory license shall be non-exclusive and shall not be transferable, even in the form of the grant of a sub-license, except with that part of the enterprise or goodwill which exploits such license.

(5) The foregoing provisions shall be applicable, mutatis mutandis, to utility models.

B.- The protection of industrial designs shall not, under any circumstance, be subject to any forfeiture, either by reason of failure to work or by reason of the importation of articles corresponding to those which are protected.

C.-

(1) If, in any country, use of the registered mark is compulsory, the registration may be cancelled only after a reasonable period, and then only if the person concerned does not justify his inaction.

(2) Use of a trademark by the proprietor in a form differing in elements which do not alter the distinctive character of the mark in the form in which it was registered in one of the countries of the Union shall not entail invalidation of the registration and shall not diminish the protection granted to the mark.

(3) Concurrent use of the same mark on identical or similar goods by industrial or commercial establishments considered as co-proprietors of the mark according to the provisions of the domestic law of the country where protection is claimed shall not prevent registration or diminish in any way the protection granted to the said mark in any country of the Union, provided that such use does not result in misleading the public and is not contrary to the public interest.

D.- No indication or mention of the patent, of the utility model, of the registration of the trademark, or of the deposit of the industrial design, shall be required upon the goods as a condition of recognition of the right to protection.

Article 5bis All Industrial Property Rights: Period of Grace for the Payment of Fees for the Maintenance of Rights; Patents: Restoration

(1) A period of grace of not less than six months shall be allowed for the **A19-009** payment of the fees prescribed for the maintenance of industrial property rights, subject, if the domestic legislation so provides, to the payment of a surcharge.

(2) The countries of the Union shall have the right to provide for the restoration of patents which have lapsed by reason of non-payment of fees.

Article 5ter Patents: Patented Devices Forming Part of Vessels, Aircraft, or Land Vehicles

In any country of the Union the following shall not be considered as infringe- **A19-010** ments of the rights of a patentee:

1. the use on board vessels of other countries of the Union of devices forming the subject of his patent in the body of the vessel, in the machinery, tackle, gear and other accessories, when such vessels temporarily or accidentally enter the waters of the said country, provided that such devices are used there exclusively for the needs of the vessel;

2. the use of devices forming the subject of the patent in the construction or operation of aircraft or land vehicles of other countries of the Union, or of accessories of such aircraft or land vehicles, when those aircraft or land vehicles temporarily or accidentally enter the said country.

Article 5quater Patents: Importation of Products Manufactured by a Process Patented in the Importing Country

When a product is imported into a country of the Union where there exists a **A19-011** patent protecting a process of manufacture of the said product, the patentee shall have all the rights, with regard to the imported product, that are accorded to him by the legislation of the country of importation, on the basis of the process patent, with respect to products manufactured in that country.

Article 5quínquies Industrial Designs

Industrial designs shall be protected in all the countries of the Union. **A19-012**

Article 6 Marks: Conditions of Registration; Independence of Protection of Same Mark in Different Countries

(1) The conditions for the filing and registration of trademarks shall be **A19-013** determined in each country of the Union by its domestic legislation.

(2) However, an application for the registration of a mark filed by a national of a country of the Union in any country of the Union may not be refused, nor may a registration be invalidated, on the ground that filing, registration, or renewal, has not been effected in the country of origin.

(3) A mark duly registered in a country of the Union shall be regarded as independent of marks registered in the other countries of the Union, including the country of origin.

Article 6bis Marks: Well-Known Marks

(1) The countries of the Union undertake, ex officio if their legislation so **A19-014** permits, or at the request of an interested party, to refuse or to cancel the registration, and to prohibit the use, of a trademark which constitutes a reproduction, an imitation, or a translation, liable to create confusion, of a mark considered by the competent authority of the country of registration or use to be well known

in that country as being already the mark of a person entitled to the benefits of this Convention and used for identical or similar goods. These provisions shall also apply when the essential part of the mark constitutes a reproduction of any such well-known mark or an imitation liable to create confusion therewith.

(2) A period of at least five years from the date of registration shall be allowed for requesting the cancellation of such a mark. The countries of the Union may provide for a period within which the prohibition of use must be requested.

(3) No time limit shall be fixed for requesting the cancellation or the prohibition of the use of marks registered or used in bad faith.

Article 6ter Marks: Prohibitions concerning State Emblems, Official Hallmarks, and Emblems of Intergovernmental Organizations

A19-015 (1)

(a) The countries of the Union agree to refuse or to invalidate the registration, and to prohibit by appropriate measures the use, without authorization by the competent authorities, either as trademarks or as elements of trademarks, of armorial bearings, flags, and other State emblems, of the countries of the Union, official signs and hallmarks indicating control and warranty adopted by them, and any imitation from a heraldic point of view.

(b) The provisions of subparagraph (a), above, shall apply equally to armorial bearings, flags, other emblems, abbreviations, and names, of international intergovernmental organizations of which one or more countries of the Union are members, with the exception of armorial bearings, flags, other emblems, abbreviations, and names, that are already the subject of international agreements in force, intended to ensure their protection.

(c) No country of the Union shall be required to apply the provisions of subparagraph (b), above, to the prejudice of the owners of rights acquired in good faith before the entry into force, in that country, of this Convention. The countries of the Union shall not be required to apply the said provisions when the use or registration referred to in subparagraph (a), above, is not of such a nature as to suggest to the public that a connection exists between the organization concerned and the armorial bearings, flags, emblems, abbreviations, and names, or if such use or registration is probably not of such a nature as to mislead the public as to the existence of a connection between the user and the organization.

(2) Prohibition of the use of official signs and hallmarks indicating control and warranty shall apply solely in cases where the marks in which they are incorporated are intended to be used on goods of the same or a similar kind.

(3)

(a) For the application of these provisions, the countries of the Union agree to communicate reciprocally, through the intermediary of the International Bureau, the list of State emblems, and official signs and hallmarks indicating control and warranty, which they desire, or may hereafter desire, to place wholly or within certain limits under the protection of this Article, and all subsequent modifications of such list. Each country of the Union shall in due course make available to the public the lists so communicated. Nevertheless such communication is not obligatory in respect of flags of States.

(b) The provisions of subparagraph (b) of paragraph (1) of this Article shall apply only to such armorial bearings, flags, other emblems, abbreviations, and names, of international intergovernmental organizations as the latter have communicated to the countries of the Union through the intermediary of the International Bureau.

(4) Any country of the Union may, within a period of twelve months from the receipt of the notification, transmit its objections, if any, through the intermediary of the International Bureau, to the country or international intergovernmental organization concerned.

(5) In the case of State flags, the measures prescribed by paragraph (1), above, shall apply solely to marks registered after November 6, 1925.

(6) In the case of State emblems other than flags, and of official signs and hallmarks of the countries of the Union, and in the case of armorial bearings, flags, other emblems, abbreviations, and names, of international intergovernmental organizations, these provisions shall apply only to marks registered more than two months after receipt of the communication provided for in paragraph (3), above.

(7) In cases of bad faith, the countries shall have the right to cancel even those marks incorporating State emblems, signs, and hallmarks, which were registered before November 6, 1925.

(8) Nationals of any country who are authorized to make use of the State emblems, signs, and hallmarks, of their country may use them even if they are similar to those of another country.

(9) The countries of the Union undertake to prohibit the unauthorized use in trade of the State armorial bearings of the other countries of the Union, when the use is of such a nature as to be misleading as to the origin of the goods.

(10) The above provisions shall not prevent the countries from exercising the right given in paragraph (3) of Article 6quinquies, Section B, to refuse or to invalidate the registration of marks incorporating, without authorization, armorial bearings, flags, other State emblems, or official signs and hallmarks adopted by a country of the Union, as well as the distinctive signs of international intergovernmental organizations referred to in paragraph (1), above.

Article 6quater Marks: Assignment of Marks

(1) When, in accordance with the law of a country of the Union, the **A19-016** assignment of a mark is valid only if it takes place at the same time as the transfer of the business or goodwill to which the mark belongs, it shall suffice for the recognition of such validity that the portion of the business or goodwill located in that country be transferred to the assignee, together with the exclusive right to manufacture in the said country, or to sell therein, the goods bearing the mark assigned.

(2) The foregoing provision does not impose upon the countries of the Union any obligation to regard as valid the assignment of any mark the use of which by the assignee would, in fact, be of such a nature as to mislead the public, particularly as regards the origin, nature, or essential qualities, of the goods to which the mark is applied.

Article 6quinquies Marks: Protection of Marks Registered in One Country of the Union in the Other Countries of the Union

A.- **A19-017**

(1) Every trademark duly registered in the country of origin shall be accepted for filing and protected as is in the other countries of the

Union, subject to the reservations indicated in this Article. Such countries may, before proceeding to final registration, require the production of a certificate of registration in the country of origin, issued by the competent authority. No authentication shall be required for this certificate.

(2) Shall be considered the country of origin the country of the Union where the applicant has a real and effective industrial or commercial establishment, or, if he has no such establishment within the Union, the country of the Union where he has his domicile, or, if he has no domicile within the Union but is a national of a country of the Union, the country of which he is a national.

B.- Trademarks covered by this Article may be neither denied registration nor invalidated except in the following cases:

1. when they are of such a nature as to infringe rights acquired by third parties in the country where protection is claimed;

2. when they are devoid of any distinctive character, or consist exclusively of signs or indications which may serve, in trade, to designate the kind, quality, quantity, intended purpose, value, place of origin, of the goods, or the time of production, or have become customary in the current language or in the bona fide and established practices of the trade of the country where protection is claimed;

3. when they are contrary to morality or public order and, in particular, of such a nature as to deceive the public. It is understood that a mark may not be considered contrary to public order for the sole reason that it does not conform to a provision of the legislation on marks, except if such provision itself relates to publicorder.

This provision is subject, however, to the application of Article 10bis.

C.-

(1) In determining whether a mark is eligible for protection, all the factual circumstances must be taken into consideration, particularly the length of time the mark has been in use.

(2) No trademark shall be refused in the other countries of the Union for the sole reason that it differs from the mark protected in the country of origin only in respect of elements that do not alter its distinctive character and do not affect its identity in the form in which it has been registered in the said country of origin.

D.- No person may benefit from the provisions of this Article if the mark for which he claims protection is not registered in the country of origin.

E.- However, in no case shall the renewal of the registration of the mark in the country of origin involve an obligation to renew the registration in the other countries of the Union in which the mark has been registered.

F.- The benefit of priority shall remain unaffected for applications for the registration of marks filed within the period fixed by Article 4, even if registration in the country of origin is effected after the expiration of such period.

Article 6sexies Marks: Service Marks

A19-018   The countries of the Union undertake to protect service marks. They shall not be required to provide for the registration of such marks.

Article 6septies Marks: Registration in the Name of the Agent or Representative of the Proprietor Without the Latter's Authorization

(1) If the agent or representative of the person who is the proprietor of a **A19-019** mark in one of the countries of the Union applies, without such proprietor's authorization, for the registration of the mark in his own name, in one or more countries of the Union, the proprietor shall be entitled to oppose the registration applied for or demand its cancellation or, if the law of the country so allows, the assignment in his favor of the said registration, unless such agent or representative justifies his action.

(2) The proprietor of the mark shall, subject to the provisions of paragraph (1), above, be entitled to oppose the use of his mark by his agent or representative if he has not authorized such use.

(3) Domestic legislation may provide an equitable time limit within which the proprietor of a mark must exercise the rights provided for in this Article.

Article 7 Marks: Nature of the Goods to which the Mark is Applied

The nature of the goods to which a trademark is to be applied shall in no case **A19-020** form an obstacle to the registration of the mark.

Article 7bis Marks: Collective Marks

(1) The countries of the Union undertake to accept for filing and to protect **A19-021** collective marks belonging to associations the existence of which is not contrary to the law of the country of origin, even if such associations do not possess an industrial or commercial establishment.

(2) Each country shall be the judge of the particular conditions under which a collective mark shall be protected and may refuse protection if the mark is contrary to the public interest.

(3) Nevertheless, the protection of these marks shall not be refused to any association the existence of which is not contrary to the law of the country of origin, on the ground that such association is not established in the country where protection is sought or is not constituted according to the law of the latter country.

Article 8 Trade Names

A trade name shall be protected in all the countries of the Union without the **A19-022** obligation of filing or registration, whether or not it forms part of a trademark.

Article 9 Marks, Trade Names: Seizure, on Importation, etc., of Goods Unlawfully Bearing a Mark or Trade Name

(1) All goods unlawfully bearing a trademark or trade name shall be seized **A19-023** on importation into those countries of the Union where such mark or trade name is entitled to legal protection.

(2) Seizure shall likewise be effected in the country where the unlawful affixation occurred or in the country into which the goods were imported.

(3) Seizure shall take place at the request of the public prosecutor, or any other competent authority, or any interested party, whether a natural person or a legal entity, in conformity with the domestic legislation of each country.

(4) The authorities shall not be bound to effect seizure of goods in transit.

(5) If the legislation of a country does not permit seizure on importation, seizure shall be replaced by prohibition of importation or by seizure inside the country.

(6) If the legislation of a country permits neither seizure on importation nor prohibition of importation nor seizure inside the country, then, until such time as the legislation is modified accordingly, these measures shall be replaced by the actions and remedies available in such cases to nationals under the law of such country.

Article 10 False Indications: Seizure, on Importation, etc., of Goods Bearing False Indications as to their Source or the Identity of the Producer

A19-024   (1) The provisions of the preceding Article shall apply in cases of direct or indirect use of a false indication of the source of the goods or the identity of the producer, manufacturer, or merchant.

(2) Any producer, manufacturer, or merchant, whether a natural person or a legal entity, engaged in the production or manufacture of or trade in such goods and established either in the locality falsely indicated as the source, or in the region where such locality is situated, or in the country falsely indicated, or in the country where the false indication of source is used, shall in any case be deemed an interested party.

Article 10bis Unfair Competition

A19-025   (1) The countries of the Union are bound to assure to nationals of such countries effective protection against unfair competition.

(2) Any act of competition contrary to honest practices in industrial or commercial matters constitutes an act of unfair competition.

(3) The following in particular shall be prohibited:
1. all acts of such a nature as to create confusion by any means whatever with the establishment, the goods, or the industrial or commercial activities, of a competitor;
2. false allegations in the course of trade of such a nature as to discredit the establishment, the goods, or the industrial or commercial activities, of a competitor;
3. indications or allegations the use of which in the course of trade is liable to mislead the public as to the nature, the manufacturing process, the characteristics, the suitability for their purpose, or the quantity, of the goods.

Article 10ter Marks, Trade Names, False Indications, Unfair Competition: Remedies, Right to Sue

A19-026   (1) The countries of the Union undertake to assure to nationals of the other countries of the Union appropriate legal remedies effectively to repress all the acts referred to in Articles 9, 10, and 10bis.

(2) They undertake, further, to provide measures to permit federations and associations representing interested industrialists, producers, or merchants, provided that the existence of such federations and associations is not contrary to the laws of their countries, to take action in the courts or before the administrative authorities, with a view to the repression of the acts referred to in Articles 9, 10, and 10bis, in so far as the law of the country in which protection is claimed allows such action by federations and associations of that country.

Article 11 Inventions, Utility Models, Industrial Designs, Marks: Temporary Protection at Certain International Exhibitions

A19-027   (1) The countries of the Union shall, in conformity with their domestic legislation, grant temporary protection to patentable inventions, utility models, industrial designs, and trademarks, in respect of goods exhibited at official or officially recognized international exhibitions held in the territory of any of them.

(2) Such temporary protection shall not extend the periods providedby Article 4. If, later, the right of priority is invoked, the authorities of any country may provide that the period shall start from the date of introduction of the goods into the exhibition.

(3) Each country may require, as proof of the identity of the article exhibited and of the date of its introduction, such documentary evidence as it considers necessary.

Article 12 Special National Industrial Property Services

(1) Each country of the Union undertakes to establish a special industrial A19-028 property service and a central office for the communication to the public of patents, utility models, industrial designs, and trademarks.

(2) This service shall publish an official periodical journal. It shall publish regularly:
- (a) the names of the proprietors of patents granted, with a brief designation of the inventions patented;
- (b) the reproductions of registered trademarks.

Article 19 Special Agreements

It is understood that the countries of the Union reserve the right to make A19-029 separately between themselves special agreements for the protection of industrial property, in so far as these agreements do not contravene the provisions of this Convention.

Berne Convention for the Protection of Literary and Artistic Works

Paris Act of July 24, 1971, as amended on September 28, 1979 of September 9, 1886, completed at PARIS on May 4, 1896, revised at BERLIN on November 13, 1908, completed at BERNE on March 20, 1914, revised at ROME on June 26, 1948, at BRUSSELS on June 26, 1948, at STOCKHOLM on July 14, 1967, and at PARIS on July 24, 1971, and amended on September 28, 1979

Article 1 Establishment of a Union

The countries to which this Convention applies constitute a Union for the A20-001 protection of the rights of authors in their literary and artistic works.

Article 2 Protected Works: 1. "Literary and artistic works"; 2. Possible requirement of fixation; 3. Derivative works; 4. Official texts; 5. Collections; 6. Obligation to protect; beneficiaries of protection; 7. Works of applied art and industrial designs; 8. News

(1) The expression "literary and artistic works" shall include every A20-002 production in the literary, scientific and artistic domain, whatever may be the mode or form of its expression, such as books, pamphlets and other writings; lectures, addresses, sermons and other works of the same nature; dramatic or dramatico-musical works; choreographic works and entertainments in dumb show; musical compositions with or without words; cinematographic works to which are assimilated works expressed by a process analogous to cinematogra-

phy; works of drawing, painting, architecture, sculpture, engraving and lithography; photographic works to which are assimilated works expressed by a process analogous to photography; works of applied art; illustrations, maps, plans, sketches and three-dimensional works relative to geography, topography, architecture or science.

(2) It shall, however, be a matter for legislation in the countries of the Union to prescribe that works in general or any specified categories of works shall not be protected unless they have been fixed in some material form.

(3) Translations, adaptations, arrangements of music and other alterations of a literary or artistic work shall be protected as original works without prejudice to the copyright in the original work.

(4) It shall be a matter for legislation in the countries of the Union to determine the protection to be granted to official texts of a legislative, administrative and legal nature, and to official translations of such texts.

(5) Collections of literary or artistic works such as encyclopaedias and anthologies which, by reason of the selection and arrangement of their contents, constitute intellectual creations shall be protected as such, without prejudice to the copyright in each of the works forming part of such collections.

(6) The works mentioned in this Article shall enjoy protection in all countries of the Union. This protection shall operate for the benefit of the author and his successors in title.

(7) Subject to the provisions of Article 7(4) of this Convention, it shall be a matter for legislation in the countries of the Union to determine the extent of the application of their laws to works of applied art and industrial designs and models, as well as the conditions under which such works, designs and models shall be protected. Works protected in the country of origin solely as designs and models shall be entitled in another country of the Union only to such special protection as is granted in that country to designs and models; however, if no such special protection is granted in that country, such works shall be protected as artistic works.

(8) The protection of this Convention shall not apply to news of the day or to miscellaneous facts having the character of mere items of press information.

Article 2bis Possible Limitation of Protection of Certain Works: 1. Certain speeches; 2. Certain uses of lectures and addresses; 3. Right to make collections of such works

A20-003   (1) The protection of this Convention shall apply to:

(a) authors who are nationals of one of the countries of the Union, for their works, whether published or not;

(b) authors who are not nationals of one of the countries of the Union, for their works first published in one of those countries, or simultaneously in a country outside the Union and in a country of the Union.

(2) Authors who are not nationals of one of the countries of the Union but who have their habitual residence in one of them shall, for the purposes of this Convention, be assimilated to nationals of that country.

(3) The expression "published works" means works published with the consent of their authors, whatever may be the means of manufacture of the copies, provided that the availability of such copies has been such as to satisfy the reasonable requirements of the public, having regard to the nature of the work. The performance of a dramatic, dramatico-musical, cinematographic or musical work, the public recitation of a literary work, the communication by wire or the

broadcasting of literary or artistic works, the exhibition of a work of art and the construction of a work of architecture shall not constitute publication.

(4) A work shall be considered as having been published simultaneously in several countries if it has been published in two or more countries within thirty days of its first publication.

Article 3 Criteria of Eligibility for Protection: 1. Nationality of author; place of publication of work; 2. Residence of author; 3: "Published" works; 4. "Simultaneously published" works

(1) The protection of this Convention shall apply to: **A20-004**
   (a) authors who are nationals of one of the countries of the Union, for their works, whether published or not;
   (b) authors who are not nationals of one of the countries of the Union, for their works first published in one of those countries, or simultaneously in a country outside the Union and in a country of the Union.

(2) Authors who are not nationals of one of the countries of the Union but who have their habitual residence in one of them shall, for the purposes of this Convention, be assimilated to nationals of that country.

(3) The expression "published works" means works published with the consent of their authors, whatever may be the means of manufacture of the copies, provided that the availability of such copies has been such as to satisfy the reasonable requirements of the public, having regard to the nature of the work. The performance of a dramatic, dramatico-musical, cinematographic or musical work, the public recitation of a literary work, the communication by wire or the broadcasting of literary or artistic works, the exhibition of a work of art and the construction of a work of architecture shall not constitute publication.

(4) A work shall be considered as having been published simultaneously in several countries if it has been published in two or more countries within thirty days of its first publication.

Article 4 Criteria of Eligibility for Protection of Cinematographic Works, Works of Architecture and Certain Artistic Works

The protection of this Convention shall apply, even if the conditions of **A20-005** Article 3 are not fulfilled, to:
   (a) authors of cinematographic works the maker of which has his headquarters or habitual residence in one of the countries of the Union;
   (b) authors of works of architecture erected in a country of the Union or of other artistic works incorporated in a building or other structure located in a country of the Union.

Article 5 Rights Guaranteed: 1. and 2. Outside the country of origin; 3. In the country of origin; 4. "Country of origin"

(1) Authors shall enjoy, in respect of works for which they are protected **A20-006** under this Convention, in countries of the Union other than the country of origin, the rights which their respective laws do now or may hereafter grant to their nationals, as well as the rights specially granted by this Convention.

(2) The enjoyment and the exercise of these rights shall not be subject to any formality; such enjoyment and such exercise shall be independent of the existence of protection in the country of origin of the work. Consequently, apart from the provisions of this Convention, the extent of protection, as well as the means of redress afforded to the author to protect his rights, shall be governed exclusively by the laws of the country where protection is claimed.

(3) Protection in the country of origin is governed by domestic law. However, when the author is not a national of the country of origin of the work for which he is protected under this Convention, he shall enjoy in that country the same rights as national authors.

(4) The country of origin shall be considered to be:

(a) in the case of works first published in a country of the Union, that country; in the case of works published simultaneously in several countries of the Union which grant different terms of protection, the country whose legislation grants the shortest term of protection;

(b) in the case of works published simultaneously in a country outside the Union and in a country of the Union, the latter country;

(c) in the case of unpublished works or of works first published in a country outside the Union, without simultaneous publication in a country of the Union, the country of the Union of which the author is a national, provided that:

(i) when these are cinematographic works the maker of which has his headquarters or his habitual residence in a country of the Union, the country of origin shall be that country, and

(ii) when these are works of architecture erected in a country of the Union or other artistic works incorporated in a building or other structure located in a country of the Union, the country of origin shall be that country.

Article 6 Possible Restriction of Protection in Respect of Certain Works of Nationals of Certain Countries Outside the Union: 1. In the country of the first publication and in other countries; 2. No retroactivity; 3. Notice

A20-007   (1) Where any country outside the Union fails to protect in an adequate manner the works of authors who are nationals of one of the countries of the Union, the latter country may restrict the protection given to the works of authors who are, at the date of the first publication thereof, nationals of the other country and are not habitually resident in one of the countries of the Union. If the country of first publication avails itself of this right, the other countries of the Union shall not be required to grant to works thus subjected to special treatment a wider protection than that granted to them in the country of first publication.

(2) No restrictions introduced by virtue of the preceding paragraph shall affect the rights which an author may have acquired in respect of a work published in a country of the Union before such restrictions were put into force.

(3) The countries of the Union which restrict the grant of copyright in accordance with this Article shall give notice thereof to the Director General of the World Intellectual Property Organization (hereinafter designated as ıthe Director Generalı) by a written declaration specifying the countries in regard to which protection is restricted, and the restrictions to which rights of authors who are nationals of those countries are subjected. The Director General shall immediately communicate this declaration to all the countries of the Union.

Article 6bis Moral Rights: 1. To claim authorship; to object to certain modifications and other derogatory actions; 2. After the author's death; 3. Means of redress

A20-008   (1) Independently of the author's economic rights, and even after the transfer of the said rights, the author shall have the right to claim authorship of the work and to object to any distortion, mutilation or other modification of, or other derogatory action in relation to, the said work, which would be prejudicial to his honor or reputation.

(2) The rights granted to the author in accordance with the preceding paragraph shall, after his death, be maintained, at least until the expiry of the economic rights, and shall be exercisable by the persons or institutions authorized by the legislation of the country where protection is claimed. However, those countries whose legislation, at the moment of their ratification of or accession to this Act, does not provide for the protection after the death of the author of all the rights set out in the preceding paragraph may provide that some of these rights may, after his death, cease to be maintained.

(3) The means of redress for safeguarding the rights granted by this Article shall be governed by the legislation of the country where protection is claimed.

Article 7 Term of Protection: 1. Generally; 2. For cinematographic works; 3. For anonymous and pseudonymous works; 4. For photographic works and works of applied art; 5. Starting date of computation; 6. Longer terms; 7. Shorter terms; 8. Applicable law; "comparison" of terms

(1) The term of protection granted by this Convention shall be the life of the **A20-009** author and fifty years after his death.

(2) However, in the case of cinematographic works, the countries of the Union may provide that the term of protection shall expire fifty years after the work has been made available to the public with the consent of the author, or, failing such an event within fifty years from the making of such a work, fifty years after the making.

(3) In the case of anonymous or pseudonymous works, the term of protection granted by this Convention shall expire fifty years after the work has been lawfully made available to the public. However, when the pseudonym adopted by the author leaves no doubt as to his identity, the term of protection shall be that provided in paragraph (1). If the author of an anonymous or pseudonymous work discloses his identity during the above-mentioned period, the term of protection applicable shall be that provided in paragraph (1). The countries of the Union shall not be required to protect anonymous or pseudonymous works in respect of which it is reasonable to presume that their author has been dead for fifty years.

(4) It shall be a matter for legislation in the countries of the Union to determine the term of protection of photographic works and that of works of applied art in so far as they are protected as artistic works; however, this term shall last at least until the end of a period of twenty-five years from the making of such a work.

(5) The term of protection subsequent to the death of the author and the terms provided by paragraphs (2), (3) and (4) shall run from the date of death or of the event referred to in those paragraphs, but such terms shall always be deemed to begin on the first of January of the year following the death or such event.

(6) The countries of the Union may grant a term of protection in excess of those provided by the preceding paragraphs.

(7) Those countries of the Union bound by the Rome Act of this Convention which grant, in their national legislation in force at the time of signature of the present Act, shorter terms of protection than those provided for in the preceding paragraphs shall have the right to maintain such terms when ratifying or acceding to the present Act.

(8) In any case, the term shall be governed by the legislation of the country where protection is claimed; however, unless the legislation of that country otherwise provides, the term shall not exceed the term fixed in the country of origin of the work.

Article 7bis Term of Protection for Works of Joint Authorship

A20-010   The provisions of the preceding Article shall also apply in the case of a work of joint authorship, provided that the terms measured from the death of the author shall be calculated from the death of the last surviving author.

Article 8 Right of Translation

A20-011   Authors of literary and artistic works protected by this Convention shall enjoy the exclusive right of making and of authorizing the translation of their works throughout the term of protection of their rights in the original works.

Article 9 Right of Reproduction: 1. Generally; 2. Possible exceptions; 3. Sound and visual recordings

A20-012   (1) Authors of literary and artistic works protected by this Convention shall have the exclusive right of authorizing the reproduction of these works, in any manner or form.

(2) It shall be a matter for legislation in the countries of the Union to permit the reproduction of such works in certain special cases, provided that such reproduction does not conflict with a normal exploitation of the work and does not unreasonably prejudice the legitimate interests of the author.

(3) Any sound or visual recording shall be considered as a reproduction for the purposes of this Convention.

Article 10 Certain Free Uses of Works: 1. Quotations; 2. Illustrations for teaching; 3. Indication of source and author

A20-013   (1) It shall be permissible to make quotations from a work which has already been lawfully made available to the public, provided that their making is compatible with fair practice, and their extent does not exceed that justified by the purpose, including quotations from newspaper articles and periodicals in the form of press summaries.

(2) It shall be a matter for legislation in the countries of the Union, and for special agreements existing or to be concluded between them, to permit the utilization, to the extent justified by the purpose, of literary or artistic works by way of illustration in publications, broadcasts or sound or visual recordings for teaching, provided such utilization is compatible with fair practice.

(3) Where use is made of works in accordance with the preceding paragraphs of this Article, mention shall be made of the source, and of the name of the author if it appears thereon.

Article 10bis Further Possible Free Uses of Works: 1. Of certain articles and broadcast works; 2. Of works seen or heard in connection with current events

A20-014   (1) It shall be a matter for legislation in the countries of the Union to permit the reproduction by the press, the broadcasting or the communication to the public by wire of articles published in newspapers or periodicals on current economic, political or religious topics, and of broadcast works of the same character, in cases in which the reproduction, broadcasting or such communication thereof is not expressly reserved. Nevertheless, the source must always be clearly indicated; the legal consequences of a breach of this obligation shall be determined by the legislation of the country where protection is claimed.

(2) It shall also be a matter for legislation in the countries of the Union to determine the conditions under which, for the purpose of reporting current events by means of photography, cinematography, broadcasting or communication to the public by wire, literary or artistic works seen or heard in the course of the event may, to the extent justified by the informatory purpose, be reproduced and made available to the public.

Article 11 Certain Rights in Dramatic and Musical Works: 1. Right of public performance and of communication to the public of a performance; 2. In respect of translations

(1) Authors of dramatic, dramatico-musical and musical works shall enjoy **A20-015** the exclusive right of authorizing:
  - (i) the public performance of their works, including such public performance by any means or process;
  - (ii) any communication to the public of the performance of their works.

(2) Authors of dramatic or dramatico-musical works shall enjoy, during the full term of their rights in the original works, the same rights with respect to translations thereof.

Article 11bis Broadcasting and Related Rights: 1. Broadcasting and other wireless communications, public communication of broadcast by wire or rebroadcast, public communication of broadcast by loudspeaker or analogous instruments; 2. Compulsory licenses; 3. Recording; ephemeral recordings

(1) Authors of literary and artistic works shall enjoy the exclusive right of **A20-016** authorizing:
  - (i) the broadcasting of their works or the communication thereof to the public by any other means of wireless diffusion of signs, sounds or images;
  - (ii) any communication to the public by wire or by rebroadcasting of the broadcast of the work, when this communication is made by an organization other than the original one;
  - (iii) the public communication by loudspeaker or any other analogous instrument transmitting, by signs, sounds or images, the broadcast of the work.

(2) It shall be a matter for legislation in the countries of the Union to determine the conditions under which the rights mentioned in the preceding paragraph may be exercised, but these conditions shall apply only in the countries where they have been prescribed. They shall not in any circumstances be prejudicial to the moral rights of the author, nor to his right to obtain equitable remuneration which, in the absence of agreement, shall be fixed by competent authority.

(3) In the absence of any contrary stipulation, permission granted in accordance with paragraph (1) of this Article shall not imply permission to record, by means of instruments recording sounds or images, the work broadcast. It shall, however, be a matter for legislation in the countries of the Union to determine the regulations for ephemeral recordings made by a broadcasting organization by means of its own facilities and used for its own broadcasts. The preservation of these recordings in official archives may, on the ground of their exceptional documentary character, be authorized by such legislation.

Article 11ter Certain Rights in Literary Works: 1. Right of public recitation and of communication to the public of a recitation; 2. In respect of translations

A20-017 (1) Authors of literary works shall enjoy the exclusive right of authorizing:
  (i) the public recitation of their works, including such public recitation by any means or process;
  (ii) any communication to the public of the recitation of their works.
(2) Authors of literary works shall enjoy, during the full term of their rights in the original works, the same rights with respect to translations thereof.

Article 12 Right of Adaptation, Arrangement and Other Alteration

A20-018 Authors of literary or artistic works shall enjoy the exclusive right of authorizing adaptations, arrangements and other alterations of their works.

Article 13 Possible Limitation of the Right of Recording of Musical Works and Any Words Pertaining Thereto: 1. Compulsory licenses; 2. Transitory measures; 3. Seizure on importation of copies made without the author's permission

A20-019 (1) Each country of the Union may impose for itself reservations and conditions on the exclusive right granted to the author of a musical work and to the author of any words, the recording of which together with the musical work has already been authorized by the latter, to authorize the sound recording of that musical work, together with such words, if any; but all such reservations and conditions shall apply only in the countries which have imposed them and shall not, in any circumstances, be prejudicial to the rights of these authors to obtain equitable remuneration which, in the absence of agreement, shall be fixed by competent authority.
(2) Recordings of musical works made in a country of the Union in accordance with Article 13(3) of the Conventions signed at Rome on June 2, 1928, and at Brussels on June 26, 1948, may be reproduced in that country without the permission of the author of the musical work until a date two years after that country becomes bound by this Act.
(3) Recordings made in accordance with paragraphs (1) and (2) of this Article and imported without permission from the parties concerned into a country where they are treated as infringing recordings shall be liable to seizure.

Article 14 Cinematographic and Related Rights: 1. Cinematographic adaptation and reproduction; distribution; public performance and public communication by wire of works thus adapted or reproduced; 2. Adaptation of cinematographic productions; 3. No compulsory licenses

A20-020 (1) Authors of literary or artistic works shall have the exclusive right of authorizing:
  (i) the cinematographic adaptation and reproduction of these works, and the distribution of the works thus adapted or reproduced;
  (ii) the public performance and communication to the public by wire of the works thus adapted or reproduced.
(2) The adaptation into any other artistic form of a cinematographic production derived from literary or artistic works shall, without prejudice to the authorization of the author of the cinematographic production, remain subject to the authorization of the authors of the original works.
(3) The provisions of Article 13(1) shall not apply.

Article 14bis Special Provisions Concerning Cinematographic Works: 1. Assimilation to "original" works; 2. Ownership; limitation of certain rights of certain contributors; 3. Certain other contributors

(1) Without prejudice to the copyright in any work which may have been **A20-021** adapted or reproduced, a cinematographic work shall be protected as an original work. The owner of copyright in a cinematographic work shall enjoy the same rights as the author of an original work, including the rights referred to in the preceding Article.

(2)

    (a) Ownership of copyright in a cinematographic work shall be a matter for legislation in the country where protection is claimed.

    (b) However, in the countries of the Union which, by legislation, include among the owners of copyright in a cinematographic work authors who have brought contributions to the making of the work, such authors, if they have undertaken to bring such contributions, may not, in the absence of any contrary or special stipulation, object to the reproduction, distribution, public performance, communication to the public by wire, broadcasting or any other communication to the public, or to the subtitling or dubbing of texts, of the work.

    (c) The question whether or not the form of the undertaking referred to above should, for the application of the preceding subparagraph (b), be in a written agreement or a written act of the same effect shall be a matter for the legislation of the country where the maker of the cinematographic work has his headquarters or habitual residence. However, it shall be a matter for the legislation of the country of the Union where protection is claimed to provide that the said undertaking shall be in a written agreement or a written act of the same effect. The countries whose legislation so provides shall notify the Director General by means of a written declaration, which will be immediately communicated by him to all the other countries of the Union.

    (d) By "contrary or special stipulation" is meant any restrictive condition which is relevant to the aforesaid undertaking.

(3) Unless the national legislation provides to the contrary, the provisions of paragraph (2)(b) above shall not be applicable to authors of scenarios, dialogues and musical works created for the making of the cinematographic work, or to the principal director thereof. However, those countries of the Union whose legislation does not contain rules providing for the application of the said paragraph (2)(b) to such director shall notify the Director General by means of a written declaration, which will be immediately communicated by him to all the other countries of the Union.

Article 14ter "Droit de suite" in Works of Art and Manuscripts: 1. Right to an interest in resales; 2. Applicable law; 3. Procedure

(1) The author, or after his death the persons or institutions authorized by **A20-022** national legislation, shall, with respect to original works of art and original manuscripts of writers and composers, enjoy the inalienable right to an interest in any sale of the worksubsequent to the first transfer by the author of the work.

(2) The protection provided by the preceding paragraph may be claimed in a country of the Union only if legislation in the country to which the author belongs so permits, and to the extent permitted by the country where this protection is claimed.

(3) The procedure for collection and the amounts shall be matters for determination by national legislation.

Article 15 Right to Enforce Protected Rights: 1. Where author's name is indicated or where pseudonym leaves no doubt as to author's identity; 2. In the case of cinematographic works; 3. In the case of anonymous and pseudonymous works; 4. In the case of certain unpublished works of unknown authorship

A20-023   (1) In order that the author of a literary or artistic work protected by this Convention shall, in the absence of proof to the contrary, be regarded as such, and consequently be entitled to institute infringement proceedings in the countries of the Union, it shall be sufficient for his name to appear on the work in the usual manner. This paragraph shall be applicable even if this name is a pseudonym, where the pseudonym adopted by the author leaves no doubt as to his identity.

(2) The person or body corporate whose name appears on a cinematographic work in the usual manner shall, in the absence of proof to the contrary, be presumed to be the maker of the said work.

(3) In the case of anonymous and pseudonymous works, other than those referred to in paragraph (1) above, the publisher whose name appears on the work shall, in the absence of proof to the contrary, be deemed to represent the author, and in this capacity he shall be entitled to protect and enforce the author's rights. The provisions of this paragraph shall cease to apply when the author reveals his identity and establishes his claim to authorship of the work.

(4)
  (a) In the case of unpublished works where the identity of the author is unknown, but where there is every ground to presume that he is a national of a country of the Union, it shall be a matter for legislation in that country to designate the competent authority which shall represent the author and shall be entitled to protect and enforce his rights in the countries of the Union.
  (b) Countries of the Union which make such designation under the terms of this provision shall notify the Director General by means of a written declaration giving full information concerning the authority thus designated. The Director General shall at once communicate this declaration to all other countries of the Union.

Article 16 Infringing Copies: 1. Seizure; 2. Seizure on importation; 3. Applicable law

A20-024   (1) Infringing copies of a work shall be liable to seizure in any country of the Union where the work enjoys legal protection.

(2) The provisions of the preceding paragraph shall also apply to reproductions coming from a country where the work is not protected, or has ceased to be protected.

(3) The seizure shall take place in accordance with the legislation of each country.

Article 17 Possibility of Control of Circulation, Presentation and Exhibition of Works

A20-025   The provisions of this Convention cannot in any way affect the right of the Government of each country of the Union to permit, to control, or to prohibit, by legislation or regulation, the circulation, presentation, or exhibition of any work or production in regard to which the competent authority may find it necessary to exercise that right.

Article 18 Works Existing on Convention's Entry Into Force: 1. Protectable where protection not yet expired in country of origin; 2. Non-protectable where protection already expired in country where it is claimed; 3. Application of these principles; 4. Special cases

(1) This Convention shall apply to all works which, at the moment of its A20-026 coming into force, have not yet fallen into the public domain in the country of origin through the expiry of the term of protection.

(2) If, however, through the expiry of the term of protection which was previously granted, a work has fallen into the public domain of the country where protection is claimed, that work shall not be protected anew.

(3) The application of this principle shall be subject to any provisions contained in special conventions to that effect existing or to be concluded between countries of the Union. In the absence of such provisions, the respective countries shall determine, each in so far as it is concerned, the conditions of application of this principle.

(4) The preceding provisions shall also apply in the case of new accessions to the Union and to cases in which protection is extended by the application of Article 7 or by the abandonment of reservations.

Article 19 Protection Greater than Resulting from Convention

The provisions of this Convention shall not preclude the making of a claim to A20-027 the benefit of any greater protection which may be granted by legislation in a country of the Union.

Article 20 Special Agreements Among Countries of the Union

The Governments of the countries of the Union reserve the right to enter A20-028 into special agreements among themselves, in so far as such agreements grant to authors more extensive rights than those granted by the Convention, or contain other provisions not contrary to this Convention. The provisions of existing agreements which satisfy these conditions shall remain applicable.

Madrid Agreement Concerning the International Registration of Marks of April 14, 1891

as revised at Brussels on December 14, 1900, at Washington on
June 2, 1911, at The Hague on November 6, 1925, at London on
June 2, 1934, at Nice on June 15, 1957, and at Stockholm on July 14,
1967, and as amended on September 28, 1979

Article 1 Establishment of a Special Union. Filing of Marks at International Bureau. Definition of Country of Origin*

* Articles have been given titles to facilitate their identification. There are no A21-001 titles in the signed, French text.

(1) The countries to which this Agreement applies constitute a Special Union for the international registration of marks.

(2) Nationals of any of the contracting countries may, in all the other countries party to this Agreement, secure protection for their marks applicable to

goods or services, registered in the country of origin, by filing the said marks at the International Bureau of Intellectual Property (hereinafter designated as "the International Bureau") referred to in the Convention Establishing the World Intellectual Property Organization (hereinafter designated as "the Organization"), through the intermediary of the Office of the said country of origin.

(3) Shall be considered the country of origin the country of the Special Union where the applicant has a real and effective industrial or commercial establishment; if he has no such establishment in a country of the Special Union, the country of the Special Union where he has his domicile; if he has no domicile within the Special Union but is a national of a country of the Special Union, the country of which he is a national.

Article 2 Reference to Article 3 of Paris Convention (Same Treatment for Certain Categories of Persons as for Nationals of Countries of the Union)

A21-002   Nationals of countries not having acceded to this Agreement who, within the territory of the Special Union constituted by the said Agreement, satisfy the conditions specified in Article 3 of the Paris Convention for the Protection of Industrial Property shall be treated in the same manner as nationals of the contracting countries.

Article 3 Contents of Application for International Registration

A21-003   (1) Every application for international registration must be presented on the form prescribed by the Regulations; the Office of the country of origin of the mark shall certify that the particulars appearing in such application correspond to the particulars in the national register, and shall mention the dates and numbers of the filing and registration of the mark in the country of origin and also the date of the application for international registration.

(2) The applicant must indicate the goods or services in respect of which protection of the mark is claimed and also, if possible, the corresponding class or classes according to the classification established by the Nice Agreement Concerning the International Classification of Goods and Services for the Purposes of the Registration of Marks. If the applicant does not give such indication, the International Bureau shall classify the goods or services in the appropriate classes of the said Classification. The indication of classes given by the applicant shall be subject to control by the International Bureau, which shall exercise the said control in association with the national Office. In the event of disagreement between the national Office and the International Bureau, the opinion of the latter shall prevail.

(3) If the applicant claims color as a distinctive feature of his mark, he shall be required:

1. to state the fact, and to file with his application a notice specifying the color or the combination of colors claimed;
2. to append to his application copies in color of the said mark, which shall be attached to the notification given by the International Bureau. The number of such copies shall be fixed by the Regulations.

(4) The International Bureau shall register immediately the marks filed in accordance with Article 1. The registration shall bear the date of the application for international registration in the country of origin, provided that the application has been received by the International Bureau within a period of two months from that date. If the application has not been received within that period, the International Bureau shall record it as at the date on which it received the said application. The International Bureau shall notify such registration without delay

to the Offices concerned. Registered marks shall be published in a periodical journal issued by the International Bureau, on the basis of the particulars contained in the application for registration. In the case of marks comprising a figurative element of a special form of writing, the Regulations shall determine whether a printing block must be supplied by the applicant.

(5) With a view to the publicity to be given in the contracting countries to registered marks, each Office shall receive from the International Bureau a number of copies of the said publication free of charge and a number of copies at a reduced price, in proportion to the number of units mentioned in Article 16(4)(a) of the Paris Convention for the Protection of Industrial Property, under the conditions fixed by the Regulations. Such publicity shall be deemed in all the contracting countries to be sufficient, and no other publicity may be required of the applicant.

Article 3bis Territorial Limitation

(1) Any contracting country may, at any time, notify the Director General of the Organization (hereinafter designated as "the Director General") in writing that the protection resulting from the international registration shall extend to that country only at the express request of the proprietor of the mark. **A21-004**

(2) Such notification shall not take effect until six months after the date of the communication thereof by the Director General to the other contracting countries.

Article 3ter Request for "Territorial Extension"

(1) Any request for extension of the protection resulting from the international registration to a country which has availed itself of the right provided for in Article 3bis must be specially mentioned in the application referred to in Article 3(1). **A21-005**

(2) Any request for territorial extension made subsequently to the international registration must be presented through the intermediary of the Office of the country of origin on a form prescribed by the Regulations. It shall be immediately registered by the International Bureau, which shall notify it without delay to the Office or Offices concerned. It shall be published in the periodical journal issued by the International Bureau. Such territorial extension shall be effective from the date on which it has been recorded in the International Register; it shall cease to be valid on the expiration of the international registration of the mark to which it relates.

Article 4 Effects of International Registration

(1) From the date of the registration so effected at the International Bureau in accordance with the provisions of Articles 3 and 3ter, the protection of the mark in each of the contracting countries concerned shall be the same as if the mark had been filed therein direct. The indication of classes of goods or services provided for in Article 3 shall not bind the contracting countries with regard to the determination of the scope of the protection of the mark. **A21-006**

(2) Every mark which has been the subject of an international registration shall enjoy the right of priority provided for by Article 4 of the Paris Convention for the Protection of Industrial Property, without requiring compliance with the formalities prescribed in Section D of that Article.

Article 4bis Substitution of International Registration for Earlier National Registrations

A21-007   (1) When a mark already filed in one or more of the contracting countries is later registered by the International Bureau in the name of the same proprietor or his successor in title, the international registration shall be deemed to have replaced the earlier national registrations, without prejudice to any rights acquired by reason of such earlier registrations.

(2) The national Office shall, upon request, be required to take note in its registers of the international registration.

Article 5 Refusal by National Offices

A21-008   (1) In countries where the legislation so authorizes, Offices notified by the International Bureau of the registration of a mark or of a request for extension of protection made in accordance with Article 3ter shall have the right to declare that protection cannot be granted to such mark in their territory. Any such refusal can be based only on the grounds which would apply, under the Paris Convention for the Protection of Industrial Property, in the case of a mark filed for national registration. However, protection may not be refused, even partially, by reason only that national legislation would not permit registration except in a limited number of classes or for a limited number of goods or services.

(2) Offices wishing to exercise such right must give notice of their refusal to the International Bureau, together with a statement of all grounds, within the period prescribed by their domestic law and, at the latest, before the expiration of one year from the date of the international registration of the mark or of the request for extension of protection made in accordance with Article 3ter.

(3) The International Bureau shall, without delay, transmit to the Office of the country of origin and to the proprietor of the mark, or to his agent if an agent has been mentioned to the Bureau by the said Office, one of the copies of the declaration of refusal so notified. The interested party shall have the same remedies as if the mark had been filed by him direct in the country where protection is refused.

(4) The grounds for refusing a mark shall be communicated by the International Bureau to any interested party who may so request.

(5) Offices which, within the aforesaid maximum period of one year, have not communicated to the International Bureau any provisional or final decision of refusal with regard to the registration of a mark or a request for extension of protection shall lose the benefit of the right provided for in paragraph (1) of this Article with respect to the mark in question.

(6) Invalidation of an international mark may not be pronounced by the competent authorities without the proprietor of the mark having, in good time, been afforded the opportunity of defending his rights. Invalidation shall be notified to the International Bureau.

Article 5bis Documentary Evidence of Legitimacy of Use of Certain Elements of Mark

A21-009   Documentary evidence of the legitimacy of the use of certain elements incorporated in a mark, such as armorial bearings, escutcheons, portraits, honorary distinctions, titles, trade names, names of persons other than the name of the applicant, or other like inscriptions, which might be required by the Offices of the contracting countries shall be exempt from any legalization or certification other than that of the Office of the country of origin.

Article 5ter Copies of Entries in International Register. Searches for Anticipation. Extracts from International Register

(1) The International Bureau shall issue to any person applying therefor, **A21-010** subject to a fee fixed by the Regulations, a copy of the entries in the Register relating to a specific mark.

(2) The International Bureau may also, upon payment, undertake searches for anticipation among international marks.

(3) Extracts from the International Register requested with a view to their production in one of the contracting countries shall be exempt from all legalization.

Article 6 Period of Validity of International Registration. Independence of International Registration. Termination of Protection in Country of Origin

(1) Registration of a mark at the International Bureau is effected for twenty **A21-011** years, with the possibility of renewal under the conditions specified in Article 7.

(2) Upon expiration of a period of five years from the date of the international registration, such registration shall become independent of the national mark registered earlier in the country of origin, subject to the following provisions.

(3) The protection resulting from the international registration, whether or not it has been the subject of a transfer, may no longer be invoked, in whole or in part, if, within five years from the date of the international registration, the national mark, registered earlier in the country of origin in accordance with Article 1, no longer enjoys, in whole or in part, legal protection in that country. This provision shall also apply when legal protection has later ceased as the result of an action begun before the expiration of the period of five years.

(4) In the case of voluntary or ex officio cancellation, the Office of the country of origin shall request the cancellation of the mark at the International Bureau, and the latter shall effect the cancellation. In the case of judicial action, the said Office shall send to the International Bureau, ex officio or at the request of the plaintiff, a copy of the complaint or any other documentary evidence that an action has begun, and also of the final decision of the court; the Bureau shall enter notice thereof in the International Register.

Article 7 Renewal of International Registration

(1) Any registration may be renewed for a period of twenty years from the **A21-012** expiration of the preceding period, by payment only of the basic fee and, where necessary, of the supplementary and complementary fees provided for in Article 8(2).

(2) Renewal may not include any change in relation to the previous registration in its latest form.

(3) The first renewal effected under the provisions of the Nice Act of June 15, 1957, or of this Act, shall include an indication of the classes of the International Classification to which the registration relates.

(4) Six months before the expiration of the term of protection, the International Bureau shall, by sending an unofficial notice, remind the proprietor of the mark and his agent of the exact date of expiration.

(5) Subject to the payment of a surcharge fixed by the Regulations, a period of grace of six months shall be granted for renewal of the international registration.

Article 8 National Fee. International Fee. Division of Excess Receipts, Supplementary Fees, and Complementary Fees

A21-013　(1) The Office of the country of origin may fix, at its own discretion, and collect, for its own benefit, a national fee which it may require from the proprietor of the mark in respect of which international registration or renewal is applied for.

(2) Registration of a mark at the International Bureau shall be subject to the advance payment of an international fee which shall include:

(a) a basic fee;

(b) a supplementary fee for each class of the International Classification, beyond three, into which the goods or services to which the mark is applied will fall;

(c) a complementary fee for any request for extension of protection under Article 3ter.

(3) However, the supplementary fee specified in paragraph (2)(b) may, without prejudice to the date of registration, be paid within a period fixed by the Regulations if the number of classes of goods or services has been fixed or disputed by the International Bureau. If, upon expiration of the said period, the supplementary fee has not been paid or the list of goods or services has not been reduced to the required extent by the applicant, the application for international registration shall be deemed to have been abandoned.

(4) The annual returns from the various receipts from international registration, with the exception of those provided for under paragraph (2)(b) and (2)(c), shall be divided equally among the countries party to this Act by the International Bureau, after deduction of the expenses and charges necessitated by the implementation of the said Act. If, at the time this Act enters into force, a country has not yet ratified or acceded to the said Act, it shall be entitled, until the date on which its ratification or accession becomes effective, to a share of the excess receipts calculated on the basis of that earlier Act which is applicable to it.

(5) The amounts derived from the supplementary fees provided for in paragraph (2)(b) shall be divided at the expiration of each year among the countries party to this Act or to the Nice Act of June 15, 1957, in proportion to the number of marks for which protection has been applied for in each of them during that year, this number being multiplied in the case of countries which make a preliminary examination, by a coefficient which shall be determined by the Regulations. If, at the time this Act enters into force, a country has not yet ratified or acceded to the said Act, it shall be entitled, until the date on which its ratification or accession becomes effective, to a share of the amounts calculated on the basis of the Nice Act.

(6) The amounts derived from the complementary fees provided for in paragraph (2)(c) shall be divided according to the requirements of paragraph (5) among the countries availing themselves of the right provided for in Article 3bis. If, at the time this Act enters into force, a country has not yet ratified or acceded to the said Act, it shall be entitled, until the date on which its ratification or accession becomes effective, to a share of the amounts calculated on the basis of the Nice Act.

Article 8bis Renunciation in Respect of One or More Countries

A21-014　The person in whose name the international registration stands may at any time renounce protection in one or more of the contracting countries by means of a declaration filed with the Office of his own country, for communication to the

International Bureau, which shall notify accordingly the countries in respect of which renunciation has been made. Renunciation shall not be subject to any fee.

Article 9 Changes in National Registers also Affecting International Registration. Reduction of List of Goods and Services Mentioned in International Registration. Additions to that List. Substitutions in that List

(1) The Office of the country of the person in whose name the international **A21-015** registration stands shall likewise notify the International Bureau of all annulments, cancellations, renunciations, transfers, and other changes made in the entry of the mark in the national register, if such changes also effect the international registration.

(2) The Bureau shall record those changes in the International Register, shall notify them in turn to the Offices of the contracting countries, and shall publish them in its journal.

(3) A similar procedure shall be followed when the person in whose name the international registration stands requests a reduction of the list of goods or services to which the registration applies.

(4) Such transactions may be subject to a fee, which shall be fixed by the Regulations.

(5) The subsequent addition of new goods or services to the said list can be obtained only by filing a new application as prescribed in Article 3.

(6) The substitution of one of the goods or services for another shall be treated as an addition.

Article 9bis Transfer of International Mark Entailing Change in Country of Proprietor

(1) When a mark registered in the International Register is transferred to a **A21-016** person established in a contracting country other than the country of the person in whose name the international registration stands, the transfer shall be notified to the International Bureau by the Office of the latter country. The International Bureau shall record the transfer, shall notify the other Offices thereof, and shall publish it in its journal. If the transfer has been effected before the expiration of a period of five years from the international registration, the International Bureau shall seek the consent of the Office of the country of the new proprietor, and shall publish, if possible, the date and registration number of the mark in the country of the new proprietor.

(2) No transfer of a mark registered in the International Register for the benefit of a person who is not entitled to file an international mark shall be recorded.

(3) When it has not been possible to record a transfer in the International Register, either because the country of the new proprietor has refused its consent or because the said transfer has been made for the benefit of a person who is not entitled to apply for international registration, the Office of the country of the former proprietor shall have the right to demand that the International Bureau cancel the mark in its Register.

Article 9ter Assignment of International Mark for Part Only of Registered Goods or Services or for Certain Contracting Countries. Reference to Article 6quater of Paris Convention (Assignment of Mark)

(1) If the assignment of an international mark for part only of the registered **A21-017** goods or services is notified to the International Bureau, the Bureau shall record it in its Register. Each of the contracting countries shall have the right to refuse

to recognize the validity of such assignment if the goods or services included in the part so assigned are similar to those in respect of which the mark remains registered for the benefit of the assignor.

(2) The International Bureau shall likewise record the assignment of an international mark in respect of one or several of the contracting countries only.

(3) If, in the above cases, a change occurs in the country of the proprietor, the Office of the country to which the new proprietor belongs shall, if the international mark has been transferred before the expiration of a period of five years from the international registration, give its consent as required by Article 9bis.

(4) The provisions of the foregoing paragraphs shall apply subject to Article 6quater of the Paris Convention for the Protection of Industrial Property.

Article 9quater Common Office for Several Contracting Countries. Request by Several Contracting Countries to be Treated as a Single Country

A21-018   (1) If several countries of the Special Union agree to effect the unification of their domestic legislations on marks, they may notify the Director General:

     (a) that a common Office shall be substituted for the national Office of each of them, and

     (b) that the whole of their respective territories shall be deemed to be a single country for the purposes of the application of all or part of the provisions preceding this Article.

(2) Such notification shall not take effect until six months after the date of the communication thereof by the Director General to the other contracting countries.

Protocol Relating to the Madrid Agreement Concerning the International Registration of Marks (as signed at Madrid on June 28, 1989)

Article 1 Membership in the Madrid Union

A22-001   The States party to this Protocol (hereinafter referred to as "the Contracting States"), even where they are not party to the Madrid Agreement Concerning the International Registration of Marks as revised at Stockholm in 1967 and as amended in 1979 (hereinafter referred to as "the Madrid (Stockholm) Agreement"), and the organizations referred to in Article 14(1)(b) which are party to this Protocol (hereinafter referred to as "the Contracting Organizations") shall be members of the same Union of which countries party to the Madrid (Stockholm) Agreement are members. Any reference in this Protocol to "Contracting Parties" shall be construed as a reference to both Contracting States and Contracting Organizations.

Article 2 Securing Protection Through International Registration

A22-002   (1) Where an application for the registration of a mark has been filed with the Office of a Contracting Party, or where a mark has been registered in the register of the Office of a Contracting Party, the person in whose name that application (hereinafter referred to as "the basic application") or that registration (hereinafter referred to as "the basic registration") stands may, subject to the provisions of this Protocol, secure protection for his mark in the territory of the Contracting Parties, by obtaining the registration of that mark in the register of the International Bureau of the World Intellectual Property Organization (hereinafter referred to as "the international registration," "the International Register," "the International Bureau" and "the Organization," respectively), provided that,

(i) where the basic application has been filed with the Office of a Contracting State or where the basic registration has been made by such an Office, the person in whose name that application or registration stands is a national of that Contracting State, or is domiciled, or has a real and effective industrial or commercial establishment, in the said Contracting State,

(ii) where the basic application has been filed with the Office of a Contracting Organization or where the basic registration has been made by such an Office, the person in whose name that application or registration stands is a national of a State member of that Contracting Organization, or is domiciled, or has a real and effective industrial or commercial establishment, in the territory of the said Contracting Organization.

(2) The application for international registration (hereinafter referred to as "the international application") shall be filed with the International Bureau through the intermediary of the Office with which the basic application was filed or by which the basic registration was made (hereinafter referred to as ιthe Office of originι), as the case may be.

(3) Any reference in this Protocol to an "Office" or an "Office of a Contracting Party" shall be construed as a reference to the office that is in charge, on behalf of a Contracting Party, of the registration of marks, and any reference in this Protocol to "marks" shall be construed as a reference to trademarks and service marks.

(4) For the purposes of this Protocol, "territory of a Contracting Party" means, where the Contracting Party is a State, the territory of that State and, where the Contracting Party is an intergovernmental organization, the territory in which the constituting treaty of that intergovernmental organization applies.

Article 3 International Application

(1) Every international application under this Protocol shall be presented on **A22-003** the form prescribed by the Regulations. The Office of origin shall certify that the particulars appearing in the international application correspond to the particulars appearing, at the time of the certification, in the basic application or basic registration, as the case may be. Furthermore, the said Office shall indicate,

(i) in the case of a basic application, the date and number of that application,

(ii) in the case of a basic registration, the date and number of that registration as well as the date and number of the application from which the basic registration resulted.

The Office of origin shall also indicate the date of the international application.

(2) The applicant must indicate the goods and services in respect of which protection of the mark is claimed and also, if possible, the corresponding class or classes according to the classification established by the Nice Agreement Concerning the International Classification of Goods and Services for the Purposes of the Registration of Marks. If the applicant does not give such indication, the International Bureau shall classify the goods and services in the appropriate classes of the said classification. The indication of classes given by the applicant shall be subject to control by the International Bureau, which shall exercise the said control in association with the Office of origin. In the event of

disagreement between the said Office and the International Bureau, the opinion of the latter shall prevail.

(3) If the applicant claims color as a distinctive feature of his mark, he shall be required

- (i) to state the fact, and to file with his international application a notice specifying the color or the combination of colors claimed;
- (ii) to append to his international application copies in color of the said mark, which shall be attached to the notifications given by the International Bureau; the number of such copies shall be fixed by the Regulations.

(4) The International Bureau shall register immediately the marks filed in accordance with Article 2. The international registration shall bear the date on which the international application was received in the Office of origin, provided that the international application has been received by the International Bureau within a period of two months from that date. If the international application has not been received within that period, the international registration shall bear the date on which the said international application was received by the International Bureau. The International Bureau shall notify the international registration without delay to the Offices concerned. Marks registered in the International Register shall be published in a periodical gazette issued by the International Bureau, on the basis of the particulars contained in the international application.

(5) With a view to the publicity to be given to marks registered in the International Register, each Office shall receive from the International Bureau a number of copies of the said gazette free of charge and a number of copies at a reduced price, under the conditions fixed by the Assembly referred to in Article 10 (hereinafter referred to as "the Assembly"). Such publicity shall be deemed to be sufficient for the purposes of all the Contracting Parties, and no other publicity may be required of the holder of the international registration.

Article 3bis Territorial Effect

A22-004   The protection resulting from the international registration shall extend to any Contracting Party only at the request of the person who files the international application or who is the holder of the international registration. However, no such request can be made with respect to the Contracting Party whose Office is the Office of origin.

Article 3ter Request for "Territorial Extension"

A22-005   (1) Any request for extension of the protection resulting from the international registration to any Contracting Party shall be specially mentioned in the international application.

(2) A request for territorial extension may also be made subsequently to the international registration. Any such request shall be presented on the form prescribed by the Regulations. It shall be immediately recorded by the International Bureau, which shall notify such recordal without delay to the Office or Offices concerned. Such recordal shall be published in the periodical gazette of the International Bureau. Such territorial extension shall be effective from the date on which it has been recorded in the International Register; it shall cease to be valid on the expiry of the international registration to which it relates.

Article 4 Effects of International Registration

(1) (a) From the date of the registration or recordal effected in accordance **A22-006** with the provisions of Articles 3 and 3ter, the protection of the mark in each of the Contracting Parties concerned shall be the same as if the mark had been deposited direct with the Office of that Contracting Party. If no refusal has been notified to the International Bureau in accordance with Article 5(1) and 5(2) or if a refusal notified in accordance with the said Article has been withdrawn subsequently, the protection of the mark in the Contracting Party concerned shall, as from the said date, be the same as if the mark had been registered by the Office of that Contracting Party.

(b) The indication of classes of goods and services provided for in Article 3 shall not bind the Contracting Parties with regard to the determination of the scope of the protection of the mark.

(2) Every international registration shall enjoy the right of priority provided for by Article 4 of the Paris Convention for the Protection of Industrial Property, without it being necessary to comply with the formalities prescribed in Section 4.D.

Article 4bis Replacement of a National or Regional Registration by an International Registration

(1) Where a mark that is the subject of a national or regional registration in **A22-007** the Office of a Contracting Party is also the subject of an international registration and both registrations stand in the name of the same person, the international registration is deemed to replace the national or regional registration, without prejudice to any rights acquired by virtue of the latter, provided that

- (i) the protection resulting from the international registration extends to the said Contracting Party under Article 3ter(1) or 3ter(2),
- (ii) all the goods and services listed in the national or regional registration are also listed in the international registration in respect of the said Contracting Party,
- (iii) such extension takes effect after the date of the national or regional registration.

(2) The Office referred to in paragraph (1) shall, upon request, be required to take note in its register of the international registration.

Article 5 Refusal and Invalidation of Effects of International Registration in Respect of Certain Contracting Parties

(1) Where the applicable legislation so authorizes, any Office of a Contracting **A22-008** Party which has been notified by the International Bureau of an extension to that Contracting Party, under Article 3ter(1) or 3ter(2), of the protection resulting from the international registration shall have the right to declare in a notification of refusal that protection cannot be granted in the said Contracting Party to the mark which is the subject of such extension. Any such refusal can be based only on the grounds which would apply, under the Paris Convention for the Protection of Industrial Property, in the case of a mark deposited direct with the Office which notifies the refusal. However, protection may not be refused, even partially, by reason only that the applicable legislation would permit registration only in a limited number of classes or for a limited number of goods or services.

(2) (a) Any Office wishing to exercise such right shall notify its refusal to the International Bureau, together with a statement of all grounds, within the period prescribed by the law applicable to that Office and at the latest, subject to subpar-

agraphs (b) and (c), before the expiry of one year from the date on which the notification of the extension referred to in paragraph (1) has been sent to that Office by the International Bureau.

(b) Notwithstanding subparagraph (a), any Contracting Party may declare that, for international registrations made under this Protocol, the time limit of one year referred to in subparagraph (a) is replaced by 18 months.

(c) Such declaration may also specify that, when a refusal of protection may result from an opposition to the granting of protection, such refusal may be notified by the Office of the said Contracting Party to the International Bureau after the expiry of the 18-month time limit. Such an Office may, with respect to any given international registration, notify a refusal of protection after the expiry of the 18-month time limit, but only if

(i) it has, before the expiry of the 18-month time limit, informed the International Bureau of the possibility that oppositions may be filed after the expiry of the 18-month time limit, and

(ii) the notification of the refusal based on an opposition is made within a time limit of not more than seven months from the date on which the opposition period begins; if the opposition period expires before this time limit of seven months, the notification must be made within a time limit of one month from the expiry of the opposition period.

(d) Any declaration under subparagraphs (b) or (c) may be made in the instruments referred to in Article 14(2), and the effective date of the declaration shall be the same as the date of entry into force of this Protocol with respect to the State or intergovernmental organization having made the declaration. Any such declaration may also be made later, in which case the declaration shall have effect three months after its receipt by the Director General of the Organization (hereinafter referred to as "the Director General"), or at any later date indicated in the declaration, in respect of any international registration whose date is the same as or is later than the effective date of the declaration.

(e) Upon the expiry of a period of ten years from the entry into force of this Protocol, the Assembly shall examine the operation of the system established by subparagraphs (a) to (d). Thereafter, the provisions of the said subparagraphs may be modified by a unanimous decision of the Assembly.

(3) The International Bureau shall, without delay, transmit one of the copies of the notification of refusal to the holder of the international registration. The said holder shall have the same remedies as if the mark had been deposited by him direct with the Office which has notified its refusal. Where the International Bureau has received information under paragraph (2)(c)(i), it shall, without delay, transmit the said information to the holder of the international registration.

(4) The grounds for refusing a mark shall be communicated by the International Bureau to any interested party who may so request.

(5) Any Office which has not notified, with respect to a given international registration, any provisional or final refusal to the International Bureau in accordance with paragraphs (1) and (2) shall, with respect to that international registration, lose the benefit of the right provided for in paragraph (1).

(6) Invalidation, by the competent authorities of a Contracting Party, of the effects, in the territory of that Contracting Party, of an international registration may not be pronounced without the holder of such international registration having, in good time, been afforded the opportunity of defending his rights. Invalidation shall be notified to the International Bureau.

Article 5bis Documentary Evidence of Legitimacy of Use of Certain Elements of the Mark

Documentary evidence of the legitimacy of the use of certain elements incor- **A22-009** porated in a mark, such as armorial bearings, escutcheons, portraits, honorary distinctions, titles, trade names, names of persons other than the name of the applicant, or other like inscriptions, which might be required by the Offices of the Contracting Parties shall be exempt from any legalization as well as from any certification other than that of the Office of origin.

Article 5ter Copies of Entries in International Register; Searches for Anticipations; Extracts from International Register

(1) The International Bureau shall issue to any person applying therefor, **A22-010** upon the payment of a fee fixed by the Regulations, a copy of the entries in the International Register concerning a specific mark.

(2) The International Bureau may also, upon payment, undertake searches for anticipations among marks that are the subject of international registrations.

(3) Extracts from the International Register requested with a view to their production in one of the Contracting Parties shall be exempt from any legalization.

Article 6 Period of Validity of International Registration; Dependence and Independence of International Registration

(1) Registration of a mark at the International Bureau is effected for ten **A22-011** years, with the possibility of renewal under the conditions specified in Article 7.

(2) Upon expiry of a period of five years from the date of the international registration, such registrationshall become independent of the basic application or the registration resulting therefrom, or of the basic registration, as the case may be, subject to the following provisions.

(3) The protection resulting from the international registration, whether or not it has been the subject of a transfer, may no longer be invoked if, before the expiry of five years from the date of the international registration, the basic application or the registration resulting therefrom, or the basic registration, as the case may be, has been withdrawn, has lapsed, has been renounced or has been the subject of a final decision of rejection, revocation, cancellation or invalidation, in respect of all or some of the goods and services listed in the international registration. The same applies if

    (i) an appeal against a decision refusing the effects of the basic application,

    (ii) an action requesting the withdrawal of the basic application or the revocation, cancellation or invalidation of the registration resulting from the basic application or of the basic registration,

    or

    (iii) an opposition to the basic application an opposition to the basic application results, after the expiry of the five-year period, in a final decision of rejection, revocation, cancellation or invalidation, or ordering the withdrawal, of the basic application, or the registration resulting therefrom, or the basic registration, as the case may be, provided that such appeal, action or opposition had begun before the expiry of the said period. The same also applies if the basic application is withdrawn, or the registration resulting from the basic application or the basic registration is renounced, after the expiry of the five-year period, provided that, at the time of the withdrawal or renunciation, the said application or registration was the subject of a proceeding referred to in item (i), (ii) or (iii) and that such proceeding had begun before the expiry of the said period.

(4) The Office of origin shall, as prescribed in the Regulations, notify the International Bureau of the facts and decisions relevant under paragraph (3), and the International Bureau shall, as prescribed in the Regulations, notify the interested parties and effect any publication accordingly. The Office of origin shall, where applicable, request the International Bureau to cancel, to the extent applicable, the international registration, and the International Bureau shall proceed accordingly.

Article 7 Renewal of International Registration

A22-012   (1) Any international registration may be renewed for a period of ten years from the expiry of the preceding period, by the mere payment of the basic fee and, subject to Article 8(7), of the supplementary and complementary fees provided for in Article 8(2).

(2) Renewal may not bring about any change in the international registration in its latest form.

(3) Six months before the expiry of the term of protection, the International Bureau shall, by sending an unofficial notice, remind the holder of the international registration and his representative, if any, of the exact date of expiry.

(4) Subject to the payment of a surcharge fixed by the Regulations, a period of grace of six months shall be allowed for renewal of the international registration.

Article 8 Fees for International Application and Registration

A22-013   (1) The Office of origin may fix, at its own discretion, and collect, for its own benefit, a fee which it may require from the applicant for international registration or from the holder of the international registration in connection with the filing of the international application or the renewal of the international registration.

(2) Registration of a mark at the International Bureau shall be subject to the advance payment of an international fee which shall, subject to the provisions of paragraph (7)(a), include,
  (i) a basic fee;
  (ii) a supplementary fee for each class of the International Classification, beyond three, into which the goods or services to which the mark is applied will fall;
  (iii) a complementary fee for any request for extension of protection under Article 3ter.

(3) However, the supplementary fee specified in paragraph (2)(ii) may, without prejudice to the date of the international registration, be paid within the period fixed by the Regulations if the number of classes of goods or services has been fixed or disputed by the International Bureau. If, upon expiry of the said period, the supplementary fee has not been paid or the list of goods or services has not been reduced to the required extent by the applicant, the international application shall be deemed to have been abandoned.

(4) The annual product of the various receipts from international registration, with the exception of the receipts derived from the fees mentioned in paragraph (2)(ii) and (2)(iii), shall be divided equally among the Contracting Parties by the

International Bureau, after deduction of the expenses and charges necessitated by the implementation of this Protocol.

(5) The amounts derived from the supplementary fees provided for in paragraph (2)(ii) shall be divided, at the expiry of each year, among the interested Contracting Parties in proportion to the number of marks for which protection has been applied for in each of them during that year, this number being multiplied, in the case of Contracting Parties which make an examination, by a coefficient which shall be determined by the Regulations.

(6) The amounts derived from the complementary fees provided for in paragraph (2)(iii) shall be divided according to the same rules as those provided for in paragraph (5).

(7) (a) Any Contracting Party may declare that, in connection with each international registration in which it is mentioned under Article 3ter, and in connection with the renewal of any such international registration, it wants to receive, instead of a share in the revenue produced by the supplementary and complementary fees, a fee (hereinafter referred to as "the individual fee") whose amount shall be indicated in the declaration, and can be changed in further declarations, but may not be higher than the equivalent of the amount which the said Contracting Party's Office would be entitled to receive from an applicant for a ten-year registration, or from the holder of a registration for a ten-year renewal of that registration, of the mark in the register of the said Office, the said amount being diminished by the savings resulting from the international procedure. Where such an individual fee is payable,

    (i) no supplementary fees referred to in paragraph (2)(ii) shall be payable if only Contracting Parties which have made a declaration under this subparagraph are mentioned under Article 3ter, and

    (ii) no complementary fee referred to in paragraph (2)(iii) shall be payable in respect of any Contracting Party which has made a declaration under this subparagraph.

(b) Any declaration under subparagraph (a) may be made in the instruments referred to in Article 14(2), and the effective date of the declaration shall be the same as the date of entry into force of this Protocol with respect to the State or intergovernmental organization having made the declaration. Any such declaration may also be made later, in which case the declaration shall have effect three months after its receipt by the Director General, or at any later date indicated in the declaration, in respect of any international registration whose date is the same as or is later than the effective date of the declaration.

Article 9 Recordal of Change in the Ownership of an International Registration

At the request of the person in whose name the international registration stands, or at the request of an interested Office made ex officio or at the request of an interested person, the International Bureau shall record in the International Register any change in the ownership of that registration, in respect of all or some of the Contracting Parties in whose territories the said registration has effect and in respect of all or some of the goods and services listed in the registration, provided that the new holder is a person who, under Article 2(1), is entitled to file international applications. **A22-014**

Article 9bis Recordal of Certain Matters Concerning an International Registration

The International Bureau shall record in the International Register **A22-015**

(i) any change in the name or address of the holder of the international registration,

(ii) the appointment of a representative of the holder of the international registration and any other relevant fact concerning such representative,

(iii) any limitation, in respect of all or some of the Contracting Parties, of the goods and services listed in the international registration,

(iv) any renunciation, cancellation or invalidation of the international registration in respect of all or some of the Contracting Parties,

(v) any other relevant fact, identified in the Regulations, concerning the rights in a mark that is the subject of an international registration.

Article 9ter Fees for Certain Recordals

A22-016   Any recordal under Article 9 or under Article 9bis may be subject to the payment of a fee.

Article 9quater Common Office of Several Contracting States

A22-017   (1) If several Contracting States agree to effect the unification of their domestic legislations on marks, they may notify the Director General

    (i) that a common Office shall be substituted for the national Office of each of them, and

    (ii) that the whole of their respective territories shall be deemed to be a single State for the purposes of the application of all or part of the provisions preceding this Article as well as the provisions of Articles 9quinquies and 9sexies.

(2) Such notification shall not take effect until three months after the date of the communication thereof by the Director General to the other Contracting Parties.

Article 9quinquies Transformation of an International Registration into National or Regional Applications

A22-018   Where, in the event that the international registration is cancelled at the request of the Office of origin under Article 6(4), in respect of all or some of the goods and services listed in the said registration, the person who was the holder of the international registration files an application for the registration of the same mark with the Office of any of the Contracting Parties in the territory of which the international registration had effect, that application shall be treated as if it had been filed on the date of the international registration according to Article 3(4) or on the date of recordal of the territorial extension according to Article 3ter(2) and, if the international registration enjoyed priority, shall enjoy the same priority, provided that

    (i) such application is filed within three months from the date on which the international registration was cancelled,

    (ii) the goods and services listed in the application are in fact covered by the list of goods and services contained in the international registration in respect of the Contracting Party concerned, and

    (iii) such application complies with all the requirements of the applicable law, including the requirements concerning fees.

Article 9sexies Safeguard of the Madrid (Stockholm) Agreement

A22-019   (1) Where, with regard to a given international application or a given international registration, the Office of origin is the Office of a State that is party to both this Protocol and the Madrid (Stockholm) Agreement, the provisions of this

Protocol shall have no effect in the territory of any other State that is also party to both this Protocol and the Madrid (Stockholm) Agreement.

(2) The Assembly may, by a three-fourths majority, repeal paragraph (1), or restrict the scope of paragraph (1), after the expiry of a period of ten years from the entry into force of this Protocol, but not before the expiry of a period of five years from the date on which the majority of the countries party to the Madrid (Stockholm) Agreement have become party to this Protocol. In the vote of the Assembly, only those States which are party to both the said Agreement and this Protocol shall have the right to participate.

Universal Copyright Convention as revised at Paris on 24 July 1971

The Contracting States.
Moved by the desire to ensure in all countries copyright protection of literary, scientific and artistic works,
Convinced that a system of copyright protection appropriate to all nations of the world and expressed in a universal convention, additional to, and without impairing international systems already in force, will ensure respect for the rights of the individual and encourage the development of literature, the sciences and the arts,
Persuaded that such a universal copyright system will facilitate a wider dissemination of works of the human mind and increase international understanding,
Have resolved to revise the Universal Copyright Convention as signed at Geneva on 6 September 1952 (hereinafter called "the 1952 Convention"), and consequently,
Have agreed as follows:

ARTICLE I

Each Contracting State undertakes to provide for the adequate and effective **A23-001** protection of the rights of authors and other copyright proprietors in literary, scientific and artistic works, including writings, musical, dramatic and cinematographic works, and paintings, engravings and sculpture.

ARTICLE II

1. Published works of nationals of any Contracting State and works first **A23-002** published in that State shall enjoy in each other Contracting State the same protection as that other State accords to works of its nationals first published in its own territory, as well as the protection specially granted by this Convention.

2. Unpublished works of nationals of each Contracting State shall enjoy in each other Contracting State the same protection as that other State accords to unpublished works of its own nationals, as well as the protection specially granted by this Convention.

3. For the purpose of this Convention any Contracting State may, by domestic legislation, assimilate to its own nationals any person domiciled in that State.

ARTICLE III

1. Any Contracting State which, under its domestic law, requires as a **A23-003** condition of copyright, compliance with formalities such as deposit, registration, notice, notarial certificates, payment of fees or manufacture or publication in

that Contracting State, shall regard these requirements as satisfied with respect to all works protected in accordance with this Convention and first published outside its territory and the author of which is not one of its nationals, if from the time of the first publication all the copies of the work published with the authority of the author or other copyright proprietor bear the symbol © accompanied by the name of the copyright proprietor and the year of first publication placed in such manner and location as to give reasonable notice of claim of copyright.

2. The provisions of paragraph 1 shall not preclude any Contracting State from requiring formalities or other conditions for the acquisition and enjoyment of copyright in respect of works first published in its territory or works of its nationals wherever published.

3. The provisions of paragraph 1 shall not preclude any Contracting State from providing that a person seeking judicial relief must, in bringing the action, comply with procedural requirements, such as that the complainant must appear through domestic counsel or that the complainant must deposit with the court or an administrative office, or both, a copy of the work involved in the litigation; provided that failure to comply with such requirements shall not affect the validity of the copyright, nor shall any such requirement be imposed upon a national of another Contracting State if such requirement is not imposed on nationals of the State in which protection is claimed.

4. In each Contracting State there shall be legal means of protecting without formalities the unpublished works of nationals of other Contracting States.

5. If a Contracting State grants protection for more than one term of copyright and the first term is for a period longer than one of the minimum periods prescribed in Article IV, such State shall not be required to comply with the provisions of paragraph 1 of this Article in respect of the second or any subsequent term of copyright.

ARTICLE IV

A23-004   1. The duration of protection of a work shall be governed, in accordance with the provisions of Article II and this Article, by the law of the Contracting State in which protection is claimed.

2. (a) The term of protection for works protected under this Convention shall not be less than the life of the author and twenty-five years after his death. However, any Contracting State which, on the effective date of this Convention in that State, has limited this term for certain classes of works to a period computed from the first publication of the work, shall be entitled to maintain these exceptions and to extend them to other classes of works. For all these classes the term of protection shall not be less than twenty-five years from the date of first publication.

(b) Any Contracting State which, upon the effective date of this Convention in that State, does not compute the term of protection upon the basis of the life of the author, shall be entitled to compute the term of protection from the date of the first publication of the work or from its registration prior to publication, as the case may be, provided the term of protection shall not be less than twenty-five years from the date of first publication or from its registration prior to publication, as the case may be.

(c) If the legislation of a Contracting State grants two or more successive terms of protection, the duration of the first term shall not be less than one of the minimum periods specified in subparagraphs (a) and (b).

3. The provisions of paragraph 2 shall not apply to photographic works or to works of applied art; provided, however, that the term of protection in those Contracting States which protect photographic works, or works of applied art in so far as they are protected as artistic work, shall not be less than ten years for each of said classes of works.

4. (a) No Contracting State shall be obliged to grant protection to a work for a period longer than that fixed for the class of works to which the work in question belongs, in the case of unpublished works by the law of the Contracting State of which the author is a national, and in the case of published works by the law of the Contracting State in which the work has been first published.

(b) For the purposes of the application of subparagraph (a), if the law of any Contracting State grants two or more successive terms of protection, the period of protection of that State shall be considered to be the aggregate of those terms. However, if a specified work is not protected by such State during the second or any subsequent term for any reason, the other Contracting States shall not be obliged to protect it during the second or any subsequent term.

5. For the purposes of the application of paragraph 4, the work of a national of a Contracting State, first published in a non-Contracting State, shall be treated as though first published in the Contracting State of which the author is a national.

6. For the purposes of the application of paragraph 4, in case of simultaneous publication in two or more Contracting States, the work shall be treated as though first published in the State which affords the shortest term; any work published in two or more Contracting States within thirty days of its first publication shall be considered as having been published simultaneously in said Contracting States.

ARTICLE IVbis

1. The rights referred to in Article I shall include the basic rights ensuring **A23-005** the author's economic interests, including the exclusive right to authorize reproduction by any means, public performance and broadcasting. The provisions of this Article shall extend to works protected under this Convention either in their original form or in any form recognizably derived from the original.

2. However, any Contracting State may, by its domestic legislation, make exceptions that do not conflict with the spirit and provisions of this Convention, to the rights mentioned in paragraph 1 of this Article. Any State whose legislation so provides, shall nevertheless accord a reasonable degree of effective protection to each of the rights to which exception has been made.

ARTICLE V

1. The rights referred to in Article I shall include the exclusive right of the **A23-006** author to make, publish and authorize the making and publication of translations of works protected under this Convention.

2. However, any Contracting State may, by its domestic legislation, restrict the right of translation of writings, but only subject to the following provisions:

    (a) If, after the expiration of a period of seven years from the date of the first publication of a writing, a translation of such writing has not been published in a language in general use in the Contracting State, by the owner of the right of translation or with his authorization, any national of such Contracting State may obtain a non-exclusive licence from the competent authority thereof to translate the work into that language and publish the work so translated.

(b) Such national shall in accordance with the procedure of the State concerned, establish either that he has requested, and been denied, authorization by the proprietor of the right to make and publish the translation, or that, after due diligence on his part, he was unable to find the owner of the right. A licence may also be granted on the same conditions if all previous editions of a translation in a language in general use in the Contracting State are out of print.

(c) If the owner of the right of translation cannot be found, then the applicant for a licence shall send copies of his application to the publisher whose name appears on the work and, if the nationality of the owner of the right of translation is known, to the diplomatic or consular representative of the State of which such owner is a national, or to the organization which may have been designated by the government of that State. The licence shall not be granted before the expiration of a period of two months from the date of the dispatch of the copies of the application.

(d) Due provision shall be made by domestic legislation to ensure to the owner of the right of translation a compensation which is just and conforms to international standards, to ensure payment and transmittal of such compensation, and to ensure a correct translation of the work.

(e) The original title and the name of the author of the work shall be printed on all copies of the published translation. The licence shall be valid only for publication of the translation in the territory of the Contracting State where it has been applied for. Copies so published may be imported and sold in another Contracting State if a language in general use in such other State is the same language as that into which the work has been so translated, and if the domestic law in such other State makes provision for such licences and does not prohibit such importation and sale. Where the foregoing conditions do not exist, the importation and sale of such copies in a Contracting State shall be governed by its domestic law and its agreements. The licence shall not be transferred by the licensee.

(f) The licence shall not be granted when the author has withdrawn from circulation all copies of the work.

ARTICLE Vbis

A23-007   1. Any Contracting State regarded as a developing country in conformity with the established practice of the General Assembly of the United Nations may, by a notification deposited with the Director-General of the United Nations Educational, Scientific and Cultural Organization (hereinafter called "the Director-General") at the time of its ratification, acceptance or accession or thereafter, avail itself of any or all of the exceptions provided for in Articles Vter and Vquater.

2. Any such notification shall be effective for ten years from the date of coming into force of this Convention, or for such part of that ten-year period as remains at the date of deposit of the notification, and may be renewed in whole or in part for further periods of ten years each if, not more than fifteen or less than three months before the expiration of the relevant ten-year period, the Contracting State deposits a further notification with the Director-General. Initial notifications may also be made during these further periods of ten years in accordance with the provisions of this Article.

3. Notwithstanding the provisions of paragraph 2, a Contracting State that has ceased to be regarded as a developing country as referred to in paragraph 1 shall no longer be entitled to renew its notification made under the provisions of paragraph 1 or 2, and whether or not it formally withdraws the notification such State shall be precluded from availing itself of the exceptions provided for in Articles Vter and Vquater at the end of the current ten-year period, or at the end of three years after it has ceased to be regarded as a developing country, whichever period expires later.

4. Any copies of a work already made under the exceptions provided for in Articles Vter and Vquater may continue to be distributed after the expiration of the period for which notifications under this Article were effective until their stock is exhausted.

5. Any Contracting State that has deposited a notification in accordance with Article XIII with respect to the application of this Convention to a particular country or territory, the situation of which can be regarded as analogous to that of the States referred to in paragraph 1 of this Article, may also deposit notifications and renew them in accordance with the provisions of this Article with respect to any such country or territory. During the effective period of such notifications, the provisions of Articles Vter and Vquater may be applied with respect to such country or territory. The sending of copies from the country or territory to the Contracting State shall be considered as export within the meaning of Articles Vter and Vquater.

ARTICLE Vter

1. (a) Any Contracting State to which Article Vbis (1) applies may substitute **A23-008** for the period of seven years provided for in Article V (2) a period of three years or any longer period prescribed by its legislation. However, in the case of a translation into a language not in general use in one or more developed countries that are party to this Convention or only the 1952 Convention, the period shall be one year instead of three.

(b) A Contracting State to which Article Vbis (1) applies may, with the unanimous agreement of the developed countries party to this Convention or only the 1952 Convention and in which the same language is in general use, substitute, in the case of translation into that language, for the period of three years provided for in subparagraph (a) another period as determined by such agreement but not shorter than one year. However, this subparagraph shall not apply where the language in question is English, French or Spanish. Notification of any such agreement shall be made to the Director-General.

(c) The licence may only be granted if the applicant, in accordance with the procedure of the State concerned, establishes either that he has requested, and been denied, authorization by the owner of the right of translation, or that, after due diligence on his part, he was unable to find the owner of the right. At the same time as he makes his request he shall inform either the International Copyright Information Centre established by the United Nations Educational, Scientific and Cultural Organization or any national or regional information centre which may have been designated in a notification to that effect deposited with the Director-General by the government of the State in which the publisher is believed to have his principal place of business.

(d) If the owner of the right of translation cannot be found, the applicant for a licence shall send, by registered airmail, copies of his application to the publisher whose name appears on the work and to any national or regional information centre as mentioned in subparagraph (c). If no such centre is notified he shall also send a copy to the international copyright information centre established by the United Nations Educational, Scientific and Cultural Organization.

2. (a) Licences obtainable after three years shall not be granted under this Article until a further period of six months has elapsed and licences obtainable after one year until a further period of nine months has elapsed. The further period shall begin either from the date of the request for permission to translate mentioned in paragraph 1(c) or, if the identity or address of the owner of the right of translation is not known, from the date of dispatch of the copies of the application for a licence mentioned in paragraph 1 (d).

(b) Licences shall not be granted if a translation has been published by the owner of the right of translation or with his authorization during the said period of six or nine months.

3. Any licence under this Article shall be granted only for the purpose of teaching,scholarship or research.

4. (a) Any licence granted under this Article shall not extend to the export of copies and shall be valid only for publication in the territory of the Contracting State where it has been applied for.

(b) Any copy published in accordance with a licence granted under this Article shall bear a notice in the appropriate language stating that the copy is available for distribution only in the Contracting State granting the licence. If the writing bears the notice specified in Article III (1) the copies shall bear the same notice.

(c) The prohibition of export provided for in subparagraph (a) shall not apply where a governmental or other public entity of a State which has granted a licence under this Article to translate a work into a language other than English, French or Spanish sends copies of a translation prepared under such licence to another country if:

(i) the recipients are individuals who are nationals of the Contracting State granting the licence, or organizations grouping such individuals;

(ii) the copies are to be used only for the purpose of teaching, scholarship or research;

(iii) the sending of the copies and their subsequent distribution to recipients is without the object of commercial purpose; and

(iv) the country to which the copies have been sent has agreed with the Contracting State to allow the receipt, distribution or both and the Director-General has been notified of such agreement by any one of the governments which have concluded it.

5. Due provision shall be made at the national level to ensure:

(a) that the licence provides for just compensation that is consistent with standards of royalties normally operating in the case of licences freely negotiated between persons in the two countries concerned; and

(b) payment and transmittal of the compensation; however, should national currency regulations intervene, the competent authority shall make all efforts, by the use of international machinery, to ensure transmittal in internationally convertible currency or its equivalent.

6. Any licence granted by a Contracting State under this Article shall terminate if a translation of the work in the same language with substantially the same content as the edition in respect of which the licence was granted is published in the said State by the owner of the right of translation or with his authorization, at a price reasonably related to that normally charged in the same State for comparable works. Any copies already made before the licence is terminated may continue to be distributed until their stock is exhausted.

7. For works which are composed mainly of illustrations a licence to translate the text and to reproduce the illustrations may be granted only if the conditions of Article Vquater are also fulfilled.

8. (a) A licence to translate a work protected under this Convention, published in printed or analogous forms of reproduction, may also be granted to a broadcasting organization having its headquarters in a Contracting State to which Article Vbis (1) applies, upon an application made in that State by the said organization under the following conditions:

    (i) the translation is made from a copy made and acquired in accordance with the laws of the Contracting State;

    (ii) the translation is for use only in broadcasts intended exclusively for teaching or for the dissemination of the results of specialized technical or scientific research to experts in a particular profession;

    (iii) the translation is used exclusively for the purposes set out in condition (ii), through broadcasts lawfully made which are intended for recipients on the territory of the Contracting State, including broadcasts made through the medium of sound or visual recordings lawfully and exclusively made for the purpose of such broadcasts;

    (iv) sound or visual recordings of the translation may be exchanged only between broadcasting organizations having their headquarters in the Contracting State granting the licence; and

    (v) all uses made of the translation are without any commercial purpose.

(b) Provided all of the criteria and conditions set out in subparagraph (a) are met, a licence may also be granted to a broadcasting organization to translate any text incorporated in air audio-visual fixation which was itself prepared and published for the sole purpose of being used in connexion with systematic instructional activities.

(c) Subject to subparagraphs (a) and (b), the other provisions of this Article shall apply to the grant and exercise of the licence.

9. Subject to the provisions of this Article, the licence granted under this Article shall be governed by the provisions of Article V, and shall continue to be governed by the provisions of Article V and of this Article, even after the seven-year period provided for in Article V has expired. However, after the said period has expired, the licensee shall be free to request that the said licence be replaced by a new licence governed exclusively by the provisions of Article V.

ARTICLE Vquater

1. Any Contracting State to which Article Vbis (1) applies may adopt the **A23-009** following provisions:

    (a) If, after the expiration of (i) the relevant period specified in subparagraph (c) commencing from the date of first publication of a particular edition of a literary, scientific or artistic work referred to in paragraph 3, or (ii) any longer period determined by national legislation of the State, copies of such edition have not been distributed in that State to the general public or in connexion with systematic instructional activities at a price reasonably related to that normally charged in the State for comparable works, by the owner of the right of reproduction or with his authorization, any national of such State may obtain a non-exclusive licence from the competent authority to publish such edition at that or a lower price for use in connexion with systematic instructional activities. The licence may only be granted if such national, in accordance with the procedure of the State concerned, establishes either that he has requested, and been denied, authorization by the proprietor of the right to publish such work, or that, after due diligence on his part, he was unable to find the owner of the right. At the same time as he makes his request he shall inform either the international copyright information centre established by the United Nations Educational, Scientific and Cultural Organization or any national or regional information centre referred to in subparagraph (d).

(b) A licence may also be granted on the same conditions if, for a period of six months, no authorized copies of the edition in question have been on sale in the State concerned to the general public or in connexion with systematic instructional activities at a price reasonably related to that normally charged in the State for comparable works.

(c) The period referred to in subparagraph (a) shall be five years except that:
  (i) for works of the natural and physical sciences, including mathematics, and of technology, the period shall be three years;
  (ii) for works of fiction, poetry, drama and music, and for art books, the period shall be seven years.

(d) If the owner of the right of reproduction cannot be found, the applicant for a licence shall send, by registered air mail, copies of his application to the publisher whose name appears on the work and to any national or regional information centre identified as such in a notification deposited with the Director-General by the State in which the publisher is believed to have his principal place of business. In the absence of any such notification, he shall also send a copy to the international copyright information centre established by the United Nations Educational, Scientific and Cultural Organization. The licence shall not be granted before the expiration of a period of three months from the date of dispatch of the copies of the application.

(e) Licences obtainable after three years shall not be granted under this Article:
  (i) until a period of six months has elapsed from the date of the request for permission referred to in subparagraph (a) or, if the identity or address of the owner of the right of reproduction is unknown, from the date of the dispatch of the copies of the application for a licence referred to in subparagraph (d);
  (ii) ifany such distribution of copies of the edition as is mentioned in subparagraph (a) has taken place during that period.

(f) The name of the author and the title of the particular edition of the work shall be printed on all copies of the published reproduction. The licence shall not extend to the export of copies and shall be valid only for publication in the territory of the Contracting State where it has been applied for. The licence shall not be transferable by the licensee.

(g) Due provision shall be made by domestic legislation to ensure an accurate reproduction of the particular edition in question.

(h) A licence to reproduce and publish a translation of a work shall not be granted under this Article in the following cases:
  (i) where the translation was not published by, the owner of the right of translation or with authorization;
  (ii) where the translation is not in a language in general use in the State with power to grant the licence.

2. The exceptions provided for in paragraph 1 are subject to the following additional provisions:

    (a) Any copy published in accordance with a licence granted under this Article shall bear a notice in the appropriate language stating that the copy is available for distribution only in the Contracting State to which the said licence applies. If the edition bears the notice specified in Article III (1), the copies shall bear the same notice.

    (b) Due provision shall be made at the national level to ensure:

        (i) that the licence provides for just compensation that is consistent with standards of royalties normally operating in the case of licences freely negotiated between persons in the two countries concerned; and

        (ii) payment and transmittal of the compensation; however, should national currency regulations intervene, the competent authority shall make all efforts, by the use of international machinery, to ensure transmittal in internationally convertible currency or its equivalent.

    (c) Whenever copies of an edition of a work are distributed in the Contracting State to the general public or in connexion with systematic instructional activities, by the owner of the right of reproduction or with his authorization, at a price reasonably related to that normally charged in the State for comparable works, any licence granted under this Article shall terminate if such edition is in the same language and is substantially the same in content as the edition published under the licence. Any copies already made before the licence is terminated may continue to be distributed until their stock is exhausted.

    (d) No licence shall be granted where the author has withdrawn from circulation all copies of the edition in question.

3.

    (a) Subject to subparagraph (b), the literary, scientific or artistic works to which this Article applies shall be limited to works published in printed or analogous forms of reproduction.

    (b) The provisions of this Article shall also apply to reproduction in audio-visual form of lawfully made audio-visual fixations including any protected works incorporated therein and to the translation of any incorporated text into a language in general use in the State with power to grant the licence; always provided that the audio-visual fixations in question were prepared and published for the sole purpose of being used in connexion with systematic instructional activities.

ARTICLE VI

"Publication", as used in this Convention, means the reproduction in tangible **A23-010** form and the general distribution to the public of copies of a work from which it can be read or otherwise visually perceived.

ARTICLE VII

This Convention shall not apply to works or rights in works which, at the **A23-011** effective date of this Convention in a Contracting State where protection is claimed, are permanently in the public domain in the said Contracting State.

ARTICLE XVII

A23-012 1. This Convention shall not in any way affect the provisions of the Berne Convention for the Protection of Literary and Artistic Works or membership in the Union created by that Convention.

2. In application of the foregoing paragraph, a declaration has been annexed to the present Article. This declaration is an integral part of this Convention for the States bound by the Berne Convention on 1 January 1951, or which have or may become bound to it at a later date. The signature of this Convention by such States shall also constitute signature of the said declaration, and ratification, acceptance or accession by such States shall include the declaration, as well as this Convention.

ROME CONVENTION, 1961

INTERNATIONAL CONVENTION FOR THE PROTECTION OF PERFORMERS, PRODUCERS OF PHONOGRAMS AND BROADCASTING ORGANISATIONS

Done at Rome on October 26, 1961

The Contracting States, moved by the desire to protect the rights of performers, producers of phonograms, and broadcasting organisations,
Have agreed as follows:

Article 1 Safeguard of Copyright Proper

A24-001 Protection granted under this Convention shall leave intact and shall in no way affect the protection of copyright in literary and artistic works. Consequently, no provision of this Convention may be interpreted as prejudicing such protection.

Article 2 Protection given by the Convention. Definition of National Treatment

A24-002 1. For the purposes of this Convention, national treatment shall mean the treatment accorded by the domestic law of the Contracting State in which protection is claimed:

(a) to performers who are its nationals, as regards performances taking place, broadcast, or first fixed, on its territory;

(b) to producers of phonograms who are its nationals, as regards phonograms first fixed or first published on its territory;

(c) to broadcasting organisations which have their headquarters on its territory, as regards broadcasts transmitted from transmitters situated on its territory.

2. National treatment shall be subject to the protection specifically guaranteed, and the limitations specifically provided for, in this Convention.

Article 3 Definitions: (a) Performers; (b) Phonogram; (c) Producers of Phonograms; (d) Publication; (e) Reproduction; (f) Broadcasting; (g) Rebroadcasting

A24-003 1. For the purposes of this Convention:

(a) "performers" means actors, singers, musicians, dancers, and other persons who act, sing, deliver, declaim, play in, or otherwise perform literary or artistic works;

(b) "phonogram" means any exclusively aural fixation of sounds of a performance or of other sounds;

(c) "producer of phonograms" means the person who, or the legal entity which, first fixes the sounds of a performance or other sounds;

(d) "publication" means the offering of copies of a phonogram to the public in reasonable quantity;

(e) "reproduction" means the making of a copy or copies of a fixation;

(f) "broadcasting" means the transmission by wireless means for public reception of sounds or of images and sounds;

(g) "rebroadcasting" means the simultaneous broadcasting by one broadcasting organisation of the broadcast of another broadcasting organisation.

Article 4 Performances Protected. Points of Attachment for Performers

1. Each Contracting State shall grant national treatment to performers if any **A24-004** of the following conditions is met:

(a) the performance takes place in another Contracting State;

(b) the performance is incorporated in a phonogram which is protected under Article 5 of this Convention;

(c) the performance, not being fixed on a phonogram, is carried by a broadcast which is protected by Article 6 of this Convention.

Article 5 Protected Phonograms: 1. Points of Attachment for Producers of Phonograms; 2. Simultaneous Publication; 3. Power to exclude certain Criteria

1. Each Contracting State shall grant national treatment to producers of **A24-005** phonograms if any of the following conditions is met:

(a) the producer of the phonogram is a national of another Contracting State (criterion of nationality);

(b) the first fixation of the sound was made in another Contracting State (criterion of fixation);

(c) the phonogram was first published in another Contracting State (criterion of publication).

2. If a phonogram was first published in a non-contracting State but if it was also published, within thirty days of its first publication, in a Contracting State (simultaneous publication), it shall be considered as first published in the Contracting State.

3. By means of a notification deposited with the Secretary-General of the United Nations, any Contracting State may declare that it will not apply the criterion of publication or, alternatively, the criterion of fixation. Such notification may be deposited at the time of ratification, acceptance or accession, or at any time thereafter; in the last case, it shall become effective six months after it has been deposited.

Article 6 Protected Broadcasts: 1. Points of Attachment for Broadcasting Organizations; 2. Power to Reserve

1. Each Contracting State shall grant national treatment to broadcasting orga- **A24-006** nisations if either of the following conditions is met:

(a) the headquarters of the broadcasting organisation is situated in another Contracting State;

(b) the broadcast was transmitted from a transmitter situated in another Contracting State.

2. By means of a notification deposited with the Secretary-General of the United Nations, any Contracting State may declare that it will protect broadcasts only if the headquarters of the broadcasting organisation is situated in another Contracting State and the broadcast was transmitted from a transmitter situated in the same Contracting State. Such notification may be deposited at the time of ratification, acceptance or accession, or at any time thereafter; in the last case, it shall become effective six months after it has been deposited.

Article 7 Minimum Protection for Performers: 1. Particular Rights; 2. Relations between Performers and Broadcasting Organizations

A24-007   1. The protection provided for performers by this Convention shall include the possibility of preventing:

(a) the broadcasting and the communication to the public, without their consent, of their performance, except where the performance used in the broadcasting or the public communication is itself already a broadcast performance or is made from a fixation;

(b) the fixation, without their consent, of their unfixed performance;

(c) the reproduction, without their consent, of a fixation of their performance:

    (i) if the original fixation itself was made without their consent;

    (ii) if the reproduction is made for purposes different from those for which the performers gave their consent;

    (iii) if the original fixation was made in accordance with the provisions of Article 15, and the reproduction is made for purposes different from those referred to in those provisions.

2.

(1) If broadcasting was consented to by the performers, it shall be a matter for the domestic law of the Contracting State where protection is claimed to regulate the protection against rebroadcasting, fixation for broadcasting purposes and the reproduction of such fixation for broadcasting purposes.

(2) The terms and conditions governing the use by broadcasting organisations of fixations made for broadcasting purposes shall be determined in accordance with the domestic law of the Contracting State where protection is claimed.

(3) However, the domestic law referred to in sub-paragraphs (1) and (2) of this paragraph shall not operate to deprive performers of the ability to control, by contract, their relations with broadcasting organisations.

Article 8 Performers acting jointly

A24-008   Any Contracting State may, by its domestic laws and regulations, specify the manner in which performers will be represented in connection with the exercise of their rights if several of them participate in the same performance.

Article 9 Variety and Circus Artists

A24-009   Any Contracting State may, by its domestic laws and regulations, extend the protection provided for in this Convention to artists who do not perform literary or artistic works.

Article 10 Right of Reproduction for Phonogram Producers

Producers of phonograms shall enjoy the right to authorize or prohibit the **A24-010** direct or indirect reproduction of their phonograms.

Article 11 Formalities for Phonograms

If, as a condition of protecting the rights of producers of phonograms, or of **A24-011** performers, or both, in relation to phonograms, a Contracting State, under its domestic law, requires compliance with formalities, these shall be considered as fulfilled if all the copies in commerce of the published phonogram or their containers bear a notice consisting of the symbol (P), accompanied by the year date of the first publication, placed in such a manner as to give reasonable notice of claim of protection; and if the copies or their containers do not identify the producer or the licensee of the producer (by carrying his name, trade mark or other appropriate designation), the notice shall also include the name of the owner of the rights of the producer; and, furthermore, if the copies or their containers do not identify the principal performers, the notice shall also include the name of the person who, in the country in which the fixation was effected, owns the rights of such performers.

Article 12 Secondary Uses of Phonograms

If a phonogram published for commercial purposes, or a reproduction of **A24-012** such phonogram, is used directly for broadcasting or for any communication to the public, a single equitable remuneration shall be paid by the user to the performers, or to the producers of the phonograms, or to both. Domestic law may, in the absence of agreement between these parties, lay down the conditions as to the sharing of this remuneration.

Article 13 Minimum Rights for Broadcasting Organizations

Broadcasting organisations shall enjoy the right to authorize or prohibit: **A24-013**
(a) the rebroadcasting of their broadcasts;
(b) the fixation of their broadcasts;
(c) the reproduction:
     (i) of fixations, made without their consent, of their broadcasts;
     (ii) of fixations, made in accordance with the provisions of Article 15, of their broadcasts, if the reproduction is made for purposes different from those referred to in those provisions;
(d) the communication to the public of their television broadcasts if such communication is made in places accessible to the public against payment of an entrance fee; it shall be a matter for the domestic law of the State where protection of this right is claimed to determine the conditions under which it may be exercised.

Article 14 Minimum Duration of Protection

The term of protection to be granted under this Convention shall last at least **A24-014** until the end of a period of twenty years computed from the end of the year in which:
(a) the fixation was made-for phonograms and for performances incorporated therein;
(b) the performance took place-for performances not incorporated in phonograms;
(c) the broadcast took place-for broadcasts.

Article 15 Permitted Exceptions: 1. Specific Limitations; 2. Equivalents with copyright

A24-015   1. Any Contracting State may, in its domestic laws and regulations, provide for exceptions to the protection guaranteed by this Convention as regards:

(a) private use;

(b) use of short excerpts in connection with the reporting of current events;

(c) ephemeral fixation by a broadcasting organisation by means of its own facilities and for its own broadcasts;

(d) use solely for the purposes of teaching or scientific research.

2. Irrespective of paragraph 1 of this Article, any Contracting State may, in its domestic laws and regulations, provide for the same kinds of limitations with regard to the protection of performers, producers of phonograms and broadcasting organisations, as it provides for, in its domestic laws and regulations, in connection with the protection of copyright in literary and artistic works. However, compulsory licences may be provided for only to the extent to which they are compatible with this Convention.

Article 16 Reservations

A24-016   1. Any State, upon becoming party to this Convention, shall be bound by all the obligations and shall enjoy all the benefits thereof. However, a State may at any time, in a notification deposited with the Secretary-General of the United Nations, declare that:

(a) as regards Article 12:

(i) it will not apply the provisions of that Article;

(ii) it will not apply the provisions of that Article in respect of certain uses;

(iii) as regards phonograms the producer of which is not a national of another Contracting State, it will not apply that Article;

(iv) as regards phonograms the producer of which is a national of another Contracting State, it will limit the protection provided for by that Article to the extent to which, and to the term for which, the latter State grants protection to phonograms first fixed by a national of the State making the declaration; however, the fact that the Contracting State of which the producer is a national does not grant the protection to the same beneficiary or beneficiaries as the State making the declaration shall not be considered as a difference in the extent of the protection;

(b) as regards Article 13, it will not apply item (d) of that Article; if a Contracting State makes such a declaration, the other Contracting States shall not be obliged to grant the right referred to in Article 13, item (d), to broadcasting organisations whose headquarters are in that State.

2. If the notification referred to in paragraph 1 of this Article is made after the date of the deposit of the instrument of ratification, acceptance or accession, the declaration will become effective six months after it has been deposited.

Article 17 Certain countries applying only the "fixation" criterion

A24-017   Any State which, on October 26, 1961, grants protection to producers of phonograms solely on the basis of the criterion of fixation may, by a notification deposited with the Secretary-General of the United Nations at the time of ratification, acceptance or accession, declare that it will apply, for the purposes of

Article 5, the criterion of fixation alone and, for the purposes of paragraph 1(a)(iii) and (iv) of Article 16, the criterion of fixation instead of the criterion of nationality.

Article 18 Withdrawal of reservations

Any State which has deposited a notification under paragraph 3 of Article 5, **A24-018** paragraph 2 of Article 6, paragraph 1 of Article 16 or Article 17, may, by a further notification deposited with the Secretary-General of the United Nations, reduce its scope or withdraw it.

Article 19 Performers' Rights in Films

Notwithstanding anything in this Convention, once a performer has **A24-019** consented to the incorporation of his performance in a visual or audio-visual fixation, Article 7 shall have no further application.

Article 20 Non-retroactivity

1. This Convention shall not prejudice rights acquired in any Contracting **A24-020** State before the date of coming into force of this Convention for that State.

2. No Contracting State shall be bound to apply the provisions of this Convention to performances or broadcasts which took place, or to phonograms which were fixed, before the date of coming into force of this Convention for that State.

Article 21 Protection by other means

The protection provided for in this Convention shall not prejudice any **A24-021** protection otherwise secured to performers, producers of phonograms and broadcasting organisations.

Article 22 Special agreements

Contracting States reserve the right to enter into special agreements among **A24-022** themselves in so far as such agreements grant to performers, producers of phonograms or broadcasting organisations more extensive rights than those granted by this Convention or contain other provisions not contrary to this Convention.

INTERNATIONAL CONVENTION FOR THE PROTECTION OF NEW VARIETIES OF PLANTS *

(* This is reproduced with the kind permission of the UPOV, the owner of the copyright)

CHAPTER I

DEFINITIONS

Article 1 Definitions

For the purposes of this Act: **A25-001**

(i) "this Convention" means the present (1991) Act of the International Convention for the Protection of New Varieties of Plants;

(ii) "Act of 1961/1972" means the International Convention for the Protection of New Varieties of Plants of December 2, 1961, as amended by the Additional Act of November 10, 1972;

(iii) "Act of 1978" means the Act of October 23, 1978, of the International Convention for the Protection of New Varieties of Plants;

(iv) "breeder" means

–the person who bred, or discovered and developed, a variety,

– the person who is the employer of the aforementioned person or who has commissioned the latter's work, where the laws of the relevant Contracting Party so provide, or

–the successor in title of the first or second aforementioned person, as the case may be;

(v) "breeder's right" means the right of the breeder provided for in this Convention;

(vi) "variety" means a plant grouping within a single botanical taxon of the lowest known rank, which grouping, irrespective of whether the conditions for the grant of a breeder's right are fully met, can be

– defined by the expression of the characteristics resulting from a given genotype or combination of genotypes,

– distinguished from any other plant grouping by the expression of at least one of the said characteristics and

– considered as a unit with regard to its suitability for being propagated unchanged;

(vii) "Contracting Party" means a State or an intergovernmental organization party to this Convention;

(viii) "territory," in relation to a Contracting Party, means, where the Contracting Party is a State, the territory of that State and, where the Contracting Party is an intergovernmental organization, the territory in which the constituting treaty of that intergovernmental organization applies;

(ix) "authority" means the authority referred to in Article 30(1)(ii);

(x) "Union" means the Union for the Protection of New Varieties of Plants founded by the Act of 1961 and further mentioned in the Act of 1972, the Act of 1978 and in this Convention;

(xi) "member of the Union" means a State party to the Act of 1961/1972 or the Act of 1978, or a Contracting Party.

CHAPTER II

GENERAL OBLIGATIONS OF THE CONTRACTING PARTIES

Article 2 Basic Obligation of the Contracting Parties

A25-002   Each Contracting Party shall grant and protect breeders' rights.

Article 3 Genera and Species to be Protected

A25-003   (1) [States already members of the Union] Each Contracting Party which is bound by the Act of 1961/1972 or the Act of 1978 shall apply the provisions of this Convention,

(i) at the date on which it becomes bound by this Convention, to all plant genera and species to which it applies, on the said date, the provisions of the Act of 1961/1972 or the Act of 1978 and,

(ii) at the latest by the expiration of a period of five years after the said date, to all plant genera and species.

(2) New members of the Union Each Contracting Party which is not bound by the Act of 1961/1972 or the Act of 1978 shall apply the provisions of this Convention,

(i) at the date on which it becomes bound by this Convention, to at least 15 plant genera or species and,

(ii) at the latest by the expiration of a period of 10 years from the said date, to all plant genera and species.

Article 4 National Treatment

(1) [Treatment] Without prejudice to the rights specified in this Convention, **A25-004** nationals of a Contracting Party as well as natural persons resident and legal entities having their registered offices within the territory of a Contracting Party shall, insofar as the grant and protection of breeders' rights are concerned, enjoy within the territory of each other Contracting Party the same treatment as is accorded or may hereafter be accorded by the laws of each such other Contracting Party to its own nationals, provided that the said nationals, natural persons or legal entities comply with the conditions and formalities imposed on the nationals of the said other Contracting Party.

(2) ["Nationals"] For the purposes of the preceding paragraph, "nationals" means, where the Contracting Party is a State, the nationals of that State and, where the Contracting Party is an intergovernmental organization, the nationals of the States which are members of that organization.

CHAPTER III

CONDITIONS FOR THE GRANT OF THE BREEDER'S RIGHT

Article 5 Conditions of Protection

(1) [Criteria to be satisfied] The breeder's right shall be granted where the **A25-005** variety is

(i) new,
(ii) distinct,
(iii) uniform and
(iv) stable.

(2) [Other conditions] The grant of the breeder's right shall not be subject to any further or different conditions, provided that the variety is designated by a denomination in accordance with the provisions of Article 20, that the applicant complies with the formalities provided for by the law of the Contracting Party with whose authority the application has been filed and that he pays the required fees.

Article 6 Novelty

(1) [Criteria] The variety shall be deemed to be new if, at the date of filing of **A25-006** the application for a breeder's right, propagating or harvested material of the variety has not been sold or otherwise disposed of to others, by or with the consent of the breeder, for purposes of exploitation of the variety

(i) in the territory of the Contracting Party in which the application has been filed earlier than one year before that date and

(ii) in a territory other than that of the Contracting Party in which the application has been filed earlier than four years or, in the case of trees or of vines, earlier than six years before the said date.

(2) [Varieties of recent creation] Where a Contracting Party applies this Convention to a plant genus or species to which it did not previously apply this Convention or an earlier Act, it may consider a variety of recent creation existing at the date of such extension of protection to satisfy the condition of novelty defined in paragraph (1) even where the sale or disposal to others described in that paragraph took place earlier than the time limits defined in that paragraph.

(3) ["Territory" in certain cases] For the purposes of paragraph (1), all the Contracting Parties which are member States of one and the same intergovernmental organization may act jointly, where the regulations of that organization so require, to assimilate acts done on the territories of the States members of that organization to acts done on their own territories and, should they do so, shall notify the Secretary-General accordingly.

Article 7 Distinctness

A25-007   The variety shall be deemed to be distinct if it is clearly distinguishable from any other variety whose existence is a matter of common knowledge at the time of the filing of the application. In particular, the filing of an application for the granting of a breeder's right or for the entering of another variety in an official register of varieties, in any country, shall be deemed to render that other variety a matter of common knowledge from the date of the application, provided that the application leads to the granting of a breeder's right or to the entering of the said other variety in the official register of varieties, as the case may be.

Article 8 Uniformity

A25-008   The variety shall be deemed to be uniform if, subject to the variation that may be expected from the particular features of its propagation, it is sufficiently uniform in its relevant characteristics.

Article 9 Stability

A25-009   The variety shall be deemed to be stable if its relevant characteristics remain unchanged after repeated propagation or, in the case of a particular cycle of propagation, at the end of each such cycle.

CHAPTER IV

APPLICATION FOR THE GRANT OF THE BREEDER'S RIGHT

Article 10 Filing of Applications

A25-010   (1) [Place of first application] The breeder may choose the Contracting Party with whose authority he wishes to file his first application for a breeder's right.

(2) [Time of subsequent applications] The breeder may apply to the authorities of other Contracting Parties for the grant of breeders' rights without waiting for the grant to him of a breeder's right by the authority of the Contracting Party with which the first application was filed.

[Independence of protection] No Contracting Party shall refuse to grant a breeder's right or limit its duration on the ground that protection for the same variety has not been applied for, has been refused or has expired in any other State or intergovernmental organization.

Article 11 Right of Priority

(3)—(1) [The right; its period] Any breeder who has duly filed an application **A25-011** for the protection of a variety in one of the Contracting Parties (the "first application") shall, for the purpose of filing an application for the grant of a breeder's right for the same variety with the authority of any other Contracting Party (the "subsequent application"), enjoy a right of priority for a period of twelve months. This period shall be computed from the date of filing of the first application. The day of filing shall not be included in the latter period.

(2) [Claiming the right] In order to benefit from the right of priority, the breeder shall, in the subsequent application, claim the priority of the first application. The authority with which the subsequent application has been filed may require the breeder to furnish, within a period of not less than three months from the filing date of the subsequent application, a copy of the documents which constitute the first application, certified to be a true copy by the authority with which that application was filed, and samples or other evidence that the variety which is the subject matter of both applications is the same.

(3) [Documents and material] The breeder shall be allowed a period of two years after the expiration of the period of priority or, where the first application is rejected or withdrawn, an appropriate time after such rejection or withdrawal, in which to furnish, to the authority of the Contracting Party with which he has filed the subsequent application, any necessary information, document or material required for the purpose of the examination under Article 12, as required by the laws of that Contracting Party.

(4) [Events occurring during the period] Events occurring within the period provided for in paragraph (1), such as the filing of another application or the publication or use of the variety that is the subject of the first application, shall not constitute a ground for rejecting the subsequent application. Such events shall also not give rise to any third-party right.

Article 12 Examination of the Application

Any decision to grant a breeder's right shall require an examination for **A25-012** compliance with the conditions under Article 5 to Article 9. In the course of the examination, the authority may grow the variety or carry out other necessary tests, cause the growing of the variety or the carrying out of other necessary tests, or take into account the results of growing tests or other trials which have already been carried out. For the purposes of examination, the authority may require the breeder to furnish all the necessary information, documents or material.

Article 13 Provisional Protection

Each Contracting Party shall provide measures designed to safeguard the **A25-013** interests of the breeder during the period between the filing or the publication of the application for the grant of a breeder's right and the grant of that right. Such measures shall have the effect that the holder of a breeder's right shall at least be entitled to equitable remuneration from any person who, during the said period, has carried out acts which, once the right is granted, require the breeder's authorization as provided in Article 14. A Contracting Party may provide that the said measures shall only take effect in relation to persons whom the breeder has notified of the filing of the application.

CHAPTER V

THE RIGHTS OF THE BREEDER

Article 14 Scope of the Breeder's Right

A25-014

(1) [Acts in respect of the propagating material]

  (a) Subject to Article 15 and Article 16, the following acts in respect of the propagating material of the protected variety shall require the authorization of the breeder:

    (i) production or reproduction (multiplication),

    (ii) conditioning for the purpose of propagation,

    (iii) offering for sale,

    (iv) selling or other marketing,

    (v) exporting,

    (vi) importing,

    (vii) stocking for any of the purposes mentioned in (i) to (vi), above.

  (b) The breeder may make his authorization subject to conditions and limitations.

(2) [Acts in respect of the harvested material] Subject to Article 15 and Article 16, the acts referred to in items paragraph (1)(a)(i) to paragraph (1)(a)(vii) in respect of harvested material, including entire plants and parts of plants, obtained through the unauthorized use of propagating material of the protected variety shall require the authorization of the breeder, unless the breeder has had reasonable opportunity to exercise his right in relation to the said propagating material.

(3) [Acts in respect of certain products] Each Contracting Party may provide that, subject to Article 15 and Article 16, the acts referred to in items paragraph (1)(a)(i) to paragraph (1)(a)(vii) in respect of products made directly from harvested material of the protected variety falling within the provisions of paragraph (2) through the unauthorized use of the said harvested material shall require the authorization of the breeder, unless the breeder has had reasonable opportunity to exercise his right in relation to the said harvested material.

(4) [Possible additional acts] Each Contracting Party may provide that, subject to Article 15 and Article 16, acts other than those referred to in items paragraph (1)(a)(i) to paragraph (1)(a)(vii) shall also require the authorization of the breeder.

(5) [Essentially derived and certain other varieties]

  (a) The provisions of paragraph (1) to paragraph (4) shall also apply in relation to

    (i) varieties which are essentially derived from the protected variety, where the protected variety is not itself an essentially derived variety,

    (ii) varieties which are not clearly distinguishable in accordance with Article 7 from the protected variety and

    (iii) varieties whose production requires the repeated use of the protected variety.

  (b) For the purposes of subparagraph (a)(i), a variety shall be deemed to be essentially derived from another variety ("the initial variety") when

    (i) it is predominantly derived from the initial variety, or from a variety that is itself predominantly derived from the initial variety, while retaining the expression of the essential characteristics that

result from the genotype or combination of genotypes of the
initial variety,

    (ii) it is clearly distinguishable from the initial variety and

    (iii) except for the differences which result from the act of derivation,
it conforms to the initial variety in the expression of the essential
characteristics that result from the genotype or combination of
genotypes of the initial variety.

  (c) Essentially derived varieties may be obtained for example by the
selection of a natural or induced mutant, or of a somaclonal variant, the
selection of a variant individual from plants of the initial variety, back-
crossing, or transformation by genetic engineering.

Article 15 Exceptions to the Breeder's Right

    (1) [Compulsory exceptions] The breeder's right shall not extend to   **A25-015**

    (i) acts done privately and for non-commercial purposes,

    (ii) acts done for experimental purposes and

    (iii) acts done for the purpose of breeding other varieties, and, except
where the provisions of Article 14(5) apply, acts referred toin Article
14(1) to Article 14(4) in respect of such other varieties.

    (2) [Optional exception] Notwithstanding Article 14, each Contracting Party
may, within reasonable limits and subject to the safeguarding of the legitimate
interests of the breeder, restrict the breeder's right in relation to any variety in
order to permit farmers to use for propagating purposes, on their own holdings,
the product of the harvest which they have obtained by planting, on their own
holdings, the protected variety or a variety covered by Article 14(5)(a)(i) or Article
14(5)(a)(ii).

Article 16 Exhaustion of the Breeder's Right

    (1) [Exhaustion of right] The breeder's right shall not extend to acts **A25-016**
concerning any material of the protected variety, or of a variety covered by the
provisions of Article 14(5), which has been sold or otherwise marketed by the
breeder or with his consent in the territory of the Contracting Party concerned,
or any material derived from the said material, unless such acts

    (i) involve further propagation of the variety in question or

    (ii) involve an export of material of the variety, which enables the propaga-
tion of the variety, into a country which does not protect varieties of the
plant genus or species to which the variety belongs, except where the
exported material is for final consumption purposes.

    (2) [Meaning of "material"] For the purposes of paragraph (1), "material"
means, in relation to a variety,

    (i) propagating material of any kind,

    (ii) harvested material, including entire plants and parts of plants, and

    (iii) any product made directly from the harvested material.

    (3) ["Territory" in certain cases] For the purposes of paragraph (1), all the
Contracting Parties which are member States of one and the same intergovernmental organization may act jointly, where the regulations of that organization so
require, to assimilate acts done on the territories of the States members of that
organization to acts done on their own territories and, should they do so, shall
notify the Secretary-General accordingly.

Article 17 Restrictions on the Exercise of the Breeder's Right

A25-017   (1) [Public interest] Except where expressly provided in this Convention, no Contracting Party may restrict the free exercise of a breeder's right for reasons other than of public interest.

(2) [Equitable remuneration] When any such restriction has the effect of authorizing a third party to perform any act for which the breeder's authorization is required, the Contracting Party concerned shall take all measures necessary to ensure that the breeder receives equitable remuneration.

Article 18 Measures Regulating Commerce

A25-018   The breeder's right shall be independent of any measure taken by a Contracting Party to regulate within its territory the production, certification and marketing of material of varieties or the importing or exporting of such material. In any case, such measures shall not affect the application of the provisions of this Convention.

Article 19 Duration of the Breeder's Right

A25-019   (1) [Period of protection] The breeder's right shall be granted for a fixed period.

(2) [Minimum period] The said period shall not be shorter than 20 years from the date of the grant of the breeder's right. For trees and vines, the said period shall not be shorter than 25 years from the said date.

CHAPTER VI

VARIETY DENOMINATION

Article 20 Variety Denomination

A25-020   1. [Designation of varieties by denominations; use of the denomination]
    (a) The variety shall be designated by a denomination which will be its generic designation.
    (b) Each Contracting Party shall ensure that, subject to paragraph (4), no rights in the designation registered as the denomination of the variety shall hamper the free use of the denomination in connection with the variety, even after the expiration of the breeder's right.

2. [Characteristics of the denomination] The denomination must enable the variety to be identified. It may not consist solely of figures except where this is an established practice for designating varieties. It must not be liable to mislead or to cause confusion concerning the characteristics, value or identity of the variety or the identity of the breeder. In particular, it must be different from every denomination which designates, in the territory of any Contracting Party, an existing variety of the same plant species or of a closely related species.

3. [Registration of the denomination] The denomination of the variety shall be submitted by the breeder to the authority. If it is found that the denomination does not satisfy the requirements of paragraph (2), the authority shall refuse to register it and shall require the breeder to propose another denomination within a prescribed period. The denomination shall be registered by the authority at the same time as the breeder's right is granted.

4. [Prior rights of third persons] Prior rights of third persons shall not be affected. If, by reason of a prior right, the use of the denomination of a variety is forbidden to a person who, in accordance with the provisions of paragraph (7), is

obliged to use it, the authority shall require the breeder to submit another denomination for the variety.

5. [Same denomination in all Contracting Parties] A variety must be submitted to all Contracting Parties under the same denomination. The authority of each Contracting Party shall register the denomination so submitted, unless it considers the denomination unsuitable within its territory. In the latter case, it shall require the breeder to submit another denomination.

6. [Information among the authorities of Contracting Parties] The authority of a Contracting Party shall ensure that the authorities of all the other Contracting Parties are informed of matters concerning variety denominations, in particular the submission, registration and cancellation of denominations. Any authority may address its observations, if any, on the registration of a denomination to the authority which communicated that denomination.

7. [Obligation to use the denomination] Any person who, within the territory of one of the Contracting Parties, offers for sale or markets propagating material of a variety protected within the said territory shall be obliged to use the denomination of that variety, even after the expiration of the breeder's right in that variety, except where, in accordance with the provisions of paragraph (4), prior rights prevent such use.

8. [Indications used in association with denominations] When a variety is offered for sale or marketed, it shall be permitted to associate a trademark, trade name or other similar indication with a registered variety denomination. If such an indication is so associated, the denomination must nevertheless be easily recognizable.

CHAPTER VII

NULLITY AND CANCELLATION OF THE BREEDER'S RIGHT

Article 21 Nullity of the Breeder's Right

1. [Reasons of nullity] Each Contracting Party shall declare a breeder's right **A25-021** granted by it null and void when it is established

   (i) that the conditions laid down in Article 6 or Article 7 were not complied with at the time of the grant of the breeder's right,

   (ii) that, where the grant of the breeder's right has been essentially based upon information and documents furnished by the breeder, the conditions laid down in Article 8 or Article 9 were not complied with at the time of the grant of the breeder's right, or

   (iii) that the breeder's right has been granted to a person who is not entitled to it, unless it is transferred to the person who is so entitled.

2. [Exclusion of other reasons] No breeder's right shall be declared null and void for reasons other than those referred to in paragraph (1).

Article 22 Cancellation of the Breeder's Right

1. [Reasons for cancellation]   **A25-022**

   (a) Each Contracting Party may cancel a breeder's right granted by it if it is established that the conditions laid down in Article 8 or Article 9 are no longer fulfilled.

   (b) Furthermore, each Contracting Party may cancel a breeder's right granted by it if, after being requested to do so and within a prescribed period,

(i) the breeder does not provide the authority with the information, documents or material deemed necessary for verifying the maintenance of the variety,

(ii) the breeder fails to pay such fees as may be payable to keep his right in force, or

(iii) the breeder does not propose, where the denomination of the variety is cancelled after the grant of the right, another suitable denomination.

2. [Exclusion of other reasons] No breeder's right shall be cancelled for reasons other than those referred to in paragraph (1).

Convention for the Protection of Producers of Phonograms Against Unauthorized Duplication of Their Phonograms of October 29, 1971 *

(* Material provided by the World Intellectual Property Organization (WIPO). The Secretariat of WIPO assumes no liability or responsibility with regard to the transformation of this data.)

The Contracting States, concerned at the widespread and increasing unauthorized duplication of phonograms and the damage this is occasioning to the interests of authors, performers and producers of phonograms; convinced that the protection of producers of phonograms against such acts will also benefit the performers whose performances, and the authors whose works, are recorded on the said phonograms; recognizing the value of the work undertaken in this field by the United Nations Educational, Scientific and Cultural Organization and the World Intellectual Property Organization; anxious not to impair in any way international agreements already in force and in particular in no way to prejudice wider acceptance of the Rome Convention of October 26, 1961, which affords protection to performers and to broadcasting organizations as well as to producers of phonograms; have agreed as follows:

Article 1 Definitions

A26-001   For the purposes of this Convention:

(a) "phonogram" means any exclusively aural fixation of sounds of a performance or of other sounds;

(b) "producer of phonograms" means the person who, or the legal entity which, first fixes the sounds of a performance or other sounds;

(c) "duplicate" means an article which contains sounds taken directly or indirectly from a phonogram and which embodies all or a substantial part of the sounds fixed in that phonogram;

(d) "distribution to the public" means any act by which duplicates of a phonogram are offered, directly or indirectly, to the general public or any section thereof.

Article 2 Obligations of Contracting States; Whom they must protect and against what

A26-002   Each Contracting State shall protect producers of phonograms who are nationals of other Contracting States against the making of duplicates without the consent of the producer and against the importation of such duplicates, provided that any such making or importation is for the purpose of distribution to the public, and against the distribution of such duplicates to the public.

Article 3 Means of Implementation by Contracting States

The means by which this Convention is implemented shall be a matter for the **A26-003** domestic law of each Contracting State and shall include one or more of the following: protection by means of the grant of a copyright or other specific right; protection by means of the law relating to unfair competition; protection by means of penal sanctions.

Article 4 Term of Protection

The duration of the protection given shall be a matter for the domestic law of **A26-004** each Contracting State. However, if the domestic law prescribes a specific duration for the protection, that duration shall not be less than twenty years from the end either of the year in which the sounds embodied in the phonogram were first fixed or of the year in which the phonogram was first published.

Article 5 Formalities

If, as a condition of protecting the producers of phonograms, a Contracting **A26-005** State, under its domestic law, requires compliance with formalities, these shall be considered as fulfilled if all the authorized duplicates of the phonogram distributed to the public or their containers bear a notice consisting of the symbol (P), accompanied by the year date of the first publication, placed in such manner as to give reasonable notice of claim of protection; and, if the duplicates or their containers do not identify the producer, his successor in title or the exclusive licensee (by carrying his name, trademark or other appropriate designation), the notice shall also include the name of the producer, his successor in title or the exclusive licensee.

Article 6 Limitations on Protection

Any Contracting State which affords protection by means of copyright or **A26-006** other specific right, or protection by means of penal sanctions, may in its domestic law provide, with regard to the protection of producers of phonograms, the same kinds of limitations as are permitted with respect to the protection of authors of literary and artistic works. However, no compulsory licenses may be permitted unless all of the following conditions are met:

(a) the duplication is for use solely for the purpose of teaching or scientific research;

(b) the license shall be valid for duplication only within the territory of the Contracting State whose competent authority has granted the license and shall not extend to the export of duplicates;

(c) the duplication made under the license gives rise to an equitable remuneration fixed by the said authority taking into account, inter alia, the number of duplicates which will be made.

Article 7 Savings: 1. Safeguard of Copyright and Neighboring Rights; 2. Protection for Performers; 3. Non-Retroactivity; 4. Substitution of the Criterion of Fixation

(1) This Convention shall in no way be interpreted to limit or prejudice the **A26-007** protection otherwise secured to authors, to performers, to producers of phonograms or to broadcasting organizations under any domestic law or international agreement.

(2) It shall be a matter for the domestic law of each Contracting State to determine the extent, if any, to which performers whose performances are fixed in a phonogram are entitled to enjoy protection and the conditions for enjoying any such protection.

(3) No Contracting State shall be required to apply the provisions of this Convention to any phonogram fixed before this Convention entered into force with respect to that State.

(4) Any Contracting State which, on October 29, 1971, affords protection to producers of phonograms solely on the basis of the place of first fixation may, by a notification deposited with the Director General of the World Intellectual Property Organization, declare that it will apply this criterion instead of the criterion of the nationality of the producer.

CONVENTION ON THE GRANT OF EUROPEAN PATENTS (EUROPEAN PATENT CONVENTION) of 5 October 1973

text as amended by the act revising Article 63 EPC of 17 December 1991 and by decisions of the Administrative Council of the European Patent Organisation of 21 December 1978, 13 December 1994, 20 October 1995, 5 December 1996 and 10 December 1998

PREAMBLE

The Contracting States,

DESIRING to strengthen co-operation between the States of Europe in respect of the protection of inventions,

DESIRING that such protection may be obtained in those States by a single procedure for the grant of patents and by the establishment of certain standard rules governing patents so granted,

DESIRING, for this purpose, to conclude a Convention which establishes a European Patent Organisation and which constitutes a special agreement within the meaning of Article 19 of the Convention for the Protection of Industrial Property, signed in Paris on 20 March 1883 and last revised on 14 July 1967, and a regional patent treaty within the meaning of Article 45, paragraph 1, of the Patent Cooperation Treaty of 19 June 1970,

HAVE AGREED on the following provisions:

PART I

GENERAL AND INSTITUTIONAL PROVISIONS

CHAPTER I

GENERAL PROVISIONS

Article 1 European law for the grant of patents

A27-001   A system of law, common to the Contracting States, for the grant of patents for invention is hereby established.

Article 2 European patent

(1) Patents granted by virtue of this Convention shall be called European **A27-002** patents.

(2) The European patent shall, in each of the Contracting States for which it is granted, have the effect of and be subject to the same conditions as a national patent granted by that State, unless otherwise provided in this Convention.

Article 3 Territorial effect

The grant of a European patent may be requested for one or more of the Con- **A27-003** tracting States.

Article 4 European Patent Organisation

(1) A European Patent Organisation, hereinafter referred to as the Organisa- **A27-004** tion, is established by this Convention. It shall have administrative and financial autonomy.

(2) The organs of the Organisation shall be:
   (a) a European Patent Office;
   (b) an Administrative Council.

(3) The task of the Organisation shall be to grant European patents. This shall be carried out by the European Patent Office supervised by the Administrative Council.

PART II

SUBSTANTIVE PATENT LAW

CHAPTER I

PATENTABILITY

Article 52 Patentable inventions

(1) European patents shall be granted for any inventions which are susceptible **A27-005** of industrial application, which are new and which involve an inventive step

(2) The following in particular shall not be regarded as inventions within the meaning of paragraph 1:
   (a) discoveries, scientific theories and mathematical methods;
   (b) aesthetic creations;
   (c) schemes, rules and methods for performing mental acts, playing games or doing business, and programs for computers;
   (d) presentations of information.

(3) The provisions of paragraph 2 shall exclude patentability of the subject-matter or activities referred to in that provision only to the extent to which a European patent application or European patent relates to such subject-matter or activities as such.

(4) Methods for treatment of the human or animal body by surgery or therapy and diagnostic methods practised on the human or animal body shall not be regarded as inventions which are susceptible of industrial application within the meaning of paragraph 1. This provision shall not apply to products, in particular substances or compositions, for use in any of these methods.

Article 53 Exceptions to patentability

A27-006 European patents shall not be granted in respect of:

(a) inventions the publication or exploitation of which would be contrary to "ordre public" or morality, provided that the exploitation shall not be deemed to be so contrary merely because it is prohibited by law or regulation in some or all of the Contracting States;

(b) plant or animal varieties or essentially biological processes for the production of plants or animals; this provision does not apply to microbiological processes or the products thereof.

Article 54 Novelty

A27-007 (1) An invention shall be considered to be new if it does not form part of the state of the art.

(2) The state of the art shall be held to comprise everything made available to the public by means of a written or oral description, by use, or in any other way, before the date of filing of the European patent application.

(3) Additionally, the content of European patent applications as filed, of which the dates of filing are prior to the date referred to in paragraph 2 and which were published under Article 93 on or after that date, shall be considered as comprised in the state of the art.

(4) Paragraph 3 shall be applied only in so far as a Contracting State designated in respect of the later application, was also designated in respect of the earlier application as published.

(5) The provisions of paragraphs 1 to 4 shall not exclude the patentability of any substance or composition, comprised in the state of the art, for use in a method referred to in Article 52, paragraph 4, provided that its use for any method referred to in that paragraph is not comprised in the state of the art.

Article 55 Non-prejudicial disclosures

A27-008 (1) For the application of Article 54 a disclosure of the invention shall not be taken into consideration if it occurred no earlier than six months preceding the filing of the European patent application and if it was due to, or in consequence of:

(a) an evident abuse in relation to the applicant or his legal predecessor, or

(b) the fact that the applicant or his legal predecessor has displayed the invention at an official, or officially recognised, international exhibition falling within the terms of the Convention on international exhibitions signed at Paris on 22 November 1928 and last revised on 30 November 1972.

(2) In the case of paragraph 1(b), paragraph 1 shall apply only if the applicant states, when filing the European patent application, that the invention has been so displayed and files a supporting certificate within the period and under the conditions laid down in the Implementing Regulations.

Article 56 Inventive step

A27-009 An invention shall be considered as involving an inventive step if, having regard to the state of the art, it is not obvious to a person skilled in the art. If the state of the art also includes documents within the meaning of Article 54, paragraph 3, these documents are not to be considered in deciding whether there has been an inventive step.

Article 57 Industrial application

An invention shall be considered as susceptible of industrial application if it **A27-010** can be made or used in any kind of industry, including agriculture.

Article 58 Entitlement to file a European patent application

A European patent application may be filed by any natural or legal person, or **A27-011** any body equivalent to a legal person by virtue of the law governing it.

Article 59 Multiple applicants

A European patent application may also be filed either by joint applicants or **A27-012** by two or more applicants designating different Contracting States.

Article 60 Right to a European patent

(1) The right to a European patent shall belong to the inventor or his **A27-013** successor in title. If the inventor is an employee the right to the European patent shall be determined in accordance with the law of the State in which the employee is mainly employed; if the State in which the employee is mainly employed cannot be determined, the law to be applied shall be that of the State in which the employer has his place of business to which the employee is attached.

(2) If two or more persons have made an invention independently of each other, the right to the European patent shall belong to the person whose European patent application has the earliest date of filing; however, this provision shall apply only if this first application has been published under Article 93 and shall only have effect in respect of the Contracting States designated in that application as published.

(3) For the purposes of proceedings before the European Patent Office, the applicant shall be deemed to be entitled to exercise the right to the European patent.

Article 62 Right of the inventor to be mentioned

The inventor shall have the right, vis-à-vis the applicant for or proprietor of a **A27-014** European patent, to be mentioned as such before the European Patent Office.

CHAPTER III

EFFECTS OF THE EUROPEAN PATENT AND THE EUROPEAN PATENT
APPLICATION

Article 63 Term of the European patent

(1) The term of the European patent shall be 20 years as from the date of **A27-015** filing of the application.

(2) Nothing in the preceding paragraph shall limit the right of a Contracting State to extend the term of a European patent, or to grant corresponding protection which follows immediately on expiry of the term of the patent, under the same conditions as those applying to national patents:

- (a) in order to take account of a state of war or similar emergency conditions affecting that State;
- (b) if the subject-matter of the European patent is a product or a process of manufacturing a product or a use of a product which has to undergo an administrative authorisation procedure required by law before it can be put on the market in that State.

(4) A Contracting State which makes provision for extension of the term or corresponding protection under paragraph 2(b) may, in accordance with an agreement concluded with the Organisation, entrust to the European Patent Office tasks associated with implementation of the relevant provisions.

Article 64 Rights conferred by a European patent

A27-016   (1) A European patent shall, subject to the provisions of paragraph 2, confer on its proprietor from the date of publication of the mention of its grant, in each Contracting State in respect of which it is granted, the same rights as would be conferred by a national patent granted in that State.

(2) If the subject-matter of the European patent is a process, the protection conferred by the patent shall extend to the products directly obtained by such process.

(3) Any infringement of a European patent shall be dealt with by national law.

Article 65 Translation of the specification of the European patent

A27-017   (1) Any Contracting State may prescribe that if the text, in which the European Patent Office intends to grant a European patent or maintain a European patent as amended for that State, is not drawn up in one of its official languages, the applicant for or proprietor of the patent shall supply to its central industrial property office a translation of this text in one of its official languages at his option or, where that State has prescribed the use of one specific official language, in that language. The period for supplying the translation shall end three months after the date on which the mention of the grant of the European patent or of the maintenance of the European patent as amended is published in the European Patent Bulletin, unless the State concerned prescribes a longer period.

(2) Any Contracting State which has adopted provisions pursuant to paragraph 1 may prescribe that the applicant for or proprietor of the patent must pay all or part of the costs of publication of such translation within a period laid down by that State.

(3) Any Contracting State may prescribe that in the event of failure to observe the provisions adopted in accordance with paragraphs 1 and 2, the European patent shall be deemed to be void ab initio in that State.

Article 66 Equivalence of European filing with national filing

A27-018   A European patent application which has been accorded a date of filing shall, in the designated Contracting States, be equivalent to a regular national filing, where appropriate with the priority claimed for the European patent application.

Article 67 Rights conferred by a European patent application after publication

A27-019   (1) A European patent application shall, from the date of its publication under Article 93, provisionally confer upon the applicant such protection as is conferred by Article 64, in the Contracting States designated in the application as published.

(2) Any Contracting State may prescribe that a European patent application shall not confer such protection as is conferred by Article 64. However, the protection attached to the publication of the European patent application may not be less than that which the laws of the State concerned attach to the

compulsory publication of unexamined national patent applications. In any event, every State shall ensure at least that, from the date of publication of a European patent application, the applicant can claim compensation reasonable in the circumstances from any person who has used the invention in the said State in circumstances where that person would be liable under national law for infringement of a national patent.

(3) Any Contracting State which does not have as an official language the language of the proceedings, may prescribe that provisional protection in accordance with paragraphs 1 and 2 above shall not be effective until such time as a translation of the claims in one of its official languages at the option of the applicant or, where that State has prescribed the use of one specific official language, in that language:

    (a) has been made available to the public in the manner prescribed by national law, or

    (b) has been communicated to the person using the invention in the said State.

(4) The European patent application shall be deemed never to have had the effects set out in paragraphs 1 and 2 above when it has been withdrawn, deemed to be withdrawn or finally refused. The same shall apply in respect of the effects of the European patent application in a Contracting State the designation of which is withdrawn or deemed to be withdrawn.

Article 68 Effect of revocation of the European patent

The European patent application and the resulting patent shall be deemed **A27-020** not to have had, as from the outset, the effects specified in Articles 64 and 67, to the extent that the patent has been revoked in opposition proceedings.

Article 69 Extent of protection

(1) The extent of the protection conferred by a European patent or a **A27-021** European patent application shall be determined by the terms of the claims. Nevertheless, the description and drawings shall be used to interpret the claims.

(2) For the period up to grant of the European patent, the extent of the protection conferred by the European patent application shall be determined by the latest filed claims contained in the publication under Article 93. However, the European patent as granted or as amended in opposition proceedings shall determine retroactively the protection conferred by the European patent application, in so far as such protection is not thereby extended.

CHAPTER IV

THE EUROPEAN PATENT APPLICATION AS AN OBJECT OF PROPERTY

Article 71 Transfer and constitution of rights

A European patent application may be transferred or give rise to rights for **A27-022** one or more of the designated Contracting States.

Article 72 Assignment

An assignment of a European patent application shall be made in writing **A27-023** and shall require the signature of the parties to the contract.

Article 73 Contractual licensing

A27-024   A European patent application may be licensed in whole or in part for the whole or part of the territories of the designated Contracting States.

Article 74 Law applicable

A27-025   Unless otherwise specified in this Convention, the European patent application as an object of property shall, in each designated Contracting State and with effect for such State, be subject to the law applicable in that State to national patent applications

PART III

APPLICATION FOR EUROPEAN PATENTS

CHAPTER I

FILING AND REQUIREMENTS OF THE EUROPEAN PATENT APPLICATION

Article 75 Filing of the European patent application

A27-026   (1) A European patent application may be filed:
- (a) at the European Patent Office at Munich or its branch at The Hague, or
- (b) if the law of a Contracting State so permits, at the central industrial property office or other competent authority of that State. An application filed in this way shall have the same effect as if it had been filed on the same date at the European Patent Office.

(2) The provisions of paragraph 1 shall not preclude the application of legislative or regulatory provisions which, in any Contracting State:
- (a) govern inventions which, owing to the nature of their subject-matter, may not be communicated abroad without the prior authorisation of the competent authorities of that State, or
- (b) prescribe that each application is to be filed initially with a national authority or make direct filing with another authority subject to prior authorisation.

(3) No Contracting State may provide for or allow the filing of European divisional applications with an authority referred to in paragraph 1(b).

Article 78 Requirements of the European patent application

A27-027   (1) A European patent application shall contain:
- (a) a request for the grant of a European patent;
- (b) a description of the invention;
- (c) one or more claims;
- (d) any drawings referred to in the description or the claims;
- (e) an abstract.

(2) A European patent application shall be subject to the payment of the filing fee and the search fee within one month after the filing of the application.

(3) A European patent application must satisfy the conditions laid down in the Implementing Regulations.

Article 79 Designation of Contracting States

(1) The request for the grant of a European patent shall contain the designation of the Contracting State or States in which protection for the invention is desired. **A27-028**

Article 80 Date of filing

The date of filing of a European patent application shall be the date on which documents filed by the applicant contain: **A27-029**
    (a) an indication that a European patent is sought;
    (b) the designation of at least one Contracting State;
    (c) information identifying the applicant;
    (d) a description and one or more claims in one of the languages referred to in Article 14, paragraphs 1 and 2, even though the description and the claims do not comply with the other requirements of this Convention.

Article 81 Designation of the inventor

The European patent application shall designate the inventor. If the applicant is not the inventor or is not the sole inventor, the designation shall contain a statement indicating the origin of the right to the European patent. **A27-030**

Article 82 Unity of invention

The European patent application shall relate to one invention only or to a group of inventions so linked as to form a single general inventive concept. **A27-031**

Article 83 Disclosure of the invention

The European patent application must disclose the invention in a manner sufficiently clear and complete for it to be carried out by a person skilled in the art. **A27-032**

Article 84 The claims

The claims shall define the matter for which protection is sought. They shall be clear and concise and be supported by the description. **A27-033**

Article 85 The abstract

The abstract shall merely serve for use as technical information; it may not be taken into account for any other purpose, in particular not for the purpose of interpreting the scope of the protection sought nor for the purpose of applying Article 54, paragraph 3. **A27-034**

CHAPTER II

PRIORITY

Article 87 Priority right

(1) A person who has duly filed in or for any State party to the Paris Convention for the Protection of Industrial Property, an application for a patent or for the registration of a utility model or for a utility certificate or for an inventor's certificate, or his successors in title, shall enjoy, for the purpose of filing a European patent application in respect of the same invention, a right of priority during a period of twelve months from the date of filing of the first application. **A27-035**

(2) Every filing that is equivalent to a regular national filing under the national law of the State where it was made or under bilateral or multilateral agreements, including this Convention, shall be recognised as giving rise to a right of priority.

(3) By a regular national filing is meant any filing that is sufficient to establish the date on which the application was filed, whatever may be the outcome of the application.

(4) A subsequent application for the same subject-matter as a previous first application and filed in or in respect of the same State shall be considered as the first application for the purposes of determining priority, provided that, at the date of filing the subsequent application, the previous application has been withdrawn, abandoned or refused, without being open to public inspection and without leaving any rights outstanding, and has not served as a basis for claiming a right of priority. The previous application may not thereafter serve as a basis for claiming a right of priority.

(5) If the first filing has been made in a State which is not a party to the Paris Convention for the Protection of Industrial Property, paragraphs 1 to 4 shall apply only in so far as that State, according to a notification published by the Administrative Council, and by virtue of bilateral or multilateral agreements, grants on the basis of a first filing made at the European Patent Office as well as on the basis of a first filing made in or for any Contracting State and subject to conditions equivalent to those laid down in the Paris Convention, a right of priority having equivalent effect.

Article 88 Claiming priority

A27-036 (1) An applicant for a European patent desiring to take advantage of the priority of a previous application shall file a declaration of priority, a copy of the previous application and, if the language of the latter is not one of the official languages of the European Patent Office, a translation of it in one of such official languages. The procedure to be followed in carrying out these provisions is laid down in the Implementing Regulations.

(2) Multiple priorities may be claimed in respect of a European patent application, notwithstanding the fact that they originated in different countries. Where appropriate, multiple priorities may be claimed for any one claim. Where multiple priorities are claimed, time limits which run from the date of priority shall run from the earliest date of priority.

(3) If one or more priorities are claimed in respect of a European patent application, the right of priority shall cover only those elements of the European patent application which are included in the application or applications whose priority is claimed.

(4) If certain elements of the invention for which priority is claimed do not appear among the claims formulated in the previous application, priority may nonetheless be granted, provided that the documents of the previous application as a whole specifically disclose such elements.

Article 89 Effect of priority right

A27-037 The right of priority shall have the effect that the date of priority shall count as the date of filing of the European patent application for the purposes of Article 54, paragraphs 2 and 3, and Article 60, paragraph 2.

PART IV

PROCEDURE UP TO GRANT

Article 90 Examination on filing

(1) The Receiving Section shall examine whether: **A27-038**

    (a) the European patent application satisfies the requirements for the accordance of a date of filing;

    (b) the filing fee and the search fee have been paidin due time;

    (c) in the case provided for in Article 14, paragraph 2, the translation of the European patent application in the language of the proceedings has been filed in due time.

(2) If a date of filing cannot be accorded, the Receiving Section shall give the applicant an opportunity to correct the deficiencies in accordance with the Implementing Regulations. If the deficiencies are not remedied in due time, the application shall not be dealt with as a European patent application.

(3) If the filing fee and the search fee have not been paid in due time or, in the case provided for in Article 14, paragraph 2, the translation of the application in the language of the proceedings has not been filed in due time, the application shall be deemed to be withdrawn.

Article 91 Examination as to formal requirements

(1) If a European patent application has been accorded a date of filing, and **A27-039** is not deemed to be withdrawn by virtue of Article 90, paragraph 3, the Receiving Section shall examine whether:

    (a) the requirements of Article 133, paragraph 2, have been satisfied;

    (b) the application meets the physical requirements laid down in the Implementing Regulations for the implementation of this provision;

    (c) the abstract has been filed;

    (d) the request for the grant of a European patent satisfies the mandatory provisions of the Implementing Regulations concerning its content and, where appropriate, whether the requirements of this Convention concerning the claim to priority have been satisfied;

    (e) the designation fees have been paid;

    (f) the designation of the inventor has been made in accordance with Article 81;

    (g) the drawings referred to in Article 78, paragraph 1(d), were filed on the date of filing of the application.

(2) Where the Receiving Section notes that there are deficiencies which may be corrected, it shall give the applicant an opportunity to correct them in accordance with the Implementing Regulations.

(3) If any deficiencies noted in the examination under paragraph 1(a) to (d) are not corrected in accordance with the Implementing Regulations, the application shall be refused; where the provisions referred to in paragraph 1(d) concern the right of priority, this right shall be lost for the application.

(4) Where, in the case referred to in paragraph 1(e), the designation fee has not been paid in due time in respect of any designated State, the designation of that State shall be deemed to be withdrawn.

(5) Where, in the case referred to in paragraph 1(f), the omission of the designation of the inventor is not, in accordance with the Implementing Regulations and subject to the exceptions laid down therein, corrected within 16 months after

the date of filing of the European patent application or, if priority is claimed, after the date of priority, the application shall be deemed to be withdrawn.

(6) Where, in the case referred to in paragraph 1(g), the drawings were not filed on the date of filing of the application and no steps have been taken to correct the deficiency in accordance with the Implementing Regulations, either the application shall be re-dated to the date of filing of the drawings or any reference to the drawings in the application shall be deemed to be deleted, according to the choice exercised by the applicant in accordance with the Implementing Regulations.

Article 92 The drawing up of the European search report

A27-040 (1) If a European patent application has been accorded a date of filing and is not deemed to be withdrawn by virtue of Article 90, paragraph 3, the Search Division shall draw up the European search report on the basis of the claims, with due regard to the description and any drawings, in the form prescribed in the Implementing Regulations.

(2) Immediately after it has been drawn up, the European search report shall be transmitted to the applicant together with copies of any cited documents.

Article 93 Publication of a European patent application

A27-041 (1) A European patent application shall be published as soon as possible after the expiry of a period of eighteen months from the date of filing or, if priority has been claimed, as from the date of priority. Nevertheless, at the request of the applicant the application may be published before the expiry of the period referred to above. It shall be published simultaneously with the publication of the specification of the European patent when the grant of the patent has become effective before the expiry of the period referred to above.

(2) The publication shall contain the description, the claims and any drawings as filed and, in an annex, the European search report and the abstract, in so far as the latter are available before the termination of the technical preparations for publication. If the European search report and the abstract have not been published at the same time as the application, they shall be published separately.

Article 94 Request for examination

A27-042 (1) The European Patent Office shall examine, on written request, whether a European patent application and the invention to which it relates meet the requirements of this Convention.

(2) A request for examination may be filed by the applicant up to the end of six months after the date on which the European Patent Bulletin mentions the publication of the European search report. The request shall not be deemed to be filed until after the examination fee has been paid. The request may not be withdrawn.

(3) If no request for examination has been filed by the end of the period referred to in paragraph 2, the application shall be deemed to be withdrawn.

Article 96 Examination of the European patent application

A27-043 (1) If the applicant for a European patent has filed the request for examination before the European search report has been transmitted to him, the European Patent Office shall invite him after the transmission of the report to indicate, within a period to be determined, whether he desires to proceed further with the European patent application.

(2) If the examination of a European patent application reveals that the application or the invention to which it relates does not meet the requirements of this Convention, the Examining Division shall invite the applicant, in accordance with the Implementing Regulations and as often as necessary, to file his observations within a period to be fixed by the Examining Division.

(3) If the applicant fails to reply in due time to any invitation under paragraph 1 or paragraph 2, the application shall be deemed to be withdrawn.

Article 97 Refusal or grant

(1) The Examining Division shall refuse a European patent application if it is **A27-044** of the opinion that such application or the invention to which it relates does not meet the requirements of this Convention, except where a different sanction is provided for by this Convention.

(2) If the Examining Division is of the opinion that the application and the invention to which it relates meet the requirements of this Convention, it shall decide to grant the European patent for the designated Contracting States provided that:

    (a) it is established, in accordance with the provisions of the Implementing Regulations, that the applicant approves the text in which the Examining Division intends to grant the patent;

    (b) the fees for grant and printing are paid within the time limit prescribed in the Implementing Regulations;

    (c) the renewal fees and any additional fees already due have been paid.

(3) If the fees for grant and printing are not paid in due time, the application shall be deemed to be withdrawn.

(4) The decision to grant a European patent shall not take effect until the date on which the European Patent Bulletin mentions the grant. This mention shall be published at least 3 months after the start of the time limit referred to in paragraph 2(b).

(5) Provision may be made in the Implementing Regulations for the applicant to file a translation, in the two official languages of the European Patent Office other than the language of the proceedings, of the claims appearing in the text in which the Examining Division intends to grant the patent. In such case, the period laid down in paragraph 4 shall be atleast five months. If the translation has not been filed in due time, the application shall be deemed to be withdrawn.

(6) At the request of the applicant, mention of grant of the European patent shall be published before expiry of the time limit under paragraph 4 or 5. Such request may only be made if the requirements pursuant to paragraphs 2 and 5 are met.

Article 98 Publication of a specification of the European patent

At the same time as it publishes the mention of the grant of the European **A27-045** patent, the European Patent Office shall publish a specification of the European patent containing the description, the claims and any drawings.

PART V

OPPOSITION PROCEDURE

Article 99 Opposition

A27-046   (1) Within nine months from the publication of the mention of the grant of the European patent, any person may give notice to the European Patent Office of opposition to the European patent granted. Notice of opposition shall be filed in a written reasoned statement. It shall not be deemed to have been filed until the opposition fee has been paid.

(2) The opposition shall apply to the European patent in all the Contracting States in which that patent has effect.

(3) An opposition may be filed even if the European patent has been surrendered or has lapsed for all the designated States.

(4) Opponents shall be parties to the opposition proceedings as well as the proprietor of the patent.

(5) Where a person provides evidence that in a Contracting State, following a final decision, he has been entered in the patent register of such State instead of the previous proprietor, such person shall, at his request, replace the previous proprietor in respect of such State. By derogation from Article 118, the previous proprietor and the person making the request shall not be deemed to be joint proprietors unless both so request.

Article 100 Grounds for opposition

A27-047   Opposition may only be filed on the grounds that:

(a) the subject-matter of the European patent is not patentable within the terms of Articles 52 to 57;

(b)   the European patent does not disclose the invention in a manner sufficiently clear and complete for it to be carried out by a person skilled in the art;

(c) the subject-matter of the European patent extends beyond the content of the application as filed, or, if the patent was granted on a divisional application or on a new application filed in accordance with Article 61, beyond the content of the earlier application as filed.

Article 101 Examination of the opposition

A27-048   (1) If the opposition is admissible, the Opposition Division shall examine whether the grounds for opposition laid down in Article 100 prejudice the maintenance of the European patent.

(2) In the examination of the opposition, which shall be conducted in accordance with the provisions of the Implementing Regulations, the Opposition Division shall invite the parties, as often as necessary, to file observations, within a period to be fixed by the Opposition Division, on communications from another party or issued by itself.

Article 102 Revocation or maintenance of the European patent

A27-049   (1) If the Opposition Division is of the opinion that the grounds for opposition mentioned in Article 100 prejudice the maintenance of the European patent, it shall revoke the patent.

(2) If the Opposition Division is of the opinion that the grounds for opposition mentioned in Article 100 do not prejudice the maintenance of the patent unamended, it shall reject the opposition.

(3) If the Opposition Division is of the opinion that, taking into consideration the amendments made by the proprietor of the patent during the opposition proceedings, the patent and the invention to which it relates meet the requirements of this Convention, it shall decide to maintain the patent as amended, provided that:

(a) it is established, in accordance with the provisions of the Implementing Regulations, that the proprietor of the patent approves the text in which the Opposition Division intends to maintain the patent;

(b) the fee for the printing of a new specification of the European patent is paid within the time limit prescribed in the Implementing Regulations.

(4) If the fee for the printing of a new specification is not paid in due time, the patent shall be revoked.

(5) Provision may be made in the Implementing Regulations for the proprietor of the patent to file a translation of any amended claims in the two official languages of the European Patent Office other than the language of the proceedings. If the translation has not been filed in due time the patent shall be revoked.

PART VI

APPEALS PROCEDURE

Article 106 Decisions subject to appeal

(1) An appeal shall lie from decisions of the Receiving Section, Examining **A27-050** Divisions, Opposition Divisions and the Legal Division. It shall have suspensive effect.

(2) An appeal may be filed against the decision of the Opposition Division even if the European patent has been surrendered or has lapsed for all the designated States.

(3) A decision which does not terminate proceedings as regards one of the parties can only be appealed together with the final decision, unless the decision allows separate appeal.

(4) The apportionment of costs of opposition proceedings cannot be the sole subject of an appeal.

(5) A decision fixing the amount of costs of opposition proceedings cannot be appealed unless the amount is in excess of that laid down in the Rules relating to Fees.

Article 107 Persons entitled to appeal and to be parties to appeal proceedings

Any party to proceedings adversely affected by a decision may appeal. Any **A27-051** other parties to the proceedings shall be parties to the appeal proceedings as of right.

Article 108 Time limit and form of appeal

Notice of appeal must be filed in writing at the European Patent Office **A27-052** within two months after the date of notification of the decision appealed from. The notice shall not be deemed to have been filed until after the fee for appeal has been paid. Within four months after the date of notification of the decision, a written statement setting out the grounds of appeal must be filed.

Article 110 Examination of appeals

A27-053   (1) If the appeal is admissible, the Board of Appeal shall examine whether the appeal is allowable.

(2) In the examination of the appeal, which shall be conducted in accordance with the provisions of the Implementing Regulations, the Board of Appeal shall invite the parties, as often as necessary, to file observations, within a period to be fixed by the Board of Appeal, on communications from another party or issued by itself.

(3) If the applicant fails to reply in due time to an invitation under paragraph 2, the European patent application shall be deemed to be withdrawn, unless the decision under appeal was taken by the Legal Division.

Article 111 Decision in respect of appeals

A27-054   (1) Following the examination as to the allowability of the appeal, the Board of Appeal shall decide on the appeal. The Board of Appeal may either exercise any power within the competence of the department which was responsible for the decision appealed or remit the case to that department for further prosecution.

(2) If the Board of Appeal remits the case for further prosecution to the department whose decision was appealed, that department shall be bound by the ratio decidendi of the Board of Appeal, in so far as the facts are the same. If the decision which was appealed emanated from the Receiving Section, the Examining Division shall similarly be bound by the ratio decidendi of the Board of Appeal.

Article 112 Decision or opinion of the Enlarged Board of Appeal

A27-055   (1) In order to ensure uniform application of the law, or if an important point of law arises:

   (a) the Board of Appeal shall, during proceedings on a case and either of its own motion or following a request from a party to the appeal, refer any question to the Enlarged Board of Appeal if it considers that adecision is required for the above purposes. If the Board of Appeal rejects the request, it shall give the reasons in its final decision;

   (b) the President of the European Patent Office may refer a point of law to the Enlarged Board of Appeal where two Boards of Appeal have given different decisions on that question.

(2) In the cases covered by paragraph 1(a) the parties to the appeal proceedings shall be parties to the proceedings before the Enlarged Board of Appeal.

(3) The decision of the Enlarged Board of Appeal referred to in paragraph 1(a) shall be binding on the Board of Appeal in respect of the appeal in question.

PART VII

COMMON PROVISIONS

Article 113 Basis of decisions

A27-056   (1) The decisions of the European Patent Office may only be based on grounds or evidence on which the parties concerned have had an opportunity to present their comments.

(2) The European Patent Office shall consider and decide upon the European patent application or the European patent only in the text submitted to it, or agreed, by the applicant for or proprietor of the patent.

Article 114 Examination by the European Patent Office of its own motion

(1) In proceedings before it, the European Patent Office shall examine the facts of its own motion; it shall not be restricted in this examination to the facts, evidence and arguments provided by the parties and the relief sought. **A27-057**

(2) The European Patent Office may disregard facts or evidence which are not submitted in due time by the parties concerned.

Article 115 Observations by third parties

(1) Following the publication of the European patent application, any person may present observations concerning the patentability of the invention in respect of which the application has been filed. Such observations must be filed in writing and must include a statement of the grounds on which they are based. That person shall not be a party to the proceedings before the European Patent Office. **A27-058**

(2) The observations referred to in paragraph 1 shall be communicated to the applicant for or proprietor of the patent who may comment on them.

Article 116 Oral proceedings

(1) Oral proceedings shall take place either at the instance of the European Patent Office if it considers this to be expedient or at the request of any party to the proceedings. However, the European Patent Office may reject a request for further oral proceedings before the same department where the parties and the subject of the proceedings are the same. **A27-059**

(2) Nevertheless, oral proceedings shall take place before the Receiving Section at the request of the applicant only where the Receiving Section considers this to be expedient or where it envisages refusing the European patent application.

(3) Oral proceedings before the Receiving Section, the Examining Divisions and the Legal Division shall not be public.

(4) Oral proceedings, including delivery of the decision, shall be public, as regards the Boards of Appeal and the Enlarged Board of Appeal, after publication of the European patent application, and also before the Opposition Divisions, in so far as the department before which the proceedings are taking place does not decide otherwise in cases where admission of the public could have serious and unjustified disadvantages, in particular for a party to the proceedings.

Article 123 Amendments

(1) The conditions under which a European patent application or a European patent may be amended in proceedings before the European Patent Office are laid down in the Implementing Regulations. In any case, an applicant shall be allowed at least one opportunity of amending the description, claims and drawings of his own volition. **A27-060**

(2) A European patent application or a European patent may not be amended in such a way that it contains subject-matter which extends beyond the content of the application as filed.

(3) The claims of the European patent may not be amended during opposition proceedings in such a way as to extend the protection conferred.

Article 125 Reference to general principles

A27-061   In the absence of procedural provisions in this Convention, the European Patent Office shall take into account the principles of procedural law generally recognised in the Contracting States.

CHAPTER II

INFORMATION TO THE PUBLIC OR OFFICIAL AUTHORITIES

Article 127 Register of European Patents

A27-062   The European Patent Office shall keep a register, to be known as the Register of European Patents, which shall contain those particulars the registration of which is provided for by this Convention. No entry shall be made in the Register prior to the publication of the European patent application. The Register shall be open to public inspection.

Article 128 Inspection of files

A27-063   (1) The files relating to European patent applications, which have not yet been published, shall not be made available for inspection without the consent of the applicant.

(2) Any person who can prove that the applicant for a European patent has invoked the rights under the application against him may obtain inspection of the files prior to the publication of that application and without the consent of the applicant.

(3) Where a European divisional application or a new European patent application filed under Article 61, paragraph 1, is published, any person may obtain inspection of the files of the earlier application prior to the publication of that application and without the consent of the relevant applicant.

(4) Subsequent to the publication of the European patent application, the files relating to such application and the resulting European patent may be inspected on request, subject to the restrictions laid down in the Implementing Regulations.

(5) Even prior to the publication of the European patent application, the European Patent Office may communicate the following bibliographic data to third parties or publish them:

(a) the number of the European patent application;
(b) the date of filing of the European patent application and, where the priority of a previous application is claimed, the date, State and file number of the previous application;
(c) the name of the applicant;
(d) the title of the invention;
(e) the Contracting States designated.

Article 129 Periodical publications

A27-064   The European Patent Office shall periodically publish:

(a) a European Patent Bulletin containing entries made in the Register of European Patents, as well as other particulars the publication of which is prescribed by this Convention;
(b) an Official Journal of the European Patent Office, containing notices and information of a general character issued by the President of the European Patent

Office, as well as any other information relevant to this Convention or its implementation.

PART VIII

IMPACT ON NATIONAL LAW

CHAPTER I

CONVERSION INTO A NATIONAL PATENT APPLICATION

Article 135 Request for the application of national procedure

(1) The central industrial property office of a designated Contracting State **A27-065** shall apply the procedure for the grant of a national patent only at the request of the applicant for or proprietor of a European patent, and in the following circumstances:

(a) when the European patent application is deemed to be withdrawn pursuant to Article 77, paragraph 5, or Article 162, paragraph 4;

(b) in such other cases as are provided for by the national law in which the European patent application is refused or withdrawn or deemed to be withdrawn, or the European patent is revoked under this Convention.

(2) The request for conversion shall be filed within three months after the European patent application has been withdrawn or after notification has been made that the application is deemed to be withdrawn, or after a decision has been notified refusing the application or revoking theEuropean patent. The effect referred to in Article 66 shall lapse if the request is not filed in due time.

CHAPTER II

REVOCATION AND PRIOR RIGHTS

Article 138 Grounds for revocation

(1) Subject to the provisions of Article 139, a European patent may only be **A27-066** revoked under the law of a Contracting State, with effect for its territory, on the following grounds:

(a) if the subject-matter of the European patent is not patentable within the terms of Articles 52 to 57;

(b) if the European patent does not disclose the invention in a manner sufficiently clear and complete for it to be carried out by a person skilled in the art;

(c) if the subject-matter of the European patent extends beyond the content of the application as filed or, if the patent was granted on a divisional application or on a new application filed in accordance with Article 61, beyond the content of the earlier application as filed;

(d) if the protection conferred by the European patent has been extended;

(e) if the proprietor of the European patent is not entitled under Article 60, paragraph 1.

(2) If the grounds for revocation only affect the European patent in part, revocation shall be pronounced in the form of a corresponding limitation of the said patent. If the national law so allows, the limitation may be effected in the form of an amendment to the claims, the description or the drawings.

Article 139 Rights of earlier date or the same date

A27-067   (1) In any designated Contracting State a European patent application and a European patent shall have with regard to a national patent application and a national patent the same prior right effect as a national patent application and a national patent.

(2) A national patent application and a national patent in a Contracting State shall have with regard to a European patent in which that Contracting State is designated the same prior right effect as they have with regard to a national patent.

(3) Any Contracting State may prescribe whether and on what terms an invention disclosed in both a European patent application or patent and a national application or patent having the same date of filing or, where priority is claimed, the same date of priority, may be protected simultaneously by both applications or patents.

PART IX

SPECIAL AGREEMENTS

Article 142 Unitary patents

A27-068   (1) Any group of Contracting States, which has provided by a special agreement that a European patent granted for those States has a unitary character throughout their territories, may provide that a European patent may only be granted jointly in respect of all those States.

(2) Where any group of Contracting States has availed itself of the authorisation given in paragraph 1, the provisions of this Part shall apply.

Article 148 The European patent application as an object of property

A27-069   (1) Article 74 shall apply unless the group of Contracting States has specified otherwise.

(2) The group of Contracting States may provide that a European patent application for which these Contracting States are designated may only be transferred, mortgaged or subjected to any legal means of execution in respect of all the Contracting States of the group and in accordance with the provisions of the special agreement.

PART XII

FINAL PROVISIONS

Article 168 Territorial field of application

A27-070   (1) Any Contracting State may declare in its instrument of ratification or accession, or may inform the Government of the Federal Republic of Germany by written notification any time thereafter, that this Convention shall be applicable to one or more of the territories for the external relations of which it is responsible. European patents granted for that Contracting State shall also have effect in the territories for which such a declaration has taken effect.

(2) If the declaration referred to in paragraph 1 is contained in the instrument of ratification or accession, it shall take effect on the same date as the ratification or accession; if the declaration is made in a notification after the deposit of the instrument of ratification or accession, such notification shall take

effect six months after the date of its receipt by the Government of the Federal Republic of Germany.

(3) Any Contracting State may at any time declare that the Convention shall cease to apply to some or to all of the territories in respect of which it has given a notification pursuant to paragraph 1. Such declaration shall take effect one year after the date on which the Government of the Federal Republic of Germany received notification thereof.

Article 172 Revision

(1) This Convention may be revised by a Conference of the Contracting **A27-071** States.

(2) The Conference shall be prepared and convened by the Administrative Council. The Conference shall not be deemed to be validly constituted unless at least three-quarters of the Contracting States are represented at it. In order to adopt the revised text there must be a majority of three-quarters of the Contracting States represented and voting at the Conference. Abstentions shall not be considered as votes.

(3) The revised text shall enter into force when it has been ratified or acceded to by the number of Contracting States specified by the Conference, and at the time specified by that Conference.

(4) Such States as have not ratified or acceded to the revised text of the Convention at the time of its entry into force shall cease to be parties to this Convention as from that time.

Protocol on the Interpretation of Article 69 of European Patent Convention, adopted at Munich Diplomatic for the setting up of a European System for the Grant of Patents on 5 October 1973

Article 69 should not be interpreted in the sense that the extent of the **A27-072** protection conferred by a European patent is to be understood as that defined by the strict, literal meaning of the wording used in the claims, the description and drawings being employed only for the purpose of resolving an ambiguity found in the claims. Neither should it be interpreted in the sense that the claims serve only as a guideline and that the actual protection conferred may extend to what, from a consideration of the description and drawings by a person skilled in the art, the patentee has contemplated. On the contrary, it is to be interpreted as defining a position between these extremes which combines a fair protection for the patentee with a reasonable degree of certainty for third parties.

Treaty on Intellectual Property in respect of Integrated Circuits (Washington, 26 May 1989)

Article 1 Establishment of a Union

The Contracting Parties constitute themselves into a Union for the purposes **A28-001** of this Treaty.

Article 2 Definitions

For the purposes of this Treaty: **A28-002**

(i) "integrated circuit" means a product, in its final form or an intermediate form, in which the elements, at least one of which is an active element, and some or all of the interconnections are integrally formed in and/or on a piece of material and which is intended to perform an electronic function,

(ii) "lay-out design (topography)" means the three-dimensional disposition, however expressed, of the elements, at least one of which is an active element, and of some or all of the interconnections of an integrated circuit, or such a three-dimensional disposition prepared for an integrated circuit intended for manufacture,

(iii) "holder of the right" means the natural person who, or the legal entity which, according to the applicable law, is to be regarded as the beneficiary of the protection referred to in Article 6,

(iv) "protected layout-design (topography)" means a layout-design (topography) in respect of which the conditions of protection referred to in this Treaty are fulfilled,

(v) "Contracting Party" means a State, or an Intergovernmental Organization meeting the requirements of item (x), party to this Treaty,

(vi) "territory of a Contracting Party" means, where the Contracting Party is a State, the territory of that State and, where the Contracting Party is an Intergovernmental Organization, the territory in which the constituting treaty of that Intergovernmental Organization applies,

(vii) "Union" means the Union referred to in Article 1,

(viii) "Assembly" means the Assembly referred to in Article 9,

(ix) "Director General" means the Director General of the World Intellectual Property Organization,

(x) "Intergovernmental Organization" means an organization constituted by, and composed of, States of any region of the world, which has competence in respect of matters governed by this Treaty, has its own legislation providing for intellectual property protection in respect of layout-designs (topographies) and binding on all its member States, and has been duly authorized, in accordance with its internal procedures, to sign, ratify, accept, approve or accede to this Treaty.

Article 3 The subject matter of the Treaty

A28-003 (1) [Obligation to Protect Layout-Designs (Topographies)]

(a) Each Contracting Party shall have the obligation to secure, throughout its territory, intellectual property protection in respect of layout-designs (topographies) in accordance with this Treaty. It shall, in particular, secure adequate measures to ensure the prevention of acts considered unlawful under Article 6 and appropriate legal remedies where such acts have been committed.

(b) The right of the holder of the right in respect of an integrated circuit applies whether or not the integrated circuit is incorporated in an article.

(c) Notwithstanding Article 2(i), any Contracting Party whose law limits the protection of layout-designs (topographies) to layout-designs (topographies) of semiconductor integrated circuits shall be free to apply that limitation as long as its law contains such limitation.

(2) [Requirement of Originality]

(a) The obligation referred to in paragraph (1)(a) shall apply to layout-designs (topographies) that are original in the sense that they are the result of their creators' own intellectual effort and are not commonplace among creators of layout-designs (topographies) and manufacturers of integrated circuits at the time of their creation.

(b) A layout-design (topography) that consists of a combination of elements and interconnections that are commonplace shall be protected only if the combination, taken as a whole, fulfills the conditions referred to in subparagraph (a).

Article 4 The legal form of the protection

Each Contracting Party shall be free to implement its obligations under this **A28-004** Treaty through a special law on layout-designs (topographies) or its law on copyright, patents, utility models, industrial designs, unfair competition or any other law or a combination of any of those laws.

Article 5 National treatment

(1) [National Treatment]   **A28-005**
Subject to compliance with its obligation referred to in Article 3(1)(a), each Contracting Party shall, in respect of the intellectual property protection of layout-designs (topographies), accord, within its territory,

(i) to natural persons who are nationals of, or are domiciled in the territory of, any of the other Contracting Parties, and
(ii) to legal entities which or natural persons who, in the territory of any of the other Contracting Parties, have a real and effective establishment for the creation of layout-designs (topographies) or the production of integrated circuits,

the same treatment that it accords to its own nationals.

(2) [Agents, Addresses for Service, Court Proceedings]
Notwithstanding paragraph (1), any Contracting Party is free not to apply national treatment as far as any obligations to appoint an agent or to designate an address for service are concerned or as far as the special rules applicable to foreigners in court proceedings are concerned.

(3) [Application of Paragraphs (1) and (2) to Intergovernmental Organizations]
Where the Contracting Party is an Intergovernmental Organization, "nationals" in paragraph (1) means nationals of any of the States members of that Organization.

Article 6 The scope of the protection

(1) [Acts Requiring the Authorization of the Holder of the Right]   **A28-006**
(a) Any Contracting Party shall consider unlawful the following acts if performed without the authorization of the holder of the right:
(i) the act of reproducing, whether by incorporation in an integrated circuit or otherwise, a protected layout-design (topography) in its entirety or any part thereof, except the act of reproducing any part that does not comply with the requirement of originality referred to in Article 3(2),
(ii) the act of importing, selling or otherwise distributing for commercial purposes a protected layout-design (topography) or an integrated circuit in which a protected layout-design (topography) is incorporated.
(b) Any Contracting Party shall be free to consider unlawful also acts other than those specified in subparagraph (a) if performed without the authorization of the holder of the right.

(2) [Acts Not Requiring the Authorization of the Holder of the Right]

(a) Notwithstanding paragraph (1), no Contracting Party shall consider unlawful the performance, without the authorization of the holder of the right, of the act of reproduction referred to in paragraph (1)(a)(i) where that act is performed by a third party for private purposes or for the sole purpose of evaluation, analysis, research or teaching.

(b) Where the third party referred to in subparagraph (a), on the basis of evaluation or analysis of the protected layout-design (topography) ("the first layout-design (topography)"), creates a layout-design (topography) complying with the requirement of originality referred to in Article 3(2) ("the second layout-design (topography)"), that third party may incorporate the second layout-design (topography) in an integrated circuit or perform any of the acts referred to in paragraph (1) in respect of the second layout-design (topography) without being regarded as infringing the rights of the holder of the right in the first layout-design (topography).

(c) The holder of the right may not exercise his right in respect of an identical original layout-design (topography) that was independently created by a third party.

(3) [Measures Concerning Use Without the Consent of the Holder of the Right]

(a) Notwithstanding paragraph (1), any Contracting Party may, in its legislation, provide for the possibility of its executive or judicial authority granting a non-exclusive license, in circumstances that are not ordinary, for the performance of any of the acts referred to in paragraph (1) by a third party without the authorization of the holder of the right ("non-voluntary license"), after unsuccessful efforts, made by the said third party in line with normal commercial practices, to obtain such authorization, where the granting of the non-voluntary license is found, by the granting authority, to be necessary to safeguard a national purpose deemed to be vital by that authority; the non-voluntary license shall be available for exploitation only in the territory of that country and shall be subject to the payment of an equitable remuneration by the third party to the holder of the right.

(b) The provisions of this Treaty shall not affect the freedom of any Contracting Party to apply measures, including the granting, after a formal proceeding by its executive or judicial authority, of a non-voluntary license, in application of its laws in order to secure free competition and to prevent abuses by the holder of the right.

(c) The granting of any non-voluntary license referred to in subparagraph (a) or subparagraph (b) shall be subject to judicial review. Any non-voluntary license referred to in subparagraph (a) shall be revoked when the conditions referred to in that subparagraph cease to exist.

(4) [Sale and Distribution of Infringing Integrated Circuits Acquired Innocently]

Notwithstanding paragraph (1)(a)(ii), no Contracting Party shall be obliged to consider unlawful the performance of any of the acts referred to in that paragraph in respect of an integrated circuit incorporating an unlawfully reproduced layout-design (topography) where the person performing or ordering such acts did not know and had no reasonable ground to know, when acquiring the said integrated circuit, that it incorporates an unlawfully reproduced layout-design (topography).

(5) [Exhaustion of Rights]

Notwithstanding paragraph (1)(a)(ii), any Contracting Party may consider lawful the performance, without the authorization of the holder of the right, of any of the acts referred to in that paragraph where the act is performed in respect of a protected layout-design (topography), or in respect of an integrated circuit in which such a layout-design (topography) is incorporated, that has been put on the market by, or with the consent of, the holder of the right.

Article 7 Exploitation; registration, disclosure

(1) [Faculty to Require Exploitation]   A28-007
Any Contracting Party shall be free not to protect a layout-design (topography) until it has been ordinarily commercially exploited, separately or as incorporated in an integrated circuit, somewhere in the world.

(2) [Faculty to Require Registration; Disclosure]
(a) Any Contracting Party shall be free not to protect a layout-design (topography) until the layout-design (topography) has been the subject of an application for registration, filed in due form with the competent public authority, or of a registration with that authority; it may be required that the application be accompanied by the filing of a copy or drawing of the layout-design (topography) and, where the integrated circuit has been commercially exploited, of a sample of that integrated circuit, along with information defining the electronic function which the integrated circuit is intended to perform; however, the applicant may exclude such parts of the copy or drawing that relate to the manner of manufacture of the integrated circuit, provided that the parts submitted are sufficient to allow the identification of the layout-design (topography).
(b) Where the filing of an application for registration according to subparagraph (a) is required, the Contracting Party may require that such filing be effected within a certain period of time from the date on which the holder of the right first exploits ordinarily commercially anywhere in the world the layout-design (topography) of an integrated circuit; such period shall not be less than two years counted from the said date
(c) Registration under subparagraph (a) may be subject to the payment of a fee.

Article 8 The duration of the protection

Protection shall last at least eight years.   A28-008

Article 12 Safeguard of Paris and Berne Conventions

This Treaty shall not affect the obligations that any Contracting Party may A28-009 have under the Paris Convention for the Protection of Industrial Property or the Berne Convention for the Protection of Literary and Artistic Works.

AGREEMENT ON TRADE-RELATED ASPECTS OF
INTELLECTUAL PROPERTY RIGHTS

Members,
Desiring to reduce distortions and impediments to international trade, and taking into account the need to promote effective and adequate protection of intellectual property rights, and to ensure that measures and procedures to

enforce intellectual property rights do not themselves become barriers to legitimate trade;

Recognizing, to this end, the need for new rules and disciplines concerning:

the applicability of the basic principles of GATT 1994 and of relevant international intellectual property agreements or conventions;

(a) the provision of adequate standards and principles concerning the availability, scope and use of trade-related intellectual property rights;

(b) the provision of effective and appropriate means for the enforcement of trade-related intellectual property rights, taking into account differences in national legal systems;

(c) the provision of effective and expeditious procedures for the multilateral prevention and settlement of disputes between governments; and

(d) transitional arrangements aiming at the fullest participation in the results of the negotiations;

(e) *Recognizing* the need for a multilateral framework of principles, rules and disciplines dealing with international trade in counterfeit goods;

Recognizing that intellectual property rights are private rights;

Recognizing the underlying public policy objectives of national systems for the protection of intellectual property, including developmental and technological objectives;

Recognizing also the special needs of the least-developed country Members in respect of maximum flexibility in the domestic implementation of laws and regulations in order to enable them to create a sound and viable technological base;

Emphasizing the importance of reducing tensions by reaching strengthened commitments to resolve disputes on trade-related intellectual property issues through multilateral procedures;

Desiring to establish a mutually supportive relationship between the WTO and the World Intellectual Property Organization (referred to in this Agreement as "WIPO") as well as other relevant international organizations;

Hereby agree as follows:

PART I

GENERAL PROVISIONS AND BASIC PRINCIPLES

Article 1 Nature and Scope of Obligations

A29-001   1. Members shall give effect to the provisions of this Agreement. Members may, but shall not be obliged to, implement in their law more extensive protection than is required by this Agreement, provided that such protection does not contravene the provisions of this Agreement. Members shall be free to determine the appropriate method of implementing the provisions of this Agreement within their own legal system and practice.

    2. For the purposes of this Agreement, the term "intellectual property" refers to all categories of intellectual property that are the subject of Sections 1 through 7 of Part II.

    3. Members shall accord the treatment provided for in this Agreement to the nationals of other Members. In respect of the relevant intellectual property right, the nationals of other Members shall be understood as those natural or legal persons that would meet the criteria for eligibility for protection provided for in the Paris Convention (1967), the Berne Convention (1971), the Rome Convention and the Treaty on Intellectual Property in Respect of Integrated Circuits, were

all Members of the WTO members of those conventions. Any Member availing itself of the possibilities provided in paragraph 3 of Article 5 or paragraph 2 of Article 6 of the Rome Convention shall make a notification as foreseen in those provisions to the Council for Trade-Related Aspects of Intellectual Property Rights (the "Council for TRIPS").

Article 2 Intellectual Property Conventions

1. In respect of Parts II, III and IV of this Agreement, Members shall comply **A29-002** with Articles 1 through 12, and Article 19, of the Paris Convention (1967).

2. Nothing in Parts I to IV of this Agreement shall derogate from existing obligations that Members may have to each other under the Paris Convention, the Berne Convention, the Rome Convention and the Treaty on Intellectual Property in Respect of Integrated Circuits.

Article 3 National Treatment

1. Each Member shall accord to the nationals of other Members treatment **A29-003** no less favourable than that it accords to its own nationals with regard to the protection of intellectual property, subject to the exceptions already provided in, respectively, the Paris Convention (1967), the Berne Convention (1971), the Rome Convention or the Treaty on Intellectual Property in Respect of Integrated Circuits. In respect of performers, producers of phonograms and broadcasting organizations, this obligation only applies in respect of the rights provided under this Agreement. Any Member availing itself of the possibilities provided in Article 6 of the Berne Convention (1971) or paragraph 1(b) of Article 16 of the Rome Convention shall make a notification as foreseen in those provisions to the Council for TRIPS.

2. Members may avail themselves of the exceptions permitted under paragraph 1 in relation to judicial and administrative procedures, including the designation of an address for service or the appointment of an agent within the jurisdiction of a Member, only where such exceptions are necessary to secure compliance with laws and regulations which are not inconsistent with the provisions of this Agreement and where such practices are not applied in a manner which would constitute a disguised restriction on trade.

Article 4 Most-Favoured-Nation Treatment

With regard to the protection of intellectual property, any advantage, favour, **A29-004** privilege or immunity granted by a Member to the nationals of any other country shall be accorded immediately and unconditionally to the nationals of all other Members. Exempted from this obligation are any advantage, favour, privilege or immunity accorded by a Member:

(a) deriving from international agreements on judicial assistance or law enforcement of a general nature and not particularly confined to the protection of intellectual property;

(b) granted in accordance with the provisions of the Berne Convention (1971) or the Rome Convention authorizing that the treatment accorded be a function not of national treatment but of the treatment accorded in another country;

(c) in respect of the rights of performers, producers of phonograms and broadcasting organizations not provided under this Agreement;

(d) deriving from international agreements related to the protection of intellectual property which entered into force prior to the entry into force of the WTO Agreement, provided that such agreements are notified to the Council for

TRIPS and do not constitute an arbitrary or unjustifiable discriminationagainst nationals of other Members.

Article 5 Multilateral Agreements on Acquisition or Maintenance of Protection

A29-005   The obligations under Articles 3 and 4 do not apply to procedures provided in multilateral agreements concluded under the auspices of WIPO relating to the acquisition or maintenance of intellectual property rights.

Article 6 Exhaustion

A29-006   For the purposes of dispute settlement under this Agreement, subject to the provisions of Articles 3 and 4 nothing in this Agreement shall be used to address the issue of the exhaustion of intellectual property rights.

Article 7 Objectives

A29-007   The protection and enforcement of intellectual property rights should contribute to the promotion of technological innovation and to the transfer and dissemination of technology, to the mutual advantage of producers and users of technological knowledge and in a manner conducive to social and economic welfare, and to a balance of rights and obligations.

Article 8 Principles

A29-008   1. Members may, in formulating or amending their laws and regulations, adopt measures necessary to protect public health and nutrition, and to promote the public interest in sectors of vital importance to their socio-economic and technological development, provided that such measures are consistent with the provisions of this Agreement.

2. Appropriate measures, provided that they are consistent with the provisions of this Agreement, may be needed to prevent the abuse of intellectual property rights by right holders or the resort to practices which unreasonably restrain trade or adversely affect the international transfer of technology.

PART II
Standards concerning the availability, scope and use of Intellectual Property Rights

SECTION 1: COPYRIGHT AND RELATED RIGHTS

Article 9 Relation to the Berne Convention

A29-009   1. Members shall comply with Articles 1 through 21 of the Berne Convention (1971) and the Appendix thereto. However, Members shall not have rights or obligations under this Agreement in respect of the rights conferred under Article 6bis of that Convention or of the rights derived therefrom.

2. Copyright protection shall extend to expressions and not to ideas, procedures, methods of operation or mathematical concepts as such.

Article 10 Computer Programs and Compilations of Data

A29-010   1. Computer programs, whether in source or object code, shall be protected as literary works under the Berne Convention (1971).

2. Compilations of data or other material, whether in machine readable or other form, which by reason of the selection or arrangement of their contents constitute intellectual creations shall be protected as such. Such protection,

which shall not extend to the data or material itself, shall be without prejudice to any copyright subsisting in the data or material itself.

Article 11 Rental Rights

In respect of at least computer programs and cinematographic works, a **A29-011** Member shall provide authors and their successors in title the right to authorize or to prohibit the commercial rental to the public of originals or copies of their copyright works. A Member shall be excepted from this obligation in respect of cinematographic works unless such rental has led to widespread copying of such works which is materially impairing the exclusive right of reproduction conferred in that Member on authors and their successors in title. In respect of computer programs, this obligation does not apply to rentals where the program itself is not the essential object of the rental.

Article 12 Term of Protection

Whenever the term of protection of a work, other than a photographic work **A29-012** or a work of applied art, is calculated on a basis other than the life of a natural person, such term shall be no less than 50 years from the end of the calendar year of authorized publication, or, failing such authorized publication within 50 years from the making of the work, 50 years from the end of the calendar year of making.

Article 13 Limitations and Exceptions

Members shall confine limitations or exceptions to exclusive rights to certain **A29-013** special cases which do not conflict with a normal exploitation of the work and do not unreasonably prejudice the legitimate interests of the right holder.

Article 14 Protection of Performers, Producers of Phonograms (Sound Recordings) and Broadcasting Organizations

1. In respect of a fixation of their performance on a phonogram, performers **A29-014** shall have the possibility of preventing the following acts when undertaken without their authorization: the fixation of their unfixed performance and the reproduction of such fixation. Performers shall also have the possibility of preventing the following acts when undertaken without their authorization: the broadcasting by wireless means and the communication to the public of their live performance.

2. Producers of phonograms shall enjoy the right to authorize or prohibit the direct or indirect reproduction of their phonograms.

3. Broadcasting organizations shall have the right to prohibit the following acts when undertaken without their authorization: the fixation, the reproduction of fixations, and the rebroadcasting by wireless means of broadcasts, as well as the communication to the public of television broadcasts of the same. Where Members do not grant such rights to broadcasting organizations, they shall provide owners of copyright in the subject matter of broadcasts with the possibility of preventing the above acts, subject to the provisions of the Berne Convention (1971).

4. The provisions of Article 11 in respect of computer programs shall apply mutatis mutandis to producers of phonograms and any other right holders in phonograms as determined in a Member's law. If on 15 April 1994 a Member has in force a system of equitable remuneration of right holders in respect of the rental of phonograms, it may maintain such system provided that the commercial

rental of phonograms is not giving rise to the material impairment of the exclusive rights of reproduction of right holders.

5. The term of the protection available under this Agreement to performers and producers of phonograms shall last at least until the end of a period of 50 years computed from the end of the calendar year in which the fixation was made or the performance took place. The term of protection granted pursuant to paragraph 3 shall last for at least 20 years from the end of the calendar year in which the broadcast took place.

6. Any Member may, in relation to the rights conferred under paragraphs 1, 2 and 3, provide for conditions, limitations, exceptions and reservations to the extent permitted by the Rome Convention. However, the provisions of Article 18 of the Berne Convention (1971) shall also apply, mutatis mutandis, to the rights of performers and producers of phonograms in phonograms.

SECTION 2: TRADEMARKS

Article 15 Protectable Subject Matter

A29-015   1. Any sign, or any combination of signs, capable of distinguishing the goods or services of one undertaking from those of other undertakings, shall be capable of constituting a trademark. Such signs, in particular words including personal names, letters, numerals, figurative elements and combinations of colours as well as any combination of such signs, shall be eligible for registration as trademarks. Where signs are not inherently capable of distinguishing the relevant goods or services, Members may make registrability depend on distinctiveness acquired through use. Members may require, as a condition of registration, that signs be visually perceptible.

2. Paragraph 1 shall not be understood to prevent a Member from denying registration of a trademark on other grounds, provided that they do not derogate from the provisions of the Paris Convention (1967).

3. Members may make registrability depend on use. However, actual use of a trademark shall not be a condition for filing an application for registration. An application shall not be refused solely on the ground that intended use has not taken place before the expiry of a period of three years from the date of application.

4. The nature of the goods or services to which a trademark is to be applied shall in no case form an obstacle to registration of the trademark.

5. Members shall publish each trademark either before it is registered or promptly after it is registered and shall afford a reasonable opportunity for petitions to cancel the registration. In addition, Members may afford an opportunity for the registration of a trademark to be opposed.

Article 16 Rights Conferred

A29-016   1. The owner of a registered trademark shall have the exclusive right to prevent all third parties not having the owner's consent from using in the course of trade identical or similar signs for goods or services which are identical or similar to those in respect of which the trademark is registered where such use would result in a likelihood of confusion. In case of the use of an identical sign for identical goods or services, a likelihood of confusion shall be presumed. The rights described above shall not prejudice any existing prior rights, nor shall they affect the possibility of Members making rights available on the basis of use.

2. Article 6bis of the Paris Convention (1967) shall apply, mutatis mutandis, to services. In determining whether a trademark is well-known, Members shall take account of the knowledge of the trademark in the relevant sector of the public, including knowledge in the Member concerned which has been obtained as a result of the promotion of the trademark.

3. Article 6bis of the Paris Convention (1967) shall apply, mutatis mutandis, to goods or services which are not similar to those in respect of which a trademark is registered, provided that use of that trademark in relation to those goods or services would indicate a connection between those goods or services and the owner of the registered trademark and provided that the interests of the owner of the registered trademark are likely to be damaged by such use.

Article 17 Exceptions

Members may provide limited exceptions to the rights conferred by a **A29-017** trademark, such as fair use of descriptive terms, provided that such exceptions take account of the legitimate interests of the owner of the trademark and of third parties.

Article 18 Term of Protection

Initial registration, and each renewal of registration, of a trademark shall be **A29-018** for a term of no less than seven years. The registration of a trademark shall be renewable indefinitely.

Article 19 Requirement of Use

1. If use is required to maintain a registration, the registration may be **A29-019** cancelled only after an uninterrupted period of at least three years of non-use, unless valid reasons based on the existence of obstacles to such use are shown by the trademark owner. Circumstances arising independently of the will of the owner of the trademark which constitute an obstacle to the use of the trademark, such as import restrictions on or other government requirements for goods or services protected by the trademark, shall be recognized as valid reasons for non-use.

2. When subject to the control of its owner, use of a trademark by another person shall be recognized as use of the trademark for the purpose of maintaining the registration.

Article 20 Other Requirements

The use of a trademark in the course of trade shall not be unjustifiably **A29-020** encumbered by special requirements, such as use with another trademark, use in a special form or use in a manner detrimental to its capability to distinguish the goods or services of one undertaking from those of other undertakings. This will not preclude a requirement prescribing the use of the trademark identifying the undertaking producing the goods or services along with, but without linking it to, the trademark distinguishing the specific goods or services in question of that undertaking.

Article 21 Licensing and Assignment

Members may determine conditions on the licensing and assignment of **A29-021** trademarks, it being understood that the compulsory licensing of trademarks shall not be permitted and that the owner of a registered trademark shall have the right to assign the trademark with or without the transfer of the business to which the trademark belongs.

SECTION 3: GEOGRAPHICAL INDICATIONS

Article 22 Protection of Geographical Indications

A29-022   1. Geographical indications are, for the purposes of this Agreement, indications which identify a good as originating in the territory of a Member, or a region or locality in that territory, where a given quality, reputation or other characteristic of the good is essentially attributable to its geographical origin.

2. In respect of geographical indications, Members shall provide the legal means for interested parties to prevent:

(a) the use of any means in the designation or presentation of a good that indicates or suggests that the good in question originates in a geographical area other than the true place of origin in a manner which misleads the public as to the geographical origin of the good;

(b) any use which constitutes an act of unfair competition within the meaning of Article 10bis of the Paris Convention (1967).

3. A Member shall, ex officio if its legislation so permits or at the request of an interested party, refuse or invalidate the registration of a trademark which contains or consists of a geographical indication with respect to goods not originating in the territory indicated, if use of the indication in the trademark for such goods in that Member is of such a nature as to mislead the public as to the true place of origin.

4. The protection under paragraphs 1, 2 and 3 shall be applicable against a geographical indication which, although literally true as to the territory, region or locality in which the goods originate, falsely represents to the public that the goods originate in another territory.

Article 23 Additional Protection for Geographical Indications for Wines and Spirits

A29-023   1. Each Member shall provide the legal means for interested parties to prevent use of a geographical indication identifying wines for wines not originating in the place indicated by the geographical indication in question or identifying spirits for spirits not originating in the place indicated by the geographical indication in question, even where the true origin of the goods is indicated or the geographical indication is used in translation or accompanied by expressions such as "kind", "type", "style", "imitation" or the like.

2. The registration of a trademark for wines which contains or consists of a geographical indication identifying wines or for spirits which contains or consists of a geographical indication identifying spirits shall be refused or invalidated, ex officio if a Member's legislation so permits or at the request of an interested party, with respect to such wines or spirits not having this origin.

3. In the case of homonymous geographical indications for wines, protection shall be accorded to each indication, subject to the provisions of paragraph 4 of Article 22. Each Member shall determine the practical conditions under which the homonymous indications in question will be differentiated from each other, taking into account the need to ensure equitable treatment of the producers concerned and that consumers are not misled.

4. In order to facilitate the protection of geographical indications for wines, negotiations shall be undertaken in the Council for TRIPS concerning the establishment of a multilateral system of notification and registration of geographical indications for wines eligible for protection in those Members participating in the system.

Article 24 International Negotiations; Exceptions

1. Members agree to enter into negotiations aimed at increasing the **A29-024** protection of individual geographical indications under Article 23. The provisions of paragraphs 4 through 8 below shall not be used by a Member to refuse to conduct negotiations or to conclude bilateral or multilateral agreements. In the context of such negotiations, Members shall be willing to consider the continued applicability of these provisions to individual geographical indications whose use was the subject of such negotiations.

2. The Council for TRIPS shall keep under review the application of the provisions of this Section; the first such review shall take place within two years of the entry into force of the WTO Agreement. Any matter affecting the compliance with the obligations under these provisions may be drawn to the attention of the Council, which, at the request of a Member, shall consult with any Member or Members in respect of such matter in respect of which it has not been possible to find a satisfactory solution through bilateral or plurilateral consultations between the Members concerned. The Council shall take such action as may be agreed to facilitate the operation and further the objectives of this Section.

3. In implementing this Section, a Member shall not diminish the protection of geographical indications that existed in that Member immediatelyprior to the date of entry into force of the WTO Agreement.

4. Nothing in this Section shall require a Member to prevent continued and similar use of a particular geographical indication of another Member identifying wines or spirits in connection with goods or services by any of its nationals or domiciliaries who have used that geographical indication in a continuous manner with regard to the same or related goods or services in the territory of that Member either (a) for at least 10 years preceding 15 April 1994 or (b) in good faith preceding that date.

5. Where a trademark has been applied for or registered in good faith, or where rights to a trademark have been acquired through use in good faith either:

    (a) before the date of application of these provisions in that Member as defined in Part VI; or

    (b) before the geographical indication is protected in its country of origin;

measures adopted to implement this Section shall not prejudice eligibility for or the validity of the registration of a trademark, or the right to use a trademark, on the basis that such a trademark is identical with, or similar to, a geographical indication.

6. Nothing in this Section shall require a Member to apply its provisions in respect of a geographical indication of any other Member with respect to goods or services for which the relevant indication is identical with the term customary in common language as the common name for such goods or services in the territory of that Member. Nothing in this Section shall require a Member to apply its provisions in respect of a geographical indication of any other Member with respect to products of the vine for which the relevant indication is identical with the customary name of a grape variety existing in the territory of that Member as of the date of entry into force of the WTO Agreement.

7. A Member may provide that any request made under this Section in connection with the use or registration of a trademark must be presented within five years after the adverse use of the protected indication has become generally known in that Member or after the date of registration of the trademark in that Member provided that the trademark has been published by that date, if such date

is earlier than the date on which the adverse use became generally known in that Member, provided that the geographical indication is not used or registered in bad faith.

8. The provisions of this Section shall in no way prejudice the right of any person to use, in the course of trade, that person's name or the name of that person's predecessor in business, except where such name is used in such a manner as to mislead the public.

9. There shall be no obligation under this Agreement to protect geographical indications which are not or cease to be protected in their country of origin, or which have fallen into disuse in that country.

SECTION 4: INDUSTRIAL DESIGNS

Article 25 Requirements for Protection

A29-025   1. Members shall provide for the protection of independently created industrial designs that are new or original. Members may provide that designs are not new or original if they do not significantly differ from known designs or combinations of known design features. Members may provide that such protection shall not extend to designs dictated essentially by technical or functional considerations.

2. Each Member shall ensure that requirements for securing protection for textile designs, in particular in regard to any cost, examination or publication, do not unreasonably impair the opportunity to seek and obtain such protection. Members shall be free to meet this obligation through industrial design law or through copyright law.

Article 26 Protection

A29-026   1. The owner of a protected industrial design shall have the right to prevent third parties not having the owner's consent from making, selling or importing articles bearing or embodying a design which is a copy, or substantially a copy, of the protected design, when such acts are undertaken for commercial purposes.

2. Members may provide limited exceptions to the protection of industrial designs, provided that such exceptions do not unreasonably conflict with the normal exploitation of protected industrial designs and do not unreasonably prejudice the legitimate interests of the owner of the protected design, taking account of the legitimate interests of third parties.

3. The duration of protection available shall amount to at least 10 years.

SECTION 5: PATENTS

Article 27 Patentable Subject Matter

A29-027   1. Subject to the provisions of paragraphs 2 and 3, patents shall be available for any inventions, whether products or processes, in all fields of technology, provided that they are new, involve an inventive step and are capable of industrial application. Subject to paragraph 4 of Article 65, paragraph 8 of Article 70 and paragraph 3 of this Article, patents shall be available and patent rights enjoyable without discrimination as to the place of invention, the field of technology and whether products are imported or locally produced.

2. Members may exclude from patentability inventions, the prevention within their territory of the commercial exploitation of which is necessary to protect ordre public or morality, including to protect human, animal or plant life or

health or to avoid serious prejudice to the environment, provided that such exclusion is not made merely because the exploitation is prohibited by their law.

3. Members may also exclude from patentability:

   (a) diagnostic, therapeutic and surgical methods for the treatment of humans or animals;

   (b) plants and animals other than micro-organisms, and essentially biological processes for the production of plants or animals other than non-biological and microbiological processes. However, Members shall provide for the protection of plant varieties either by patents or by an effective sui generis system or by any combination thereof. The provisions of this subparagraph shall be reviewed four years after the date of entry into force of the WTO Agreement.

Article 28 Rights Conferred

1. A patent shall confer on its owner the following exclusive rights: **A29-028**

   (a) where the subject matter of a patent is a product, to prevent third parties not having the owner's consent from the acts of: making, using, offering for sale, selling, or importing for these purposes that product;

   (b) where the subject matter of a patent is a process, to prevent third parties not having the owner's consent from the act of using the process, and from the acts of: using, offering for sale, selling, or importing for these purposes at least the product obtained directly by that process.

2. Patent owners shall also have the right to assign, or transfer by succession, the patent and to conclude licensing contracts.

Article 29 Conditions on Patent Applicants

1. Members shall require that an applicant for a patent shall disclose the **A29-029** invention in a manner sufficiently clear and complete for the invention to be carried out by a person skilled in the art and may require the applicant to indicate the best mode for carrying out the invention known to the inventor at the filing date or, where priority is claimed, at the priority date of the application.

2. Members may require an applicant for a patent to provide information concerning the applicant's corresponding foreign applications and grants.

Article 30 Exceptions to Rights Conferred

Members may provide limited exceptions to the exclusive rights conferred by **A29-030** a patent, provided that such exceptions do not unreasonably conflict with a normal exploitation of the patent and do not unreasonably prejudice the legitimate interests of the patent owner, taking account of the legitimate interests of third parties.

Article 31 Other Use Without Authorization of the Right Holder

Where the law of a Member allows for other use of the subject matter of a **A29-031** patent without the authorization of the right holder, including use by the government or third parties authorized by the government, the following provisions shall be respected:

   (a) authorization of such use shall be considered on its individual merits;

   (b) such use may only be permitted if, prior to such use, the proposed user has made efforts to obtain authorization from the right holder on reasonable commercial terms and conditions and that such efforts have not been successful within a reasonable period of time. This requirement may be waived by a Member in the case of a national emergency or other circumstances of extreme urgency or in cases of public non-commercial use. In situations of national emergency or other circumstances of extreme urgency, the right holder shall, nevertheless, be notified as soon as reasonably practicable. In the case of public non-commercial use, where the government or contractor, without making a patent search, knows or has demonstrable grounds to know that a valid patent is or will be used by or for the government, the right holder shall be informed promptly;

(c) the scope and duration of such use shall be limited to the purpose for which it was authorized, and in the case of semi-conductor technology shall only be for public non-commercial use or to remedy a practice determined after judicial or administrative process to be anti-competitive;

(d) such use shall be non-exclusive;

(e) such use shall be non-assignable, except with that part of the enterprise or goodwill which enjoys such use;

(f) any such use shall be authorized predominantly for the supply of the domestic market of the Member authorizing such use;

(g) authorization for such use shall be liable, subject to adequate protection of the legitimate interests of the persons so authorized, to be terminated if and when the circumstances which led to it cease to exist and are unlikely to recur. The competent authority shall have the authority to review, upon motivated request, the continued existence of these circumstances;

(h) the right holder shall be paid adequate remuneration in the circumstances of each case, taking into account the economic value of the authorization;

(i) the legal validity of any decision relating to the authorization of such use shall be subject to judicial review or other independent review by a distinct higher authority in that Member;

(j) any decision relating to the remuneration provided in respect of such use shall be subject to judicial review or other independent review by a distinct higher authority in that Member;

(k) Members are not obliged to apply the conditions set forth in subparagraphs (b) and (f) where such use is permitted to remedy a practice determined after judicial or administrative process to be anti-competitive. The need to correct anti-competitive practices may be taken into account in determining the amount of remuneration in such cases. Competent authorities shall have the authority to refuse termination of authorization if and when the conditions which led to such authorization are likely to recur;

(l) where such use is authorized to permit the exploitation of a patent ("the second patent") which cannot be exploited without infringing another patent ("the first patent"), the following additional conditions shall apply:

  (i) the invention claimed in the second patent shall involve an important technical advance of considerable economic significance in relation to the invention claimed in the first patent;

  (ii) the owner of the first patent shall be entitled to a cross-licence on reasonable terms to use the invention claimed in the second patent; and

  (iii) the use authorized in respect of the first patent shall be non-assignable except with the assignment of the second patent.

Article 32 Revocation / Forfeiture

A29-032   An opportunity for judicial review of any decision to revoke or forfeit a patent shall be available.

Article 33 Term of Protection

The term of protection available shall not end before the expiration of a **A29-033** period of twenty years counted from the filing date

Article 34 Process Patents: Burden of Proof

1. For the purposes of civil proceedings in respect of the infringement of the **A29-034** rights of the owner referred to in paragraph 1(b) of Article 28, if the subject matter of a patent is a process for obtaining a product, the judicial authorities shall have the authority to order the defendant to prove that the process to obtain an identical product is different from the patented process. Therefore, Members shall provide, in at least one of the following circumstances, that any identical product when produced without the consent of the patent owner shall, in the absence of proof to the contrary, be deemed to have been obtained by the patented process:

    (a) if the product obtained by the patented process is new;
    (b) if there is a substantial likelihood that the identical product was made by the process and the owner of the patent has been unable through reasonable efforts to determine the process actually used.

2. Any Member shall be free to provide that the burden of proof indicated in paragraph 1 shall be on the alleged infringer only if the condition referred to in subparagraph (a) is fulfilled or only if the condition referred to in subparagraph (b) is fulfilled.

3. In the adduction of proof to the contrary, the legitimate interests of defendants in protecting their manufacturing and business secrets shall be taken into account.

SECTION 6: LAYOUT-DESIGNS (TOPOGRAPHIES) OF INTEGRATED CIRCUITS

Article 35 Relation to the IPIC Treaty

Members agree to provide protection to the layout-designs (topographies) of **A29-035** integrated circuits (referred to in this Agreement as "layout-designs") in accordance with Articles 2 through 7 (other than paragraph 3 of Article 6), Article 12 and paragraph 3 of Article 16 of the Treaty on Intellectual Property in Respect of Integrated Circuits and, in addition, to comply with the following provisions.

Article 36 Scope of the Protection

Subject to the provisions of paragraph 1 of Article 37, Members shall consider **A29-036** unlawful the following acts if performed without the authorization of the right holder: importing, selling, or otherwise distributing for commercial purposes a protected layout-design, an integrated circuit in which a protected layout-design is incorporated, or an article incorporating such an integrated circuit only in so far as it continues to contain an unlawfully reproduced layout-design.

Article 37 Acts Not Requiring the Authorization of the Right Holder

1. Notwithstanding Article 36, no Member shall consider unlawful the perfor- **A29-037** mance of any of the acts referred to in that Article in respect of an integrated circuit incorporating an unlawfully reproduced layout-design or any article incorporating such an integrated circuit where the person performing or ordering such acts did not know and had no reasonable ground to know, when acquiring

the integrated circuit or article incorporating such an integrated circuit, that it incorporated an unlawfully reproduced layout-design. Members shall provide that, after the time that such person has received sufficient notice that the layout-design was unlawfully reproduced, that person may perform any of the acts with respect to the stock on hand or ordered before such time, but shall be liable to pay to the right holder a sum equivalent to a reasonable royalty such as would be payable under a freely negotiated licence in respect of such a layout-design.

2. The conditions set out in subparagraphs (a) through (k) of Article 31 shall apply mutatis mutandis in the event of any non-voluntary licensing of a layout-design or of its use by or for the government without the authorization of the right holder.

Article 38 Term of Protection

A29-038 1. In Members requiring registration as a condition of protection, the term of protection of layout-designsshall not end before the expiration of a period of 10 years counted from the date of filing an application for registration or from the first commercial exploitation wherever in the world it occurs.

2. In Members not requiring registration as a condition for protection, layout-designs shall be protected for a term of no less than 10 years from the date of the first commercial exploitation wherever in the world it occurs.

3. Notwithstanding paragraphs 1 and 2, a Member may provide that protection shall lapse 15 years after the creation of the layout-design.

SECTION 7: PROTECTION OF UNDISCLOSED INFORMATION

Article 39

A29-039 1. In the course of ensuring effective protection against unfair competition as provided in Article 10bis of the Paris Convention (1967), Members shall protect undisclosed information in accordance with paragraph 2 and data submitted to governments or governmental agencies in accordance with paragraph 3.

2. Natural and legal persons shall have the possibility of preventing information lawfully within their control from being disclosed to, acquired by, or used by others without their consent in a manner contrary to honest commercial practices so long as such information:

    (a) is secret in the sense that it is not, as a body or in the precise configuration and assembly of its components, generally known among or readily accessible to persons within the circles that normally deal with the kind of information in question;

    (b) has commercial value because it is secret; and

    (c) has been subject to reasonable steps under the circumstances, by the person lawfully in control of the information, to keep it secret.

3. Members, when requiring, as a condition of approving the marketing of pharmaceutical or of agricultural chemical products which utilize new chemical entities, the submission of undisclosed test or other data, the origination of which involves a considerable effort, shall protect such data against unfair commercial use. In addition, Members shall protect such data against disclosure, except where necessary to protect the public, or unless steps are taken to ensure that the data are protected against unfair commercial use.

SECTION 8: CONTROL OF ANTI-COMPETITIVE PRACTICES IN CONTRACTUAL LICENCES

Article 40

1. Members agree that some licensing practices or conditions pertaining to **A29-040** intellectual property rights which restrain competition may have adverse effects on trade and may impede the transfer and dissemination of technology.

2. Nothing in this Agreement shall prevent Members from specifying in their legislation licensing practices or conditions that may in particular cases constitute an abuse of intellectual property rights having an adverse effect on competition in the relevant market. As provided above, a Member may adopt, consistently with the other provisions of this Agreement, appropriate measures to prevent or control such practices, which may include for example exclusive grantback conditions, conditions preventing challenges to validity and coercive package licensing, in the light of the relevant laws and regulations of that Member.

3. Each Member shall enter, upon request, into consultations with any other Member which has cause to believe that an intellectual property right owner that is a national or domiciliary of the Member to which the request for consultations has been addressed is undertaking practices in violation of the requesting Member's laws and regulations on the subject matter of this Section, and which wishes to secure compliance with such legislation, without prejudice to any action under the law and to the full freedom of an ultimate decision of either Member. The Member addressed shall accord full and sympathetic consideration to, and shall afford adequate opportunity for, consultations with the requesting Member, and shall cooperate through supply of publicly available non-confidential information of relevance to the matter in question and of other information available to the Member, subject to domestic law and to the conclusion of mutually satisfactory agreements concerning the safeguarding of its confidentiality by the requesting Member.

4. A Member whose nationals or domiciliaries are subject to proceedings in another Member concerning alleged violation of that other Member's laws and regulations on the subject matter of this Section shall, upon request, be granted an opportunity for consultations by the other Member under the same conditions as those foreseen in paragraph 3.

PART III

ENFORCEMENT OF INTELLECTUAL PROPERTY RIGHTS

SECTION 1: GENERAL OBLIGATIONS

Article 41

1. Members shall ensure that enforcement procedures as specified in this **A29-041** Part are available under their law so as to permit effective action against any act of infringement of intellectual property rights covered by this Agreement, including expeditious remedies to prevent infringements and remedies which constitute a deterrent to further infringements. These procedures shall be applied in such a manner as to avoid the creation of barriers to legitimate trade and to provide for safeguards against their abuse.

2. Procedures concerning the enforcement of intellectual property rights shall be fair and equitable. They shall not be unnecessarily complicated or costly, or entail unreasonable time-limits or unwarranted delays.

3. Decisions on the merits of a case shall preferably be in writing and reasoned. They shall be made available at least to the parties to the proceeding without undue delay. Decisions on the merits of a case shall be based only on evidence in respect of which parties were offered the opportunity to be heard.

4. Parties to a proceeding shall have an opportunity for review by a judicial authority of final administrative decisions and, subject to jurisdictional provisions in a Member's law concerning the importance of a case, of at least the legal aspects of initial judicial decisions on the merits of a case. However, there shall be no obligation to provide an opportunity for review of acquittals in criminal cases.

5. It is understood that this Part does not create any obligation to put in place a judicial system for the enforcement of intellectual property rights distinct from that for the enforcement of law in general, nor does it affect the capacity of Members to enforce their law in general. Nothing in this Part creates any obligation with respect to the distribution of resources as between enforcement of intellectual property rights and the enforcement of law in general.

SECTION 2: CIVIL AND ADMINISTRATIVE PROCEDURES AND REMEDIES

Article 42 Fair and Equitable Procedures

A29-042   Members shall make available to right holders civil judicial procedures concerning the enforcement of any intellectual property right covered by this Agreement. Defendants shall have the right to written notice which is timely and contains sufficient detail, including the basis of the claims. Parties shall be allowed to be represented by independent legal counsel, and procedures shall not impose overly burdensome requirements concerning mandatory personal appearances. All parties to such procedures shall be duly entitled to substantiate their claims and to present all relevant evidence. The procedure shall provide a means to identify and protect confidential information, unless this would be contrary to existing constitutional requirements.

Article 43 Evidence

A29-043   1. The judicial authorities shall have the authority, where a party has presented reasonably available evidence sufficient to support its claims and has specified evidence relevant to substantiation of its claims which lies in the control of the opposing party, to order that this evidence be produced by the opposing party, subject in appropriate cases to conditions which ensure the protection of confidential information.

2. In cases in which a party to a proceeding voluntarily and without good reason refuses access to, or otherwise does not provide necessary information within a reasonable period, orsignificantly impedes a procedure relating to an enforcement action, a Member may accord judicial authorities the authority to make preliminary and final determinations, affirmative or negative, on the basis of the information presented to them, including the complaint or the allegation presented by the party adversely affected by the denial of access to information, subject to providing the parties an opportunity to be heard on the allegations or evidence.

Article 44 Injunctions

1. The judicial authorities shall have the authority to order a party to desist **A29-044** from an infringement, inter alia to prevent the entry into the channels of commerce in their jurisdiction of imported goods that involve the infringement of an intellectual property right, immediately after customs clearance of such goods. Members are not obliged to accord such authority in respect of protected subject matter acquired or ordered by a person prior to knowing or having reasonable grounds to know that dealing in such subject matter would entail the infringement of an intellectual property right.

2. Notwithstanding the other provisions of this Part and provided that the provisions of Part II specifically addressing use by governments, or by third parties authorized by a government, without the authorization of the right holder are complied with, Members may limit the remedies available against such use to payment of remuneration in accordance with subparagraph (h) of Article 31. In other cases, the remedies under this Part shall apply or, where these remedies are inconsistent with a Member's law, declaratory judgments and adequate compensation shall be available.

Article 45 Damages

1. The judicial authorities shall have the authority to order the infringer to **A29-045** pay the right holder damages adequate to compensate for the injury the right holder has suffered because of an infringement of that person's intellectual property right by an infringer who knowingly, or with reasonable grounds to know, engaged in infringing activity.

2. The judicial authorities shall also have the authority to order the infringer to pay the right holder expenses, which may include appropriate attorney's fees. In appropriate cases, Members may authorize the judicial authorities to order recovery of profits and/or payment of pre-established damages even where the infringer did not knowingly, or with reasonable grounds to know, engage in infringing activity.

Article 46 Other Remedies

In order to create an effective deterrent to infringement, the judicial authorities **A29-046** shall have the authority to order that goods that they have found to be infringing be, without compensation of any sort, disposed of outside the channels of commerce in such a manner as to avoid any harm caused to the right holder, or, unless this would be contrary to existing constitutional requirements, destroyed. The judicial authorities shall also have the authority to order that materials and implements the predominant use of which has been in the creation of the infringing goods be, without compensation of any sort, disposed of outside the channels of commerce in such a manner as to minimize the risks of further infringements. In considering such requests, the need for proportionality between the seriousness of the infringement and the remedies ordered as well as the interests of third parties shall be taken into account. In regard to counterfeit trademark goods, the simple removal of the trademark unlawfully affixed shall not be sufficient, other than in exceptional cases, to permit release of the goods into the channels of commerce.

Article 47 Right of Information

Members may provide that the judicial authorities shall have the authority, **A29-047** unless this would be out of proportion to the seriousness of the infringement, to order the infringer to inform the right holder of the identity of third persons involved in the production and distribution of the infringing goods or services and of their channels of distribution.

Article 48 Indemnification of the Defendant

A29-048   1. The judicial authorities shall have the authority to order a party at whose request measures were taken and who has abused enforcement procedures to provide to a party wrongfully enjoined or restrained adequate compensation for the injury suffered because of such abuse. The judicial authorities shall also have the authority to order the applicant to pay the defendant expenses, which may include appropriate attorney's fees.

2. In respect of the administration of any law pertaining to the protection or enforcement of intellectual property rights, Members shall only exempt both public authorities and officials from liability to appropriate remedial measures where actions are taken or intended in good faith in the course of the administration of that law.

Article 49 Administrative Procedures

A29-049   To the extent that any civil remedy can be ordered as a result of administrative procedures on the merits of a case, such procedures shall conform to principles equivalent in substance to those set forth in this Section.

SECTION 3: PROVISIONAL MEASURES

Article 50

A29-050   1. The judicial authorities shall have the authority to order prompt and effective provisional measures:

(a) to prevent an infringement of any intellectual property right from occurring, and in particular to prevent the entry into the channels of commerce in their jurisdiction of goods, including imported goods immediately after customs clearance;

(b) to preserve relevant evidence in regard to the alleged infringement.

2. The judicial authorities shall have the authority to adopt provisional measures inaudita altera parte where appropriate, in particular where any delay is likely to cause irreparable harm to the right holder, or where there is a demonstrable risk of evidence being destroyed.

3. The judicial authorities shall have the authority to require the applicant to provide any reasonably available evidence in order to satisfy themselves with a sufficient degree of certainty that the applicant is the right holder and that the applicant's right is being infringed or that such infringement is imminent, and to order the applicant to provide a security or equivalent assurance sufficient to protect the defendant and to prevent abuse.

4. Where provisional measures have been adopted inaudita altera parte, the parties affected shall be given notice, without delay after the execution of the measures at the latest. A review, including a right to be heard, shall take place upon request of the defendant with a view to deciding, within a reasonable period after the notification of the measures, whether these measures shall be modified, revoked or confirmed.

5. The applicant may be required to supply other information necessary for the identification of the goods concerned by the authority that will execute the provisional measures.

6. Without prejudice to paragraph 4, provisional measures taken on the basis of paragraphs 1 and 2 shall, upon request by the defendant, be revoked or otherwise cease to have effect, if proceedings leading to a decision on the merits of the case are not initiated within a reasonable period, to be determined by the judicial authority ordering the measures where a Member's law so permits or, in the absence of such a determination, not to exceed 20 working days or 31 calendar days, whichever is the longer.

7. Where the provisional measures are revoked or where they lapse due to any act or omission by the applicant, or where it is subsequently found that there has been no infringement or threat of infringement of an intellectual property right, the judicial authorities shall have the authority to order the applicant, upon request of the defendant, to provide the defendant appropriate compensation for any injury caused by these measures.

8. To the extent that any provisional measure can be ordered as a result of administrative procedures, such procedures shall conform to principles equivalent in substance to those set forth in this Section.

SECTION 4: SPECIAL REQUIREMENTS RELATED TO BORDER MEASURES

Article 51 Suspension of Release by Customs Authorities

Members shall, in conformity with the provisions set out below, adopt **A29-051** procedures to enable a rightholder, who has valid grounds for suspecting that the importation of counterfeit trademark or pirated copyright goods may take place, to lodge an application in writing with competent authorities, administrative or judicial, for the suspension by the customs authorities of the release into free circulation of such goods. Members may enable such an application to be made in respect of goods which involve other infringements of intellectual property rights, provided that the requirements of this Section are met. Members may also provide for corresponding procedures concerning the suspension by the customs authorities of the release of infringing goods destined for exportation from their territories.

Article 52 Application

Any right holder initiating the procedures under Article 51 shall be required **A29-052** to provide adequate evidence to satisfy the competent authorities that, under the laws of the country of importation, there is prima facie an infringement of the right holder's intellectual property right and to supply a sufficiently detailed description of the goods to make them readily recognizable by the customs authorities. The competent authorities shall inform the applicant within a reasonable period whether they have accepted the application and, where determined by the competent authorities, the period for which the customs authorities will take action.

Article 53 Security or Equivalent Assurance

1. The competent authorities shall have the authority to require an applicant **A29-053** to provide a security or equivalent assurance sufficient to protect the defendant and the competent authorities and to prevent abuse. Such security or equivalent assurance shall not unreasonably deter recourse to these procedures.

2. Where pursuant to an application under this Section the release of goods involving industrial designs, patents, layout-designs or undisclosed information

into free circulation has been suspended by customs authorities on the basis of a decision other than by a judicial or other independent authority, and the period provided for in Article 55 has expired without the granting of provisional relief by the duly empowered authority, and provided that all other conditions for importation have been complied with, the owner, importer, or consignee of such goods shall be entitled to their release on the posting of a security in an amount sufficient to protect the right holder for any infringement. Payment of such security shall not prejudice any other remedy available to the right holder, it being understood that the security shall be released if the right holder fails to pursue the right of action within a reasonable period of time.

Article 54 Notice of Suspension

A29-054   The importer and the applicant shall be promptly notified of the suspension of the release of goods according to Article 51.

Article 55 Duration of Suspension

A29-055   If, within a period not exceeding 10 working days after the applicant has been served notice of the suspension, the customs authorities have not been informed that proceedings leading to a decision on the merits of the case have been initiated by a party other than the defendant, or that the duly empowered authority has taken provisional measures prolonging the suspension of the release of the goods, the goods shall be released, provided that all other conditions for importation or exportation have been complied with; in appropriate cases, this time-limit may be extended by another 10 working days. If proceedings leading to a decision on the merits of the case have been initiated, a review, including a right to be heard, shall take place upon request of the defendant with a view to deciding, within a reasonable period, whether these measures shall be modified, revoked or confirmed. Notwithstanding the above, where the suspension of the release of goods is carried out or continued in accordance with a provisional judicial measure, the provisions of paragraph 6 of Article 50 shall apply.

Article 56 Indemnification of the Importer and of the Owner of the Goods

A29-056   Relevant authorities shall have the authority to order the applicant to pay the importer, the consignee and the owner of the goods appropriate compensation for any injury caused to them through the wrongful detention of goods or through the detention of goods released pursuant to Article 55.

Article 57 Right of Inspection and Information

A29-057   Without prejudice to the protection of confidential information, Members shall provide the competent authorities the authority to give the right holder sufficient opportunity to have any goods detained by the customs authorities inspected in order to substantiate the right holder's claims. The competent authorities shall also have authority to give the importer an equivalent opportunity to have any such goods inspected. Where a positive determination has been made on the merits of a case, Members may provide the competent authorities the authority to inform the right holder of the names and addresses of the consignor, the importer and the consignee and of the quantity of the goods in question.

Article 58 Ex Officio Action

A29-058   Where Members require competent authorities to act upon their own initiative and to suspend the release of goods in respect of which they have acquired prima facie evidence that an intellectual property right is being infringed:

(a) the competent authorities may at any time seek from the right holder any information that may assist them to exercise these powers;

(b) the importer and the right holder shall be promptly notified of the suspension. Where the importer has lodged an appeal against the suspension with the competent authorities, the suspension shall be subject to the conditions, mutatis mutandis, set out at Article 55;

(c) Members shall only exempt both public authorities and officials from liability to appropriate remedial measures where actions are taken or intended in good faith.

Article 59 Remedies

Without prejudice to other rights of action open to the right holder and **A29-059** subject to the right of the defendant to seek review by a judicial authority, competent authorities shall have the authority to order the destruction or disposal of infringing goods in accordance with the principles set out in Article 46. In regard to counterfeit trademark goods, the authorities shall not allow the re-exportation of the infringing goods in an unaltered state or subject them to a different customs procedure, other than in exceptional circumstances.

Article 60 De Minimis Imports

Members may exclude from the application of the above provisions small **A29-060** quantities of goods of a non-commercial nature contained in travellers' personal luggage or sent in small consignments.

SECTION 5: CRIMINAL PROCEDURES

Article 61

Members shall provide for criminal procedures and penalties to be applied at **A29-061** least in cases of wilful trademark counterfeiting or copyright piracy on a commercial scale. Remedies available shall include imprisonment and/or monetary fines sufficient to provide a deterrent, consistently with the level of penalties applied for crimes of a corresponding gravity. In appropriate cases, remedies available shall also include the seizure, forfeiture and destruction of the infringing goods and of any materials and implements the predominant use of which has been in the commission of the offence. Members may provide for criminal procedures and penalties to be applied in other cases of infringement of intellectual property rights, in particular where they are committed wilfully and on a commercial scale.

PART IV

ACQUISITION AND MAINTENANCE OF INTELLECTUAL PROPERTY RIGHTS AND RELATED INTER-PARTES PROCEDURES

Article 62

1. Members may require, as a condition of the acquisition or maintenance of **A29-062** the intellectual property rights provided for under Sections 2 through 6 of Part II, compliance with reasonable procedures and formalities. Such procedures and formalities shall be consistent with the provisions of this Agreement.

2. Where the acquisition of an intellectual property right is subject to the right being granted or registered,Members shall ensure that the procedures for grant or registration, subject to compliance with the substantive conditions for acquisition of the right, permit the granting or registration of the right within a reasonable period of time so as to avoid unwarranted curtailment of the period of protection.

3. Article 4 of the Paris Convention (1967) shall apply mutatis mutandis to service marks.

4. Procedures concerning the acquisition or maintenance of intellectual property rights and, where a Member's law provides for such procedures, administrative revocation and inter partes procedures such as opposition, revocation and cancellation, shall be governed by the general principles set out in paragraphs 2 and 3 of Article 41.

5. Final administrative decisions in any of the procedures referred to under paragraph 4 shall be subject to review by a judicial or quasi-judicial authority. However, there shall be no obligation to provide an opportunity for such review of decisions in cases of unsuccessful opposition or administrative revocation, provided that the grounds for such procedures can be the subject of invalidation procedures.

PART V

DISPUTE PREVENTION AND SETTLEMENT

Article 63 Transparency

A29-063   1. Laws and regulations, and final judicial decisions and administrative rulings of general application, made effective by a Member pertaining to the subject matter of this Agreement (the availability, scope, acquisition, enforcement and prevention of the abuse of intellectual property rights) shall be published, or where such publication is not practicable made publicly available, in a national language, in such a manner as to enable governments and right holders to become acquainted with them. Agreements concerning the subject matter of this Agreement which are in force between the government or a governmental agency of a Member and the government or a governmental agency of another Member shall also be published.

2. Members shall notify the laws and regulations referred to in paragraph 1 to the Council for TRIPS in order to assist that Council in its review of the operation of this Agreement. The Council shall attempt to minimize the burden on Members in carrying out this obligation and may decide to waive the obligation to notify such laws and regulations directly to the Council if consultations with WIPO on the establishment of a common register containing these laws and regulations are successful. The Council shall also consider in this connection any action required regarding notifications pursuant to the obligations under this Agreement stemming from the provisions of Article 6ter of the Paris Convention (1967).

3. Each Member shall be prepared to supply, in response to a written request from another Member, information of the sort referred to in paragraph 1. A Member, having reason to believe that a specific judicial decision or administrative ruling or bilateral agreement in the area of intellectual property rights affects its rights under this Agreement, may also request in writing to be given access to or be informed in sufficient detail of such specific judicial decisions or administrative rulings or bilateral agreements.

4. Nothing in paragraphs 1, 2 and 3 shall require Members to disclose confidential information which would impede law enforcement or otherwise be contrary to the public interest or would prejudice the legitimate commercial interests of particular enterprises, public or private.

Article 64 Dispute Settlement

1. The provisions of Articles XXII and XXIII of GATT 1994 as elaborated **A29-064** and applied by the Dispute Settlement Understanding shall apply to consultations and the settlement of disputes under this Agreement except as otherwise specifically provided herein.

2. Subparagraphs 1(b) and 1(c) of Article XXIII of GATT 1994 shall not apply to the settlement of disputes under this Agreement for a period of five years from the date of entry into force of the WTO Agreement.

3. During the time period referred to in paragraph 2, the Council for TRIPS shall examine the scope and modalities for complaints of the type provided for under subparagraphs 1(b) and 1(c) of Article XXIII of GATT 1994 made pursuant to this Agreement, and submit its recommendations to the Ministerial Conference for approval. Any decision of the Ministerial Conference to approve such recommendations or to extend the period in paragraph 2 shall be made only by consensus, and approved recommendations shall be effective for all Members without further formal acceptance process.

PART VI

Article 65 Transitional Arrangements

1. Subject to the provisions of paragraphs 2, 3 and 4, no Member shall be **A29-065** obliged to apply the provisions of this Agreement before the expiry of a general period of one year following the date of entry into force of the WTO Agreement.

2. A developing country Member is entitled to delay for a further period of four years the date of application, as defined in paragraph 1, of the provisions of this Agreement other than Articles 3, 4 and 5.

3. Any other Member which is in the process of transformation from a centrally-planned into a market, free-enterprise economy and which is undertaking structural reform of its intellectual property system and facing special problems in the preparation and implementation of intellectual property laws and regulations, may also benefit from a period of delay as foreseen in paragraph 2.

4. To the extent that a developing country Member is obliged by this Agreement to extend product patent protection to areas of technology not so protectable in its territory on the general date of application of this Agreement for that Member, as defined in paragraph 2, it may delay the application of the provisions on product patents of Section 5 of Part II to such areas of technology for an additional period of five years.

5. A Member availing itself of a transitional period under paragraphs 1, 2, 3 or 4 shall ensure that any changes in its laws, regulations and practice made during that period do not result in a lesser degree of consistency with the provisions of this Agreement.

Article 66 Least-Developed Country Members

1. In view of the special needs and requirements of least-developed country **A29-066** Members, their economic, financial and administrative constraints, and their

need for flexibility to create a viable technological base, such Members shall not be required to apply the provisions of this Agreement, other than Articles 3, 4 and 5, for a period of 10 years from the date of application as defined under paragraph 1 of Article 65. The Council for TRIPS shall, upon duly motivated request by a least-developed country Member, accord extensions of this period.

2. Developed country Members shall provide incentives to enterprises and institutions in their territories for the purpose of promoting and encouraging technology transfer to least-developed country Members in order to enable them to create a sound and viable technological base.

Article 67 Technical Cooperation

A29-067   In order to facilitate the implementation of this Agreement, developed country Members shall provide, on request and on mutually agreed terms and conditions, technical and financial cooperation in favour of developing and least-developed country Members. Such cooperation shall include assistance in the preparation of laws and regulations on the protection and enforcement of intellectual property rights as well as on the prevention of their abuse, and shall include support regarding the establishment or reinforcement of domestic offices and agencies relevant to these matters, including the training of personnel.

PART VII

INSTITUTIONAL ARRANGEMENTS; FINAL PROVISIONS

Article 68 Council for Trade-Related Aspects of Intellectual Property Rights

A29-068   The Council for TRIPS shall monitor the operation of this Agreement and, in particular, Members' compliance with their obligations hereunder, and shall afford Members the opportunity of consulting on matters relating to the trade-related aspects of intellectual property rights. It shall carry out such other responsibilities as assigned to it by the Members, and it shall, in particular, provide any assistance requested by them in the context of dispute settlement procedures. In carrying out its functions, the Council for TRIPS may consult with and seek information from any source it deems appropriate. In consultation with WIPO, the Council shall seek to establish, within one year of its first meeting, appropriate arrangements for cooperation with bodies of that Organization.

Article 69 International Cooperation

A29-069   Members agree to cooperate with each other with a view to eliminating international trade in goods infringing intellectual property rights. For this purpose, they shall establish and notify contact points in their administrations and be ready to exchange information on trade in infringing goods. They shall, in particular, promote the exchange of information and cooperation between customs authorities with regard to trade in counterfeit trademark goods and pirated copyright goods.

Article 70 Protection of Existing Subject Matter

A29-070   1. This Agreement does not give rise to obligations in respect of acts which occurred before the date of application of the Agreement for the Member in question.

2. Except as otherwise provided for in this Agreement, this Agreement gives rise to obligations in respect of all subject matter existing at the date of application of this Agreement for the Member in question, and which is protected in that Member on the said date, or which meets or comes subsequently to meet the criteria for protection under the terms of this Agreement. In respect of this paragraph and paragraphs 3 and 4, copyright obligations with respect to existing works shall be solely determined under Article 18 of the Berne Convention (1971), and obligations with respect to the rights of producers of phonograms and performers in existing phonograms shall be determined solely under Article 18 of the Berne Convention (1971) as made applicable under paragraph 6 of Article 14 of this Agreement.

3. There shall be no obligation to restore protection to subject matter which on the date of application of this Agreement for the Member in question has fallen into the public domain.

4. In respect of any acts in respect of specific objects embodying protected subject matter which become infringing under the terms of legislation in conformity with this Agreement, and which were commenced, or in respect of which a significant investment was made, before the date of acceptance of the WTO Agreement by that Member, any Member may provide for a limitation of the remedies available to the right holder as to the continued performance of such acts after the date of application of this Agreement for that Member. In such cases the Member shall, however, at least provide for the payment of equitable remuneration.

5. A Member is not obliged to apply the provisions of Article 11 and of paragraph 4 of Article 14 with respect to originals or copies purchased prior to the date of application of this Agreement for that Member.

6. Members shall not be required to apply Article 31, or the requirement in paragraph 1 of Article 27 that patent rights shall be enjoyable without discrimination as to the field of technology, to use without the authorization of the right holder where authorization for such use was granted by the government before the date this Agreement became known.

7. In the case of intellectual property rights for which protection is conditional upon registration, applications for protection which are pending on the date of application of this Agreement for the Member in question shall be permitted to be amended to claim any enhanced protection provided under the provisions of this Agreement. Such amendments shall not include new matter.

8. Where a Member does not make available as of the date of entry into force of the WTO Agreement patent protection for pharmaceutical and agricultural chemical products commensurate with its obligations under Article 27, that Member shall:

    (a) notwithstanding the provisions of Part VI, provide as from the date of entry into force of the WTO Agreement a means by which applications for patents for such inventions can be filed;

    (b) apply to these applications, as of the date of application of this Agreement, the criteria for patentability as laid down in this Agreement as if those criteria were being applied on the date of filing in that Member or, where priority is available and claimed, the priority date of the application; and

    (c) provide patent protection in accordance with this Agreement as from the grant of the patent and for the remainder of the patent term, counted from the filing date in accordance with Article 33 of this Agreement, for those of these applications that meet the criteria for protection referred to in subparagraph (b).

9. Where a product is the subject of a patent application in a Member in accordance with paragraph 8(a), exclusive marketing rights shall be granted, notwithstanding the provisions of Part VI, for a period of five years after obtaining marketing approval in that Member or until a product patent is granted or rejected in that Member, whichever period is shorter, provided that, subsequent to the entry into force of the WTO Agreement, a patent application has been filed and a patent granted for that product in another Member and marketing approval obtained in such other Member.

Article 71 Review and Amendment

A29-071   1. The Council for TRIPS shall review the implementation of this Agreement after the expiration of the transitional period referred to in paragraph 2 of Article 65. The Council shall, having regard to the experience gained in its implementation, review it two years after that date, and at identical intervals thereafter. The Council may also undertake reviews in the light of any relevant new developments which might warrant modification or amendment of this Agreement.

2. Amendments merely serving the purpose of adjusting to higher levels of protection of intellectual property rights achieved, and in force, in other multilateral agreements and accepted under those agreements by all Members of the WTO may be referred to the Ministerial Conference for action in accordance with paragraph 6 of Article X of the WTO Agreement on the basis of a consensus proposal from the Council for TRIPS.

Article 72 Reservations

A29-072   Reservations may not be entered in respect of any of the provisions of this Agreement without the consent of the other Members.

Article 73 Security Exceptions

A29-073   Nothing in this Agreement shall be construed:

(a) to require a Member to furnish any information the disclosure of which it considers contrary to its essential security interests; or

(b) to prevent a Member from taking any action which it considers necessary for the protection of its essential security interests;

(i) relating to fissionable materials or the materials from which they are derived;

(ii) relating to the traffic in arms, ammunition and implements of war and to such traffic in other goods and materials as is carried on directly or indirectly for the purpose of supplying a military establishment;

(iii) taken in time of war or other emergency in international relations; or

(c) to prevent a Member from taking any action in pursuance of its obligations under the United Nations Charter for the maintenance of international peace and security.

WIPO Copyright Treaty and Agreed statements Concerning the WIPO Copyright Treaty

WIPO Copyright Treaty (adopted in Geneva on December 20, 1996) *

(* Material provided by the World Intellectual Property Organization (WIPO). The Secretariat of WIPO assumes no liability or responsibility with regard to the transformation of this data.)

Preamble

The Contracting Parties,   A30-001

Desiring to develop and maintain the protection of the rights of authors in their literary and artistic works in a manner as effective and uniform as possible,

Recognizing the need to introduce new international rules and clarify the interpretation of certain existing rules in order to provide adequate solutions to the questions raised by new economic, social, cultural and technological developments,

Recognizing the profound impact of the development and convergence of information and communication technologies on the creation and use of literary and artistic works,

Emphasizing the outstanding significance of copyright protection as an incentive for literary and artistic creation,

Recognizing the need to maintain a balance between the rights of authors and the larger public interest, particularly education, research and access to information, as reflected in the Berne Convention,

Have agreed as follows:

Article 1 Relation to the Berne Convention

(1) This Treaty is a special agreement within the meaning of Article 20 of the   A30-002
Berne Convention for the Protection of Literary and Artistic Works, as regards Contracting Parties that are countries of the Union established by that Convention. This Treaty shall not have any connection with treaties other than the Berne Convention, nor shall it prejudice any rights and obligations under any other treaties.

(2) Nothing in this Treaty shall derogate from existing obligations that Contracting Parties have to each other under the Berne Convention for the Protection of Literary and Artistic Works.

(3) Hereinafter, "Berne Convention" shall refer to the Paris Act of July 24, 1971 of the Berne Convention for the Protection of Literary and Artistic Works.

(4) Contracting Parties shall comply with Articles 1 to 21 and the Appendix of the Berne Convention.

Article 2 Scope of Copyright Protection

A30-003   Copyright protection extends to expressions and not to ideas, procedures, methods of operation or mathematical concepts as such.

Article 3 Application of Articles 2 to 6 of the Berne Convention

A30-004   Contracting Parties shall apply mutatis mutandis the provisions of Articles 2 to 6 of the Berne Convention in respect of the protection provided for in this Treaty

Article 4 Computer Programs

A30-005   Computer programs are protected as literary works within the meaning of Article 2 of the Berne Convention. Such protection applies to computer programs, whatever may be the mode or form of their expression.

Article 5 Compilations of Data (Databases)

A30-006   Compilations of data or other material, in any form, which by reason of the selection or arrangement of their contents constitute intellectual creations, are protected as such. This protection does not extend to the data or the material itself and is without prejudice to any copyright subsisting in the data or material contained in the compilation.

Article 6 Right of Distribution

A30-007   (1) Authors of literary and artistic works shall enjoy the exclusive right of authorizing the making available to the public of the original and copies of their works through sale or other transfer of ownership.

(2) Nothing in this Treaty shall affect the freedom of Contracting Parties to determine the conditions, if any, under which the exhaustion of the right in paragraph (1) applies after the first sale or other transfer of ownership of the original or a copy of the work with the authorization of the author.

Article 7 Right of Rental

A30-008   (1) Authors of
    (i) computer programs;
    (ii) cinematographic works; and
    (iii) works embodied in phonograms, as determined in the national law of Contracting Parties,
shall enjoy the exclusive right of authorizing commercial rental to the public of the originals or copies of their works.

(2) Paragraph (1) shall not apply
    (i) in the case of computer programs, where the program itself is not the essential object of the rental; and
    (ii) in the case of cinematographic works, unless such commercial rental has led to widespread copying of such works materially impairing the exclusive right of reproduction.

(3) Notwithstanding the provisions of paragraph (1), a Contracting Party that, on April 15, 1994, had and continues to have in force a system of equitable remuneration of authors for the rental of copies of their works embodied in phonograms may maintain that system provided that the commercial rental of works embodied in phonograms is not giving rise to the material impairment of the exclusive right of reproduction of authors.

Article 8 Right of Communication to the Public

Without prejudice to the provisions of Articles 11(1)(ii), 11bis(1)(i) and (ii), **A30-009** 11ter(1)(ii), 14(1)(ii) and 14bis(1) of the Berne Convention, authors of literary and artistic works shall enjoy the exclusive right of authorizing any communication to the public of their works, by wire or wireless means, including the making available to the public of their works in such a way that members of the public may access these works from a place and at a time individually chosen by them.

Article 9 Duration of the Protection of Photographic Works

In respect of photographic works, the Contracting Parties shall not apply the **A30-010** provisions of Article 7(4) of the Berne Convention.

Article 10 Limitations and Exceptions

(1) Contracting Parties may, in their national legislation, provide for limita- **A30-011** tions of or exceptions to the rights granted to authors of literary and artistic works under this Treaty in certain special cases that do not conflict with a normal exploitation of the work and do not unreasonably prejudice the legitimate interests of the author.

(2) Contracting Parties shall, when applying the Berne Convention, confine any limitations of or exceptions to rights provided for therein to certain special cases that do not conflict with a normal exploitation of the work and do not unreasonably prejudice the legitimate interests of the author.

Article 11 Obligations concerning Technological Measures

Contracting Parties shall provide adequate legal protection and effective legal **A30-012** remedies against the circumvention of effective technological measures that are used by authors in connection with the exercise of their rights under this Treaty or the Berne Convention and that restrict acts, in respect of their works, which are not authorized by the authors concerned or permitted by law.

Article 12 Obligations concerning Rights Management Information

(1) Contracting Parties shall provide adequate and effective legal remedies **A30-013** against any person knowingly performing any of the following acts knowing, or with respect to civil remedies having reasonable grounds to know, that it will induce, enable, facilitate or conceal an infringement of any right covered by this Treaty or the Berne Convention:

(i) to remove or alter any electronic rights management information without authority;

(ii) to distribute, import for distribution, broadcast or communicate to the public, without authority, works or copies of works knowing that electronic rights management information has been removed or altered without authority.

(2) As used in this Article, "rights management information" means information which identifies the work, the author of the work, the owner of any right in the work, or information about the terms and conditions of use of the work, and any numbers or codes that represent such information, when any of these items of information is attached to a copy of a work or appears in connection with the communication of a work to the public.

Article 13 Application in Time

A30-014   Contracting Parties shall apply the provisions of Article 18 of the Berne Convention to all protection provided for in this Treaty.

Article 14 Provisions on Enforcement of Rights

A30-015   (1) Contracting Parties undertake to adopt, in accordance with their legal systems, the measures necessary to ensure the application of this Treaty.

(2) Contracting Parties shall ensure that enforcement procedures are available under their law so as to permit effective action against any act of infringement of rights covered by this Treaty, including expeditious remedies to prevent infringements and remedies which constitute a deterrent to further infringements.

AGREED STATEMENTS CONCERNING THE WIPO COPYRIGHT TREATY

adopted by the Diplomatic Conference on December 20, 1996 *

(* Material provided by the World Intellectual Property
Organization (WIPO). The Secretariat of WIPO assumes no
liability or responsibility with regard to the transformation of this
data.)

Concerning Article 1(4)

A31-001   The reproduction right, as set out in Article 9 of the Berne Convention, and the exceptions permitted thereunder, fully apply in the digital environment, in particular to the use of works in digital form. It is understood that the storage of a protected work in digital form in an electronic medium constitutes a reproduction within the meaning of Article 9 of the Berne Convention.

Concerning Article 3

A31-002   It is understood that in applying Article 3 of this Treaty, the expression "country of the Union" in Articles 2 to 6 of the Berne Convention will be read as if it were a reference to a Contracting Party to this Treaty, in the application of those Berne Articles in respect of protection provided for in this Treaty. It is also understood that the expression "country outside the Union" in those Articles in the Berne Convention will, in the same circumstances, be read as if it were a reference to a country that is not a Contracting Party to this Treaty, and that "this Convention" in Articles 2(8), 2bis(2), 3, 4 and 5 of the Berne Convention will be read as if it were a reference to the Berne Convention and this Treaty. Finally, it is understood that a reference in Articles 3 to 6 of the Berne Convention to a "national of one of the countries of the Union" will, when these Articles are applied to this Treaty, mean, in regard to an intergovernmental organization that is a Contracting Party to this Treaty, a national of one of the countries that is member of that organization.

Concerning Article 4

A31-003   The scope of protection for computer programs under Article 4 of this Treaty, read with Article 2, is consistent with Article 2 of the Berne Convention and on a par with the relevant provisions of the TRIPS Agreement.

Concerning Article 5

The scope of protection for compilations of data (databases) under Article 5   **A31-004**
of this Treaty, read with Article 2, is consistent with Article 2 of the Berne
Convention and on a par with the relevant provisions of the TRIPS Agreement.

Concerning Articles 6 and 7

As used in these Articles, the expressions "copies" and "original and copies,"   **A31-005**
being subject to the right of distribution and the right of rental under the said
Articles, refer exclusively to fixed copies that can be put into circulation as
tangible objects.

Concerning Article 7

It is understood that the obligation under Article 7(1) does not require a Con-   **A31-006**
tracting Party to provide an exclusive right of commercial rental to authors who,
under that Contracting Party's law, are not granted rights in respect of
phonograms. It is understood that this obligation is consistent with Article 14(4)
of the TRIPS Agreement.

Concerning Article 8

It is understood that the mere provision of physical facilities for enabling or   **A31-007**
making a communication does not in itself amount to communication within the
meaning of this Treaty or the Berne Convention. It is further understood that
nothing in Article 8 precludes a Contracting Party from applying Article
11bis(2).

Concerning Article 10

It is understood that the provisions of Article 10 permit Contracting Parties   **A31-008**
to carry forward and appropriately extend into the digital environment limitations and exceptions in their national laws which have been considered
acceptable under the Berne Convention. Similarly, these provisions should be
understood to permit Contracting Parties to devise new exceptions and limitations that are appropriate in the digital network environment.

It is also understood that Article 10(2) neither reduces nor extends the scope
of applicability of the limitations and exceptions permitted by the Berne
Convention.

Concerning Article 12

It is understood that the reference to "infringement of any right covered by   **A31-009**
this Treaty or the Berne Convention" includes both exclusive rights and rights of
remuneration.

It is further understood that Contracting Parties will not rely on this Article
to devise or implement rights management systems that would have the effect of
imposing formalities which are not permitted under the Berne Convention or
this Treaty, prohibiting the free movement of goods or impeding the enjoyment of
rights under this Treaty.

WIPO Performances and Phonograms Treaty and Agreed Statements Concerning the WIPO Performances and Phonograms Treaty WIPO Performances and Phonograms Treaty* (adopted in Geneva on December 20, 1996) *

(* Material provided by the World Intellectual Property Organization (WIPO). The Secretariat of WIPO assumes no liability or responsibility with regard to the transformation of this data.)

Preamble

A32-001 *The Contracting Parties,*

Desiring to develop and maintain the protection of the rights of performers and producers of phonograms in a manner as effective and uniform as possible,

Recognizing the need to introduce new international rules in order to provide adequate solutions to the questions raised by economic, social, cultural and technological developments,
Recognizing the profound impact of the development and convergence of information and communication technologies on the production and use of performances and phonograms,

Recognizing the need to maintain a balance between the rights of performers and producers of phonograms and the larger public interest, particularly education, research and access to information,

Have agreed as follows:

CHAPTER I

GENERAL PROVISIONS

Article 1 Relation to Other Conventions

A32-002 (1) Nothing in this Treaty shall derogate from existing obligations that Contracting Parties have to each other under the International Convention for the Protection of Performers, Producers of Phonograms and Broadcasting Organizations done in Rome, October 26, 1961 (hereinafter the "Rome Convention").

(2) Protection granted under this Treaty shall leave intact and shall in no way affect the protection of copyright in literary and artistic works. Consequently, no provision of this Treaty may be interpreted as prejudicing such protection.

(3) This Treaty shall not have any connection with, nor shall it prejudice any rights and obligations under, any other treaties.

Article 2 Definitions

A32-003 For the purposes of this Treaty:
(a) "performers" are actors, singers, musicians, dancers, and other persons who act, sing, deliver, declaim, play in, interpret, or otherwise perform literary or artistic works or expressions of folklore;

(b) "phonogram" means the fixation of the sounds of a performance or of other sounds, or of a representation of sounds, other than in the form of a fixation incorporated in a cinematographic or other audiovisual work

(c) "fixation" means the embodiment of sounds, or of the representations thereof, from which they can be perceived, reproduced or communicated through a device;

(d) "producer of a phonogram" means the person, or the legal entity, who or which takes the initiative and has the responsibility for the first fixation of the sounds of a performance or other sounds, or the representations of sounds;

(e) "publication" of a fixed performance or a phonogram means the offering of copies of the fixed performance or the phonogram to the public, with the consent of the rightholder, and provided that copies are offered to the public in reasonable quantity;

(f) "broadcasting" means the transmission by wireless means for public reception of sounds or of images and sounds or of the representations thereof; such transmission by satellite is also "broadcasting"; transmission of encrypted signals is "broadcasting" where the means for decrypting are provided to the public by the broadcasting organization or with its consent;

(g) "communication to the public" of a performance or a phonogram means the transmission to the public by any medium, otherwise than by broadcasting, of sounds of a performance or the sounds or the representations of sounds fixed in a phonogram. For the purposes of Article 15, "communication to the public" includes making the sounds or representations of sounds fixed in a phonogram audible to the public.

Article 3 Beneficiaries of Protection under this Treaty

(1) Contracting Parties shall accord the protection provided under this Treaty **A32-004** to the performers and producers of phonograms who are nationals of other Contracting Parties.

(2) The nationals of other Contracting Parties shall be understood to be those performers or producers of phonograms who would meet the criteria for eligibility for protection provided under the Rome Convention, were all the Contracting Parties to this Treaty Contracting States of that Convention. In respect of these criteria of eligibility, Contracting Parties shall apply the relevant definitions in Article 2 of this Treaty.

(3) Any Contracting Party availing itself of the possibilities provided in Article 5(3) of the Rome Convention or, for the purposes of Article 5 of the same Convention, Article 17 thereof shall make a notification as foreseen in those provisions to the Director General of the World Intellectual Property Organization (WIPO).

Article 4 National Treatment

(1) Each Contracting Party shall accord to nationals of other Contracting **A32-005** Parties, as defined in Article 3(2), the treatment it accords to its own nationals with regard to the exclusive rights specifically granted in this Treaty, and to the right to equitable remuneration provided for in Article 15 of this Treaty.

(2) The obligation provided for in paragraph (1) does not apply to the extent that another Contracting Party makes use of the reservations permitted by Article 15(3) of this Treaty.

CHAPTER II

RIGHTS OF PERFORMERS

Article 5 Moral Rights of Performers

A32-006 (1) Independently of a performer's economic rights, and even after the transfer of those rights, the performer shall, as regards his live aural performances or performances fixed in phonograms, have the right to claim to be identified as the performer of his performances, except where omission is dictated by the manner of the use of the performance, and to object to any distortion, mutilation or other modification of his performances that would be prejudicial to his reputation.

(2) The rights granted to a performer in accordance with paragraph (1) shall, after his death, be maintained, at least until the expiry of the economic rights, and shall be exercisable by the persons or institutions authorized by the legislation of the Contracting Party where protection is claimed. However, those Contracting Parties whose legislation, at the moment of their ratification of or accession to this Treaty, does not provide for protection after the death of the performer of all rights set out in the preceding paragraph may provide that some of these rights will, after his death, cease to be maintained.

(3) The means of redress for safeguarding the rights granted under this Article shall be governed by the legislation of the Contracting Party where protection is claimed.

Article 6 Economic Rights of Performers in their Unfixed Performances

A32-007 Performers shall enjoy the exclusive right of authorizing, as regards their performances:

(i) the broadcasting and communication to the public of their unfixed performances except where the performance is already a broadcast performance; and

(ii) the fixation of their unfixed performances.

Article 7 Right of Reproduction

A32-008 Performers shall enjoy the exclusive right of authorizing the direct or indirect reproduction of their performances fixed in phonograms, in any manner or form.

Article 8 Right of Distribution

A32-009 (1) Performers shall enjoy the exclusive right of authorizing the making available to the public of the original and copies of their performances fixed in phonograms through sale or other transfer of ownership.

(2) Nothing in this Treaty shall affect the freedom of Contracting Parties to determine the conditions, if any, under which the exhaustion of the right in paragraph (1) applies after the first sale or other transfer of ownership of the original or a copy of the fixed performance with the authorization of the performer.

Article 9 Right of Rental

A32-010 (1) Performers shall enjoy the exclusive right of authorizing the commercial rental to the public of the original and copies of their performances fixed in phonograms as determined in the national law of Contracting Parties, even after distribution of them by, or pursuant to, authorization by the performer.

(2) Notwithstandingthe provisions of paragraph (1), a Contracting Party that, on April 15, 1994, had and continues to have in force a system of equitable remuneration of performers for the rental of copies of their performances fixed in phonograms, may maintain that system provided that the commercial rental of phonograms is not giving rise to the material impairment of the exclusive right of reproduction of performers.

CHAPTER III

RIGHTS OF PRODUCERS OF PHONOGRAMS

Article 11 Right of Reproduction

Producers of phonograms shall enjoy the exclusive right of authorizing the **A32-011** direct or indirect reproduction of their phonograms, in any manner or form.

Article 12 Right of Distribution

(1) Producers of phonograms shall enjoy the exclusive right of authorizing **A32-012** the making available to the public of the original and copies of their phonograms through sale or other transfer of ownership.

(2) Nothing in this Treaty shall affect the freedom of Contracting Parties to determine the conditions, if any, under which the exhaustion of the right in paragraph (1) applies after the first sale or other transfer of ownership of the original or a copy of the phonogram with the authorization of the producer of the phonogram.

Article 13 Right of Rental

(1) Producers of phonograms shall enjoy the exclusive right of authorizing **A32-013** the commercial rental to the public of the original and copies of their phonograms, even after distribution of them by or pursuant to authorization by the producer.

(2) Notwithstanding the provisions of paragraph (1), a Contracting Party that, on April 15, 1994, had and continues to have in force a system of equitable remuneration of producers of phonograms for the rental of copies of their phonograms, may maintain that system provided that the commercial rental of phonograms is not giving rise to the material impairment of the exclusive right of reproduction of producers of phonograms.

Article 14 Right of Making Available of Phonograms

Producers of phonograms shall enjoy the exclusive right of authorizing the **A32-014** making available to the public of their phonograms, by wire or wireless means, in such a way that members of the public may access them from a place and at a time individually chosen by them.

CHAPTER IV

COMMON PROVISIONS

Article 15 Right to Remuneration for Broadcasting and Communication to the Public

A32-015 (1) Performers and producers of phonograms shall enjoy the right to a single equitable remuneration for the direct or indirect use of phonograms published for commercial purposes for broadcasting or for any communication to the public.

(2) Contracting Parties may establish in their national legislation that the single equitable remuneration shall be claimed from the user by the performer or by the producer of a phonogram or by both. Contracting Parties may enact national legislation that, in the absence of an agreement between the performer and the producer of a phonogram, sets the terms according to which performers and producers of phonograms shall share the single equitable remuneration.

(3) Any Contracting Party may in a notification deposited with the Director General of WIPO, declare that it will apply the provisions of paragraph (1) only in respect of certain uses, or that it will limit their application in some other way, or that it will not apply these provisions at all.

(4) For the purposes of this Article, phonograms made available to the public by wire or wireless means in such a way that members of the public may access them from a place and at a time individually chosen by them shall be considered as if they had been published for commercial purposes.

Article 16 Limitations and Exceptions

A32-016 (1) Contracting Parties may, in their national legislation, provide for the same kinds of limitations or exceptions with regard to the protection of performers and producers of phonograms as they provide for, in their national legislation, in connection with the protection of copyright in literary and artistic works.

(2) Contracting Parties shall confine any limitations of or exceptions to rights provided for in this Treaty to certain special cases which do not conflict with a normal exploitation of the performance or phonogram and do not unreasonably prejudice the legitimate interests of the performer or of the producer of the phonogram.

Article 17 Term of Protection

A32-017 (1) The term of protection to be granted to performers under this Treaty shall last, at least, until the end of a period of 50 years computed from the end of the year in which the performance was fixed in a phonogram.

(2) The term of protection to be granted to producers of phonograms under this Treaty shall last, at least, until the end of a period of 50 years computed from the end of the year in which the phonogram was published, or failing such publication within 50 years from fixation of the phonogram, 50 years from the end of the year in which the fixation was made.

Article 18 Obligations concerning Technological Measures

A32-018 Contracting Parties shall provide adequate legal protection and effective legal remedies against the circumvention of effective technological measures that are used by performers or producers of phonograms in connection with the exercise of their rights under this Treaty and that restrict acts, in respect of their performances or phonograms, which are not authorized by the performers or the producers of phonograms concerned or permitted by law.

Article 19 Obligations concerning Rights Management Information

(1) Contracting Parties shall provide adequate and effective legal remedies **A32-019** against any person knowingly performing any of the following acts knowing, or with respect to civil remedies having reasonable grounds to know, that it will induce, enable, facilitate or conceal an infringement of any right covered by this Treaty:

(i) to remove or alter any electronic rights management information without authority;

(ii) to distribute, import for distribution, broadcast, communicate or make available to the public, without authority, performances, copies of fixed performances or phonograms knowing that electronic rights management information has been removed or altered without authority.

(2) As used in this Article, "rights management information" means information which identifies the performer, the performance of the performer, the producer of the phonogram, the phonogram, the owner of any right in the performance or phonogram, or information about the terms and conditions of use of the performance or phonogram, and any numbers or codes that represent such information, when any of these items of information is attached to a copy of a fixed performance or a phonogram or appears in connection with the communication or making available of a fixed performance or a phonogram to the public.

Article 20 Formalities

The enjoyment and exercise of the rights provided for in this Treaty shall not **A32-020** be subject to any formality.

DIPLOMATIC CONFERENCE ON CERTAIN COPYRIGHT AND NEIGHBORING RIGHTS QUESTIONS

Geneva, December 2 to 20, 1996

agreed statements concerning WIPO PERFORMANCES AND PHONOGRAMS TREATY

adopted by the Diplomatic Conference on December 20, 1996

Concerning Article 1

It is understood that Article 1(2) clarifies the relationship between rights in **A33-001** phonograms under this Treaty and copyright in works embodied in the phonograms. In cases where authorization is needed from both the author of a work embodied in the phonogram and a performer or producer owning rights in the phonogram, the need for the authorization of the author does not cease to exist because the authorization of the performer or producer is also required, and vice versa.

It is further understood that nothing in Article 1(2) precludes a Contracting Party from providing exclusive rights to a performer or producer of phonograms beyond those required to be provided under this Treaty.

Concerning Article 2(b)

A33-002   It is understood that the definition of phonogram provided in Article 2(b) does not suggest that rights in the phonogram are in any way affected through their incorporation into a cinematographic or other audiovisual work.

Concerning Articles 2(e), 8, 9, 12, and 13

A33-003   As used in these Articles, the expressions "copies" and "original and copies," being subject to the right of distribution and the right of rental under the said Articles, refer exclusively to fixed copies that can be put into circulation as tangible objects.

Concerning Article 3

A33-004   It is understood that the reference in Articles 5(a) and 16(a)(iv) of the Rome Convention to "national of another Contracting State" will, when applied to this Treaty, mean, in regard to an intergovernmental organization that is a Contracting Party to this Treaty, a national of one of the countries that is a member of that organization.

Concerning Article 3(2)

A33-005   For the application of Article 3(2), it is understood that fixation means the finalization of the master tape ("bande-mère").

Concerning Articles 7, 11 and 16

A33-006   The reproduction right, as set out in Articles 7 and 11, and the exceptions permitted thereunder through Article 16, fully apply in the digital environment, in particular to the use of performances and phonograms in digital form. It is understood that the storage of a protected performance or phonogram in digital form in an electronic medium constitutes a reproduction within the meaning of these Articles.

Concerning Article 15

A33-007   It is understood that Article 15 does not represent a complete resolution of the level of rights of broadcasting and communication to the public that should be enjoyed by performers and phonogram producers in the digital age. Delegations were unable to achieve consensus on differing proposals for aspects of exclusivity to be provided in certain circumstances or for rights to be provided without the possibility of reservations, and have therefore left the issue to future resolution.

Concerning Article 15

A33-008   It is understood that Article 15 does not prevent the granting of the right conferred by this Article to performers of folklore and producers of phonograms recording folklore where such phonograms have not been published for commercial gain.

Concerning Article 16

A33-009   The agreed statement concerning Article 10 (on Limitations and Exceptions) of the WIPO Copyright Treaty is applicable mutatis mutandis also to Article 16 (on Limitations and Exceptions) of the WIPO Performances and Phonograms Treaty.

Concerning Article 19

The agreed statement concerning Article 12 (on Obligations concerning **A33-010** Rights Management Information) of the WIPO Copyright Treaty is applicable mutatis mutandis also to Article 19 (on Obligations concerning Rights Management Information) of the WIPO Performances and Phonograms Treaty.

INDEX

Learning Resources
Centre